TYNESIDE
SCOTTISH

**This book is dedicated to the memory of all ranks of
102 (TYNESIDE SCOTTISH) BRIGADE 1914 –18**

102 (Tyneside Scottish) Brigade Headquarters
102 Light Trench Mortar Battery
102 Machine Gun Company

20th(Service) Battalion Northumberland Fusiliers (1st Tyneside Scottish)
21st(Service) Battalion Northumberland Fusiliers (2nd Tyneside Scottish)
22nd(Service) Battalion Northumberland Fusiliers (3rd Tyneside Scottish)
23rd(Service) Battalion Northumberland Fusiliers (4th Tyneside Scottish)
29th(Reserve) Battalion Northumberland Fusiliers (Tyneside Scottish)

'HARDER THAN HAMMERS'

TYNESIDE SCOTTISH

20th, 21st, 22nd & 23rd (Service) Battalions
of the Northumberland Fusiliers
A HISTORY OF THE TYNESIDE SCOTTISH BRIGADE
RAISED IN THE NORTH EAST IN WORLD WAR ONE

GRAHAM STEWART
JOHN SHEEN

Pen & Sword Books Limited

Also available in the same series:

Accrington Pals: The 11th (Service) Battalion (Accrington)
The East Lancashire Regiment *by William Turner*

Barnsley Pals: The 13th & 14th (Service) Battalions (Barnsley)
The York & Lancaster Regiment *by Jon Cooksey*

Sheffield City: The 12th (Service) Battalion (Sheffield)
The York & Lancaster Regiment *by Paul Oldfield and Ralph Gibson*

Liverpool Pals: A History of the 17th, 18th, 19th & 20th Service Battalions
The King's (Liverpool Regiment) *by Graham Maddocks*

Leeds Pals: A History of the 15th (Service) Battalion
The Prince of Wales's Own (West Yorkshire Regiment) *by Laurie Milner*

Salford Pals: A History of the 15th, 16th, 19th & 20th Battalions
Lancashire Fusiliers *by Michael Stedman*

Manchester Pals: The 16th, 17th, 18th, 19th, 20th, 21st, 22nd & 23rd
Battalions of the Manchester Regiment *by Michael Stedman*

Birmingham Pals: The 14th, 15th & 16th
Battalions of the Royal Warwickshire Regiment *by Terry Carter*

Tyneside Irish: The 24th, 25th, 26th & 27th
Battalions of the Northumberland Fusiliers *by John Sheen*

**First published in Great Britain in 1999 by Pen & Sword Books Limited,
47 Church Street, Barnsley, South Yorkshire S70 2AS**

Copyright © Graham Stewart, John Sheen 1999

*For up-to-date information on other titles produced under Pen & Sword
and Leo Cooper imprints, please telephone or write to:*
Pen & Sword Books Ltd
FREEPOST
47 Church Street
Barnsley
South Yorkshire
S70 2BR
Telephone (24 hours): 01226 734555

ISBN 0-85052-587-X

British Library Cataloguing in Publication Data

Printed by Yorkshire Web
47 Church Street, Barnsley, South Yorkshire S70 2AS

Contents

Acknowledgements

Thanks are due to the following who have assisted with photographs and documents:
Martin Atwell once again freely gave his help with the nominal roll officers and the citations for gallantry awards saving many hours of extra work and deserves much more than his name here. Pamela Armstrong yet again gave transcripts of interviews with veterans long dead and pointed the way towards other material. Andrew Brooks again came to the rescue with postcards and the photograph of Pte Cummings. From Maurice Wilkinson came photographs of men from the Seaham area. Sue Wood at Northumberland Record Office, Dillys Harding and the staff of the Local Studies Department of Newcastle Central Library. The staff at Gateshead Central Library and Durham Central Library. Professor Norman McCord gave permission to use material from his collection at Newcastle University. J Deveruex, J Lappin, F Bromilow, Sam Eedle, Matthew Richardson, Ralph J Whitehead (USA) provided the German material, Gordon Weston, Lieutenant Colonel R R James RA Officer Commanding 101(Northumbrian) Regt RA(Volunteers), who provided copies of the Battalion War Diaries.Staff at the Public Record Office, The Imperial War Museum and the Commonwealth War Graves Commission all were as ever very helpful. The Ministry of Defence PS4(ARMY) for permission to include information in the epilogue. Last but far from least Roni Wilkinson at Pen & Sword for his help and advice and those immortal words 'jus ger on wi' it'.

Mrs M Ash	Sgt W Stokoe 22nd Bn,
Mrs F Anderson	Pte W Barton 21st Bn,
Grenville Arnott	Captain Spencer Arnott 23rd & 2nd Garrison Bns,
Mr B Barton	Drmr A Barton 23rd Bn,
Mr G Barton	Sgt J Barton, Pte W Barton Snr 23rd Bn & RE,
Mr D Bell	Pte G Bell 29th Bn,
Geoff Baty	Second Lieutenant Reg Baty MC 21st Bn & RFC,
Mr J Brady	Pte D Prior 20th BN & Lcpl W Brady 22nd Bn,
Sue Bright,	Private Edward O'Connell 21st & 2nd Garrison Bns,
Mrs A Brown	Sgt J Peacock & Pte G Peacock 23rd Bn,
Mrs M Brown	Sgt J Brown 21st Bn,
Mr T Cassidy	Pte J Cassidy 20th Bn,
Col J A Charlton	Pte H F Rowell 29th Bn,
Mr D Christie	Lcpl F Robinson 21st Bn,
Mr J W Clark	Pte J Earle 23rd Bn,
Mr T Clifford	Pte T Smith 22nd Bn,
David Coates	Sergeant William G Wright 23rd Bn,
Mrs V Conneely	Cpl A Lynch 22nd Bn,
Miss R I Curry	Pte R Curry 22nd Bn,
Mr & Mrs Davey	Lieutenant R J Dougall 21st Bn,
Mrs M A Davison	Captain A Turnbull ,
Mr R T Dawson	Pte R Dawson 23rd Bn,
Mr T D Dunn	Sgt T Dunn MM 20th Bn,
Mrs R Durkin	Pte G Alexander 20th Bn,
Charles Eagles	Pte W A Leighton 29th Bn,
Iris Edmonds,	Piper Garnet W Fyffe 20th Bn &
	Piper Frank Wilson Northern Cyclists, & Tyneside Scottish,
Mrs S Fleming	Pte W N Goodfellow 22nd Bn,
Mr A Fitzpatrick	Pte J Fitzpatrick 20th Bn,
Mr E Forrest	Pte J Forrest 23rd Bn,
Mr J Fox	Pte W Denton DLI & 22nd Bn,
Mrs S Gilhespy	Sgt E Young 21st Bn,
Bill Gibson	Sgt Bill Estell MM 1/6th Bn & Tyneside Scottish.
Mrs S Grieves	Piper E R Grieves 22nd Bn,
Douglas Harris	Sgt J O Harris 21st Bn,

Mr W L Hedley	Pte N R Hedley,
Mr R Hermiston	Pte T Dixon 23rd Bn,
Mrs L Hirst	Lt A R Hunter MC, Legion of Honour, C de D(Belguim),
Mr G Hodges	Pte W H Hodges 23rd Bn,
Mr A Jackson	Ptes G Buglass, Sgt J Hamblin 21st Bn, A Wood 23rd Bn,
Mrs L Jackson	Ptes D Cutter 21st Bn & Pte E Cutter 22nd Bn,
Mr G Kitchen	Pte S Kitchen 20th Bn,
Mr C Land	Pte C Griffiths 22nd Bn,
Mr D A Main	Pte A Main 23rd Bn,
Mrs F Matthews	Pte T H Lee 23rd Bn,
Mrs J Matthews	Pte J Markwell 23rd Bn,
Mrs D T Mawer	Pte G Welch, 23rd Bn,
Mr S McGuire	Pte W H McGuire 21st & 1st Garrison Bns,
Mrs M A McNab	Pte F C Reid 20th Bn,
Terry McNamara	Pte Daniel Pearce 23rd, 1st & 12/13th Bns,
Mrs D McPherson	Pte T Atkinson & Pte G E Waddell 21st Bn,
Mr A Middlemiss	Sgt W A Middlemiss 22nd Bn,
Ted Milburn	CSM Richard Dale 20th Bn,
Mrs H Mitchell	Pte W Hall 21st Bn,
Maurice Morallee,	Pte George Morallee 23rd Bn,
Mrs S Mulhern	Pte F Blythe 21st Bn,
Mr J Muter	CQMS Muter 23rd Bn,
Mr W Neale	Pte G Neale 22nd Bn,
Mr J O'Keefe	Pte J O'Keefe 8th, 21st, 3rd & 1st Bns,
Mrs C Pattison	Pte J H Finn 21st Bn,
Mr R W Pattison	Pte W R Pattison 20th Bn,
Mrs E Poll	Sgt J T Dodds 21st Bn,
Lawrence Quinn	Pte Francis Quinn 22nd Bn,
Mr S J Read	Pte J S Lauder 23rd Bn,
Mr W Reece	Private B Coy 22nd Bn The last surviving Tyneside Scot,
Mrs G Reid	Pte J S Hunter 29th & 22nd Bns,
Mr S Richardson	Pte J W Richardson 20th Bn,
Mr W Rigby	Pte W Rigby 20th Bn,
Mr J F Robe	Pte J H Robe 21st Bn,
Mrs E Robinson	Pte A Bates 20th Bn,
Mr J G Schultz	Pte Schultz 23rd Bn,
Mrs M Scott	Pte G Barnfather 21st Bn,
Mr J T Simpson	Pte J Simpson 23rd Bn,
Mrs C Smith	Sgt J Johnston & Pte J R Robertson 20th Bn,
Mrs L Smith	CQMS W A B MacDonald 20th Bn,
Mrs G Spratt	Pte J Foster 20th Bn,
Kieth Strom,	LCpl Charlie Hope 20th Bn & Labour Corps,
Mr J Taylor	Cpl E J Taylor 20th Bn,
Lorna Young.	Ptes James & John Osbourne 23rd Bn,
Mr R A Walker	Pte J Glaister 20th Bn,
Alan Wallace	Pte Harry Allan 23rd, 24th, 8th and 1/5th Bns,
Mrs M Wallace	Pte W Ray 20th Bn,
Wng Cmdr A Watson	Pte F S Watson 23rd Bn,
Mr R Watson	Pte A Watson 22nd Bn,
J A Wilkinson	Pte Harry Wilkinson 29th and 12/13th Bns,
Mrs J Williams	Pte S H Wray 20th Bn,
John Wilson.	Pipe Major John Wilson MM 20th Bn.

Foreword

THE STORY OF THE TYNESIDE SCOTTISH BRIGADE goes side by side with the story of the Tyneside Irish Brigade, wherever I looked for information about the Tyneside Irish, I could be sure to find something about the Tyneside Scottish. Having completed Tyneside Irish it seemed a natural follow on to write about the Tyneside Scottish. That's when I met Graham who had been researching the Tyneside Scottish for a number of years.

Today, eighty years after the end of the Great War, many people are very proud to say that their grandfathers and great grandfathers took part in the gallant but tragic advance of the 34th Division on 1 July 1916. Many visitors every year walk down the slopes of the Tara – Usna Ridge and up to La Boisselle, following in the foot steps of relatives they probably didn't know, trying to work out positions of trenches and how far an ancestor may have got before being wounded or killed. It was here across this small piece of the French countryside on that Saturday in 1916 that, 'Never a man faltered,' and where pinned down in No Man's Land an unknown bomber shouted, 'Hey I've been shot in the arse,' with Sergeant Billy Grant shouting back, 'Haven't we all.' Yet still they tried to move forward, as ordered, only to be added to the list of casualties. After the Somme battle the Brigade was rebuilt with men from many parts of the country, who became proud to call themselves Tyneside Scots, and with the surviving originals, fought on until the end of the war. This is their story, for both Graham and myself it has been a privilege to tell it.

John Sheen
Durham City
2/1/1999

Chapter One

Origins of the Tyneside Scottish
Number 4 (Highland) Company 1860
Tyneside Scottish Volunteer Rifle Corps 1900

'He's a braw, braw Heilan' lad is Private Jock McDade,
There's no another like him in a' the Scots Brigade'

ANON

THE TYNESIDE SCOTTISH are probably unique among all of the Kitchener battalions raised during the Great War of 1914-1918, because unlike most of those battalions raised during the war the Tyneside Scottish came into being some fifty-four years earlier in 1860.

At that time Europe was again in turmoil, once again France, under Napoleon III, and Great Britain, under Queen Victoria, were at the brink of war. The danger was so great that the outbreak of a second Napoleonic War seemed imminent. Prominent men throughout Britain began to petition Parliament and the War Office for the raising of a volunteer force for the defence of the nation should a French invasion ever take place.

The man who saw the need for a home defence force was in fact the Duke of Wellington, who began campaigning for such a force as early as 1847, but it was not until 1852 that the first Corps to be sanctioned by the War Office was raised in Exeter. By 1855 a second formation was well under way in Liverpool, but it was not until 1859 that the main recruiting effort of volunteers was to be seen up and down the country.

The North East of England was not slow in taking up the challenge of raising such rifle volunteer corps, because the east coast of Great Britain had always been seen as the natural route for invaders from the continent. One of the first towns in the region to approve of the raising of a rifle corps was Tynemouth, in May 1859.

Towards the end of May the city of Newcastle was to follow with an initial meeting being held in the Chamber of Commerce, Guildhall, Newcastle. Mr E Glynn chaired this first meeting with another twenty gentlemen in attendance. Letters were read to them by the Hon Secretary Mr R T Green, from those corps which had already been sanctioned and were proving successful in other parts of the country. With this in mind it was decided that should a Corps be raised in Newcastle, that the expense for each volunteer should not exceed ten pounds, for uniforms, arms and equipment and that an annual subscription of two guineas be paid which would be sufficient to defray such costs.

On adjournment it was decided that lists would be placed in Mr M S Dodds bookshop on the quayside as well as the newsrooms at Central Exchange and Sandhill, with the view of obtaining the names of one hundred would-be volunteers. Sadly the citizens of Newcastle seemed loath to join such a Corps and at the next meeting it was announced that the lists had produced only thirty-one signatures. This caused some consternation among the committee members and Mr R T Green and M L Jobling proposed that meetings be adjourned until it was seen what Parliament would do to aid Rifle Volunteer Corps.

Other committee members Mr R L Watson, Mr Kelly, Sir John Fife and Mr E Glynn were all in favour of the formation of a Corps in the city, with Mr Watson suggesting that Sir M W Ridley be invited to act as officer of the Corps. The next meeting was to take place a fortnight later and it was hoped that better times lay ahead and by 3 June, 1859, another nineteen names had been added to the lists on public display.

What happened next will remain a mystery as there appears to be no further references to the raising of a rifle corps in Newcastle after 3 June, 1859. Indeed it would appear that Sir John Fife took matters into his own hands over the raising of the Corps. As chairman of the Newcastle Rifle Club he summoned a meeting of its members, with the view to forming themselves into a Rifle Corps. The club had only been in existence since the summer of 1859 and had many leading citizens of Newcastle as members, including those who were advanced in years and some who were described as infirm, but who were enrolled as honorary members. A contemporary member of the club said:

> *It may be well to observe that the club remains totally independent of Government, but should such encouragement be*

*given as the club deems satisfactory there
can be little doubt but that it would most
willingly enrol itself as a Rifle Volunteer
Corps.*

These assurances were apparently forthcoming and
the 1st Newcastle-Upon-Tyne Rifle Volunteer Corps
appears to have been sanctioned on 22 February,
1860, with Sir John Fife as Lieutenant Colonel and
a Sergeant Smillie as 'Drill Master'. The official
number of the Newcastle Rifle Volunteer Corps in
the Volunteer Force List was 81, because as each
Corps was sanctioned by the War Office it received
a number in the order of precedence in which it
was raised. Within the Corps itself, No 1 and No 2
Companies consisted of gentlemen from the City
Rifle Club, who supplied their own arms and accou-
trements, while the Government supplied some
fifty percent of the unit's rifles. Number 3 Company
was termed the 'Quaysiders' Company as it was
formed from the white-collar workers of businesses
located on Newcastle Quayside.

On 30 March, 1860, a fourth company was
added to the Corps. Number 4 (Highland)
Company, 1st Newcastle Rifle Volunteer Corps was
enrolled on a Monday evening at the Riding School,
Newcastle before Lieutenant Colonel Sir John Fife.
From the very beginning this was a kilted company
and it was more popularly known as 'The Newcastle
Scottish'. This small company was so popular
amongst the citizens of Newcastle that a
proposition was made to form another independent
corps to be known as 'The Northern Counties
Scottish Rifle Brigade'. It was hoped this new corps
could drill in Newcastle but would be composed of
volunteers not only from Newcastle and Gateshead,
but also the outlying districts.

The uniform of No 4(Highland) Company, 1st
Newcastle Rifle Volunteer Corps is of particular
interest since only one photograph seems to exist
from that particular period. The photograph is of
Archibald N Fraser, who was a former member of
the company. In the photograph he is wearing a
rifle grey doublet which is edged and braided with
black material. A black glengarry is worn with
possibly a single red feather behind a badge of
unknown design. Both the crossbelt (bearing a
badge of unknown design) and the waistbelt are of
brown leather, whist grey spats are worn over boots
of an unknown colour. Three white tassels are
noted on the sporran, which bears a similar badge
to that worn in the glengarry. Both the plaid and the
kilt are the sett of the 42nd Foot, The Black Watch.
Mr Fraser records the company as being about 170
strong with its armoury in Hood Street, Newcastle
and drills held at the Corn Exchange in Newcastle.
Captain Hugh L Pattinson of Scotts House, Boldon,
County Durham, who was assisted by Lieutenant
Alexander Laing and Ensign Adamson, of the
Howdon-on-Tyne shipbuilding family, commanded
the company. The company's senior NCOs' were
Colour Sergeant Rougier and Sergeant G G Taylor.
On 6 April 1860 resolutions were finally adopted

for the formation of an independent corps which was to be known as 'The Northern Counties Scottish Rifle Brigade'. A governing body was elected which included the Lord Mayors' of Newcastle and Gateshead and the Corps first drill took place at the Guildhall, Newcastle on the following Monday, which was attended by seventy members. Sadly no further records of this corps can be found and it is presumed that its existence was short lived – possibly its formation did not meet with the approval of the War Office.

The demise of the Northern Counties Scottish Rifle Brigade as an independent movement had no effect on No 4(Highland) Company, NRVC or on the Corps as a whole, which went from strength to strength and which eventually was to have thirteen companies under its control. Like No 4 (Highland) Company others were also to have sub-titles; No 8 Company was designated 'Oddfellows' Company and No 12 Company which consisted of men who were no less than six feet in height was known as the 'Guards' Company.

On 7 August, 1860, the 1st Newcastle-upon-Tyne Rifle Volunteer Corps took part in the great Volunteer Review held at Edinburgh which was reviewed by Queen Victoria. It is recorded that No 4 (Highland) Company took part in this review and a subsequent review held at York in 1866 and the company possibly took part in the great 'Sham Fight' on Newcastle Town Moor in 1868 in which some 5,000 troops took part. Sadly the days of No 4 (Highland) Company appear to have been numbered, as were many other companies up and down the country. The decreasing likelihood of war with France and a possible invasion of Great Britain resulted in a lack of interest and decline in the Volunteer movement. The end result was a scaling down in the number of companies in the larger urban corps and the disbandment of some of the smaller rural corps. In the case of the NRVC it was reduced to eight companies, four of which amalgamated with other companies while Number 13 Company left as a whole and joined a neighbouring Volunteer Artillery Corps. One of those which appears to have disbanded totally was Number 4(Highland) Company of which there is no record after 1868.

There was no further attempt to raise a kilted company or an Independent Scottish Corps in Newcastle until the end of the century, when another war in another land once again prompted the leading Anglo-Scottish citizens of Newcastle to press for a Scottish Volunteer Rifle Corps.

The war which began this new movement, had begun in South Africa in 1899. It was principally a war of independence fought between South Africa's Dutch settlers, the Boers, led by Paul Kruger, and Great Britain. As Great Britain's regular army was mobilized and began embarking for South Africa, the average Briton was under the impression that the up-start Boers would soon be put in their place by an army which had carved for Great Britain the largest empire the world had ever seen.

Sadly it was an illusion, as the army had been neglected for many years and, although successful in many minor wars against natives, they had not fought a major campaign since the Crimean War in 1854. The Boers were to be a difficult adversary, because they fought a guerrilla war, mostly on horseback. The Boers were both excellent shots and horsemen, being used to the hardships of farming and settling in a foreign land. Poor leadership and tactics, as well as being tied to a vast logistic train, which kept it in the field of battle, encumbered the British Army.

The initial stages of this war were to see numerous reverses for the British forces in the field with some extremely embarrassing defeats, showing neglect and poor leadership. These defeats also began to show up a manpower shortage back home once Army Reservists had been called forward, this in turn led to the call up of men in the Militia Reserve and in January 1900 the war Office prepared for the embodiment of the nation's Militia battalions in order to free regular battalions from overseas garrison duty.

As with the scares in Europe some fifty years earlier, so Great Britain once again saw an outbreak of patriotic fervour with the prominent of the land pursuing the War Office for permission to raise new Volunteer units. One such unit was the Liverpool Scottish, formed by Scotsmen resident in the City of Liverpool, sanctioned on 4 October, 1900, and officially known as the 8th (Scottish) Volunteer Battalion King's (Liverpool) Regiment. Another unit was the City Imperial Volunteers formed by gentlemen for gentlemen in London towards the end of 1899 and which eventually served in South Africa.

To those Anglo-Scots based on Tyneside the opportunity for raising a kilted Volunteer Rifle Corps was not to be missed and the campaigning for the raising of a Corps began in January 1900 with the appearance of a letter in the 'Newcastle Daily Chronicle' proposing the formation of a Tyneside Scottish Volunteer Corps and signed by J Graham Duff. Apparently this was not his first proposal for such a corps to be raised and he had made a similar suggestion long before this, but the idea never caught on. Mr Duff's letter caught the imagination of many fellow Scots on Tyneside and within a short time there were enough willing applicants to join that the formation of a proper committee and an approach to the War Office for sanction was considered. Towards the end of February 1900 a meeting was held in the Eldon Hotel, Grey Street, Newcastle which was to put forward proposals to approach the War Office for the sanctioning of the Tyneside Scottish Rifle Volunteer Corps. Mr Farquahar M Laing presided and among those present were: - Councillor Hugh Morton, Mr Farquahar A Ogilvie Laing, Mr H Cuthbertson, Mr Johnstone Wallace, Mr R J D Brown, Mr John M Campbell, Dr Dougall, Mr A T

Martin, Mr Dougald McPherson, Prof Thomas Oliver MD, Mr John M McGregor with Mr James Lawrence and Mr J Graham Duff acting as joint secretaries.

The meeting was full of Scottish patriotism with Mr F M Laing pointing out that he had been a member of the original Highland Company in 1859. Mr J Graham Duff said that he reckoned, 'that they had over 700 names for the Corps and that the great majority of them had already seen some discipline in the Volunteers.' It was intimated that the corps would require at least thirty-five officers and 1,000 other ranks and the chairman proposed that a Corps fund of about £4000 to £5000 would put the Corps on a sound basis. They had also secured the services of Mr Walter Smith as a bandmaster and thirty bandsmen plus a pipe band numbering sixteen. Uniforms were also discussed and they were unanimous in their choice - that the kilt should be worn.

So ended the first meeting of the Tyneside Scottish Rifle Volunteer Corps whose next step was to approach the War Office for official sanctioning. For some unknown reason this did not take place

Right: Trooper William George Wright, joined the South African Constabulary and served throughout the Boer War after which he returned to England and managed a public House in Stanley. On the outbreak of the Great War he joined the Tyneside Scottish.

until the end of May 1900.

31 Malvern Street
Newcastle upon Tyne
30/5/1900

To The Most Noble, The Marquis of
Lansdowne
Secretary of State for War
My Lord,
PROPOSED SCOTTISH RIFLE VOLUNTEER CORPS FOR NEWCASTLE UPON TYNE & DISTRICT.

I am instructed by the Committee of the above movement to approach your Lordship and ask your sanction for the formation of the above Corps.

As your Lordship will perceive by the accompanying lists, 900 men have appended their names as being desirous of joining, the minimum height as fixed by the committee is five feet six inches, they are all of Scotch nationality or of Scotch parentage: the majority have at one time been local volunteers and in no instance has a member of any other local Volunteer Corps been accepted.

As you will also perceive twenty-five gentlemen have signed their names as being wishful of holding commissions and many others have signified a similar intention on the formation of the Corps.

With regard to finance, the committee has the support of several influential gentlemen in the district in guaranteeing the necessary funds.

The Committee has been successful in securing the use of a large hall in every way suited for the purpose of drill and is also negotiating for a suitable Rifle Range. In addition to the services of a full Military Band a Highland Pipe Band of sixteen members is already enrolled.

It is the unanimous desire of all concerned in the movement that the highland dress is adopted and a decided preference has been expressed for the tartan of the Argyll and Sutherland Highlanders. The movement has the hearty support of Earl Grey, The Lord Lieutenant of the County of Northumberland; the Members of Parliament for the City; the Mayor and members of the City Council; the Commanding Officer of the District and many prominent citizens.

It is earnestly hoped your Lordship will grant the petition, I have
The honour to be
Your Lordships most obedient servant
Mr J G Duff
Secretary to the Committee.

The War Office made no immediate reply to the committee and so a further letter was sent on 14

June 1900. On 22 June the War Office sent a reply, which read:

> V/Northumb/695
> War Office
> London SW 22
> June 1900
>   Sir
>   With reference to your letters of 30th and 14th instant, I am directed by the Secretary of State for War to acquaint you that the application for authority to raise a Scottish Battalion of Volunteer Rifles at Newcastle on Tyne is under consideration and that a further communication will be made to you on the subject.
>   I am
>   Sir
>   Your Obedient Servant
>   Evelyn Wood
>   Adjutant General

There was a genuine reason for the delay by the War Office to reply, it was because opposition was being voiced by the Lieutenant Colonels of some of the Volunteer units in both Northumberland and Durham. Their objections were, firstly that there were already sufficient Volunteer Battalions in the area with vacancies to fill and, secondly that the attraction of a kilted battalion would possibly cause some men to leave their present units for the new battalion and the kilt would prove irresistible to men who might have otherwise joined other units.

Against this argument the supporters of the Tyneside Scottish Volunteer Corps pointed out that the increased population of Tyneside would be able to support all the current volunteer units and the Tyneside Scottish which was eventually to have 970 members enrolled, none of whom had resigned

from other units to enlist with them. Those that had enrolled into the Tyneside Scottish Volunteer Corps had come from the following areas, Newcastle-upon-Tyne 600, Gateshead 100, South Shields 100, Tyneside in general 150 and twenty-five gentlemen from various areas who wished to be considered for a commission in the Corps.

In the meantime the committee had already approached Isaac Walton, tailors of Grainger Street, Newcastle, for a quote regarding the fitting of uniforms for the Corps. The uniform chosen to clothe the Corps was that of the Argyll and Sutherland Highlanders and although quotes were

given for kilts and trews, no overall cost was given.

The committee sent a further letter to the War Office on 18 August, 1900, but the reply from the War Office on the 21st wasn't exactly what was expected.

V/Northumb/698
War Office
London SW
21 August 1900
Sir,

With reference to your letter of the 18th instant I am directed by the Secretary of State for War to acquaint you that the proposal for the establishment of a Scottish battalion of Volunteer Rifles for Newcastle-upon-Tyne has received full and careful consideration, that in view of the strong objections which have been raised on recruiting grounds by corps in the locality, Lord Lansdowne much regrets that he cannot advise Her Majesty to accept the services offered by those who have interested themselves in the project – I have the honour to be Sir your obedient servant.

J W Laye
Deputy Adjutant General

By September 1900 tension between the Tyneside Scottish Volunteer Corps and the dissenting Colonels had grown so much that Mr J R Hall wrote to the 'Newcastle Daily Journal' asking Lieutenant Colonel A Angus, commanding the 1st Newcastle Artillery Volunteers, Lieutenant Colonel Downing, commanding 3rd Volunteer Battalion Northumland Fusiliers and Lieutenant Colonel Proctor, commanding 5th Volunteer Battalion Durham Light Infantry to resign from their units. Earl Grey the

Lord Lieutenant of Northumberland tried desperately to mediate with the Lieutenant Colonels in question, but their replies 'did not encourage me to be very hopeful of success'. Despite Earl Grey's doubts as to what mediation would bring, there was no doubt about the unanimous support that the corps was receiving from various quarters within the region. Encouraged by this support the Committee once again petitioned the War Office for official sanction with a further letter on 5 October. The reply was as uncompromising as that of August,

V/Northumb/703
War Office
London SW
8 October 1900
Sir,

With reference to your letter of 5th ultim and former correspondence upon the subject of a proposed Scottish Battalion of Volunteer Rifles at Newcastle upon Tyne. I am directed by the Secretary of State for War to acquaint you that the question has again been under consideration and the local military authorities have been further consulted, but that the objections on recruiting grounds still exist and that in the circumstances Lord Lansdowne regrets that he must adhere to his former decision that a new battalion in Newcastle cannot be approved.

I have the honour to be
Sir
Your Obedient Servant
E Fleetwood Wilson

Undeterred by this further rejection the committee

of the Tyneside Scottish movement, supported by the Lord Lieutenant, the local City Council, Members of Parliament and many members of the public began to petition all of the commanding officers of Volunteer Units in the area, asking for their objections to the Tyneside Scottish Volunteer Corps. The surprise was that Lieutenant Colonel Angus withdrew his objections, while the Officer Commanding 1st Newcastle Engineer Volunteers raised his objections for the first time, but said he would withdraw them once his new companies had been raised. The bulk had no objection as long as the new Corps did not encroach upon their recruiting boundaries and it was with high hopes that a letter was sent to the Secretary of State for War on 20 February, 1901.

Also in late February 1901 Colonel C S Gordon commanding 5/68 Regimental District wrote to the Chief Staff Officer North Eastern District advising support for the Tyneside Scottish Volunteer Corps, as he believed that, ' the men exist and that once started the corps will not suffer from want of recruits.' However there was added caution to his letter, 'But I express the same opinion now as then, That it will directly affect the welfare of corps located in Newcastle, I do not possibly see how it can be otherwise.' The battle for the formation of the Tyneside Scottish Volunteer Corps was to continue throughout 1901 to the point of even a deputation from the committee travelling to the War Office. The Secretary of State for War was adamant that no sanction would be given to a Tyneside Scottish Volunteer Corps despite active lobbying for the formation of the Tyneside Scottish Volunteers. The final nail in the coffin was driven home by a War Office letter on 1 August, 1901,

War Office
London SW
1 August, 1901

With reference to the proposed formation of a Newcastle upon Tyne and Tyneside Scottish Infantry Volunteer Corps which was the subject of previous correspondence and the desirability of which was subsequently urged upon the Secretary of State by a deputation of those interested in the scheme, I am directed by Mr Broderick to express his deep regret that he is unable after further consideration to give the affirmative reply for which the deputation pressed. While fully appreciating the patriotic moves which are inducing those who were represented by the deputation he is unable to add further to the inequality that exists in the propor-

tion of the three arms in the forces available for home defence – an inequality which is especially marked in Newcastle where the infantry arm so largely predominates. The C-in-C has most strongly urged upon him the necessity of supplementing the present great mass of infantry in the Volunteer Force by the increased body of mounted troops which is required for the proper defence of the country. Under these circumstances Mr Broderick most sincerely trusts that the same patriotic motives which induced the council and the committee to propose the establishment of the infantry corps will cause them to organise an Imperial Yeomanry Corps of Scottish Horse.'

Yours etc E C Ward.

Following the letter the committee held a meeting at the Royal Exchange Hotel, Newcastle on 9 October, 1901. It was with heavy hearts that they decided to abandon the movement for the formation of the Tyneside Scottish Volunteer Corps both the corps and the committee were to be dissolved on 1 November, 1901. One final letter was written to the Officer Commanding 5/68 Regimental District and the following was inserted into the local press:

The Committee having decided after consideration of the reply received by the Town Clerk from the Secretary of State for War to abandon the movement, beg most heartily to tender their warmest thanks to all those who have fostered the scheme so strenuously; to the men who eagerly volunteered to join the corps, to the band and pipers, who for two years have kept themselves efficient and to the local press for all their support.

The Tyneside Scottish Volunteer Corps had faded into history. The Boer War was to last a further year before it to came to a close and it was won by the British army who had adopted tactics not unlike the Boers, using masses of mounted infantry and mobile columns. Other innovations such as the machine gun, barbed wire, block houses and better marksmanship were to play a more prominent roll in later years, while the use of colonial troops, the Militia and Volunteer Service Companies on active service overseas was to be a sign of the times ahead. Queen Victoria died in 1901 and King Edward VII came to the throne but by May 1910 he too was dead and his son King George V led Great Britain and her Empire as dark war clouds once again gathered over Europe.

Above: The Consett Iron Company's works. Consett provided Iron and steel for the ship builders on the Tyne.

The Emma Pit at Ryton. Many miners from this colliery enlisted in the Tyneside Scottish.

Left: Many famous warships were constructed at yards on the Tyne. Here the *Yashima* of the Imperial Japanese Navy passes through the Swing Bridge at Newcastle on her way to the sea (with a slight list to port). High above, crowds line the High Level Bridge. The *Yashima* went on to fight in the Sino-Japanese War and the Russo-Japanese War.

Above: A coalminer typical of many of the Northumberland and Durham men who joined the Tyneside Scottish.

Chapter Two

The North East at the Outbreak of War

'Now Geordie and Bob Johnson both lay in the shem bed,
In a little lodgin' hoos doon by the shore,'

KEEP YER FEET STILL GEORDIE HINNIE.

To TELL THE STORY of the north east at the time of the outbreak of the First World War could fill many volumes. The region, in particular County Durham and Northumberland along the north bank of the River Tyne, was highly populated, owing to the large amount of labour intensive industry that was located there. To understand the story of the Tyneside Scottish Brigade one needs to know a little of where the men came from, what their occupations were and why they should enlist into the army.

THE COALFIELD

By 1914 the north east of England was an industrial powerhouse, the area was covered with inter-related heavy industry. From the south west of County Durham to the Northumberland coast there was a vast coalfield with a huge number of mines. In County Durham alone there were 335 coalmines working in 1912. These mines employed thousands of men underground and still more were employed on the surface. The sole reason for the existence of many villages was that they were built as dormitories for the miner and his family, the houses being built as close to the pithead as possible. Many miners had large families and their young sons

would start work at the pit at the age of eleven. As they grew older they became 'putters' filling the tubs of coal to be sent to the surface or 'hewers' actually cutting the coal from the face. The work was hard and dangerous, in many places the face would be only three-foot high and the miners would be lying in inches of water as they hewed the coal from the face and loaded the tubs. From the face the tubs were taken by the drivers and their pit ponies to the shaft to be sent to the surface. Output was measured in thousands of tons daily, yet miners struggled to make a living wage, whilst the coal owners made vast fortunes from their mines.

Poor industrial relations between the owners and the miners led to many strikes and to break these strikes the owners brought in men from many parts of the country. The Irish were probably the largest immigrant community, but there were tin miners from Cornwall brought by sea, Welshmen from the valleys', some who came by sea and others who made their way by land. Other men came from the Staffordshire potteries, along with unemployed farm labourers from East Anglia. All these workers were brought to the region to ensure that coal was brought to the surface and that the cost of wages was kept low. Disaster was always close to the miner; an accidental spark could cause an

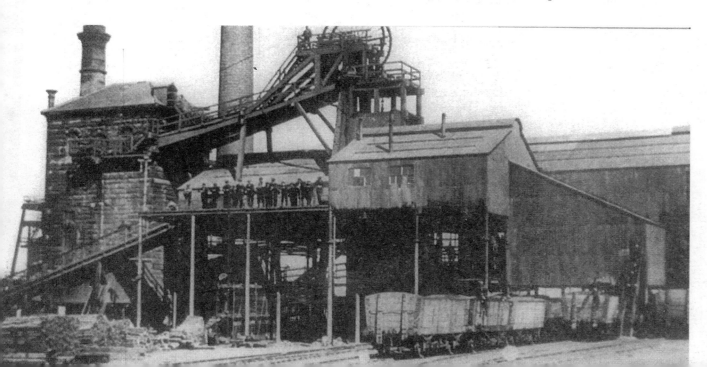

Left: Doctor Pit, Bedlington, Northumberland. A large number of men, mainly miners, volunteered from this village.

Above: Loading colliers on the Tyne. The export of coal from Northumberland and Durham coalfield was a major activity on the river.

explosion that would kill or bury alive all the men in the mine. At West Stanley on 16 February, 1909, one such explosion occurred that wrecked the Townley, Tilley and Busty seams. No less than 168 men and boys were killed and only thirty survivors were rescued, One of whom, Edward Pace, had been involved in a similar explosion at Wingate Colliery. Danger was ever-present, a wire rope could snap suddenly, a tub come off the rails or a roof could cave in and, if not killed outright, the miner could be trapped alive to die slowly as the oxygen ran out.

If the shift went well and he came out, tired and hungry, he would have to walk home, to a tin bath on the kitchen floor.

The accommodation for the miner and his family was poor, to say the least; in many cases two or sometimes three families would share a house with rudimentary toilet and washing facilities, for many the 'double raa' and the 'back to back' built close to the colliery would be the only home they ever knew. To improve living conditions local water companies, such as the Sunderland and South Shields Water Company, built huge steam driven pumps to improve the water supply to the towns and colliery villages. But in many places a single tap shared with other families would be the only water supply.

The smoke and grime from the mine would keep out the sunlight. But when the sun broke through, the shadow of the 'pitheap' would be cast over the village streets, a constant reminder to villagers of why they were living there. From these colliery villages railway lines were laid to carry the coal to the rivers, where huge staithes had been built for loading the colliers that lined the riverbanks. One coastal port, Seaham Harbour, owes its existence to the coal trade, Lord Londonderry, with extensive colliery ownership, mainly in the Penshaw area, found he was paying large amounts of money to ship his coal through Sunderland. With the coming of the railways, easing the transportation problems, he had his own port built at Seaham. Over two million tons of coal were exported through Sunderland, and over five million tons from the Tyne, as well as coal that was shipped to other British ports.

THE SHIPYARDS

The banks of the Rivers Tyne, Wear and Tees were also home to large shipyards. On the Tyne from Shields to Newcastle there were no less than twenty five yards, on the Wear fourteen, and in Middlesborough on the Tees two, with others at Blyth and Hartlepool. Many famous ships were to begin their lives by sliding into the murky, coal dust-covered waters of the Tyne and Wear. Some yards specialized in cargo vessels, others in huge passenger vessels, such as the *Mauritania* built by Swan, Hunter and Wigham's yard at Wallsend. When she was launched in 1907 the *Mauritania* was the largest ship afloat, displacing 42000 tons.

For many years she held the Blue Riband for the fastest crossing of the Atlantic. Her sister ship, built on the Clyde, was the ill-fated Lusitania which was torpedoed by a U-boat in May 1915.

Another famous shipbuilding firm was Hawthorn and Leslie's which had yards at Hebburn, St Peter's and Forth Banks. The St Peter's yard was responsible for HMS Ghurka the first Torpedo Boat Destroyer to be propelled by steam turbine, which

had its speed trials in 1907. The battleship HMS *Warspite* which was ordered in 1912 was built by Hawthorn Leslie, but they also made warships for foreign navies, the *Hai Chi* and the *Hai Tien* for the Chinese Navy, the *General Baquedano* for the Chilean Navy as well as a cruiser for Portugal and although orders were placed by the Turkish Navy the events of 1914 prevented them being built. By 20 October, 1914, 409 men had left the Hebburn yard, 198 from St Peters and 110 from Forth Banks to join His Majesty's Forces, and within a few months the total figure was nearly 1000.

Not far from the Hawthorn Leslie yard at Hebburn was Palmer's Shipbuilding at Jarrow, another firm with a world class reputation. Palmer's works covered over one hundred acres and comprised the shipbuilding yard, graving dock, slipway, engine works, boiler works, steel works and smelting plant. In fact the whole works was self-sufficient, from smelting the ore and making pig iron to converting that pig iron into steel and rolling steel plates and bars. Indeed it was the proud boast at Palmer's that, 'ore went in one end and a battleship came out of the other'. Battleships such as HMS *Russell* and HMS *Queen Mary* both went down the slipway at Jarrow and felt the cold waters of the Tyne beneath their keels; both would be lost in action in 1916. Another famous battleship built by Palmer's was HMS *Resolution* which was completed in 1915, Destroyers like HMS *Leonidas* and HMS *Lucifer*, light cruisers, submarines and monitors were built for the navy at Jarrow but the yard also made large merchant vessels. Well known shipping companies such as the Ellerman Line placed orders and ships like the *City of Bombay*, *City of Durham* and the *City of Lincoln* began their working life on the north east coast. Over 1500 men would eventually leave this company to serve with the forces.

Probably one of the most famous yards was that of Lord Armstrong at Elswick in Newcastle. Armstrong has been described as the genius that revolutionized modern ordnance with his breechloader. As with the other yards, many famous names were launched at Armstrong's Elswick yard, the light cruiser HMS *Achilles* was one, another was HMS *Agincourt*, a ship that

Above: Palmer's works at Jarrow where it was the proud boast of this company that 'Ore went in one end and a battleship came out of the other'.

Far left: Chilian cruiser *O'Higgins* taking the water.

19

began life as the *Rio de Janeiro* for the Brazilian Navy. During a financial crisis, before she was finally finished, the ship was sold to Turkey and became the *Sultan Osman 1*. When war broke out with Germany the ship was seized for use by the Royal Navy. Many of the guns for these warships came from Armstrong's Ordnance factory at Elswick, but ships and guns have one thing in common - steel!

THE IRON and STEEL WORKS

The coal produced in the Durham coalfield produced exceptional coke of the finest quality, ideal for the production of iron and steel. Accordingly, iron production flourished in the region; as early as 1747 Hawks' Iron works was

operating in Gateshead so that by 1808 coal was being transported on cast iron rails. When Stephenson laid the tracks for the Stockton to Darlington railway in 1822 the track was made from iron rolled at Bedlington. Many companies operated in the iron and steel trade and at different times there were blast furnaces at Washington, Felling, Seaham and Witton Park. Around the Middlesborough district there were works at Port Clarence, Linthorpe and West Hartlepool which had its own Iron and Steel Company. As well as Armstrong's and Palmer's shipyards with their own blast furnaces already mentioned, on the Tyne there was Spencer's at Newburn and at Lemington there had been the Tyne Iron Company. At Tudhoe near Spennymoor, there was the Weardale Iron and

Right: Armstrong's 6 inch Quick Firer, Armstrong's breech loading mechanism revolutionised modern ordnance, not only for Naval but also Military Field Artillery.

Left: Torpedo tubes under construction in 1898.

Coal Company's works and at Sunderland S Tyzack had established an Iron and Steel works to support the shipbuilding on the Wear. Along with these there was of course the Consett Iron Company's works in the North West of County Durham.

OTHER INDUSTRIES

Hand in hand with these main regional industries there were many smaller works operating in the region, lead ore was raised in Weardale and Teesdale, whilst to the north, in Northumberland, there had been a small textile industry and at Acklington Park there was a blanket mill which was located in a disused iron works. Fire clay and brick clay was dug in various locations and in Newcastle C A Parsons at Heaton manufactured steam turbines and high speed dynamos for the shipbuilding and electricity industry. Electric lighting had come early to the northeast and Newcastle was one of the first cities in the country to be lit by electric street lighting. The region was well provided with railways, the main line from London to Edinburgh running due north from Darlington to Newcastle and on to Berwick. Each colliery had its branch line that connected into the main line for the transportation of coal. The North East Railway Company was not slow to use electricity either, as early as 1907 sections of the line around Newcastle were operating electric trains and in Newcastle, Gateshead, South Shields and other towns in the region electric trams ran along the streets. One of the larger industries, although in decline at the time, were the chemical works. Factories at Wallsend, Felling and Friars Goose had at their peak employed upwards of 10000 workers and at this same peak were exporting thousands of tons of alkali, bleaching powder and soda. But much of the output was sold to other local traders such as glass, paper and soap manufacturers. Copper piping was manufactured at Rowlands Gill, Walkergate and Pelaw, whilst tanneries were producing leather goods and clothing manufacturers made various clothing products. On Wearside glass was made, rope and sail making were to be found and paper making was carried on to some extent. However there was a high degree of multiple ownership, many of the leading industrialists of the day had their fingers in many pies, taking a leading part in the financing and control of two or three major manufacturing

Below: Friars Goose Chemical works. this industry was in decline by the outbreak of the Great War.

21

industries of related interest, leading to the integration and eventual total control of vital supplies.

If accommodation for the miner was poor, it was just as bad (in some cases worse) for many other workers. In the towns large tenement houses were built; tall, ugly structures and in many cases damp and overcrowded. Two or three families would share toilet and washing facilities in blocks joined by narrow, dark, claustrophobic passageways.

But the region was not just about work since there were some famous seats of learning here also. Durham University was well established and in Newcastle there was the School of Medicine and Armstrong College. Newcastle Royal Grammar School, and Durham School to mention but two, would both provide many officers for the Army and Navy in the conflict that lay ahead.

By the summer of 1914 there were large stockpiles of coal, and in consequence of this in some places collieries were only working two, sometimes three days in a fortnight. It seemed a long hot summer then, and not many miners were interested when an assassin shot an Austrian Archduke in a faraway place called Sarajevo. As one member of the Tyneside Scottish was to recall,

'I joined up not through any sense of patriotism but as a means of getting out of the pit. I was a hand putter and men were hewing in a two foot seam.'

(Lance Corporal J G Barron 21st Battalion)

THE CALL TO ARMS

On the 28 June, 1914, the two fatal shots fired at the Archduke Ferdinand of Austria, in Sarejevo, in Bosnia-Herzegovina, which resulted in the death of his wife and the Archduke himself, started the bugles blowing in barracks and camps throughout Europe.

From that moment on, Europe began to spiral into one of the bloodiest wars ever fought on the continent. It was to absorb nearly all of the major European nations and by its end many of Europe's leading families would be swallowed up in its wake and the face of Europe changed forever.

For Germany, under the leadership of Kaiser Wilhelm II the assassination was seen as an Act of God, and the mobilization of its massive army was considered. Austria sent an ultimatum to Serbia on 23 July 1914 and although Serbia accepted almost all clauses of the ultimatum, Austria deemed this inadequate and declared war. On 30 July Great Britain ordered mobilization and, more by luck than planning, this was aided by the fact that most of the Territorial Force was attending its annual camp. Tsar Nicholas of Russia tried in vain to maintain peace, but inevitably Russia's great army began mobilization too and Germany replied by declaring war on Russia on 1 August, 1914. France was offered the opportunity to remain neutral, but under the terms of her treaties refused and Germany declared war on her on 3 August.

Germany then contravened the treaty with Luxembourg and threatened Belgium, who in turn appealed to Great Britain and France to protect her neutrality under past treaties. Germany declared war on Belgium too and invaded both countries on the same day. Of the major powers only Great Britain under her Sovereign King George V had not up to then been involved and so an ultimatum was sent to Germany which received no reply. Accordingly the British Empire declared war on Germany on 4 August 1914.

Thanks to the Haldane reforms in the years prior to 1914 the British Army was in its prime and, although small in comparison to some of its European neighbours, was a true professional army as there was no conscription in Great Britain.

With the call up of the regular army reservists it was possible to field one cavalry and six infantry divisions, although not all deployed immediately. The regulars were supported by fourteen mounted brigades and fourteen infantry divisions of the Territorial Force, which had been created in 1908 from the Volunteer Force by the Haldane reforms.

Territorial Force training was not up to regular army standards nor were its battalions up to war establishment, but they were as fit for action as any of their European counterparts. One problem lay in the fact that the Territorial Force was a home defence organization with no obligation to serve overseas and so its primary function was to man the coastal defences.

Lord Kitchener was made Secretary of State for War and he immediately made it plain that this was to be a long struggle and that Germany could only be defeated in major land battles. One problem lay in the fact that Kitchener did not have great confidence in the Territorial Force and so decided to create six more divisions, from regular troops serving in overseas garrisons.[Two cavalry and four infantry]. He also planned to raise New Armies, initially of six divisions from civilian volunteers and he appealed for 100,000 of them on 7 August. By the end of his appeal five new armies would be created[eventually reduced to four] and twenty new divisions would take to the field.

On 7 August 1914 Army Council Instruction 37 was issued which read 'Lord Kitcheners appeal for raising 100,000 men'.

The response to Kitchener's call, 'Your Country Needs You', was phenomenal and men began pouring into regimental depots and recruiting offices, with some 10626 men enlisting up and down the country between 4 and 9 August, 1914. Soon the strain began to tell on recruiting offices and recruiting staff as more and more men came forward and the only solution to the problem was to open more recruiting offices, using any premises that were suitable. The problem was relieved in the short term, but soon the signs of potential breakdown began to show once again and it is recorded that at some offices it was taking up to eight hours for volunteers to enlist

By early September 1914, as the inability of the War Office to cope with the recruiting flood continued, Lord Kitchener became forced to rely more and more upon civilian help. The history of the 1860 Volunteer movement was repeating itself, as many of Britain's leading citizens came forward with offers of help to raise battalions for the New Armies and eventually a new phrase was to enter the English language 'Pals Battalions'.

On the continent the British Regular Army entered the fray, when the British Expeditionary Force under Sir John French began landing in France on 9 August, 1914, which was completed by 22 August 1914. By this time the French Army was in desperate straits feeling the full weight of the German Army operating the Schlieffen Plan. The first shots fired by the British were at Mons; the presence of these troops was much to the Germans' surprise, but despite superior British marksmanship they could not prevent the French

from giving way on their right and so began the epic 'Retreat from Mons', which was followed by the Battle of Le Cateau. Casualties were not light and soon there would be an urgent need for reinforcements.

Tyneside was not to be omitted in the great recruiting rush of 1914 and it is recorded that 1100 men enlisted into the 8th (Service) Battalion of the Northumberland Fusiliers in the first eleven days of August 1914, with surplus recruits sent to York to fill out a battalion forming there. Of the 1766 reservists expected to be called back to the regimental depot of the Northumberland Fusiliers at Fenham Barracks, in Newcastle, only forty four failed to turn up, and those that had arrived came from every part of the country. The Depot was instrumental in the formation of the early service battalions and as quickly as men enlisted they were gathered together into battalions and sent to join their respective brigades and divisions. The 8th

Above: Northumberland
Fusiliers recruits learning
drill. Possibly men of the
4th Battalion at Hexam,
note some of them already
wear puttees with their
civilian clothing.

(Service) Battalion was soon followed by the
9th(Service) and 10th(Service) Battalions, which
were despatched from Newcastle on 7 September,
1914.

The 'Pals Battalion' phenomenon had its
beginnings in late August 1914 and although Lord
Derby is often credited with its beginnings in
Liverpool, its original foundations actually lie with
the raising of the 'Stockbrokers Battalion' of the
Royal Fusiliers raised at the instigation of Major
the Hon Robert White from the City of London
business corporations. The City of Liverpool, under
the guidance of Lord Derby, was soon to follow with
the raising of the 1st, 2nd 3rd and later the 4th '
City Battalions', of the Kings Liverpool Regiment.
Argument as to who began the 'Pals' movement will
continue, but what is certain is that it soon became

rooted in Northern tradition as cities and towns
across the North began raising their own
battalions.

The North East of England and in particular the
City of Newcastle-upon-Tyne, was not to be left
behind in the raising of local battalions, the first of
which to be recorded was the 'Newcastle
Commercials' raised by the Newcastle and
Gateshead Chamber of Commerce, from the city's
white collar workers. This battalion began life on 2
September, 1914, but was not officially recognized
until 8 September, the day after it sent a company
[the 'Quayside Company'] of 250 men to join the
9th (Service) Battalion Northumberland Fusiliers.
With men rushing to join the colours it was not long
before a call to the immigrants of Tyneside to join
their own units came.

Right: Northumberland
Fusilier recruits doing
physical training.

Chapter Three

Raising the Tyneside Scottish Brigade

*'Get a feather te yer bonnet and the kilt abain yer knee
and list bonnie laddie and cam awa' wi' me.'*

'TWA RECRUITIN' SERGEANTS.

HAD IT NOT BEEN for the outbreak of war in August 1914 there would have been no further attempts to raise a Tyneside Scottish unit on Tyneside and the War Office would have been as adamant as ever that no such unit would be raised.

It was on 8 September, 1914, that proposals for the raising of a Tyneside Scottish battalion began to appear in the local papers. Sir Thomas Oliver MD, supported by Major Innes-Hopkins [who had been the prospective commanding officer of the Tyneside Scottish in 1900], had been in touch with Mr H J Tennant, the Parliamentary Secretary, on the matter of raising a battalion. The reply was that the War Office was considerably keener than it had been in 1900 and should a battalion of 1000 men be recruited then the Tyneside Scottish would probably enjoy the same status as the London Scottish and that kilts would be worn.

Mr Tennant also implied in his letter that they would accept applications up to the age of forty-five years, but it was presumed this would only apply to ex-regulars, ex-territorials and ex-volunteers. Until the latter was confirmed, new recruits would only be accepted up to the age of thirty-five years. It was also emphasized that there must be 1000 otherwise the battalion would not be formed and the men drafted elsewhere. In order to ascertain exactly how they stood with the raising of a Tyneside Scottish Battalion intended recruits were asked to send a postcard to Sir Thomas Oliver at Ellison Place Newcastle.

The appeal for recruits was made direct to Scotsmen living and working on Tyneside, but although Newcastle's social elite was made up of quite a number of Scotsmen, the number of ordinary Scots folk living and working on Tyneside was not as great as the raisers possibly thought. Northumbrian/English was the dominant social group, followed by the Irish, who had been settling in the region since the 1850's, the Scots followed in smaller numbers with the Welsh having the smallest numbers of all. This social grouping was to play an important fact in the raising of local battalions.

The first 'other rank' to take up the call of the Tyneside Scottish was H G Hendrie of 45 Dilston Road, Newcastle on 8 September, 1914, he was to head a list of thirty eight names which included Pipe Major Munro Strachan of 20 Diamond Street, Wallsend. Three applications for commissions were

Below: Tyneside Scottish recruiting poster.

"SCOTLAND FOR EVER."

Tyneside Scottish

"Harder than Hammers."

SCOTSMEN ON TYNESIDE

are given the opportunity to defend their Country's honour and to throw back into the Kaiser's teeth his statement that Britons are "pestilent" and "contemptible."

ENROL NOW

in this fine Battalion which is quickly being filled with the **Toughest, Hardest, and Best Tyneside Fighting Men.**

AGE LIMIT 19 TO 45

:: a special concession to this Battalion only ::

HEIGHT, 5 ft. 3 ins.   CHEST, 34 ins.

Central Recruiting Office:

17 Grainger Street West, Newcastle

BRANCHES IN MOST TYNESIDE TOWNS

One man to-day worth Three in three months.

GOD SAVE THE KING

accepted but unfortunately their names were not recorded. A further forty-nine rank and file indicated their willingness to enlist on 10 September, 1914. On 11 September only fourteen names came forward, but one of them Robert Henry Jackson of 40 Faraday Close, Bensham, Gateshead in County Durham not only offered himself but twenty other men also, bringing the day's total to thirty-four. Within four days of starting enlistments the Tyneside Scottish had the names of 165 rank and file on their books, which would soon rise to 200, and among them were reported to be many veterans of the South African War who had served in Highland units.

Despite the fact that official sanctioning had not been received from the War Office, a meeting to promote the Tyneside Scottish was held at Hebburn, County Durham on 11 September, 1914, Mr Cockburn, manager of the local Palmer's Shipyard presided, and Major Innes-Hopkins spoke as a representative of the Tyneside Scottish.

At 4pm on 14 September, 1914, the Tyneside Scottish committee held a meeting in the Lord Mayor's Chambers, Town Hall, Newcastle. Present were the Lord Mayor, Johnstone Wallace, Lord Armstrong, Sir Thomas Oliver, Messrs T M Turnbull, F Deuchar, F A O Laing, F W Laing, Dr Mackay, W B Lauder, Dr McCracken, Dr Napier-Burnett, Dr Dougal, Major Innes-Hopkins, E E McClintock and J R Hall. On the proposal of the Lord Mayor, seconded by Mr F A O Laing, Sir Thomas Oliver was elected to the chair.

J R Hall
Hon Secretary

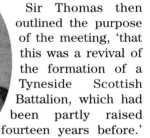

Major E E McClintock
Hon Secretary

Colonel W M Angus CB

Lord Armstrong
Vice Chairman

Prof J Wight Duff

J T Steele

Angus Watson

Sir Thomas then outlined the purpose of the meeting, 'that this was a revival of the formation of a Tyneside Scottish Battalion, which had been partly raised fourteen years before.' He stated that he had already received a large number of applications if the battalion was to be raised. The meeting was to consider the proposals of the War Office with whom Sir Thomas had been in communication and he had obtained the sanction of Lord Kitchener. Correspondence between Sir Thomas and Mr Tennant at the War Office, and General Bellfield were read out, together with the conditions laid down by the War Office with regard to raising the battalion.

Major Innes-Hopkins explained the nature and effect of the conditions should the battalion be accepted by the War Office, in particular the financial responsibility which the committee would have to undertake. Even after reimbursement of expenditure by the authorities the committee would have about £500 of extra expenditure to defray themselves or by public subscription. The cost of raising the battalion in his view would be anything from £5000 to £10000. He went on to add that as regards uniform the conditions stated that, apart from a distinctive cap, the battalion would wear the same uniform as the Northumberland Fusiliers, and that 'Highland uniform would neither be provided or expected.'

These two points caused considerable discussion among the committee and it was felt that the War Office was 'too onerous and not in harmony with general expectation'. Sir Thomas Oliver pointed out that his letter to Mr Tennant earlier in September stated that the battalion, ' would be raised on the same lines as fourteen years ago, being the same as the London Scottish' and that Mr Tennant had in his reply virtually agreed to the same.

The following resolution was then laid before the meeting, which stated:

'In view of the onerous nature of the terms stipulated in the letter from the War Office of 10 September 1914 with the conditions attached thereto particularly as to the financing of the battalion and uniform(non-kilt) this committee requests the chairman to write to the War Office and Mr Tennant that this committee feels the duty of the raising of the battalion cannot at present be proceeded with.'

Sir Thomas said he would contact the authorities immediately with the view of the committee.

The Lord Mayor, in conference with the Town Clerk, then offered part of the Corn Exchange as well as the use of clerks and general organization to the committee. The Lord Mayor also stated that further committee meetings would have the use of the Town Hall. The meeting was then adjourned pending the outcome of Sir Thomas Oliver's contact with the authorities. Once it became known to the public that the War Office would not accept the wearing of the kilt letters began appearing in the local press from local Scotsmen showing disbelief:

'Sir,

The London Scottish don the kilt and also the Liverpool Scottish so why shouldn't the 'Tynesiders' do the same. I am sure the adoption of so distinguishing a dress would bring in a better class of recruit. Only a Scotsman knows the feeling of national pride awakened by the sight of the kilt.'

Yours a Tyneside Scot.

'Sir,

No kilts for the Tyneside Scottish? Has the War Office forgotten the Piper of Dargai? We cannot expect such deeds in mere trousers after the brilliant exploits of Scotia's sons in national garb.'

Yours 'A Dumfries lad'

Subsequent events illustrate exactly the state of confusion existed during this period of almost non-stop recruitment and the effect this was to have on locally raised battalions. In the case of the Tyneside Scottish, Sir Thomas Oliver received a reply from the War Office, which can be said to have been totally unexpected. It read

18 September 1914

Sir,

With reference to your application to raise a battalion in Newcastle upon Tyne, I am commanded by the Army Council to inform you that owing to the number of local battalions already authorised they have decided that no more such battalions can be authorised. I am to express to you the sincere thanks of the Army Council and to say that whilst they appreciate the patriotic spirit which has prompted your proposal they much regret they are unable to accept it.'

Yours etc   B B Cubitt.

In essence it was a repeat of the events of 1900 when attempts were made to raise the Tyneside Scottish Volunteer Corps, but there is an added twist to the Army Council's refusal, because no such instruction exists in Army Council Instructions which refuses the acceptance of further local battalions! In fact the opposite can be said as there are indications for the further recruitment of such battalions, so was the decision on the Tyneside Scottish made on the strength of the letter sent by Sir Thomas Oliver? The answer is probably yes; and that as it was a national emergency, if committees could not or would not comply with the conditions laid down by the War Office then they would not be sanctioned.

Sadly there was a knock on effect on Tyneside because not only was the Tyneside Scottish Battalion not accepted, but also the Tyneside Irish was refused sanction. They had begun recruiting and by the time they received the telegram of refusal they had around 600 men on the books. It is said that Kitchener had a cautious attitude towards semi-nationalist formations, but as he had already sent Sir Thomas Oliver word that he would sanction the Tyneside Scottish, then the reasons for the refusal of these two units are debatable. What is more, only Newcastle-upon-Tyne seems to have been affected by the Army Council decision.

Fortunately the committee members of both the Tyneside Scottish and Tyneside Irish did not disband as one would have expected after such a rebuttal, but seemingly went into abeyance, with Sir Thomas Oliver still corresponding with the War

A CALL TO THE TYNESIDE SCOTTISH.

The Call of the Pipes.

The fiery cross is out, now
  There's a beacon on each hill,
The Scottish pipes are sounding,
  'Tis the Slogan wild and shrill.

REFRAIN :—

  Don't you hear the pipes a calling ?
  Don't you hear their martial strain ?
  O'er Tyneside the sound is falling,
  Scottish pipes ne'er call in vain.

Clansmen, your country calls you ;—
  You are wanted over there,
Mid shriek of shell and bullet,
  You will gladly do your share.

You've come from hill and hamlet,
  City street, and village green ;
Eager to serve your Country
  As the Scots have always been.

Onward ! the Tyneside Scottish,
  " Scotland for Ever " crying ;
Still in face of every foe
  We'll keep the Old Flag flying.

W.B.L.

Left: Postcard sent from Newcastle by Pipe Major John Wilson. Sold for recruiting purposes to attract men to the Colours.

Office. Sadly both were unable to hold on to many of their recruits who drifted away to join other units, although some seemed to hang on to the ideal that their desired battalion would eventually be formed.

Recruiting in general had not declined on Tyneside and those who had no desire to join a Scots or Irish battalion chose other units. By this choice the 11th and 12th (Service) Battalions of the Northumberland Fusiliers came into existence on 17 September, 1914, whilst the 13th (Service) Battalion supposedly came into being on the 16th. The Newcastle Commercial Battalion was complete with 1100 men on 16 September 1914 having had to recruit extensively to replace the company sent to the 9th Battalion. The 14th (Service) Battalion was added to the list on 25 September 1914 and it is possible that it contained many of the original Scottish and Irish recruits. Other battalions were to be added to the list of Fusilier battalions, one in particular was the North East Railway Battalion made up entirely of employees of the North East Railway Company.

When the idea was first put to the workforce that 1100 men would be needed, there were 3,000 applications and so the battalion was sanctioned on 11 September 1914 and began recruiting on 14 September. What is unique about this Northumberland battalion is that 52% of those men

Above: Lord Haldane
'I've brought to the city of Newcastle a message from Lord Kitchener, whom I saw yesterday. Lord Kitchener is asking you to say that you will raise two more battalions in Newcastle – two good Tyneside battalions, and one of them, I think might consist of the Scots, who are my own countrymen'.

Above right: Lord Kitchener

attested came from Yorkshire.

September soon passed into October and there were signs that the recruiting boom was beginning to slow down. Although men were still coming forward, the numbers were not enough. The Army Council were already making plans to increase the number of service battalions available with the publication of Army Council Instruction 76 of 8 October, 1914, which announced 'That a service battalion will be formed from each reserve and extra reserve battalion of each infantry regiment of the line.' In the case of the Northumberland Fusiliers, this new battalion, the 15th(Service) Battalion would not form until 6 November, 1914.

Lord Haldane and Kitchener's message

With the slowing down of recruitment there seems to have been a drastic change of attitude by the War Office towards Newcastle-upon-Tyne and its efforts to raise Scottish and Irish Battalions. This came in the form of a personal visit to Newcastle by Lord Haldane (the Lord Chancellor) to assist in recruiting, bearing a message from Lord Kitchener himself. Lord Haldane came to Newcastle on 10 October 1914 where he met the Lord Mayor and other dignitaries. During his visit he inspected the Newcastle Commercials at the Royal Grammar School and visited wounded soldiers in Armstrong College and the Royal Infirmary.

Later he would visit the Tyne and Pavilion Theatres where crowds of up to 8000 gathered. It was an event full of patriotic fervour, of the kind which is unlikely to be seen again, bands played, people sang and eloquent speeches were made by those present. Then Lord Haldane spoke – but it was the end of his speech which caught the crowd's attention. He stated that,

> *'I bring to the city of Newcastle a message from Lord Kitchener, whom he had seen yesterday.'* He went on *'Lord Kitchener is asking you to say that you will raise two more battalions in Newcastle – two good Tyneside battalions, and one of them, I think might consist of the Scots, who are my own countrymen'. 'Make it three – English, Irish and Scottish',* interjected one of the audience. *'That is what we are going to do.'* responded Haldane *'We are going to give you a Scottish Battalion here. We are giving every encouragement to the Irish, who are a splendid fighting race to make their battalions together, and as for the English – they will have no difficulty. There are lots of famous North Country regiments and we can provide for those who have national or a clannish feeling to be together.'*

He went on to give assurances over separation allowances and resumed his seat amid a great demonstration of cheers. The stage was now set for a recruiting battle, which was second to none.

Curiously none of the press reports indicated

that Sir Thomas Oliver, the principal raiser and chairman of the Tyneside Scottish committee, had met Lord Haldane during his visit, although in the minutes for the next meeting of the Tyneside Scottish committee on 12 October, 1914, Sir Thomas says that he conferred with Lord Haldane and one can only presume this was in private. Lord Haldane repeated Lord Kitchener's authority to go ahead with the formation of the Tyneside Scottish to Sir Thomas and handed him a letter from the Adjutant General dated 9 October, 1914, which was accompanied by conditions of raising.

During the meeting some of the conditions were pointed out the first being that the height of recruits had been reduced to 5´5˝ with a chest dimension of 34½˝ minimum. Condition 2 specified the age limit as 19 - 45 years of age and condition 4 required the battalion to be completed at 1100 all ranks after medical examination, with an allowance of 10% for rejections. Condition 5 again related to the committees liability to finance the battalion, but in this case the Lord Mayor said he had the support of certain persons, while Major Innes-Hopkins had been in communication with a bank which would give them 'favourable terms'.

With regard to recruitment, Major Innes-Hopkins pointed out that they could have joint use of the two Commercial Battalion offices located in Grey Street and Sandhill, whereas the Lord Mayor said he preferred that they use the Corn Exchange. It was at this point that Mr J R Hall, one of the joint secretaries, intimated that he had seen the executors of Sir Walter Scott's estates and they had offered the use of a shop at 17 Grainger Street for a period of ten days. This property would eventually become the Tyneside Scottish Central Recruiting Office.

Mr Hall also read out a circular and postcard, which was to be sent to the men already enrolled by that evening's post. This was agreed to and also that printing and circulation should begin. The

Lord Mayor said that no other steps beyond the recruiting circular should go ahead, while Major Hopkins Innes that enlistment should only be proceeded with until the approximate numbers were obtained. Sir Thomas Oliver had arranged with Lord Haldane that he would write to Lord Kitchener stating the Committee would undertake the raising of the battalion on the conditions of the letter of 9 October 1914. With regard to uniform the views expressed by the committee were:

'That the battalion should be known as the Tyneside Scottish Battalion and while it is recognised that the kilt might not be practicable at present, the committee hope that reasonable assurance will be given that the kilt will be allowed at the expiration of the war if the battalion became a permanency and that in the meantime a distinctive head-dress be allowed such as a Glengarry or a Dice bordered cap.'

The meeting was finally adjourned after the voting of further committee members while other subjects were left over to the following meeting. The committee, which was to play a crucial roll over the next few months, was to consist of the following members:

Sir Thomas Oliver, Chairman, Lord Armstrong, Vice Chairman, Mr J R Hall and Mr G T Hall, Joint Secretaries, The Lord Mayor of Newcastle, Councillor Johnstone Wallace, Colonel William M Angus CB, Dr E Napier, Mr J A C Brumwell, Professor J Wight-Duff, Dr Dougall, Mr Farquhar Deuchar, The Lord Mayor of Tynemouth, Colonel Hicks, Mr W B Lauder, Mr F M Laing, Mr F A O Laing, Dr N MacLay, Major E E McClintock, Dr McCracken, Sir Andrew Noble, Sir Walter Runciman, Mr Joseph Reed, Mr G T Steel, Mr Alex Wilkie MP for Dundee, Mr Angus Watson, Mr T K White, Mr R C Whitfield, Mr J H B Noble.

Two members of the committee, Mr Whitfield and Sir Andrew Noble, both died at this time and Major Innes-Hopkins resigned later from the committee in order to take up military duties.

It can also be recorded that up until the visit of Lord Haldane the Tyneside Scottish Committee was in direct communication with the War Office on matters concerning the raising of the battalion. After the visit of Lord Haldane it was found that the War Office was no longer reporting direct to the Tyneside Scottish Committee, but to the Lord Mayor whom the War Office had termed the 'nominal raiser' contrary to the fact that it was Sir Thomas Oliver.

In fact it soon became known that the Lord Mayor was the 'raiser' of all those locally raised battalions in Newcastle and this was to include the Irish and Commercial battalions, again contrary to fact. The general excuse is the War Office needed an authoritative representative, usually a municipal official to communicate with, but this was not a requirement mentioned in Army Council Instructions, which specifically refer to 'locally raised battalions, raised by individuals or committees'. It is more likely that the previous dealings with the Tyneside Scottish committee in September caused the War Office to shy away from all of the original raisers in Newcastle.

At the next meeting on 14 October 1914 it was announced by the Lord Mayor that Mr Joseph Cowen of Stella Hall had provided the sum of £10000 to be divided equally among the Scottish, Irish and second Commercial battalions. The Lord Mayor then announced he had approached Barclays Bank and as guarantor had secured a further £40000, again to be divided between the three battalions until the War Office took over control. The Lord Mayor was duly thanked for his efforts, and the committee now being free from financial responsibility and accompanying anxiety, a letter of thanks was drafted to Mr Cowen for his generosity. Through his gesture the committee then voted the Lord Mayor the treasurer and Barclays the unit's bankers.

The Committee had agreed to concentrate its recruiting efforts solely on enrolments and not attestation until 500 - 600 names were received, a sign that they were obviously testing the water. The Lord Mayor had also approached the Evening Chronicle with a view to publishing a daily list of men enrolled in the three battalions in an effort to stimulate recruitment. Those who applied for commissions would not be included in the lists for fear of rejection, and the other ranks would be given the choice of withholding their names from publication.

Mr J R Hall reported he had thirty applications for commissions and that the circulars had produced a further 110 replies of about which eighty would enrol, while thirty had withdrawn their names and had gone to other units, but names were coming in steadily and the recruiting would cover Berwick, Alston, Sunderland and Stockton. It

Below: Northumberland Veterans Pipe Band played at many recruiting drives for the Tyneside Scottish Brigade.

was also reported that the Automobile Association had offered a motor car for any purposes the committee wished and it was decided it was to be used at recruiting meetings throughout the area.

They agreed to the use of Sir Walter Scott's shop at 17 Granger Street as a recruiting office and that during attestation Captain Poulett be in charge, and that the Corn Exchange be used for this purpose. The medical members of the committee offered their services for the examination of recruits.

With the go ahead from the War Office to recruit the three local battalions in Newcastle and with the Newcastle Commercial Battalion already under training it was hoped that all four battalions would be brigaded together. (The Tyneside Brigade was initially formed from the First Commercial Battalion, Second Commercial Battalion, Tyneside Scottish Battalion, Tyneside Irish Battalion.) It was proposed that as the Newcastle Commercials would soon be moving into the hutted camp then being built at Alnwick that their place at the Royal Grammar School would be handed to the Second Commercial Battalion who had already begun some training at the Northumberland County Cricket Ground. The Tyneside Scottish hoped to use similar places to the Commercials for training purposes, while nothing positive had been announced for the Irish, although it was suggested they may be offered to the Irish Division then in the process of forming in Ireland.

By 19 October, 1914, some 250 men had enrolled into the Tyneside Scottish and it was soon hoped to have enough of the 1100 required to begin attestation at the Corn Exchange. Arrangements were also being made to open Tyneside Scottish recruiting Offices in other districts, which would make it easier for those living outside Newcastle to enlist. Offices were opened as follows:

Gosforth, 160 High Street, Mr A F Hough,

North Shields, 65 Saville Street, Messrs Graham Noble,

Wallsend, 34 High Street,

Hebburn, Carr Street,

Jarrow, Ormonde Street,

South Shields, 36 King Street,

with other offices at Prudhoe, Wallsend, Blaydon, Durham City and Crawcrook.

Recruiting meetings were also on the agenda for the purposes of further recruitment, one of the first being held in the Town Hall, Newcastle. To give it an authentic Scottish air the Caledonian Pipe Band paraded through the streets of Newcastle before the meeting, playing many of Scotland's national songs. Most of the Tyneside Scottish committee was present as speakers and it was hinted that, although the kilt would not be worn, a distinctive cap badge and headdress would be viable. For this purpose Sir Thomas Oliver and the Lord Mayor were to visit the War Office. As an added incentive to recruitment it was hoped to form platoons and companies of men from the districts in which they

were recruited, with brothers and friends being especially catered for. Of the 370 names received up to that date Major Hopkins had secured twenty-nine from a single village in the Ryton area of County Durham, and more were promised. On the same day the first list of names for the Tyneside Scottish appeared in alphabetical order in the local press, the first being Peter Leach Adams of Garden House, Mitford, Northumberland.

At the next committee meeting held on 20 October 1914 Sir Thomas reported the events of the meeting that he and the Lord Mayor had had in London with Lord Haldane, Mr Tennant, General Bellfield KCB DSO and Sir Henry Slater. The Tyneside Scottish Battalion would not be part of the Territorial Force, but part of Lord Kitcheners New Armies, and the age limit of forty-five was a special concession. The unit would be definitely known as the 'Tyneside Scottish Battalion' and a distinctive badge and head dress would be allowed, but the question of kilts would be stood over, while the question of a Commanding Officer would be settled by the War Office at a later date.

With everything seemingly going to plan the committee decided that on the formation of the battalion arrangements should be made to house the men in the hutments at Alnwick. Should the battalion only manage to raise 800 men then the War Office had agreed to find the remainder.

Some members of the committee wished to go ahead with the attestation of recruits, but it was soon pointed out that there was at present no separation allowance for the battalion. As each recruit was only allowed three shillings per day in allowances this would cause the men some hardship travelling backwards and forwards to their homes while training and since no accommodation was available it was better to delay attestation. It was agreed that those recruits who lived in Bedlington and Cramlington districts should attest in their own areas, while the others attest at 65 Westgate Road Newcastle.

Mr J R Hall was instructed to have a poster ready for circulation, while he in turn reported that arrangements for recruiting meetings had been made for Westerhope, Wallsend, Willington Quay, West Moor, Holystone and North Shields.

The Lord Mayor of Tynemouth reported he was conducting meetings at Ryton, Crawcrook and Greenside in County Durham and pipe bands had been engaged for the purpose. The pipe bands were seen as a crucial aid to recruitment and it was reported that the meeting held in Newcastle on 17 October, 1914, had brought in 170 men to add to the 632 already enrolled.

It was at this point that Johnstone Wallace questioned the nationality of those enrolling, as the press had reported that those other than Scots would be admitted. J R Hall replied that he was responsible for the press reports, because so many men had come forward from areas as friends it would have been unwise to accept only those of

Scottish birth or parentage. Although he foresaw the danger of sticking to a Scots only policy, others present in the committee would have preferred a Scots only battalion. Mr Hall received the full backing from the majority of members who decided not to emphasize the 'Scots only' line due to the fact other battalions were being recruited locally.

Among the other battalions, recruitment was on the move as far as the Second Commercial Battalion was concerned, with medical examination and attestation in full swing, but it appears that only 116 recruits had been accepted up to 20 October, 1914. The Tyneside Irish Battalion had not begun recruiting at all but was, like the Scottish, accepting names of those wishing to enrol. Once they had 500 - 600 names they too would begin attestation and training, but in the meantime they were preparing a vigorous recruiting campaign.

On 21 October, 1914, instructions were at last being sent out to enrolled members of the Tyneside Scottish for batches of 100 men to make their way to 65 Westgate Road for medical examination and attestation, under the guidance of Captain Poulett. Everyone was keen to point out the physique of those who would be examined and how few rejections or withdrawals were expected. Sir Thomas Oliver was particularly keen on the medical health of the men and he was to publish a paper for the Lancet that pointed out the variation in those examined. The paper certainly makes interesting reading as it strips away the gloss of the earlier reports(see Appendix 1).

Recruiting for the Tyneside Scottish was really beginning to take off and on this day a list was forwarded from Lord Armstrong of men from the Cragside and Rothbury districts. The rapidity in which men were coming forward to enlist caught the newspapers wrong footed and on 22 October, 1914, the second list of 297 names appeared in the local press, the first of whom was James Armstrong of 265 High Street, Wallsend. This was followed on 24 October by a third list of 112 enrolled men, which included Henry Loverow of 34 Letchiman Street, Kentish Town, London, who was probably the first man to enlist from outside the region.

Those listed in the newspapers amounted to 544 but in reality 833 had enrolled in little over a week and it was soon hoped that the 1100 target would be reached. Among the latest were twenty-two men from North Shields and nine from Cramlington. The interest being shown in the Ryton, Crawcrook and Greenside area of County Durham drew twenty-seven recruits, while postal enrolments were being received from as far away as Stockton, Durham City and Coldstream in Berwickshire. Further meetings were to take place in Hebburn and at the Mechanics Institute in Jarrow. Consett in County Durham was said to be showing an interest in the Tyneside Scottish with a view to sending some company sections from those who wished to enlist.

By 23 October, 1914, Sir Thomas Oliver could declare, 'At the rate at which things are going now

it almost looks as if there would be an opportunity given for a second battalion of Scottish, and this is the opinion of several members of the committee.'

One important new factor was that the Tyneside Scottish committee had at last secured premises for the accommodation and feeding of the growing battalion and this was Tilleys Restaurant, New Market Street, Newcastle, which could accommodate at least half the battalion. Arrangements for the remaining half had yet to be made, and for the purposes of training premises were still being viewed at Newcastle, Wallsend and Hebburn.

Andrew Reid and Co had completed free of charge the Tyneside Scottish posters, which were probably one of the best ever printed for an individual unit at this time. The motto of the Tyneside Scottish was displayed for the first time as 'Harder than Hammers' and the poster went on to claim that, 'this fine battalion which is quickly being filled with the Toughest, Hardest and Best

Above: Tilleys Restaurant Blackett Street Branch, the New Market Street branch of Tilleys was used as a billet for half of the first battalion.

Tyneside Fighting Men, and which will if given the opportunity cover itself with Renown and Glory as every man feels he is striking the right'.

By 25 October, 1914, the Tyneside Scottish Battalion was complete and a letter was issued to all of the leading newspapers from Sir Thomas Oliver:

'To the men of the Tyneside Scottish Battalion

Gentlemen - by Saturday evening over 1150 men had been enrolled. On Tyneside, as in Scotland, our countrymen have come well to the front in the matter of recruiting, for in one week our battalion has been raised. I take this the earliest opportunity, on behalf of the committee and myself, of thanking all the men who have so promptly come forward in obedience to the call of duty, and who have so patriotically inscribed themselves under the badge of the Tyneside Scottish.

We have many friends to whom we are indebted- Mr Joseph Cowen for his handsome gift, and the Lord Mayor for his kind assistance and urbanity.

Although somewhat anticipating, I know that the committee feels it cannot adequately enough express its gratitude to the Hon secretaries, Mr J R Hall and Mr E E McClintock, for their supreme efforts; also to the various speakers at, and the chairman of, various meetings, the motor scouts, the pipe major and the pipe band and last but not least the evening and morning press for the great assistance all have personally rendered.

Yours etc
Sir Thomas Oliver'

Raising the Second Battalion

So great was the response for the initial battalion that the Tyneside Scottish committee made an application to the War Office for permission to

Right: 21/836 Sergeant John Owen Harris, born in Great Yarmouth in 1887, his father a fisherman 'lost his boat' so brought the family to Newcastle to find work. When he was old enough John started work in the local colliery and in 1914 enlisted into 2nd Tyneside Scottish. He was killed in action on 1 July 1916 and is commemorated on the Thiepval Memorial, France.

raise a Second Tyneside Scottish Battalion, but no response had been received. At this time a Ladies Committee had also began to function with the aim of providing comforts and garments for members of the Tyneside Scottish Battalion who were already beginning to occupy Tilleys Restaurant. Mr Angus Watson had provided £500 for the comforts fund being run by Miss Kathleen E Oliver (Sir Thomas' youngest daughter) and Miss J R Hall, while Drums and Bugles were to be presented to the battalion by Mrs W Scott of The Mount, Ryton, County Durham. In turn her daughters offered to present the same to the Second Battalion, if formed.

At a committee meeting held on 26 October 1914, J R Hall was to report that 1268 men had enrolled into the Tyneside Scottish of whom 78 had been applications for commissions. With regard to the application to the War Office for the raising of a second battalion, Sir Thomas had received a telegram which read 'Secretary of State sends his acknowledgement and gratefully accepts a Second Tyneside Scottish Battalion.' Years of disappointment had at last come to an end and not only had one Tyneside Scottish Battalion been raised, but now they were sanctioned to raise a second.

Having raised a battalion, the question of uniform and equipment arose and this matter needed to be settled quickly now that they had been told to go ahead with a second battalion. It was agreed to settle the clothing contract immediately, but that any such contract would be made locally and the battalion should be in khaki rather than have a dark blue uniform as some early service battalions had been wearing. After examining the tenders and patterns submitted, the committee decided on Adelman and Thompson of Newcastle as clothing contractors, subject to War Office approval.

This particular contractor promised to supply up to 600 suits of clothing per week from 24 November, 1914, at the cost of £2-5s-0d for two serge jackets and two pairs of serge trousers. The greatcoat contract went to Messrs Herbert Nisbet who promised to supply 200 coats per week at 27/9d each. Both of these clothing contracts fell well within the allowances of the War Office plus 20% and although J R Hall felt they should wait for War Office approval, it was agreed by other members to proceed with the contracts in order to save time. As for the remainder of the equipments for the men it was decided to award contracts subject to a sub committee approval.

It was then made known that the War Office had approved the glengarry cap for wear by the battalion, and although Major Innes-Hopkins suggested a bronze cap badge for wear with it, they decided to leave the matter in the hands of the sub-committee, as was the question of an armlet for wear in civilian clothes until uniforms were issued.

As regards billeting for the men Tilleys said they could accommodate and feed 500 men at the rate

of 2/3d per day and that they could also supply 100 mattresses at 1/101/2 d each. Messrs Lowes had already been contracted to supply 100 pairs of blankets at 6/9d each plus twelve dozen towels. Although the authorities had initially disapproved of the use of Tilleys, they eventually agreed that the men could remain there until the move into huts at Alnwick.

The remaining half of the battalion was to be accommodated at Simpson's Hotel, Wallsend at the same rate of 2/3d per day, but there was no need for the provision of mattresses blankets or towels as these were already provided. As for parades and drills, the men located at Tilleys would have the use

Above: Men of the 1st and 2nd Company's of the 1st Tyneside Scottish. Note the early issue brown leather belts. fifth from the right in the second row from the front is 20/1152 Private S H Wray.

Left: Simpson's Hotel, Wallsend. this was used as billets for the Tyneside Scottish in 1914. the building was finally demolished in July 1998.

Above: Men of the 1st and 2nd Company's of the 1st Tyneside Scottish. Standing behind the motorcycle combination is 20/480 John Thistle.

of Newcastle City Football Club Ground while the men at Wallsend had the use of Wallsend Cricket Club Ground.

To make the attestation of the men easier it was agreed that North Shields men and those from other districts could attest locally, whereas in Newcastle the Lord Mayor agreed to the use of the Corn Exchange and the supply of officers and magistrates, who would assist the committee's medical members who would carry out medical examinations.

The question of who would command the First Battalion was put forward and it was unanimously agreed that Major Innes-Hopkins command the battalion and this would be recommended to Lieutenant General Sir H C O Plumer C-in-C Northern Command at York. Major Innes-Hopkins then suggested that a circular be sent to the other applicants who wished for commissions informing them of the formation of an officers' squad, from which the best would be selected. He also reported that he had appointed a Sergeant McKenzie in charge of the men, along with several other NCOs.

Among the other two battalions of the Tyneside Brigade recruiting was going slowly as far as the Tyneside Irish Battalion was concerned where up to 21 October, 1914, only twenty recruits had come forward. With more and more recruiting meetings taking place for the Irish, enrolments began to pick up and by 27 October it was estimated to have over 200 men enrolled. The Second Commercial Battalion was making much steadier progress,

although not on the scale of the Scottish, who had leapt ahead of their recruiting rivals. By 26 October, 1914, the second Commercials had attested 315 men and this was to increase quickly over the next few days as the Commercials were driven to compete with the Scottish.

Such was the enthusiasm being generated in the area, especially for the Tyneside Scottish, that recruits were coming forward at a steady rate and by 28 October some 350 men had enlisted into the Second Battalion. Seventy-one had been enrolled in a single evening at Ashington, where a recruiting meeting was presided over by G T Hall (brother of J R Hall) aided by Mr Alex Wilkie MP, the Reverend Siddon Cooper, Councilor Gilbertson and Mr Farquhar Deuchar. Further meetings were arranged for Gosforth, Prudhoe, Eltringham and Mickley in Northumberland and at Sunderland, Dunston, Swalwell and Whickham in County Durham. All of these would be attended by a pipe band. As a further boost, the Tyneside Scottish committee had received notice from Sir Walter Scott's executors that 17 Grainger Street could be used as a recruiting office for a further fourteen days.

So successful was the organisation of the Tyneside Scottish committee that an unidentified NCO of the First Battalion was to write:

'The record organisation and formation of the Tyneside Scottish is now almost history but I am pleased to be able to say that the preliminary stages of cementing good feeling and comradeship amongst

this body of men have been passed with equal success. Since the occupation of Monday morning of the local billet obtained for these recruits, it is most gratifying to find the men settling down so keenly to their new conditions in life and making such satisfactory progress in their military duties. This is indeed very complimentary to that body of gentlemen responsible for the creation of the battalion, but I am able to still further testify to the excellent conditions, the comfort and entertainment they are receiving at the hands of the same committee. On Monday evening an enjoyable gramophone concert was provided by the kindness of Dr McCracken, who occupied the chair, and he took an early opportunity of mentioning that the committee who he represented were specially keen upon sparing no effort in attaining the highest possible feelings of esprit de corps amongst the men in the leisure moments as well as on parade. Last night Dr McCracken again brought a party of ladies and gentlemen and provided a first rate programme of vocal and instrumental selections, which was highly appreciated by all present. The NCO in charge Quarter-Master Sergeant McKenzie in proposing a hearty vote of thanks to the committee, to Dr MacCracken and to the musical contributors spoke in very appreciative terms of the kindness displayed in providing so well for the men's enjoyment in this way and said as long as such displays of genuine consideration were forthcoming their objects were sure to be obtained.'

The following day saw the arrival of a postbag at 17 Grainger Street containing big batches of enrolments from North Shields, Hebburn and Jarrow, putting great pressure on the staff there. At the Jarrow recruiting office of the Tyneside Scottish it was revealed they had enrolled fifty-one recruits up to that date and the committee made it known that further recruiting meetings would be held South of the Tyne at Consett, Annfield Plain and surrounding districts.

Widespread interest was also being shown in the fortunes of the Tyneside Scottish and a large package containing Rowans was received from Loch Rannoch in Perthshire to be used as window decoration.

By 31 October, 1914, it was announced that the numbers enlisted into the Second Battalion had reached just over 600 with no let up, as a further nine were recruited in North Shields and fourteen from Eltringham and district. J R Hall was recorded as saying:

'If we go on as we are doing, in my view we shall have our second battalion full by the middle of next week. The enthusiasm shows no signs of abating and the organisation is complete. Meetings are arranged for the next ten days and the committee no doubt will seriously consider whether they should tackle the problem of a third battalion. There are big centres where I know we should find substantial support. I do not see why we should not have a Tyneside Scottish Brigade of four battalions.'

With this the seeds were sown and as if pre-empting the formation of such a brigade, half a dozen special clerks were employed to help relieve the constant pressure of work placed upon the recruiters. Billeting arrangements were already in hand for the Second Battalion as were contracts for the provision of clothing, as it was hoped to have both battalions clothed as soon as possible. On a lighter note seven pipers had been enlisted, but the Veterans' Band and Caledonian Pipe Band still provided the stirring pipe music at the various recruiting meetings.

Even at weekends there was no sign of recruiting slackening off on Tyneside and on Monday 2 November 1914 local press reports showed how well things were going not only for the Tyneside Scottish but also for the Tyneside Irish Battalion and the Second Commercial Battalion. The recruiting efforts of these latter two battalions had shown they were no slouches either, with 900 men enlisted into the Irish Battalion and 722 into the Second Commercials, whilst the Tyneside Scottish still remained in the lead with one battalion full and 756 men enlisted into the second battalion. For the Irish and Commercials this was a jump forward and the Irish policy of tapping into the second and third generation Irish living in County Durham was to prove highly successful.

Confidence was beginning to boom in the Tyneside Scottish camp and Sir Thomas Oliver went into communication with the War Office over the possibility of raising a third battalion. At a committee meeting held on 3 November Mr J R Hall reported that the Second Battalion was 'now substantially at strength'. In reply to this the Lord Mayor said that the War Office had sent him a wire with regard to proceeding with a proposed third battalion, enquiring whether he (the Lord Mayor) approved of the raising of the third battalion.

Sir Thomas confided that it was he who had been in touch with the War Office over the matter. But both the Lord Mayor and Major Innes-Hopkins expressed their doubts as to the wisdom of proceeding with a third battalion, except on the lines of merely enrolment with a possible view to attestation at a later date, possibly January. Their doubts did have some foundation, since the recruiting office was already under great pressure and there was also the question of billeting, officers and hutments for a further battalion.

Both J R Hall and Sir Thomas supported by

others on the committee argued, 'that such difficulties ought not to stand in the way, considering the spirit of the men'. It was then agreed to continue with enrolment and that some members would meet with Colonel Dashwood in an effort to clear away the difficulty regarding billeting. As regards the hutments then under construction at Alnwick the Lord Mayor reported that the first full battalion would get the huts and that he had given Major Innes-Hopkins a list received by him that very day of requirements for the huts. Mr J R Hall then pointed out that of the First Battalion 550 men were currently attested and billeted at Messrs Tilleys in Newcastle and 241 men were at Simpson's in Wallsend.

It was on this occasion that the question of some form of insignia arose and Major Innes-Hopkins produced a design. After some discussion by the committee members it was decided to have him produce a further design to submit at the next meeting. What was decided was that the badges of the officers would be in silver. As regards regimental shoulder titles, the committee decided to confine it to two letters 'T.S.'. With the enlistment of the seven pipers for the pipe band it was decided on the request of Major Innes-Hopkins that they would be in kilts and the Shepherds plaid, which is a distinctive black and white check associated with Northumberland, was suggested and eventually adopted. Major Innes- Hopkins also reported he would possibly be able to get the cost of seven sets of pipes defrayed by a friend, but if not the cost would be defrayed by the Cowen Fund, which would also be used for the raising of the third battalion if proceeded with.

On 4 November, 1914, the Tyneside Irish Battalion was complete and on the 5th a message of congratulation was forwarded by Mr J R Hall at a soldiers' concert being held at Tilleys which read:

'The Tyneside Scottish are delighted to hear of the successful recruiting campaign for the Tyneside Irish Battalion and desire to take this early opportunity of wishing them the best of luck. The Tyneside Scottish look forward to the time when, with the Tyneside Irish, they will be together as chums and fellow Tynesiders in camp for training and later on during a stern grim task, shoulder to shoulder in the fighting line of His Majesty's forces.'

The response to this message from the men of the Tyneside Scottish was like a bomb going off as every man sprang to his feet cheering wildly for a full five minutes.

On the following day it was announced that the Tyneside Brigade was complete, with the Second Commercial Battalion recorded as being fully recruited. Already there was talk of a second Tyneside Brigade, as all the relevant committees had decided to carry on recruiting.

Mr J R Hall's previous statement of 'now substantially at strength' for the Second Battalion was quite true with 1158 men actually enlisted by this date. It was hoped to begin attestation the following week and this was aided by a recent Army Order, which simplified the attestation procedure. It also added that, although conditions of enlistment remained unchanged, all future enlistments other than those for the Territorial Force would be as for the regular Army and for the duration of the war, which at its end would see those enlisted discharged with all convenient speed. It also emphasized that men with no previous military experience would be accepted from the ages of nineteen to thirty-eight years. This was followed by a further Army Order on 7 November 1914 which reduced the height for enlistment to five feet.

The Third Battalion sanctioned

On 9 November the Lord Mayor of Newcastle received a War Office wire authorizing the committee to proceed with the Third Battalion of the Tyneside Scottish, which he announced at that evening's meeting. This was immediately followed by the committee announcing that Colonel V M Stockley had been approved as temporary commanding officer of the Second Battalion. (He had already accepted command of the Tyneside Irish Battalion and the Irish had to find a new CO.)

Things had also moved on as regards billeting of the Second Battalion, with Mr Hall reporting that 216 men of that battalion were in quarters in Tower House, Newcastle, or in other billets. At the same time negotiations were once again under way with Simpson's Hotels Ltd with a view to billeting the first half of the Second Battalion in Rowton House, which once agreed to, would see the transfer of men from Tower House to Rowton House.

Major Innes-Hopkins had also submitted his second design of cap badge to the committee at this meeting and after some discussion the committee approved its design, subject to the addition of the motto 'Quo Fata Vocant' (Where ever the fates call), the motto of the Northumberland Fusiliers. So the first pattern cap badge was born of the four that were eventually to be worn by the Tyneside Scottish. This first pattern badge was eventually replaced with one that was more Scottish in nature. The men were allowed to keep the old badge as a souvenir, but it was published in Battalion Orders that a replacement for the new badge would cost the men 3½d if the new badge were lost.

The sanctioning and recruitment of the Third Battalion Tyneside Scottish proved to be Tyneside's finest hour and within twenty-four hours of the announcement to proceed the Third Battalion enrolments numbered over 700 men. The following day on 11 November 1914 it was announced with great pride that the battalion was already full with 1169 men enlisted into the battalion. This is likely to be a recruiting record that remains unsurpassed in the history of the British Army; nowhere in the

Left: November 1914, Second Lieutenant Reginald Beaumont leads his platoon of the 3rd Tyneside Scottish along the Ryton to Newcastle road. The River Tyne can be seen in the background.

United Kingdom was recruitment being carried out on the same scale as it was on Tyneside. The following day the exact number of enlisted men in the Tyneside Scottish was given in the local press as 1280 in the first battalion, 1370 in the second battalion and 1269 in the third battalion. It was also recorded that there were a number of rejections and withdrawals but figures were not given; what was clear though was that there was enough surplus to be carried into a possible fourth battalion. This was because large groups of men from outlying districts were still coming forward although the three established battalions were full and the general opinion was that if a fourth battalion was authorized it would be well on the way to being full also. The advice being given to would be recruits was that if you wanted to be in the Tyneside Scottish, get in as quickly as possible because it was unlikely that the committee would recruit beyond a Brigade of Tyneside Scottish.

Completing the Brigade

On 12 November, 1914, a wire was received from Mr Wilkie MP who acted as an agent for the committee and had been to the War Office to try to secure sanction for a fourth battalion. His wire was simple and to the point, 'Seen Under Secretary. He is favourable for a fourth battalion.' All that was needed was one final push and the undreamt of would take place and a Tyneside Scottish Brigade would take its place in the British Army Order of Battle.

Meanwhile there had been some rearrangements as far as billeting was concerned and half the First Battalion had been moved into Rowton House, Newcastle, allowing half of the Second Battalion to occupy Tilleys Restaurant. The other half of the First Battalion remained at Simpson's Hotel, Wallsend, while the other half of the Second Battalion was being quartered in four halls in the Heaton Road district of Newcastle.

Among those members of the Second Battalion who were originally quartered in Tilleys was 21/1000 Private Thomas Easton. Tom had enlisted underage with his elder brother Joe at Blyth and to ensure that they would be enlisted together they increased their ages by one year. After enlisting they were both sent home until such times as they were wanted. A few days later word came by post informing them (and many others) to be at Blyth railway station, where a train took them to Newcastle Central Station. From there they were

eventually marched to Tilleys which was to be their first billet.

> 'The building was bursting with over 1000 men, but we got down to sleep on the ballroom floor. For many days we were pushed about until we got recorded, surprisingly though after a few more days, came a semblance of order.'

The stay was not permanent as Tom was in the half of the battalion destined for billets on Heaton Road:

> 'Our company was sent to Heaton and we slept in the Church Hall but had to walk to New Bridge Street every morning and in the evening return. So we trod the streets of Byker up along the old Shields Road and just for a change they would send us up by City Road.'

Basic training was begun almost immediately, but feeding the battalion was a problem as it was centralized at Tilleys:

> 'We trained up on the Town Moor, but were fed at Tilleys Rooms. We leaned against the Old Gaol Wall until everyone was served then off again to the Town Moor until it was time for tea. After that fell in

again and off we go to Heaton, the rest of the day we could call our own.'

Another recruit to the 21st Battalion, although under age when he enlisted that November, was Private T W Bowman, who also recalled being billeted in Newcastle:

> 'While stationed in Tilleys, we were still wearing our civilian clothing with the tartan Tyneside Scottish armbands. I borrowed a drum from my old Boy Scout troop and with this we were able to keep in step when marching in fours to the Town Moor, much to Colonel Stockley's satisfaction. Later on I did a spell in the Battalion band as a drummer.'

By 13 November, 1914, no word had been received from the War Office sanctioning the fourth battalion, but the Tyneside Scottish committee had already recruited 400 men in anticipation. As regards the First and Second battalions, the equipment contractors had made good their contracts and stores and personal equipment were already being delivered, with a warehouse in Thornton Street being set up as a Quartermasters stores. So confident was the committee in the contractors that it was hoped the battalions would be equipped within a fortnight. As it was, the NCOs of the First Battalion were already in uniform and it was reported that they looked 'decidedly smart'.

On 16 November, 1914, a wire from the War Office finally arrived it said simply, ' To Lord Mayor Newcastle upon Tyne Fourth Tyneside Scottish and Second Tyneside Battalion sanctioned: War Office.'

Within twenty-four hours of the sanctioning being announced, Sir Thomas Oliver proudly proclaimed that the Fourth Battalion Tyneside Scottish was full, with 1920 men enlisted into the battalion. The Tyneside Scottish Brigade was now a reality and it had taken exactly thirty-four days in which to complete it and with that the Tyneside Scottish Committee proposed that no more men would be enrolled. This was to prove a mistake by the Tyneside Scottish Committee, who went about the business of tying up loose ends, winding down recruiting meetings and organizing the return of 17 Grainger Street to Sir Walter Scott's executors.

Among those volunteering at this time were two brothers from Silksworth, Jack and William Barton, who were both from a musical family and joined the pipe band, where Jack did well and was soon promoted to Sergeant. Shortly after their enlistment, their father, William Senior also enlisted and became a member of the band. This put Jack in a somewhat difficult position, as his father did not like being told what to do by his son. The company they were in bought a cow to provide fresh milk every morning but no one wanted to look after the beast. Jack had to charge his father on several occasions for insubordination and finally to get him out of the way he put him in charge of the company cow, which did not go down too well with William senior. (A third son, William junior, was to join the 21st Battalion.)

Billeting, equipping and the smooth running of the Tyneside Scottish Brigade were now the priority of the committee and on 18 November it was recorded that 470 men of the Third Battalion had been billeted at Newburn in Northumberland under Colonel Hicks. At the same time the committee was offered a full company of 250 men from an unspecified mining district, with the proviso that it serve as a company in the Fourth Battalion. Sadly the committee had to decline the offer, which they would later regret. One thing the committee was prepared to do and that was ensure each battalion had its own pipe band and that the pipers at least would wear the kilt and plaid.

Among their rivals recruiting was carrying on steadily with over 1000 already enlisted into the Third Commercial Battalion, while over 400 men had enlisted into the Third Tyneside Irish which was still waiting for sanction from the War Office. The First Commercial Battalion was preparing to move to the hutments at Alnwick Castle from their location in Newcastle.

The Composite Battalion

It was about this time that there was an invasion scare with the possibility of German troops landing on the North East coast. This resulted in the manning of the North East coast defences by the Territorial Force units stationed in the area, but even these were not enough to cover all areas of possible invasion. As an emergency measure all of those new army units then in training in the region were asked to provide men with knowledge of musketry. As a result a census was begun among the various battalions calling for those who knew how to shoot to come forward. The result was phenomenal as various battalions were besieged with those who professed knowledge of the art of musketry. Gradually those who were eligible to join specially formed companies were weeded from the hundreds of would-be's and a Composite Battalion was formed from men of the Commercials, Tyneside Scottish and Tyneside Irish. Unlike their comrades there were no weekends off and, even worse for those who had been returning to their

homes in the evening after training, they had to stay with their respective company with no return home.

The overall command of the Composite Battalion was given to Colonel V M Stockley of the Second Tyneside Scottish and on 20 November, 1914, the battalion mobilized and was issued with emergency rations and ball ammunition. It was however a false alarm and the companies stood fast in their respective billets and 'Stood to' every morning from 6 am to 7am. Three days later the battalion was gathered at Gosforth Station where many thought 'things looked promising'. They soon came down to earth when ordered to pick up picks and shovels and began another march to Benton where a trench system was begun. This then continued on a daily basis, billets to Benton and back, with a shift system of two hours work and two hours stood easy when sports were played to keep out the cold and wet.

During the digging of the trenches it was quickly noted how easy such work proved among the Northumberland and Durham miners with most of them reaching four foot six inches within an hour, while the non miners struggled. Within a short space of time the Benton trenches began to look businesslike, with proper parapets and machine-gun emplacements, a reserve line and communication trench. The Composite Battalion carried on this work until 7 December 1914, when the battalion was disbanded and the companies returned to their respective units.

Towards the end of November the Tyneside Scottish Brigade concentrated on the billeting and training of the four battalions; the Fourth Battalion having begun attestation by 21 November. The present billeting arrangements were regarded as satisfactory and the men settled down into training although many were still in their civilian clothing. At least there was no problem with equipping the pipers, of whom twenty had been recruited for the Tyneside Scottish Brigade, as they were sponsored. Donations included £140 from Mrs Hopkins while Mr J T Nisbet of Ryton also covered the cost of clothing and equipping one piper.

As a result of another visit to the War Office

TYNESIDE SCOTTISH BATTALION.

191

ORDERS FOR THE DAY — THURSDAY — DEC. 3rd. 14.

X-X-X-X-X-X-X-X-X-XX-

Orderly Officer:-   Acting-Lieut. P. C. Longhurst

:-:-:-:-:-:-:-:-:-:-:-:-

6-30	a.m.	Reveille
7-15	"	Physical Drill, doubling and walking exercises
7-45		First Breakfast Call
8-0	"	Second Breakfast Call
9-0	"	Orderly Room
9-0 : 10-30		Parade
11-0 : 12-30		"
12-45	p.m.	First dinner call
1-0	"	Dinner
2-0 : 3-30		Parade
3-45 : 4-15		Lecture
5- 0		Tea

Guard mounting parade   10 a.m.

9-30	p.m.	First Post
10-0	"	Second Post
10-15	"	Lights out.

By Order

[signature]

Acting Adjutant.

40

regarding the Tyneside Scottish Brigade the Lord Mayor and Sir Thomas Oliver returned with the news that the Brigade was to be known officially as 60(Tyneside Scottish) Brigade. This was possibly an error by the War Office as 60 Brigade was already then in formation and serving as part of 20th (Light) Division. It is possible that the Tyneside Scottish Brigade had been allocated to a New Army division from Northern Command, but that its introduction to a division was delayed.

At the same time as the formation of the Brigade there should have been a Brigade commander appointed, but no such appointment was made.

Meanwhile the Tyneside Scottish committee had agreed to appoint Major Macarthy Morrough of the 4th (Extra Reserve) Battalion Royal Munster Fusiliers, then based in Cork, as Commanding Officer of the Third Tyneside Scottish and accordingly informed the War Office of their choice. The War Office was to reply some two weeks later that Major Morrough could not be relieved from his present duties and would not be taking up the appointment.

The committee also suspended recruitment for the Fourth Battalion at this time, hoping to have the battalion attested to full strength in a few days. Within a week however they had to reverse this decision and reopen the battalion for recruitment. The reason for this was because many men had moved onto other units thinking they were surplus to requirements when recruiting for the battalion had ceased. Since then many had been rejected on medical grounds, while others had not turned up to join the battalion and so the battalion was short of the required numbers of men. Men were being asked to enrol at 17 Grainger Street, the old Tyneside Scottish recruiting office, but this had been handed over to the committee recruiting on behalf of the Tyneside Company of the Royal Inniskilling Fusiliers, on 5 December 1914.

Meanwhile it was announced the band of the First Tyneside Scottish was now complete and applications were being considered for the band of the Fourth Battalion. Training was now in full swing, but within twenty four hours of these announcements the Tyneside Scottish were to be thrown into confusion.

The Depot Companies

On 5 December, 1914, the War Office announced that all locally raised battalions formed throughout the country were to be supplemented by the further recruitment of a Depot Company for each battalion. In effect a further 250 men had to be found for each battalion, whose war establishment was raised from 1100 to 1350, and in the case of the Tyneside Scottish brigade another 1000 men had to be enlisted. This was to be a stumbling block for the Tyneside Scottish committee, for although they had won the initial race against the Commercials and the Tyneside Irish, recruiting had slowed down in the region, the

Tyneside Scottish committee had closed its recruiting offices and ceased to hold recruiting meetings. Now they had to start all over again, whereas the Tyneside Irish had enlisted Depot Companies as they went along.

Ten days later the Tyneside Scottish committee announced that Sir Thomas Oliver had been appointed Colonel of the First Tyneside Scottish Battalion and Mr Joseph Reed, Colonel of the Second Tyneside Scottish, it was hoped that appointments would soon be made for the third and fourth battalions, but in the meantime the committee were pre-occupied with the recruitment and formation of four Depot Companies. New premises were eventually found at 9 Grainger Street, Newcastle, for the purpose of recruiting for the Depot Companies and a new poster was printed for that purpose by Andrew Reid & Company.

By 9 December, 1914, up to fifteen applications a day were being received for the Depot Companies, while the Tyneside Scottish executive committee was evolving ways to stimulate recruiting into the Brigade including the recommencing of recruiting meetings. With this in mind Sir Thomas Oliver and Mr J R Hall paid a further visit to the War Office on 12 December in connection with the recruitment, they in turn were in agreement for a further recruiting drive, which was carried out as speedily as possible, without interfering with the training of those already enlisted.

By 16 December, 1914, the Tyneside Scottish Brigade was renumbered as 123 (Tyneside Scottish) Brigade forming part of the 41st Division, new battalions titles were also given which reflected the association with the county regiment as follows:

20th(Service) Battalion Northumberland Fusiliers (1st T.S.)
21st(Service) Battalion Northumberland Fusiliers (2nd T.S.)
22nd(Service) Battalion Northumberland Fusiliers (3rd T.S.)
23rd(Service) Battalion Northumberland Fusiliers (4th T.S.).

By 21 December, 1914, the War Office confirmed that Lieutenant Colonel A P A Elphinstone had been appointed to command the 22nd Battalion. The Colonel had served in the Indian Army, commanding both 7/Bombay Native Infantry and 106/Hazara Pioneers and had seen active service in Burma and Somaliland. Lieutenant Colonel Elphinstone was not the only addition to the 22nd Battalion as a Mrs Davidson of Gateshead presented the battalion with a mascot in the form of a monkey. The monkey was handed over to the battalion by Sir Thomas Oliver and was described as, 'a particularly lively little monkey' and the men of the battalion were said to be very fond of it. What eventually became of it is unknown and only one press photograph is known to exist of it.

The following message to the soldiers of the

Above: Bedlington village, Northumberland. It was from the the local colliery that over 300 men volunteered for the Tyneside Scottish.

Tyneside Scottish Brigade was sent by the Tyneside Scottish committee:

TYNESIDE SCOTTISH COMMITTEE

Christmas message to the troops

Soldiers - To you is now entrusted the rare and glorious privilege of going forth to crush the power of a military despotism 'The German Hun.' On all sides we hear the remark, 'What a fine body of men the Tyneside Scottish have secured,' Men, we know this, and are proud of you! Together with your comrades 'The Tyneside Irish and Commercials, you will soon join our brave Allies in avenging and redressing the unspeakable and hellish atrocities perpetrated upon the gallant little Belgian nation by the blasphemous and 'Kultured' Teuton. Stay not your triumphal march until the arsenals of Krupp's are razed to the ground: forward to the roll of the drums and sound of the pibroch, on through the gates of Berlin to the overthrow of the Hohenzollern throne. Cease not till over the German citadel the Union Jack floats on the breeze. That is the task, which is set you. Will you accomplish it? The finger of destiny has beckoned and brought into being the mighty British Force, casting the lie in the teeth of the German autocrat. 'That contemptible little army' has grown and become a mighty force the wonder of the world. To the call of the Mother Country the sons of the Empire have nobly responded. From every quarter of the globe they come, 'every race and every creed' are marching shoulder to shoulder under the British Standard, so proudly unfurled, to destroy oppression and maintain the law of Liberty and Justice to all the nations upon earth.

You have lived in the most progressive age the world has witnessed. The introduction of steam and electricity brought into being the facilities of railway travel, the birth of 'ocean greyhounds' and has established more firmly our Navy, 'Britannia's bulwark,' as Mistress of the Seas. In medical and surgical science marvellous strides have been made including the use in hospitals of X-rays and radium. In commerce we see introduced the telegraph and telephone systems, wireless telegraphy, the turbine and displacement of horse vehicles by motor cars. The sea and air have been conquered by submarine and aeroplane and the countless other creative inventions of man's brains too numerous to mention. Now we are face to face with the greatest war the world has known and it is the proud privilege of the 'Tyneside Scottish' to be created, so that you will be enabled to take your place, not in a 'contemptible little army' but in a mighty and ever increasing host, marching from victory to victory against the trained hordes of Germany and Austria, brave, brainy but unscrupulous foes, until their hearts are broken, their hopes shattered, their homes and country desolate, their bragging ceased and until they drain the cup of bitter defeat. That is the inevitable, the task you are given to accomplish. You have freely volunteered your services, relinquished position, the comforts of home, the association of father, mother, wife, children, sweethearts and friends, to endure hardship and suffering in the cause of humanity and the defence of your empire. Guard jealously your birthright of liberty and justice, obey those in authority, who are both your friends and counsellors, and who as British officers will maintain the heroic traditions of their predecessors. This is the making of history which will be read by your children's children, by generations yet unborn 'Let the record of the Tyneside Scottish' and their kindred battalions be engraven on its scroll grasp the opportunity and return victorious bearing the title deeds of the name with which we now endow you. 'Heroes All.'

This Christmas Day of 1914 recalls the anniversary of the birth of the Saviour to bring ' Peace on earth, goodwill towards men.' As a unit of the British Army you are sent to save the world from a despotic military tyranny. In anticipation we shall wait and listen to the Christmas chimes of 1915. How far will you be on the journey to Berlin, or will your task be then accomplished? We will wait and see. We have faith in you.

Forward to victory, We will not be disappointed.

TYNESIDE SCOTTISH COMMITTEE

For all four battalions special Christmas and New Year arrangements had been made which would allow half of the men to have Christmas Day leave with their families, allowing the other half to have New Year's Day with theirs. Those still in camp were to be treated to a traditional Christmas Dinner accompanied by special entertainments, which would be repeated on New Year's day. Although recruitment had slackened off in the City of Newcastle, the City was proud to announce that it had recruited some 21000 men since 15 August 1914. The new Tyneside Scottish recruiting campaign was to begin at the Albion Hall, North Shields, which was to be addressed by Sir Thomas Oliver, Alex Wilkie MP, Mr H Gregg (Chairman), Dr Burnett and Mr J Steel. New branch offices were also opened up for the Tyneside Scottish at West Moor, Wallsend, North Shields and in Sunderland.

A further forty men were recruited from the Bedlington district, making a total of 257 men recruited from that area alone. The meeting held in the Albion Hall on 22 December added a further sixty men to the Depot Companies. Steady progress was once again being made and it was noted that Ashington was proving fruitful as regards recruits. To add impetus to the campaign it was decided to add a 'Wearside Company' of men from Sunderland and district, a meeting being held in the Victoria Hall, Sunderland. This was infringing on a successful recruiting area for the Tyneside Irish, but the Sunderland area had not been fully exploited resulting in uncomplimentary letters in the press.

It was later reported in the *Sunderland Echo* on 8 January, 1915, that not only was one 'Wearside Company' of 250 men raised but two. Major Byrne, the Sunderland recruiting officer, then received a letter from the Tyneside Scottish Committee asking if he could possibly supply a further 500 men. Indeed a large number of men from the Sunderland district served in the Tyneside Scottish.

On Christmas Day all three recruiting committees, Commercial, Scottish and Irish, called a recruiting truce to be ended on 29 December, 1914. A day later it was announced that Brigadier General Trevor Ternan had been appointed as General Officer Commanding 123 (Tyneside Scottish) Brigade.

Brigadier General Ternan was at this time Assistant Adjutant and Quartermaster General of the Northumbrian Territorial Division at Newcastle, he was in fact classed as a 'dug-out' having retired in 1907 as a Brigadier General. He had been informed of his appointment by the War Office as early as 16 December 1914 but was unable to take up the appointment until 28 December, when his successor as AAQMG Northumbrian Division arrived. His first impressions of his new command were favourable despite it being a New Army Brigade:

The men in those days were all keen volunteers, most of them miners, a large

Hurrah for the TYNESIDE SCOTTISH!

Left: Postcard for the soldiers to send home from camp. The name of the unit was changed according to which regiment was in camp at the time.

portion of whom were married with families. It was soon evident that here was in my hands all the material for a magnificent brigade, the physique of the men, after the necessary weeding out of the crocks had been attended to, left nothing to be desired and I quickly came to the conclusion that though the bulk of the officers had had little or no previous military experience their keenness to learn and intelligence would soon rectify that matter.'

Commanding a brigade like the Tyneside Scottish did have one drawback, as any one unfamiliar with the working class dialects of Northumberland and Durham can testify:

What did puzzle me very much at first was the Tyneside speech. Many a time when attempting to talk to a man in the ranks I knocked up against a, to me, perfectly unintelligible reply and I must confess that in spite of my best endeavours, though I improved to some extent, I have never yet reached any degree of proficiency in the language of the Tyne.

With the recruiting truce taking place over Christmas and New Year, large numbers of men from the Tyneside Scottish Brigade were allowed home to be with their families. For those left in billets the proprietors of Tilleys provided a sumptuous dinner which consisted of Turkey and Goose with all the trimmings followed by plum pudding and fruit. Yet again Dr McCracken provided the troops with suitable entertainment, Farquahar Deuchar and others provided fruit, pipes and tabbaco and cigarettes and beer.

The cessation of recruiting over the holiday period did not prevent those wishing to join the Tyneside Scottish Brigade coming forward to enlist and it is recorded that at least eighty men were coming forward every day up to 1 January, 1915. Once the holidays were over the raising committee decided on a vigorous recruiting campaign for the Depot Companies which was to focus on the north west of County Durham around the Stanley and Blaydon districts. Sunderland had also proved to be a good area in which to recruit and by 4 January, 1915, a further sixty men there had come forward for the Wearside Company.

Northumberland was also still providing recruits, especially Bedlington, under the direction of Mr C A Nicholls who was manager of the Prince of Wales Picture Hall. Originally asked to provide a company of 250 men, his enthusiasm was such that he managed to recruit a further 100 from Bedlington for the Brigade. For his recruiting endeavours on behalf of the Tyneside Scottish Brigade, Mr Nicholls received a commission in the 23rd Battalion.

Over the next few days recruiting for the Depot Companies was brisk with up to 100 men a day enlisting even though no recruiting meetings had taken place. In Newcastle the Tyneside Scottish Committee had taken partial use of its old HQ at 17 Grainger Street, but it was being shared with the committee recruiting a Tyneside Company on behalf of the Royal Inniskilling Fusiliers. By 9 January recruiting took a drastic dip and although half of the men required had come forward, still more were required and it was hoped that the recruiting meeting at Stanley would boost the numbers.

On Sunday, 10 January, 1915, the Tyneside Scottish had its first uniformed church parade at St Nicholas's Cathedral, Newcastle. Since the cathedral could not hold the whole Brigade, numbers were restricted to 700 officers and men from the 20th and 21st Battalions and 300 from the 22nd and 23rd Battalions. There were no families present although several local dignitaries and members of the committee were, as well as Brigadier General Ternan and the Honorary Colonels of the 20th and 21st Battalions, Sir Thomas Oliver and Joseph Reed. The sermon, preeched by Canon Gough, the Vicar of Newcastle,

was taken from Timothy, III. 17 'That the man of God may be complete, furnished completely unto every good work'.

Prior to the start of the march to the Cathedral the 20th Battalion had paraded at the Boer War Memorial at Barras Bridge where Mrs Henry Armstrong of The Grove. Jesmond presented Sir Thomas Oliver with a Scottish Deerhound as a battalion mascot. The Deerhound was a pedigree animal registered at the Kennel Club as 'Bruce of Abbotsford', whose pups were fetching up to 100 Guineas; later the dog name was shortened to 'Hammer'.

After the presentation the battalion marched to the Haymarket and joined up with the other battalions. From the Haymarket all four detachments, headed by their pipe bands marched via Northumberland Street, Blackett Street, Grey Street and Mosley Street to the Cathedral. After the service men of the 20th and 23rd Battalions were entertained to tea at the Town Hall by the Honorary Colonels.

By mid January the first batches of the emergency leather equipment were being issued, shared equally between the 2nd Commercial, 1st Scottish and 1st Irish Battalions. Finally on 18 January, 1915, it was announced in the press that the Tyneside Scottish Brigade was complete, but this could have been a premature report for 29 January is the date given in other sources.

Now both the Tyneside Irish and Scottish committee's received a request from the War Office to recruit Artillery and Engineer units, possibly to complete the 41st Division. However alarm bells began to ring among the committee members, who realized that they were at the edge of the recruiting limit having recruited 14850 men for the Tyneside Brigades.

A deputation from the various committees headed by the new Lord Mayor Alderman John Fitzgerald went to the War Office to explain the problems of the request. It was explained that 20 - 30000 men were required on Tyneside to assist with government work, mainly in the shipyards and if the War Office insisted on the units being recruited then a drastic shortage of manpower would occur.

By 9 March, 1915, weeding out once again had taken its toll and strengths were given as follows:

Batt.	20th	21st	22nd	23rd	Total
Strength	1301	1314	1315	1322	5252
shortage	49	36	35	28	148

But by this time the Tyneside Scottish Brigade was on the move at the beginning of a great adventure.

Below: Tyneside Scottish church parade, here the 2nd Battalion march to St Nicholas Cathedral, Newcastle.

"SCOTLAND FOR EVER."

TYNESIDE SCOTTISH BRIGADE

"Harder than Hammers"

SCOTSMEN ON TYNESIDE

are given the opportunity to defend their Country's honour by

ENROLLING NOW

in this fine Brigade which is quickly being filled with the **Toughest, Hardest and Best Tyneside Fighting Men.**

AGE LIMIT 19 TO 45

HEIGHT, 5ft. 3ins. CHEST, 34ins.

Central Recruiting Office:

9 Grainger Street West, Newcastle

BRANCHES IN MOST TYNESIDE TOWNS

ONE MAN TO-DAY WORTH THREE IN THREE MONTHS.

GOD SAVE THE KING.

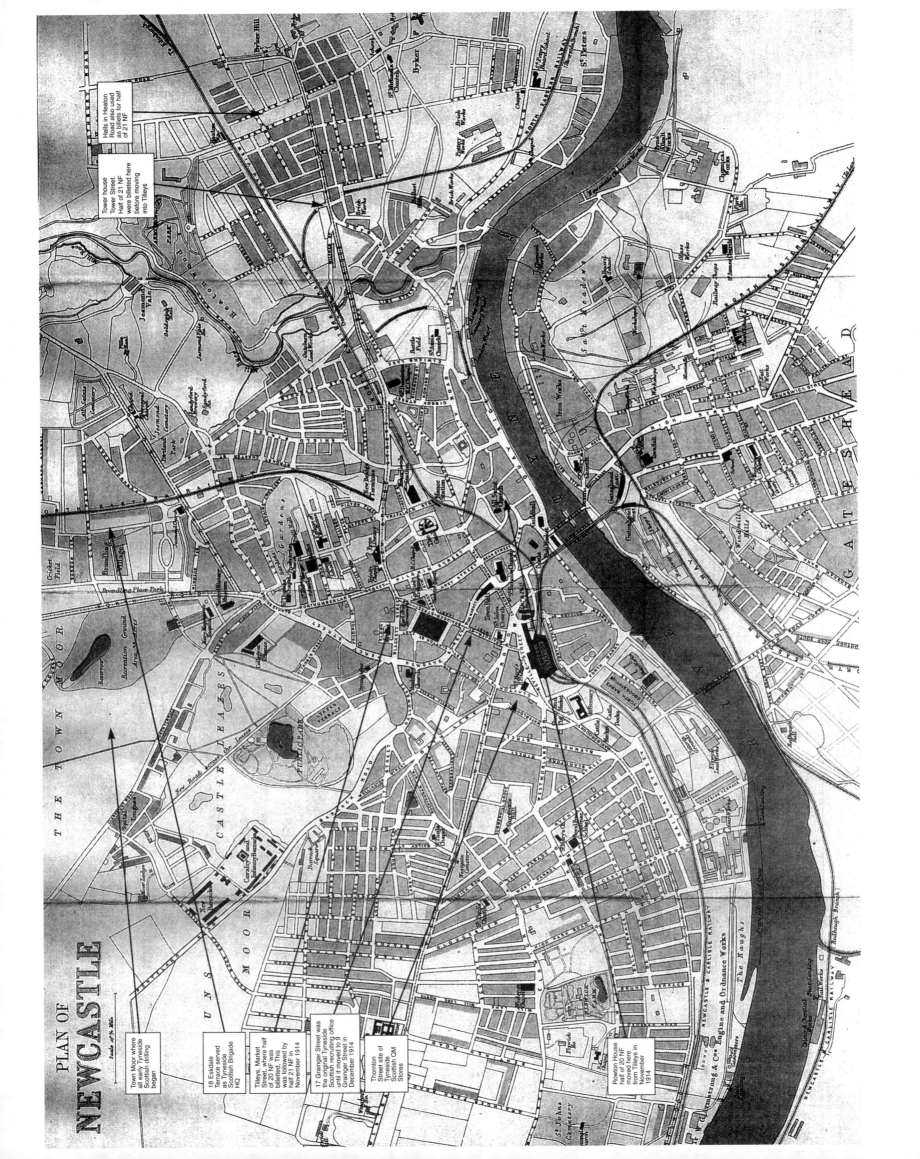

PLAN OF
NEWCASTLE

Scale of 1/2 Mile.

Town Moor where all early Tyneside Scottish drilling began

19 Eskdale Terrace served as Tyneside Scottish Brigade HQ

Tilleys, Market Street, where half of 20 NF was billeted. This was followed by half 21 NF in November 1914

17 Grainger Street was the original Tyneside Scottish recruiting office until moved to Grainger Street in December 1914

Thornton Street site of Tyneside Scottish QM Stores

Rowton House half of 20 NF moved here from Tilleys in November 1914

Halls in Heaton Road also used as billets for half of 21 NF

Tower house Tower Street. Half of 21 NF were billeted here before moving into Tilleys

Chapter Four

Training, Tragedy and Discipline

(Alnwick and Salisbury Plain 1915)

'I heard the bugles callin' an' join I felt I must,
Now I wish I'd let them, go on blowin' till they bust.'

ANON

OWING TO THE MANY difficulties encountered along the way, the training of the Tyneside Scottish Brigade, as with all of the battalions of Kitchener's New Army, was an uphill task. Initially, when the battalions were located in and around Newcastle, the facilities were adequate for only the most basic form of training. But as training progressed, the limitations of being quartered in a large town became apparent. Also being in a city such as Newcastle offered too many distractions to the men from the colliery villages, while many of those who lived in Newcastle were still living at home, the officers trusting them to turn up for training every morning.

Brigadier Ternan realised that the scattering of his Brigade over a wide area was restricting its progress. Once aware of the construction of a hutted camp at Alnwick he hoped to have some, if not all, of the Brigade sent there,

'There was much rejoicing and some anxiety as to which if any of the battalions of the Tyneside Scottish would be lucky enough to get there. I was very desirous of getting my Brigade concentrated in camp somewhere and the possibility of a camp at Alnwick seemed almost too good to be true.'

The anxiety was caused by the fact that the 16th Battalion (The Newcastle Commercials) had occupied the camp or at least part of it since 8 December, 1914. Since they were the senior battalion of 122 Brigade it was thought that the other battalions of that brigade would take up residence before the Tyneside Scottish Brigade.

Fortunately this was not the case and it was with great satisfaction that Brigadier General Ternan learned that the Tyneside Scottish Brigade was

Below: Huts at Alnwick under construction by the contractors Messers J and W Lowry.

47

Above: Infantry training on the pastures with Alnwick Castle dominating the background.

eventually to be concentrated at Alnwick. Orders were issued to the 20th Battalion that they would leave Newcastle and march there. This was seen as a feather in the cap of the battalion, as the 16th Battalion had done the journey by train.

Alnwick Camp was completed to the specific design of the War Office (WO Type Plan BD85A/14 Authorised by Army Council Instruction 352/Sept/14). This allowed for thirty-nine huts, each sleeping twenty-six men. On the completion of the sleeping accommodation authority was granted for the erection of recreation rooms, officers' and sergeants' messes, harness rooms, wagon sheds and mobilization stores. At Alnwick the camp was built to house a full infantry Brigade of four battalions, each camp was eventually given an identifying letter A, B, C or D. The 20th Battalion moved into what would become C Camp, with the 16th Battalion in B Camp and the 24th Battalion going into A Camp.

The following table shows the firms involved in the construction of Alnwick Camp:

Messrs Graham and Hill	Architects
Messrs J and W Lowry	Building Contractors
Messrs Falconer and Cross	Electrical Installations
Messrs H Walker and Sons	Cooking Ranges & Heating
Mr A E Green	Plumbing
Messrs Briggs and Co	Aqualite Hut Covering
Messrs A Robinson & Son	Painting and Glazing
Mr John Jeffery	Carters
Mr T Coxon	Carters
Mr Jos Davidson	Carters
Messrs Smart and Robinson	Transport
Mr Green	Freestone
Northumberland Whinstone Co	Road Metal

The building of the camp commenced in the Autumn of 1914 but the first huts were not ready for occupation until December, when the 16th Battalion arrived from Newcastle. The huts should have been ready by November but after repeated delays the Pioneer Section of the 16th Battalion was sent to help with the completion of the first camp. These delays had a knock-on effect and both the Tyneside Scottish and Tyneside Irish had to send their Pioneer Sections to Alnwick to assist with the completion of the camp.

Prior to the departure of the 20th Battalion from Newcastle, the civic dignitaries gave a farewell banquet at the Mansion House. The Lord Mayor was the first to make a speech, and commenting on the 20th Battalion's march to Alnwick the next day he added 'I am sure that the whole brigade carries with them the best wishes of all Northumbrians', he then proposed the toast, '123 Brigade and Brigadier General Ternan.'

In response Brigadier General Ternan replied that,

> 'It is entirely due to the patriotism of the citizens of Newcastle, that such a Brigade as 123 exists. In that matter mere military people took a back seat. But for the extraordinary hard work of the Tyneside Committee in raising recruits the work of the military would have been no use. The committee has taken on their own hands the labours usually performed by the headquarters' staff. I am astonished to find that the committee have shown such a grasp of military detail and formula. They seem to

Above: Alwick Camp completed and ready to receive the men.

Left: As the 20th Battalion prepare to leave Newcastle the Honorary Colonel Sir Thomas Oliver shakes hands with Lieutenant Colonel C H Innes Hopkins. Between the two is the new Lord Mayor of Newcastle upon Tyne, Alderman John Fitzgerald and looking on from the left is Brigadier General Trevor Ternan CB, CMG, DSO Commanding 123 Tyneside Scottish Brigade.

have assimilated it and treated it as a mere matter of business routine.'

He concluded by proposing the health of the Lord Mayor whose kind hospitality they appreciated so much.

Lieutenant Colonel Innes-Hopkins on behalf of the 20th Battalion said,

'The departure of the battalion has been postponed from time to time and I will not say if this is due to certain gentlemen whom Wellington would have been delighted to hang in the Peninsular.' He then went on, *'Brigadier General Collings has told me that he has met a large collection of doors and windows on the road to Alnwick, It is hoped they will be in position when the battalion arrives.'* He concluded, *'However despite all the trials of training, I hope the battalion when on active service will prove itself not unworthy of the efforts made by the patriotic citizens of Newcastle.'*

In reply to the toast of his health the Lord Mayor said,

'It has been a great privilege to have the company of so many distinguished officers. I trust I might have the pleasure of taking part in the reception of the Brigade on its return to the city after the war.'

He then went on to say it was his intention to entertain the officers of the Tyneside Irish and the Commercials, before toasting Brigadier General Collings and Sir Thomas Oliver, to which he added

'It is owing to Sir Thomas' great efforts that this country is indebted for the raising of four magnificent battalions.

On 29 January 1915, the 20th Battalion, less the advance party which had left on 26 January, paraded outside the Town Hall where it received a civic benediction before departure. To one observer the battalion appeared, 'uncommonly fit and quite capable of accomplishing the long march of nearly forty miles to Alnwick.' The march itself was to be completed in two stages, the first from Newcastle to Morpeth with a halt for lunch at Seaton Burn. The second day would see them leave Morpeth, halt for lunch at Felton and arrive at Alnwick.

Despite the early hour of nine-o-clock the area was crowded with onlookers, many of them delaying starting work to watch the parade. The Lord Mayor, accompanied by the Lady Mayoress inspected the battalion while the Tyneside Scottish Committee members and civic dignitaries looked on. After the inspection the Lord Mayor complimented the men on their soldierly appearance, he added

'during your stay in the city you have conducted yourselves in a gentlemanly manner. As the civic head of the community I wish you God speed and the best of luck and I trust that I will be in a position to give you a warm welcome on your return to the city. All at home will follow your career with a very great interest fully confident that whatever task you are called upon to undertake, you will do your duty in a way worthy of the glorious traditions of the Fighting Fifth.'

In a few sentences Lieutenant Colonel Innes-Hopkins thanked the Lord Mayor on behalf of the battalion for his kind wishes and then amidst the

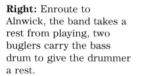

Right: Enroute to Alnwick, the band takes a rest from playing, two buglers carry the bass drum to give the drummer a rest.

cheers of the onlookers, the Battalion Pipe Band, resplendent in their Shepherds' plaid, swung round and to the sound of a stirring pipe tune the battalion began its march.

Unfortunately the weather did not fit the occasion and the battalion marched into a shower of hail, which alternated with bursts of sunshine and rain. Despite this and the muddy state of the road the battalion made steady progress with the Commanding Officer, Lieutenant Colonel Innes-Hopkins, at its head, maintaining the regulation three and a half miles per hour.

The first halt was made near Seaton Burn where the inhabitants gave a rousing welcome. The men were served a hot meal and refreshments and some men received gifts from the well wishers of the district. After a halt of forty-five minutes the men were back on their feet as the column took the road again. It was observed that there was no lack of music on the march, when the pipers rested an unofficial mouth organ band played and at the slightest provocation the troops sang the marching songs of the new armies of the Empire.

By late afternoon the battalion had reached Morpeth where they received an overwhelming welcome from an immense crowd. Not a single man had dropped out on the march although one or two were limping, hence it was an empty medical cart carrying Doctor Neil MacClay of the Tyneside Scottish Brigade Medical Committee that brought up the rear of the battalion. The billets that they stayed in that night were described as luxurious quarters, but unfortunately the billet was not named. Many men prayed for a heavy overnight fall of snow in the hope that they could remain in Morpeth for a day or two.

The following morning the battalion paraded at 8.30 a.m. for the next stage of the march, and at 9 o clock sharp, led by the Pipe Band, they headed north out of Morpeth. Every village en-route turned out to welcome the battalion as it passed by. Flags were waved, crowds cheered and many men had gifts pressed on to them. At Felton the welcome was no less enthusiastic, as the battalion halted on the recreation field for its midday meal, which the local populace augmented with tea, coffee, cocoa, sandwiches and cake. The departure from Felton was described as, 'as inspiring as the march into the village', and that 'they entered and left at a pace that would have done credit to the most seasoned troops in the Army.' More cheers echoed, but these were drowned out as the battalion began to sing.

Above: The 20th Battalion march to Alnwick.

Above: On arrival in Alnwick cooks report to the stores to draw food for their respective companies.

Above: Private Alex Cummings, 21st Battalion, of Morton Colliery, County Durham. He was wounded 1 July, 1916 and discharged in April 1917.

By 4.30 p.m. the battalion had reached the outskirts of Alnwick which was alerted by the chorus of 'Tipperary'. From the direction of the old town came an equally stirring sound as the band and drums of the 16th Battalion struck up and marched towards the 20th Battalion. On reaching the pipe band of the 20th Battalion, the men of the 16th Battalion about turned and led the marching column into Alnwick. As the column reached the railway station the pipes and drums of the 20th Battalion struck up again. The town had turned out in force, and cheers as loud as any along the route welcomed the newcomers to the town. At the head of the battalion marched Lieutenant Colonel Innes-Hopkins, who although getting on in years had marched all the way with his men. Only three men had dropped out on the final leg of the march and the 16th Battalion acknowledged that the 20th Battalion had brought nothing but credit to Newcastle and district.

That night the 20th Battalion settled into brilliantly lit huts, complete with pot bellied stoves that glowed red hot, and after a meal of stewing steak, potatoes and carrots the men settled down for the night. When the bugler sounded 'Lights Out' the general feeling was, 'that there were worse things than soldiering.'

The following day, 1 February, 1915, the following telegram was received by the battalion,

'The Tyneside Irish Brigade sends heartiest congratulations on the success of the battalion march to Alnwick,' signed Mulcahy secretary.

The day after the following was printed in the local press,

'Dear Sirs,
On behalf of the officers, NCOs and men of the battalion, I thank you for your kind telegram of today. The march was a great success and people in Morpeth where we were billeted on Friday and all along the road were most cordial. To have arrived here with only three men in the ambulance is something I am proud of.
C H Innes-Hopkins Lieutenant Colonel
Commanding 20th Battalion
Northumberland Fusiliers
(1st Tyneside Scottish)'

With the departure of the 20th Battalion to Alnwick, the men of the 21st Battalion were shuffled round and some were moved into better accommodation in Tilleys rooms. 21/1381 Private Alex Cummings of Murton wrote to his uncle, Thomas Carver:

'Dear Uncles and Aunts, pleased to hear you are all keeping champion. Sorry for Uncle Jack, I hope he will not be long in improving, I got your kind and welcome letter + pleased to receive one. You must excuse me for not visiting you last week as I have a lot of friends to see, hope it is not long before I see you. I have shifted now as 750 of the Tyneside Scottish left this morning to march thirty-four miles to Alnwick, my new address is,
1381 Pte A Cummings
Tilleys Rooms
Market Street
Newcastle.'

Despite the arrival of the 20th Battalion at Alnwick the completion of the huts still created a problem and it was nearly a month later before the 21st and 24th Battalions were to follow. The Tyneside Scottish camp was not completed until 17 February and to mark the occasion a small presentation was held in the contractors' hut of the Tyneside Scottish

Right: 20th Battalion on parade at Alnwick, 18 May 1915.

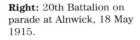
20th Northumberland Fusiliers.

camp. Mr George Ward, agent for the contractors, was presented with a valuable gold watch and chain suitably inscribed for the occasion. Also presented was a large framed photograph of the 180 men who had worked on the erection of the Tyneside Scottish camp. Among those present was 20/423 Sergeant George Kirk of the 20th Battalion Pioneer Section, who had assisted the contractors in their work. On the following evening Sergeant Kirk was entertained to a supper by the pioneers of the battalion at the White Hart Hotel in Alnwick, where at the end of the proceedings he was presented with a handsome oak smoking cabinet by the pioneer section.

On 12 March, 1915, the 21st Battalion commenced its march to Alnwick, preceded by an advance party of 250 men whose job it was to prepare the camp for the main body. Following the same route as the 20th Battalion, the Commanding Officer, Lieutenant Colonel V M Stockley, together with the pipe band, led the 21st Battalion north to Alnwick.

At around 5.30 p.m. on Saturday 13 March, the 21st Battalion reached the outskirts of Alnwick and about one mile from the town they were met by the pipe band of the 20th Battalion, who fell in to accompany the 21st battalion in to town. The Battalion had not gone much further when the bands of the 16th and 24th Battalion's (the 24th Battalion had arrived in Alnwick by train on 12 March 1915) joined in, each band playing alternately until they reached the camp. The reception from both townsfolk and soldiers was tremendous as they marched through the town and it was felt that, 'the 21st battalion were a hardy, well built and warlike class of men, fit for any hardship.' On marching through Bondgate Without, one bystander was heard to shout, 'Are ye no tired', to which came a cheery reply, 'Whey no, we're fit for another twenty miles yet.'

All four battalions, 16th, 20th, 21st and 24th were beginning to settle into the strenuous camp routine when the camp was hit by a blizzard on 18 March which forced the cancellation of training and sports. Training was reduced to lectures on military tactics, which could be held indoors, but the fall of snow did cause one light-hearted moment. Snow had been falling for a day and a half and stopped by the end of training on the second day. Three soldiers of the 16th Battalion were near the boundary of their camp with the camp of the 20th Battalion, when they spotted three soldiers of the Tyneside Scottish. In an instant they were challenged to a snowball fight, a challenge readily accepted by the men of the Tyneside Scottish. Before more than a few snowballs had been thrown however reinforcements arrived for both sides, and a full-scale battle ensued with the Scottish repeatedly attacking the gate dividing the two camps. In the end both sides declared a victory.

Another feature of life in Alnwick Camp concerns the naming of the huts which appears to have started with the huts in the Tyneside Irish camp and spread to those of the 16th Battalion. However the 20th Battalion seem to have been reluctant to join in and to follow the trend, but at least one hut in their camp was named 'The Police Hut', not a popular place by all accounts. The camp of the 21st Battalion was a totally different story, since nearly every hut in the camp had a name, many named after the public houses in the men's home villages such as The Crown Hotel, The Pig and Whistle, The County Hotel, Free Trade Inn, and The Three Horse Shoes Hotel. Other huts bore comic names like, Knock Out Villa or The Crackers Hut, but Simonside Cottage gave away the home location of the men inside.

This helped establish moral and esprit-de-corps among the men and a further moral booster was the contribution in The Alnwick and County Gazette, 'Hut Town News'. This became a firm favourite among the troops, with up to-date news items from the camp, as well as sports and social items. One of the regular features was 'The soldiers letter' addressed Dear Flaxman and signed P Latoon. Many aspects of daily camp and town life were related in the column, liberally sprinkled with the humour of the day. Unfortunately the identity of the writer remains a mystery, but he is thought to have been an officer of the Tyneside Scottish. Camp life seemed to be suiting the men of both battalions, and after a visit by Sir Thomas Oliver to Alnwick he declared,

'I saw all the men of our first two battalions and they looked very much better for their change into the country. Living in good air and getting excellent food, life seemed to be passing quite pleasantly for them there.' He then went on to say, 'There are a few vacancies in each battalion, the committee are certain that there are men on Tyneside who hitherto have been prevented for many reasons from coming in and will now be glad of the opportunity.'

This last comment was made owing to the fact that the vigorous training programme was beginning to show up flaws in the health of the men, not picked up at the medical examination during attestation. Miners in particular seemed to suffer, mainly owing to their physical build and the poor diet that they had.

The training of the new armies has often been criticized as being inadequate, but the training programme was the same as laid down for the pre war regular soldier. Alnwick made a good training ground, as Brigadier Ternan was later to recall,

'I have always looked upon this concentration of the Brigade in such a perfect camp as a huge stroke of good fortune, and as the main factor resulting beyond any other in the undoubtedly very high standard of training and discipline to which the Brigade so rapidly attained. Officers and men had most comfortable accommo-

Above: Captain and Quartermaster Charles Young Adamson. Educated at Durham School he represented England in the 1899 XV that toured Australia. Served in Boer War with the Queensland Volunteers.

Below: Trooper William Wright served with the Hussars in Ireland in the 1890s. He brought experience gained in the Boer War to the Tyneside Scottish.

Right: 20/106 Corporal 'Charlie' Hope, of Gateshead, enlisted in November 1914 age 42. He had previously served as a boy seaman in the Royal Navy and then he went on to serve in the Durham Light Infantry in Ireland, India and Burma.

LEO LEGGE & Co

Below: Constable Richard Dale served with the Royal Irish Constabulary and Newcastle City police, prior to becoming CSM of A Company, 1st Tyneside Scottish.

1889, in Cockatoo Dockyard, Australia. He afterwards joined the Durham Light Infantry in 1893 and served in India for ten years and Ireland for a further two years, before transferring to the Army Reserve. Furthermore there were others like 20/639 Private William Herbert Robson of Hexham and 20/640 Private William Robson of Bedlington who had served in the volunteer and territorial forces and their experience was to prove invaluable. Yet many eminent authors and historians persist in the myth that the Kitchener Battalions lacked experienced NCOs. With the release of some of the soldiers personal documents to the Public Record Office a much clearer picture is emerging, but it may be that the Tyneside Brigades had a larger portion of re-enlistments.

Along with the direct enlistments other NCOs were posted in for training purposes and the Part Two Orders for the 20th Battalion recorded that, on 14 April, 1915, Company Sergeant Major A Short was taken on strength from the 10th Battalion Northumberland Fusiliers to become CSM of D Company. Two days later Colour Sergeants A Copeland, H Henderson and W Redman along with Sergeant F T Watson joined the Battalion from the 11th Battalion Northumberland Fusiliers. They were all allotted Tyneside Scottish Regimental Numbers, 20/1534, 20/1535, 20/1536, 20/1537 and 20/1538 Sergeant Watson was promoted to Company Sergeant Major of B Company. These are only some of the experienced men that are known about, the information coming mainly from family sources, Battalion Orders and newspaper reports.

In an effort to build up the strength and stamina of the men route marches were regularly carried out, usually covering a distance of twenty miles or more. For those taking part it was a case of forming sections in platoons and then platoons into companies, the companies formed fours and then it was a steady tramp, tramp, tramp over hill and dale. Occasionally the routine would be broken by a humorous incident as happened to the 21st Battalion one day:

> *'The company was marching along the country lanes headed by the Officer Commanding, when suddenly he called a halt and the following ensued,*
>
> *OC Coy, 'Sergeant Carr! Who is that man in that field?'*
>
> *Sgt Carr 'Its a scarecrow Sir.'*
>
> *OC Coy 'A What?'*
>
> *Sgt Carr 'A scarecrow Sir'*
>
> *OC Coy 'Nothing of the kind its a spy, a spy! Fall in two men and bring that man in.'*
>
> *This was done and when the scarecrow was brought back for his inspection, the company now in a state of hysterics heard the shouted command, "Take it back, Take it back, the farmer will go mad!"*
>
> *(21/1119 Sergeant Edward Young, The Yellow Diamond)*

dation in magnificent surroundings and the facilities for training left nothing to be desired. Steadily drill was carried out in the park, a range for musketry was available within three or four miles, and later on the extensive moors in the neighbourhood provided ample room for digging trenches and carrying out schemes for attack and defence.'

Another reason for the high level of training and discipline could be ascribed to the number of ex-regular soldier's and policemen among the ranks. 20/8 CSM Richard Dale (His brother RSM J H Dale 10/R Irish Rifles, would win the MM before being killed in action on 21st March 1918) of Killevan, County Monaghan, had served in the Royal Irish Constabulary prior to joining the Newcastle City Police. 23/1338 Sergeant William George Wright of Gilesgate, Durham City, had seen service in the Hussars and during the Boer War served in the South African Constabulary, whilst 22/1653 RSM John Wadge of Kelloe, County Durham served in the Coldstream Guards in the same conflict, as had 20/25 Private William Bond of Newcastle, another ex-Coldstream Guardsman. The Durham Light Infantry was also represented, 21/231 John W Robson of Winlaton had served with the Durhams for two-and-a-half years. One of the most experienced was 20/106 Corporal Charles Hope, who had enlisted as a boy seaman into the Royal Navy in 1887 at North Shields. He was on board HMS Egria when some of the crew mutinied on Christmas Day

C Company of the 23rd Battalion regularly marched for training to the coast at Alnmouth, where Grenfell Arnot, the four year old son of Captain Arnot, was taken to see his fathers men training.

'I was taken on a walk, with my mother pushing my sister in the pram, and I recall the men doing leapfrog, one man in particular was making a back, with blood streaming from a wound on the side of his head, this must have been caused by a boot as someone leapt over him. On asking why he stayed down I was told soldiers had to be brave and not cry when they were hurt. The blood on the man's neck made me feel very sombre and I remember it to this day.'

Captain Arnot and his men also made an impression on the ladies at Alnmouth, for when they marched past a group of ladies holding a service, at a 'seaside mission' for children, Captain Arnot always ordered 'off caps' until the company was clear - a gentlemanly gesture always appreciated by the ladies.

Sport of all kind was a major feature in the lives of the men stationed at Alnwick. Football was a firm favourite with all units in the area, as well as inter-company matches the four battalions and the Northern Cyclists all played inter-battalion matches against each other. Competition with the Tyneside Irish was particularly strong and there were several matches between them, the 20th Battalion winning 1-0 on one occasion and 3-2 on another. The 21st Battalion managed to draw 1-1 on one occasion, but in the return match received a 'severe drubbing' at the feet of the Tyneside Irish. Rugby however seems to have been limited to the 16th and 24th Battalions, with the Tyneside Scottish taking no part in this sport.

The competitors on battalion sports days were always keen and the competitions varied. On the sports day held by the 20th Battalion the results were as follows:

100 Yards foot races	Sergeant Ormsby, *A Company*
120 yard hurdles	L/Cpl J E Philipson, *C Company*
Tug of War	B Company
Quarter Mile race	Private McDonald, *A Company*
Three Legged race	Privates Tyler and Nicholson, *A Company*
100 yard kit race	Corporal Bessford, *A Company*
Half Mile race	Lance Corporal Davidson, *C Company*

Far Left: Lieutenant S J Arnott and his young son Grenfell, promoted to Captain and transferred to the 2nd Garrison Battalion Northumberland Fusiliers, Captain Arnott served in India throughout the war. He eventually commanded the 2nd Garrison Battalion.

Above: Many ex-regular NCOs served in the Tyneside Scottish, probably attracted by newspaper advertisements such as the above.

ALNWICK CAMP.

B. X.

Left: Men of the 20th Battalion at Alnwick in early 1915. Note the 1st pattern cap badge is being worn. Bottom row, first left, 20/1346 Private W R Pattison, second left, 20/1279 Private J Foster, fourth left, 20/1299 Private J W Hills, Centre row, fifth left 20/1241 Private Bob Chilton. Of the four named only Private Hills would survive the war.

100 yard sack race	Private F W Pond, *C Company*
High Jump	Private Campbell, *B Company*
Long Jump	Private Lord
Pipers 100 yard race	Piper McLean, *A Company*
Buglers race	Bugler J Bell *A Company*

In the last two events both pipers and buglers had to play their respective instrument as they ran the course. Boxing matches were organized too, there being no less than twenty-six entrants for the 20th Battalion tournament, watched by hundreds of spectators. Lists of all competitors were published and details of two exhibition bouts given. In the first, Corporal Waugh met Private Morton, the latter being the ex-lightweight champion of England, and in the heavyweight class, Lance Corporal Dixon fought Private Stewart. The Boxing programme ended with a Buglers' contest between Bugler Forster and Bugler Hutchinson, which was declared a draw.

On 21 April, 1915, the 16th Battalion left Alnwick by train for a new camp at Cramlington. On 29 April the 23rd Battalion, under the command of Lieutenant Colonel Gamble, arrived in Alnwick on two special trains from Gosforth and immediately marched into B Camp. On the following day the 24th Battalion left Alnwick to join the rest of the Tyneside Irish Brigade in camp at Woolsington.

The advance party of the 22nd Battalion then arrived and took over A Camp, soon followed by the remainder of the battalion.

The 22nd Battalion had been quartered outside of Newcastle at Newburn with one platoon at Throckley, this platoon is remembered in the following anecdote:

> '*Throckley school was used in 1915 to billet soldiers of the Tyneside Scottish and when they left they were given a tea at the Wesleyan Chapel. Aunt Eva said that the soldiers were no bother in Throckley, they marched and drilled and the children imitated them and of course the lasses loved it and they* [the soldiers] *lapped it up.*'

It was reported in the *Police Gazette* that 22/138 Private Thomas Corner of the 22nd Battalion had deserted on the night of 13 March, however a report in the Football Pink stated that 'He was last seen on guard duty at the Newburn Steel Works at about 9 o'clock and that it was feared he had fallen in the River Tyne.' No further clues have turned up about the fate of Private Corner, who was a coalminer aged twenty-four and resided at 161 Talbot Street, Tyne Dock. If he did fall in the river his body was never recovered.

So now by the beginning of May 1915 the Brigade was finally brought together. The concentration of the Brigade accelerated the need for specialist training as it was thought that it would be going overseas by August or September at the earliest. Every hour of the day was taken up with some form of training or instruction in musketry, signalling, machine gunnery, telephones, sanitation and transport. Luckily each battalion had a first class signalling instructor and so keen were the signallers to learn their trade that they soon reached a remarkable degree of proficiency. The same applied to the battalion transport sections, where the transport officers, who were said to have been 'men accustomed to horses in civil life,' soon brought their sections up to a high standard. Besides the specialists, intensive training was also taking place for the rifle sections, day and night they were trench digging, practising trench reliefs and attacking and defending outposts.

Route marching and physical training gave the men 'a splendid physique' and Brigadier Ternan was to describe the Tyneside Scottish Brigade as a 'truly hard lot'. He also said that their discipline and morale were excellent and that his officers were 'bright, cheery and intelligent and had, reached a high state of professional proficiency. These were indeed high words of praise from a professional soldier for a brigade of men who until recently had been civilians with no thought of being soldiers.

A cottage industry grew up in the Alnwick area, with local tradesmen selling mementoes for each of the battalions stationed in the town. Tyneside Scottish ties were on sale in the Bondgate Hill shop of A R Smith for 1/6p. A memento for lady friends, a specially manufactured brooch was also available. Obviously some of the men made an impression on the local female population, and it was said locally that a few months after the Tyneside Scottish left there was an increase in the population.

It was while the Tyneside Scottish were at Alnwick that fundamental changes to the British Army Order of Battle took place, these changes had a direct effect on the Tyneside Battalions of the 41st Division.

The six infantry divisions, authorized on 5 November, 1914, which were numbered 30th - 35th Divisions and comprised the Fourth New Army, were broken up. The six divisions authorized on 10 December, 1914, which comprised the Fifth New Army, and were numbered 37th to 41st Divisions were then renumbered 30th - 35th Divisions. In the case of the 41st Division, it was renumbered as the 34th Division. The Infantry Brigades were also renumbered using the numbers allocated to the new divisional number, 101, 102 and 103 Brigades. The battalions of 122 Brigade that should have become 101 Brigade were dispersed and new battalions were allocated to the Division. 123 Brigade became 102 Brigade and 124 Brigade became 103 Brigade, The Divisional Infantry Order of Battle now was:

41st Division renumbered on 27/4/15, 34th Division.

122 Brigade dispersed
101 Brigade new formation
    16th Northbld Fus to 32nd Div
    15th Royal Scots (1st Edinburgh)
    18th Northbld Fus to 34th Div
    16th Royal Scots (2nd Edinburgh)
    19th Northbld Fus to 35th Div
    10th Lincolns (Grimsby Chums)
    18th Durham LI to 31st Div
    11th Suffolks (Cambridge Bn)
123 Brigade renumbered 102 Brigade
20th Northbld Fus (1st Tyneside Scottish)
21st Northbld Fus (2nd Tyneside Scottish)
22nd Northbld Fus (3rd Tyneside Scottish)

Below: 18 May 1915, the Tyneside Scottish Brigade parade for His Grace The Duke of Northumberland.

Above: 20th Battalion Transport Section at Alnwick. Note the use of mules.

23rd Northbld Fus (4th Tyneside Scottish)

124 Brigade renumbered 103 Brigade
24th Northbld Fus (1st Tyneside Irish)
25th Northbld Fus (2nd Tyneside Irish)
26th Northbld Fus (3rd Tyneside Irish)
27th Northbld Fus (4th Tyneside Irish)

18th Northbld Fus (1st Tyneside Pioneers) Divisional Pioneer Battalion.

The battalions that made up 101 Brigade were scattered up and down the country and it was not until June that they were brought together as a Brigade at Ripon in North Yorkshire. This brought the problem of the 34th Division being scattered, 101 Brigade in Ripon, 102 Brigade in Alnwick and

Right: Kneeling with the flag is 20/480 John Thistle, by the end of the war he was the Signals Sergeant of the 23rd Battalion.

103 Brigade at Woolsington, with the Artillery, Engineers and support arms even further apart. Divisional training was impossible and was not resolved until the Division came together on Salisbury Plain.

It was during May that 102 Brigade took part in two major inspections, the first of which took place on 18 May in the pasture at Alnwick, where the Brigade was inspected by the Honorary Colonel, His Grace the Duke of Northumberland KG, Lord Lieutenant of the County. Proceedings began at 9 O'clock when the brigade was assembled and put through preliminary movements by their respective commanding officers. The assembling of the battalions on the parade ground at 11 O'clock followed, when each battalion was formed up in columns of close companyies with the battalion bands in the rear. On the arrival of the Duke he was greeted by Brigadier General Ternan and received the General Salute whilst the combined pipe bands played 'Highland Laddie'. Accompanied by Brigadier General Ternan the Duke then carried out an inspection of each battalion riding between the lines, before mounting the dais to take the salute on the march past of the Brigade. The march past was 'executed with admirable steadiness and precision', said one onlooker and on completion each battalion marched back to its respective camp headed by its pipe band.

The whole process was repeated two days later on 20 May, 1915 when the Tyneside Scottish Brigade took part in the King's Review on the Town Moor, Newcastle. All four battalions were conveyed to Newcastle by rail from Alnwick and took their place among 18000 troops gathered for the occasion. It was during this parade that thousands of old pattern rifles were issued to the Brigade to give

Above: Sergeant Jack Barton, as a boy, had won several competions and played cornet solo at the Crystal Palace in London.
Left: The Barton family, *standing left*, Sergeant Jack Barton, *right*, the father Private William Barton, *seated*, Privates Adam and William junior.

it a look of uniformity, prior to this all they had been given was Drill Purpose rifles for arms training.

His Majesty, King George V was accompanied by Lord Kitchener on this review and the King's great satisfaction at the 'extremely soldierly appearance of the Tyneside Scottish', was expressed to Brigadier Ternan. The King went on to suggest to Lord Kitchener that Balmoral caps would be an improvement on the Brigade's Glengarry, the former giving better shade to the eyes. Lord Kitchener then directed Brigadier Ternan to indent for the

Below: 'Jim' the monkey mascot of the Tyneside Scottish. His antics lived on when Mrs Barton made a glove puppet monkey which was christened 'Jim'.

Left: The Band and drums lead a battalion through Alnwick, only two pipers are present. Note either Tyneside Irish or Newcastle Commercials standing watching on the left.

59

Right: 1st Tyneside
Scottish Sports Day.

Below: On the extreme
right is 20/257 CQMS
William Archie Byron
MacDonald, 20th
Battalion, with his
platoon.

Bottom: Signallers of the
20th Battalion and two of
the 16th Battalion at
Alnwick 1915.
Back row left to right,
1?, 2 Wm Milburn, 3?, 4?,
5 'Tiny' Thompson, 6?, 7
Bill Robson.
Centre row left to right,
1?, 2 Ned Mather, 3 John
Thistle, 4 Wm Marshall, 5
Sandy Grant, 6 Cornelius
Bowring.
Front row left to right,
1?, 2 Alf Lord, 3 Rob
Halliday, 4 Hardy, 5 Geo
Lord, 6 Ned Mitchell, 7 G
W Killen MM.

Balmorals, which he did on the following day, but it was months before they actually materialized.

One of the interesting reports written in *The Alnwick and County Gazette*, by P Latoon concerned musical instruments.

'One of our chaps has a cornet and on Sunday afternoons he and his pals go down to the riverside. He plays hymns. It has a real fine effect. The sound seems to hit the smooth water and fly off in a beautiful crystal tone, then it goes rap up against the walls of the castle and comes echoing round the river in distant silvery notes. There are plenty of instruments among 'the boys'. Another goes over the parade ground with an accordion, and so on.'

The mention of the soldier with the cornet is interesting in that a member of the 23rd Battalion Band was Sergeant Jack Barton. As a young boy he had won several competitions and was the youngest person to give a cornet solo at the Crystal Palace in London. A silver cornet he won was mounted in a glass case and for many years was displayed in Silksworth Working Men's Club.

Another character written about by P Latoon was 'Jim'. As a fighting soldier he was second to none, one of the best in the 22nd Battalion, 'Jim' the Battalion's monkey mascot was always in trouble!

'For real 'divilment' in Camp you want to see 'Jim' the monkey in one of his real

anti-German rampages. He can do some damage. We took him out on Sunday for a walk down the North Road to the Lion Bridge. He followed us along like a lap dog, except where he sprang on to the iron railing, ran along it and performed his acrobatic antics on the rails, very much to the amusement of the Sunday afternoon Alnwickers who were walking that way. We are training a jackdaw to talk and there are some very fine canaries in Camp.'

The soldiers must have talked of the stories of the monkey and his tricks when home on leave, for in Silksworth Mrs Barton made a glove puppet monkey that was christened 'Jim'. After the war the antics of 'Jim' and his 'monkey business' were the centre of family entertainment on the dark winter nights in the colliery village.

Tragedy

May soon passed into June and with it a notable increase in temperatures, which soon saw the men training in shirt sleeve order. Training did not slacken for the battalions, but the heat did make the long route marches and general training hot work. Within a short space of time three deaths occurred in the Brigade, which were to mar what was previously an untroubled Camp. The first death was that of 21/409 Sergeant John Nevo Rowan, formerly of Dundee and lately manager of the Western Hotel in Durham City. He was forty-six years of age and had previously seen service in the Volunteer Force, he rapidly rose the promotion ladder and was appointed officers' mess catering sergeant.

Sergeant Rowan had contracted tonsillitis, which in itself was not fatal, but pneumonia set in and this resulted in him being sent to hospital at Armstrong College, Newcastle, which was in use as a military hospital. It was there on 21 May, 1915, that Sergeant Rowan passed away. His funeral took place the following Tuesday, and was reported in the local press as 'an impressive spectacle'. A party of twenty-six officers, NCO's and men of the 21st Battalion travelled from Alnwick by train to Durham to take part in the funeral proceedings. The party included Lieutenant Buskie and members of the Warrant Officers' and Sergeants' mess, including Sergeant Major Hodson, RQMS Stanley, CQMS Burton and Sergeants McDonald, Fraser, Pattison and Swindon. The interment took place at St Bede's RC Cemetery, Redhills, Durham and the Reverend Father Rowan, the deceased man's brother, conducted the service. On completion of the service, a firing party fired three vollies over the grave and a bugler sounded the Last Post, before the party fixed bayonets and marched from the burial ground. The coffin bore the simple inscription 'John Nevo Rowan, Died 21 May 1915 – aged 46 years'.

The second death occurred on 1 June, 1915, and could possibly be attributed to training in the hot weather. 20/1577 Private Frederick Fair was among a party of men returning to camp in the late afternoon, after instruction in squad drill, when he fell down dead on the march. Private Fair was thirty-

Below: D Company, 20th Battalion marching through Alnwick in shirt sleeve order and at ease, carrying large packs. The method of carrying their Lee Metfords by the stock with the butt to the rear is reminiscent of the technique adopted by British troops in the Boer War.

Above: Cooks, orderlies and mess waiters, 20th Battalion at Alnwick.

Below: Men at each end are the Raisbeck twins from Hexam, second left is 23/398 Private Thomas Dixon. He and five other signallers would be killed by a single shell 29 June 1916.

eight years old and lived at 28 Moor Street Sunderland. He had recently joined the battalion, having enlisted on 22 May he had spent a few days on the strength of the Depot Company. A post-mortem was carried out by Doctor C E L Burman, who gave the opinion that Private Fair had died of natural causes. The body was then taken to Alnwick mortuary, while arrangements were made for a mil-

itary funeral in Private Fair's hometown of Sunderland.

Two days later the body was sent on its way home, being laid upon a horse drawn wagon and covered with the Union Flag, along with Private Fair's belt and bayonet, and a wreath. Escorting the coffin was a firing party of twelve men with arms reversed, under the command of Sergeant Major Watson. Leading the way were eight pipers and five drummers, playing 'Lord Lovat's Lament', under the direction of Pipe Major John Wilson and Drum Major James Wilson. A further 200 NCOs and men of Private Fair's company under the command of Captain Laing and Lieutenants Kerr and Sanby followed the procession in slow time to Alnwick railway station.

The whole route was lined with townsfolk and soldiers who had been given a break from training to attend. On reaching the railway station the coffin was borne onto the platform by six under-bearers and then placed in a special carriage. Here the final military rites were carried out as the firing party presented arms before fixing bayonets and marching back to camp. Sergeant Major Watson and a small party accompanied the coffin to Sunderland, where the interment of Private Fair took place at Bishopwearmouth Cemetery.

On 12 June a third death occurred of a more unusual nature when 22/674 Lance Corporal George Gardiner of A Company, 22nd Battalion was badly injured when he fell off his bicycle on the path near the Lion Bridge, after colliding with Corporal Robert Gordon of the 23rd Battalion. Private Gardiner received a large cut to the back of his head and was semi-conscious, when Corporal Gordon and another soldier helped him into the car

Above: 21st Battalion officers taking a meal break, Alnwick 1915. *Seated left to right*, Captain A G Niven, Lieutenant G Robertson, Second Lieutenant Telford, Lieutenant L R Raines, Second Lieutenant G H Buscke. Walking at the rear is Captain S A White who became Battalion Adjutant February 1915.

Left: 21st Battalion junior officers at Alnwick 1915.

Above: Major C J H Gardner 6th Yorkshire Regiment, with revolver, Second Lieutenant V Pinnington, Second Lieutenant H R Telford and an unknown sergeant on the ranges at Alnwick.

Right: 21st Battalion officers on the range. *Left to right*, unknown, Second Lieutenant H R Telford, Second Lieutenant V Pinnington.

of a passing officer. He was taken back to camp but on being seen by a doctor was transferred to the Red Cross Hospital in Alnwick, where he died of his injuries the following morning.

At a coroners inquest on the same evening of his death an eye witness, Sergeant John Riddle, of the 23rd Battalion stated he was standing at the north end of the Lion Bridge when he saw Gardiner riding down from the top of the far peth 'at a big rate'. He thought he saw him lose control of the machine and after he saw him fall off, assisted Corporal Gordon to get him up. The witness did not hear Gardiner sound his bell and the coroner concluded that if Private Gardiner had not struck Corporal Gordon with the bicycle he would have collided with the bridge, the verdict being accidental death

Right: 21st Battalion boxing tournament Alnwick 1915.

caused by injuries received from his fall.

Private Gardiner, who was married, was twenty-eight years of age and resided at 48 Hunter Street, East Hendon, Sunderland. He was accorded the same military funeral as Private Fair, his remains being transported to Sunderland on 14 June, accompanied by Sergeant Major William Bowman and a small party of men from A Company. He too was buried in Bishopwearmouth Cemetery.

Since January there had been a steady stream of deaths among the men of the Tyneside Scottish, at least one a month, although none were as widely reported as the deaths at Alnwick and none as tragic as a death in June. This story was reported in most local newspapers on 16/17 June, 1915, under the heading, 'Tyneside Scots Suicide', followed by the sub-heading 'Muderous attack on Woman.' The facts surrounding the event were tragic and even the police were unsure as to what triggered the event.

22/1618 Private Alfred Hobbs was to die from a wound to the throat on 15 June as a result of a quarrel with his common law wife Florrie Knowles of Chirton. Private Hobbs had actually cut his own throat after attempting to cut the throat of Florrie. She was to survive the incident but Alfred died of his injuries and had he not committed the act of suicide, he would have certainly been charged with attempted murder. Private Hobbs seems to have had compassionate grounds for being at home at

Above: Men of A Company 23rd Battalion Northumberland Fusiliers (4th Tyneside Scottish) at Alnwick 1915. The corporal standing second left is 23/1338 William George Wright, who died of wounds 9 July 1916. Note the soldier with the Boer War medals.

Left: Non commissioned officers of A Company, 4th Tyneside Scottish.

Above: Alnwick Camp. As gardens begin to shown signs of producing the Tyneside Scottish prepare to move to Salisbury Plain.

this time, he does not appear to have been an absentee or a deserter. He was staying with his mother at 115 Bedford Street North Shields and was visiting Florrie at Chirton. What ensued at Chirton caused him to return home in grief, crying all night that Florrie did not care for him.

Florrie then came to the mothers house in North Shields on the Tuesday with their baby, but the quarrelling continued, until Alfred asked his mother to leave with the child while he and Florrie 'made it up'. His mother made an attempt to leave but returned and hid under a bed upstairs. Events happened quickly after that. A witness, Mary Wood,

who lived on the ground floor of 115 Bedford Street, saw Florrie run down the stairs, fall in the passage, get up and run outside. When Mary Wood brought Florrie back she asked her what was the matter, to which Florrie replied, 'Alf has cut my throat.' Immediately Mary was called upstairs where she found Alfred Hobbs lying on the second landing. He spoke a few words then died, a blood stained razor was found on the floor by the police during a search. The inquest found that he had died from a self-inflicted wound to the throat, but concluded that there was no evidence to prove his state of mind at the time. Private Alfred Hobbs, who was

Right: Officers of the Tyneside Scottish at Alnwick Railway Station. *Left to right,* Unknown, Captain F G Trubridge, 20th; Second Lieutenant Ian Campbell, 23rd; Captain Hector Whitehead 23rd; unknown; Lieutenant Robert Dougal, 21st.

34 years old, was laid to rest in Preston Cemetery, Tynemouth.

Tragedy can come in many guises and it was not only the soldier who suffered but also the families, as in the headline, 'Children neglected in Newcastle – Mother sent to Prison'. Elizabeth Sims was 32 years old when she was sent to gaol for three months in December 1914, for being found drunk in Walker Road, Newcastle and for having neglected her five children, who were aged from eleven months to ten years old. Police evidence showed that Elizabeth was the wife of a former miner who had enlisted into the Tyneside Scottish. She was reported to be of drunken habits, and had been told repeatedly to mend her ways. She had used the £3-1s-6d from the Lord Mayor's relief fund to buy drink and was spending 4/- a week on beer. She had previously been found drunk in bed lying with the five children, who were often left alone in the house. The bed was filthy and the children neglected and on one occasion when a police sergeant visited the house, he was so overcome with the stench he had to retire outside and vomit. One wonders what happened to those poor children of the Tyneside Scot and if he was discharged to look after them.

A similar case involved Private Robert Short Temple, who before the war was a bricklayer living at 253 Raby Street, Byker. Having enlisted in November 1914, when he was billeted at home he came home drunk every night, except Fridays, which was pay night, then he stayed out all night. By March 1915 he had been discharged because he refused to go out on long route marches. He did very little work and got drunk twice a day, and kept his wife living in two rooms of squalor. The wife was sick of his behaviour and applied for, and got, a separation.

South to Salisbury Plain

July 1915 saw the first changes of command within the Tyneside Scottish Brigade when Lieutenant Colonel V M Stockley relinquished command of the 21st Battalion and assumed command of the Depot Companyies, which were being formed into the 29th (Reserve) Battalion. Lieutenant Colonel Dunbar-Stuart, formerly the second-in-command of the 20th Battalion, took his place as commanding officer of the 21st Battalion.

It was around this time that 102 Brigade received orders that it was to move to Ripon, North Yorkshire where the 34th Division would be concentrated for Brigade and Divisional training. The Brigade Staff Captain, Wallace Mars, was sent to reconnoitre the area and married officers began making arrangements for their wives and families to move into accommodation in the Ripon area. The landladies of the properties actually demanded payment in advance, when further orders were received saying that the move was cancelled and that 102 Brigade would remain in Alnwick. It is recorded that the landladies of Ripon were not too upset by this decision, nor did they repay the advanced rents.

The new orders called for 102 Brigade to assemble on Salisbury Plain, where along with 101 and 103 Brigades and all the Divisional troops, the 34th Division was to concentrate. The move for the Tyneside Scottish began on 1 August 1915 and eventually no less than ten trains were used to

Below: 23rd Battalion camp at Windmill Hill, Luggarshall, Salisbury Plain.

Above: 21st Battalion Sergeants Mess cooks and waiters at Windmill Hill Camp.

Below: Cooks of 21st Battalion at Windmill Hill Camp.

move the Brigade south.

Prior to the move the Honorary Colonels, Sir Thomas Oliver and Joseph Reed entertained to dinner Brigadier General Ternan and the senior officers of the 22nd and 23rd Battalions, as well as officials up to sixty officers were present from the four battalions of the brigade. The dinner was held at the Star Hotel, Alnwick and the pipe band of the 21st Battalion led by 21/1147 Pipe Major Munro Strachan played for the guests outside the building.

After the wining and dining and toasts, came the speeches and even at this stage the Tyneside Scottish Committee were still pursuing the War Office for permission to wear the kilt. Colonel Johnstone Wallace, the Honorary Colonel of the 24th Battalion said,

'A promise has been given to the Tyneside Scottish that if they distinguish themselves they will have the privilege, when they come back, of wearing the kilt'. He concluded *'when the time of trial comes this Brigade will not be found wanting and the people of Tyneside will share in the*

glory they bring back from the field of battle.'

The Honorary Colonel of the 20th Battalion, Sir Thomas Oliver, backed up Colonel Wallace's claims saying,

'I have made it a point if the Tyneside Scottish went to the front and distinguish themselves they should be allowed to wear the kilt and I am determined the matter should be pressed because I know that when they go to the front they will distinguish themselves.'

He then went on to make rather an unusual claim,

'The King has been very gracious in granting to us in respect of our caps, a distinctive mark in the form of a dice board around the border, which will put us into very much the same position as many other Scottish regiments.'

It is known that King George V approved the wearing of the Balmoral and if he also approved the diced border, then it was never officially sanctioned or taken into use.

102 Brigade left Alnwick on 1 August, 1915, and arrived at Ludgershall, Wiltshire on 2 August and from there marched to Windmill Hill, where they were accommodated in tented camps. The general routine was no different from that at Alnwick, but greater emphasis was given to musketry, bombing and ever lengthening route marches. One additional feature was the inclusion of a Brigade exercise, which took place at least once a week. Postal arrangements seemed to go wrong whilst at Windmill Hill and Private R Turnbull wrote to his wife Mary at 12 Third Street, Wallsend on 3 September,

'Dear Wife
I write these few lines asking if you sent me that parcel and if you have I have not got it yet. So it will pay you to see about it.

68

So write straight away and tell them it has to come to Windmill Hill, Andover Tyneside Scottish, and be sure to put Tyneside Scottish on my letters. So no more now.

Your loving husband R Turnbull.'

During the stay at Windmill Hill, 102 Brigade made the acquaintance of the Divisional Commander, Major General Ingouville-Williams CB CMG DSO late East Kent Regiment, The Buffs. 'Inky Bill' as he became known to the troops of the 34th Division, was a regular soldier, who had previously served in France as Brigadier General Commanding 16 Infantry Brigade of the 6th Division, from mobilisation in 1914 until he returned to England to take up his post as commander of the 34th Division on 5 July 1915. He was often seen being driven round the various camp locations of the 34th Division, in his open topped motor car, chauffeured by his aide-de-camp, Captain J Needham, Northamptonshire Regiment, who had also seen service in France before returning home wounded.

'Inky Bill' was described as having an eye like a hawk, and was a wonderful judge of men, he wielded the axe rarely, but deservedly. He was also rather dynamic and both his young ADCs had a job keeping up with him. Not long after the arrival of the Division on Salisbury Plain, they nearly lost the services of their GOC, when he crashed his car head on into a traction engine. He suffered a fractured skull and was unconscious for days. Badly bruised and shaken, on recovery he could not remember the incident and it was feared he would lose command of the Division, but he returned to duty within three weeks and eventually made a full recovery.

In late August, Lieutenant Colonel Innes Hopkins and Lieutenant Colonel Dunbar Stuart

crossed the channel, to carry out a reconnaissance of the conditions that would face the Tyneside Scottish in France and Flanders. They were attached to Headquarters 149 Brigade of 50th (Northumbrian) Division, at that time serving in the Armentières sector. On 23 August 1915 they both joined Headquarters of 4/Northumberland Fusil-

Above: 21/1302 Sergeant John Finn, Love Street, Belmont, Durham, transferred to 1st Garrison Battalion, Northumberland Fusiliers.

Left: 20/61 Private Jacob Stubbs, 22 West Street, Whickham, transferred to the 2nd Garrison Battalion, Northumberland Fusiliers and served in India.

Below: The 2nd Garrison Battalion, Northumberland Fusiliers, parade in Newcastle prior to embarking for India. Among their ranks are 276 ex-Tyneside Scots.

Right: 20/77 Private John Roscoe, 4 Lane Row, West Cramlington, after his transfer to a Tunnelling Company of the Royal Engineers.

iers, who had been in the line since 19 August. The next day, shortly after a German bombardment, the two commanding officers were taken on a visit to the front line, which had been damaged by the enemy artillery. They remained with 4/Northumberland Fusiliers for forty-eight hours and the visit concluded with an exchange of artillery fire as they returned to England.

But back in the North East recruiting was still being undertaken, Captain Charles Anderson led one particular drive through the streets of Durham City that was well reported in the local papers, as were his exploits as a Sergeant of the Scots Guards at the Battle of Mons.

Weeding Out the unfit

With the increased pace in the training of 102 Brigade since their arrival in Wiltshire it was becoming apparent that many of the enlisted men, through no fault of their own, were unfit for active service.

The problem emerged as to what to do with the 'crocks' once it was discovered they were no longer fit for active service. Fortunately the problem was solved by the formation of the Garrison battalions, which would accept medically downgraded men for service overseas as part of the Empire's garrison.

In the case of the Northumberland Fusiliers the formation of the 1st Garrison Battalion, Northumberland Fusiliers, took place in August 1915. Among its ranks were many former Tyneside Scottish, Irish and Pioneers as well as men from the Barnsley Pals and Sheffield City Battalion. From the Tyneside Scottish 21/298 Private William McQuire served with the battalion in Malta throughout the war.

A 2nd Garrison Battalion, Northumberland Fusiliers was formed in October of the same year, at Newcastle. Among those transferred to this unit was Captain S J Arnot of the 23rd Battalion who was given command of A Company. The battalion sailed for India from Devonport on 20 February, 1916, arriving at Karachi on 12 March. Among its ranks were 276 other ranks of the Tyneside Scottish, who had transferred into the battalion from the 29th Battalion Northumberland Fusiliers, the Tyneside Scottish reserve battalion.

As the war progressed many of these ex-Tyneside Scottish found themselves being re-transferred to active service units. Those who were sent to Malta found themselves serving in either Salonika, Italy or France, while the Indian contingent could find themselves on the North West Frontier or being sent to Mesopotamia. For those sent out to India, even garrison duty could prove fatal in the vile, unsanitary conditions, especially older men whose health was already suspect. Eleven ex-Tyneside Scots died with the 2nd Garrison Battalion and six with the 1st Garrison Battalion. Ironically the soldiers of the Garrison Battalions found that their time for demobilization was not as rapid as their former comrades who served in France, the shortage of troopships ensured that many served well into 1920 before returning home.

The Move to Sandhill Camp

Sadly the fine weather which accompanied the Brigade south began to change dramatically towards the end of September, with frequent rain storms and high winds. These winds were violent enough to level the tents on several occasions and cause general discomfort to the men. In the end the decision was taken to move 102 Brigade to Sandhill Camp, a hutted camp near the village of Longbridge Deverill near Warminster. This move took place on 26 September, all battalions of the Brigade moving by train to the new camp.

While at Sandhill Camp there was a constant battle with the elements, which caused Brigadier General Ternan to write,

'Here we lived through a prolonged battle with the mud. The huts for officers and men were sufficiently comfortable, but to get to one's abode was the difficulty, however as time went on, duckboards were laid down and roads were made and the approach became a less exhausting labour.'

He concluded,

'Longbridge Deverill was memorable to me as a time of wet and mud – what we didn't know about mud wasn't worth knowing.'

In October orders were received that men were to be transferred to the Royal Engineers Tunnelling companies, the Battalion Part Two Orders for the 20th Battalion on 13 October list the following as posted to the Tunnelling Depot,

20/1470 Private A Leighton, 20/946 Private T Walters, 20/77 Private J Roscoe, 20/411 Private M Hall, 20/1126 Private J Ridge, 20/953 Private J Welsh and 20/932 Private T Tatters.

Also sent to the Tunnelling Depot from the 23rd Battalion were father and son Private William and Sergeant Jack Barton, they were allotted consecutive numbers in the Royal Engineers. Posted to a Tunnelling Company they were sent to Gallipoli, where they arrived on 22 November 1915. Jack Barton was later to win the Military Medal with 254 Tunnelling Company, after being posted to France in March 1916. Not only were drafts found for the Royal Engineers but the 34th Divisional Cyclist Company, Army Cyclist Corps was formed, every battalion in the Division sent men to join its ranks. Later, in 1916, when the Company disbanded, many of those who had previously served in the Tyneside Scottish Battalions were re-transferred to the 1st Tyneside Irish. Other entries on the 20th Battalion orders indicated that some men who were machine gun limber drivers were transferred to the 26th Battalion the 3rd Tyneside Irish.

It was around this time that officers commanding the infantry battalions of the 34th Division began to feel that the unreadiness of the 34th Divisional Artillery was the main reason for the division not being posted overseas.

Among the Tyneside Scottish it was felt that 'staleness' was beginning to set in as fighting men can only stay at a mental and physical peak for so long before boredom sets in. It was also about now that 'The Sandhill Lyre' made its appearance, this was a newspaper for the Tyneside Scottish, and it became an outlet for the frustrations being built up at not being sent to the front. This was done through composition and prose of the subtlest nature. One particular piece of verse, which made its way into the 'Sandhill Lyre' was 'The Forgotten Brigade.'

While at Sandhill Camp the number of Lewis guns issued to each Battalion was increased from two per battalion to one per company, Captain J W E Murray was selected from the 21st Battalion to become Brigade Machine Gun Officer, responsible for the training of the Brigade Lewis gunners. Once in France however the value of the Lewis guns was soon to be realized and the number of guns per battalion would eventually reach sixteen.

Not only were there changes in equipment but further command changes took place. Shortly after 102 Brigade arrived in Wiltshire Major J C Campbell handed over command of the 23rd Battalion to Major E K Purnell. The latter only commanded the Battalion until October when he was invalided out, to be replaced by Major W Lyle. The

Above: Duty Piper, Duty Bugler and the Quarter Guard of the 20th Battalion at Number 11 Camp, Sandhill, Longbridge Deveral, Wiltshire, late 1915.

Above: Lieutenant Colonel C H Innes Hopkins and officers, 20th (Service) Battalion, Northumberland Fusiliers (1st Tyneside Scottish).

Below: Lieutenant Colonel Dunbar Stuart and officers, 21st (Service) Battalion, Northumberland Fusiliers (2nd Tyneside Scottish).

labour at the Petty Sessions in Westbury. The sentence was reduced to fourteen days, which he served in the military prison in Devizes.

What was constant during the autumn months was the extremely wet weather, which on occasions caused the men great discomfort during field exercises. During one event the 34th Division had to carry out an attack on a series of trenches in the Sutton Veny area for a party of visiting Japanese officers. Previously the weather had been fine then followed a continuous downpour, which turned the training area into a quagmire. Everyone thought the exercise would be cancelled owing to the adverse weather conditions, but it was not to be and the men of the Tyneside Scottish lay for hours on the sodden ground until the arrival of the Japanese, who were amazed at the hardiness of the British troops.

Brigadier General Ternan was impressed enough to write,

'The drenched and dripping companies having wallowed for several hours on the soaked ground, each man became a moving mass of mud from head to toe. Though the language used at the time was regrettably strong it was however satisfactory afterwards to be informed that the Division had gained great kudos by its distinctly amphibian performance, which had unmistakably impressed our Japanese friends.'

What the men had to say about it though, was never recorded.

Held about this time was the Divisional cross country race, recalled by 21/561 Private Bill Robinson,

'It was at such short notice that not even a trial run was held. Tommy Weddell, of Ovingham, who was a well-known harrier, led C Company's contingent, I was whipper-in to see that at least ten men finished. How the legs had stiffened the day after, when it was easier to walk backwards than forwards.'

It was at Longbridge Deverill that the Tyneside Scottish Brigade adopted its Battle Patch, a piece of coloured cloth stitched on to the tunic in order to identify a soldier's unit in battle. The Tyneside Scottish adopted the shape of a diamond, but strangely though this was positioned to the rear of the shoulder next to the seam of the sleeve. The colours chosen were;

20th Battalion, Red, 21st Battalion, Yellow, 22nd Battalion Black and the 23rd Battalion Blue. The regimental transport had the Divisional sign, a black and white checked board, and a Thistle with St Andrews Cross in the battalion colour, painted on each wagon. Cloth for the Battle patches was procured locally in Warminster or Salisbury, Battalion Quartermasters being authorized to arrange for the patches to be sewn on to tunics, helmets and greatcoats.

23rd Battalion came in for some criticism from the Brigade Staff who thought the condition of the battalion was not altogether satisfactory and it was only after the appointment of Major Purnell that the battalion reached a high state of proficiency. One fact that was affecting both Tyneside Brigades was the high rate of absenteeism. Local court registers give the names of those who were arrested by the police but this does not show the true picture. By far the best evidence comes from the Part Two Orders of the 20th Battalion which show every absentee by name rank and number, as well as the punishment, normally stoppage of pay, which the soldier received. In October, November and December long lists were published on Orders, with persistent offenders being sentenced to undergo Field Punishment or detention in the unit guardroom. The odd man out was 20/1371 Private J Shaw of D Company, who was given six weeks' hard

At Christmas many towns and villages collected money and gifts which were distributed to those serving in the armed forces, Chester le Street in County Durham was no exception and the following letter of appreciation was published in the Chester le Street Chronicle:

'Sir

On behalf of the men in my battalion from Chester le Street, who have received your much esteemed parcel and are unable to thank the people personally. I take this our only course. We wish to thank you very much for your kindness towards the men who have come from your midst to do their duty, and I feel sure that the committee or someone must have done a lot of hard work. It goes to show that the people at home are proud of us and we are equally proud of those who are left behind and to know their hearts and thoughts are with us. We wish to thank them very much for trying to brighten our Xmas and we can only wish you all a bright and prosperous New Year.

Yours Sergeant B Cooke
B Company, 3rd Tyneside Scottish,
Warminster, Wilts.'

Towards the end of the year preparations were made for an inspection of the Division, by His Majesty the King, which would have been the second occasion on which 102 Brigade was presented to His Majesty. Sadly this event never took place owing to the King having a bad fall in France a week before he was due to take the inspection. However as so much effort had gone into the preparation of the Division for the event, the GOC Major General Ingouville-Williams decided to carry out the inspection himself near Codford St Mary.

Captain Needham his ADC was to recall,

'It was a great success and a really most amazing performance. The massed Bands, Pipes and Drums of the Division put up a fine show. The gunners were marvellous, it was impossible to believe that when they had come to the Plain five months before hardly any of them had been on a horse! They marched past and trotted past and grand they looked. The whole parade was most impressive – the whole Division was on parade. Battalions complete with first line transport, the RE Divisional Signal Company, the ASC Divisional Train, Divisional Ammunition Column, Field and Howitzer Batteries RFA. The General was most awfully pleased at everything.'

Previous to this the Division had been put into a flap by a War Office telegram. The Division had been equipped for France, but the telegram instructed, 'Cancel preparations- re-equip for East.' This meant horses had to be exchanged for unbroken mules and the men had to exchange their woollen serge service dress uniforms for the lighter khaki drill dress and swap the steel helmet for foreign service helmets.

Even the troops were convinced that they were due for the off, but not to France. 22/1139 Private Thomas Smith of the Battalion Machine Gun Section wrote to his mother in Byker,

'Dear Mother

I received your welcome letter and am glad to hear that you are all in the best of health. I have ordered a photo of the Machine Gun Section, which will be sent through to you. I have sent it to a house in Heaton because it will save us 6d each and I have given him the address to send it through. We have to pay for them on Monday and I don't know whether they are 2/6 or 3/- so would you send me some money through as soon as possible as I will

Above: Lieutenant Colonel A P A Elphinstone and officers, 22nd (Service) Battalion, Northumberland Fusiliers (3rd Tyneside Scottish).

Below: Lieutenant Colonel W Lyle and officers, 23rd (Service) Battalion, Northumberland Fusiliers (4th Tyneside Scottish).

need all the money I have for going abroad. I think we will next week or the week after be for Egypt. We have received our pith helmets for going out and very funny we look in them. I must now leave hoping everyone is in the best of health, I remain your loving son.

Tom

Very sorry to have troubled you but I could not pay for it as this is the last week we are paid.'

Another who wrote home with news of going overseas was 20/702 Private Gibson Alexander, but his letter gave a completely different destination,

'Just a few lines to you hoping that you're keeping well at present. Mother I was very sorry I couldn't get back again to see you before I went away, but never mind I wont give up. I will see you after this great struggle of a war. I'm sure to come back. Mother keep your heart up – we are going to the Serbian frontier in three weeks time.

Your loving son

Gib   By by all.'

The Division was re-equipped in record time and trains and troop transports were arranged to take the Division overseas. With that the men were allowed a few days embarkation leave, to say their last farewells to their families. There is one well-known story of this period. When a party of men, with their wives and families were gathered on Newcastle station, at the end of their embarkation leave for the last journey back to Warminster, a young Bugler climbed up above the crowd and produced his bugle. He could have sounded any call, but he chose to sound the Last Post, immediately many of the women were reduced to tears and this was regarded as a bad omen by many of those present.

No sooner had the arrangements for service in the East been made, when a further War Office telegram was received which read, 'Cancel everything – re-equip for France'. Then on 4 January 1916 on the authority of 34th Division HQ Order No/1329/A12 102 (Tyneside Scottish) Brigade was mobilised for service in France.

Before the Brigade left representatives of the raising committee made a farewell visit to the Brigade. Among them was Lord Armstrong, Mr Alex Wilkie MP, Colonel Sir Thomas Oliver, Colonel Johnstone Wallace, Colonel Joseph Reed and Mr J R Hall. A dinner was laid on in honour of the occasion by the Brigade Headquarters mess and on the Sunday some attended the Brigade Church of England service. After the service, Colonel Sir Thomas Oliver, as chairman of the Tyneside Scottish Committee, gave a speech to the Brigade and took the salute at the subsequent march past. In honour of the occasion every man of the Brigade was given a printed message from the committee, entitled, 'To the Men of the Tyneside Scottish Brigade'.

Sadly, though, during the stay in the south of England a further seven members of the Brigade had died, from illness, accident or suicide and were left at home for ever, as the Brigade left for foreign shores.

Chapter Five

France, The early days
January to June 1916

*'When you're first under fire and wishful to duck,
Don't look nor take heed of the man that is struck.'*

KIPLING

Embarkation

After a period of continual alarms about the impending departure of the Brigade to Egypt, word was received that the destination was to be France after all. Tropical kit was handed in and the mobilization plan put into effect. All the required stores were drawn.

The first members of the Brigade to depart were the Transport and Machine Gun sections of the 23rd Battalion, under the command of Major Burge, who with Lieutenants Hunter and Nelson along with 106 other ranks, drivers, grooms, cooks and machine gunners, paraded at midnight on Saturday, 8 January 1916 and marched to Warminster Station. They boarded a train for Folkestone, which left Warminster at 3.35 a.m. Meanwhile back in Number 15 Camp Sandhill, reveille had sounded at 2.30.a.m. and at 3.a.m. hot tea had been served out. Then the remainder of the battalion paraded in full marching order ready to depart. Next to leave were A and B Companies with the Battalion Headquarters' element, followed at 4.45.a.m. by C and D Companies. They too marched into Warminster and boarded trains bound for Folkestone. The trains carrying the battalion main party arrived ahead of time at Folkestone and the battalion quickly detrained and marched aboard a small paddle steamer. At 2.p.m. this paddle steamer, accompanied by a destroyer, departed for France. Air cover for the small convoy was provided in the shape of an Airship, which eventually parted company with the ships about half way across the English Channel.

Also parading to depart on that Sunday in January, 1916, was the 20th Battalion, who travelled via Southampton to Le Havre. They left Warminster station at 9 a.m. and arrived at Southampton docks at 1 15 p.m. where for some unknown reason there was a delay. The boat did not leave until 6.10 p.m. Having crossed the channel and arrived in Le Havre at 1.15 a.m. the battalion

.. TO ..
THE MEN OF THE "TYNESIDE SCOTTISH BRIGADE."

On the point of your departure to the Front, in the name of the COMMITTEE of the "TYNESIDE SCOTTISH" we send you this MESSAGE :—

"We are proud of our Brigade: we think it is "second to none. We firmly believe it will add fresh "lustre to the glory of the British Army. Such hard-"ships and sacrifices as may await you, we feel will be "patiently and heroically borne, while your spirit of "determination to overcome the enemy, we believe, will "never falter.

"You will be much in our thoughts and in "our prayers.

"Finally when, your task accomplished, you return "amongst us once more, a warm welcome will await you. "It will be "THE DAY" in Newcastle.

"On your part you are leaving behind those who "are dear to you. On our part we wish you to know "that so far as is possible we want to be a real help to "those here who will be frequently in your thoughts. "Let us know how we can do this. Tell us frankly what "you would like us to do, so that you may feel that those "who are left at home may not be without friends to "whom, in your absence, they may turn. Give them this "message so that they may come to us in any difficulty."

On behalf of the Committee,

THOS. OLIVER, Kt., Chairman.
ARMSTRONG, Vice-Chairman.
J. R. HALL, Honorary Secretary.
JOHNSTONE WALLACE,) Administrators
Honorary Treasurer. } of the Col. Cowen
JOSEPH REED,) Fund.

9 GRAINGER STREET WEST,
NEWCASTLE-UPON-TYNE,
DECEMBER, 1915.

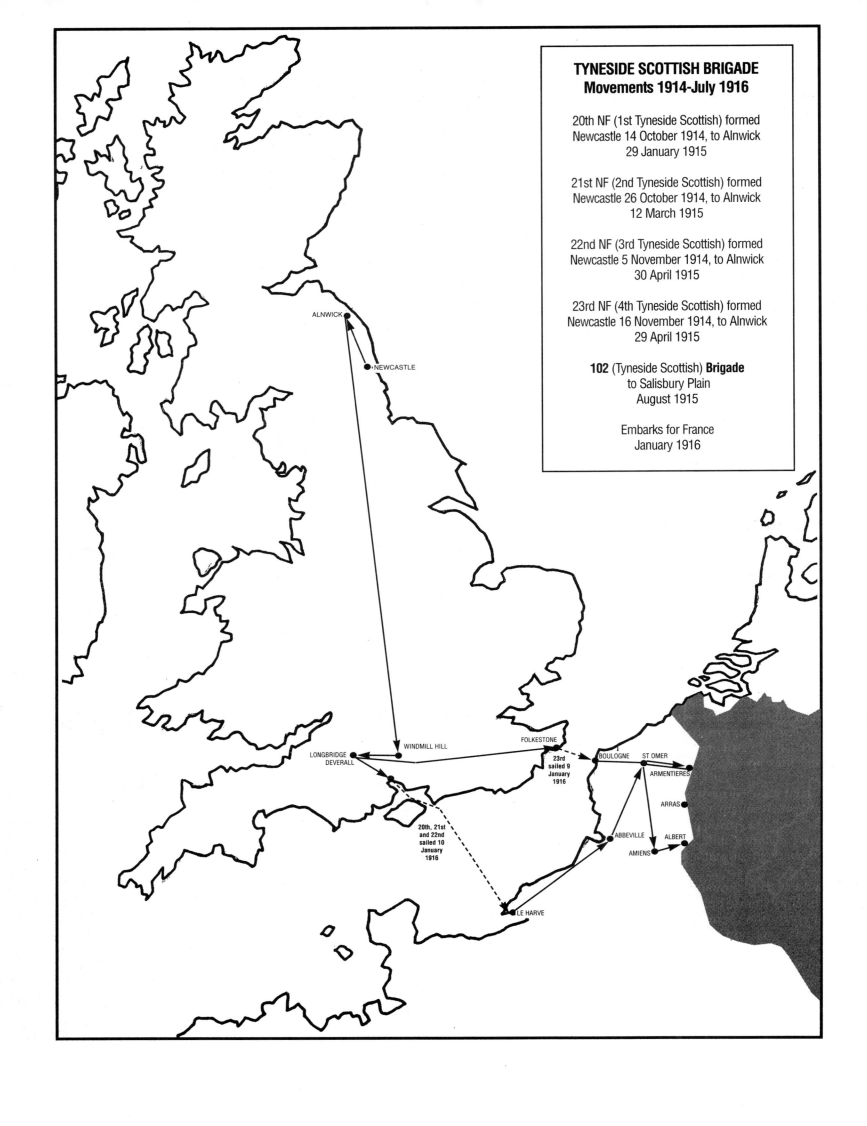

TYNESIDE SCOTTISH BRIGADE
Movements 1914-July 1916

20th NF (1st Tyneside Scottish) formed
Newcastle 14 October 1914, to Alnwick
29 January 1915

21st NF (2nd Tyneside Scottish) formed
Newcastle 26 October 1914, to Alnwick
12 March 1915

22nd NF (3rd Tyneside Scottish) formed
Newcastle 5 November 1914, to Alnwick
30 April 1915

23rd NF (4th Tyneside Scottish) formed
Newcastle 16 November 1914, to Alnwick
29 April 1915

102 (Tyneside Scottish) **Brigade**
to Salisbury Plain
August 1915

Embarks for France
January 1916

ALNWICK

NEWCASTLE

WINDMILL HILL

FOLKESTONE

LONGBRIDGE
DEVERALL

23rd
sailed 9
January
1916

BOULOGNE

ST OMER

ARMENTIERES

ARRAS

20th, 21st
and 22nd
sailed 10
January
1916

ABBEVILLE

ALBERT

AMIENS

LE HARVE

had to remain on board and were not allowed to disembark until 8 a.m. when they marched to Number 5 rest camp.

A much fuller account of the 21st Battalion's travels is contained in the battalion's war diary. The 21st Battalion, Thirty officers and 991 men strong, all wearing their new mobilization boots, left Warminster station on 10 January 1916 in three trains. The trains were allocated numbers and pulled out, and arrived on time as follows:

X986 3.35 a.m. arrived Southampton 6.15 a.m.
X988 5.05 a.m. arrived Southampton 7.30 a.m.
X990 6.20 a.m. arrived Southampton 8.25 a.m.

After resting some time on the dockside the battalion Transport section, six officers and 320 men boarded the *African Prince*, the remainder embarking on the *Empress Queen*. Last but not least was the 22nd Battalion departing at 8.50 a.m. on 10 January and also travelling at two hourly intervals from Warminster via Southampton, to Le Havre, who also made little mention of their journey.

After the Channel crossing the various battalions of the brigade disembarked and were marched to rest camps near the docks, except for those on board the *African Prince*, this vessel missed the tide and had to wait some time before she could come alongside and discharge her load. Those members of the 21st Battalion on board did not rejoin their unit until 6 p.m. As one old soldier was to comment many years later, 'So our Brigade missed the 1914/15 Star by ten days.' (Lance Corporal Tommy Easton 21st Battalion).

Having rested in the base camps it was now time to begin moving inland, towards the front. At Boulogne, reveille for the 23rd Battalion was at 5.30 a.m. but they overslept and the War Diary records that they left St Martin's Camp in a dirty condition. At the railhead, Major Burge with the Transport and Machine Gun sections rejoined the battalion prior to entraining for Blendeques. As the train carrying the main party passed through St Omer the Anti-Aircraft artillery opened fire and members of the battalion were treated to the sight of an enemy aircraft, described as a Taube in the War Diary, dropping bombs on the town.

Upon arrival at Blendeques it took a long time to unload the transport and the guides allotted to the battalion disappeared. With no one to show them the way the battalion had to wait until a Staff Captain turned up and took the Adjutant, along with the battalion's French interpreter, to Wardrecques to arrange billets. The officers were quartered in the local monastery, with A, B and D Companies in barns and C Company in a small village nearby. At Havre the other battalions paraded at various times and entrained. They followed the route via Abbeville, where coffee laced with rum was served, to St Omer and on to Blendeques. But 150 men of the 21st Battalion had to travel with 175 Brigade, Royal Field Artillery and had to detrain at Ebblinghem, not rejoining until 4

p.m. on 13 January 1916. When the battalions arrived at Blendeques they were allotted villages as billets and training areas, the 20th Battalion to Wardrecques, the 21st Battalion marched to Campagne and the 22nd Battalion to Racquinghem, some five miles distant. Training started in earnest now, all battalion specialists, signallers, machine gunners and stretcher-bearers received extra training. The battalion snipers of the 23rd Battalion were given 'Hyperscopes' for their rifles and spent time on the range getting used to them. Various parades and inspections took place, on 21 January General Joffre inspected the 34th Division, drawn up along the roadside on a cold wet and windy day. The men had to wait from 11 a.m. until 2.10 p.m. because the General was running late. The Duke of Northumberland also paid a visit to the men of the county regiment, being entertained at Brigade Headquarters by Brigadier Ternan. On 23 January Lieutenant General W Pultney, General Officer Commanding III Corps, inspected the Brigade and spoke to the men. The highlight of this period of training appears to be when hot baths were taken in a tile factory. Gas lectures, machine gun and bombing courses were held at various Army and Divisional schools and with training progressing it was now time to move nearer to the front and for the men of the Tyneside Scottish to go into the firing line at last.

Trench Warfare begins

The battalions had moved forward to the Steenbecque area in preparation for the instruction in trench warfare, to take place under the guidance of the regular army battalions of the 8th Division. The 23rd Battalion took over Number Four Camp and having recorded that his battalion had left St Martin's Camp in a dirty condition, the officer writing the battalion war diary complained bitterly that, 'This camp was left by its late occupants in a disgustingly filthy condition. Fatigue parties were at once put to work to clean up – a week's work!'

The 20th Battalion was allocated to 23 Brigade for instruction and the companies were allocated as follows,

A Company, to 2/Scottish Rifles,
B Company, to 2/Devonshire Regiment,
C Company, to 2/West Yorkshire Regiment and
D Company, to 2/Middlesex Regiment.

On 26 January, 1916, C and D Companies paraded and marched up to the trenches in the Fleurbaix sector for a three-day tour of duty. Shortly before they were due to be relieved the first casualties occurred when Privates R Kirby, J R Paxton and J W Mavin were wounded by shrapnel, the latter two men were only slightly wounded and rejoined after treatment at the battalion aid post. These two companies were relieved by A and B Companies on 29 January and the following morning B Company had the battalion's first fatal casualty when 20/1215 Private R Armstrong was shot through the head by a sniper whilst on sentry duty.

Above: High command trenches at Fleurbaix a 'quiet part of the line' where fresh troops to the Western Front could be acclimatised. The Tyneside Scottish served here in January 1916.

to have new boots issued already. The companies of the 21st Battalion rotated with B and D going into the line on a very foggy night on 31 January. The following morning the battalion's first fatality occurred when 21/1568 Private Cree was wounded by a machine gun bullet, whilst on a working party, and died the following day. After being relieved the battalion paraded to march back to billets in Estaires and on the way they met, coming the other way, the 22nd and 23rd Battalions on their way up to the line for the first time. We can only imagine now the chaffing and calling out from the 'veterans' of the 21st to the 'new boys' of the other two battalions.

The 22nd also came under command of 25 Brigade and over a four-day period between 3 and 7 February all the men spent some time in the front line. This first spell in the line was recalled by 22/1139 Private Thomas Smith of the 22nd Battalion, Machine Gun Section in a letter home:

> 'We have just come out of the trenches and are back for a short rest, but I think I would sooner be in the trenches as we have a nice big fire in our dugout and there is plenty food for us. Whereas back here we are not allowed a light after dark and we have a lot of trouble with our grub. So you see there are worse places than the trenches.'

On the other hand the 23rd Battalion came under command of 70 Brigade, a New Army formation, originally part of the 23rd Division, but had been exchanged for 24 Brigade. After Officers and NCOs had received instruction, the companies moved into the line, A and B were split among 9/York and Lancaster Regiment and C and D among 11/Notts and Derby Regiment. The men of the Tyneside Scottish battalion took their turn at sentry duty alongside the men of the other two regiments, also taking their turn at wiring and on patrol. During one patrol into No Man's Land, Sergeant Bell received a slight leg wound, becoming the first casualty of the 23rd Battalion. Then during the relief of 11/Notts and Derby Regiment, Private Harrison of C Company, 23rd Battalion, was accidentally shot and killed by a man of the Notts and Derby's and two other men died of wounds they received the previous day. The period of instruction was now over and in future the battalions would have to hold the line by themselves.

After being relieved the Brigade began marching back towards Steenbecque via Estaires, the 23rd battalion recorded these marches as 'very tiring, with a number of men falling out and having to be transported in ambulances.'

Things started to go wrong for the 22nd Battalion, they marched past the 23rd at 9.00 a.m. Then later in the day they passed again, the guides of the 22nd having lost their way, causing the 22nd to march many needless miles. To add to the confusion the 23rd Battalion's blankets got lost and

Meanwhile the 21st Battalion had come under command of 25 Brigade for its instruction by 2/Royal Berkshire Regiment and 2/Royal Irish Rifles. On the night of 25 January, 1916, half of the officers and NCOs went into the trenches, followed by the other half on 27 January. The following day, at 5.30 p.m, the battalion proceeded by half companies into the line. The first casualty to the 21st Battalion was not in the trenches but behind the line. At 12 noon on 29 January, the enemy shelled Battalion Headquarters and the Officers' Mess Cook, 21/1080 Private Johnson, had his leg broken by shrapnel. This battalion convened a Court of Inquiry about the issue and wearing of the mobilization boots. The court condemned the issue of the boots, for these boots were wearing out very fast and over ten per cent of the battalion had had

the men spent a very cold and frosty night. It was not until 7 p.m. the following day that the blankets turned up and in addition each man was then given an extra blanket.

On 11 February, Lord Kitchener was to inspect elements of the 34th Division, namely 101 Brigade, and on hearing this Brigadier Ternan made up his mind that Lord Kitchener should at least see the Tyneside Scottish. The event was recalled in *The Story of the Tyneside Scottish* by Brigadier Ternan:

'I had known Lord Kitchener for many years, having served in the Egyptian Army and in South Africa under him. I was anxious that the Tyneside Scottish Brigade should at least have the honour of being inspected by the great Field Marshal. I therefore obtained permission for the Brigade to line the road by which he would approach on his way to see 101 Brigade. When his car came up to the right of my line I ventured to stop it, and opening the door asked him if he would like to see a fine Brigade though it was not on the programme. Lord Kitchener at once agreed, and got out, walking along the entire front, and was received by vociferous cheers by each company as he passed. He was in the best of spirits, laughing and talking, and said he was delighted with the look of the men.'

However pleased Lord Kitchener may have been, the Corps and Divisional Commanders, Lieutenant General Pultney and Major General Ingouville-Williams were not, and Brigadier Ternan was told

Far left: 22/1139 Private Thomas Smith, 46 Norfolk Road, Byker, served with 22nd Battalion Machine Gun Section. He wrote to his parents, 'There are worse places than the trenches', he was killed 1 July 1916 and has no known grave.

Below: Behind the trenches at Fleurbaix. The trenches in this sector were little more than breastworks of sandbags built up above ground level, owing to the waterlogged ground. When this was taken the York and Lancs were holding the line.

he was in their bad books. But some of the Tyneside Scottish were not bothered about seeing Lord Kitchener, preferring the warmth of the billet, to standing in the cold and the rain, waiting to be inspected as the war diary of the 23rd Battalion records:

> 'We were ordered to parade for Lord Kitchener at 10 a.m. but luckily for our comfort this was postponed.'

After the inspection by Lord Kitchener the Tyneside Scottish Brigade began marching back towards the front line and was initially billeted behind the line in the village of Estaires. Attached to the 8th Division, the battalions were to take over the line in the Estaires sector themselves. Accordingly a conference was held at Brigade Headquarters and the system of reliefs worked out. First to go in was the 21st Battalion, who relieved 2/Royal Irish Rifles in the line on 14 January.

Also going into the front line was the 22nd Battalion, who by 8.25.p.m. had completed the relief of 2/Royal Berkshire Regiment. The other battalions were in support, the 20th Battalion at Windy Farm and the 23rd Battalion at Jerry Villa. The trenches in this sector were little more than breastworks of sandbags built up above ground level, owing to the waterlogged ground. The newcomers of the Tyneside Scottish seem to have had trouble keeping their heads down below the parapet, for the early reported casualties, 21/142 Private Tweddle and 20/1393 Private J T Taylor were killed by gunshot wounds to the head. Among the casualties at this time were a number of men who were accidentally shot by their comrades, and it is very apparent that the standard of weapon handling needed improving.

On 17 February the 20th and 23rd Battalions commenced the relief of the front line, company commanders, adjutants, signal officers and machine gun officers all went forward and carried out a reconnaissance of the front line, the men meanwhile moved forward by platoons and the relief was completed without casualties. Although the men settled in the diarist of the 23rd Battalion noted:

> 'This is the first time the battalion has been in the trenches as a single unit and the men seem quite keen, they were not quite "at home" yet.'

The weather was dull, cold and wet and the enemy artillery and trench mortars were active, shelling the line and causing casualties, knocking the breastworks down, the men having to work hard to keep them built up. It was during this shelling that 20/346 Private J Stewart working in the signals dugout at Trou Post won the first Military Medal awarded to the Tyneside Scottish. When the enemy started shelling and his post was set on fire, he immediately sent all the other men to safety. He then sat at the Morse key sending messages to the front line, warning that the communication trench was under fire. That day there was also a report of the Germans using gas to the south of 102 Brigade in the Givenchy sector, while overhead the German airforce was making its presence felt. Now units of the 8th Division commenced to take over the front line again, 2/Rifle Brigade replaced the 20th Battalion and 2/Lincolshire Regiment took over from the 23rd Battalion. The Tyneside Scottish Brigade moved back towards Erquinghem into billets and began supplying working parties for the front line and the Royal Engineers. It was about this time that members of the Tyneside Scottish Committee came out from England to visit the Brigade in the field. The Brigade Commander, Brigadier Ternan, described their visit at some length,

> 'The members of the committee who came to see us were, Sir Thomas Oliver, Colonel Joseph Cowan, Colonel Johnstone Wallace and Colonel Joseph Reed. They arrived one afternoon in motor cars and remained with us until the following day. Owing to the want of accommodation in the house it was decided that our guests should occupy two little Armstrong Huts that the Royal Engineers had put up on piles in the dung pit. To get to them one had to walk along a narrow, slippery plank causeway across the pit. That evening we had a cheery little dinner, and in view of a projected visit to the front trenches next morning our guests turned in early. It was a dark, wet and bitterly cold night and the journey across the pit was a somewhat formidable undertaking. All went well until one of the guests, who was following the guide, Captain Murray, along the plank, slipped off and with a yell rolled into the unsavoury depths below, followed by Captain Murray, who clutched tight had no chance. I had not left the house and was not an eyewitness to this incident but I gathered next morning that the spectacle presented when the two unfortunate gentlemen eventually suc-ceeded in extricating themselves was beyond words to describe.'

The following morning the Committee Members were shown round the front line trenches, where Colonel Joseph Reed fired a few rounds towards the German lines. Returning to Brigade Head-quarters they had lunch with the staff, before a visit to Armentières and returning to England.

The 34th Division had now taken over the front line, with 101 and 103 Brigades actually in the line and 102 Brigade in Divisional reserve. New equipment such as boots, gas capes and PH Gas helmets were issued as and when they became available and a wet, cold snowy February passed into March.

The Tyneside Scottish and indeed the 34th Division as a whole were now ready to settle down to the rigours and routines of trench warfare. The next sector to be taken over by the Tyneside Scottish was further north, in the Bois Grenier Sector. This was a quiet area where new divisions were given time to settle down and learn the craft of the front line soldier. Word was received that 102 Brigade would now relieve 103 Brigade and arrangements were made forthwith. On 3 March, 1916, the signallers, under the command of Second Lieutenant R MacDonald and machine gunners of the 23rd Battalion, relieved those of the 25th (2nd Tyneside Irish) Battalion in the line. Followed the next day by the men of the rifle companies, the occupation of the front line was not completed until 10.45 p.m. owing to the guide leading A Company losing his way. Simultaneously the 22nd Battalion was relieving the 24th Battalion, the 1st Tyneside Irish, in the Bois Grenier Line, where the trenches were in an appalling condition owing to the prevailing weather. On the plus side the weather did at least stop all enemy activity for the next couple of days. Brigadier Ternan described the front line in this sector as follows:

'No Man's Land between our front trenches and the Boches front trench varied in this sector from fifty to four hundred yards. The support line was about seventy yards in the rear of the front line, and the reserve line was about a thousand yards from the front line. About another thousand yards further back was the lines of the Divisional Artillery, usually posted in sheltered spots mostly in houses or under artificial cover in order to escape observation by enemy aeroplanes. Deep trenches were impossible, water being so near the surface and the trenches therefore were breast works similar to those found in the area we previously held. There were four or five communication trenches leading up from the reserve line to the support of the front trenches. The length of the Brigade front was about one thousand two hundred yards and on our right we joined with 101 Brigade. The country on our side of No Man's Land was very flat.'

The battalions in reserve were located in the village of Rue Marle and it was from here that 22/501 Corporal Andrew Lynch wrote:

'I must say that the weather out here is something dreadful as we have had snow all the time we were in the trenches, by the time you receive this letter we expect to be in again. You will also be glad to hear that every time we come out of the trenches that I make it my business to visit the church either on the first or second night. I must say that it is beautiful inside some of them.'

Other Companies were located forward, one in a position known as the Bois Grenier Loop, and another in the village of La Chappelle d'Armentières, although these latter billets were eventually abandoned owing to enemy shelling, the men being moved forward into the support line. The German shelling was also described to his wife and children by Corporal Andrew Lynch, who wrote on 10 March:

'You will be surprised to hear that I had

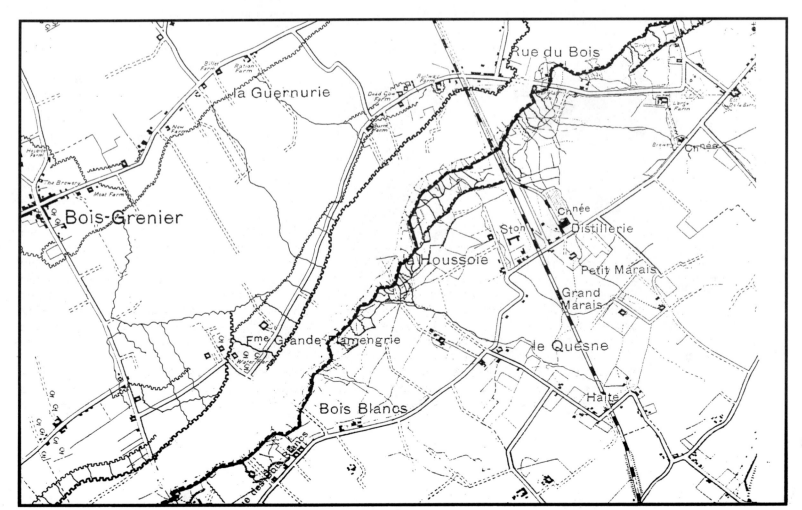

Above: British artillery moving up to the front through muddy terrain.

Below: British artillery position camouflaged against enemy observation.

a lucky escape on Sunday afternoon as they shelled us for all the afternoon and we had a few wounded. But they sent one just at the back of our dugout where me and my men were resting. But there was only one wounded so you can judge how lucky I was to miss such an awful death, as no doubt we would have all been blown to atoms if it had been a few yards shorter.'

Another man of the Tyneside Scottish who was writing home about the Germans at this time was Sergeant George Hood, of the 23rd Battalion, who wrote to his wife and family,

'The Alleman is very quite about here just now, he does not seem as if he wants to fight, but perhaps when he does he will make things hot a little, he has not got a good temper when he starts.'

Reinforcements from the reserve battalion in England were now beginning to arrive, for due to what was known as 'daily wastage' the battalions were now under strength. As many as ten men daily were being killed and wounded and others were being sent sick to hospital.

On 7 March, Lieutenant Williams and six men of the 23rd Battalion patrolled No Man's Land, and the same battalion reported that Captain T A Anderson of B Company had been placed under arrest for being drunk at 7.30 in the morning, his Court-Martial taking place at the Headquarters of 11/Suffolk regiment on the morning of 20 March. Having re-enlisted and served as a Sergeant at Mons with 1/Scots Guards, Captain T A Anderson suffered loss of seniority, his seniority to date from 20 March 1916. He was again court martialled for drunkeness on 16 November 1916 and dismissed the service. He was immediately called up under the National Service Act and served as 73799 CSM 52nd Battalion Royal Fusiliers.

At the same time the funeral of Second Lieutenant F O Dunn took place in Erquinghem Churchyard. He was killed in an accident at the Brigade Bombing School the previous day, when an experiment with a catapult launched grenade went wrong; there was a premature explosion which caused his death.

As well as other rank reinforcements, officer replacements also began to arrive. Captain Amos and Second Lieutenant Smith joining the 22nd Battalion for duty on 14 March and the 21st

Battalion recorded the arrival of Second Lieutenants S De Redder, W J Bourne, T B Spearing, C Bulman, and A W McCluskey towards the end of the month. The battalions in reserve took over the front line, reporting that the enemy artillery was active, with the British artillery and trench mortars replying. Working parties continued but the work was made easier when a light railway track was taken in to use, with mules also employed to ease the infantrymen's burden. Patrols were frequently out, with wiring parties working in bright moonlight in No Man's Land. After some late snow the weather turned bright and sunny, but the spell of the brigade in the line was extended from sixteen to twenty days and the 22nd and 23rd battalions again took over the line of trenches previously held.

Of course the Germans were not the only enemy with which the men of the Tyneside Scottish had to contend, Rats and lice needed to be treated to a constant offensive. There was plenty for the rats to live on and the rat population of the trenches multiplied to incredible numbers.

'At night in the trenches rats in some areas abounded to such an extent that they got under the feet and were frequently trodden upon, and even by day they ran about as if the place belonged to them. They did much damage to boots, clothes and equipment, while the lawful owner slept in them. In one case an officer on awakening found that every one of the bone buttons of his clothes had been chewed off by rats while he rested for a few hours in the night. Many rats were killed but still they increased.'

Thus wrote Brigadier Ternan, who also recorded the attempts to deal with the lice:

'It was practically impossible to deal with the lice; the trenches themselves were full of them. Every man on coming out of the line was, however, marched to the baths especially erected in the area, where he was adequately treated and was given a complete clean outfit of clothing, so that while he was out of the line he was clean and free from vermin.'

Leave was a subject that came up for discussion at

Left: Soldiers 'chatting' hunting for lice in the seams of their clothing. A necessary task for men of all the armies involved in the conflict.

4. Geschütz

Above: German gun crew take a break from shelling British positions.

about this time; Private Thomas Smith of the 22nd Battalion, was writing home to Byker:

'I am keeping all right and am hoping to be just the same when our leave starts. But I don't think that will be for a bit yet as we have to be out here for three months before we are entitled to a leave and then we may have to wait another month or two before our turn comes around. But I have heard that the headquarters staff are first for leave so that I will be among the first to go.'

Sergeant George Hood, serving in the 23rd Battalion, also mentioned this,

'The leave has started and our Company Quartermaster Sergeant is going away tomorrow, I think I will get mine in about three weeks time. I hope I am lucky enough to keep clear of those 'Dirty Dogs' until I get away, but you can never be sure here. You are safe one minute and the next you are blown to pieces.'

For the battalions in support there was plenty of fatigue work to do, carrying stores up to the line, whilst also the Royal Engineers called for manpower. To add to this training was also undertaken, often in the form of the assault course, and those reinforcements who had arrived recently were marched to the rifle range and put through a musketry course, during which they fired fifteen rounds per man.

April started badly for the 21st Battalion; on the first a heavy barrage by the German Artillery was kept up for most of the day, then at 8 p.m. a shell landed near A Company mess and wounded many men. However word came through that 102 Brigade was to be relieved by battalions of the 2nd Australian Division in order that the Brigade could begin training for the coming offensive further south. Australian officers arrived and visited the line and were given lunch at the various battalion headquarters that they were to relieve. In the meantime the Tynesiders were busy returning fur coats, mufflers and gloves to the stores, and as the weather was improving each man had to hand in his second blanket to the Divisional Salvage Company. After the relief was completed, and the Australians were safely holding the line, the battalions of 102 Brigade began their march by daily stages to the training area.

'Our march occupied eight days, and we were very pleased to find that the country round about the villages in which our battalions were to be billeted was very different from the uninteresting, low lying flat lands which we had left. Here we found undulating country prettily wooded and a better class of farm. The weather became bright and warm and life took on a very different aspect.',
wrote Brigadier Ternan.

The daily marches of approximately ten miles a day ended when the battalions reached their allotted billets. The 20th Battalion was quartered in the small village of Recques. It was on this march that Pipe Major John Wilson felt ill and was forced to fall out. When he arrived in the village he went to bed and when examined by the Doctor was then ordered to hospital with tonsillitis. Admitted initially to 102 Field Ambulance and then 104 Field Ambulance he was out of action for nearly a week before being discharged. On his return to duty however, he did not return to the Tyneside Scottish, but was attached to the 25th Battalion, the Second Tyneside Irish. This latter unit had started a pipe band and he was to give instruction to the pipers. But the GOC 103 Brigade, Brigadier General N J G Cameron an ex-Cameron Highlander, did not like the Irish war pipes. He ordered John Wilson to get Scottish Pipes but none were available so, on the Brigadier's instruction, Pipe Major John Wilson fitted a third drone into one set of Irish Pipes, thereby converting them into Scottish pipes. John Wilson returned to his own battalion shortly afterwards.

The 21st Battalion meanwhile had made their home at Nordasques, the 22nd Battalion found accommodation in Nortleulinghen and last but not least the 23rd Battalion made use of some very good barns in Bayenghem. This unfortunate battalion once again had trouble, this time the lorries carrying A and B Companies blankets and kit got lost, then when trying to turn round they got stuck in a ditch. Handcarts had to be taken out and the equipment cross-loaded. The lorries when they were unstuck, returning to the previous billet to collect C and D Company's equipment, not arriving back at the new location until almost midnight.

Training now commenced in earnest, starting with physical training, basic platoon drill, saluting, guard mounting and the like, then working up to company and battalion attacks. A rifle range was constructed in a sandpit, whilst in a nearby brewery a furnace was repaired, coal purchased and a vat was pressed into service as a bath for the men. This bath was at one time hired out to the 34th Divisional Train, Army Service Corps, at the cost of 2d per head. After the training had reached the required standard, brigade and divisional tactical training took place. The Tyneside Scottish Brigade began practising the assault over a trench system

Above: A group of men from the Tyneside Scottish wearing goat skins. These were handed back to stores at the end of March 1916.

that had been spit locked out on the ground. The training was described by 21/373 Private William Hall, to his brothers and sisters:

'Talk about rest they nearly killed us, big days and skirmishing and squad drill, we get no rest, I only wish it was all over.'

Part of the training was route marching; the 23rd Battalion organized this in the form of an inter-company competition, over a ten-mile course. This was won by D Company, who completed the march in two hours eleven minutes, followed by C, A and B Companies in that order. The afternoons were

Below: Tyneside Scots and men of 3rd Australian Division (note the oval battle patch) swap headress. Also present is a member of 18/NF.

now given over to football matches, the 23rd Battalion in particular running a well supported inter-platoon competition.

Each battalion also formed a bombing platoon, which went to the Divisional Bombing School for instruction under the guidance of the Divisional Bombing Officer. The 21st Battalion received word that Captains D J Simpson and E H White, who had been admitted to hospital suffering from shellshock, had now been evacuated to England, but by way of replacement a steady stream of officers were arriving from the reserve battalion.

Move to the Somme

The coming Somme Offensive had its origins in December 1915, when General French had a attended an inter-allied conference at Chantilly. The French initially wanted the British to make a series of preparatory attacks, beginning in April. After a series of meetings it was decided to attack on a broad front, the French with forty divisions on a twenty-five mile front and the British with twenty-five divisions on a fourteen mile front. However before plans were settled the Germans attacked at Verdun in February of 1916, which caused the French to ask the British to take over that part of the line held by the French Tenth Army in the Arras area. The British now held a continuous line from Ypres to the Somme and as the pressure on the French at Verdun increased, so its share of the coming offensive was reduced to an attack with fourteen divisions on an eight mile front.

General Haig allotted the main part of the attack to the British Fourth Army, under the command of General Sir Henry Rawlinson. The plan was for an infantry attack on a ten mile front, which would capture the Pozières Ridge. All along this front the British would be attacking uphill, against strongly prepared enemy positions. For the offensive, General Rawlinson had under his command five Army Corps. In line from south to north there were XIII commanded by Lieutenant General W C Congreve VC, XV Corps commanded by Lieutenant General H S Horne, III Corps commanded by Lieutenant General Sir W P Pultney, X Corps commanded by Lieutenant General Sir T L N Morland, and VIII Corps commanded by Lieutenant General Sir A G Hunter-Weston.

III Corps during April was on the move from the Bois Grenier – Fleurbaix sector to the Somme, and took over the line in the area in front of Albert, astride the old Roman road that runs from Albert to Bapaume. The Corps commander, Sir W P Pultney, had under his command 8th, 19th and 34th

Below: British heavy artillery moving through Albert with the Brasilica and its famous leaning Madonna and child.

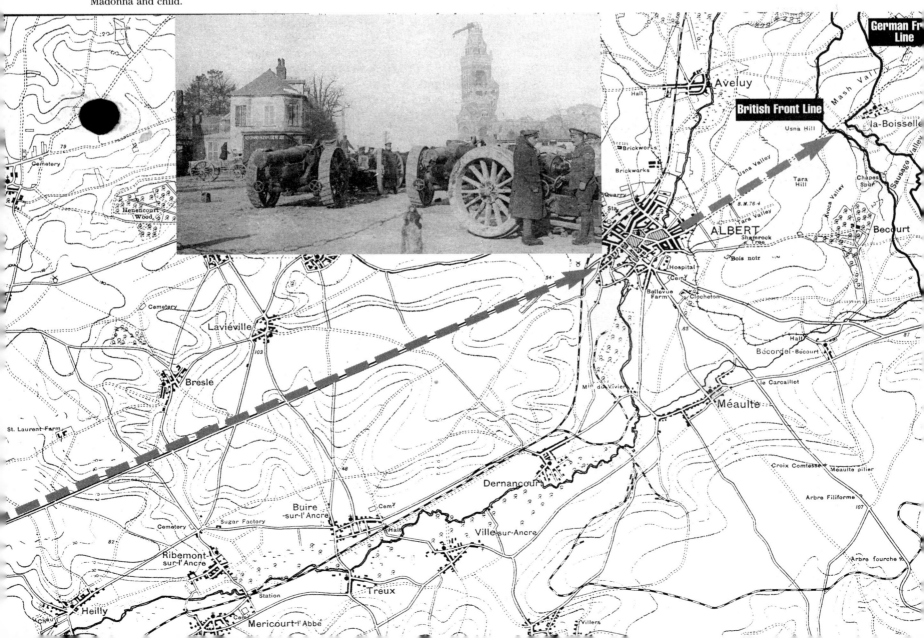

Divisions, whilst further back, available to come up in support, was the 23rd Division. Serving in 34th Division, of course, was the Tyneside Scottish Brigade, who after spending the last days of April and the early part of May on the training area, began to move south to the Somme front.

On 4 May advance parties left for St Gratien to prepare billets for the battalions. On 6 May, the battalions began entraining at St Omer and were transported in cattle trucks to Longau. From there there was a hot and exhausting march to St Gratien, where they arrived tired, thirsty and dirty. This march was recalled by 21/373 Private William Hall,in a letter to his father:

'Well we have had a torturous week last week, we have been marching three days and mind we got some stick with distance, pack and heat and eating rich food, such as nice cake and fruit (dog biscuits) and then we rode twenty four hours in cattle trucks.'

For the thirsty troops the supply of water was quite a problem, about a mile from the billets of the 23rd Battalion was a government water tank, but the battalion had to bring water in carts so that the men could fill their water bottles. This lack of water and the attitude of the French villagers were a cause for much bitterness amongst the troops.

'The last village we rested at, the people there were rotten pigs, we marched twelve miles to it and were dying for a drink and they took the handles off the taps and tried to stop up all the wells, but they were soon stopped at that game. They even tried to charge double on the beer, but the French interpreter stopped them, they are worse than the Germans.'

(21/373 Private William Hall)

Pipe Major John Wilson also echoed the complaints about the French populace in his diary:

'Marched through Amiens to St Gratien – 12 miles – into billets. Rotten place and rotten people, the most unfriendly people I have met in France.'

The billets taken over by the 23rd Battalion in the village of Behencourt were in a very dirty condition. From this place leave parties began departing for England and other groups were sent away on bombing, sniping and trench mortar courses.

The Brigade was now supplying working parties for the area behind Albert; the 21st Battalion had parties of one officer and fifty men and one officer and two hundred men working on different tasks in Dernancourt. It was now that a tragic mystery was recorded in the war diary of the 22nd Battalion. The facts are fairly straightforward; the war diary clearly states that on 23 May 1916 one soldier of the battalion shot and killed himself. However, despite searches of all the War Grave Registers for the area where the battalion was billeted, no trace has been found of a soldier from the 22nd Battalion

Left: 21/373 Private William Hall of Southmoor, County Durham, KiA 3 June 1916 and buried in Becourt Military Cemetery.

Below: Home made identity disc returned to his family.

buried at that time.

The beginning of June found the battalions carrying out divisional training in preparation for the coming offensive. A trench system that resembled the enemy trenches near La Boisselle, was constructed and the battalions trained where possible. The village of Heilly represented La Boisselle, the main road through the village representing the Albert – Bapaume road, this gave the men the general idea of what they would have to do and allowed the brigade and battalion staffs to rectify minor problems with the battle plans. However, working parties carrying stores up to Albert had to be provided and probably as much time, if not more was spent on these work details. On the night of 3 – 4 June the 20th Battalion went into the line and relieved 15/Royal Scots of 101 Brigade, which was to be a strenuous tour of duty when heavy casualties caused by enemy shelling occurred daily. One unfortunate soldier, 20/43 Private C W Ferguson, was wounded in the chest, head, legs, thighs, knees, as well as losing his left eye, eventually died from these wounds at Number 36 Casualty Clearing Station. That night, rations were brought forward by a party under the command of Pipe Major Wilson, who recorded in his diary the terrible shelling they received:

'Sunday morning 2 a.m. 4/6/16, first experience of tear shells, terrible artillery duels during the night. We were twice under shellfire with the rations. Hottest experience I have had in France so far.'

The 21st Battalion also went forward, to Becourt Château and commenced the relief of 10/Lincolnshire Regiment. They too suffered from heavy shelling, but the enemy, intent on gathering information about the coming attack, carried out

Right: 21/960 Private George Anderton, born at Morpeth but was resident at Barrington Colliery when he enlisted. He died of wounds 9 June 1916 and was buried at Heilly Station Cemetry, France.

Below: 20/1279 Private James Foster, born at Cambois and enlisted at Bedlington. KiA 11 June 1916 and buried at Albert the following day.

two raids on their front. The first was beaten off, leaving one dead and one wounded German soldier in Tyneside Scottish hands. However that night; after an hour-long bombardment, the Germans raided the centre company, this was very successful and they succeeded in capturing nineteen Tynesiders. It would seem that some of the bombers of the 21st Battalion actually followed the enemy back into No Man's Land, where they met a stronger party of Germans and were captured there, unable to fight their way back. Among those taken prisoner was 21/1727 Private Charles Coulter who recalled the front line at the time:

> 'We were far too busy piling sandbags and reveting the parapet and keeping our heads down to see much of what was going on but I did see a haccy great belt of uncut wire out in front.'

Another of those captured that night was 21/876 Private George Barnfather, a bomber serving with B Company, who hailed from Holywell, Northumberland. As early as 7 June the Germans allowed him to write home to his wife and family:

> 'My dear Wife
>
> Just a line or two hoping to find you well, as it leaves me at present. You will see I am a prisoner here but going on all right. But we are getting treated all right up to now. There is... of us here so keep your heart up and I hope I will see you again before long. Tell the children I am kindly asking after them. So good day from
>
> Your loving husband XXXXX to you all.'

But among those killed by the German raiders was

R. Lelong, 21, Rue St-Martin, Amien

571. Albert (Somme) — Le Cimetière Anglais - The English Cemetery

21/939 Corporal John Welsh, a married man with six children, who was born in Bishop Auckland, but at the time he enlisted was living at Sixth Pit, Lamesly. Mrs Welsh received the news of her husband's death in a letter from her husband's Company Commander, Captain J M Charlton:

'Dear Mrs. Welsh

I expect by now you will have heard of the death of your husband Corporal Welsh. I write these few lines to express my admiration of your husband. The day previous to his death, he held out with his section against the enemy and by rapid firing, under heavy shellfire, he helped greatly in maintaining the position. I congratulated him on the way he had held on and he replied his motto was "Never say die". I only wish I had more like him in the company and I want you to try and feel that in laying down his life as he has done, he has won the admiration and love of his comrades and officers. My brother officers and myself wish to express to you our deepest sympathy to yourself and your children in your great sorrow.

Yours sincerely

J M Charlton Captain.'

The following night the Tyneside Irish carried out an unsuccessful raid from the Tyneside Scottish lines, and in the ensuing counter bombardment, the 21st Battalion had four officers wounded and five other ranks killed and forty-four wounded.

A Spy in the Camp

But the Germans did not just try raids to gather information, they also seem to have managed to slip some men over No Man's Land dressed as officers of the Tyneside Scottish. The story is related in Chequers by Captain D H James of the 24th Battalion, who was employed as the Divisional Trench Mortar Officer.

'One morning, shortly before the 1st July, a Trench Mortar Officer met me as I was making for the front line in 102 Brigade sector. He was accompanied by a private of one of the Trench Mortar Batteries, and – to my surprise – he jerked out the information that a German spy had wandered into our line and had, through the agency of Private 'X' been captured by an officer of the Tyneside Scottish and marched off to headquarters.

'I questioned Private 'X' who was very excited, but quite definite about what had transpired a few minutes earlier. He was coming down, from his battery to the support line, when an officer (in the uniform of the Tyneside Scottish) stopped him and asked him, "Where are you going?" Private 'X' told him, then the officer asked him where his Battalion

Left: Left: Seated 21/976 Private George Barnfather taken prisoner in June 1916.

Below: George Barnfather later in the war when a PoW in Germany. He is wearing NF shoulder titles.

Headquarters were located and added in an aside, "You're in Trench Mortars, I see. Where's your Battery position?"

Private 'X' was suspicious, he gave an evasive reply and was about to move on when the officer demanded, "Your Battery position, where is? Answer me – where are the guns?"

'At that moment another officer, also in the uniform of the Tyneside Scottish came striding down the duckboards, so he shouted to him, "Oh Sir! He's been asking questions – I don't think he's one of our officers. I think he's acting strange like." In a flash the newcomer whipped out his revolver, covered the bogus officer and exclaimed "You're right! I've been looking for him – hands up! Now march down the trench. Right! I'll take care of him now, don't you worry about him," Or words to that effect. Private 'X' was excited and could not remember exactly because it was all over in a few seconds and the 'spy' was marched off before he had time to collect his thoughts.

'When the two officers had gone a few paces they turned right out of the trench Private 'X' was in, so he hurried on to report to his superior officer Lieutenant 'Z' who had taken down his story and made out a report which he handed me to read. I

asked a few leading questions, then added my commendation on the good work done by Private 'X'.

'As the matter seemed to me important, to Divisional Headquarters I scribbled out a message and sent it on – for information and action, please! Alas – that was my undoing. Some hours later, while on my belly in an advanced OP beyond the front line, I was amazed to see a messenger wriggling his way to me. He brought an urgent order from General Williams to report immediately to 102nd Brigade Headquarters regarding the German spy.

'I went there, but no one had seen or heard of the spy and no officer of the Tyneside Scottish had made a report concerning any arrest that morning. From there I went to other Headquarters and at last came to face the music at Divisional Headquarters where the report of Lieutenant 'Z' had been received – confirming my message about the spy! To add to the complications, the 'news' had been relayed to Army and other higher places, and they wanted news of the body.

'General Ingouville-Williams was very angry – I felt very stupid, it was all rather confusing, but there was no getting away from the detailed report of Lieutenant 'Z' and Private 'X's' statement. However, the very irate General ordered me to return to the front line, with the APM, Captain H A Coombe, make a thorough investigation and report back to headquarters. Well to cut a long story short – we went – we questioned Lieutenant 'Z' and cross-examined Private 'X' in a candle lit dugout. But the more we examined the more the facts remained, one officer arrested another officer, they were both wearing Tyneside Scottish uniforms and they went out of the trench to the right! We followed their trail, which could have taken them back into No Man's Land at the head of the maze of shell holes'.

No further information has been traced about this incident. The question remains whether these two men were German spies, but if they were, they were certainly brave men, knowing they could face a firing squad if captured in enemy uniform.

The 22nd Battalion meanwhile had moved into reserve positions at Dernancourt and Becourt Château, relieving 11/Suffolk Regiment and after one night at Dernancourt the half battalion there moved up into the front line, B Company coming under command of the 21st Battalion. Although working parties had to go on, the 23rd Battalion instigated a court of inquiry on 2 June. Lieutenants Young and Williams had taken working parties up to the front line, set them to work and left them. The two subalterns had then been found in Albert having lunch some mile and a half from their men. This battalion also moved forward to Albert and placed two platoons in Usna Redoubt and one platoon in Tara Redoubt. As the battalion made its way forward they were heavily bombarded with lachrymatory shells, which made everyone weep and delayed the takeover from the 20th Battalion, who returned to billets in Albert. The 21st Battalion was relieved in the front line by the 22nd Battalion at the same time, and the latter battalion reported that the front line trenches were very badly knocked about and much work had to be done to repair them. This was the pattern for the next two weeks, with the Tyneside Scottish first holding the right sector of the front, next to Becourt Wood, then taking over the left sector alongside the 8th Division. Many men of the Brigade remembered this time spent in the trenches in front of La Boisselle.

'We seemed to spend most of our time in Keats Redan and Elie Street carting stuff around. Once we were sent to carry Ammonal tins to the mine shaft.'
(Private J Elliot 20th Battalion)

'We spent most of our time carrying Ammonal to the big mine shaft at La Boisselle.'
(Private J G Barron 21st Battalion)

A steady stream of casualties occurred to the men of the brigade, and on the night of 23 - 24 June, twenty-five men were accidentally gassed as they placed gas cylinders in position in the front line. The weather had turned and rain caused the trenches to become very muddy, this making hard work for those on the carrying parties. Cooking was not allowed in the line, so all food had to be brought up from the cookhouse in containers, three times daily. Large parties for carrying gas cylinders were detailed by the 23rd Battalion and there were casualties among this and the other working parties. By 23 June special stores for the advance were being issued: picks, shovels, bombs, bomb buckets, wire cutters and sandbags, all adding to the load that the individual soldier would have to carry into battle.

It was about this time that a very large shell hit the 23rd Battalion signals dugout. When the shell exploded the Battalion RSM, John Wadge, went out immediately under the heavy fire and commenced to dig out the survivors. Thirty-five year old RSM Wadge, a widower, was a coalminer and came from Kelloe, County Durham. An ex-regular soldier of the Coldstream Guards, he had seen active service in South Africa, during the Boer War. On the outbreak of the First World War he joined the Tyneside Scottish and assisted in the training of the first three battalions, before being appointed RSM of the fourth battalion. For his gallant conduct in trying to save the signallers he was awarded the Military Cross. Sadly he never lived to wear the decoration, for he died in hospital in Woolwich of wounds received on 1 July 1916 and his two young

Above: German machine gun teams and their weapons.

children had to go into an orphanage. Brigadier Ternan witnessed the effects of the shelling of the 23rd Battalion Headquarters and wrote:

'One day on arriving at Lyle's Headquarters I found that a very big shell had crashed through into a deep dugout next door to his own, used by the Battalion Signallers, all picked men, six of whom were killed instantly. This was a very serious loss to his battalion and Lyle was much cut up about it.'

Conferences were being held at Brigade Headquarters for Battalion and Company Commanders to clear up any points about the forthcoming operation. Each Brigade and Battalion Commander issued detailed instruction to the units below them. In the case of 102 Brigade, Operation Order Number 64, issued on 23 June, 1916, detailed the move into the line.

Secret
102 (TYNESIDE SCOTTISH) BRIGADE
Operation Order No 64

1 The following moves will take place on the night of 23/24 June.

2 Six platoons of 21/NF will take over and hold front line and support line from the junction of X.20.4 & X.20.5 to Inch Street exclusive, from 101 Brigade.

3 C Company 18/NF (Pioneers) will take over and hold the crater area [The Glory Hole] from Inch Street to Dunfirmilne Street South inclusive.

4 Five platoons of 23/NF will take over and hold the front and support line from Dunfirmilne Street South exclusive to Keats Redan inclusive.

5 Five platoons of 20/NF will take over and hold the front and support line from Keats Redan exclusive to Argyll Street exclusive and be responsible for the defense of Elie Street and Bray Street to Port Louis exclusive, and Hydrocroft Street to Argyll Street exclusive.

6 With the exception of the move of the five platoons of 21/NF, who will relieve a corresponding portion of 101 Brigade, and the extension of the present line to Argyle Street, all the above moves are to relieve 22/NF.

7 The distribution at 4 a.m. on the morning 24 June will be as follows:

21/NF six platoons holding front and support line,
Battalion HQ and remainder at Bresle.

8 C Company 18/NF holding the crater area.

9 23/NF five platoons in the line, D Company + one platoon A.
One Platoon A Company, Tara Redoubt.
Four platoons defense work Fir Wood, C Company.
Six platoons Sunken Garden, Albert, B Company + two platoons A Company.

10 20/NF five platoons in line,
Three platoons, Usna Redoubt,
Four platoons Sunken Garden, Albert.
Four platoons and Battalion HQ, Tara – Usna line.

11 102 Machine Gun Company in the line.

12 The OC 23/NF to take over command of the front system of trenches on completion of relief and establish headquarters at St Monan's Street.

13 Guides from 15/Royal Scots will meet the incoming platoons of 21/NF at Becourt Chateau at 10 p.m. on 23 inst.

Guides from 22/NF will meet the platoons of 23/NF at midnight and C Company 18/NF at 11 p.m.

22/NF on relief will proceed to Bresle. The billeting party will proceed to Bresle and report to the Town Major who will allot accommodation.

14 The special carrying parties detailed in Operation Order No 32 will proceed to Sunken Garden and will remain there until the night W/X, when they will report to Lieutenant Bowker OC 102 Light Trench Mortar Battery. The Brigade Bombing Company will also proceed to the sunken Garden and move into the line on W/X night

15 Signallers will be relieved between the hours of 12 – 3 p.m. and Lewis gunners between the hours of 3 6 p.m.

16 All further details to be arranged by OC's concerned.

17 Completion of relief to be reported to Brigade HQ by telegraphing the word 'TYPE' and the hour at which completed.

18 The advanced Brigade report centre will be at W.24.b. from 7 p.m. on 23 inst.

19 On night W/X the tails of all battalions will close up and be East of the Tara – Usna Line.

20 22/NF will move from Bresle to the Sunken Garden on W/X night and into positions in the line on X/Y night.

No troops are to be quartered in the town of Albert after 9 p.m. on 23 inst. For this purpose the Sunken garden is not included in the town of Albert. 23 June 1916

Brigade Major
Issued at 6 a.m.
102 (Tyneside Scottish) Brigade

The moves detailed in the above order were duly carried out and the men moved into the front line trenches, which for some would be their home for the next week. All the men's packs were labelled and stored at Albert, officers' kits were packed and sent back to Franvillers, whilst battalion cookers and water carts were removed to the transport lines. 26 June was designated U Day and the bombardment of the German lines commenced, confirmation to all that the time for action was nigh. The following day Lieutenant Leech of the 23rd Battalion was responsible for the release of smoke over the enemy trenches, although it was reported that the wind was unfavourable for the release of gas. The trenches were crowded and conditions for the men were cramped and uncomfortable. At 5 a.m. on 28 June, gas was released towards the German lines, and this was said to have been very successful. The same day word was received that Z Day had been delayed two days, owing to the rain making the ground very muddy, and the attack would now take place on 1 July.

On the night of 29 – 30 June the 21st Battalion sent two officers and twenty men to raid the enemy lines. But they were unable to reach their objective, owing to heavy fire and had to return to the British lines. Further to the right the 23rd Battalion sent a raiding party of forty-five men out under Captain Todd assisted by Captain Bolton, Lieutenant Nelson and Second Lieutenant Campbell, the latter was subsequently reported wounded and missing. At the same time a party of Royal Engineers went out to cut the enemy wire. A covering party was required to escort the engineers and volunteers were called for. Second Lieutenant Percy Hall immediately offered and was accepted, the men of his platoon being eager to go with him. As he led his men over the parapet Second Lieutenant Hall was killed, shot by a German sniper. Percy Hall had been serving in the Merchant Navy and was at sea when war broke out but upon his return to England in 1915 he

Below: Panorama of the battlefield looking towards the German lines around the village of la Boisselle.

obtained a commission in the Tyneside Scottish and gave his life in their cause. The second-in-command of the covering party, 23/1106 Lance Sergeant Andrew Davison of Seaham, immediately took over command and carried out the work, bringing back all his men safely. He was to be awarded the Military Medal for his bravery in the following August. Writing to Lance Sergeant Davison's wife after her husband had been wounded on 1 July, Captain T B Coull said:

> 'The Colonel was very pleased with the way your husband did the work and had he (the Colonel) not been killed he would have recommended your husband for a decoration. Fortunately one or two of us who knew the circumstances are still left, and put his name forward. I write to tell you that your husband has been awarded the Military Medal. I do not know which hospital your husband is in, but I hope he will have a rapid recovery and soon be back with his old company again,'

Lance Sergeant Andrew Davison was one of seven brothers serving in the army at the time. Further to the raids by these two battalions, the 22nd Battalion was also to send a party out. Timed to leave Number Six sap at 11 p.m. they were unable to do so owing to the fact that the British artillery were shelling the saphead. This caused a delay of half an hour and at 11.30 p.m. the raiders, protected by a machine gun, started forward. No sooner had they got going than a Very light was sent up by the Germans opposite, followed by about a dozen more. The raiders must have been spotted for immediately an array of red rockets and flares lit the night sky, bringing down a heavy artillery and trench mortar barrage and a lot of rifle fire. The men of the 22nd Battalion out in No Man's Land took cover and were eventually able to withdraw in good order and without casualties to the British front line. There were, however, two casualties once they were safely in the British trench. It was a source of disappointment to the raiding party that they had been driven back, and they appealed for permission to go again. An officer's patrol of one officer and five men was detailed to:

> 'Examine and report on the state of the Hun wire. Report on the garrison of the Hun front line. If possible enter and secure a prisoner'.

At 1.55 a.m. this patrol left the British front line at a point 300 yards south of the previous attempt and worked their way from shell-hole to shell-hole towards the enemy line. As they reached the German wire they came under intense rifle fire and bombs were thrown right which landed in the middle of the patrol. The officer, Second Lieutenant McDonald, was immediately wounded as were two other soldiers, one seriously. Second Lieutenant McDonald along with one NCO and a wounded man returned to the British front line to get assistance.

Left: Germans in one of their strongpoints, confident that they will be able to deal with any British attack.

Another officer's patrol came forward to try and find the missing members of the original patrol, but the search proved fruitless and no trace of the wounded man or his comrades was found. Once again the enemy sent up the red rockets and flares and within five minutes a heavy barrage came down on the British lines which lasted for nearly an hour.

As the time to go over the top was drawing near the Tyneside Scottish Brigade RC Padre, Father Joseph McHardy CF went forward into the front line and had this to say,

> 'I was in the trenches with them – heard the confessions of all the catholics before they crossed the parapets.'

In the lines of the 20th Battalion Private J Elliot watched one man removing his trade badges from his uniform:

> 'There was a sniper just behind Largo Street, a canny lad from Prudhoe. Ridley was his name I think, but everyone, even the officers knew him as 'The Mickley Vulture'. He would have a bit crack to us, though he was in another company. He collected cigarette cards so we did quite a bit of swapping, he was also a souvenir supplier – really good stuff like German officers' equipment. I remember seeing

him un-pick his marksman's badge the night before we went over saying, "Well I don't want to get caught with this bugger on my shoulder do I". Well I didn't think that was a very good omen.'

The battalions of the Brigade were now in position and the barrage was continuing; several times the enemy put down a counter-barrage, causing casualties to the waiting British infantry. The 23rd Battalion reported that CSM Corbett was wounded by shrapnel just before midnight, whilst in the 21st Battalion Lieutenant Colonel Dunbar-Stuart was evacuated with shellshock and Major Heniker was brought over from the 20th Battalion to assume command. This waiting in the trenches was beginning to tell on the men as it left them time to think, as Private Elliot commented,

'The guns seemed to be all round us, it's then you begin to wonder. As the night wore on we knew it was going to be tough but it was in the early hours that I was scared stiff. I wasn't afraid to die but I didn't want to be maimed or left lying in agony. I was more scared of the heavy guns than of going over, those big guns would be turned on us.'

As the night wore on the 22nd Battalion reported that as well as Second Lieutenant McDonald wounded on the patrol, they had four other ranks killed, twelve wounded and three missing. Thus 30 June passed into history and the dawn rose on that sad historic day the First of July 1916.

Below: German trench mortar crew. Their constant bombardments ensured that the British army experienced a daily 'wastage' in dead and wounded.

Chapter Six

The First of July 1916

'A bomber shouted, 'I've been shot in the Arse',
Billy Grant called back 'Haven't we all.'

PRIVATE J ELLIOT 20TH BATTALION

MAJOR GENERAL Ingouville-Williams had developed a simple and straightforward plan of attack for the 34th Division. The Division held the Front Line with 101 Brigade on the right and 102 (Tyneside Scottish) Brigade on the left; in support along the Tara - Usna line were the four battalions of 103 (Tyneside Irish) Brigade. The divisional attack would be in four columns; each column made up of two battalions of the leading brigade and one battalion of 103 Brigade. The objectives for the 34th Division were as follows:

First Objective, the German front line system, comprising four successive lines of trenches. Marked on maps as the Green Line. This required an advance of two thousand yards and it was to be reached forty-eight minutes after zero hour.

Second Objective, the enemy intermediate line known as the Kaisergraben in front of Pozières and Contalmaison villages, marked on maps as the Yellow Line. This line was to be reached at 8.58 a.m. At this point 101 and 102 Brigades would halt and start to consolidate. 103 Brigade would then pass through the leading brigades and move on and take the;

Third Objective, the consolidation of a zone of defence to the east of Contalmaison and then facing east and then extending northwards to the outskirts of Pozières. Marked on maps as the Violet Line. To aid the men in keeping direction as they began to advance, white tapes were laid in No Man's Land.

The German front line had been under artillery and trench mortar fire since 24 June and the Bavarians opposite were reporting that trenches, barbed wire entanglements, deep dugouts as well as the best observation posts had all suffered badly and had been speedily demolished. It was only with utmost effort that the Bavarian infantrymen could keep their trenches and dugouts clear. But those Bavarians were well drilled at manning their posts

and when the time came it would be a race between them and the advancing British infantry to be first to the German parapet. The British had been told to advance at a walk and furthermore they would be heavily weighed down with their personal equipment. The Operation Order for the 23rd Battalion written by Lieutenant Colonel W Lyle lists in paragraph 6 the equipment to be carried:

6. Dress and Equipment

Every man will carry.

Rifle, Bayonet and equipment.

2 extra bandoliers of ammunition.

2 Mills grenades.

1 Iron ration and rations for the day of the assault.

Haversack and waterproof cape.

Four sandbags.

2 Gas helmets.

Either a pick or a shovel.

Full water bottle.

Mess tins to be carried in the haversack.

Bomb buckets, Bomb waistcoats and wire cutters to be distributed under supervision of OC Companies.

Bombers to carry equipment ammunition only.

Added to this, a yellow triangle was to be fastened to each man's back, to aid the artillery observation officers.

To further slow the men down they were crossing broken ground strewn with barbed wire. Those in the second and other waves also had to cross the British trenches. In many places these trenches had been bridged, but the bridges acted as a funnel and became aiming points for the German machine gunners.

The village of La Boisselle was a strong point in the German line which would be costly to take by a frontal assault and the plans for its capture had to take this into account.

The plan for the Tyneside Scottish Brigade was

Above: Major General Ingouville-Williams commander of 34th Division.

Below: A German listening post tapping in to British telephone communications. In La Boisselle the Germans had a listening post, code named 'Moritz'; the members of the listening team were very alert and picked up a message as it was transmitted to the Tyneside Scottish in the front line.

that the right column, the 21st Battalion, followed by the 22nd Battalion, with the 26th (3rd Tyneside Irish) Battalion in support would pass south of La Boisselle. The left column comprised the 20th Battalion, followed by the 23rd Battalion, with the 25th (2nd Tyneside Irish) Battalion in support and would pass to the north of the village. A Brigade Bombing Company had been formed specially for the storming of the village and so when the columns had passed the village those detailed for its capture would turn and try to take the village from the sides and rear. In the early hours of the morning the Army Commander's message of good wishes for the coming attack arrived at Brigade Headquarters. This message had to be passed on to the forward battalions. The message should have gone by runner, but one of the Brigade Staff Officers worried that the front line troops would not receive the message, decided to send it by telephone or telegraph. In La Boisselle the Germans had a listening post, code named 'Moritz'; the members of the listening team were very alert and picked up the message as it was transmitted to the Tyneside Scottish in the front line. At 3.45 a.m. German time, on the morning of 1 July 1916, the German 56th Infantry Brigade, from its battle headquarters in Contalmaison reported to Headquarters 28th Reserve Division a fragment of an order from the 34th British Division overheard by the listening post 'Moritz' at the tip of La Boisselle. 'The infantry is to stubbornly defend each yard of ground that it has gained. It is brilliant artillery behind you.' This order, apparently identified as coming from Fourth Army, confirmed to the Germans that the general attack would be delivered that day.

Furthermore German intelligence had identified the 34th Division and its Brigades, and the fact that three brigades would be used in the attack at La Boisselle.

Word was quickly passed to the machine gun crews of Bavarian Reserve Infantry Regiments 110 and 111 and they were ready and waiting for the British barrage to lift.

Back in the British lines men were also waiting for the barrage to lift. Writing to his father in Newcastle, Captain Herries of the 22nd Battalion said:

'We moved up into the reserve line on the Friday night. On the way we passed dozens of our batteries, all of them firing as hard as they could go. The din was terrific, so great in fact was the noise that although twenty feet down in dugouts we were unable to sleep. During the day we were able to snatch a little sleep, but on the whole everyone was so excited that it was time to move down to our battle positions

before we at last realised that we were at last under way. I was in command of my old platoon with three others from other companies and our special place for the night was a narrow trench about three feet deep and 500 yards from our front line. Again owing to the din and general discomfort there was no sleep for us. About dawn we had tea and biscuits which freshened us up a lot.'

The time for the assault to begin was very close now. With five minutes to go the men were standing waiting for the mines at Y Sap and Lochnagar to explode,

Private Elliot of the 20th Battalion recalled:

'At five minutes to go we were to stand at the bridge ready for the mine to blow.... We had short ladders. Then someone called NOW! Get hold of the parapet boys, she's going up.'

Above: Machine gunners moving up to assist in the attack at La Boisselle.

Below: British carrying party moving up in front of La Boisselle.

Above: German trench which ran through the village cemetery.

Below: German troops keep a watch on the British lines with the aid of a mirror.

Just along the line to the right Private J Barron of the 21st Battalion was also standing waiting and remarked:

'At five minutes to we were to stand beside the short ladders and get right under the parapet ready for the mine to go up.'

Close behind Private Barron's position was Captain Herries with his men of the 22nd Battalion who wrote:

'As the time approached I passed the word along for the men to get their hats on and for the pipes to get going.' As in the other Scottish battalions of the 34th Division and also the Tyneside Irish, the Pipers would be leading their respective companies 'over the top'.

As the morning sun warmed the ground and broke through the mist, rays of sunshine lit the battlefield the British barrage reached a crescendo. At exactly 7.28 a.m. the mines were fired and for some minutes soil, stones and debris rained down on the surrounding area. The Germans had spotted the mine at Y Sap and the area had been evacuated but the Lochnagar mine caused many casualties to the defenders. 110th Regiment reported that half of the 7th Company had become casualties, the 5th Company numbered only one NCO and fifteen men and the 2nd Company was completely wiped out. However these surviving defenders were to make the British infantry pay dearly for any ground that they captured. They waited with their machine guns, silent, watching for the approach of the British infantry.

The explosion of the mines was observed by Brigadier General Ternan from an observation post inside the British Lines on the forward slope of the Tara Usna ridge:

'As the watches marked the half hour the two huge mines on the flanks of La Boisselle exploded with a concussion that shook the ground for miles around, and the attack began. The mine on the right had been charged with thirty tons of ammonal, and that on the left with twenty tons, so that the effect of the explosion was terrific. The bottom of the valley was quickly obliterated from our view by the dust thrown up and the smoke of countless shells, so that one could see little or nothing except the movement of the companies of the reserve Brigade as they went forward.'

Also watching as the mines exploded was Captain Herries who recorded the following:

'Well, at 7.28 prompt the mine opposite us was exploded and we witnessed a most wonderful spectacle. A huge column of chalk was thrown up several hundred feet into the air and came down in a beautiful white cascade. By that time we were out of our own particular trench and passed over others very rapidly.'

Over to the left, with the 20th Battalion, Private Elliot also was ready to go:

'We had to wait to let the debris fall. We only had these narrow places to go through and the fear was that if we weren't quick about it the Germans might reach the mine first.'

These narrow gaps in the wire were also recalled by Private Barron:

'We only had narrow places to go

through and by the time the debris fell, the Germans had reached the mine.'

Company and Platoon commanders blew their whistles, NCOs shouted and as the leading companies left their trenches, that brave band of unarmed men, the Pipers, commenced to play. Watching from positions inside the lines of the 8th Division, most likely 2/Middlesex Regiment, an unnamed officer reported:

'The pluckiest thing I ever saw was a piper of the Tyneside Scottish playing his company over the parapet in the attack on the German trenches near Albert. The Tynesiders were on our right, and as their officers gave the signal to advance I saw the piper – I think he was the Pipe Major [20/290 Piper Major John Wilson] – jump out of the trench and march straight over No Man's Land towards the German lines. The tremendous rattle of machine gun and rifle fire, which the enemy at once opened on us and completely drowned the sound of his pipes. But it was obvious he was playing as though he would burst the bag, and just faintly through the din we heard the mighty shout his comrades gave as they swarmed after him. How he escaped death I can't understand for the ground was literally ploughed up by the hail of bullets. But he seemed to bear a charmed life and the last glimpse I had of him, as we too dashed out, showed him still marching erect, playing furiously, and quite regardless of the flying bullets and the men dropping all around him.'

Of the pipers of the 20th Battalion, Private Elliot said that:

'I never heard the pipes but I did see poor 'Aggy' Fife. [20/237 Lance Corporal Piper, Garnet Wolsley Fyfe, the uncle of Pipe Major Wilson.] *He was riddled with bullets, writhing and screaming. Another lad was just kneeling, his head thrown right back. Bullets were just slapping into him knocking great bloody chunks off his body.'*

21/558 Piper George Griffiths was waiting for the order to advance and gave this account of what happened:

'At the given signal we jumped from our trenches and struck up our pipes. It was like all hell let loose. I got so far and then got caught on some barbed wire. After I got disentangled I had to abandon my pipes and take up my rifle. Fellow piper Willie Scott, a shipyard worker from Elswick in Newcastle, was still ahead of me playing. When I reached the German trenches and jumped in, the first man I saw was Willie – dead, but still holding his pipes. If ever a man deserved the VC Willie did.' [21/1230

Above: The advance at a walk against the German lines and machine guns is underway.

Below: 20/290 Piper Major John Wilson, who was to win the Military Medal 'For Conspicuous Bravery and Devotion to Duty on 1 July 1916'.

Above: One of a well known series of photographs showing the Tyneside Irish walking towards the German front line at 0730, 1 July 1916.

Piper William Alexander Scott has no known grave, and is commemorated on the Thiepval Memorial France.]

Piper James Philips of the same battalion, after piping his way across No Man's Land, had his pipes shattered, he immediately took up a rifle and started fighting and then obtaining some bombs, he then proceeded to bomb the Germans out of their trenches.

Captain Herries also mentioned the pipers of his 22nd Battalion:

'Men were dropping now fairly thickly, but our pipers stuck to their playing and on we went.'

The War Diary of the 23rd battalion also contains information on the part played by the pipers of that battalion:

'Each Company was played over into No Man's Land by its pipers who continued to play until killed or wounded.'

But Piper Alexander Boyd of Newcastle, of the 22nd Battalion wrote from the First Eastern General Hospital in Cambridge, to his mother after the battle:

'The only thing the matter with me is I have a finger blown off. The only thing disabled is the pipes, I got them blown away when I was playing the charge. You would see in the papers about a piper playing in No Man's Land – that is between our trenches and those of the Germans, it was I. I was playing Tipperary and all the boys were singing and shouting. I could see them falling all about me. It was a lucky day for me that I was not blown away, I shall never forget it as long as I live.'

Watching the advance from a post in the rear was the French interpreter of the 34th Division, several variations of his account exist. The main theme, however, was,

'I saw the Tyneside Scottish go into action, pipes playing, and the men cheering wildly as they advanced towards the enemy trenches in the teeth of a blizzrd

Right: 20/237 Lance Corporal Piper, Garnet Wolsley Fyfe, the uncle of Pipe Major Wilson.
'I did see poor "Aggy" Fife. He was riddled with bullets, writhing and screaming.'
He was killed as he piped the 20th Battalion over No Man's Land. He is buried in Ovillers Military Cemetery.

100

of bullets, bombs and shells. They might have been going out for a bean feast for all the difference it made to them.'

The two minute gap between the explosion of the mines and the beginning of the advance had given the Bavarian machine gunners a head start, they quickly manned their positions and waited, watching, and allowing the waves of British infantry to reach a point of no return.

'You know Fritzie had let us come on just enough so that we were exposed coming down that slope. That way we would cop it if we came forward and cop it just as bad if we tried to go back. We were just scythed down. We found out later that they must have aimed their machine guns at our thighs so that when we went down, we got hit again as we fell.'

(Private J Elliot 20th Battalion)

'It was hell on earth; that is the only name I can give it. We were the first over the trenches after the signal to advance and never a man faltered. It was like going to a picnic, the way the men marched on, but it was only for a few yards, until the Hun got sight of us. Then every kind of shell they possess was dropped amongst us and their machine guns also got in on the act.'

(23/696 Private William Bloomfield)

On the left the advance of the 20th and 23rd Battalions was heroically pressed forward. The German front line followed the contours of Mash Valley and there was nearly eight hundred yards of No Man's Land to be crossed. Immediately the two battalions crossed the parapet they came under accurate cross fire from machine guns in Ovillers and La Boisselle. This was recalled by 23/180 Private Thomas Grant, a compositer at the Cooperative printing works before the war, who wrote to his wife in Harbottle Street, Byker:

'The Tyneside Scottish Brigade made the move forward towards the enemy at a certain place, we swarmed over the parapets at a given time and we went over the ground as if on parade, but it was a tough job. Numerous German machine guns thinned the Scottish ranks, but still the men went forward, it was glorious!'

It was to be seen later, from the position of the dead that many fought their way through to the second line before they were wiped out. Private William Bloomfield, who hailed from Netherton Colliery also, mentioned this:

'A few of us got up to their second line but I dropped before I got to the wires as my knee gave way.'

The party detailed to take La Boisselle from the flank had tried in vain to force an entry before meeting a similar fate. The men had been told that they must at all costs leave the wounded behind, no assistance had to be given. Private J Elliot also recalled this horrible experience:

'That was awful, hearing men who were your mates pleading with you and pulling at your ankles for help but not being able to do anything. One lad alongside me was chanting 'Mother of God No! Mother of God No!' just like that. Others were effing and blinding. I don't know how I got through it. I could see men dropping all around then Billy yelled, "Down on your bellies".'

Below: German machine gunners. Machine Gun Company of 55/Landwehr Regiment, commanded by Hauptmann Von Rohr, were brave men who stood their ground under the tremendous British barrage and threw back the oncoming Tyneside Scottish.

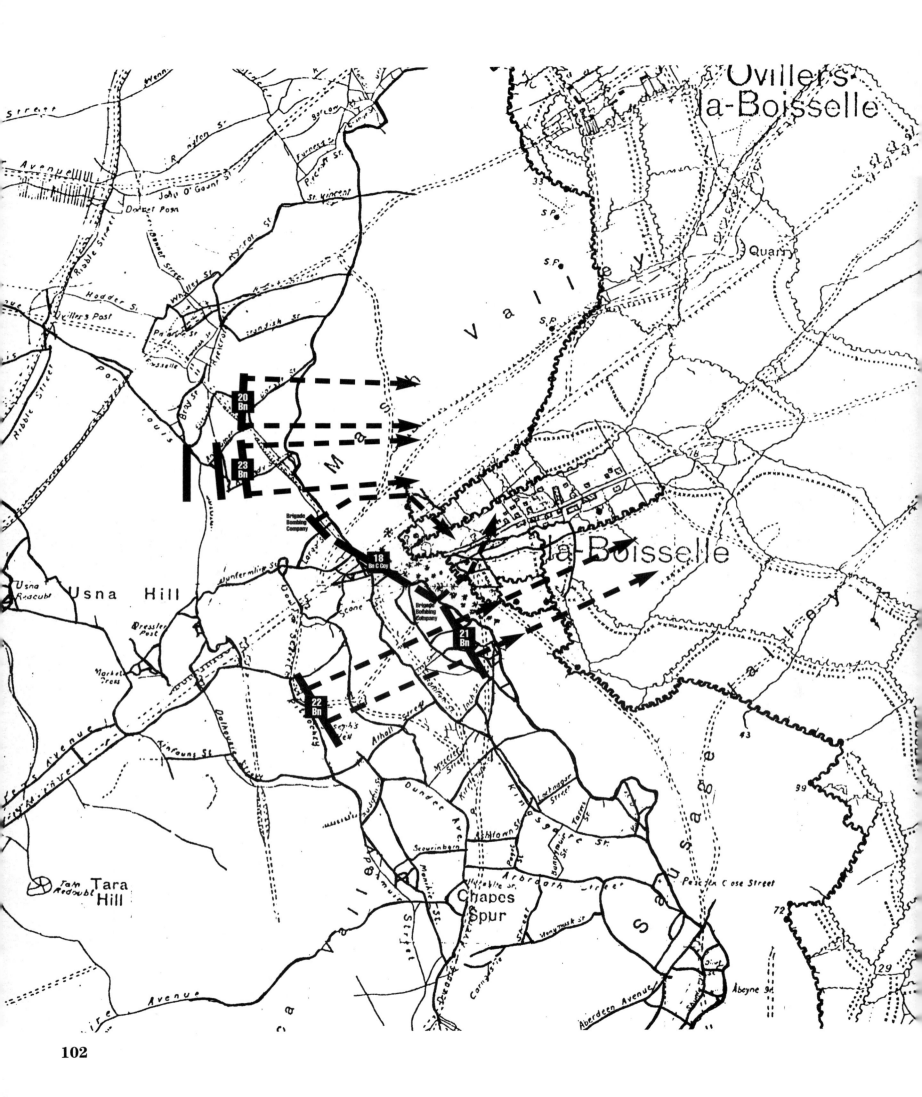

Compare trench map (left) with aerial photograph (below) which clearly shows Y Sap crater and Lochnagar Crater, blown 1 July 1916. It was over this ground that the Tynesiders attacked on that Saturday morning at the onset of the 'Big Push'.

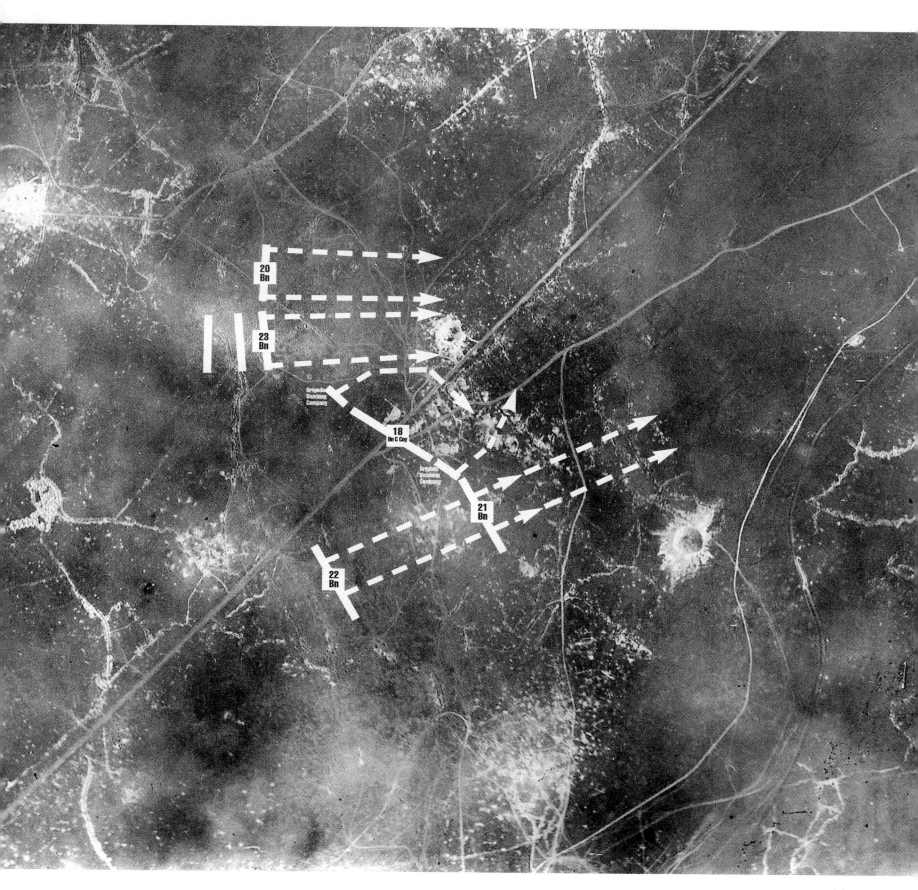

They were pinned down, unable to move, over their heads the machine gun bullets whistled, if a man showed himself he immediately became a casualty.

'PZZING, PZZING, those machine gun bullets came buzzing through the grass all around us. Through the din we could hear screams behind us but no one dared look round. It would have been suicide just to raise yourself up to look. At one moment there was silence – maybe Fritzie boy was changing his ammunition belts. At any rate for a few moments above it all we could hear was the larks. A bomber near me shouted 'Hey I've been shot in the arse!' Billy Grant shouted back, "Haven't we all!"'

(Private J Elliot)

It would appear that 'Fritzie boy' was a gunner of the Machine Gun Company of 55/Landwehr

Regiment, commanded by Hauptmann Von Rohr, brave men who stood their ground under the tremendous British barrage and threw back the oncoming Tyneside Scottish.

However these Bavarians were not going to have it all their own way, an unknown Tyneside Scottish Corporal, reported in the *Evening Chronicle*:

'One of our chaps did an amazingly plucky thing. He was a bit of a sprinter and easily outdistanced the rest of us, so he dashed right up to a machine gun that was worrying us and put it out of action on his own.'

The officer casualties caused by the German gunners were staggering, in the 20th Battalion every officer who went over became a casualty, with the Commanding Officer Lieutenant Colonel C C A Sillery killed and the Adjutant, Captain A E Kerr wounded. In the 23rd Battalion Lieutenant Colonel W Lyle was last seen alive with a walking stick in his hand, amongst his men in No Man's Land about two hundred yards from the German trenches. Many officers of this battalion fell as they crossed No Man's Land, Major M Burge before he had gone a good many yards, whilst the officers commanding A and B companies, Captains J B Cubey and J G Todd, both died before they reached the British wire. One officer reported to have reached the German trenches on this flank was Lieutenant W B Tytler, who was seen there badly wounded, but he was subsequently reported missing, believed killed. Writing to the wife of Lieutenant Alfred Shapely, Major S H Macintosh said:

'No one could possibly have carried out his duty more faithfully than your husband. His platoon advanced over the parapet first and the last I saw of him was leading his men most gallantly in the direction of the German lines.'

Meanwhile on the right the 21st and 22nd Battalions were leaving their trenches, before they

had scarcely gone a hundred yards Second Lieutenant James Fryer of C Company fell with a bullet in his head. This was reported by his Platoon Sergeant 22/415 John T Henderson, of Kitchener Street, Gateshead, who made the following statement to the Red Cross,

'We had only gone about one hundred yards when I saw Second Lieutenant Fryer fall. I went over and had a look at him and found he had a wound in the temple and was dead. He fell in our second line and was probably buried by a shell explosion. I took over command of the platoon and carried on.'

Another Sergeant must have seen Second Lieutenant Fryer go down for Lance Corporal Thomas Downs of D Company who was lying wounded in the British Front Line reported this from The County of London War Hospital Epsom,

'I was lying in the British Front Line and I was informed by a Sergeant that he had seen Second Lieutenant Fryer wounded, this was just before noon but I can give no further information.'

Others were able to get across No Man's Land and enter the enemy lines but some fell as they made their way forward.

Captain Laing of the 22nd Battalion was killed as he crossed No Man's Land, the news being relayed to his father by the Company Sergeant Major.

'When the order was given to advance, Captain Laing and myself were over at once, the men following smartly. Five minutes after, the Captain was wounded in the neck and fell, and had to be left. He came round, however and came on again, and was again bowled over and was not seen to move anymore. Later on his orderly went out to try and get him brought in, but reported him as dead, and could not get the body moved. I am sorry

not to be able to give you further information. I myself was badly wounded and could do nothing to help. The Captain was one of the best, liked by his brother officers, and he held the respect and esteem of the men, and to me it was as though I had lost a friend let alone my Captain'.

Some men of these two battalions managed to fight their way through to the enemy second line, where a party set off for the third line, but owing to heavy fire and being under-manned they had to retire. Captain Herries was on this side of the brigade advance and he wrote:

'Crossing No Man's Land the enemy machine guns got to work, but we were into their trench in a remarkable short time and passed quickly to their second line. Beyond that they were very strong and several of us who got over the parapet had a hot time of it.'

Also crossing No Man's Land near here was 21/1000 Private Tommy Easton; of the 21st Battalion:

'Your concentration is on self-preservation and you are only interested in what is ahead of you. You can't stop to give succour to pals; you've got to press on. People fell on all sides – blown up – but we just persevered, the wire was reasonably destroyed and we tumbled into the first German trench we came to.'

The fight to get into the enemy trenches on this flank was also recorded by the unnamed corporal mentioned earlier who wrote:

'The Huns fought desperately and we had a tough job clearing them out. They simply crushed us with machine gun fire. It was real red blistering hell hot and make no mistake.'

The right flank of this column was exposed owing

Above: Second James W Fryer, NF of Fenham, formerly of Hawes. *'I saw Second Lieutenant Fryer fall. I went over and had a look at him and found he had a wound in the temple and was dead. He fell in our second line and was probably buried by a shell explosion. I took over command of the platoon and carried on.'*

Above: 'I passed through successive lines of dead Tyneside Scots lying as regularly as if on parade.'

to 101 Brigade, through no fault of their own, being slow to move off at zero hour. This led to casualties among the advancing Tynesiders.

'We got over the trenches down and up – no planks. I don't know how I got through it. I could see men dropping all around, and then someone yelled, 'Get down! Get down!' and I was on my belly for the next eleven hours. I crawled, if you stood up the machine guns would get you for sure.'

(Private J Barron 21st Battalion)

Having reached the German trenches Tommy Easton had time to reflect on the crossing of No-Mans-Land and he said:

'How I ever got across there I'll never know – bearin' in mind we had to traverse three lines of trenches before we came to our original front line and started over No Man's Land. As we went an officer says "You're all right lads, they're firing over our heads", but that fire was decimating

the Tyneside Irish who were coming in behind us.'

The Brigade Bombing Company were trying to fight their way into La Boisselle and, lying out in No Man's Land, Private Elliot could see them:

'Over in the village you couldn't see much of what was happening because of the dust and smoke but I could see some of our lads chucking bombs. They were beckoning towards us, trying to get us to come forward. They couldn't see that Fritzie boy had a machine gun on us. Billy Grant, the Sergeant, wanted to get forward to the crater to support them. He said that if we didn't get forward the barrage would paste us. We waited until the machine gun had passed. One... Two... Three, we tried to get to our feet to charge but as soon as we rose, that gun was on us. Billy was caught in the side by machine gun fire. That was it, we durst not move, it was belly down for

Above: Germans manning a substantial front line trench, well constructed with firing loop holes and an armour-plated sniper position.

Left: The killing ground in front of La Boisselle after the attack by the Tynesiders – No Man's Land is littered with the dead and wounded.

Right: Captain J M Charlton 21st Battalion, killed while attempting to charge a German strongpoint.

the rest of the day after that. I often wonder if we could have done more to get forward but we were possed, well and truly possed. The lads up in front must have put up a good fight because we could hear bombs and shouting and Lewis guns well into the afternoon. So if the lads in front went down, they went down fighting.'

La Boisselle had the appearance of being completely obliterated, however the Germans, safe underground, manned the ruins of the village in strength and the bombers were unable to force an entry and hang on. On the other side of the village the bombers of the 21st and 22nd Battalions, under the cover of a trench mortar barrage, also attempted to gain a foothold in La Boisselle. Here, too, the Germans emerged from their deep dugouts and poured enfilade fire into the flanks of the Tynesiders and also drove back the bombers from the village. The leader of the 21st Battalion bombers, 21/840 CSM J E Patterson of Gateshead,

was awarded the Distinguished Conduct Medal for leading this bombing attack, and later showing conspicuous gallantry in repulsing the enemy counter attacks.

'Charlton and I lay in a hollow in the ground with half a dozen men, but could not get on. Most of the men were killed and the only thing to do was to get a machine-gun up, which we were fortunate enough to do. Then we gave it to them hot. Further along Forster, McIntosh and Lamb got over with a party of men, but the whole lot were mown down by a machine-gun'

(Captain W Herries)

Private Thomas Grant mentioned the officers of the 23rd Battalion in a letter to his wife:

'The officers went through the same as the men, they knew no fear. The Germans are retiring and I believe this move will shorten the war.'

Despite their losses, the remnants of all three

battalions making up the column advancing on this side of the village pushed on towards the German intermediate line, *Quergraben III*, near the Contalmaison road. But other brave souls were reported as far east into the German lines as Bailiff Wood, quite close to Contalmaison village; who they were will probably never be known.

Trying to continue the advance, Captains Herries and Charlton kept their gun firing, but not for long, and Captain Herries recorded how Charlton fell,

'For a while we did great execution but the gun jammed at a critical moment. Poor Charlton was shot down while attempting to charge a German strong-point and the initiative passed to the enemy who tried, unsuccessfully, to work their way around us.'

Nearby the battalion bombers also fought their way

Right: Lieutenant L R Raines, B Company, 21st Battalion, seen here holding a non-issue revolver (private purchase) at Alnwick. Killed on the morning of the 'Big Push'.

forward, but through a shortage of bombs and ammunition they were gradually forced back by repeated German counter-attacks. Captain Herries also mentioned these men:

'In the meantime our bombers were at work and reached their third line which they held for a short time, but out of which we were bombed step by step – all our bombs being used up. While this was happening we were consolidating the other two lines, which we held against repeated bombing attacks. The men were splendid but very tired, I had to pull myself together with a mouthful of brandy once or twice. We were now busy digging the Bosches out of their dugouts. They all threw their hands up and yelled 'Mercy Kamerad.''

Watching the attack of the Division in an OP was Captain D H James of the 1st Tyneside Irish who was employed as the Divisional TMO.

'From my advanced OP, I reported (very bluntly I am afraid) to General Williams that no objectives had been gained and the left wing, 102 Brigade, had suffered heavily in the attack.'

Further on he wrote,

'After the attack I went down to 102 Brigade Headquarters – to send messages to Divisional Headquarters, and I had a few words with Brigadier General Ternan. He had read some of my earlier messages and was inclined to think I was in error about the failure on the left, his Brigade, and in my estimation of the way the battle was going, but I gave him details which did nothing to relieve his anxiety.'

For those able to observe the advance it was easy to see the failure, but, at the dugout being used as a temporary Brigade Headquarters, Brigadier General Ternan was completely in the dark. Owing to the dust and the smoke it was impossible to observe the leading troops. The Brigade Staff, desperate for news from the front line, sent runners forward, from where some never returned, to try and locate the position of the men in the enemy lines. One route to the German front line was through the tunnel dug by the miners for the Lochnagar mine and another was through a shallow gallery dug by Lieutenant Nixon and his platoon of B Company 18/Northumberland Fusiliers. However these tunnels were narrow, not very high and they soon became blocked with wounded and dying men trying to get back, and ammunition parties trying to get forward. They were therefore a painfully slow route for the runners to travel, but gradually they brought back a picture that became clearer to those in the rear and the news that was sent back to Divisional Headquarters was that of a disaster. The 20th and 23rd Battalions on the left had practically ceased to exist, despite the gallant attempts already described, the survivors were pinned down in No Man's Land, where Private

Elliot was trying to help Sergeant Billy Grant:

'During a lull we tried to dress Billy's wound but Fritzie was on his toes and every movement attracted fire. Anyway the wound was a big mush, the flies were on him as soon as he got hit and he was helpless on his back, poor Billy was soon beyond human help. The Germans started searching the battlefield with artillery and I think that did for a lot of our fellows who were stuck out there without cover. Certainly those shells were lashing us late afternoon. We could do absolutely nothing. There was about ten of us just stuck there flat on our bellies, heads down as far as they would go. We were thirsty but none dared reach for his water bottle. For me it was the longest day of my life and I never thought it would end.'

Near to where Private Elliot was lying was 20/614 Corporal J E Philipson who, as part of a Lewis gun team, was trying to get his gun forward. Each time he moved he would be wounded, showing conspicuous bravery and devotion to duty, four times he tried to get the gun forward and four times he was wounded. His gallant conduct resulted in the award of the Distinguished Conduct Medal.

On the other flank the survivors of the 21st and 22nd Battalions did at least hold some of the enemy trenches, but these two battalions had also had tremendous casualties.

Major Acklom now commanded the remnants of these two battalions, as both Major F C Henniker and Lieutenant Colonel A P A Elphinstone had become casualties. With seven officers and approximately 200 men, Major Acklom was managing to hold on with the enemy on both flanks. On his left La Boisselle had not been taken

and on the right there was an enemy held gap of some hundred yards or more between him and the men of 101 and 103 Brigades. The positions were held on to and where possible consolidated, patrols being sent out to link up with the other parties holding sections of the line. The arrival of Major Acklom had put new spirit into the men. Tommy Easton recalled him:

'We got a CO from our 3rd Battalion who was a very great officer, Major Acklom. He got us to make defensive positions should they try to counter attack. Later some R.E,s got us linked to Brigade HQ using a field observer's telephone.'

With the attack grinding to a halt and no reserves available Brigade Headquarters received orders to order forward a company of 18/Northumberland Fusiliers, the Divisional Pioneer Battalion, to attack La Boisselle. The orders were issued, but before the pioneers could move the order was countermanded, as two battalions of the 19th Division had been made available for the task.

All this time the German artillerymen of Artillery Group Pozières, under the command of Oberst Pawlowski, kept up a stiff barrage on the British, which meant the men of the Brigade spent the remainder of the day under very trying conditions. The war diary of the 22nd Battalion recorded that the men were greatly fatigued and in much need of water. No one will ever know the true happenings of the 1 July, 1916, as it states in the war diary of the 23rd Battalion:

'Many heroic deeds were performed during the day, and though only about six came to special notice there were undoubtedly very many gallant deeds performed that will never come to light.'

Among the acts of bravery that did come to light

Above: German 10 cm field gun and crew. German artillerymen of Artillery Group Pozières kept up a stiff barrage on the British, for the remainder of the day.

Above: Many acts of bravery occured on that day – 1 July 1916 – as wounded men were located and brought back to safety, more often than not under fire.

open, under fire, many times to bring in wounded comrades. For this work and piping the Battalion over the top, he was awarded the Military Medal. Medical officers worked continuously to try and clear the wounded from the congested trenches and as dusk arrived the men of the 20th and 23rd Battalions in No Man's Land were brought, tired and thirsty, back to the British front line, where they remained until the morning of 2 July. They were moved back to dugouts in the Tara - Usna line, where the battalion rolls were called. Of the 20th Battalion, every officer and sergeant that crossed the parapet had become a casualty, whilst of the 23rd only about 100 men answered their names, a further twenty turning up later in the day.

In the German front line, Major Acklom and Captain Herries and their men spent a weary night, waiting for the German counter-attack that never came. During 2 July the Germans shelled the trenches, causing some casualties among the men who were gradually improving their positions. Then in the afternoon men of 9/Cheshire Regiment began to arrive in preparation for a further advance. The group of the Tyneside Scottish then started to move back, but on the way Major Acklom received a message that they must return to the front line and hold it at all costs, so back they went. At 5.10 p.m. two Lewis guns arrived, followed at 7.0. p.m. by three Vickers guns of 102 Machine Gun Company which were immediately placed in defensive positions; still later two Stokes guns of the Light Trench Mortar Battery arrived along with food, water and ammunition. The arrival of these reinforcements and rations brought about an improvement in morale and by midnight they were able to report that the position was secure and that the strength of the party was now five officers and 155 men.

About noon on 3 July Lieutenant Rutherford and Corporal Burns of the 22nd Battalion carried out a patrol under heavy machine gun fire. Their mission was to select a route to enable a link up with the

were those of Lieutenant George Nelson of the 23rd Battalion, who during the advance came upon some men of the 20th Battalion in No Man's Land near the enemy wire. He gathered them together and led them forward until only two or three remained alive and unwounded, then later in the day under extremely heavy fire he assisted in bringing in the wounded. For his actions he received the Military Cross.

As the day wore on the stretcher bearers were busy and conspicuous by their gallant attempts to bring in the wounded. Pipe Major John Wilson worked as a stretcher-bearer and went out in the

20th (s) Bn
North'd Fus:
(1st Tyneside   No. 20/290.   Pipe Major
Scottish).   J. Wilson

For conspicuous bravery and devotion to duty. This N.C.O. continually went out under fire to assist in recovering the wounded at LA BOISELLE. July 1st 1916.

Awarded MILITARY MEDAL.

troops of 101 Brigade on the right, which was achieved when Captain Longhurst arrived to supplement the defence with about one hundred men of the 23rd Battalion. During the day Brigadier General Ternan managed to cross No Man's Land and have a look at the position for himself, observing: 'I passed through successive lines of dead Tyneside Scots lying as regularly as if on parade.'

Then at midnight on 3 July, 58 Brigade began the relief of the remnants of the Brigade and the tired and weary survivors commenced making their way back over No Man's Land to collecting points in the British lines.

Captain Herries wrote to his father:

'We were a weary crowd as we moved out on Monday night released at last. None of us had had a wash since Friday or a shave. I was a sight for the gods – uniform white with chalk and splashed with blood, puttees in shreds and with only half my things. I lost my compass, water bottle and gas helmet. We spent the night in a reserve trench again and the next morning moved back to a village.'

The battalions of 58 Brigade could have come up sooner and helped the Tyneside Scottish; the Colonel of one battalion, 9/Cheshire Regiment, offered his battalion's assistance several times but the offer was refused. This was recalled by one of the Battalion Signaller's, Private J Gerrard:

'I was there as a Battalion Signaller in the 58 Brigade, we waited in the assembly trench all day. Our Colonel wired several times asking if he must come up in support and he was told each time he was not needed – just another brass hat stupid action wanting the honour for themselves, which caused the Division to be cut up. They went to the fourth German line, so we were told on the phone leaving the Germans down the dug outs, to come up afterwards and machine gun them from the rear.'

The refusal of the assistance of 58 Brigade probably led to many more casualties than were necessary.

THE CASUALTIES

The casualties sustained by the Tyneside Scottish Brigade during the period 1- 3 July 1916 were among the highest for any brigade involved in the attack. However collating accurate figures has proved difficult for every source consulted gives different totals. Divisional, Brigade and Battalion war diaries all present the casualty figures in a different way, thus leading to some confusion. The number of casualties initially reported to the Tyneside Scottish Committee are given in Committee Book Number Two, on page 181 as:

		Killed	Missing	Wounded	Total
20th	Bn	197	57	310	564
21st	Bn	114	76	388	578
22nd	Bn	100	144	384	628
23rd	Bn	64	212	392	668
		475	**489**	**1474**	**2438**

Far left: 21/595 Sergeant William Taylor of Leeds, killed in the attack on La Boisselle, commemorated on the Thiepval Memorial.

Above: Lance Corporal John Russell, Seaton Burn, KiA 1 July, buried Ovillers Military Cemetery.

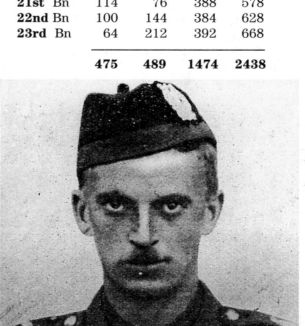

Left: Captain John George Todd, 23rd Battalion KiA 1 July 1916 at La Boisselle.

111

Captain William Nixon, 20th Battalion, killed in the German first line trench. Naval architect by trade.

Second Lieutenant L Williams, 23rd Battalion KiA 1 July 1916.

Captain J P Forster, 22nd Battalion KiA 1 July 1916.

Lieutenant Robert J Dougal, 21st Battalion KiA 1 July 1916.

Captain David Douglas Horne, 21st Battalion KiA 1 July 1916.

The Divisional history, published in 1921 also presents the figures in a different way, taking the figures from the brigade war diaries and separating the officers from the other ranks thus:

	Officers			Other Ranks			Total
	Kd	Wnd	Msg	Kd	Wnd	Msg	
20th Bn	16	10	0	337	268	0	631
21st Bn	11	10	0	161	296	0	478
22nd Bn	7	14	1	198	319	0	539
23rd Bn	9	7	2	178	444	0	640
	43	41	3	874	1327	0	2288

Right: 20/919 Private Thomas Stephenson, 9 Frank Street, Greenside, KiA 1 July 1916, commemorated on the Thiepval Memorial.

If we compare the figures for just one battalion the discrepancy becomes readily obvious, the 22nd Battalion reported in the Battalion war diary on 31 July 1916 as follows:

Officers			Other Ranks			Total
Kd*	Wnd	Msg	Kd*	Wnd	Msg	
8	11	1	38	324	155	537

*Includes died of wounds

There is a difference of two officers and two other ranks, from the Divisional History and ninety-one men in total from the figure reported to the committee. Quite obviously there were some men wounded who would soon succumb to their wounds and possibly some of those missing who were possibly prisoners of war, however the Brigade Commander, Brigadier General Ternan states in his history on page 111 that, 'no officers or men were taken prisoner.' Yet other accounts tell of Tyneside Scottish as well as Tyneside Irish held prisoner in dugouts in Contalmaison.

Among the dead were the four battalion commanding officers, three of whom would be buried side by side in Bapaume Post Military Cemetery. The body of Lieutenant Colonel Lyle was found by the Divisional Commander Major General Ingouville-Williams on 13 July, the General wrote to his wife:

> 'I have just been reconnoitering and found poor Colonel Lyle's body, surrounded by Tyneside Scottish, North-umberland Fusiliers, all dead, a most grievous sight to me, who loved my faithful soldiers.'

The General also wrote to the Chairman of the Tyneside Scottish and Tyneside Irish Committees:

> 'To the Tyneside Committee, – It is with the greatest pride and the deepest regret that I wish to inform you that the division which included the Tyneside Irish and Tyneside Scottish covered itself with glory on July 1 1916, but its losses were very heavy.

Everyone testifies to the magnificent work they did that day and it is the admiration of all. I, their commander, will never forget their splendid advance through the German curtain of fire. It was simply wonderful and they behaved like veterans. Tyneside can well be proud of them, and although they will sorrow for all my brave and faithful comrades, it is some consolation to know they died not in vain, and that their gallant attack was of the greatest service to the Army that day.'

Two or three versions of the letter were printed in the local press in the northeast, some under the heading 'MY GALLANT TYNESIDERS', but he had also written to his wife on 3 July:

'My men did glorious deeds. Never have I seen men go through such hell of a barrage of artillery. They advanced as if on parade, and never flinched. I can't speak too highly of them. They earned a great record, but alas! At a great cost.'

In a further letter on 20 July, General Ingouville-Williams wrote,

'Never shall I cease singing the praises of my men and I shall never have the same grand men to deal with again. I think they have done their parts well and their attack made all this possible.'

Two days later, at 7 p.m. on 22 July, whilst returning from reconnoitring in the vicinity of Mametz, the General was killed by shellfire as he walked back to his car. At 4 p.m. on 23 July he was buried in Warloy cemetery.

Replying to a letter of sympathy from Colonel Johnstone Wallace on behalf of the Tyneside Committees, Mrs Ingouville-Williams wrote:

'The most kind letter of sympathy from yourself and the members of the Tyneside Scottish and Irish committee has touched me deeply in my overwhelming sorrow,

and I shall be most grateful if you will convey to them the warm thanks of a broken-hearted woman, whose only consolation is to know that her beloved husband was appreciated by those who had an opportunity of judging of his great worth and noble character.

He loved his dear men and his whole heart and soul was given for their welfare and perfect training and his pride was immense in their glorious response to his affectionate care. My heart bleeds for all the poor widows and mothers, who like me, have lost their dearest and best, and I would like to send a message of deepest sympathy to them in their anguish, which indeed I realise only too well

To my daughter and me our loss is a life-long sorrow. Our hearts go out to those who speak kindly of our beloved. Yours, most gratefully and sincerely

T Ingouville-Williams.'

Sad though the death of the General was, Mrs Ingouville-Williams would hardly have to face the hardships of many of the mothers and widows of the men of the Tyneside Scottish. In the harsh colliery villages of Northumberland and Durham the sight of the postman or telegraph boy was enough to strike fear into many a heart. In many villages every other house would have the curtains

Far left: 20/409 Private Cyril D Guy, A Company 20th Battalion, KiA 1 july 1916, buried at Ovillers Military Cemetery.

Above: 22/204 Private Thomas Philipson, 16 Emmaville, Ryton, wounded 1 July 1916 died 12 July, buried at the Casualty Clearing Station at Heilly Station.

Left: General Ingouville-Williams wrote, 'Never shall I cease singing the praises of my men and I shall never have the same grand men to deal with again.' On 22 July, whilst returning from reconnoitring in the vicinity of Mametz, the General was killed by shellfire as he walked back to his car.

113

Above: Hall's Corner, West Sleekburn, taken in the first weeks of July 1916. The postman, in the hat, is waiting for the post to be delivered from Newcastle. The women and children are waiting for letters from the front. Some of these women will receive an Army Form B104 stating that a husband or son had been killed. Of those serving with the Tyneside Scottish from the village, no less than eight men were killed and ten wounded 1 July, 1916.

drawn in mourning after the delivery of an Army Form B104, Casualty on Active Service Form. Many would have to survive on next to nothing, others would take in washing and ironing, and in one case, a widow with three children, married a soldier-widower with three children. When her second husband was also killed in action she was left with six children to look after. Again she remarried, her third husband a Royal Engineer came home gassed and unable to go back to the mines. To say life was hard or difficult is an understatement.

In the first week of July, at Hall's Corner, West Sleekburn, in Northumberland, a photographer took a picture of the postman as he waited for the delivery of his mailbags from Newcastle. A small crowd of women, girls and boys gathered around him, desperately waiting for news of a loved one. The sad fact is that this photograph shows women who are already widows but do not know it, and for most of their husbands there would be no known grave. The majority of the men of the Tyneside Scottish who were killed in action on 1 July, 1916, have their names recorded on the Thiepval Memorial to the missing in France. Those who do have known graves lie in places named, Gordon Dump, Bapaume Post and Ovillers Military Cemetery. Many of the missing also lie in these cemeteries, with gravestones that say, 'A Soldier of the Great War, Known unto God', or 'A Soldier of the Great War, Unknown Sergeant or Unknown Corporal, Tyneside Scottish NF.' Others whose remains were identified later, in the 1920s and 1930s, were taken further afield to Serre Road Number 2 Cemetery, but there are only a few. Many

were never identified because they were wearing their identity discs on their braces.

What of the wounded? Many of these had to struggle themselves to the Battalion Aid Posts just behind the front line. From there they were evacuated to Casualty Clearing Stations, where they were given further rudimentary treatment, wounds cleaned and dressed and if need be stabilized, before onward evacuation to General and Stationary Hospitals on the French Coast, for further treatment and if need be an operation, prior to transfer to a Hospital Ship or a convalescent camp.

Working at the Battalion Aid Post of the 21st Battalion was Father Joseph McHardy who had the sad task of writing to the families of the fallen soldiers. In late August he wrote to Mrs Lynch, the widow of 22/501 Corporal Andrew Lynch of the 22nd Battalion.

'Dear Mrs Lynch
I am exceedingly sorry that I can give you no further information regarding your husband, I knew him very well indeed + there is one thing I can tell you which will help very much to lessen your great sorrow. I received him into the church the day before the attack. I went to your husbands company on Friday afternoon, said some prayers with them, heard their confessions in the trenches + asked your husband to wait till I had finished the others. We then went to a quiet spot where I baptised him + heard his confession. He was very proud of being received +

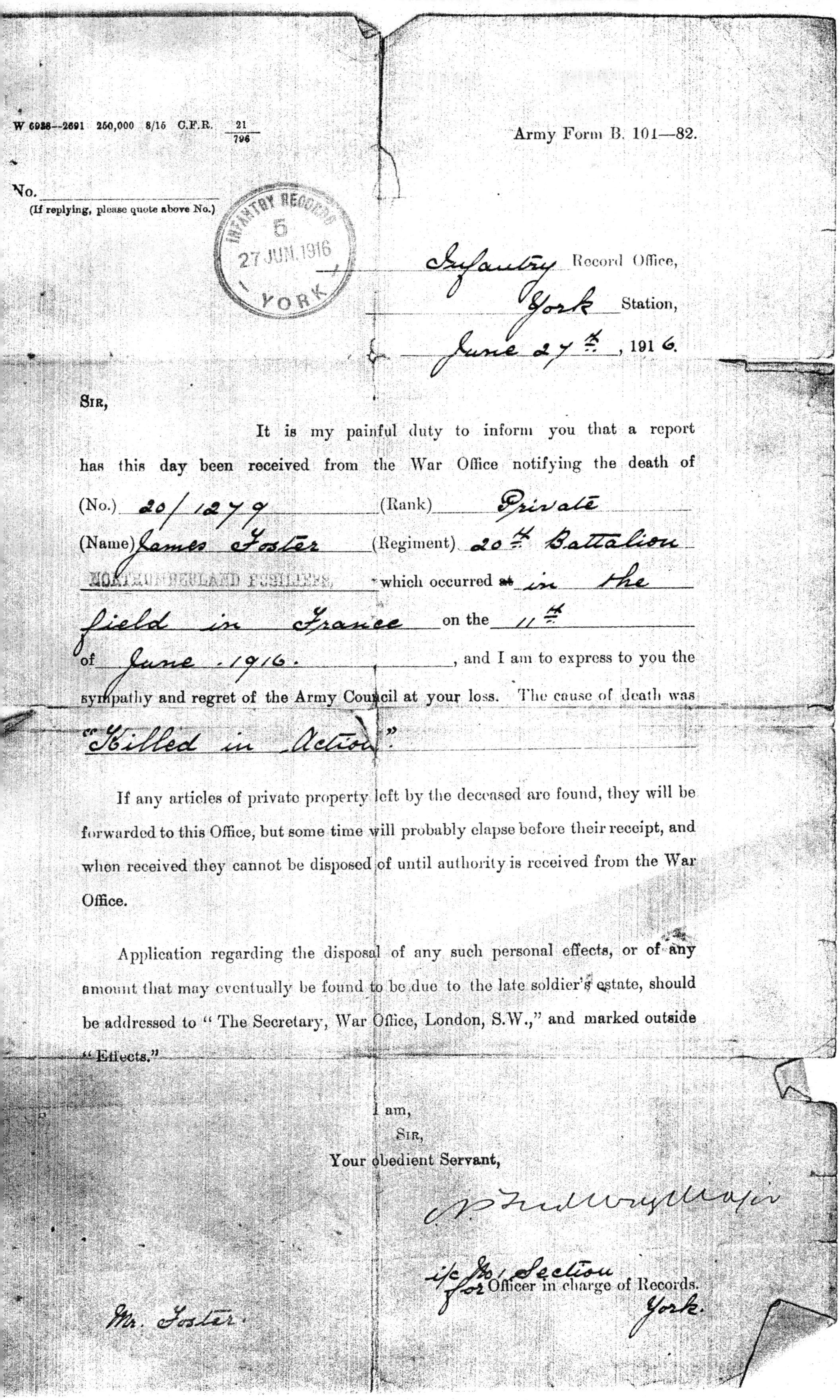

W 6938—2691 250,000 8/15 C.F.R. 21/796

Army Form B. 101—82.

No. _____
(If replying, please quote above No.)

[stamp: INFANTRY RECORDS 5 27 JUN. 1916 YORK]

Infantry Record Office,

York Station,

June 27th, 1916.

Sir,

It is my painful duty to inform you that a report has this day been received from the War Office notifying the death of

(No.) 20/1279 (Rank) Private

(Name) James Foster (Regiment) 20th Battalion

NORTHUMBERLAND FUSILIERS, which occurred at in the field in France on the 11th of June 1916, and I am to express to you the sympathy and regret of the Army Council at your loss. The cause of death was "Killed in Action"

If any articles of private property left by the deceased are found, they will be forwarded to this Office, but some time will probably elapse before their receipt, and when received they cannot be disposed of until authority is received from the War Office.

Application regarding the disposal of any such personal effects, or of any amount that may eventually be found to be due to the late soldier's estate, should be addressed to "The Secretary, War Office, London, S.W.," and marked outside "Effects."

I am,

Sir,

Your obedient Servant,

[signature]

i/c No. Section
for Officer in charge of Records.
York.

Mr. Foster.

Left: How the news of the death of a loved one arrived. This AF B104 for James Foster notified the next of kin of his death ten days prior to the 'Big Push'.

115

Captain James Muirhead RAMC, a general practitioner from North Shields, who between the beginning of the advance at 7.30 a.m. and 10.00 a.m. estimated that he treated almost 750 men. At one stage during a lull in the fighting his orderly said, 'Have a look Doc', and as the Doctor looked over No Man's Land the orderly said 'It's just as if they shot up the crowd going to see Newcastle United.' A month later Captain Muirhead would be evacuated with typhoid.

Lying out among the 'football crowd' was Private William Bloomfield of Netherton Colliery, who told of how he was wounded and how he got himself back to the Dressing Station in the British lines,

'I had been wounded previously in the knee and as soon as I dropped a machine gun put a bullet through my shoulder. The next one took my steel helmet off, and a third my haversack from my shoulders. All this happened in about half a second. After that the bullets were pinging about me just as if I was an attraction for them. I thought discretion the better part of valour; so I slid on my stomach as best I could into some thistles and took cover there for some time. I then slid along as my strength allowed me for about 200 yards and then lay down until I could get my bearings taken so that

Above: 23/1338 Sergeant William G and Mrs Wright, 26 Magdelene Street, Gilesgate, Durham City, died of wounds 9 July 1916, buried Saint Sever Cemetery, Rouen.

Far right: 23/911 Private James Simpson lay wounded in No Man's Land for three or four days and was eventually brought into the British lines by a German padre.

intended writing to you with the good news. I had instructed him before that + he was one of the best attendees of my church. He had his rosaries round his neck and after that I never saw him again. He did not come to the doctors dressing station where I was, nor did I see his body among the dead, but there were hundreds that I did not see. It was a glorious attack, but the cost in the lives of our very bravest lads was very heavy. I read the service for all the dead but unfortunately got my arm put out of joint at the shoulder and had to go to hospital. I am sure however it will be some consolation to you to know that he was received into the church.
I am yours sincerely
Joseph McHardy.

At the Battalion Aid Post of the 23rd Battalion was

I could return at dusk.'

All day long William Bloomfield lay out in the hot summer sun, the German counter barrage crashing around him, then late in the evening he began to make his way back across No Man's Land.

'I was wounded at about 9 a.m. on 1 July and it was 2 a.m. the next morning by the time I had crawled back to the dressing station in our front line. All the time I was crawling back they were shelling heavily, as the advance had begun again on our front. When our men got up to the Germans they shouted, 'Mercy Kamerade!' I think Tyneside will have made a name for itself this time. I cannot use my arm, but if I never get to use it again I am thankful that I am here to tell my story as many of my comrades are lying "somewhere in France".'

On 11 July the *Sunderland Echo* carried a report from an unnamed private of the Royal Army Medical Corps who stated,

'The Tyneside Scottish did wonders. They took four lines of trenches without turning a hair, although met with a tremendous hail of whizz-bangs and bullets and other specimens of German Kultur. Two days before a chance shell had plumped into their trenches and injured one or two fellows. It made them so mad that there and then they wanted to get over the top and take their revenge. They've got spirit have those North Country lads. When their chance to advance did come they made the best of it. The Colonel was the first to get over the parapet and I think he was hit the moment he showed himself.'

Unfortunately the position on the battlefield or the name of this soldier is not recorded, therefore the accuracy of his statement about the Colonel could

Above: 22/1681 Private Francis Joseph Quinn, who was wounded by machine bullets in the legs and suffered from gas poisoning at the same time. He lay wounded in No Man's Land and when he regain consciousness he thought that the whole of the British Army had been wiped out. He was picked up by some Germans and taken prisoner.

Above: 21/34 Private Joseph Graham, of Ryton, who was reported shellshocked in August 1916 and later, in November 1916, he was reported missing.

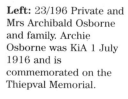

Left: 23/196 Private and Mrs Archibald Osborne and family. Archie Osborne was KiA 1 July 1916 and is commemorated on the Thiepval Memorial.

117

Right: 21/43 Sergeant Joseph Brown, 1 Jubilee Terrace, Seaton Delaval, and relatives. Kia 1 July 1916, buried in Gordon Dump Military Cemetery

Below: 20/8 CSM Richard Dale, A Company, 20th Battalion, KiA 1 July 1916, buried in Ovillers Military Cemetery.

Below: 20/1310 Private Isaac Johnson (age 19) 3 Melbury Street, Dawdon Colliery, KiA 1 July 1916, commemorated on Thiepval Memorial.

Right: Unknown soldier from Durham City area KiA 1 July 1916.

be questioned.

Men who returned to the British trenches were questioned about the fate of the missing officers and men, in order to establish their fate. 20/1415 Private G R Bell, from Bedlington made a statement that he and Private James Cranney had been evacuated together and that in the hospital Cranney had told him of the death of Lieutenant A Coleman.

Likewise the statements made by Sergeant Henderson and Lance Corporal Downs about Second Lieutenant Fryer were added to by the Officer Commanding 22nd Battalion, who wrote,

'The evidence of men returning from the operations on July 1st and the following days shows that Second Lieutenant J W Fryer was killed by shellfire both his legs having been blown off.'

Obviously the young officers body had been hit by a shell after Sergeant Henderson had seen him shot in the head.

The death of 20/8 CSM Richard Dale was reported by Privates Gibbons and Roxborough, who both stated he was killed instantaneously by a shell.

Likewise 23/520 Lance Corporal Simpson Wallace who came from Baker Street, Leadgate, having been captured at Arras in 1917 reported the following, when he was released from a German Prisoner of War Camp in March 1918.

'On 1 July 1916 I saw a German soldier deliberately aim and fire at one of our wounded who was on the parapet of a trench, being brought into the trench for safety by a stretcher bearer named Gibson of the 23rd Battalion. The wounded man at whom the German fired was killed. This took place in front of La Boisselle.'

This soldier was probably 23/849 Private Stephen Gibson who was awarded the Military Medal for his work that day.

Another man of the 23rd Battalion, thirty-five year old Private James Simpson from Back Clayton Street, Bedlington Station, lay wounded among his dead comrades for three or four days. He survived by eating the rations he found in the haversacks and drinking the water bottles of his dead friends, he was finally found and carried into the British lines by a German Padre,[so the family story goes] to whom he owed his life. The wounds in his leg were so bad that it was eventually amputated, this prevented him from working underground again and he spent the rest of his working life on the screens at the Winning Colliery, West Sleekburn.

One man who was lying waiting for the stretcher bearers told a reporter of *The North Star*

'The Boches delivered a counter-attack pouring on our men big 'Jack Johnson's' shells of lesser weight and shrapnel. They chucked everything at us except half-crowns, and us chaps who were wounded had to lie for a long time in the open because the stretcher bearers could not get near us.'

The unwounded survivors were eventually withdrawn to the rear area and the work of rebuilding the shattered brigade commenced.

20/933 Lance Corporal Joseph Taylor aged 38, left a widow and nine children when he was killed 1 July 1916. Commemorated on Thiepval Memorial.

21/289 Corporal George Lowes, 250 Chestnut Street, Hirst, KiA 1 July 1916. Commemorated on Thiepval Memorial.

20/257 Company Quarter Master Sergeant W A B MacDonald, who only had one eye when he enlisted, was wounded 1 July 1916.

20/1152 Samuel Wray, 15 Stephenson Street, Walbottle, wounded 1 July, 1916, transferred to 16th and 9th battalions Northumberland Fusiliers.

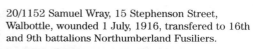

Standing is 20/350 Bugler Thompson Robson, Scotswood, wounded 1 July 1916. Seated is Private James Green 6/Seaforth Highlanders.

23/1121 Private Thomas Henry Lee, 6 Percy Court, Morpeth, KiA 1 July 1916. Commemorated on Thiepval Memorial.

Gateshead War Honour Board

20/140 Sergeant Thomas Barnes age 41 of St Mary's Terrace, Ryton, DoW 13 July 1916. Buried in St Sever Cemetery Rouen.

20/238 Private George Hall, Pond Cottages, Ryton, wounded 1 July 1916, KiA 11 August 1917 with 16th Battalion NF. Buried Adinkerke Military Cemetery, Belgium.

20/248 Private Richard Hogg, stretcher bearer C Company, resident of Ryton, KiA 1 July 1916. Commemorated on Thiepval Memorial.

20/283 Corporal Joseph Spinks, A Company, of Dyke Heads, Ryton, wounded 31 March 1916, returned to Battalion and killed 1 July 1916. Commemorated Thiepval Memorial.

20/430 Corporal William Liddle, C Company, born in Ryton, resident in Blaydon, KiA 1 July 1916. Commemorated Thiepval Memorial.

20/790 Lance Corporal John Graham, Ryton, County Durham, KiA 1 July 1916.

22/780 Private James Burrows, 41 Clifford Terrace, Crawcrook, KiA 10 June 1916, buried in Becourt Military Cemetery.

22/534 Private Arthur Tremble, B Company, of 10 High Grove, Ryton. He worked as a hewer at Stella Colliery and was KiA 1 July 1916. Commemorated on Thiepval Memorial.

22/769 Private William Cook, West Ryton, KiA 1 July 1916. Commemorated on Thiepval Memorial.

Private J R Bulmer, Tyneside Scottish. No further information available.

22/874 Private Robert Forster, C Company of Ryton, County Durham, KiA 1 July 1916. Commemmorated on Thiepval Memorial.

Private W Walker, Tyneside Scottish. No further information available.

120

Chapter Seven

Reorganization and Raiding Parties at Armentières

*'If you're looking for the Battalion.
I know where they are, I know where they are.'*

SOLDIERS' SONG 1914-18

OVER THE PERIOD 2 - 4 July survivors were brought out of the line in dribs and drabs moving via the Tara - Usna line to the sunken garden in Albert. With the remnants of the 21st Battalion was Piper George Griffiths, whose own pipes had been shot to pieces, so he acquired another set of pipes in No Man's Land. George found that his brother John, who was a drummer, had also survived. John managed to get hold of a drum and a stick, and together they 'played' the survivors of the 21st Battalion back to Albert.

After a short rest in Albert the battalions moved to Millencourt where the process of reforming the shattered remnants commenced. At 11 a.m. on the morning of 5 July the four battalions of the brigade fell in for an inspection by the Corps Commander, Lieutenant General Pultney, who expressed his satisfaction and congratulated the brigade on their magnificent conduct during the attack at La Boisselle. Brigadier Ternan wrote of this:

'The whole Brigade when formed up now barely occupied the space of one battalion, and the absence of so many old familiar faces made the occasion a sad one. But the men when asked the old tag if they felt down hearted roared out a stentorian "NO!" General Williams who was present, expressed his intense gratification with the splendid gallantry displayed, and hoped that we should soon rejoin his command.'

The news was now received that the shattered Tyneside Scottish and Irish Brigades and 18/Northumberland Fusiliers (Pioneers) were to be transferred from the 34th Division to the 37th Division, in exchange for 110 and 111 Brigades and the 37th Divisional Pioneer Battalion. The 37th Division was holding the line to the north and the Tyneside Scottish moved to Pommier to join them. Embussing on the afternoon of 6 July they were transported to the Pommier and La Cauchie areas

and arrived in billets there about midnight. With the deaths in action of all four commanding officers on the first of the month, command now passed as follows:

20th Battalion (1st Tyneside Scottish)
Lieutenant Colonel F A Farquhar Royal Scots
21st Battalion (2nd Tyneside Scottish)
Lieutenant Colonel H W Blair-Imrie, replaced by
Lieutenant Colonel P B Norris
22nd Battalion (3rd Tyneside Scottish)
Lieutenant Colonel S Acklom 22NF
23rd Battalion (4th Tyneside Scottish)
Major C P Porch 18/Northumberland Fusiliers.

The time at Pommier was spent resting and cleaning up, waiting for reinforcements to arrive. The officer replacements began to arrive first and then on 9 July the first draft of forty-four other ranks joined the 21st Battalion from 1/Northumberland Fusiliers. Among the draft was Private Tommy O'Keefe, a fit, athletic runner and a miner by trade, who had seen a lot of fighting at Gallipoli with the 8th Battalion, Northumberland Fusiliers, prior to being evacuated wounded to England. When he was again fit he was drafted to France and ended up in the 21st Battalion.

After an inspection on 12 July by the GOC 37th Division, Major General Count Gleichen KCVO CB CMG DSO, the brigade began marching towards Divion, which was reached on 16 July. The 37th Division now formed part of First Army under the command of General Sir Charles Monro GCMG KCB, who carried out an inspection on the 22nd of the month. On this parade awards for gallant conduct on 1 July, 1916, were made as follows;

Lieutenant R W Rutherford, 22nd Battalion, Military Cross; Second Lieutenant A W McCluskey, 21st Battalion, Military Cross; CSM E J Patterson Distinguished Conduct Medal.

Military Medals went to the following NCOs and men: Private R Ditchburn, Sergeant G A Kirk, Sergeant J Malcomb, Corporal J T Kempster,

Below: 4566 Private Thomas O'Keefe was wounded with the 8th Battalion NF at Gallipoli. He was among the replacements for the 21st Battalion, joining them 5 July 1916.

Above: German infantrymen. By the summer of 1916 the steel helmet was in regular use by both sides. After the losses of 1 July the Tynesiders were moved to a relatively quiet part of the front, however, enemy activity ensured a steady drain in killed and wounded.

Corporal T Patterson, Private G Johnson, Lance Sergeant R Davison, Private C Maddison, Private A A Bell, Private S Gibson.

Owing to the fact that the battalions were under strength the decision was taken to amalgamate the battalions in order to take over the line, consequently the 20th and 21st Battalions joined forces, likewise the 22nd and 23rd came together, each battalion providing two companies of the new battalion.

Officers from each battalion were taken forward by motor bus in order to reconnoitre the front line in the Carency sector, a thorough tour of the line was undertaken and all details for the relief agreed prior to the party returning to their own units. Specialists were trained in Lewis guns, bombing and signalling in preparation for going back into the front line, which was ordered for the night of 27/28 July. On that date the relief of 21/London Regiment by 20/21 Northumberland Fusiliers in the right sector of the line commenced. Combined battalion HQ was opened in Villers au Bois under Major Farquhar, 20th Battalion, as Lieutenant Colonel Blair-Imrie had been evacuated to the 23rd Casualty Clearing Station. Likewise the combined 22/23 Battalion, under the command of Major Porch, relieved 24/London Regiment in centre sector, the left sector being held by a combined

Tyneside Irish Battalion.

The weather was really hot and the number of dead bodies and flies made the trenches very unhealthy. These front line trenches were in a very bad state of repair and work was commenced to improve them. The drafts of new men were beginning to arrive; the 23rd Battalion reporting the arrival of 109 men on the 25th, 175 on the 26th and 45 on 27 July, whilst the 20th Battalion recorded the arrival of 190 men on the 25th and 111 on 26 July, 1916. Neither unit gave any details of the previous units the draftees came from, but it is highly likely that the majority came from Yorkshire regiments and had only been in the army a few months.

August began with only a little enemy trench mortar activity so the days in the line were described as quiet, the battalions once more began to supply men for working parties, carrying stores and ammunition up to the front. On the morning of 10 August at 6.57 a.m. the Germans blew a mine in front of the 20th/21st Battalion near Kennedy Crater and a bombing fight, which lasted for some two hours, took place before the enemy were driven back to their front line. During this action 20/825 Corporal J W Liddle of B Company, from Rowlands Gill, immediately carried two boxes of bombs to the head of the sap, and proceeded to throw the bombs at the enemy. For some time Corporal Liddle held the sap single-handed and prevented the Germans from gaining a foothold in the British line, this resulted in the award of the Distinguished Conduct Medal. Casualties from this action were described as light, then on 12 August the experience was repeated when another mine was exploded by the Germans near Number One Sap, once again the enemy were driven back and the crater lip consolidated after a short, sharp fight. A large draft of 221 men from 1/Northern Cyclists, 4/Northumberland Fusiliers and 10/Kings Own Yorkshire Light Infantry joined the 20th Battalion whilst it was in the line. Within a few days Cyclist R P Burrell was killed in action and a dozen or so of the draft wounded.

Also killed in action at this time was Captain Robert Knott, who fell on 14 August and who was a favourite with all who knew him. Originally a CQMS in B Company 9/Northumberland Fusiliers, he was commissioned into 28/Northumberland Fusiliers, and later he became the signalling officer of 19/Northumberland Fusiliers. He had to remain in England to undergo an operation for appendicitis and eventually joined the 20th Battalion in France on 11 July 1916. The Commanding Officer of the 20th Battalion wrote of him: 'I loved him as my own son'.

Questions were being asked in Parliament about the Tyneside Scottish in August 1916. It transpires that in December 1915, when the 22nd and 23rd Battalions were given their embarkation leave, the men were told their fares would be paid. Therefore when they went to the station to get the train, on being asked to pay, the men had refused. The Army authorities had also refused to pay and the railway company was chasing the men for the fare. Mr Wilkie MP, speaking in support of the men, had asked if the Financial Secretary was aware that the correspondence had been taking place ever since the previous January and that up to the present a settlement seemed to be as far off as ever. Mr Foster speaking on behalf of the Financial Secretary said: 'the investigation of the claims had been rather difficult but hoped that the matter would be dealt with very shortly.' The sad truth is that the railway company could never get the money from some of the men, for they were now dead.

Back in the line the enemy artillery and trench mortars were very active at this time and the men of the Tyneside Scottish were pleased when men of 11/Royal Scots and 9/Scottish Rifles arrived to begin the relief. The combined battalions were now reformed in their original order of battle and moved to the rear area, the 20th to Fresnicourt, the 21st, 22nd and 23rd to Estree Gauchie, further reorganisation and refitting taking place. The reinforcements that were arriving were no longer Tyneside Scottish and the north-country identity of the brigade was being lost. Many of the original members of the brigade, when they had recovered from their wounds, were posted to other regiments. This was commented on by Brigadier Ternan in his book:

'The reorganisation of the Brigade was now pushed on, and officers and men were sent to us from a variety of units to bring us up to strength. At first very few of our own wounded returned to us, and I got letters from men complaining that they had, on recovering from their wounds, been posted to units in which they were entire strangers. As one Corporal who had been posted to a south country battalion wrote, "They don't understand what I say, and I can't understand them". I tried hard to get our own men back, and was fortunate enough to enlist the sympathies of the Second Army Commander, Sir Herbert Plumer, with the result that a certain number of our men did eventually return to us, but in nearly every case the man, to his annoyance, was posted to the wrong Battalion, not the one in which he and his friends enlisted and with which he had his home associations.'

This state of affairs was bad for morale and a great mistake by the higher authorities, a fact recognized by the Brigadier who tried in his own way to rectify the situation, realizing that his soldiers would be happier and probably fight better if they were sent back to their own battalion.

'This I remedied by transferring the men to their own units until orders were received from the Adjutant-General's branch at General Headquarters that this could not be permitted. In order to comply with this order and at the same time fall in with the very natural wish of the men to serve with their old friends, I "re-transferred" the men to the wrong unit and "attached" them to their old one.'

However General Headquarters would not be beaten and this move was also blocked on the grounds that it made the clerical work 'unnecessarily complicated'. This meant that the men of the Tyneside Scottish would be sent to other regiments and the Brigade brought up to strength with men from other units. One large draft of the Tyneside Scottish were sent after the Somme battle to join 9/Cheshire Regiment in 58 Brigade of the 19th Division They were recalled by Private J Gerrard, a signaller in the above battalion, who wrote:

'What remained of the Tyneside Division we received as reinforcements. My company got a platoon of Tyneside Scottish and some of them were with us until the end of the war. These men included some fine fighting soldiers indeed, mostly colliers from the Durham coalfield.'

Orders were now received that 102 Brigade would

Above: Captain R C Knott attached 20 Battalion KiA, August 1916, his CO wrote: 'I loved him as my son'.

move to the Château de la Haie, to provide working parties for the 9th (Scottish) Division, but before this could take place the order was countermanded, with new orders being issued for the Brigade to rejoin the 34th Division. With the death in action of General Ingouville-Williams, the command of the 34th Division had passed to Major General C L Nicholson CMG, who would remain in command until 1919.

The various battalion transport sections left first and got the horses and wagons on to the train, the battalions themselves marching via Houdain and Divion to Calonne-Ricouart where they entrained for La Gorgue. On arrival at the last named place they were met by motor bus and transported to Erquinghem. Arriving at around 8.30.p.m. they went into billets, except the 21st Battalion who took over the subsidiary line from 11/Royal Fusiliers.

The 20th Battalion who took over the line from 6/Northamptonshire Regiment, had a rather quiet tour in the line except for the occasional *Strafe* by the German artillery and trench mortars. Prior to being relieved on the 31st they reported that 153 Brigade on the left had released gas towards the enemy trenches, which was supported by a heavy artillery bombardment, as well as rifle and machine-gun fire. In retaliation the Germans shelled the Bois Grenier line, but did little damage. The 22nd Battalion had marched to the trenches in the Bois Grenier sector on the same day as the 20th Battalion, and on 24 August their Battalion Headquarters was heavily shelled, the officers'

mess receiving a direct hit, burying the four occupants. When they were eventually dug out, Second Lieutenant T C Whitlock was found to be dead and Captain E Roscoe, Lieutenant S Bryson, the battalion doctor, and Second Lieutenant J H Faulder all wounded. Meanwhile the 23rd Battalion found billets in the laundries and these were described in the war diary as 'good accommodation.' The same battalion reported sending eight men to Divisional HQ to work with pigeons, given the Geordie coalminers interest in racing these birds; this is not such an unusual entry in the war diary. Another entry from the same unit records the assembly on the 25 August of a Court Martial to try five men of the battalion, and again on 29 August to try men of the 22nd Battalion. Although no actual case files have been seen, Courts Martial registers in WO/217 at the PRO Kew record that Privates W McKering, J Turnbull and J H Barron, of the 23rd Battalion, were tried for 'quitting their post in the face of the enemy'. All were found guilty and sentenced to one year's hard labour. At the same time Private F Barnett, of the same battalion, was tried for being drunk and was found guilty. His sentence was twenty-eight days Field Punishment Number One. The men of the 22nd Battalion were also tried for 'quitting their post in the face of the enemy', but in their case, Lance Corporal G W Alderson was found not guilty, unlike Lance Corporal J Blakey who received a sentence of one year hard labour. On the same day Private G W Maitland was tried and convicted under section 40 of the Army Act and sentenced to

Below: Aftermath of an attack, unburied corpses litter the ground making life in the trenches very unhealthy.

forty-two days Field Punishment Number One. Bearing in mind the harsh regime of military discipline in place at the time, these members of the Tyneside Scottish who allegedly 'quit their post', and were found guilty were lucky not to be executed.

Men were now being found for working parties, training undertaken where possible and the men medically examined for scabies and other skin complaints. The 23rd Battalion noted that two 'Old Men' were to be permanently attached to the Royal Engineers, for work in the communication trenches. This work involved the setting up of rest houses in the support line behind each battalion. These places are recorded in the Divisional History as follows,

'These were in cellars very close to the front line. In a rest house a man who had collapsed from cold after being some hours in a listening post, where no movement was possible, or one who had fallen into a shell hole and got wet through, could be brought. He was given soup or cocoa while his clothes were dried, and sent on his way, generally fit again, after a few hours. Finally we had an "up and down canteen", also near the front line. In this canteen all through the night a man or officer could get hot soup, tea or cocoa on his way up to or down from the trenches. The old light duty men who got the much sought after job of taking care of these places could live in a fug which is indescribable, and that is what everyone wants at the front.'

The Tyneside Scottish Brigade also established a soup-kitchen, in the village of Chappelle d'Armentières with two old soldiers running it, this was mentioned by Brigadier Ternan in his Brigade History,

'When we returned to Armentières we established in the village of Chappelle d'Armentières a soup-kitchen, and found a ruined shop in the main street which answered the purpose admirably. It had a real counter, over which the soup and biscuits were handed out to applicants in the most approved style. A bench or two were knocked up and the men could sit down and eat in some comfort. On cold nights the kitchen was much used by the transport men and by carrying parties returning from the trenches.'

The end of the month found the 23rd Battalion relieving the 20th in the B II sector of the front line. At 2.15 p.m. all signallers, snipers, observers and Lewis gunners paraded and proceeded to the trenches, followed at 8 p.m. by the men of the rifle companies, the relief being complete at 11 p.m. At the same time the 22nd Battalion were taking over the BI sector from the 21st Battalion. During the time in the line the 20th Battalion reported that NC/1203 Cyclist J A Bell accidentally shot himself.

Also 4/3546 Private J Danby attached from 4/Northumberland Fusiliers was accidentally killed. Both, 6120 Lance Corporal Rouse, East Yorks attached, and 20/1575 Private J J Carr, were wounded. The battalion diary also recorded the awarding of the Military Cross to Captain A E Kerr the DCM to Corporal Philipson, and four Military Medals to Sergeant Piper J Wilson, Piper G H Taylor, Privates J Ferguson and H Jackson along with a Divisional Card of Honour to Sergeant G Bestford. All these awards were for the gallant conduct of the individuals named at La Boisselle on 1 July.

It was about this time that Private Tommy O'Keefe found himself on duty in a forward position:

'I was in an OP in the front line sitting on the fire step, off to one side above my head was a opening, but a German sniper was zeroed in on it, they clamped the rifle in a vice and lay watching through binoculars, so we didn't dare look through the opening. Well, eventually I was joined by a very young officer, who kept trying to look through the opening. Several times he was told don't do it and the reason why. The time came when for some reason I had to leave him alone in the trench for a few minutes, when I came back he had his face pressed up against the opening, I put my hand on his shoulder and he slumped sideways, dead! Shot straight between the eyes! He just wouldn't be told.'

102 Light Trench Mortar Battery had bad luck on 30 August when an enemy shell landed in a fire bay and killed 22/126 Lance Corporal George Neale, a miner at Cambois Colliery, who lived in Blyth. For his bravery in action on 1 July he had been awarded the Military Medal. The Officer Commanding 102 LTMB, Captain Edmund Bowkett, wrote with the news of her husbands death to Mrs Neale:

FRANCE 8/9/16
'Mrs George Neale
112 Bowes St
Waterloo
Blyth
Northumberland

Dear Madam
I expect by this time you will have heard of the death in action of your husband L/Cpl G Neale. On behalf of the officers and men of the Trench Mortar Battery, I offer our deepest sympathies.

He was killed by a shell while working his gun and would suffer no pain as he died instantly.

He was a brave, cheerful, hard working soldier, respected and liked by both officers + men. When under heavy fire he was always cool and collected and a splendid

Above: 22/250 Corporal Martin Henderson.

Below: Private A McDowell, 20th Battalion.

125

example to younger and less experienced soldiers.

A parcel and several letters have arrived since his death. The former I have handed over to his comrades in the Battery and the letters I am returning to you. A parcel of his personal belongings has been forwarded which you will receive in due course. Again expressing deepest sympathies with you in your loss, believe me to be

Yours very truly
Edmund F Bowkett Capt
Commdg 102 Bde LTMB

PS You will have heard that your husband had been awarded the Military Medal and I am glad yet sorry to inform you that the day after his death he was awarded an additional bar to the above medal. These you will receive in due course.

EFB Capt'

Below: Second Lieutenant Reginald Baty joined the 21st Battalion after service with B Company of 9/Northumberland Fusiliers. He is pictured here pumping water from a trench in the Armentieres Sector.

Mrs Neale also received a letter from the secretary of the Tyneside Scottish Committee, and arrangements were made for her to be presented with her late husband's Military Medal and Bar.

September began quietly, with the battalions in the line carrying out repairs and building new dugouts, there was little shelling and casualties on the whole were light. There were frequent patrols out into No Man's Land and wiring parties to strengthen the British wire, but nothing untoward was reported. Portions of the British front line were in a terrible state and were undefended, having been blocked off with wire and obstacles. Word was now received that these positions had to be reopened and placed in a state of defence. To this end the battalions in the line extended their frontage and linked up with their neighbours. This left a shortage of manpower and the battalion in support was called on to supply carrying parties to deliver the rations for those in the front line. It was on the night of 11/12 September, on one of these carrying parties, that Second Lieutenant Catto of the 23rd Battalion was shot through the heart, being buried in Erquinghem Churchyard the following day.

It was in mid-September that Corporal Reginald Baty of B (The Quayside) Company, of the 9th Battalion was commissioned. Reg had spent some time at 17th Divisional Headquarters making maps prior to attending a commissioning course at the General Headquarters of the BEF. On completion of the course he was posted to the 21st Battalion. In one of his first letters home he complained about the 'Balmoral' and said he preferred his service cap, he also wrote about his orderly and described him to his mother:

'My orderly is a chap about 27 I should think, married with three children. His address here is Pte Craig R S, 21/111, 21st NF. His wife's address is 2 Brown's Buildings, Tyne Street, off City Road N/c. He is quite a canny chap. He would at a pinch make two of me in size. He has the honour of cleaning my buttons, belt, boots etc, gets my washing done for me, gets my valise when we come out of the trenches, lays my bed out and pinches as much stuff for me as can be done creditably, for instance if I am short of hair oil, say, he 'borrows' some from another officer. I believe if my revolver ammunition ran short he would empty another officers last six rounds out for me to slay rats.'

On 15 September at 11.30.p.m, after a preparatory bombardment, Captain Waugh of the 22nd Battalion led a raiding party of 150 men against the enemy trenches at La Houssoie. The Germans however replied by putting a heavy barrage down on his own front line, and although some of the raiders reached the enemy parapet, no prisoners were taken. In fact most of the party were stopped at the enemy wire. At the same time Lieutenant

Robson led a party of thirty men out from the Rue du Bois trenches, but again the Germans put down a strong barrage that prevented identification of the enemy unit opposite being obtained. These raids cost the 22nd Battalion two killed and eight wounded other ranks. Two days later, on 17 September, Second Lieutenants Begg and Mcrea, who had both been on the previous raid, again went over and again the Germans prevented an entry to their line by shelling it, which resulted in Second Lieutenant Begg being wounded.

The next day it was the turn of the 20th Battalion to raid the enemy lines and Second Lieutenants G W Sandeman and B Wilmot, along with 25 other ranks, went over to the enemy lines opposite Chard's Farm. Yet again the raid was unsuccessful, owing to the enemy employing the same tactics as before, and placing a heavy bombardment on his own front line. Brigadier Ternan devotes a chapter of his book to the work of these raiding parties, describing at length the preparations, the tactics and composition of the raiding parties:

'In order that the enemy should not get accustomed to any particular form of raid, variety in method was necessary. Some raids were carried out by small parties others by much larger ones. Sometimes a raid would be made on a front trench only, sometimes both the front and support trench would be raided. The times for the raids had to vary, as well as the particular bit of trench to be raided, but all our raids took place after dark.'

He also described the ideal weather conditions for a raid as being, 'A dark windy night with the wind blowing from the Boche lines to ours.'

Invariably a practice trench, resembling the area to be raided in the enemy lines, was dug well to the rear in the Brigade area. Then the raiding party would practise until every man knew what was expected of him. Prior to the raid taking place those officers and NCOs in charge would go out and make several patrols into No Man's Land, in order that they would be able to find their way safely to the objective.

Second Lieutenant Reg Baty described being on patrol in a letter to his parents:

'The night scouting as you call it, I don't do so much now as we are teaching the NCOs to take them and so use a little initiative. The job is hardly horribly weird now that one has done it for seventeen months off + on. Though possibly there is nothing more weird to a novice than crawling out between the lines at night + wandering about for a couple of hours. I was jolly nervous on my first stunt I remember + I almost sweated myself to death before I went out, it was cold as well, but once out + doing a walk and a crawl soon got warmed up. Every time the Boche fired across at our trench I thought it was meant for me, but one or two patrols soon knocks that out of one. As a matter of fact No Man's Land is quite a safe place to be.'

One reasonably successful raid carried out at this time took place on the night of 30 September, when two parties of the 23rd Battalion raided the German trenches. The raid was split into two groups, the right group of fifteen men under the command of Lieutenant Cowley and Second Lieutenant Broach actually reached the enemy trenches. Here during a short fight, one German soldier was killed, and one, a member of 10/Bavarian Regiment, was captured, being brought safely back to the British lines. The left party however, again made up of fifteen other ranks, under the command of Second Lieutenants Freeman and Coyne, were held up by a ditch full of wire and did not have time to penetrate the enemy defences. The artillery co-operation for this raid was excellent, and the Germans did not send a single shell over during the time in the enemy lines. This raid brought the name of the Tyneside Scottish to the attention of the Army Commander, General Sir Herbert Plumer GCMG KCB, and the following message was received by the 23rd Battalion.

'The Army Commander wishes to congratulate all concerned in the results of last night's raid. The identifications gained are very valuable, and the damage inflicted on the enemy is very satisfactory at this stage.'

Added to the message were the congratulations of Sir Arthur Godley, Commander of 2nd ANZAC Corps. It also brought the award of the Military Cross to Second Lieutenant Cowley, for his able leading of the party and his coolness in bombing an enemy dug-out.

October began with the 23rd Battalion being relieved in the front line by the 20th Battalion, whilst the 21st Battalion were relieved by the 22nd Battalion. Little is reported for this period, the usual working parties, and officers proceeding on leave, with new officers arriving. Lieutenant Wilmot and thirty-two men of the 20th Battalion began training for a raid. Lieutenant Colonel W A Farquhar prepared plans for the raid, but meanwhile the weather changed to rain and frost. These two elements contrived to make life difficult for those trying to maintain the trenches, the mud destroying the good work previously done. Routine events such as men being inoculated, new gas masks fitted and, of course, large working parties, were noted in the various war diaries throughout the month, but the events that take up most space are the raids against the enemy positions.

The Germans were getting jittery, due to the number of raids taking place, and they started to bomb their own wire at night, but during the day they were described as fairly quiet.

On the night of 12 October, at 7.30.p.m., the party that had been training under Second Lieutenant Wilmot left the British trenches in front

Above: 20/1234 (B Coy) 20th Battalion of Browney Colliery, transferred to the Labour Corps.

Above: Captain J H Philips, 21st Battalion in the trenches at Armentieres.

Below: 20/1203 Michael Price a stretcher bearer of Old Pit, Ryton.

of the right company of the 23rd Battalion, who were holding the line. With great dash and determination the raiders crossed No Man's Land and entered the enemy trench. They killed a large number of German soldiers and captured some, however owing to their reluctance to accompany the men of the Tyneside Scottish, and their own counter barrage, they had to be killed. For his conspicuous gallantry during the raid, Second Lieutenant Wilmot was awarded the Military Cross, whilst six NCOs and men were given the Military Medal. This raid succeeded in obtaining a number of identifications at the cost of only five men wounded, but in the ensuing German counter-barrage on the British front line, the 23rd Battalion had Second Lieutenant King and one other rank killed, with eight other men wounded. The Corps Commander made a visit to the front line on 11 October, followed on 13 October by Brigadier Ternan, who visited the line in the morning.

Each battalion in turn was given the task of carrying out raids on the trench dwellers opposite. The 21st Battalion had a go on 20 October, the enemy meeting the raiders at the parapet and driving them back, costing the 21st Battalion Second Lieutenant Grice and two men wounded, with two others missing. To co-operate in this scheme, at the same time the 20th Battalion carried out a dummy raid. This involved Second Lieutenant R F Williams and four men going out with Second Lieutenants Hayward and Letherer and two sappers of 208 Field Company, Royal Engineers. Early in the evening they placed a Bangalore Torpedeo under the German wire and then at Zero Hour,

10.30 p.m, this was fired. The party in No Man's Land exposed dummy figures, and Vickers and Lewis gunfire opened on the enemy trenches. This was instrumental in bringing down a strong counter-barrage from the German artillery and trench mortars. A large number of these trench mortar bombs fell in the vicinity of Chard's Farm, a number of which were blinds. After the firing had died down Second Lieutenant R F Williams took a strong fighting patrol out to where the Bangalore Torpedeo had been fired in the hope of finding some enemy dead for identification purposes. This proved fruitless and the patrol eventually returned safely but empty-handed to their own trenches.

As previously stated, Brigadier Ternan devoted quite some space to the work of the raiding parties in late 1916, and one story well worth repeating is that of a prisoner being brought back over No Man's Land:

'On one occasion a very truculent prisoner was being hustled, fighting and kicking, across No Man's Land, and an officer with the party noticed that it might be impossible, time being pressing, to get him over alive. He knew that live prisoners, capable of giving information, were particularly required just then, so he said to the men bringing the prisoner in, "Try coaxing", whereupon one of our men, a bit of a wag, called out in a "call-the-dog-voice," "Come along Fritzy, old boy, come along, good old Fritz you shall have such a good dinner." At the word "dinner" the struggle instantly ceased, and the Hun walked in like a lamb amid the roars of laughter from his captors.'

Always after a raid there would be a roll call followed by a patrol into No Man's Land to search for those missing, but normally the enemy were alert and made this a difficult task, giving rise to a number of men reported missing, believed killed.

The routine work in the trenches continued as before, with the battalions in reserve and support, supplying working parties, and on top of this each night sending two platoons up into the front line to strengthen the garrison against attack, for rumours quickly spread in the Tyneside Scottish Brigade, when their comrades and next door neighbours, the 2nd Tyneside Irish, lost a Lewis gun and its team during a German raid on the British trenches.

A parade took place at Croix du Bac in late October, each battalion of the Brigade sent a small party of men to it, when the Second Army Commander, General Sir Herbert Plumer, presented medal ribbons to those officers and men who had won them in the recent fighting. Also present that day were Sir Thomas Oliver and Colonel Joseph Reed who were making another visit to the Brigade in the field.

The weather turned wet and the rain got progressively worse, when on 24 October the Divisional Trench Mortars, manned by the Royal

Field Artillery, carried out a bombardment. Many of the shells fired fell in the British trenches, causing the diarist of the 23rd Battalion to write:

'Fortunately no one was hit (much to the disgust of the Boche), The enemy retaliated with minenwerfers all of which fell into our lines, some of which caused considerable damage.'

November began badly, in preparation for a forthcoming raid, the 23rd Battalion sent out a patrol of three officers, Second Lieutenants Pinnington, Common and Falcy, along with four NCOs, on the night of 4 November. This patrol reached the German wire, making a thorough reconnaissance of the wire right up to the enemy held parapet. At this point the patrol began to withdraw and when they had reached a point about fifty yards from the German lines they came upon a hostile enemy fighting patrol. The Germans were lying in wait and their sudden onslaught caught the Tyneside Scottish patrol unawares. A sharp bombing fight began, during which the Tynesiders became separated. They made their way individually back to the British lines, and here it was found that Second Lieutenant Pinnington was missing, also that the other two officers and three of the four NCOs were wounded. A German soldier who had lost his way in No Man's Land was found and taken prisoner. A fighting patrol under Second Lieutenant Common was immediately assembled and set out to search for the missing Tyneside Scottish officer. A thorough search was made of the ground where the fight had taken place, even going up to the enemy wire, but no trace was found of the missing officer.

Within a day or two the 20th Battalion moved back into the line relieving the 23rd Battalion, placing three companies in the front line and one, D Company, in reserve. That afternoon a heavy barrage was opened up on B Company the left, and A Company in the centre. The Germans seemed to be throwing everything they had at the British front line, and in the centre A Company had three men killed outright and some wounded. However B Company fared even worse, for a 5.9″ shell landed straight on the Company Headquarters dug-out, killing two, and severely wounding four officers, at the same time killing one other rank. When the debris was cleared and the bodies dug out of the ruins, it was found that Captain A H Jeffreys and Second Lieutenant W H Dodds were dead; Whilst Second Lieutenants N H Richardson, T Rowell, C J Mackintosh and L H Cowper were wounded, the latter dying of his wounds later. Lieutenant Cowper had served in the Artists Rifles OTC before being commissioned into the Northumberland Fusiliers. His parents received a very long letter from Second Lieutenant George A Riding, who served with the 6th Entrenching Battalion prior to being posted to the 24th Battalion.

'If by his death I am stunned and sore, you must find the blow well-nigh un-
bearable. We came from the same battalion, the 32nd, and crossed together. At the Base we shared a tent, and our first billet here in this little French village was in a garret together, and our lives ran together until he was called up to his new battalion. We became the very closest of friends.'

George Ridings, who was a schoolmaster, then mentioned all the homely things that Leonard Cowper talked about and how happy he had been; he then went on to describe the last time he saw his friend.

'The last time I saw him he was sitting on the front of a lorry alongside his kit going out to 'The Wood', and I harked back to the joy-ride we had had together on our arrival here on a motor lorry as near to the line as we could get, "to see the war". All who knew him showed the deepest sorrow "the fair young officer who was always smiling", was the way they described him and as a man said, "He had a smile and a word for everybody: it's always the finest chaps that are taken!"and the officers here from the Colonel downwards are genuinely distressed.'

Shortly after the shelling of the Company HQ dugout at about 7 p.m. another barrage was opened up on the front line, this time without causing further casualties, the enemy ceasing to fire when British artillery replied in kind.

The only entry from the 22nd Battalion diary worthy of note in November is that Second Lieutenant Piegrove and a party of men carried out a raid, when they entered the German trenches and brought back identification of the German unit opposite. This was carried out without loss to the raiding party.

With the constant drain of manpower due to casualties reinforcements were required, but only the 21st Battalion record the arrival of these men during this period, when on 10 November twenty two other ranks joined, but no previous unit was given., A few days later RSM W Hodson joined the Battalion for duty, but the strain of trying to keep the trenches in a reasonable condition was beginning to tell and the 23rd Battalion diarist wrote:

'A great deal of work requires to be done in this sector now. There are not sufficient men in the front line or detailed for the front line to carry on with the necessary work there, with the result that it becomes more uninhabitable every day. Drainage is bad and in bad weather it will be difficult to find a place which does not take one over the shoe tops. [Was he really wearing shoes in the trenches?] *Too many men are detailed for work in dugouts in the reserve lines and posts. There are*

Above: Second Lieutenant Victor Pinnington, KiA 5 November 1916 with 23rd Battalion.

Above: Second Lieutenant Leonard Cowper after being commissioned in the 32nd NF. Drafted to France he was posted to the 20th Battalion. He died of wounds 7th November 1916.

Above: 20/410 Private Jeremiah Hair of Ryton who was killed in action 30 November 1916 and is buried in Ration Farm Military Cemetery.

Above: 241924 Private Frederick Jackson, 49 Red Lion Street, Earby, Yorkshire KiA 14 November 1916, with 1/5 Battalion NF (formerley 29th Reserve Battalion NF).

Above: 40556 Private Walter king, Tubber Hill, Barnoldswick, Yorkshire, KiA 23 November 1916, with 16th Battalion NF (formerley 29th Reserve Battalion NF).

many places in our sector where there is no accommodation for officers or men. The only places where officers can sleep or get their food, are mere shelters, which would not even keep the rain out, never mind a shell.'

The raid planned by the 23rd Battalion was progressing well, Second Lieutenants Common and Falcy with their men were training at Rue Marle. Brigade Headquarters in the meantime were completing the arrangements for the artillery barrage, orders were issued on 12 November. On the night 11/12 November the raiders arrived in the front line, and completed preparations, ready to go over the top at 4.30.a.m. The raid was divided into three parties: Second Lieutenant Falcy and twelve men; Second Lieutenant Common and ten men; and Sergeant Russell with eight men. The route through the wire was cut by X Trench Mortar Battery, who had done a thorough job, providing the raiders with a clear gap. The night was very misty and very favourable for an approach to the enemy trenches. As the moonlight broke through the mist, under cover of the barrage, the raiders got to within thirty yards of the entry point. Immediately the barrage lifted the leading section, under Second Lieutenant Falcy, rushed forward through the gap and found a barrow pit, fifteen foot wide and five feet deep, full of water. Somehow the party crossed this obstacle, crossed the parapet, worked along the trench to the left. The German Artillery now put a heavy barrage down on their front line, and the three leading men were wounded by this shellfire. The officer and a slightly wounded man pushed on followed by those members of the party who were unwounded. Further along the trench they met four or five Germans in front of them and the young officer threw two bombs then opened fire with his pistol, as the enemy retired, wounding at least one. Losing sight of the retreating enemy in the maze of trenches, Second Lieutenant Falcy gathered his men together ready to withdraw. They collected some rifles and equipment passed the wounded over the parapet then came back to the British lines.

The second party, in the meantime, had followed the first through the barrow pit and over the parapet, and on entering the trench Second Lieutenant Common took his men to the right. They searched all the dugouts they came across, finding them of a similar style to the British 'Dog Kennel', although they were empty and nothing of importance was found. This party too withdrew on time.

The third group under Sergeant Russell crossed the barrow pit and lay down on the parapet, to assist with the evacuation of any prisoners and those of the other two groups who were wounded. They successfully evacuated all the wounded, under heavy fire in difficult conditions before they too withdrew. All those who entered the enemy line noted with satisfaction that it was in a far worse state than the British line. The CO of the Battalion also wrote in his report that:

'I have every reason to believe that Second Lieutenant Falcy, Second Lieutenant Common and Sergeant Russell led their men with courage and ability, and also that all their men behaved very well.'

Once more congratulations were received, the Brigade Commander signalling: 'Last night's raid reflects great credit on all who took part.' The GOC 34th Division General Nicholson added that: 'He considered the arrangements and execution reflects great credit on officers and men.'

The same battalion noted on 15 November that,

'The only accommodation is a rat-infested dugout, which is foul smelling – one that has not been occupied for months. The value is now being realised of concrete dugouts in reserve trenches and posts. A move is to be made to build a decent company headquarters in the centre sector, and the Chard Farm sector.'

Divisional artillery was active on the 20th Battalion front, heavily shelling the foe in his communication trenches, whilst 102 Machine Gun Company fired several belts of ammunition at enemy infantry who were seen to leave the communication trench owing to the barrage.

The weather, which had been wet and cold, now turned extremely foggy, this allowed the 20th Battalion to spend time repairing the wire. Much energy and time was also spent repairing damaged trenches and dugouts, the enemy trench mortars and artillery being inactive at the time. When not engaged on working parties, those in reserve behind the line found time to have a bath, with parades taking place for physical training, drill and gas inspections. One event of note was the arrival of a draft of fifty-eight men to the 23rd Battalion, all of them old Tyneside Scottish men who had been wounded on 1 July.

A sad occurrence took place for the same battalion when, on 21 November, Second Lieutenant H H Falcy, who had just become Battalion Intelligence Officer, was shot in the head by a sniper. Two days later the award of his Military Cross was announced, along with the award of the Distinguished Conduct Medal to 3811 Sergeant E Russell.

One amusing incident took place about this time which was related in 'The Yellow Diamond' by 23/492 Private Martin Cudlipp of Cramlington. When at Armentières he went to a house in Erquinghem to see a CQMS of the 1st Battalion, who was billeted in a house there. Martin went in and, no seat being available, he sat on the edge of the CQMS's bed. Martin said he was thirsty and was invited to put his hand under the bed and pull out the usual receptacle (a chamber pot) which reposes there. Mystified, he did so, and found it full of SRD (RUM). Hesitatingly, he lifted it, but his thirst overcame his scruples! So that's where the rum ration went! However, the CQMS explained that the battalion was well under strength, hence the surplus rum, and possible scroungers were not likely to look for it there.

The 21st Battalion also raided the German lines, their raid took place on the night 22/23 November, with similar results to the previous raid. Enemy helmets and equipment were brought back, but no prisoner. On the last day of the month the 20th Battalion reported the arrival of two drafts, one of thirty men and the second of fifty-eight men and so December arrived cold and dull.

The Brigade Staff were preparing still more raids for the weary men of the Tyneside Scottish, so that even when out at rest they were kept busy training for raids. The 20th Battalion began training a party of four officers and ninety men on 1 December. The battalion was under strength at this time, having left so many men behind training, and so when they went back into the line, B Company had to be divided up to bring the other three companies up to strength. Owing to this lack of manpower C Company of the 23rd Battalion was placed in support, disposed in Paradise Alley and Queen Street.

On 8 December, 1916, Reg Baty described in a letter to his mother the billets in the rear to where the 21st Battalion had moved:

'We are now billeted in the regulation Bairnsfather farm. We have one decent room with a mahogany round table, over-mantel candelabra in a typical old farmhouse. We have a gramophone in our mess which, though a more or less disdained affair in civil life – works overtime here.'

On the night of 10/11 December 1916 at 1.10 a.m. the 20th Battalion party that had been in training commenced their raid on the enemy trenches. The party was made up of four officers and eighty-four other ranks of the 20th Battalion, three Royal Engineers of 208 Field Company, and three men of 102 Light Trench Mortar Battery. These men were divided into two main groups under the command of Second Lieutenant Macnaught and Second Lieutenant Browning. Both groups attacked simultaneously and managed to take three men of 18/Bavarian Infantry Regiment prisoner, along with much valuable information. This was one of the most successful raids carried out by men of the Tyneside Scottish Brigade.

The relief of the Tyneside Scottish Brigade now took place and for the next two weeks they went into Divisional rest at Rue Domoire. Bayonet fighting drill and musketry took place, along with a Brigade football competition in which the 21st Battalion team was unbeaten. Drafts were also arriving to bring the depleted battalions back up to strength, the 21st Battalion noting that ' A draft of 116 men was added to our strength on 20 December, these men consisted mostly of Army Service Corps personnel.'

Above: 34th Division Christmas card 1916.

Preparation for an inspection by General Sir Douglas Haig, began on 19 December, when battalions started practising ceremonial drill. As the 23rd Battalion would be in the trenches on Christmas day, on 20 December they were given a Christmas dinner. This consisted of roast Beef, Onions, potatoes, beans and cabbage, followed by Christmas pudding and fruit and nuts. The following day saw more ceremonial drill followed by football in the afternoon and that evening the officers had their Christmas dinner. Similar arrangements were made for the 21st Battalion, who had their meal on 28 December.

Second Lieutenant Reg Baty was on leave over Christmas; when he arrived in Newcastle he found that the Christmas cards he had given to his batman Private Craig to post had not arrived. On his return to the front he found the cards still inside his valise. This resulted in Private Craig's return to duty in the line and the appointment of 21/158 Private John Beavis as his new batman. He was able to send the cards to his mother, remarking in the letter,

'I am not enclosing the Xmas card but sent it along in its own envelope, having acquired a new batman, Beavis by name, who seems a jolly good man + hasn't lost

Above: Lieutenant H S Matthews MC 23rd Battalion attached 21st Battalion in the Armentières trenches late 1916.

Right: Christmas 1916 21/876 Private George Barnfather sent this card from Giessen PoW camp in Germany.

anything yet, though I have had him six hours. Also enclosed was a copy of the menu for B Company, Officers Mess Christmas Dinner.

SOMEWHERE IN FRANCE
21(S) BATTN. NORTHLD FUSILIERS 'B'
COMPANY
Christmas 1916.
M E N U

SOUPS
Creme des Tranchees
POISSONS
Clod au Mudde
JOINTS
L'Ami de l'Allemagne
Les Yeux des Armees
Le Cochon qui vole
VEGETABLES
Pommes au Mush Mush
Brussels en 1917
SWEETS
Les Delices du 102nd
Sauce de 'Stand To'
La specialite 'MATTHEWS'
DESERT
Pommes, Oranges, Pates de Noel
NOIX - de toutes sortes
Esperances de Flapperes
CAFÉ et LIQUEURES

The other two battalions did not mention their arrangements, but it is safe to assume that the men were given as good a time as possible. The parade for General Sir Douglas Haig took place on the main road This event is well recorded in all the battalion war diaries and the 34th Divisional History.

'The force was drawn up along the Armentières - Estaires road. This road was in many places visible from the ridge behind the Boche lines, but as the Huns had hitherto shown themselves complacent as

GREETINGS ~ MEILLEURS VŒUX
Xmas - Noël
~ 1916 ~
Giessen.

regards traffic passing to and fro, this fact had been overlooked when the road was selected for the inspection. The morning before the review was uncommonly fine, and General Nicholson, motoring into Armentières, noticed how much it was under observation. Not wishing to put too great a temptation in the Boche's way, he called on the Pioneers to get the whole length screened before the next morning, which they managed to do.'

The troops were formed up along the south side of the road between Erquinghem and Fort Rompu. There were all the Divisional Artillery; 208 Field Company Royal Engineers; HQ and one company of 18/Northumberland Fusiliers and 10/Lincolns representing 101 Brigade; the whole of 102 (Tyneside Scottish) Brigade; and the 24th Battalion representing 103 (Tyneside Irish) Brigade. The support arms were represented by elements of all the Field Ambulance Units and the Army Service Corps of the Divisional train was there too. Congratulatory messages came in from all quarters, from General Haig, from the Corps Commander, Lieutenant General Sir A J Godley, and the GOC of the Division, Major General Nicholson.

After the parade the men of the Tyneside Scottish were on their way back to the line. On 23 December the 20th Battalion relieved 25th Battalion, and then on 27 December they took over the front line from the 23rd Battalion. The last named had taken over the front line from the 26th Battalion, in very wet and windy conditions, on the morning of 23 December.

On Christmas day the Germans caused some damage to the trenches, when they replied to a trench mortar and artillery barrage. Likewise the 21st and 22nd Battalions were taking over from Tyneside Irish Battalions, and then relieving each other in the front and support lines. Working parties continued right up until New Year's Eve, the last reported fatality from the 20th Battalion, was 20/1573 Private Edward Anderson, of Shiney Row, on 28 December. The following day four other men were wounded, one of them 37427 Private J S Smith, accidentally. Enemy aircraft were extremely active at this time, three of their heavy machines came over the 23rd Battalion lines at the end of the month, but hastily retired when a British machine put in an appearance whilst the anti-aircraft fire against the enemy was described as erratic.

So the year 1916 came to a close the Tyneside Scottish, after the fight to raise the Brigade, had at long last made their mark on the field of battle. They had learned their trade the hard way, suffering the deaths of many brave and gallant men, but had gone on to become proficient at trench raiding, as borne out by the number of gallantry medals won in the last few months of the year. But they were still where they started from, manning the trenches near Armentières, some wondering, no doubt, if 'Madame had any good wine' left for 1917.

Chapter Eight

Arras and Greenland Hill

'Their objective is taken, they must prepare to resist,
The counter-attack which will come through the mist.'

THE BURNING QUESTION,
ANON, IN THE WIPERS TIMES

ON NEW YEAR'S EVE the 21st Battalion took over from the 22nd Battalion in the B1 sub sector, the 22nd moving back to the subsidiary line. Likewise the 23rd Battalion moved up into the B2 sub sector, replacing the 20th Battalion, who moved back into Brigade reserve, in billets at Rue Marle.

So began 1917, for those in the line the trenches were badly flooded, and movement proved difficult. This hampered those on working parties, which still had to be supplied by the battalions out at 'rest'. The artillery and trench mortars were particularly active on 1 January, and then the next day there was a concentrated artillery shoot on the whole of the Corps front. Every gun of 2nd ANZAC Corps took part, the enemy replying in kind, giving the church at La Chappelle d' Armentières frequent attention. Enemy aircraft were often over the lines too but seldom went any further than the front line. After a few days the battalions again rotated, with the 20th replacing the 23rd yet again.

Each night standing patrols were positioned out in No Man's Land, but the enemy were very quiet, that is until the night of 6/7 January, when a large fighting patrol was observed making its way towards the British line. Immediately the men of the 20th opened a rapid fire on the Germans. From the screams and cries for stretcher-bearers, which were plainly heard, it appeared that the German patrol had suffered several casualties. About this time the 21st Battalion was detailed to raid the German lines, but owing to a bright moonlit night, the party were unable to form up in No Man's Land accordingly the raid had to be cancelled.

As the month wore on the weather changed and once more thick mists descended across the whole of the front. On 14 January men of the 20th Battalion had more excitement when out in No Man's Land. A wiring party from the battalion was out at work covered by a party that included a Lewis gun. This second party noticed a German

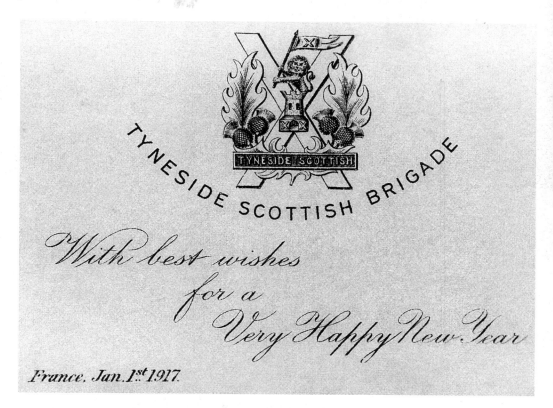

patrol approaching slowly through the mist, and the signal was given for the wiring party to cease work and quietly withdraw to the British front line trench. Once the working party was clear, the covering party poured Lewis gun and rifle fire into the enemy patrol. Sometime later a strong fighting patrol from the battalion, under the command of an officer, was sent out to check No Man's Land. They stealthily approached the German line and got to within about fifty yards of it, when through the mist the patrol could see two enemy soldiers assisting a third man, who was wounded. The British patrol then fired two rounds rapid fire at the three men, but they disappeared into the mist. Almost immediately the German front line was ablaze with rifle and machine-gun fire, but the Tynesiders withdrew in good order without casualties to their own lines.

Above: Tyneside Scottish Brigade Greetings Card New Year 1917.

Above: 22/803 Private William Stenhouse was discharged sick 19 January 1917.

Above: 40749 Private David Walling, 20 Clifford Street, Barnoldswick, Yorkshire, KiA 11 February 1917 with 23rd Battalion NF. One of several men transferred in from the Duke of Wellington's (West Riding Regiment).

Drafts were arriving daily to bring the battalions back up to strength and of three drafts that joined the 23rd Battalion, the first, of sixty men, had no front line experience, the second of one hundred men were described as, 'not very enthusiastic,' whilst the third were 'all trained men, several of our old men who were wounded on 1 July amongst them.'

The Tyneside Scottish Brigade was relieved in the line by the Tyneside Irish Brigade, and moved out to a welcome rest. After a complete day doing nothing, a programme of training began. Musketry was carried out on two ranges, a 200-yard range at Fort Rompu being used for the normal rifle practice, with a thirty-yard range at Erquingham being used for shooting in respirators. The Yellow Diamonds, the theatrical troupe of the 21st Battalion gave four performances at the Divisional Theatre in Erquinghem at this time. They received a mention in Brigadier Ternan's history owing to the leading 'Lady', Lance Corporal Charles, who took the female parts most successfully, being poached by the 34th Divisional concert party The Chequers. The Concert Party was also mentioned by Reg Baty who wrote to his parents that: 'The Brigadier was awfully bucked up by the show and so was everyone else.' About this time Reg spent some time attached to 102 Brigade Headquarters as Brigade Bombing Officer, this allowed him to move about quite a bit, and he met up with and passed on news of old members of the 'Quayside Company'.

'*I have seen Tommy Catnach* [Lieutenant 26th Battalion] *he is as fit as anything + quite cheerful as ever, so Noel Murton is 'missing' jolly bad luck. Hope good news will be to hand soon* [Sergeant, 9th Battalion, actually a POW]. *I have seen 'Billie' McQuillan he has a job now of Divisional Claims Officer, so will be allright'.*

Others that were mentioned were Jack Slater, who was a Lieutenant with The Scottish Horse, and Freddy Wilson MC, serving as a Major in 18/Northumberland Fusiliers. Of course many of the Battalion officers were also mentioned in his letters home, in particular Captain Waller, for whom he had a great regard.

In the meantime the 23rd Battalion, also out at rest, had been training for another raid. Each company in the battalion was to supply three officers and sixty men for the coming action. The raid was to be commanded by Lieutenant Colonel Porch in person. All levels of higher command were showing great interest in this raid, as it was to be the first of its type, by the division, no larger raid having been carried out up to this time. Snow had fallen and a keen frost covered the ground; this was seen to present a problem for the raiders to cross No Man's Land. On 25 January Major General Nicholson spent the morning watching them practise and that afternoon an officers' conference

took place. The next afternoon, very suddenly, orders were received to pack up and move to Mont des Cats. After the late arrival of the motor buses, which were to transport the battalion, the men were taken to the wrong area. This caused a great deal of trouble as the billets were also allocated to 10/Lincolnshire Regiment. By doubling up, the men were quartered overnight, but word was received that the raid would still take place. The next day the 23rd Battalion moved on to billets in Godewaersvelde and training for the raid recommenced. The other battalions of the brigade were also billeted in the area, the idea being to make the Germans think that troops were being concentrated for an offensive at Ypres.

At 9.30 a.m. on the morning of 30 January, 1917, 326 men left in lorries for Erquinghem. Those left behind were formed into two companies and that afternoon had a long route march.

Having moved back to the Erquinghem area, the raiders again started practising. On 1 February, General Plumer, commanding Second Army, came and watched.

The raid was organized in four parties based on the four companies. A Company was under Captain C H Daggett MC, accompanied by Second Lieutenants J Common and S Milley, with sixty-seven other ranks. B Company was led by Lieutenant W H Thompson assisted by Second Lieutenants Morris and Young with sixty men. C Company, with Lieutenant T E Heron in command, was being assisted by Second Lieutenants Watson and Algie. The Commanding Officer went over with this group. Last, but not least, D Company was led by Second Lieutenant J Freeman, under his command was Second Lieutenant S C Kerridge and sixty-six other ranks.

Zero Hour was planned for 10.30 p.m. on the night of 11 February with the parties lining up from left to right as follows: A Company, D Company, C Company and B Company.

At precisely Zero Hour the men of the Tyneside Scottish stormed forward. On the left A Company met with very heavy hostile fire. However Second Lieutenants Common and Milley, with some of their men, got into the enemy trench. Second Lieutenant Milley proceeded to bomb some dugouts, killing at least three German infantrymen later he shot another. Unfortunately Second Lieutenant Common was severely wounded and a great act of gallantry was carried out. Private Wearmouth, Second Lieutenant Common's orderly, on seeing his officer wounded, picked him up and started out across No Man's Land with him. The enemy on this flank now left their trenches and came forward, firing across No Man's Land. Private Wearmouth placed Mr Common in a safe place and began to bomb the Germans and eventually forced them to fall back.

A machine-gun firing on this side of the raid caused many casualties to the second group of A Company and they were unable to penetrate the German wire. Captain Dagget was forced to order his party to retire, owing to the machine-gun, the counter attack and the number of casualties. On arrival back in their own lines the men of A Company found that their OC was missing.

The next party, D Company were also unable to get through the German wire, and the officer leading this group, Second Lieutenant J Freeman, was seen to fall, mortally wounded. His second in command, Sergeant Alsop, took over and ordered the evacuation of all the wounded, before withdrawing the party.

C Company also met with resistance at the wire, but brushing it aside stormed into the German front line, but here Second Lieutenant Watson was wounded. Lieutenant Colonel Porch was with them and some good work was done bombing dugouts. Second Lieutenant Algie, meanwhile, with great dash and determination led his party straight on into the enemy support line. A large fight developed in this line, Algie personally accounting for several enemy soldiers. CSM L Moore and Lance Corporal W Mitchell were also in great evidence in this fight. Prior to withdrawing from the second line an ammunition store and a company headquarters dugout were blown up, this task being carried out by Sappers Brady and Morrow of 209 Field Company, Royal Engineers. Second Lieutenant Algie's party captured seven prisoners. This included two officers, a third officer being shot by Algie, with his pistol. In the front line Lieutenant Colonel Porch was wounded, but contact was made with D Company when Second Lieutenant Kerridge managed to establish communication.

When the raid commenced the enemy sent up rockets which brought down a prompt and very heavy barrage on the right hand party of the Tyneside Scottish. The barbed wire on this flank was not cut correctly and this held the party up. Second Lieutenant Thompson forced his way into the German line but had to retire very soon after. The raiding party had a good deal of casualties, one officer missing six officers wounded. Of the other ranks, twelve were killed, thirteen missing and thirty-seven wounded. Second Lieutenant Algie was immediately recommended for a Victoria Cross, however this was reduced to a Distinguished Service Order. Lieutenant Colonel Porch received the same decoration. Praise was poured on the 23rd Battalion, General Plumer wrote:

'The operation was well planned and carried out and reflects great credit on all concerned.'

Both Corps and Divisional Commanders added their comments and after the raiders had rejoined their battalion, both generals came and inspected the men. As well as the Distinguished Service Orders previously mentioned, there were five Military Crosses awarded; A bar to the Distinguished Conduct Medal went to 21/377 Sergeant A F Jackson, attached for the raid from his own battalion. Three Distinguished Conduct Medals went to CSM Moore, CSM Watson and

Private Craighill. Private Wearmouth won a Bar to his Military Medal and there were no less than twelve Military Medals given to members of the raid, one each to Sappers Brady and Morrow.

Orders were received that the 34th Division was to leave Second Army and move south to the Arras front, another offensive was in the offing and once again the Tyneside Scottish battalions would be in the line at Zero Hour.

The move to the Third Army commenced on the morning of 18 February at 8.45. a.m, the Tyneside Scottish marched in Brigade formation, passing through Le Brearde, Hazebrouck, Morbecque and spending the night in billets at Steenbecque. The next day's march took them via Aire to St Hilaire. On 20 February a footsore day was spent marching to Bours. After this halt the battalions proceeded independently towards the Arras front, each day moving a little closer to the area behind the line. The huts at Ecoivres were reached, these were new Nissen Huts made of corrugated iron sheets and much more comfortable than the barns that the men were used to; however, some were not pleased to have left their previous billets.

'Settled back into the old routine and awfully sorry to have left that billet I mentioned to you where Madam and her daughters! were so good to us. Custards when I was inoculated, Rum and hot milk before going to bed. I was known as Gosse! which is "Little Boy" and another chap was "Baby", the daughters were "Les mechantes et terribles". Some billet, but some days of marching + then we were a long way from such a nice spot. My French has improved

Above: 29/454 Private Peter Hodgson, Hill Top Farm, Wennington, Lancashire DoW 17 February 1917 with 9th Battalion NF.

Below: Men of the 21st Battalion February 1917, prior to leaving the Armentières sector for the Arras front. Seated 2nd row, second from left is 37884 Private Joseph Ray, from Tynemouth, KiA 1917.

Above: Captain Arthur Preston Ker, Brigade Transport Officer. Transferred to the Labour Corps in 1918.

Above: 40685 Private John Dean, Brook Cottage, Earby, Yorkshire, DoW 26 February 1917 with 23rd Battalion NF. Formerley Duke of Wellington's (West Riding Regiment).

a little during the fortnight we stayed there.'

(Second Lieutenant Reg Baty 21st Battalion.)

Parties of officers and NCOs were sent forward to reconnoitre the front line positions. On 24 February 102 Brigade began the relief of 27 Brigade of 9 (Scottish) Division in front of Arras. The 21st Battalion relieved 11/Royal Scots and 22nd Battalion relieved 12/Royal Scots both battalions being in the front line. Word was received that on the Fifth Army front the Germans had withdrawn, within a short time of the receipt of this news, patrols were pushed forward. The patrols found that in front of the Tyneside Scottish, at least, the Germans were wide-awake and very alert. In anticipation of a withdrawal on the Arras front the divisions in the line were placed on twenty-four hours notice to attack. It was about this time that the following incident occurred in the 21st Battalion, as recalled by Private Tommy O'Keefe:

'A lad from Walker, by the name of Chadwick, was sent to draw the rations for the company and on the way back he managed to substitute the officers bacon for some of the bacon that was for the men. A little later I was cooking the bacon when the company commander came along, and on smelling our bacon cooking he said, "By jove that smells good O'Keefe", to which I replied "Would you like a sandwich Sir and a pot of Tea". He replied "yes" of course and two thick slices of bread were cut and a huge sandwich made with freshly cooked bacon, a pot of strong tea completed the feast. Having finished his sandwich the company commander was about to leave when he said, "You chaps get jolly good bacon, much better than the rubbish they sent us". How we never choked I'll never know, no one even batted an eyelid as he went out of the dugout, Ah didn't like te tell him it was "is arn bacon he enjoyed".

Behind the front line in the meantime the 20th Battalion took over billets in Arras, where enemy shelling killed Private E Turner and wounded two other men. With an offensive due to start, working parties had to be found and every available man was out working, but tragedy struck C Company of the 23rd Battalion on 25 February. A large group of men from the company were drawing tools from a store when, without warning, an enemy shell landed amongst them. There were many casualties, six men were killed outright, and thirty-two wounded, of whom nine later died of wounds. The 21st Battalion also suffered from German shelling.

The South African Scottish, serving in 9th (Scottish) Division, carried out a raid on the night of 27 February and in the ensuing enemy counter-bombardment the communication trenches to the 21st Battalion were cut, damage was caused to the

front line and there was several casualties amongst the men.

So February passed into March and the 20th Battalion billeted in Arras had several casualties when the enemy shelled the town, but the 21st Battalion in the front line reported that the enemy was quiet. Having moved into the front line and settled down, Private Tommy O'Keefe, serving with the 21st Battalion, set off down an old trench to do some exploring.

'I had gone a little way and stopped to listen, I felt uneasy as if I was being watched. After a short time I moved on and then again stopped to listen, then I heard a noise and looked round to find myself staring down the barrel of a German rifle. I had no chance! Before I could raise my rifle I would be dead. Then suddenly the barrel of the German soldier's rifle was lowered, the young German smiled at me, then he waved his hand as if saying "next time Tommy", and before I knew it he had shouldered his rifle and disappeared out of sight round a traverse in the trench.'

Not many stories have survived about working parties but one is told in The Yellow Diamond by T B Brown of Newcastle:

"'You, You and you, Parade for a working party at 10 o'clock", said the Corporal, pointing to the three of us brewing some char over the stove in the hut. "But I was on last night corporal." "Can't help that" said the corporal. We were always unlucky, five minutes earlier and he would have found the hut empty.

Off we trudged with seven other unfortunates, at 10 o'clock, to the RE Dump. During the day this place was as though dead, but with the coming of night it sprang to life, a ghostly population arising from the dugouts and cellars.

We were shepherded in single file into the dump and there encumbered with picks, shovels and sandbags. The Royal Engineer led the way and off we went up past the Farm where the transport and at least a battalion of men were making an awful row unloading limbers.

It was very dark, and it was only possible to keep in touch with the dim shape in front by keeping close up. It was a very sticky chalky trench, typical of this sector, and my pal had covered his lower legs with sandbags. This hardly helped progress. One of the sandbags worked loose and came off and I tripped on it, crashing like a five nine shell into his back. The resulting language was noisy, choice and all embracing. The gas blanket of a nearby dugout was raised and a voice enquired sweetly who was making all the bloody noise. My pal replied, "The Bloody Tyneside

Above: German infantry in support line.

Scottish what about it?" The voice subsided at that.

"Get a move on", came from the rear, and another party carrying Flying pigs came scrambling past in the narrow trench. We eventually got to a traverse behind the front line, were told to be as quiet as possible and get on with the job of digging out a trench mortar pit about ten foot square and deep. The ping of machine-gun bullets close by was not comforting, and the occasional glare of Very lights brought us immediately to a standstill. We got down below the surface and soon had a covering of earth and chalk beside us. I thought frighteningly that it seemed like digging one's own grave. Luck was with us and there were no casualties that night; sandbags were filled and placed to strengthen the emplacement. Jerry was wakening up and a nightly strafe got going, and then the "wind" was decidedly vertical in the gun pit.

After what seemed hours, our job was completed, and we staggered back well caked with the chalky clay of the trenches. My pal's spirits were not dampened however and with his Red Hussar glowing in defiance of orders, he besought us to join him in chanting, "I have no pain dear Mother now".

Our burdens were dumped, all Royal Engineers consigned to a warmer place, and we reached the old hut at last. The other occupants are sleeping and snoring, and stumbling over them we get down to it. Ah well, there cannot be another working party until to-morrow.'

In the meantime the 22nd Battalion was relieved in the Roclincourt trenches by the 23rd Battalion. The latter unit placed A Company on the right, B Company on the left, C Company in support and in reserve, at Roclincourt village, was D Company, along with Battalion Headquarters. To the front of the position taken there were, two mine craters known as, King and Kite, very unhealthy places as they came in for a lot of mortar fire. On 6 March at 6 a.m. the Gordon Highlanders, on the right of the 23rd Battalion, carried out a raid in which they took one German Officer and twenty of his men

Above: The Kitchen brothers; George and Stephen in the Tyneside Scottish and James in the Royal Naval Division.

Above: Second Lieutenant Percy Chaston Young, 22nd Battalion, from Osbourne Road, Newcastle.

prisoner. This brought down a heavy artillery barrage onto the 23rd Battalion, causing four casualties. That night the enemy began sending up rockets, green and red in colour and as soon as they lit a heavy barrage was opened up. But the Germans too were busy with trench raids, on the evening of 6 March after a quiet day, the Germans launched an attack against the 23rd Battalion. At about 7.30 p.m. an estimated sixty to seventy Germans crossed No Man's Land opposite the left sub sector, now occupied by D Company. After a barrage of rifle Grenades and light mortars that lasted five minutes, the Germans came forward, throwing smoke bombs, towards the Tyneside Scottish held trenches. They were immediately engaged with Lewis guns, rifles and grenades and only in two places did they succeed in reaching the British wire. When the enemy realized that they were pinned down, an order was shouted out in German, most likely by the officer in command, and a red rocket was fired into the sky. In a matter of minutes a trench mortar barrage was landing on the British trenches and under its cover the enemy party withdrew to their own lines.

The routine of the working parties continued, the 21st Battalion having three officers and ninety-eight men based at a large dugout in Anzin for work, whilst the remainder of the battalion were training at Ecoivres. On the night of 7/8 March this unit sent two officers and forty-two other ranks to carry out yet another raid. The enemy was ready for them, having repaired the gaps previously cut in the wire. They had also barricaded their front line and it was strongly manned. Despite all the difficulties that they encountered, the men of the raiding party entered the German trench, and succeeded in bombing several dugouts, but unfortunately no prisoner was taken. On return to the British held line it was found that three men were missing and that one officer and four other ranks had been wounded. This raid eventually resulted in the award of the Military Cross to Second Lieutenant Reg Baty, the wounded officer, who had been admitted to Number 10 Red Cross Hospital at Le Treport, from where he was able to write home to his parents on 14 March:

'I managed to get a small wound in each leg, left thigh it missed the artery by a fraction and wasn't very deep. The right got a small piece in the shin bone which can stay there, both are giving no trouble at all, in fact I am having a delightful rest cure.'

Further on the young officer wrote:

'I know your burning curiosity re the wounds, well – a raid same old game! The wily old Hun was just too wily for us so we got the baccy instead of the Hun, though he didn't get off for nothing. I got into the trench after I was hit so you can judge my wounds weren't too bad. Should be glad of an occasional box of State Express 555 cigarettes and 50 Francs and a writing pad. I landed here with nothing except a Tommy's tunic, a revolver and a black face. I am trusting my goods and chattels will follow me here, so in the meantime I depend on charity for shaves. If I wanted to get up – I don't think I could – my pants were burnt and my breeches also as they were cut to ribbons to get at my wounds. The old Hun hasn't done much to me in twenty months has he? Twenty months tomorrow since I landed and still going strong.
Regards to all
Cheerio
Reg.'

Reg Baty was evacuated to hospital in Torquay from where he was able to write to his mother another letter, he was anxious about his wallet and the money in it and also his personal belongings:

'You see as I said I have no kit yet save my revolver which is rather an awkward thing to shave with, in fact it is only done in the best circles. I haven't wrote to Beavis at all when I get my pocket book I shall send him some French notes, however, I hope he doesn't get pinched by someone else, I want him back when I rejoin.'

Reginald Baty never rejoined, for whilst he was still in England his transfer to the Royal Flying Corps came through and he went off to learn to fly.

On 9 March both raiding and working parties rejoined the main battalion. The Brigade was now moved in motor transport to the training area at Chelers, where a model of the German trenches had been marked out with flags. For twelve days the assault was practised across this mock battlefield until the men knew precisely what they had to do. An innovation to these exercises was the inclusion of an aeroplane that co-operated with the advancing infantry. The diarist of the 22nd Battalion was impressed with the men, so much so that he wrote:

'The men showed intelligence and soon got a grip of the scheme in spite of numerous alterations and amendments. The Black, Blue and Brown lines were invariably captured.'

During the time on the training area the General Officer Commanding XVII Corps, Lieutenant General Sir Charles Ferguson, inspected the Brigade. During the parade a number of officers and men were presented with the ribbon of their gallantry award. The withdrawal of the Germans from lines south of Arras to the Hindenburg Line resulted in XVII Corps being placed at twenty-four hours' notice to attack. However the battalions that were holding the line reported that at times the enemy were increasing their bombardment and that the telephone wires were being repeatedly cut.

For a period of ten days at the end of March the Tyneside Scottish Brigade were quartered behind

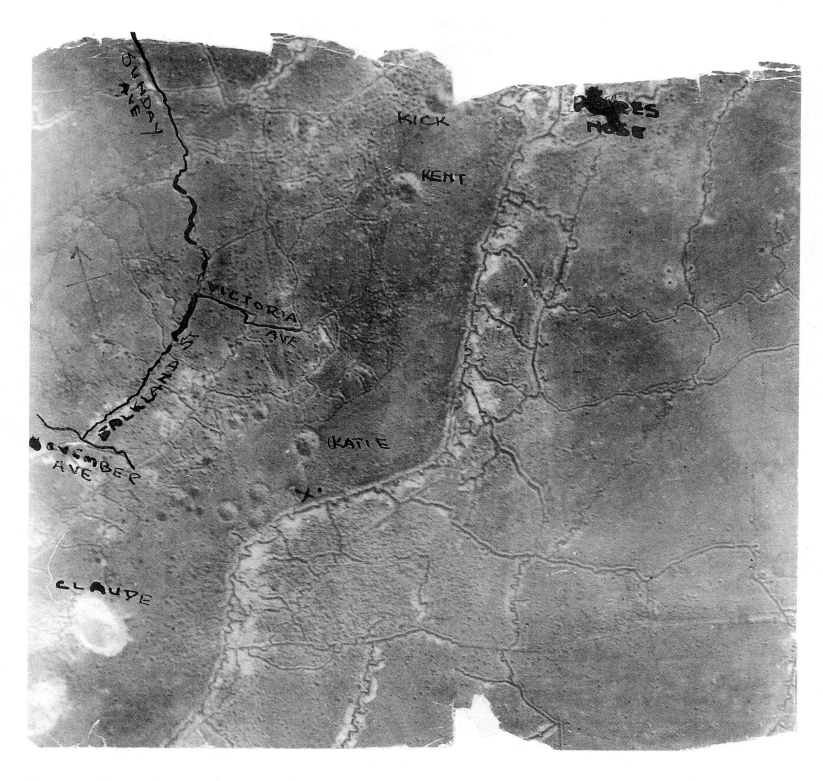

Arras, supplying working parties for the line. As they had been employed in the same way the previous July, the work was familiar to many of the old hands and this made the task much easier. Daily large parties of men made their way to forward dumps, carrying with them all the stores and equipment required to fight a war. These working parties, just before the battle of Arras, received special mention from Brigadier Ternan:

'The experience that we had had at Albert was very valuable to us now; the routine preparation was similar, though some of the arrangements were not identical.'

Raids by all the Brigades of the 34th Division were used to keep up a constant pressure on the German defenders, with the objective of identifying the enemy unit opposite. Drafts of new men were arriving to keep the battalions up to strength, but the drain of casualties was constant and some of the most experienced officers and men were evacuated at this time. The 21st Battalion reported Major A D M Napier had been evacuated on 24 March, whilst the 23rd Battalion, who had received a draft of forty-eight other ranks on 13 March, had evacuated sick between 13 and 30 March no less than thirty-six other ranks. In the same period the battalion suffered seven other ranks wounded and

Above: An aerial photograph of the Arras front kept by Second Lieutenant Reginald Baty. X marks the section in front of the German trenches where he was wounded and won the MC.

Above: 29/618 Private Robert Hebden, 41 Church Street, Barnoldswick, Yorkshire, KiA 2 April 1917, with 12th Battalion, NF.

one killed. Therefore the draft really only represented four extra men.

In the forward area the trenches were filled with wet clinging mud, which was knee deep in places; the falls of sleet and snow did nothing to improve matters, and the men's feet were beginning to suffer. The 23rd Battalion reported on 29 March, when they went back into the line, that:

'There are only fifty pairs of gum boots for the Battalion and owing to our bad boots the men are beginning to suffer unduly because of the wet, muddy trenches.'

The first week of April was spent in very bad weather, snow and rain, preparing for the advance that was soon to take place. Working parties kept the men in an exhausted condition, and the number of men reporting sick was higher than usual owing to the servere weather conditions.

Officer reinforcements arrived from 31 Infantry Base Depot among them Second Lieutenant Jack Lakeman who was posted to the 20th Battalion, shortly after his arrival he wrote to Wycliffe, his old school in Gloucestershire;

'I am doing very well billeted in a farm house. The men are packed like sardines in barns, which just at present are extremely draughty and cold. The rum ration helps to keep them warm, but an officer must always attend and keep a

sharp lookout lest the mess tin, spoon, rum and all disappear in addition to the two tablespoon rations. The men always grumble at the quantity but never go to sleep before it comes round.'

On 6 April all battalions were notified that Z Day had been delayed by twenty four hours, then the following day the 21st Battalion, having left a nucleus of men out of action, relieved the 20th Battalion in the front line. They took over the sector between Kite and Kate craters and then had Captain A V Curry evacuated owing to shellshock.

9 April 1917

Planning for a battle in the Arras area had been considered the previous year, in June 1916; however because of the heavy casualties incurred during the Battle of the Somme, the opening of an offensive on the Arras front was delayed.

The GOC Third Army, General Allenby, had under his command from right to left VII, VI and XVII Corps and on his left flank, under the command of First Army, detailed to assault and capture Vimy Ridge, was the Canadian Corps.

XVII Corps had been given the task of assaulting and capturing the land north from the left back of the River Scarpe to the southern edge of Vimy Ridge. Under his command the Corps commander, Lieutenant General Sir Charles Ferguson, had 4th, 9th (Scottish), 34th and 51st (Highland) Divisions.

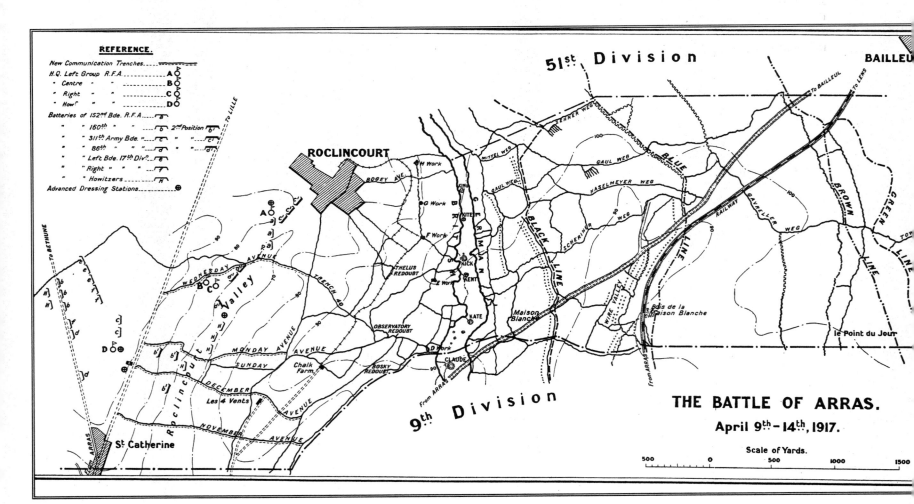

THE BATTLE OF ARRAS.
April 9th – 14th, 1917.

The Corps had a distinctive Scottish flavour about it, for as well as the two Scottish divisions, it contained the South African Scottish, 102 (Tyneside Scottish) Brigade, the 15 and 16/Royal Scots in 101 Brigade and 2/Seaforth Highlanders serving in the 4th Division. The 9th Division was given the task of covering the low ground on the right flank, from the River Scarpe to the low slopes where the Bailleul ñ St Nicholas road crossed the front line. Behind the 9th Division lay the 4th Division, ready to come up in support. From the Bailleul – St Nicholas road, north to the Bailleul – Roclincourt road, the ground was held by the 34th Division and on their left the 51st (Highland) Division. Then on the slopes of Vimy Ridge on the Highlanders left, with the hardest task of all, was the Canadian Corps. The success of the Canadian Corps depended on the XVII Corps taking its objectives and the success of the latter Corps depended on the 9th (Scottish) Division securing its objectives. The 9th Division could only succeed if the 34th Division captured and held the ridge on which stood the strongpoint, le Point du Jour Farm, which commanded all the low ground to the south and west into Arras itself.

The objectives for the British were the three main enemy trench systems, known as the Black, Blue and Brown lines. These three lines had to be taken and then a further advance made and a new line, the Green Line, had to be dug well forward to give good observation over the German positions. Once again the Germans had a good idea that an offensive was to take place. Against the wishes of General Allenby, GHQ had ordered that a three week long artillery 'wire cutting' barrage was to take place, followed by a five day bombardment. General Allenby had only wanted a two-day bombardment.

For the 34th Divisions part in the attack, Major General Nicholson decided to use all three Brigades in the line. On the right 101 Brigade, in the centre 102 Brigade, and on the left 103 Brigade. Each Brigade would have two battalions forward, one in support and the fourth in reserve. In his history of the Brigade Brigadier Ternan states, however, that he had in the line from right to left the 20th, 21st and then 22nd Battalions with the 23rd Battalion in support. Yet the War Diaries and the Divisional History state that the 21st and 22nd Battalions were in the line with the 20th in support and the 23rd in reserve.

On the night 8/9 April 1917 those battalions in the rear began to make their way forward into the firing line. At 7.30 p.m. the 20th Battalion, with 20 officers and 550 other ranks under command, marched off from their billets. When the battalion reached the trenches the men were positioned in a specially constructed assembly trench. The 22nd Battalion trooped up from Arras into the left-hand portion of the Brigade front line. In the front line were posted A and B Companies, with in support C Company in New Street and in reserve, in Spook Street, D Company. On the right flank lay the 21st Battalion, who as we have seen took over the line from the 20th Battalion on the night 7/8 April. The 21st Battalion was employed throughout the day bringing forward stores from the dumps, picks, shovels, bombs and sandbags were all distributed to the men of the battalion. Then at 2. 30 a.m. Second Lieutenant L A Woodcock from B Company led a small patrol out to inspect the German barbed wire. On return he was able to report that this was now practically non-existent on the battalion front. The 23rd Battalion left the village of Louez on the evening of 8 April and proceeded to their assembly positions in Wednesday Avenue.

The leading waves of the 21st and 22nd Battalions, at about 4.30 a.m, crept quietly out into No Man's Land close up to the German wire, in order to be as near as they could possibly be to the barrage. No Man's Land was between seventy and one hundred yards wide in this area and when the barrage lifted both battalions, advancing on a two company front, rushed forward into the enemy lines.

On the right the 21st Battalion captured their first objective within an hour, then at 6.30 a.m. Battalion Headquarters received a message from Captain H W Waller, Officer Commanding A Company, that he had fought his way into and captured Kuchen Weg, a German trench beyond the Black Line. This trench was taken with small loss but the Officer Commanding Number Three Platoon, Second Lieutenant MacNeill was killed in the German Second Line. Three other platoon commanders, Second Lieutenants Corlett, Donaghy and Woodcock, commanding Numbers One, Two and Five Platoons respectively, were wounded before reaching the first objective.

On the left flank the 22nd Battalion meanwhile also took the Black Line on time. Enemy resistance was overcome in the first line of trenches and the advance went smoothly and on time. The barrage on this portion of the front was very effective and the German Infantry surrendered without too much of a fight. The 22nd Battalion pushed on towards the Blue Line and were able to report that by 8.30 a.m. they were in possession of this objective too. Members of the battalion were behaving with great gallantry, both 22/980 CSM John Duffy, of New Delaval, and 22/1410 Sergeant Joseph Glendinning, from Mickley, Northumberland, were awarded the Distinguished Conduct Medal for taking large numbers of Germans prisoner. It was here that Captain G Charlton distinguished himself when greatly assisting the battalion to achieve its aims by the skilful way in which he handled his reserves. Another gallantry award was gained when Sergeant Bill Estell of Newcastle won the Military Medal, for going out and bringing in wounded men under fire. Originally enlisted in the 6th Territorial Battalion, Bill had been posted to the Tyneside Scottish after recovering from wounds received at Ypres in April 1915.

Above: 37325 Sergeant Bill Estell wounded at Ypres in April 1915 with 6th NF, posted to the Tyneside Scottish he won the MM at Arras in 1917. This photograph was taken later in the war when he was serving with 20th Reserve Brigade in England. Note the '20' arm patch.

Below: 29/595 Private John William Rodgers, of Cononley, Yorkshire, KiA 9 April 1917 with 21st Battalion.

Le Touquet, his parents were able to visit him and be at his bedside when he died. His parents received many letters of condolence from the officers of the Battalion, the Commanding Officer wrote:

> *'He possessed a charming disposition and his brightness and cheerfulness quickly made him a favourite with his brother officers and the men.'*

The 20th Battalion did find, however, that the German soldiers who gave themselves up were totally demoralized, the majority only too glad to surrender.

The 23rd Battalion left Wednesday Avenue as late as 8 a.m, when they moved forward in artillery formation until they reached the Blue Line. On passing through the 22nd Battalion, the 23rd Battalion moved into extended line, suffering only a few casualties owing to a weak enemy barrage and the battalion began to form up ready to advance. They were a little to the right of where they should have been owing to the troops of the Tyneside Irish Brigade being pushed across to their right by men of the 51st (Highland) Division. The British barrage started to drop short and the 23rd Battalion had several casualties from their own artillery shells. On the left, the Tyneside Irish were held up by a German machine gun, which caused the 23rd Battalion to push on with their flank in the air, until they encountered a thick uncut belt of barbed wire in front of the Western Brown Line. It was here that Captain T E Heron MC did some sterling work, setting a fine example to the men when, under sniper fire and British shellfire, he cut a lane through the barbed wire thereby gained a bar to his MC. Once there was a lane through this belt of wire the Western Brown Line was captured with ease. However the Germans put up a stiffer fight for the Eastern Brown Line, having been able to reorganize, and they made the men of the 23rd Battalion fight hard for their objective. By careful approach work in short rushes, they got close enough to deliver a bayonet charge and the Brown Line was carried at the point of the bayonet. During the latter part of the operation Captain T E Herron MC, Second Lieutenant S C Kerridge and Second Lieutenant F Ashworth were wounded; the latter eventually dying from his wounds. For his skilful handling of the battalion, Lieutenant Colonel Porch received a bar to his Distinguished Service Order.

As the day went on the weather turned very cold. The Brown Line was consolidated that night as snow came down on the victorious men of the Tyneside Scottish.

On the left, with the failure of 103 Brigade to get forward a protective flank had to be thrown back along the Gravelle Weg to link up with the Blue Line. In the early hours of 10 April a conference was held at the Headquarters' dugout of the 27th Battalion, at which plans were finalized for a further attack upon the uncaptured part of the Brown Line.

Meanwhile back on the right flank, at 7.45 a.m. the 21st Battalion had commenced to advance towards the Blue line also, which required an advance of some 1200 yards. Casualties in other ranks were light but the toll on the officers was quite heavy and it was not until 11 a.m. that the objective was captured and they were in possession of the Blue line. The Officer Commanding Number Fourteen Platoon, Second Lieutenant T E Bainbridge, was killed, along with his platoon sergeant, as they established a bombing post in the Railway Cutting. Hostile snipers too were causing trouble at this point and the men of the 21st Battalion had to begin work to ferret them out. Captain Waller, along with a party of men from his company, succeeded in capturing a German light field gun, along with its crew. Others of the Battalion also captured a German machine-gun emplacement, with the gunner still at his post.

It was now time to move on and take the Brown Line and for this task the 20th and 23rd Battalions passed through the leading battalions, in order to continue the advance. The 20th Battalion reached and captured the Brown Line but at some cost. The Battalion lost a total of 289 all ranks representing over half of the men that had started the day. One of the first to fall was Second Lieutenant Jack Lakeman who was wounded in the head almost as soon as he crossed the parapet. He had only been out at the front three weeks and had come down with a bad case of influenza. Ordered to report sick he had replied that he could not do so with the battle about to commence. Evacuated to hospital at

The 21st Battalion was detailed to take part in this attempt and, starting at 5.30 a.m, their attack was completely successful, meeting little resistance. Later on, however, as the battalion consolidated the position, they came under sniper and machine-gun fire. Patrols were pushed forward towards the Green Line and it was while carrying out a reconnaissance, in front of the position held, that Captain H W Waller was killed. The 23rd Battalion also sent forward reconnaissance parties towards the Green Line and they were instrumental in the capture of two batteries of 77mm Field Guns, along with five of the German gunners. Once the reconnaissance parties returned an advance to the Green Line was made at 7 a.m. and digging in commenced. However there was no time to rest, ammunition was brought forward, and the dead had to be buried. The weather was appalling, there had been a number of snowstorms and the men were totally exhausted by the miserable conditions. Owing to the effects of exposure a number of men were evacuated, while the remainder crowded into captured dugouts to try and get what little sleep they could.

103 Brigade was now moved into a reserve position and the Tyneside Scottish Brigade side stepped to the left and took over a portion of the line previously held by that brigade. At the 22nd Battalion Headquarters the position in the Green Line was unclear, therefore Second Lieutenant Simson was sent forward with a patrol to find out what was happening. He found that the enemy was holding an important trench junction in the area of the next division. The battalion on the left, 1/King's Royal Rifle Corps, sent up a Sergeant and four men to take the position, but this was not enough. The 21st Battalion then arranged to support them with a Stokes gun of 102 Light Trench Mortar Battery. When it arrived in position the Stokes gun failed to fire, so the attack had to be cancelled until later that night. At 1 a.m. Second Lieutenant Simson led a group of men towards the trench junction, where an alert German sentry challenged him then opened fire with his rifle, before throwing a number of bombs. Second Lieutenant Simson tried to return fire with his pistol, but this failed to fire, so he led his men forward, throwing bombs at the Germans and driving them from their position.

At dawn the men under Second Lieutenant Simson's command observed the surviving German soldiers leave some shell holes and retire towards Bailleul. The captured position was then handed over to troops of the 2nd Division, who later evacuated it and, on discovering this fact, the position was reoccupied by the 22nd Battalion. The other battalions in the reserve positions were suffering from the hostile weather, so much so that on 12 April Divisional Headquarters ordered forward three companies of 18/Northumberland Fusiliers (Pioneers), to take over from the 23rd Battalion in order that the last named could be rested.

The 22nd Battalion pushed a patrol forward towards Gavrelle to keep in touch with the enemy and the 2nd Division on the left. Despite being fired on this patrol managed to return without loss. Then at 8 p.m. on 14 April 4/Bedfordshire Regiment commenced to relieve the 22nd Battalion. Similarly other units of the 63rd (Royal Naval) Division relieved the rest of the Tyneside Scottish Brigade, which was withdrawn to billets in Arras, where a hot meal was ready for the men when they arrived.

The Brigade was then transported to the area around Monchy Breton in order to begin the usual re-organization after a battle. Reinforcements were taken in and classes to train specialists started. Inspections by Corps and Divisional commanders took place and letters of congratulations from HQ Third Army, HQ XVII Corps and HQ 34th Division were received. It was now that Brigadier Ternan, who had commanded the Tyneside Scottish Brigade since its formation, had to leave the Brigade, in his own words:

Above: Germans in well constructed trenches.

Above: Second Lieutenant John Pearce Lakeman, educated at Wycliffe School and commissioned into the NF in March 1917. He was wounded in the head during the first hours of the battle of Arras. Taken to hospital at Le Touquet he died of his wounds on 20 April and was buried in Etaples Military Cemetery, he was just 19 years old.

'I had come to the end of my tether, and reluctantly had to acknowledge that there comes a time when one must step aside for a younger man. While arrangements were being made as to my successor, Lieutenant General Sir Charles Ferguson paid us a visit, and made a congratulatory speech to the Brigade drawn up on parade, and he was good enough to say pleasant things about myself, which I much appreciated. The Brigade, a day or two later, moved to the village of La Thieuloxe, and while there I took the opportunity of thanking officers and men for their splendid services and saying goodbye to each Battalion on parade and wishing them good luck.'

THE CHEMICAL WORKS AT ROUEX

Command of 102 (Tyneside Scottish) Brigade now passed to Brigadier General N H T Thomson, late Seaforth Highlanders, who assumed command on 22 April, 1917, just as the Brigade began to make its way back towards the front line. The Brigade moved forward through Arras at 7.55 p.m. and on St George's Day 1917 the 22nd Battalion took up positions in the old German front line in the neighbourhood of St Laurent Blangy. The battalion found it difficult to find dugouts, but eventually cover was found for about 150 of the men, and fortunately the weather was improving, making conditions for those without cover bearable. The other battalions and Brigade Headquarters moved forward into the Railway Cutting east of St Laurent Blangy, the 21st Battalion relieving 16/Royal Scots at 5 30 p.m. on 24 April.

After three days spent in the Cutting, word was received that the Tyneside Scottish would relieve 103 Brigade in the Oppy Line, north of the Fampoux Road. 34th Division had been given the task of capturing the village of Rouex where the enemy was dug-in in some strength. The Chemical works and the Château inparticular were held in strength, both sites being considered as ideal for turning into strong-points. The 20th Battalion was now loaned to 101 Brigade to assist with their part in the divisional attack. The Battalions of 101 Brigade were disposed from right to left: 15/Royal Scots, 10/Lincolshire Regiment and 11/Suffolk Regiment, and behind them, employed in a mopping up role, were 16/Royal Scots. As soon as these battalions advanced, the 20th Battalion was to move into the vacated trenches. Starting at 4.25 a.m. the day started badly, the barrage being described as ragged and not heavy enough to put paid to the German machine guns. The infantry of 101 Brigade did their best but in the circumstances they could not get very far. The 20th Battalion had gone forward and it was now that they came into their own. Some men were seen to be retiring from Mount Pleasant Wood closely followed by large numbers of Germans. This counter attack, by men of 65/Reserve Infantry Regiment, was pushed hard and they succeeded in entering the British lines, although they came under fire from both the 20th Battalion and the Lincolns. Lieutenant Colonel N A Farquhar, commanding the 20th Battalion, now ordered A Company to bomb the Germans out of the positions they had just taken and as the enemy were driven out the Lewis gunners of the battalion opened fire causing a great deal of casualties among the retreating enemy. Lieutenant Colonel Farquhar took over command of the remnants of 101 Brigade and started to repair the British front line. With the failure of 101 and 103 Brigades the 22nd and 23rd Battalions were brought up into the line, the 22nd taking over the right of 103 Brigade and the 23rd Battalion taking over the trenches previously held by the Suffolks. Owing to the distance the battalions had to travel from the rear, they did not receive their orders until late, confirming that this was to be a surprise attack, without any artillery bombardment. The objective was the houses north and south of the railway and the Château and Chemical works in Rouex. The two Tyneside Scottish battalions had not had time to carry out any form of reconnaissance, nor had they been in these trenches before, added to those facts there was little definite information about the enemy.

There was an almighty foul-up now, because the 23rd Battalion was too far back and unable to reach the jumping off point for the allotted start time of 3 a.m. At 2.30 a.m. Brigadier Thomson sent word to the 22nd Battalion to delay their attack, but the message did not reach them. Then at 3 a.m. the battalion began their assault, with D Company on the right, B Company on the left, C Company in support and A Company held back in reserve. The Germans continuously put up flares and then opened fire with rifles, but much of this fire was wasted as it was aimed too high. In Calabar Trench a strong party of the enemy was encountered and driven out, then the advance continued towards the houses. Further progress could not be made owing to the amount of machine-gun fire and apart, from some men of B Company in the northern part of Calabar Trench, the remainder fell back on Cawdor Trench. However, in an isolated section of trench about eighty yards in front of the main position, Lieutenant Robson and Second Lieutenant Simson with six men were hanging on. The 22nd Battalion eventually received the message not to attack at 3.20 a.m. and realized that they were alone. A message was sent to Brigade Headquarters stating the facts and they also tried to get in touch with the 23rd Battalion but were unable to do so. Communication with the 23rd was eventually made when Lance Corporal Reay, leading a patrol, broke through an enemy bombing post and crossed the railway line and got in touch with the left hand men of the battalion. The 23rd Battalion, when it eventually reached the start line, placed from right to left A, B and C Companies with D in support. The

position the battalion was to assault was strongly defended and only about seventy to eighty yards away. But in the houses south of the railway there were four or five heavy machine-guns. Between these buildings and the northern boundary of the Château the Germans had dug a trench, which was occupied by riflemen and bombers. The instant the 23rd Battalion left the trenches to begin the assault the two left hand companies came under a withering machine-gun fire. Very soon these two companies had lost nearly all of their officers and over half of the other ranks. On the right A Company advanced along Corona Trench and initially had some success driving the enemy back. But as soon as they left the trench they too came under heavy machine-gun fire. Well forward in an isolated position, A Company was ordered to retire back down Corona Trench. The survivors of the 23rd Battalion lay exhausted in shell holes out in No Man's Land for most of the day. On at least one occasion German soldiers were seen to be carrying wounded soldiers of the Tyneside Scottish to safety and these men were not shot at, however others who did expose themselves were fired upon and several were reported hit.

Meanwhile back in their exposed position Lieutenant Robson and Second Lieutenant Simson came under attack. Between thirty and forty of the enemy attacked the position but were driven off with rifle fire and bombs. Lieutenant Robson sent a runner off to Battalion Headquarters and he managed to get through. This man then led a small patrol, under the command of Second Lieutenant Taylor back to the trench held by Lieutenant Robson. As the patrol moved out the Germans let off some gas and it was under cover of the gas cloud, which obscured them from view, that Second Lieutenant Taylor and his men reached Lieutenant

Robson and brought him and his men back without loss.

On 30 April the relief of the 34th Division by 4th Division began, the 20th Battalion being relieved along with 101 Brigade. The 23rd Battalion was not relieved until 1 May and prior to the relief the enemy heavily shelled the road where battalion headquarters was situated. During this shelling a dump of gas cylinders was hit, causing the gas to escape, which caused a number of men to be gassed, several of whom later died from gas poisoning. The battalion was then relieved and proceeded to the rear area, on the following day they were transported in motor buses to the training area at Sombrin.

Training and re-equipping commenced, several games of football were played and a move was made to another training area at Autheux where church parades were held and platoons fired a short musketry course. Owing to a shortage of reinforcements the Brigade had to reduce the number of companies in a battalion from four to three. The 20th Battalion reported that in order to strengthen discipline, and to teach the new men to work together, the battalion started doing squad drill. Visits and inspections took place and Staff Sergeant Instructors from General Headquarters supervised Lewis Gun drill and bayonet fighting. Throughout May 1917 the Tyneside Scottish Brigade stayed on the training area, working hard to absorb the reinforcements that had joined. Eventually word came that the 34th Division was to move back to the front; thankfully Rouex and the dreaded Chemical Works had fallen while 102 Brigade had been out of the line.

GREENLAND HILL

The various battalions of the Brigade left their camping grounds on the morning of 30 May and marched to Candas Station. Here they entrained and were transported, in warm sunny weather, by rail back to Arras, where they arrived that afternoon. On alighting from the train they were marched to St Nicholas where they bivouacked. On the night of 31 May the 23rd Battalion reported that they could see shells falling on Arras. In conjunction with 27 (Lowland) Brigade of 9th (Scottish) Division, 102 (Tyneside Scottish) Brigade was now detailed to take part in its next attack, which was to be against German positions on Greenland Hill, the idea being to force the enemy off the crest of the hill.

Accordingly the battalions made their way into the front line, the 20th on the right, in the centre the 21st Battalion and on the left the 22nd Battalion with the 23rd taking up positions in support. The first objective was two trenches known as Curly and Charlie and the second objective another two trenches known as Cod and Cuthbert. The attack was to be well supported by artillery for there was available no less than one hundred and twenty-six eighteen pounder guns,

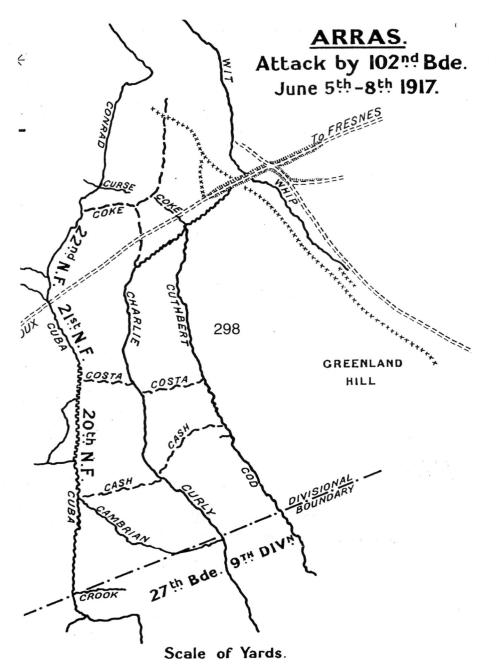

ARRAS.
Attack by 102nd Bde.
June 5th–8th 1917.

TO FRESNES

GREENLAND HILL

298

DIVISIONAL BOUNDARY

27th Bde. 9th DIVN.

Scale of Yards.

21st Battalion this barrage lasted eight minutes and the 23rd Battalion reported that this was a very prompt and heavy barrage.

Then at 8 p.m. on the evening of 5 June a four-minute barrage blasted the defenders of Greenland Hill, and the leading waves of the Tyneside Scottish advanced over No Man's Land. On the right the 20th Battalion stated that its companies on the flanks were successful, but the centre-company did not even reach the first objective owing to the heavy opposition. The flank companies then dug in and formed bomb blocks to protect their flanks. In the centre of the Brigade advance the 21st Battalion found that the enemy in front were very strong. The leading waves fought their way into the first objective and began to consolidate, followed by the third and fourth waves who established themselves in two strong points. On the left flank the 22nd Battalion also came under fire as they began to advance, the extreme left-hand platoon being almost wiped out, only two of its men and the platoon commander remaining unwounded. The other companies were also faring badly and the situation was described as critical, until a Lewis gun eliminated two German machine-guns that were causing havoc, whilst rifle grenadiers did a similar job on a third enemy machine-gun post. Hand to hand fighting was taking place and the right hand company had a stubborn fight on its hands before they managed to link up with men of the 21st Battalion. Again the following platoons detailed to capture the second objective passed through the first position and carried out their task, before starting to dig in.

At 11 p.m. the Germans began a counter-attack towards the 22nd Battalion, however an alert sentry was able to give a warning that the enemy were coming, so little trouble was experienced in dealing with the attack. At this stage no carrying parties had reached the forward troops; short of trench stores they had difficulty in erecting barbed wire emplacements. At 2 a.m. the enemy were seen massing for an attack and they were showered with rifle grenades and trench mortars. This did not prevent a very determined attack from taking place and it was some time before the Germans could be driven off. Casualties in the 22nd Battalion were mounting as the enemy repeatedly tried to recapture the lost position.

During the night the flank companies of the 20th Battalion tried to turn inwards and bomb the Germans out of the piece of trench they occupied. It was not until the following morning that a reconnaissance carried out by the Royal Flying Corps showed that there were only about twenty Germans holding this trench, so a further attack was planned. At 2.30 p.m. on 6 June a short barrage by a trench mortar was opened on the Germans and as soon as the mortar stopped firing the men of the 20th Battalion stormed into the position. The enemy were taken by surprise and the trench was captured with little resistance. However

thirty-eight howitzers and twelve sixty pounders and in addition some of XVII Corps heavy artillery was made available.

Just before the advance began the German artillery began shelling the British front line, which caused some casualties amongst the waiting British infantry, notably in the 22nd Battalion where the sergeant commanding the leading platoon of the left-hand company was killed. On the front of the

Below: Private Thomas Preston, 7 Wynyard Street, Dawdon Colliery, KiA 5th June 1917, buried Sunken Road Cemetery, Fampoux.

Servant of God, well done!
   Rest from thy loved employ;
The battle fought, the victory won,
   Enter thy Master's joy.

The voice at midnight came,
   He started up to hear,
A mortal arrow pierced his frame,
   He fell—but felt no fear.

The pains of death are past,
   Labour and sorrow cease;
And life's long warfare closed at last,
   His soul is found in peace.

HE DID HIS DUTY.

the report from the Royal Flying Corps was proved to be wrong, for two officers and over seventy other ranks were captured, along with two heavy machine guns, two light machine guns and a light trench mortar. The position was consolidated and patrols pushed forward to link up with the other positions. All night long the Germans kept up a constant barrage and at 1 a.m. they drove in the 20th Battalion outposts.

The 21st Battalion was also attacked by strong enemy patrols but succeeded in driving them off with strong rifle fire.

On the left however, the enemy kept on coming and at 2.15 a.m. it was estimated that the Germans in about battalion strength were massing for another attack. They came on across the open ground heading for the junction of Cuthbert and Charlie trenches but were met with rifle and machine-gun fire and driven back. All through the early hours of 6 June the 22nd Battalion was repeatedly attacked, but each time they were driven off, only to come back again. Then at 6 a.m. rations at last got through although by this time the men were suffering from thirst. Ammunition was also a problem, but enough was found to resupply the front line. The 22nd Battalion front went quiet during 6 June but the 23rd Battalion was called upon to assist the 20th Battalion. Upon receiving the request for assistance A Company, under

Captain Leech, were detailed to go forward and clear a pocket of Germans. Owing to a misunderstanding the men of the 23rd Battalion were caught in the British trench mortar barrage and forced to withdraw, Second Lieutenant Scaife being badly shaken by the experience. A further unfortunate incident befell this battalion later in the day when Lieutenant Colonel Porch DSO and Second Lieutenant S Millay MC were wounded by shellfire and had to be evacuated.

Then in the early hours of 7 June the enemy suddenly launched a very heavy barrage of trench mortars, on the 22nd Battalion defending Charlie - Cuthbert Trench junction. A determined and strong group of the enemy attacked the position and the majority of the garrison became casualties when the Germans forced an entry and succeeded in occupying the trench for a length of about ninety yards. The left post was driven back towards the centre post, but the Germans did not have things all their own way and the survivors began to fight back. Rifle grenades were used to hold the Germans up and this gave the Officers and NCOs time to sort things out. Within half an hour a counter attack was organized and as soon as the Tyneside Scottish attacked, across open ground, the Germans broke and fled back to their own front line. As this was happening another party of Tyneside Scots was restoring the situation in

Above: The great killing machine – the Maxim Machine Gun – and its German crew.

Below: 29/469 Private Thomas Dent Wright, 4 Back Park Road, Barnoldswick, Yorkshire, transferred to 8th Battalion, Yorkshire Regiment, KiA 7 June 1917.

Above: 45905 Private James Smith, 7 Rowland Street, Skipton, Yorkshire, KiA 16 June 1917 with 10th Battalion NF (formerly 29th Reserve Battalion).

Cuthbert Trench. Prominent among the defenders was Second Lieutenant A W D Mark MC, who although he was wounded, gallantly led his platoon, and was able to repel many enemy counter attacks, thus helping his battalion regain the trenches so nearly lost.

The morning of 7 June passed quietly but in the afternoon large numbers of the enemy formed up in front of the 21st Battalion, but were dispersed by the fire of the Divisional artillery and the machine gunners. Later that evening, at 9.45 p.m, a strong enemy patrol attacked the left hand post of the 21st Battalion, advancing under the cover of a heavy barrage, only to be driven back yet again. Then after almost two days of continuous fighting 11/Suffolk Regiment and 16/Royal Scots of 101 Brigade commenced the relief of 102 Brigade. The Brigade moved back to camps in the St Nicholas area and the next week was spent on working parties when water and Small Arms Ammunition were given priority and these were taken up to the front line as soon as possible. Information came back from the prisoners, that the enemy opposing 102 Brigade on Greenland Hill, the 1st and 3rd Battalions of the German 463 Infantry Regiment, had practically ceased to exist. In the 23rd Battalion, with Lieutenant Colonel Porch evacuated wounded, command passed to Major C R Longhurst. Officer casualties had again been heavy, sixteen killed, thirty-two wounded and one, Lieutenant H McDonald of the 21st Battalion, was missing believed killed. Likewise the toll in other ranks left many gaps to be filled, but in the Battles of Arras the Brigade had gone over the top three times, and twice had taken the objectives they had been given. The men were given two days off on 9 and 10 June, no training except a little physical training was done and time was spent cleaning up and generally resting. The battalions of the Brigade

spent a few days back in line, but the front had fallen quiet, so that improvements to the fire trench were made, bays and fire steps put in and wire put out. At night the enemy was very alert sending up many rockets and flares, opened fire with rifles and machine guns, but the diaries report that this tour was relatively quiet. The 21st Battalion came under observation from German balloons, and the Gavrelle and the Point du Jour received a fair number of shells. The relief of the 34th Division by the 17th Division started and the Brigade was moved back to the rear area. It was now time to move to pastures new, so there can be few who were sorry to say goodbye to the Chemical Works at Rouex and farewell to Greenland Hill. Among the officers that were wounded was Father Joseph McHardy MC; CF his replacement joined whilst the battalion was in the line.

The new Padre was Ernest Molineux, and when he had time he wrote to friends in England,

'I was sent right up to the line as soon as I came out and attached to a service battalion – we were in the trenches through that hot spell and our part of the line was hot from another point of view too. We have come out for a few days rest now and are a good many miles behind. Our depleted numbers are being made good. Its a great relief to be away from the continual crash and bang of shellfire for a bit. The sights and smells in the line were horrible, but the spirits of the Tommies are wonderful. The Regiment is a Border and Scottish one, beside a servant I have an excellent horse and groom.'

At the end of June, with the time spent refitting and training in the Buneville area, orders were received from Headquarters 34th Division to prepare to move south to the Hagricourt sector.

Below: Damage caused to the town of Arras by German artillery.

Chapter Nine

'No rest for the wicked'

*'Two Tommies sat in a trench one day,
Discussing the war in the usual way.'*

'THE BURNING QUESTION' ANON

Above: Second Lieutenant Basil Peacock joined 22nd Battalion in Late 1917 and was posted to A Company.

THE FIRST DAYS of July 1917 were spent training in the rear area of XVII Corps. Here more reinforcements arrived to join the depleted brigade; among them was Second Lieutenant Basil Peacock who, although commissioned in the 3rd Battalion of the Northumberland Fusiliers, was posted to the 22nd Battalion. In his memoirs, *Tinkers Mufti* he recalled the journey out from England.

'I had been placed in charge of a draft of mixed details, and with the help of a sergeant I collected the soldiers and marched them down the road to embark on the old paddle-steamer Brighton Belle. It was a raw drizzly day and a few on board were seasick, but I was too interested in our escort vessels and my first view of a foreign coastline to suffer. As we waited to disembark, and for baggage to be slung ashore, some of the newcomers began to sing, "Pack up your troubles in your old kit bag" and others shouted, "Are we downhearted? No!" A very old soldier on shore, who looked as if he had been out since Mons and with Kitchener at Khartoum before that, paused in his task of sweeping the quay, looked up leaning on his broom and shouted back, "And you soon effing will be". The song and shouting died away.'

From the docks the draft went up to the Bull Ring, a most depressing place that soldiers were very happy to leave even though they were on their way to the front. Second Lieutenant Peacock also recorded his time there in the following way.

'I handed over my draft to a receiving officer and was directed to an orderly room to report, thence to a bell tent which had five other occupants, all second lieutenants, whose sleeping valises lay on the ground round the pole. Most young officers like myself spent about ten days at the base awaiting posting to their units, and we were given some final training on what was called 'The Bull Ring'. This was an area of sand dunes on which were field works, bombing ranges, and covered trenches in which one experienced small doses of poison gas. The instructors were ancient sergeants thankful that if their luck held out their fighting days were over.'

After his stay at the Bull Ring Second Lieutenant Basil Peacock was glad to get a posting to the 22nd Battalion and to be on his way up the line.

'It took us nearly all day to travel the forty miles to Mercatel where a driver with a limber for our baggage took us to

Below: New respirators were fitted and gas training carried out behind the lines.

Battalion HQ. The commanding officer, Acklom, who interviewed us, was a pre-war regular captain of the Highland Light Infantry, now holding the temporary rank of Lieutenant Colonel. He was very pleasant, he looked keenly at me as he queried my age and sent me to A Company.'

He then went on to describe his company commander and platoon sergeant:

'The company was then commanded by Captain Charlton, who I thought was a middle-aged man but years later discovered he was only twenty-eight at the time. He was a sedate chap with charming manners, a pipe constantly in his mouth and very soon I admired him as a fine soldier. He too queried my age and appointed me to Number One Platoon. My sergeant, Soulsby, came from Blaydon, he had been a pitman and I was extremely fortunate to have the guidance of this fine man.'

Not long after he joined the battalion word came through that the 34th Division was to move south to Peronne to the Hagricourt Sector. On 1 July at least one of the battalions, the 21st, held a church parade to commemorate the attack at La Boisselle the previous year. In the evening all those who were

original members of the 21st (Service) Battalion Northumberland Fusiliers (2nd Tyneside Scottish), and had fought at La Boisselle, sat down to a dinner. The Officer Commanding, Lieutenant Colonel Norris, second in command, Major Jobson and the adjutant, Captain McCluskey, all addressed the assembled men. RSM Hodson replied on behalf of the other ranks.

The training continued. Because of the terrain in the next area of operations, special attention was given to patrolling, outpost drill and rapid wiring. Musketry, fire direction and fire control were also taught in depth, with the new men receiving basic weapon handling and close order drill as well. The afternoons were given over to sport, battalions running various competitions. In the 21st battalion football competition HQ beat D Company by 2 goals to nil.

The move south began on 4 July, at 9 30p.m. when the 21st Battalion marched to Tinques Station, followed at 10 p.m. by the 20th Battalion. In the early hours of 5 July the 22nd Battalion left their billets in Buneville and followed the other two battalions to Tinques. The 20th Battalion entrained first, arriving at Peronne at 7 a.m, closely followed by the 21st Battalion who arrived at 10 a.m. When the 22nd Battalion arrived they immediately set off by march route for Hervilly where they arrived and went into billets at 3 p.m. The journey of the 23rd Battalion was made in two parties, A Company departing on 4 July and the remainder, along with the transport section, not leaving until 5 July. Unfortunately no timings are given for their journey, but they did record that the village that was to be their home, 'was very badly damaged, not a single house left standing.' This was owing to a deliberate scorched earth policy by the Germans when they withdrew to the Hindenburg Line. A couple of days were spent assisting in the clean up of Peronne before 102 Brigade was given the task of relieving troops of the Cavalry Corps in the line in the Hagricourt Sector. This part of the front was unlike any other section of trenches that the Tyneside Scottish had previously held. It is well described in the 34th Divisional History:

'The country here, and the lines held by the opposing forces, were quite different to any we had been in before. The country had been wilfully laid to waste.

All the villages round here have suffered the same fate, practically every house ruined. The country is open and undulating like Salisbury Plain and we hold some high ridges with low ground in front. In most places, however, we are some little way from the Boche, and the lines are not dug in or organized in the way that we have been used to. Everything is more opened and scattered and we walk about in the open in what seems to be an extraordinary reckless fashion.'

On the night 8/9 July the relief of 4 (Dismounted)

Brigade of 4th Cavalry Division commenced; the troops being replaced came mainly from Indian Cavalry Regiments. The 22nd Battalion took over from the 2/Lancers, the 23rd Battalion from The Inniskilling Dragoons and 38/Empress of India's Horse and 21st from 19/Lancers, who belonged to the 6th Cavalry Division. The battalions were distributed as follows, on the right the 21st, in the centre the 22nd Battalion and on the left the 23rd Battalion, with the 20th in the rear as brigade reserve. The 21st Battalion had sent men up into the line prior to the relief in order that they could accompany the men of 19/Lancers on patrol out into No Man's Land. Their take over of the line was quiet and accomplished with speed, the relief taking place without incident. The 22nd Battalion reported nothing except that the time spent in the line was quiet, but Second Lieutenant Basil Peacock recorded the take over in his memoirs as follows:

'My first introduction to real warfare was when our battalion took over a curious part of the line from an Indian cavalry regiment, temporarily unhorsed. It was a dark night and we could see little of the troopers except their bright eyes shining in the faint light. The officers were white, rather casual, much cleaner and better dressed than ourselves. Captain Charlton with me in attendance took over the company headquarters dugout which was only sunk half way in the ground and was roofed with curved corrugated iron.'

The 23rd Battalion, also taking over a section of the front, stated that their left flank was held by 19/Durham Light Infantry, a bantam battalion of men under the height of five feet-two inches tall. The front comprised a series of isolated posts and Unnamed Farm was a very vulnerable point in the battalion's defences.

Taking over the line in the dark was a tricky business and it was not until first light that the actual layout of the ground became obvious. This too was recorded by Basil Peacock:

'When dawn came Captain Charlton was very concerned by the sketchy field works occupied by the company. Headquarters' dugout was immediately behind the ruined village of Vileret with three platoons in unconnected posts in front of it, but there was only one communication trench through the buildings. So he immediately gave orders that there must be no movement in daytime, although the enemy was very quiet. He was right, as usual, for during the afternoon a German shell screamed towards us and went clean through the curved roof of our HQ dugout, passed over my head as I lay resting, missed by inches our cook who lay on the opposite side, penetrated the far wall and buried itself in the ground, where we found it when we fled outside. Luckily, it

was a dud and did not explode, and when Captain Charlton came running up he found me looking at it laughing hysterically. He told me sharply to shut up! This was my baptism of fire, which if the shell had exploded would have also been my demise.'

Two weeks were spent in these positions, the usual reliefs from reserve into the line and back to reserve took place, but there was little to report except enemy artillery activity. On the morning of 14 July a German Lance Corporal, who had lost his way, wandered into the lines of the 23rd Battalion. Men of the left-hand company took him prisoner and under interrogation he revealed that there was going to be a raid that afternoon on two British posts, Number 9 (Unnamed Farm) and Number 11. This was to take place at 2 p.m. English time. Just before that time a heavy barrage was opened on the front line and a strong party of Germans attacked the two posts. At Unnamed Farm they were quite easily driven off, but at Number 11 Post they vastly outnumbered the garrison. Leaving behind one of their number dead, the German raiding party managed to capture a Lewis gun and its six man crew before retiring to their own lines.

A few days later, in the early hours of 21 July a German machine gunner approached a post of the 20th Battalion, and the garrison took the man prisoner. Later, that night the front line trenches occupied by the right hand company were, on two occasions heavily bombarded with gas shells. The gas shells were fired by trench mortars and mixed in the barrage were some 77mm shrapnel shells. The gas in the first barrage was reported to smell of musk, that in the second barrage of garlic. As this shelling took the battalion by surprise and occurred during an inter-company relief, casualties did occur. Two officers and twelve other ranks were affected by the gas, the worst cases were those who did exercise after being gassed, there were however no fatalities from this gas barrage, the new box respirator giving the men complete protection.

Nightly patrols went out into No Man's Land to observe the enemy and to try and get information,

'We employed two sorts of patrols, one of three to six men for listening and reconnaissance, and a fighting patrol of about twenty men and an officer. I rarely received precise orders for the objectives of the patrols I led, except to listen, or if possible take a prisoner. It was extremely difficult to catch one, as there were few loose Germans about. They came in large parties to erect barbed wire, and they made a good job of it as their entanglements were sometimes colossal and yards deep.'

(Second Lieutenant Basil Peacock 22nd Battalion.)

It was not long before the powers that be decided that the Tyneside Scottish should carry out a raid. Accordingly on the night 24/25 July Second

Above: Three of 21st Battalion; standing left 21/58 Private John T Dodds, 139 Bothal Terrace, Pegswood, promoted sergeant and discharged in January 1919.

Below: 45874 Private William Mitchell, 5 James Street, Salterforth, Yorkshire, KiA 17 July 1917 with 13th Battalion, NF (formerly 29th Reserve Battalion NF).

Below: 29/543 Private Herbert Healey, 12 Mill Brow, Earby, Yorkshire, transferred to the Machine Gun Corps, DoW 24 July 1917.

Above: German infantry carrying out a search for lifestock in the seams of their clothing – a practice carried out by men of both sides. Note the act being carried out by the soldier with the axe and block of wood.

Above: Private Robinson Waterworth, 26 Melbourne Mount, Barnoldswick, Yorkshire, transferred to 7th Battalion, East Yorkshire Regiment, KiA 25 August 1917 (formerly 29th Reserve Battalion) NF.

Lieutenant A Woodhead of the 20th Battalion, along with fifteen men, carried out a surprise attack. Their objective was to capture the garrison of an enemy held bombing post in Enfilade Trench. Under the cover of a trench mortar barrage they went over No Man's Land and entered the position. But there was no one there! Despite a search being made no enemy could be found and the raiders had to return empty handed.

The same day, in the 21st Battalion Lieutenant Colonel P B Norris, who had commanded since the Somme battle the previous year, left for England. Command of the battalion initially passed to Major J T Gracie from the 20th Battalion, but on 31 July he handed over to Major E P Lloyd, who was promoted to Lieutenant Colonel to fill the post. It was also reported that leave for the men was given at this time, and that only three men who had come out with the battalion had not yet been home. Then on 25 July the leading troops of 101 Brigade arrived to take over the front line. 102 Brigade was withdrawn to the rear for training and, of course, working parties. After several days in the rear area orders came through to go back to the line. This time 102(Tyneside Scottish) Brigade, less 102 Machine Gun Company and 102 Light Trench Mortar Battery, would relieve 103 (Tyneside Irish) Brigade in the Vandencourt sector. The 22nd Battalion received a warning order to take over from the 25th Battalion. Accordingly arrangements were made for members of the battalion to accompany Tyneside Irish patrols, in order to learn the layout of the area to be taken over. Second Lieutenant Dickinson along with ten men of the 22nd Battalion was detailed to carry out this task.

On the night of 2 August a mixed patrol of Tyneside Irish and Tyneside Scottish set off into No Man's Land. But suddenly the patrol was ambushed by a German patrol and was forced to withdraw. Owing to lack of communication and the fact that the sentries were also from mixed units and had not been briefed properly, the patrol fired at its own sentry post. This post was commanded by a Lance Corporal of the 25th Battalion, who had under his command one of his own men and two members of the 22nd Battalion. In the rapid exchange of fire the Tyneside Irish Lance Corporal was killed and one of the Tyneside Scottish privates wounded. This caused the diarist of the 22nd Battalion to write, 'These mixed patrols are highly unsatisfactory and the system of grouping parties of different units in a single patrol is altogether bad.'

On taking over from the 25th Battalion the 22nd Battalion disposed B Company on the right C Company on the left and A Company in support. The right flank rested on the Omignon River and on the other bank the French 118th Regiment was dug in. It was said that the last man on the right was the 'Right Marker' for the British Expeditionary Force.

The 23rd Battalion had also taken over a section of the front, relieving the 24th Battalion in the Grand Priel Farm – Ned Wood – Ascension Farm area. Here they found that the trenches were very dilapidated and because of the weather were very wet and dirty, the usual work being required just to maintain them as passable. The 21st Battalion took over from the 27th Battalion at Vandencourt Château were in support to the right sub sector. Because the battalions were still organized on a three company basis, one company of the 27th Battalion remained in position to assist the 21st Battalion. Likewise the 20th Battalion took over in the intermediate line from the 26th Battalion. The main landmark in this area was in No Man's Land, a large wood known to the British as Somerville Wood, which dominated No Man's Land which was very wide hereabouts, and had to be defended by a standing patrol from the battalion in the line. The Germans opposite were very confident and every night they wandered about No Man's Land as though they owned it, that is until the Tynesiders arrived.

On 3 August another mixed patrol of 22nd and 25th Battalion men met a German patrol near Somerville Wood; the enemy retired after returning fire for only a few minutes. The next night an enemy patrol, approximately fifty strong, was observed by a patrol led by Second Lieutenant Corriel. When the Tyneside Scots opened fire the Germans ran for it, not stopping to return fire and it was thought they had suffered several casualties as squeals and groans were heard by the British patrol. The next night the same officer took another patrol out and lay up in an ambush position. Fortunately he had chosen a different spot from the previous night, for his first position was heavily shelled by the German gunners. Another patrol, creeping into Dogleg Wood, came across an enemy position, but after a silent approach it was found to be unmanned.

The 23rd Battalion was also actively patrolling No Man's Land. Although their patrols encountered no enemy on 4 or 5 August on the night of 6 August a patrol led by Second Lieutenant R P Horsley did. The officer led his men out towards Big Bill Wood where a party of Germans was observed, this group of the enemy being dispersed by rifle and Lewis gun fire. After the brief action the British patrol continued on its way and made a reconnaissance of Big Bill Wood, on their way back to the British lines the patrol was ambushed, coming under fire from the enemy. When the Germans opened fire Second Lieutenant Horsley picked up a wounded NCO and began to carry him to safety but unfortunately the officer became a casualty also. It was now that an act of conspicuous gallantry was displayed when, 23/689 Corporal T W Allison returned and picked up Second Lieutenant Horsley and carried him back to their own positions to gain the Distinguished Conduct Medal.

Sergeant Wright of the 22nd Battalion also had a bit of a fight on his hands in Somerville Wood, when on 7 August, having been on a standing patrol in the wood throughout the day, the relief was late turning up owing to an enemy artillery barrage. Suspecting something was afoot, Sergeant Wright pushed his sentry posts further out towards the enemy and one of the advanced posts reported that an enemy patrol was coming. Sergeant Wright let them get near enough then opened fire, wounding at least one German and driving the rest back with Lewis gun and rifle fire. Almost simultaneously another enemy party had advanced against them from the north east, however Sergeant Wright had covered that angle by deploying an NCO with two men, which group of three Tyneside Scots promptly drove the second German patrol off by using rifle grenades. The barrage had now ceased and Second Lieutenant Stubbs was able to come out with some men and take over from Sergeant Wright.

Identification of the German unit opposing the Tyneside Scottish Brigade was at last obtained. On 9 August a patrol from the 22nd Battalion moving through the German wire, found an enemy tunic hanging in the barbed wire. On examination a diary was found in the pocket which had been written up until 6 August and belonged to a soldier, of 61/Infantry Regiment, who was most likely wounded during the encounter with Second Lieutenant Horsley's patrol.

Over the next few days patrols from the 22nd and the 23rd Battalions went out but no further enemy were encountered and the enemy no longer had the run of No Man's Land. Owing to a shortage of reinforcements the 24th and 27th Battalions amalgamated and this left a small surplus of men in 103 Brigade. These Tyneside Irishmen were now transferred to the Tyneside Scottish Brigade, being allotted to the battalions as follows, 20th Battalion – sixty-six, 21st Battalion – forty-nine, 22nd Battalion – thirty-five and the 23rd Battalion forty-four. With the arrival of a draft from the base that was also split between the battalions, the Tyneside Scottish battalions were now able to reform on a four-company basis. For once the draft from the base was made up of men who had been at the front before, the 21st Battalion recording that,

'A draft of fifty-six received from the

base, with the exception of five all have seen previous service with the BEF.'

This was indeed a bonus as it would make training a lot easier and the basic lessons of living at the front would not have to be taught at all. Another bonus for the 23rd Battalion was the return of Lieutenant Colonel Porch who, now recovered from his wounds, rejoined and assumed command on 11 August.

On the night of 17 August a fighting patrol from the 20th Battalion under the command of Second Lieutenant Friend had a fire-fight with some Germans in No Man's Land. When they returned to their own lines it was found that two other ranks were missing. Despite searches on two consecutive nights no trace of the men was found until 27 August when the body of one of them, 37286 Lance Corporal J A Bell, of Ashington, was found.

The weather was turned nasty in the middle of August 1917, heavy rain making the going difficult, and the mud was deep making the task of taking over the line very slow indeed. The posts taken over by the 21st Battalion at this time were under constant observation by the enemy and therefore could only be visited in the hours of darkness. These posts in front of Quarry Wood and overlooked by Farm trench, were waterlogged and the communication trenches had caved-in in several places. In other places the posts were only lightly held at night, the support company being detailed to counter attack vigorously and retake any post should the Germans make an attack and capture them.

Plans were being made for the capture of the German positions on Cologne Ridge, about two thousand yards west of the Hindenburg line and overlooking the British positions in the Hagricourt Valley. This task was given to 101 Brigade, but owing to the nature of the ground, Brigadier General Gore, the GOC 101 Brigade, was given the assistance of the 20th and 23rd Battalions. The 21st and 22nd Battalions were also to be involved by supplying carrying parties for each of the battalions of 101 Brigade. At 4.30 a.m. on 26 August, Zero Hour, A Company of the 23rd Battalion left Rifleman Post and attacked Rifle Pit trench. Crossing No Man's Land with only three minor casualties, the company took six Germans prisoner without a fight. As soon as they were in possession of the trench A Company started to dig in and consolidate. German artillery commenced a heavy barrage on Rifleman and Hussar posts as C Company moved forward. Two platoons of this company then proceeded to put wire out in front of Rifle Pit trench, but they came under intense and accurate fire from enemy snipers who caused a number of casualties. The rest of the attack carried out by 101 Brigade was very successful, Corporal S J Day of 11/Suffolk Regiment won the VC during the day. The 20th Battalion was not employed until the night 27/28 August when they relieved 15/Royal Scots in the captured line.

Above: 13476 Private Percy Freestone, 22 Eskdale Street, Darlington. Wounded earlier in the war with another NF battalion, he came as a reinforcement to the 22nd Battalion, subsequently transferred to the East Yorkshire Regiment.

The Royal Scots battalion had A Company of the 21st Battalion attached as a carrying party. After receiving a report that all objectives were taken A Company moved off with their loads of ammunition, but encountered a lot of difficulties owing to the German artillery barrage. On top of that snipers troubled them, and the heavy rain had made the trenches very muddy. After the hand-over was complete at about 10 p.m. the enemy made an attack on the left company of the 20th Battalion, but they were eventually beaten off, being prevented from getting into the British trenches by rifle and Lewis gun fire. Again on 30 August, prior to the 20th Battalion being relieved, the Germans made another attempt to bomb along the trench and again they were driven back. The 22nd Battalion then took over this sector of the front, the forward companies having to spend a great deal of time keeping the trenches in a reasonable state.

At the beginning of September the brigade received a large draft which was made up of experienced officers and men from the 1st and 12/13th Battalions of the Northumberland Fusiliers. The 21st Battalion war diary remarked that: 'All the other ranks had previously seen service with the BEF and were above the usual standard.'

Training was carried out on a large scale, for the divisional staff had another attack lined up for 102 Brigade; rapid wiring by night was practised, as well as anti-gas drill and the use of rifle grenades. The Germans held positions along a low ridge which gave them an excellent view over the British lines, accordingly the decision was taken to remove them from these trenches and the job was given to 102 Brigade.

The training complete, 102 Brigade started back towards the front line on 7 September, stores for the coming attack were issued and those who were to be left out of the battle fell out and remained behind. The 21st Battalion embussed at 7.00 p.m. and moved forward to take over the line from 10/Lincolnshire Regiment and 16/Royal Scots. Before the 23rd Battalion moved off they held a parade at which the Commanding Officer decorated four men with the Military Medal for digging out a buried comrade at Rifle Pit Trench under heavy fire. That afternoon there was time to complete the inter-platoon football competition, which was won by 5 Platoon of B Company. At 7.30 p.m. C and D Companies left by bus for Templeux followed at 11.30 p.m. by A, B and HQ Companies. The 20th Battalion also made their way forward and relieved 11/Suffolk Regiment in the left hand sector of the front line. The 22nd Battalion remained in support to provide carrying parties for the assaulting battalions. Throughout 8 September the enemy heavily shelled the area of the assaulting battalions, the front line and the dumps receiving particular attention.

By 11.45 p.m. both assaulting battalions, the 21st and 23rd, were formed up ready to go. Both were to attack on a two-company front, each company consisting of four waves. The first wave was to cross the enemy trench and form a screen, the second wave was to clear the trench and the third and fourth waves were to consolidate the position. The following companies were to cross the captured line and begin the process of putting up barbed wire entanglements.

At 12.15 a.m. a creeping barrage, from 18 pounders and 4.5″ Howitzers, coupled with an overhead machine gun barrage, opened precisely on time. The leading companies of the 21st Battalion, C and D, both moved forward under its cover and took their objective without too much trouble, however owing to thick fog the right-hand company lost direction and did not take the whole length of Farm Trench. Likewise the 23rd Battalion also moved forward, on their front the Germans were seen to retire in disorder and the objective was occupied without opposition. Consolidation at once commenced, and whilst this work was in progress the Commanding Officer, Lieutenant Colonel Porch, was yet again wounded. The wiring parties, working hard and fast, completed a system of wire entanglements before dawn, and the 23rd Battalion were able to get in touch with the 21st Battalion on the right. There were only a few casualties during the attack, but as the day wore on enemy shelling increased and with this so did the list of casualties. The 20th Battalion was then ordered forward, to clear the remaining portion of Railway Trench. Only forty men, working in four groups of ten, carried out this attack by the 20th Battalion. Three of these groups advanced along the top of a communication trench and established posts at the far end, the fourth group worked their way along the trench bombing the enemy out and mopping up as they went. This small group of men carried out this task without any loss to themselves and linked up with the 23rd Battalion.

On the right flank the 21st Battalion twice repulsed enemy attacks, but heavy shelling prevented the carrying parties reaching the front line. All day long the Germans kept up the shelling and at 5 p.m. they again prepared to counter attack. Unbeknown to the Germans, though, at exactly the same time the 21st Battalion was preparing a bombing attack. Owing to this the enemy attack was easily repulsed and the British barrage on Farm Trench must have caused heavy casualties. In order to secure the position taken and to prepare for a further advance Brigadier Thomson now ordered the 22nd Battalion forward to dig a jumping off trench.

This task was given to A and C companies and to assist them the Divisional pioneer battalion, 12/Green Howards, sent up two platoons; this last named unit had replaced 18/Northumberland Fusiliers who were working on roads and railways in the Ypres Salient. Basil Peacock describes the digging of the jumping off trench in quite a lengthy passage in *Tinkers Mufti*.

'Our battalion was not engaged in the preliminaries or the first attacks but was eventually used to capture and consolidate the remaining two hundred yards of enemy trench. To do this it was necessary to dig a jumping off trench in front of our position, and on the night of 9 September two companies, including mine, were sent forward to do this. We had dug down about two-and-a-half feet, making a straight ditch, when the Germans hearing our activities, fired an intensive and accurate artillery bombardment on top of us. Although I had often experienced desultory shelling before this was my first experience of a bombardment and it was terrifying. We skulked in the shallow trench, trying to deepen it, and some men hacked narrow slits in the sides to try and gain extra protection, as the shells fell thick and close, bursting with vicious explosions and emitting the acrid stink of high explosive. Curiously, in addition to terror, the bombardment induced a slight exhilaration such as is sometimes felt in the first drenching rain of a thunderstorm, probably caused by additional adrenalin being pumped into the veins. I felt slightly intoxicated and wanted to shout aloud, but the feeling soon passed and gave place to deep fear and profound weariness. I had pushed my right shoulder and body into a newly dug slit when I noticed a soldier looking at me in disdain, and I realized that he had dug it and relinquished it to him. A moment later a shell fell on top of us knocking all the breath out of my body, and I thought I was badly hit. The soldier in the slit and another leaning against me were both killed and several others were wounded. As I lay half-stunned, I heard the cry of stretcher-bearers and then the anxious voice of Captain Atkinson saying gently, "Pip(his nickname for me), where are you hit?"

I was just able to say, "I don't know yet."

I had blood on me from the other casualties but eventually discovered that I was only winded. "Thank God," said Atkinson, "I had a message that you were killed." I still treasure the memory of his coming over the open during that bombardment in his concern for his boy officer.'

In the early hours of the morning the GOC 102 Brigade, Brigadier Thomson decided to recall the two companies of the 22nd Battalion, along with their attached pioneers, to the intermediate line. Basil Peacock was among those to come back to the British lines and he recalled:

'Further operations were called off that night and we dribbled back to our reserve line. Atkinson looked entirely done in, and I think was partly shell shocked, so I made my way to battalion HQ to make a report. I remember swaying on my feet while talking to the colonel and someone saying, "a proper balls up," and the next thing I remember was waking up on the adjutant's bunk to be told I had flaked out after reporting.'

Late in the afternoon carrying parties managed to get through and re-supply the front line troops, who were in need of ammunition and stores. Further plans had been made at a conference attended by the officers commanding 21st and 22nd Battalions, in which it was decided that the 21st Battalion would bomb south down Farm Trench and the 22nd Battalion would carry out a frontal attack and then, if needed, bomb north up Farm Trench.

The 21st Battalion attack was allotted to C Company, who employed three bombing parties for the task. Two parties were on top of the trench, one either side, with a third party actually bombing along inside the trench. After a barrage by Stokes mortars and rifle grenades the action commenced. But the attack met with heavy resistance and shellfire, so much that the assistance of the carrying parties was needed to complete the link up with the 22nd Battalion. To accomplish the consolidation of the captured position the aid of men from the 23rd Battalion was needed, as there were not enough men left to do the work and man the defences. On the front of the 22nd Battalion all the objectives were taken and several prisoners captured among them a Hauptfeldwebel (Company Sergeant Major) of the 187th Infantry Regiment.

Back in command of his platoon was Basil Peacock who recalled the part he and his men played that night.

'Two nights later the attack was on, and we formed up in the open on a taped line in silence, champing on pieces of chewing gum with which we were issued. My platoon had been detailed to carry barbed wire and screw pickets to erect an entanglement in front of the new position when captured. I have never understood why we were not detected, we made a great deal of noise getting on to the start line carrying these in addition to our arms and equipment. The affair was to be a sudden surprise assault so there was no preliminary bombardment. But at zero hour scores of our heavy machine guns opened up, firing to our flanks and over our heads, and the vicious "swish" "swish" of bullets was almost more frightening than the artillery barrage which followed.'

Heavily laden down the assaulting infantry staggered their way across No Man's Land, the German infantry had not emerged from their dugouts as expected probably owing to the heavy

Above: 29812 Private James Cragg, Settlebeck, Sedburgh, Yorkshire, KiA 9 September 1917 with the 21st Battalion.

Above: Captain Hilton Roberts Telford, 21st Battalion NF, 38 Beech Grove Road, Newcastle. Educated at Durham School and was reading for his solicitors final exam in London when the war broke out. He became a trooper in the Northumberland Hussars Yeomanry and went to France in October 1914. January 1915 he obtained a commission in the Tyneside Scottish and returned to France with them in 1916. He was invalided in 1916 but returned to the front in February 1917 and was wounded at Villeret in September and died from these wounds. He is buried in the British Military Cemetery, Tincourt.

Above: 45840 Private William Groves, 5 Chapel Square, Earby, Yorkshire, DoW 26 September 1917 with 21st Battalion, formerly Duke of Wellington's (West Riding Regiment).

Above: 20/93 Private John Chipchase, transferred to 23rd Battalion and discharged in October 1917.

Above: 202174 Private Edward Carr Dawson, Coldcotes, Ingleton, Yorkshire, died 26 October 1917, with 1/4th Battalion NF, formerly 29th Reserve Battalion NF.

machine gun barrage and only a few men became casualties. The enemy front line trench was taken right on schedule and the supporting platoons crossed it and began erecting the barbed wire barricade that would hopefully stop any counter attack.

Second Lieutenant Basil Peacock recalled the advance:

> 'Sergeant Soulsby as ever was the first to get to work, screwing in pickets and erecting the entanglement. We worked feverishly, anticipating a counter-attack and counter barrage. The latter was a little slow in coming, but we were stimulated to further speed by enemy machine guns firing at short range and as soon as the job was done we tumbled back into the newly won trench where the other platoons were building parapets. There were a number of enemy dead lying in contorted positions and we took their bayonets as trophies. The Captain ordered me to return with my platoon to the reserve trenches escorting the prisoners, about a score in all of very shaken and frightened men, and we made our way to the rear along a shallow sunken road. We were about half way back when German guns plastered the road with heavy shells, and escort and prisoners went to earth for cover. I found myself with a German Feldwebel, both of us clawing into the side of a shell hole with our bare hands to escape the shrapnel. At one time we had our arms around each other, no longer enemies, but terrified human beings expecting death at any moment.'

Eventually when the bombardment ceased the prisoners were taken back and handed over for interrogation. After resting in a dugout and sleeping through the enemy counter-attacks, Basil Peacock and his men were relieved and moved back into rest. It was here that he heard the news that he and three other officers had been awarded the Military Cross for the part they had played in the attack.

> 'A few days later, I was playing pontoon with my company officers and holding a lucky bank, when the adjutant arrived and handed me a bit of purple and white ribbon, saying, "You had better wear this, it's a spare piece of my own. We have just heard that you are to have a Military Cross"'.

However in his book Basil Peacock readily admits he did not feel the decoration had gone to the right person.

> 'I have always felt that Sergeant Soulsby should have been the man to receive it, but military decorations do not always go to the most deserving soldiers.'

The Brigade went into rest for a few days prior to returning to the lines. A number of patrols went out and only on one occasion were the enemy encountered and then they retired very quickly when fired upon.

The Corps Commander, Lieutenant General Pultney visited the Division a number of times near the end of the month, each time presenting awards for gallant conduct to those men who had earned them.

Prior to the relief of the Brigade in the front line by 73 Brigade the enemy shelled the 23rd Battalion with gas shells, a large number of which fell near the post located in 'Hardy Banks', although fortunately no casualties occurred to the defenders. At the end September a large reorganization took place, Battalions reforming with four companies once again. The 21st Battalion recorded all the drafts that arrived and added comments about them,

'40 from 1st NF	All have previously served
40 from 9th NF	in BEF and are above standard.
10 from 25th NF	All have previously served
51 from 26th NF	in BEF and are up to the
49 from 18th NF	average standard of recent drafts.

137 from 9 Training Reserve Battalion (originally 11/South Staffordshire Regt) – Very few have served with the BEF. Average is below the standard of recent drafts as regards physique.

72 from ASC Labour Company – All transferred from Labour Units. Majority only partially trained.

The 20th Battalion also received drafts over the period 21 – 28 September, these totalled 345 men but the diary records that the majority, were only partially trained.

On relief the battalions were moved by motor bus from Mervilly to Doingt were they went into rest billets and started training the drafts. After two days they then paraded and marched to Peronne station from where they were moved in cattle trucks to Boisleux. On detraining the battalions proceeded by march route to billets in the area of Baileullval, arriving there on 30 September 1917.

The Ypres Salient

After spending time refitting and training 102 Brigade received orders to move north to the Ypres Salient. On the afternoon of 7 October 1917 the battalions of 102 Brigade commenced to march to the railway stations where they entrained for the journey north. On arrival in Belgium they moved into camps near the railway station where they had detrained. The 20th Battalion to Plumstead Camp, Proven, the 21st Battalion to Paddock Wood Camp, two miles west of Proven, the 22nd Battalion to Poll Hill Camp, Peselhoek and the 23rd Battalion to Plurendon Camp, Proven. Here they spent time training, a particular feature of which was attacking and capturing pillboxes.

The Tyneside Scottish Brigade were not required

straight away and for a number of days they remained in the rear area, whilst 103 Brigade went into the line. On 13 October orders came to move forward to commence the relief of the Tyneside Irish, the Battalions entraining at Proven station for Elverdinghe, from where they moved into bivouac camps. The conditions in the Salient that October were horrendous, the whole area was a vast sea of deep mud, in which some men drowned. There were insufficient bivouacs for the men and it was some time before all the men were under cover. In the early hours of 14 October a large group of German bombers, accompanied by sixty scout aircraft, came over the line. They proceeded to drop their bombs on the camps occupied by 102 Brigade: casualties occurred in all except the 20th Battalion. The 21st Battalion received particularly heavy treatment from the bombers, suffering six men killed outright, one officer, Second Lieutenant J Bryson and thirteen men died of wounds and Lieutenant M Donaghy and seventy-one men were wounded.

Moving forward by platoons at two hundred yard intervals, the 21st Battalion made its way up the Pilkem - Langemarck road, which was heavily congested with transport taking rations to the dumps and shells for the artillery. The road was under constant shellfire which made progress very slow, but they went forward until they were met by guides just west of Langemarck. The path they now trod was along a single line of wet, greasy, badly laid duckboards and progress became slower still as the column was delayed by casualties caused by the artillery fire.

The 22nd Battalion was also moving forward in a similar fashion, led by guides from the 24/27th Battalion who had only been in the line twenty-four hours. Owing to the fact that the landscape was devoid of landmarks these guides became lost and a lot of delay and difficulty in completing the relief was experienced by the 22nd Battalion, who were unable to relieve two platoons of the 24/27th Battalion. Indeed Number 10 Platoon of the 22nd Battalion did not arrive in the line until twenty-four hours later.

The 23rd Battalion had been given instructions to relieve three companies of 10/West Yorkshire Regiment and two companies of 7/Green Howards of the 17th Division. At 6 p.m. on 16 October the battalion moved forward into the front line, which was really a series of defended pill boxes and shell holes. Here they were subjected to a heavy artillery barrage which caused the deaths of three men and the wounding of a further ten.

The 20th Battalion experienced the same problem with the guides and shelling which the other battalions had suffered.

Initially in reserve the 20th Battalion moved forward on the night of 18 October and relieved parts of the 21st and 22nd Battalions in the front line. Prior to part of the battalion being relieved, the 22nd Battalion reported that the Middlesex Regiment on their right had fallen back leaving the flank of the Tyneside Scottish battalion exposed, Although from later information it was found out that they had fallen back because the British artillery was firing two hundred yards short.

On 20 October the enemy subjected those holding the line to a two hour barrage of gas shells. This was a new type of Mustard Gas which initially caused few casualties, but later when the ground was churned up by high explosive shells , the gas, which had saturated the ground, was released a second time which caused a number of casualties.

Low flying enemy aircraft also caused problems and made movement by day impossible, communications between posts did not exist and the routes between battalion and company headquarters were hard to find, which made life very difficult for the men employed as runners. Those who were holding the line suffered from exposure and lack of food and water, whilst weapons were clogged with so much mud that they were practically useless. The relief of most of the Brigade by 101 Brigade was indeed a relief. By the time the men of the Brigade reached the rear they were totally worn out and exhausted, both from the long march and the terrible conditions.

The only unit left in the line was D Company of the 20th Battalion, who was to be involved in a small attack by units of 101 and 103 Brigades. The plan was that on the right the 24/27th Battalion would advance and pivot on D Company, who would stand fast. Similarly on the left flank 15th and 16th Royal Scots would advance in an effort to straighten the line. The two Royal Scots battalions had lost their commanding officers and many men on their way up to the line. It is sufficient for this story to say that the attack of the Tyneside Irish battalion was very successful, but for the Royal Scots the day was a disaster. A huge sigh of relief must have been given when the news came that the 34th Division was to leave the Salient and return to France. On 25 October leading units of the 50th and 57th Divisions commenced to take over from the 34th Division. In the rear area time was spent cleaning up and resting, with hardly any work at all being done.

Casualties during the time in the Ypres Salient had been very heavy considering that the brigade had not been involved in an attack. The 20th Battalion, for instance, reported that the strength of the battalion had fallen from 42 Officers and 1007 other ranks, to 33 Officers and 653 other ranks. The casualty list was made up as follows:

	Killed	Died	Wounded	Missing	Sick
Officers	1		5	1	2
O/Ranks	11	3	192	9	146

The other battalions would have had similar casualty lists, the 23rd Battalion had forty-three men go sick between 28 and 31 October.

The move back into France, to join VI Corps of the Third Army, began on 28 October. The

Above: 22/969 Private Archibald Watson of Cowpen was transferred to the 1/4th Battalion NF and was KiA at Passchendaele on 26 October 1917.

Above: 32247 Private Sam Butler, 31 Highfield Road, Earby, Yorkshire, KiA 14 October 1917 with the 21st Battalion.

Below: 29/778 Private Arthur Ingham, 30 Devonshire Street, Skipton, Yorkshire, transferred to 15th Battalion Durham Light Infantry, KiA 3 November 1917.

Above: 45920 Private Harry Wilkinson from Wibsey near Bradford, enlisted in 29th Battalion. He was KiA 4 October 1917 with 12/13th NF.

Above: 202174 Private Edward Carr Dawson, Coldcotes, Ingleton, Yorkshire, KiA 26 October 1917 with the 1/4th Battalion, NF. Formerly 29th Reserve Battalion NF.

Below: German 13 cm Artillery piece with its crew.

battalions of 102 Brigade entrained at Hopoutre station and were transported to Boisleux au Mont, from where they marched to Northumberland Lines at Mercatel, where they rested for three days.

On 31 October the forward area was reconnoitred, Company officers prepared advance parties of signallers and Lewis gunners for the move forward to take over the line. On the morning of 1 November the 23rd Battalion took over from 2/Lancashire Fusiliers in the Cojuel Sector. After the struggle to get into the line at Ypres, the war diary records that this was:

'a quick and easy relief, complete by 12 noon. Splendid weather and the day passed quietly.'

On the next three nights patrols were out in No Man's Land but none of the enemy were encountered. The 22nd Battalion had took over in the front line from 2/Duke of Wellington's Regiment. The battalion deployed with D and A companyies in the line, B in support and C in reserve, whilst Battalion Headquarters were located in Buck Reserve trench. Casualties were light, only six men wounded, four of whom remained at duty.

Prior to relieving the 23rd Battalion in the line, the 21st Battalion football team managed to beat a VI Corps Siege Artillery XI 2 -1. The 20th Battalion relieved the 22nd Battalion and reported a quiet tour. Throughout this period the German artillery was active but 'a marked decrease in the use of trench mortars' was noted. Active patrolling and wiring was undertaken but, like the 23rd Battalion, they did not come across the enemy. When the 23rd Battalion went back into the line on 9 November they reported that it was an excellent relief, completed by 11.20 a.m. Two days later, in the early hours of 11 November, 1917, a German raiding party cut their way through the British wire. They attacked a post held by an officer along with one NCO and the officer, Second Lieutenant John Hewitson of Hartlepool, was killed and the NCO reported missing. All through the month the battalions rotated from front line into reserve and

back into the line. When in reserve training was carried out and owing to the battle taking place at Cambrai, 102 Brigade was put on standby in case the enemy suddenly withdrew.

The enemy probably because of the fighting at Cambrai, were very alert and when a patrol from the 21st Battalion, under the command of Second Lieutenant W T Lewis, was out in No Man's Land, the officer set off a trip flare. This immediately brought down an artillery barrage from the enemy gunners but fortunately the patrol was able to return to the British lines without casualties. At the same time the 22nd Battalion were reporting that Gas projectors were being used, and later on the night of 28 November, at around midnight, the garrison of H post encountered and captured two Germans near the British barbed wire. The next day an aeroplane with British markings dropped bombs on the support company.

As November passed into December the Corps Commander presented awards for gallantry earned during the operations at Ypres the previous month. Apart from this December was much the same as November: patrols, working parties, and training. The German artillery activity remained constant, the enemy gunners registering targets in the trenches and the back areas. Large working parties carrying wire were at work nightly because of an expected German attack, which imposed a heavy strain on the men who were, on average, wiring 700 yards a night. Also the battalions in the rear were standing to from 6.30 a.m. until 8 a.m. every morning. Towards the end of the month the weather turned cold and frosty.

On Christmas Day an inter-battalion relief took place. The 20th and 22nd Battalions changed places, and the 21st and 23rd followed suit. The next day, Boxing Day, snow fell which made active patrolling difficult, and when at night there was bright moonlight it became impossible. On Christmas Day the men of the 23rd Battalion, when relieved, were accommodated in the Hindenburg Tunnel, this being described in the war diary as follows:

'Everybody extremely comfortable, each man having a bunk, and the whole lit by electricity. Men much appreciated the warmth and comfort of their quarters. A distribution of sweet stuff was made to each man during the morning.'

Christmas dinner was held on 28 December, an excellent feast of turkey, ham, christmas pudding and dessert and inside the tunnel it was warm and cosy, whilst outside it was very cold and more snow fell. Drafts that arrived were considered to be good, as over fifty percent of the men had seen active service before. On New Year's Eve listening patrols were out in No Man's Land and the situation was reported as 'Quiet'. Thus 1917 came to a close.

Chapter Ten

The Fight to the finish

'We've done with mud and shells, and stench,
Hope ne'er again to see a trench.'

ANON IN 'THE WIPER'S TIMES'

JANUARY 1918 began with the Tyneside Scottish Brigade disposed of as follows: the Brigade was holding the centre sector of the Divisional front, on the right stood the 23rd Battalion, who had taken over from the 21st Battalion at 11.40 p.m. on the night of 29 December. During 31 December they had experienced some trench mortar activity, but generally their portion of the front was 'quiet'. Captain A Morlidge had joined the Battalion from 3/5Northumberland Fusiliers on New Year's Eve. At dawn patrols from the battalion were in No Man's Land but again the Germans were 'quiet'.

In the left sub-sector was the 22nd Battalion. The Commanding Officer had placed three companies in the line, from right to left B Company, A Company and C Company with D Company in support positions in Mallard Reserve Trench. Listening posts from the battalion were established in No Man's Land and patrols went out up to the enemy wire, but found nothing significant to report.

The 21st Battalion was in support in the Divisional centre, supplying working parties for the front line. On New Year's Day 1918 the battalion 'stood to' at 6 a.m. but no attack came and they eventually stood down. The 20th Battalion was well back in reserve in the Hindenburg Tunnels sheltering from the weather and, where possible, keeping warm. The weather at the beginning of January 1918 was severe, hard frosts and bitter cold made life in the line unbearable. The hardness of the ground made digging and wiring impossible and the bright white snow silhouetted any officer or man who dared to venture into No Man's Land on patrol.

On 2 January Headquarters of the 20th Battalion moved into a dugout in Cuckoo Reserve Trench and three companies of the battalion took over the front line from the 22nd Battalion. Likewise the 21st Battalion relieved the 23rd Battalion in the right

sub-sector. That night the Germans put down a heavy barrage on the left company C Company who suffered two men killed, one wounded and one missing was believed to have been taken prisoner. The enemy airforce was active over the lines at this time, as well as heavy artillery barrages on the rear area. Casualties were sustained when a wiring party came under fire from an enemy machine gun, with one man being killed and a sergeant severely wounded.

The 22nd Battalion, now in reserve, sent working parties into the front line to assist with keeping the trenches clear, they also sent an officer's patrol under Second Lieutenant Anderson out to have a look at an enemy sap. No enemy were encountered on this occasion, but the patrol was repeated on successive nights and on the night of 6 January the enemy were encountered and a fire fight took place. Unfortunately it proved impossible to take a prisoner or to secure any identification of the German unit in the opposite trenches.

Second Lieutenant Basil Peacock also mentioned this time in the line in the early part of 1918 in his book:

'during Christmas and New Year 1917 – 18 we were in the front lines and had our Christmas dinner in one of the deep tunnels of the Hindenburg Line, part of which was now in our hands. Bitterly cold weather persisted for six weeks, and our tour occupied four of them. The ground was so frozen that little digging could be done, and we spent our days trying to keep warm. Apparently the Boche were trying to do the same, for there was little shooting apart from a few whizbangs or light shells morning and evening to denote their presence.'

However the cold spell did not last and eventually a thaw set in, causing portions of those trenches which were unrevetted to collapse. Of course this caused extra work for the men in reserve and further working parties had to be found to rebuild the line and keep communication trenches clear. These conditions also put an extra strain on the men because it was nigh on impossible to get wet clothing dry. The war diaries of both the 20th and 21st Battalions also give credit to the hard work of the Divisional Pioneers, 18/Northumberland Fusiliers and the Brigade Engineers, 208 Field Company Royal Engineers.

But now events behind the lines and in England were to do to the Tyneside Scottish what the German Army had failed to do.

The casualties caused by the Battles of Passchendaele and Cambrai needed to be replaced, but there was an acute shortage of manpower and it was estimated that in 1918 the BEF would need at least 615,000 men to keep it up to strength. The Ministry of National Service calculated that there would only be 100,000 men available and suggested two methods to deal with the shortfall. (A) by reducing the wastage, and (B) by making more men available for front-line service.

The committee made the proposal that Infantry Divisions be reduced from twelve battalions to nine , and at the same time the Divisional Pioneer Battalion be reduced to a three company establishment. The Army Council protested at these drastic measures when many arguments against the reductions were put forward and even the prospect of losing the war was used as a lever but to no avail. The fact that many divisions were worn out, and the prospect of a large enemy offensive still did not delay the axe falling. One temporary stop-gap that was suggested was the incorporation of an American Battalion in each British Brigade, or an American Brigade in a British Division. This idea

was rejected for various reasons, the main one appears to have been that American servicemen would have been serving under a foreign flag. The American Commander in Chief General Pershing pointing out that Canadians, Australians, New Zealanders and even the Irish and Scottish served in their own Divisions.

As early as 10 January, 1918, orders for the reorganization of the BEF were issued by the War Office. These orders were not straightforward for it was laid down that no Regular, First Line Territorial or Yeomanry battalions were to be disbanded, those that were to be selected were to be Second Line Territorial or New Army (Service) battalions – those men who had responded to Kitchener's call to arms in 1914. The Commander in Chief was given a list of 145 battalions from which to choose, many of which had made a fighting reputation for themselves by gallant conduct on the battlefield. In the 34th Division the axe was to fall on the Tyneside battalions of 102 and 103 Brigades, in the Tyneside Irish Brigade the 24/27th and 26th Battalions were to disband and the 25th Battalion would move to 102 Brigade.

In the Tyneside Scottish Brigade the 20th and 21st Battalions were chosen, how or why is unknown. On the Somme had they not advanced as gallantly as the others? At Arras had they not taken their assigned objectives? In truth their men had fought and died at Greenland Hill and Hagricourt, but still they had to go.

The news of the disbandments was received at the end of January, when after spending thirty-seven days in the line the Brigade came out into rest. It is interesting to note that the replacements to the 20th Battalion are given in the war diary as eleven officers and twelve men.

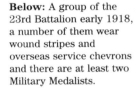

Below: A group of the 23rd Battalion early 1918, a number of them wear wound stripes and overseas service chevrons and there are at least two Military Medalists.

The men were given replacement equipment for items that were worn out or unserviceable. Baths were available to the men and, in the 21st Battalion, at least a lot of football was played as inter-company games took place and the highlight of the tournament was when an Other Ranks XI beat the Officers XI by ten goals to nil. The battalion team in the meantime defeated the 20th Battalion three goals to nil but this was only delaying the final act for these two gallant units, who undefeated by the enemy were wiped out by Whitehall. They paraded and were read the news by their respective commanding officers, and marched off into history.

The 22nd and 23rd Battalions were joined in Blairville by the 25th Battalion and 102 Brigade lost its pure Tyneside Scottish affiliation, however, on 3 February some of the men from the two disbanded battalions were transferred to the 22nd and 23rd Battalions. The latter reported that they received drafts of five Officers and eighty-eight other ranks from the 20th Battalion, seven officers and one hundred and fifty other ranks from the 21st Battalion and one officer and forty-eight other ranks from the 26th Battalion. Shortly afterwards the same battalion received a draft of seventeen signallers from the 24/27th Battalion, bringing it back to nearly peacetime establishment. There was, though, a steady trickle of men reporting sick, who were evacuated to hospital.

The working parties continued and large numbers of men had to be provided for the digging of the Heninel Switch, part of the defensive system that was being constructed.

On 26 February 1918 the war diary of the 22nd Battalion records that they were inspected by the Corps Commander prior to being sent back into the line, however, Basil Peacock recorded this as an inspection by the Army Commander, General Rawlinson.

'We stood in the mud on a drizzling morning, a bedraggled body of troops muffled in drab, muddy greatcoats near the ancient field of Agincourt, trying to look soldierly. We did not succeed, for by this time in the war the quality of reinforcements was extremely poor, many of them of low medical categories, and we were sadly under strength. My platoon numbered twenty-two all ranks, and in one of my sections the lance corporal was the only fit man – of the three privates one was deaf, one almost blind and one mentally sub-normal.

When the great man appeared on horseback with his aide and with two outriders holding pennants, the battalion pulled itself up to attention with a loud squelch. "Stand your men at ease," commanded the general to our colonel. "I wish to address them but have no time to inspect the ranks." Though we were not keen on inspections we felt aggrieved that he was not going to look at us after our efforts to clean ourselves up.

Still sitting on his horse, the great man continued,

"I regret that I must cut short your period of rest and return you to the front line tomorrow. As you know by intelligence reports, the Russians have made a separate peace with Germany which has freed many German Divisions for action on the Western Front. They are under the command of the famous victorious General Ludendorff who has placed them opposite our positions, which are not fully manned as we have had to take them over from the French Army. We shall be greatly out-numbered and outgunned, Ludendorff will use many tanks and probably a new type of gas of a most penetrating type. The supporting trenches, which you have been digging, are not yet complete but our orders are to hold on to every inch of ground. It is doubtful if I shall visit you in the trenches but I shall be waiting to welcome you when you return having repulsed the greatest military onslaught in history. Good luck to you all."

He turned his horse and rode away over the field of Agincourt leaving a stunned silence, until one of my platoon spoke up in a loud voice [in the Geordie dialect],

"That general felly missed a bit oot. He nivor telt us it wes gannin te rain as weel."

The battalions had another visit from Sir Thomas Oliver in February 1918 and although no details of what actually took place have been found, he did accompany the Brigadier on an inspection of the 23rd Battalion. There can have been only a few men present who had been inspected by Sir Thomas before.

Another occurrence at this time was that the village estaminet was opened in the afternoon as a reading and writing room and was allowed to stay open until 9 p.m., although the sale of alcoholic drink ceased at 8 p.m.

On 1 March the battalions began moving forward into the Corps reserve line, where they were held at one hours' notice to move. The 34th Division took over the front line and on the second of the month the, 22nd Battalion moved into the right sub sector of the divisional front. In view of the expected enemy attack, flank defences were prepared and positions and tactics rehearsed whilst nightly patrols tried to locate the enemy in order to learn what they were up to. The 23rd Battalion in the meantime had been placed in Brigade reserve and was employed sending working parties into the front line. On 7 March, 102 Brigade moved back to divisional reserve and further training was carried out, battle stores were issued and extensive

Above: 50242 Private John Cassidy enlisted Newcastle 5 October 1916 and served with the Royal Field Artillery and the 3rd Training Reserve Battalion, eventually posted to the 1st Tyneside Scottish he was discharged in Catterick 18 October 1918. He has borrowed a Highland Light Infantry Glengarry for the photograph.

Above: 37987 Private John Dodd, 23rd Battalion from Hexam KiA 20 March 1918, commemorated on the Arras Memorial.

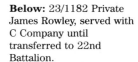

Below: 23/1182 Private James Rowley, served with C Company until transferred to 22nd Battalion.

reconnaissance of the second and third line system of trenches was undertaken. Routes into and out of the battle area were inspected and all ranks familiarized with them. Everyone in the battalions was shown how to load and fire the Lewis gun and the men's kits were inspected and brought up to scale.

The German Offensive

On 19 March, with rain falling steadily, the trek back to the front line began. As in all Scottish regiments, pipers, who played the stirring tunes of glory, led their respective companies towards the front. This also was recorded by Lieutenant Basil Peacock:

'As usual, when we were due for battle, our pipers played us up, and so two rather inexpert pipers marched in front of my company blowing their pipes almost without ceasing for five miles, directly into the ears of my men. When we arrived at the entrance to the communication trench they stood aside and saluted, and one remarked, "Good-bye sor, good luck, lads. I hope its not gannin to be too bad for ye."

One of my platoon, I believe it was Smash, replied briskly, "Ye bugger, if it's any worse than ye've put us through in the last five miles it'll be bloody murder."

I can still see the look on the breathless piper's face.'

The battalion deployed with D and C Companies in the front line, B Company in support and A Company in reserve.

Likewise the 23rd Battalion also took over a portion of the front line, on the left of the 22nd Battalion. The third battalion of 102 Brigade, the 25th Battalion was deployed in brigade support, but all three battalion headquarters were located close together in Bunhill Row, which was a trench in the second line system.

The afternoon of 20 March was warm and sunny, on top of the rain this caused overnight fog, ideal for those who were to patrol No Man's Land that night.

'The Colonel sent for me and ordered me to take the platoon over the top that night, 20 March, and to enter the German lines to take a prisoner. At 2000 hours we set off towards the front line trench, lightly equipped, with our faces blacked, carrying rifles, clubs and grenades. I reported to the company commander in the front line, who said that all was suspiciously quiet; his men would give us covering fire if necessary and would try not to shoot us on the way back. It was a dark murky night, suitable for this nefarious work, we crawled in and out of shell holes until we came to the German wire, which we found in poor repair and about twenty yards deep. Picking our way through we came to

the enemy firing trench, which was a proper trench, not an abandoned field work and had a typical German smell about it, so different from our own. Leaving a sentry we dropped into it and made our way cautiously along it for about fifty yards. All was deathly quiet and spooky, but there were plenty of recent traces of the Boche – bits of equipment, water bottles and stick grenades, but no bodies alive or dead.'

Having examined the enemy trench and taken some papers and equipment as evidence the patrol carefully withdrew across No Man's Land and back into the British line. After a mug of tea laced with rum supplied by the officer commanding the front line company, they made their way to Battalion Headquarters where Basil Peacock reported to the Commanding Officer. The CO was disappointed by the lack of a prisoner and the patrol was dismissed to return to its own company. Basil Peacock was just making his report to his company commander when the German offensive began:

'I was relating my experiences to my Captain when there came a sudden flash which lit up the whole sky, then a tremendous crash, as thousands of German shells landed at the same moment on the British lines. We ducked for cover, and my OC shouted, "You damned little liar, you said there were no Germans over there".'

The time was 5 a.m. and one of the heaviest artillery barrages of the war had just been unleashed. Consisting primarily of HE and gas shells, which fell mainly on the support lines around Bunhill Row. In some parts of the line, owing to this heavy shelling, casualties were heavy but others were more fortunate.

'We flattened ourselves against the forward walls of the dugouts, we could communicate only by signs, for most of the time we could not hear ourselves speak. Fortunately most of the projectiles hit the far bank of the cutting and at first we escaped with few casualties.'

(Lieutenant Basil Peacock 22nd Battalion.)

The story now becomes somewhat sketchy. The barrage continued for nearly five hours, but the thick fog made it impossible for the German artillery observers to correct their fire, which probably saved the lives of many Tyneside Scottish soldiers. Casualties from the gas were evacuated with the wounded where possible, but the confused situation remained unclear. On the front of the 23rd Battalion, on the left, no attack took place initially, but on the right the 22nd Battalion found their right flank unprotected as the Germans forced back the left hand battalion of the 59th Division. As had been previously rehearsed the right forward company threw back a defensive line and two

platoons from the Reserve Company were sent to extend the line westwards. Captain McLachlan's company of the 25th Battalion was brought forward and extended this flank along the Ecoust switch line. Rifle Grenadiers were sent up to assist the forward company but by 1 p.m. the 102nd Light Trench Mortar Battery was reporting that the Germans were as far into the British lines as the village of Ecoust and they were also moving along the Hogs Back.

The German storm troopers had also by now managed to force an entry into the section of the front line held by the 22nd Battalion, from where they proceeded to bomb northwards. However, the enemy was reported to have been held and two companies of the 25th Battalion were ordered to counter-attack. Also ordered forward from his position with the Reserve Company was Basil Peacock:

> '*I heard a runner call my name, and I was told to report to Battalion HQ. I groped my way into Bunhill Row, where I found my captain with his mask off his face but with the mouth and nose piece in situ. I removed mine and found the gas less dense and that it did not affect the eyes. ... The barrage seemed to be lifting so I ran down to Battalion HQ and reported to the Colonel. "Peacock" he ordered, "You will take two platoons and form a flank down Pelican Avenue to the right of our area and try and join up with our forward companies".*'

Trying to link up with the forward line, the first troops he saw were British prisoners moving eastwards. Using his binoculars he next observed German troops, but these were behind him, on his right. Then he came across stragglers from the 59th Division who were moving into the 34th Division area and these men were very quickly

followed by the Germans who were throwing bombs to keep the British heads down. Sergeant Soulsby tried to make a fight of it with a Lewis gun which very soon jammed, but he was able to dismantle the gun and dispose of the parts before he was taken prisoner.

The 23rd Battalion meanwhile did not come under direct attack and at noon they reported that they could hear the fighting on the high ground towards Ecoust and St Leger. It was not long before the headquarters of all three battalions in Bunhill Row were under pressure. Having made an attempt to retreat, and finding his numbers gradually reduced, Basil Peacock by now slightly wounded decided to try and report to the Battalion Headquarters in Bunhill Row:

> '*I could assemble only five men now and thought it my duty to report back to Battalion HQ, a foolish decision as it turned out, for the enemy had nearly surrounded it. I put myself into the bag just before the Boche closed the opening.*'

Above: 40525 Private Edward Forrest, 17 Shuttleworth Street, Earby, Yorkshire, KiA 21 March 1918 with 22nd Battalion.

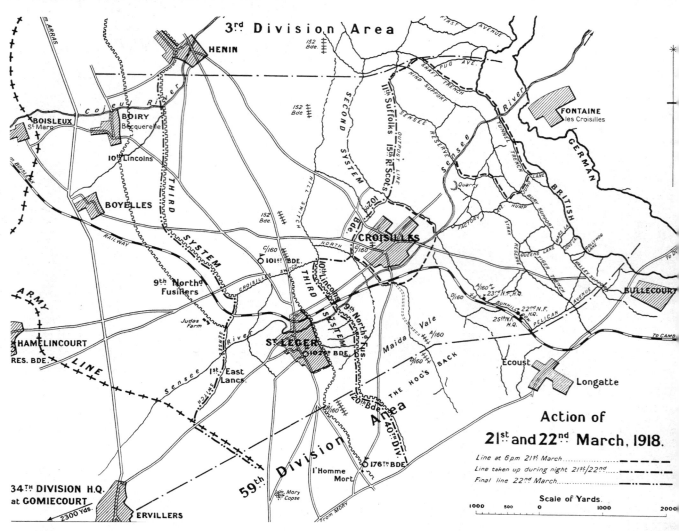

3rd Division Area

Action of 21st and 22nd March, 1918.

Line at 6pm 21st March ....
Line taken up during night 21st/22nd .... — — —
Final line 22nd March .... — · — · —

Scale of Yards
1000   500   0   1000   2000

34TH DIVISION H.Q. at GOMIECOURT

Above: 35805 Private Richard Handley, Dent, Yorkshire, KiA 29 March 1918 with 23rd Battalion. Previously served with the Lincolnshire Regiment.

The situation at the Battalion HQs was critical but an all round defence was established and the papers and documents in the headquarters dugout were burnt. Colonel Acklom and his Adjutant were killed as they tried to escape being cut off, then later the Germans sent a message that if the garrison did not surrender they would be killed. The remaining two Commanding Officers, Lieutenant Colonel Charlton of the 22nd Battalion and Lieutenant Colonel Leith-Hay-Clark commanding the 25th Battalion reluctantly took the decision to surrender. Owing to the fact that there was scarcely an unwounded or un-gassed man left standing, the defence of Bunhill Row became untenable, and the garrison capitulated.

The moment of surrender was recalled by the padre of the 22nd Battalion:

'By five in the afternoon we were surrounded, and as we were still in telephone contact with Brigade HQ we were ordered to surrender as we had so many wounded, and there was no possibility of a relief force. It had been a terrible day. We wore gasmasks from about 4.30 a.m. to 10 a.m. I could do little except occasionally provide some of our men with a cup of tea and so on. Once during the day a shell burst almost at my feet, and I was blown by the blast off the duckboard into a sea of mud. I thought I was killed and so did the others. When we had orders to surrender, I was in a dugout

with a lot of wounded. As I came out, I said to the German NCO "Ich pastor" I knew no German. However, the words acted like magic and I was allowed to go back to the wounded. This was Thursday, and we were not evacuated or attended to until Sunday. I could only give them water out of shell holes, which we were not supposed to drink, and bits of broken meat and biscuits.'

Some of the defenders fought until the last possible moment and among them was Basil Peacock who wrote of his capture:

'I had just thrown a grenade and had turned to pick up another from the box; when I straightened up, I saw a dozen Germans a few feet away in the cutting. I was so appalled that I stood paralysed, until a black bearded Feldwebel pointed a Luger at my stomach and remarked threateningly "Sie werfen granaten"(You throw grenades). Fortunately, I had not drawn the pin of the grenade I was holding, so I dropped it. Then to my everlasting gratitude, a German officer, who may have been the one we were trying to shoot, pushed away the NCO's pistol and told me to take off my belt. Other officers and men were as dumbfounded as I and probably were receiving the same treatment, but no one actually raised their hands in surrender. I do distinctly

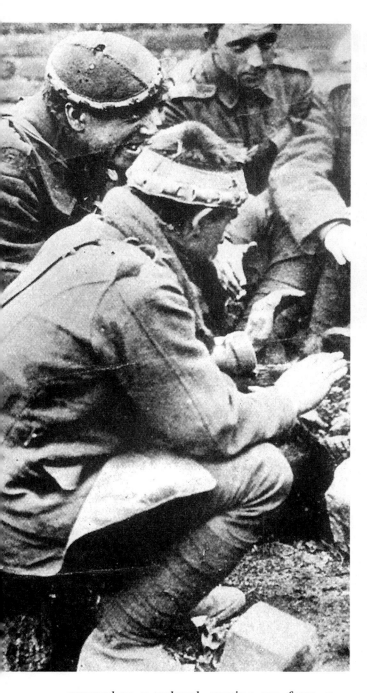

Above: British Prisoners wait to be escorted to the rear March 1918.

Far left: Tyneside Scots taken prisoner probably during the German March offensive. The Lance Corporal wearing the greatcoat has the impression of a 3rd Tyneside Scottish shoulder title on his epaulette. The black diamond battle patch can also be seen.

Below: 20/702 Private Gibson Alexander, 22nd Battalion was taken prisoner 21 March 1918.

kept getting round on the right and further retirement had to be undertaken. By the morning of 22 March parties from all three battalions as well as men from J Special Company Royal Engineers, and the Brigade Pioneer Company of 18/Northumberland Fusiliers eventually manned the Croiselles Switch. The thick fog still hung in the air and this allowed parties of German soldiers to keep outflanking the defenders.

Unfortunately very little information about the Tyneside Scottish part in the battle has survived. Second Lieutenant Pigg and forty men of the 23rd Battalion, having manned the Croiselles Switch, received word that they had been outflanked and retired to Hill Switch and then again, at 3 p.m., to the third line system where they dug in. It was here that the leading troops of the 31st Division began the relief of the 34th Division at 3 30 a.m. on the morning of 23 March 1918. During the relief Second Lieutenant Pigg lost touch with Captain Morledge and was unable to pass word of the retirement of the 23rd Battalion. Captain Morledge, along with three officers and about ten men remained with 2/Scots Guards and fought on throughout the day until they were relieved and allowed to retire.

The defence of Bunhill Row and the stubborn fighting retreat of the Tyneside Battalions of 102 Brigade brought special praise from the Divisional Commander, Major General Nicholson, who wrote in Divisional Orders on 29 March:

'On my own behalf I wish to record my high appreciation of the gallantry and the stubborn power of resistance shewn by all ranks and arms of the Division on the 21st and 22nd March.

When the full story of those days is known the gallant fight of the 102nd and part of the 101st Brigade on the 21st of March when outflanked and almost surrounded, the stubborn and protracted

remember a colonel coming up from a dugout and exclaiming, "Shall we surrender or die like English gentlemen?" and the thought flashing through my brain, "If he decides to fight, I shall be one of the first dead!" In the end we were marshalled into a column and escorted back through the enemy lines.'

Those who were not surrounded began a fighting retreat northward, the left company of the 22nd Battalion had only suffered a few casualties and with the survivors of the other companies a fighting withdrawal was made. Trying to link up on either flank, men would find just as they got dug in the enemy would get round the flank and a further retirement would have to be made. By 6 p.m. the survivors of the 23rd Battalion were manning Factory Avenue and were in touch with 15/Royal Scots of 101 Brigade on the left, but the enemy

Above: 23/546 CQMS Robert Muter, 100 North Row, Bedlington Colliery, discharged on 15 April 1918 from gunshot wounds.

Above: 64911 Private Wilf Denton joined 22nd Battalion from the DLI.

Above: 45922 Sergeant Norman Robert Hedley enlisted into the Tyneside Scottish 5 January 1915, by 1919 he was serving with the 3rd Battalion NF.

resistance of the 11th Suffolks on the left of the Division on the 21st and 22nd March and the steady disciplined gallantry of the 103rd Brigade will go down in history among the achievements of the war.'

Brigadier Thomson, the Brigade commander, was delighted by the comments of the GOC 34th Division and sent the following letter to the Officer Commanding the 22nd Battalion,

'It is with great pride in my Brigade that I read our Divisional Commander's appreciation of the good work done by it. Your Battalion did magnificently against great odds and I am full of admiration for the fine fighting spirit, which it displayed. I very much regret your losses but I am confident that the Germans suffered far more heavily at your hands.

N Thomson

Brigadier General

Cmdg 102nd Infantry Brigade'

The survivors of the depleted 23rd Battalion gathered in huts near Bucquoy under the command of Captain Morledge; in dribs and drabs men rejoined but many were simply 'missing'. The first reinforcements to arrive were 135 men from the 26th Battalion, who had been attached to the 9th Entrenching Battalion after the 26th Battalion disbanded. The next few days were spent moving from village to village in the rear area and on 25 March Major H H Neeves DSO MC and Bar of the 27th Battalion took over command of the 23rd Battalion on promotion to Lieutenant Colonel. The 22nd Battalion was also moving at this time, each night spent in a different billet, until on 27 March the two battalions entrained at Frevent to move north to Steenbeque, where they went into billets, the 23rd Battalion in Rue Du Bois, and the 22nd in Tannay. Drafts were arriving to begin the process of rebuilding the shattered battalions; 140 men on 29 March and 106 men on 31 March were recorded by the 22nd Battalion's diarist. This last draft contained sixty men of the 51st (Graduated) Battalion Durham Light Infantry, among them Private Wilf Denton from York, who had left their billets in Durham City and had been rebadged as Northumberland Fusiliers along the way. They were described in the war diary as follows: 'They were well disciplined and a good class of young lads – their musketry was excellent.'

The area taken over was in the sector known as the Bois Grenier Line, which had been allowed to deteriorate, so that trenches had collapsed and the line was only held by a series of disconnected posts very badly wired. There was no time to train the new men, every spare man being put to work strengthening the defences. On 3 April the Germans began shelling with a new type of mustard gas, but only a few of these shells fell near the Tyneside Scottish battalions.

By 5 April 102 Brigade was back in the front line, on the left the 22nd Battalion relieved 11/Suffolks, in the centre the 23rd Battalion took over from 16/Royal Scots and the 25th Battalion on the right replaced 15/Royal Scots.

Immediately the relief was complete patrols were sent out into No Man's Land to try and locate the enemy, from the 23rd Battalion Second Lieutenants Viner, Hughes and Hannington all carried out patrols but could find no trace of the enemy. On 8 April the enemy shelled Armentières with 25000 gas shells, this was a carefully planned barrage which caused many casualties to the support troops but left the front line untouched. Two companies of the 25th Battalion, who were badly gassed, had to be replaced in Brigade reserve but the two Tyneside Scottish Battalions were basically unaffected.

On the evening of 8 April the enemy started a heavy barrage and then at 4.14 a.m. commenced an attack on the right, where they made progress against the Portugese divisions. Things remained quiet on the front of the Tyneside Scottish, but they did report enemy air activity along with the fact that the 23rd Battalion had captured four German prisoners. On the morning of 10 April it was the turn of the division on the left to be attacked and by 2 p.m. 102 Brigade HQ was under shellfire. The decision was taken to withdraw and word was passed to the troops in the line, although it took some time for the word to reach the forward elements of the Brigade. The 22nd Battalion withdrew by companies, under enemy fire, which increased as time went on, but an unexpected bonus was a thick mist which prevented observation by the enemy aircraft overhead. The withdrawal of the 23rd Battalion took place after that of the 22nd, all trench stores and anything likely to be of use to the enemy was destroyed prior to the move. As the men began to move back Private Wilf Denton had a lucky escape:

'We were moving in single file along a road when a German machine gun opened fire, hitting and killing the man behind me. He fell forward and hit me in the back, the force of his body knocking me to the ground. Another burst of fire came and killed the man in front of me, if it hadn't been for the man behind me knocking me down, that burst would have killed me.'

When the two battalions reached the Estaires – Lys line they were placed in defensive positions, the 23rd Battalion put B Company, under Captain Douglas, in to Manchester Post and D Company, under Lieutenant Pigg, into Burnley Post. Between them, commanded by Second Lieutenant Coxon, was C Company. On the left though the 22nd Battalion were in difficulty, owing to heavy machine-gun fire from the enemy; D Company was unable to take up its allotted positions and had to withdraw their left flank. This meant that B Company, the reserve company, had to be brought up to extend the flank to form a switch line, facing north, from the Nieppe trench system to the River

Lys. During the night many stragglers passed through the line held by 102 Brigade, but the enemy was quiet, then as dawn rose the attack started again.

The Germans attacked from the south and forced their way into the area of Pont de Nieppe which allowed them to open fire into the rear of the Tyneside Scottish Battalions. C Company of the 22nd Battalion was detailed to cover the withdrawal of that battalion and although A, B and D Companies got away practically all of C Company became casualties, after they had held the enemy up for some time.

The highlight of the morning was the shooting down of a German aircraft by British machine gunners after the brigade withdrew to the Nieppe system. Here the enemy was held, despite repeated attacks, but eventually due to the fact they were outflanked, 102 Brigade was withdrawn to Pont d'Achelles. Marching straight down the Bailleul – Armentières road, the battalions rendezvoused at the junction of the De Seule – Neuve Eglise road, where they bivouacked in open fields for the night.

On the morning of 12 April, just before dawn, the 22nd Battalion were ordered into support positions just north of Steenwerck, where they spent a quiet day until late in the afternoon when the enemy again launched an attack at around 5 30 p.m. The Germans managed to break through the front line and the survivors of A and B Companies of the 22nd Battalion were ordered to restore the situation. The enemy tried throughout the night to establish positions in the houses in the 22nd Battalion area but was held off without too much trouble. In the meantime the 23rd Battalion were ordered forward to try and restore the front line to the east of Pont d'Achelles. The 23rd moved forward and spent the night digging and wiring a new line. All the next morning the Germans repeatedly attacked and each time were driven back, until late in the afternoon the Worcesters on the left flank were forced to withdraw which caused the left of the 23rd Battalion to be swung back to form a defensive flank. The enemy launched a violent attack and drove the men in the front line back on to the second line. The left-hand company, under the command of Lieutenant Pigg, put up a gallant resistance until the last moment.

The 22nd Battalion, meanwhile, was under heavy shellfire and all the Battalion Headquarters officers became casualties, except the Signals Officer, but stayed in position until nightfall, when they were ordered to withdraw. On the morning of 14 April, owing to the severe casualties incurred over the last few days, the three battalions of 102 Brigade were formed into a composite battalion, each of the original battalions forming a company of 102 Composite Battalion. Command of the battalion was given to Lieutenant Colonel H H Neeves DSO MC and the companies were commanded as follows;

22nd Composite Company, Lieutenant Hardy,

23rd Composite Company, Second Lieutenant Viner,
25th Composite Company, Second Lieutenant Coleby MM.

The Composite Battalion moved into support positions and dug in, the men being rested as much as possible. That night the 59th Division moved up and relieved the front line, until they retired the following morning and the 34th Division once more became the front line troops. The Composite Battalion was withdrawn into reserve positions on 16 April when throughout that day and 17 April heavy intermittent shelling took place during which Second Lieutenant H S Hardy was slightly wounded. The strength of the Tyneside Scottish Battalions at this time was very low, the 22nd Battalion numbered 11 Officers and 359 Other Ranks and the 23rd Battalion 9 Officers and 225 Other Ranks. On 18 April Second Lieutenant Viner was gassed; and 18/Northumberland Fusiliers erected a barbed wire apron along the front line. However the front fell quiet and the Composite Battalion was eventually relieved by 3rd Battalion of 401 Infantry Regiment of the French Army on 20 April.

Some time between the fighting on 21 March and 18 April, Lieutenant A R Hunter of the 23rd Battalion was captured by the enemy but after being held for two days he managed to escape and rejoin his battalion. On 18 May he was at last able to get a letter away giving news of his whereabouts:

'I have had a severe time of it since the 21st of March last, but thank God I have had the luck to get through it all. Although I was taken prisoner by Fritz, but managed to escape again two nights later, and then I was slightly wounded again a fortnight later. I am quite alright again, but still feel my arm a bit sore at times.

I am due for leave again whenever it opens and trust that may be soon as I am longing to get away from all this and see all at home again. The weather during the last five days has been excellent which makes everything else a pleasure, but during the advance we had some wretched times. I lost all my kit on 17 April last owing to a shell landing in my billet blowing everything up, but may say I had another stroke of luck to escape so easily myself, so can't complain. At present I am back in rest, which I may candidly say I have earned, as my nerves are somewhat shaky at present.
Yours very sincerely
A R Hunter'

The last nine days had been spent in continuous fighting; although the line had been broken, and often outflanked, the men of the Tyneside battalions, along with the other units involved, had managed to stop the enemy advance. Praise came from on high, Army, Corps and Divisional Commanders all sent messages of congratulations to the men under their command.

Above: 36686 Private William Henry Hodges a reinforcement to the 23rd Battalion from Kent. When he was wounded he thought that his pal had accidently bayoneted him. He was reported 'missing' and his name was included on the village war memorial.

Below: 23/683 Private Harry Allan of Ashington. After being wounded 1 July 1916, he served with 24th and 8th NF. He was transfered to 1/5th Territorial Battalion. He was KiA 27 May 1918.

Above: Standing left rear is Lieutenant A R Hunter, wounded and taken prisoner in March 1918 he managed to evade his captors and return to his battalion. He was eventually awarded the Military Cross, Belgium Croix de Guerre and the French Legion of Honour. Sadly he died of sickness in 1919.

Below: 37122 Private John Thomas Ideson, High Gamsworth, Barden, Yorkshire, 23 Battalion, died as a PoW 28 July 1918.

Typical of these messages is the one from the General Officer Commanding First Army, General H S Horne,

'I wish to express my appreciation of the great bravery and endurance with which all ranks have fought and held out against overwhelming numbers.

It has been necessary to call for great exertions and more must still be asked for, but I am confident that, at this critical period when the existence of the British Empire is at stake, all ranks of the First Army will do their very best.

H S Horne General

Commanding, First Army.'

The battalions of 102 Brigade were ordered to move by march route to the Poperinghe area to begin work digging the Poperinghe Line. Here the 22nd Battalion sustained several casualties owing to enemy shelling on 26 April and on 27 April both Tyneside Scottish Battalions moved into the Brandhoek Line. The next few days were spent working for the Royal Engineers constructing outposts and emplacements', although at times the enemy shelled the area only a few casualties were reported. The last days of April and the first two weeks of May passed in this way, until, on 16 May

1918 the sad news was received that the Tyneside Scottish was to be reduced to a training cadre and all surplus personnel were transferred to the base and thence to other units. The cadre would be employed training troops of the American Expeditionary Force who were now arriving in France in growing numbers.

On 16 May Lieutenant Colonel J T Jansen commanding the 22nd Battalion paraded his men and read out a farewell message.

FAREWELL ADDRESS

Officers, NCOs and men on the eve of the break up of the Battalion, I want to say how sorry I am that the 3rd Tyneside Scottish has got to go.

For many who have been with the Battalion for a long time I know how hard a blow it will be and probably things will never be the same again.

But wherever you go and whatever you are called upon to do I am certain that you will remember that you belonged to a Battalion with as fine a record as any in France, and will carry on elsewhere with that same splendid fighting spirit that you have shown here.

To all who are leaving, Good-bye and the very best of luck.

J T Jansen Lt Col

Comdg 22nd NF

3rd Tyneside Scottish.

As the parade was dismissed Colonel Jansen screwed up the piece of paper on which he had written the farewell address, probably in frustration and anger, and had thrown it to the ground. It was picked up and kept by 22/314 Sergeant W A Middlemiss of South Shields as a souvenir of his time with the Tyneside Scottish.

On the morning of 18 May Captain G W Atkinson, along with five subalterns and 463 other ranks, left the 22nd Battalion and proceeded to the base for re-posting. The 22nd Battalion Training Cadre was affiliated to the 109 Infantry Regiment US Army and training commenced.

The 23rd Battalion was engaged on a similar exercise, sending four officers and 407 other ranks to the base, the strength of the Training Cadre being twenty-four officers and 151 other ranks. They to went to work training men of 1st and 3rd Battalions 110 Infantry Regiment and 108 Machine Gun Battalion of the US Army. These Americans, fresh and free of the horrors of war, were described by the 23rd Battalion as, 'All ranks very keen to learn, very enthusiastic and intelligent.' Thus May passed into June, the training of the units of the 28th American Division was completed and preparations made for the reception and training of the 78th American Division. There was however some delay and it was not until 9 June that 307, 308 and 309 Machine Gun Battalions US Army arrived. On 11 June Lieutenant Colonel H H Neeves DSO MC and Bar left to command 102 Brigade for two weeks. Then on 17 June the sad news was received that the 34th Division was leaving to be reformed and that the 23rd Battalion would come under command of 116 Brigade of 39th Division. The 22nd Battalion was also transferred, but in their case to the 16th (Irish) Division, which was moving back to UK to reform, more of which later.

The 23rd Battalion spent the remainder of June all of July and the first weeks of August training various American units. Schools of instruction for signallers, machine gunners and other specialists were all started, but staleness and frustration was beginning to creep in, comments in the war diary such as, 'Rumours of another move. AEF is a mess,' and 'AEF unable to make their minds up re billets,' tell their own story. The most telling statement though is on 31 July, when the 23rd Battalion diarist writes:

> 'The end of an uninteresting month – all want to be made up – scrapping is ten times better than this.'

Various moves took place, until 23 August found the battalion in Queens Camp, Maudricourt, where preparations were made to receive reinforcements from the Salonika and Palestine fronts. These reinforcements were mainly men suffering from malaria, the first arrivals being from the Lancashire Fusiliers and Manchester Regiment of the 22nd Division. Various changes of commanding officer took place during these last months of 1918, whilst the drafts leaving the battalion went mainly to the 50th and 66th Divisions. November found the 23rd Battalion in Number 1 Lines of Communication, Area Reception Camp where they ended the war on 11 November. The only mention of this event was the fact that Brigadier J H Hall CMG DSO, the Brigade Commander, cancelled all parades to celebrate the armistice.

The 22nd Battalion and the 16th (Irish) Division

The 22nd Battalion was last heard of as transferred to the 16th Division on 17 June. The Battalion Cadre embussed at Boursin and were transported by lorry to Boulogne, where they were billeted in Oostrohove Camp for the night. The next day, 18 June, they embarked for Folkestone, from where they were transported by train to Bourley Camp, Aldershot. The next move was to Margate, in Kent, and here the 22nd Battalion Cadre took over the establishment of 38/Northumberland Fusiliers, re-organization took place, drafts arrived daily and training commenced. By the end of June the Battalion returned to Bourley Camp and formed part of 48 Brigade. By the end of July the 22nd Battalion was back in France and on 1 August began moving inland from Boulogne. Initially the 16th Division formed part of XXII Corps, but they were kept well back in training until 22 August, when they embussed for the forward area.

Gradually they moved closer to the front line,

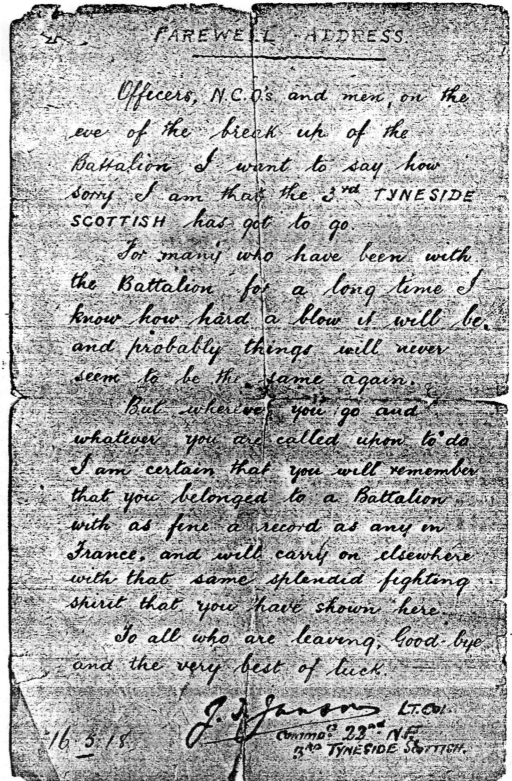

Left: 22/314 Sergeant Walter Middlemiss MM, 22nd Battalion Machine Gun Section. Walter picked up Lieutenant Colonel Jansen's farewell speech paper (above).

Above: 21/485 CSM and Mrs Harry Drury, 29 Market Street, Alnwick, commissioned into Black Watch September 1918

Below: 23/46 Private Daniel Pearce of Jarrow, employed as a miner at Hebburn Colliery. Daniel enlisted 23 November 1914. He was KiA whilst carrying rations and water to the line 8 October 1918 whilst serving with 12/13th Battalion NF and is buried in Prospect Hill Cemetery, Gouy.

until on 26 August the 22nd Battalion once again came under German fire, when the enemy shelled the camp at Noeux les Mines with HE and gas, however there were no casualties. The battalion Second in Command and the specialist officers, Lewis guns, Signals and Scouts all went forward and carried out reconnaissance of the front line in preparation for the move back into the line. Prior to the move all companies fired the Lewis gun on the nearby range and every individual was told his exact position and duty in the defence scheme. The lessons of the previous March and April had been well learned.

On 1 September the battalion relieved 18/Gloucesters in the left sub sector of the divisional front, with A and B Companies in the line, C in support and D in reserve. Strong patrols were sent out all along the front for the Germans were withdrawing, hand to hand fighting took place and the battalion once again experienced casualties. Patrols were out every night between 2 and 6 September; on 3 September Second Lieutenant Orange captured a German prisoner and on the same day Second Lieutenant J F Cree was killed whilst on patrol. On 5 September Second Lieutenant G O Gibson was posted missing. The following day a set piece attack took place with three companies in the line the attack being carried out without artillery preparation, over difficult ground, which was strewn with barbed wire. The weather for this attack was described as perfect, with a slight mist. Most of the casualties; thirty-four, were caused by gas, of a total which included six dead, eleven missing and twenty-four wounded. All objectives were taken and the battalion was heavily shelled in its new position.

On 8 September the 22nd was relieved by 18/Gloucestershire Regiment and moved back into support. The period from 8 to 13 September was spent cleaning up and resting, until the 18/Gloucesters were relieved once more. The momentum of the forward movement was maintained and by 15 September the 22nd Battalion was holding a series of posts near the railway south of the La Bassèe Canal where they were heavily shelled, mainly with gas. The Germans were described as 'Active' but the battalion snipers located some machine guns and enemy positions and kept them pinned down. An attack on 17 September by B Company resulted in the capture of five prisoners and some enemy positions, but this annoyed the Germans. After a very intense bombardment they immediately counter-attacked and re-took the positions lost, driving B Company back to its start line. A Company then came up to replace B Company and without any artillery preparation stormed forward and again took the German positions, without losing a single casualty and capturing three machine guns into the bargain.

The Gloucesters arrived and took over the front line, the 22nd moving back to support positions, and then they replaced 6/Somerset LI in divisional reserve in Cambrin. Between 18 and 25 September the Tyneside Scottish were out at rest, when cleaning up and baths were provided in Annequin. Training of reinforcements and a tactical exercise with aircraft took place prior to going back into the support positions on 27 September. Carrying parties for the front line were provided and the battalion was put on standby to reinforce the front line, but fortunately were not called up.

At the beginning of October, 5/R Irish Rifles were relieved in the front out-post line on a two-company front. However the enemy were gradually pulling back and the 22nd Battalion followed them and maintained close contact. The advance continued and several prisoners were taken and some machine guns captured but on 4 October heavy opposition was met. The Dynamite Factory in Berclau was captured and the advance was pushed on towards the canal at this stage the men, although very tired, were described as 'cheerful'. On 5 October 18/Scottish Rifles relieved the Tyneside Scottish and they moved back to the Augny area into Brigade Reserve. For the next four days the battalion was employed on salvage work cleaning up old trenches and collecting discarded ammunition. Later on they were employed as navvies repairing roads, filling in craters and where possible more training was done. The battalion was employed in this way until 4 November when they headed back towards the front. On 6 and 7 November they came under shellfire but there were no casualties, and in very wet weather on 8 November they prepared to attack again. The 22nd Battalion leapfrogged through 5/Royal Irish Rifles but found that the Germans had vacated their positions. Bridges were erected across the canal and the Battalion crossed and moved on towards their objective, which was the line of a railway and the village of Antoing, which was occupied on 10 November. The battalion scouts made a thorough search of all likely places for any Germans who could have remained behind, but no one was found. The following morning the Armistice was declared and the 22nd (Service) Battalion Northumberland Fusiliers had fired their last shots of the war. All that was left to do was to get demobilized and to get home as fast as possible.

Chapter Eleven

End of Conflict, and the Post-War years

'Once again I heard the music of the pipers from afar
They tramped and tramped the weary men,
returning from the war.'

THE GALLANT FORTY TWA, TRAD

FOR THE TWO BATTALIONS of the Tyneside Scottish in France on 11 November 1918, the end of the greatest conflict civilization had ever seen, ended with a feeling of anti-climax. Both battalion war diaries record little in the way of celebration, for the 22nd Battalion the diary reads:

11 November, 11 a.m. Companies at disposal of Company Commanders, Armistice commenced.'

Whilst the diary of the 23rd Battalion has no entry at all. However, within twenty-four hours things were back to normal and the 22nd battalion commenced 'specialist training', and battalion parades and ceremonial drill began. Three days later, on 15 November, the battalion began moving west from Antoing to Taintignies, where the night was spent. In bitterly cold weather the march continued to Genech Chateau, where they went into billets for the night. The next day, after an evening's rest, the march continued to the Templeuve area. The Battalion Headquarters was located in the village of Les Rues, where it was to remain for several months. On 18 November the battalion commenced cleaning up uniforms and equipment and platoon and company drill commenced on 19 November with the Regimental Sergeant Major instructing all the battalion NCOs. To break the monotony, education classes and recreational activities took place with the odd route march thrown in.

The 23rd Battalion meanwhile was still located on the Lines of Communication serving in 197 Brigade and after the armistice small drafts began leaving the battalion cadre.

December saw little change for the 22nd Battalion, the education classes continued and general infantry training took place, as well as inspections and drill. Everything possible was done to keep the men occupied, classes in reading, writing and arithmetic, shorthand, French, book-keeping and shoemaking were all carried out.

Instruction in tailoring, carpentry and horse-shoeing was also given, as well as plenty of sport. Inter-platoon and inter-company competitions were organized with football and boxing well to the fore. The strength of the battalion at this time was not recorded but, from 11 December, coal miners began to be demobilized in large numbers; there were, however, very few of the original miners left to be demobilized.

For the 23rd Battalion Cadre, December began with training for the reinforcements, but on 3 December all 163 malarial reinforcements were transferred to 16/Sherwood Foresters. The War Diary records for this period 'Awaiting orders for move. Nothing to do.' Then on 10 December what was left of the 23rd Battalion left Haudricourt for Havre, where they went into Number Two Rest Camp. The following day saw them move into Number One Camp to begin the demobilization of miners. In no time at all large numbers of men were passing through the hands of the 23rd Battalion and during the period 10 - 29 December no less than 104 Officers and 5172 were sent to dispersal centres at Oswestry, Chisledon and Duddington. Christmas dinner was provided by the Royal Flying Corps and was described as 'Very satisfactory'. Then on 30 December a further ten officers and 366 other ranks were sent to Duddington for demobilization, among them were sixteen miners from the 23rd Battalion Cadre, which was now reduced to a strength of ten officers and thirty-seven men.

The New year of 1919 saw little change, the 22nd Battalion remained in Templeuve carrying out the same programme of drill, training and inspections, and for those who were not involved in education classes there was a working party at Templeuve Station. Sport was an almost daily activity; C Company won the Brigade inter-company Football Competition on 8 January 1919, whilst the Battalion cross country teams took second and third places in the Brigade cross country run held on 10 January. In the Brigade Boxing Competition, held on 14 January, Private Maloney took the Featherweight title for the Tyneside Scottish. Whist drives and dances were also held and the Battalion Concert Party performed regularly in the Tyne Theatre.

Meanwhile the 23rd Battalion Cadre carried on with its duties at Number 1 Despatching Camp, (formerly Number 1 Rest Camp) and the number of dispersal centres in the UK to which it was sending men was increased to six so that on average 800 men a day were being sent home for demobilization.

With the arrival of February the 22nd Battalion had an informal visit by His Royal Highness, The Prince of Wales. Following the visit, owing to the reduction in numbers because of demobilization, the Battalion merged its four companies into a single company commanded by Captain A F Davies. On 5 February at 11.00 a.m. this company of the 22nd Battalion paraded to receive its King's Colour from General Holland commanding I Corps. The colour was a plain Union Jack and no Battle Honours were added until years later when a Special Army Order was published on 4 September, 1922. Nearly three weeks later Lieutenant McKennis MC and Lieutenant Maughan, along with 176 other ranks, left the battalion and proceeded to join 36/Northumberland Fusiliers, to serve with the Army of Occupation in Germany.

Throughout February the 23rd Battalion remained at Number 1 Despatching Camp, Havre. At one stage Lieutenant Colonel Irwin DSO 5/Northumberland Fusiliers was appointed as Commanding Officer, but the order was countermanded and he assumed the post of Commanding Officer 18/Lancashire Fusiliers. Another event at this time was a Grand Dinner for the remaining officers and men of the Cadre, which took place in the Grand Hotel, Havre, on 1 February. Five officers and sixteen men sat down to the meal, but how many were original Tyneside Scots is unknown.

Sadly the end of the war did not see an end to the dying, as many men were to perish from either wounds, gas poisoning or sickness long after the guns fell silent. The Tyneside Scottish were no different from many other units in this respect and many good men who survived the fighting and the horrors of warfare died shortly after the war. All deaths are sad but perhaps one of the saddest was that of Lieutenant Albert Richmond Hunter who had been wounded twice while serving with the 23rd Battalion. On both occasions the wound had been slight and did not warrant evacuation to England although his one wish was to return home and see his young daughter, Rona, who was almost two years old and whom he had never seen apart from photographs. Posted from the 23rd Battalion to the Base, he was on 30 October, 1918, gazetted with the Belgium Croix de Guerre. On 4 January, 1919, he was admitted to the 48th Casualty Clearing Station dangerously ill with pneumonia. Towards the end of the month he had improved enough to send a telegram to a family friend saying he, 'had got over the worst and would soon pull round.' Sadly, though, it was not to be and on 11 February, 1919, Lieutenant Albert Richmond Hunter passed away. On 3 June, 1919, he was

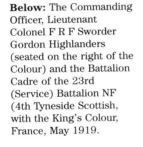

Below: The Commanding Officer, Lieutenant Colonel F R F Sworder Gordon Highlanders (seated on the right of the Colour) and the Battalion Cadre of the 23rd (Service) Battalion NF (4th Tyneside Scottish, with the King's Colour, France, May 1919.

awarded the Military Cross, but nearly seventy years were to pass before Rona eventually retrieved her father's medals, which also included a French Legion of Honour. In May 1998 she and her family made a pilgrimage to the grave of the father she never knew.

Several of the other ranks were also to die in the months following the signing of the Armistice. Fortunately they were not destined to lie in 'some foreign field' but were buried at home nearer their loved ones. They include,

20/1394 Private Robert Tuck
      Died 23/2/19 buried New Seaham
21/1301 Private William Summers
      Died 27/11/20 buried Penshaw
22/1136 C/Sgt Jacob Pattison
      Died 15/10/19 buried Castleside
23/707 Private John Daley
      Died 28/3/21 buried Boldon

The Colours

For what remained of the 22nd Battalion their long journey home to their native North East began around 6 June 1919, but owing to circumstances beyond anyone's control, they did not arrive in Newcastle until the early hours of Sunday 8 June 1919. Everything had been laid on by a very grateful and proud city for their reception, but alas at 5.45 a.m. on a Sunday morning they slipped quietly into Newcastle Station with no one to meet them.

The Cadre consisted of Lieutenant Colonel J T Janson DSO, Captain and Adjutant A C Neill. Lieutenant and Quartermaster T B Foster, Lieutenant C J Robson and thirty-six men. They brought with them the colour, which had been presented on 5 February and of the party only Lieutenant and Quartermaster T B Foster and CQMS Robson were originals who had gone to France in January 1916.

In the absence of a civic welcome the cadre were entertained to breakfast in the YMCA Army and Navy Hostel. From there they proceeded to Fenham Barracks here they were to rest before returning to Catterick, where they were to be formally disbanded. Prior to the move to Catterick the cadre laid up their battalion colour in St Nicholas' Cathedral on 10 June, 1919. This proved to be a solemn and impressive occasion for all those who attended.

The colour was borne from Fenham Barracks to the Cathedral through the streets of Newcastle for all to see, carried by Lieutenant C J Robson and escorted by Sergeants Ellis and Tindall. The Cathedral was full to capacity with families and friends and veterans of the Tyneside Scottish. Many dignitaries were among the congregation as well as members of the Tyneside Scottish Committee. Canon Newsom (Vicar of Newcastle) took up the service after the Colour entered by the west door and moved down the central aisle to the Nave. He said:

'We are here in this ancient home of religion in the presence of God to receive the Colour of the 3rd Battalion Tyneside Scottish. The name of the Northumberland Fusiliers is a proud name in Newcastle and in its ancient home, this church. We solemnly receive your Colour here today. We shall always think of it, as we have it before us in this Church, as the symbol of generous readiness for self-sacrifice. It will be in our hearts, near to that symbol of our holy religion, the cross of Jesus Christ our Savior, the supreme and eternal symbol of generous love and self-sacrifice. May this Battalion maintain its identity and remain as an integral part of our national forces in the future. May its unity with the whole of that great regiment, the Northumberland Fusiliers continue as close as it is today, the same spirit, the same mind, the same temper which have been passed down through hundreds of years of glorious history. That is our hope, we thank you, who have fought and suffered for us with all our hearts and together with you we thank, as we ought to do on this occasion, all the hundreds and thousands who have been left, as to their bodies, in a foreign field and whose spirits have been

received into the hands of the merciful Father.'

The Canon and the Colour then moved to the altar where Lieutenant Robson handed it to Colonel Jansen, who then passed it to Canon Newsom with the words,

'I present this colour in the name of the Officers and men of the 3rd Battalion Tyneside Scottish to the safe keeping of this church.'

The Canon replied

'In the name of the Father, and of the Son and of the Holy Ghost we accept this Colour to be laid up in this church, as a token of the faithful service and duty well performed. Amen.'

Later that afternoon the cadre of 22/Northumberland Fusiliers were entertained to tea by the Lord Mayor, Councilior A Munro Sutherland in the Soldiers' Hostel, Westgate Road, Newcastle. The Lord Mayor apologized to the men for not meeting them at the railway station, as they owed their arrival in the early hours to War Office arrangements. At five o'clock the cadre departed Newcastle by train for Catterick and on 14 June, 1919, the 22nd (Service) Battalion Northumberland Fusiliers (3rd Tyneside Scottish) ceased to exist.

A month earlier, on 2 May, 1919, the cadres of 18, 23 and 25/Northumberland Fusiliers serving with 39th Division received their King's Colour from Major General Uniacke, commanding Lines of Communication. On 6 June these battalions disbanded and on 12 June they made their final journey home to Newcastle.

Their welcome was as warm and enthusiastic as one would have expected, as many had gathered at the Central Station to welcome them home. Among the officials was the Lord Mayor, the Sheriff and civic dignitaries, as well as their old friends the Tyneside Scottish Committee, plus the Military Committee of the Chamber of Commerce and the Tyneside Irish Committee, who had been responsible for the raising of the battalions in the dark days of 1914.

Pipers of the Tyneside Scottish Brigade Pipe Band[1] played the Colour parties out of the station through the streets of Newcastle to the Corn Exchange. Cheer after cheer went up, handkerchiefs and hats were waved as the men proudly made their way through the throng. At the Corn Exchange many speeches were made and Colonel Methuen, commanding 18/Northumberland Fusiliers, speaking on behalf of the three colour parties, thanked the Lord Mayor for the cordiality of the reception and asked him to accept an Iron Cross taken from a German PoW.

For the 23rd Battalion cadre the journey did not end in Newcastle, as it had been decided that the resting-place of the colour would be the Jesmond Presbyterian Church. Jesmond was chosen because the Tyneside Scottish Brigade Headquarters had been located there in late 1914 and the colour was finally laid to rest there on 28 June 1919.

As the 20th and 21st battalions had both been disbanded in early 1918 they did not receive their King's Colours until March 1920. The Colours arrived at the Northumberland Fusiliers Depot as part of a batch for disbanded Northumberland Fusilier battalions. There were no representatives of the battalions in Newcastle to receive the Colours, but as the Tyneside Scottish Committee was still functioning, they were presented with them.

Later that year, on 24 July, 1920, the colours of no fewer than nineteen Northumberland Fusilier Battalions were unfurled on the Town Moor, Newcastle where they were consecrated before being taken to their final resting places. Among them were the colours of the 20th Battalion, with Sir Thomas Oliver in Command and Lieutenant Gibson MC as Colour Officer. Colonel Joseph Reed with Captain Alan Martin DSO as Colour Officer represented the 21st Battalion, whilst Captain Atkinson of the 22nd Battalion both commanded the party and carried his battalion colour. Survivors of all those battalions taking part fell in at the rear of the parade.

The Colour of the 21st Battalion had in fact been laid up in Bedlington Parish Church on 10 July by a small party of Tyneside Scottish soldiers, but as it had not been consecrated it was brought to the ceremony, to be returned to Bedlington at a later date. Bedlington was chosen for the final resting-place as a compliment to the district that had provided many recruits for the Tyneside Scottish Brigade.

Canon Newsom, Vicar of Newcastle acting on behalf of the Bishop, read the consecratory prayers aided by the Reverend F F Crossdale, Vicar of St Lukes. The order was then given 'Take up Colours', and the senior officers then collected their Colour from two sets of piled drums. The Lord Lieutenant, the Duke of Northumberland, received each colour in turn and handed it to the Colour Officer who went down on his right knee to receive it.

As the colours unfurled in the breeze they presented an inspiring site. The order was given to 'Order arms and colours,' then medals were presented to several recipients by the Duke. At the conclusion of the ceremony the Colour Parties formed groups and marched to St Nicholas Cathedral headed by a Fusilier band and the Tyneside Scottish Brigade Pipe Band led by Pipe Major Munro Strachan, with a large number of veterans following in the rear.

The pageant was as solemn as that for the 22nd Battalion the year before and as the parade entered by the west door they were met by the clergy and choir as the Cathedral organ poured forth the strains 'Oh God our help in ages past'.

The Colours were borne slowly up the aisle and the Vicar of Newcastle gave a short address:

'It is the hope of many that before long

we will have a memorial in the Cathedral bearing the names of all those who represented Northumbria in the Great war. Meanwhile we have the Colours of those glorious battalions that have won for us peace and victory. Their's was the example to follow and, forgetting our first shock of grief, let us thank God for their sacrifices. Might these Colours laid up in this Church remind us all that Christ has taught us that life meant service to humanity.'

Following the address came a prayer for the departed and then the hymn 'God of the living in whose eyes' in memory of the dead. Then followed the handing over ceremony as each Commanding Officer delivered up his colour with the words,

'I present this Colour of the .....Battalion Northumberland Fusiliers to the safe keeping of the church.'

Again the Colour was accepted with the words,

'In the name of the Father and of the Son and of the Holy Ghost we accept these Colours to be laid up in this Church as tokens of faithful service and duty well performed.'

The ceremony was concluded by the singing of the regimental hymn of the Northumberland Fusiliers, St Georges Hymn followed by the blessing, which concluded a solemn and impressive service.

Only the Colour of the 22nd Battalion was to remain in Newcastle Cathedral, where it still hangs today. That of the 20th Battalion was finally laid to rest in Holy Cross Church, Ryton, County Durham on 31 July, 1920. The Colour of the 21st Battalion returned to Bedlington and then on 21 October, 1920, the final act was carried out when the Tyneside Scottish Committee was wound up and dissolved with little ceremony.

Post War Years

The post war years were not kind to Britain's ex-servicemen as the nation struggled to change its economic outlook from a war footing to peacetime recovery. A land fit for heroes or what remained of them, was in reality a myth and much hardship and suffering was to be endured by the survivors and their families, and worst off of all were the widows and children of the fallen.

For some ex-Tyneside Scottish soldiers it was all too much and under land schemes organized by the government and the empire nations they fled the shores of Britain, to try and rebuild their lives and seek a future for their families. For others the drudgery and uncertainty of civilian life was not attractive and they re-enlisted into the post-war Regular Army.

Among those to emigrate was Private John Osborne of the 23rd Battalion who took his wife and children to Australia. Frank Wilson, the younger brother of John and Jim Wilson, and also a Piper in the Tyneside Scottish, was captured in March 1918. After release from the prison camp he eventually emigrated to Canada to find work. During the Second World War he enlisted into the Veteran Guard of Canada and was employed guarding German Prisoners of War. One of his last jobs in the Canadian Army was escorting German prisoners across the Atlantic back to Europe at the end of the war. Of the officers Lieutenant Colonel V M Stockley went to Uganda, where ill fortune struck and a charging buffalo killed him. He was buried with full military honours in The King's African Rifles Cemetery in Kampala on 9 March, 1921.

Second Lieutenant Reginald Baty MC, having transferred to the Royal Flying Corps, stayed with the Royal Air Force. During World War Two he held command positions on several airfields.

Above: 365136 Piper Frank Wilson, enlisted 12 June 1914, in the Northern Cyclists, discharged 23 March 1919.

Below: The opening of the 'Tyneside Seat' at La Boisselle, the memorial to the Tyneside Scottish and Irish who fought on the Somme. A place of pilgrimage for the survivors and the relatives of those killed.

175

Above: John Osbourne took his family to Australia after the war. Note the Tyneside Scottish sweetheart broach worn by Mrs Osbourne.

Above: Thomas Easton the longest surviving original member of the Tyneside Scottish.

One of the Tyneside Scots who chose to re-enlist was Lieutenant Denis Ward MC who served with the 20th and 23rd Battalions. His award of the Military Cross had come in 1918, for conspicuous gallantry and devotion to duty. He re-enlisted into the Army in the Royal Corps of Signals around 1925. After completion of his training as a Signalman, he was posted to India, in April 1926, and was later that year promoted to Lance Corporal. Two years later, while still serving in India he was promoted to Corporal and by December 1932 was a Lance Sergeant and the initials MC were added to his documents. Tragically Lance Sergeant D E Ward MC was killed on 1 February 1936 when the motorcycle combination on which he was travelling collided with a bullock cart.

Alas, for the majority there was no escape and it was a long hard road for many Tyneside Scots in the 1920s and 1930s. Perhaps their only escape was with the formation of the Old Comrades Associations that sprang up throughout the country during those hard times.

Only one Tyneside Scottish Old Comrades Association seems to have been formed and that, surprisingly, was for the 23rd Battalion (4th Tyneside Scottish), which appears not to have been formed until 1930, with former CSM William Patterson as its secretary and Sir Thomas Oliver as President. All former Tyneside Scottish soldiers were eligible for membership no matter what battalion they served in and by 1936 some thirty-six officers and 328 other ranks were members of the association.

Regular features of the Old Comrades activities were the reunion dinners, which were an annual event. Once the formal business was over members and guests made speeches. Some form of light entertainment followed, which was normally contributed by the members themselves, be it songs, poems, jokes or recitations, nearly all a reminder of days gone by when, Madame served the wine in the estaminet in Armentières. There were three 'special' days for the Old Comrades Association: 23 April, St George's Day, the Regimental day of all Northumberland Fusiliers; 1 July a day never to be forgotten by those who were there in 1916; and finally 11 November, Armistice Day, when the whole nation remembered its 'Glorious Dead' and the survivors of the Tyneside Scottish paraded to lay their wreaths at the War Memorial in Newcastle.

Strong links were maintained by all OCAs that had served together as the 34th Division during the Great War. As a result a year-book was published and sent to all members entitled 'The Chequers'. This booklet followed the fortunes of all the OCAs and was filled with notes of events and memoirs of its former soldiers. One of the sadder aspects of the OCAs was the listing of former comrades who passed away as the years rolled on. Some of them, although still young in years, obviously died because of their wounds or recurring illness brought on by the strains of active service.

Meetings for Old Comrades fell off during the advent of the Second World War, and it is known that many former members of the Tyneside Scottish tried to re-enlist, or owing to their age, joined the Home Guard or ARP.

The former secretary of the Tyneside Scottish Brigade, Mr J R Hall, even tried to approach the War Office with the idea of raising a new Tyneside Scottish Brigade. On being turned down he approached Northumberland Territorial Army Association with the idea of creating a single battalion but met with no success. Turning to County Durham Territorial Army Association, he found agreement and on 31 March, 1939, 2/9th Battalion Durham Light Infantry was renumbered and renamed the 12th (Tyneside Scottish) Battalion Durham Light Infantry. On 1 February, 1940, this battalion was transferred to the Black Watch as 1st Tyneside Scottish Battalion, The Black Watch (Royal Highland Regiment) with J R Hall as its Honarary Colonel. The proud name lived on and went on to fight in Normandy and the Low Countries, but that is another story.[2]

At the end of hostilities the 23rd Battalion OCA was resurrected and in 1951 the 21st Battalion OCA was reborn after ceasing its activities for the war[3]. It had the hindsight to produce an annual bulletin The Yellow Diamond which recorded stories and anecdotes of the times in France. As membership dwindled both OCAs amalgamated as the Tyneside Scottish Old Comrades Association which eventually affiliated to that of The Royal Northumberland Fusiliers in July 1959. Towards the end only Tom Easton remained of the original Tyneside Scottish that had enlisted in late 1914. The last known survivor to die had been an eighteen-year old reinforcement in 1918, 87265 Private Bill Reece, who had served with 8 Platoon, B Company, 22nd Battalion in the 16th (Irish) Division. He passed away on 22 June, 1994, and was the North East's last remaining link with one of the finest Brigades ever raised and who will forever be known as the men who were,

'HARDER THAN HAMMERS'

1. The Tyneside Scottish Brigade Pipe Band was formed in 1919 by Pipe Major Munro Strachan formerly Pipe Major of the 21st Battalion. Campbell kilts were to be worn but later 25 kilts of Hunting Stuart tartan were presented by Colonel Innes Hopkins.
2. The title Tyneside Scottish can still be found today as an honour title for 204(Tyneside Scottish) Battery 101(Northumbrian) Regiment Royal Artillery. The only surviving 'Pals' title to be found in todays British Army Order of Battle.
3. The exact date of the formation of this OCA is unknow

Chapter Twelve

The 29th Reserve Battalion and The Pipes and Drums of the Tyneside Scottish

The Reserve Battalion

Like all reserve battalions created in late 1915 as Depot Battalions for the locally raised battalions of Kitchener's New Armies, the 29th (Reserve) Battalion Northumberland Fusiliers (Tyneside Scottish) began life as the Depot Companies of the Tyneside Scottish battalions. These companies were authorized under ACI 13 of 2 December, 1914, to assist in maintaining the war establishment of the parent service battalions, which were shedding recruits mainly owing to illness or because their skills were needed by industry to assist the war effort.

Originally the call had been for one Depot Company of 250 men for each battalion of 1100 all ranks, but on the completion of these numbers the ACI called for a further depot company so that two depot companies would feed one battalion. As explained in Chapter Three this caused problems within the Tyneside Scottish because of the closure of the recruiting offices. The 5th and 6th Depot Companies[1] were administered as part of the parent battalion and were even quartered with or near to the battalion, so that the men did not feel outsiders in any way. This also meant that they were easily absorbed into the parent battalion as and when required.

This all changed however with the publication of Army Council Instruction 30 of 4 June, 1915, which suggested 'formation of 2nd Reserve Battalions to provide drafts for locally raised battalions'. The two depot companies were to be treated as the nucleus of a reserve unit and could be combined with others to form a 2nd Reserve Battalion which would have an establishment of 1525 or 2084 all ranks.

Above: 29th Reserve Battalion march into Barnard Castle led by a Drum and Bugle Band.

Below: 23/921 CSM J Rafferty and men of 19 Platoon, 5 Company, 84th Training Reserve Battalion. Note the cloth 84 cap badge. CSM Rafferty was posted back to the UK from France in April 1916.

177

Above: 29th Reserve Battalion late 1916. Eleven men in the first two rows are wearing wound stripes. Those wearing Balmorals will have served overseas with the Brigade.

Below: The family of a Tyneside Scottish soldier taken at Barnard Castle indicating that his father served with the 29th (Reserve) Battalion.

In the case of the Tyneside Scottish Brigade the eight depot companies within the suggestion of the ACI, and ACI 109 of 13 July 1915 confirmed the formation of the 29th (Reserve) Battalion Northumberland Fusiliers at Alnwick. Sadly as this was an independent battalion with little likelyhood of being called to active service there was no requirement for the battalion to keep a war diary, so that details about events concerning the battalion are few and far between.

From July 1915 the battalion acted as an independent unit and therefore was no longer subject to the influence of the other Tyneside Scottish Battalions. Its role was to recruit, train and draft men to the four service battalions of the brigade and when 102 Brigade moved to Salisbury Plain in August 1915 the 29th Battalion remained at Alnwick.

Before the Brigade left Alnwick a certain amount of exchanging took place between the service battalions and the reserve battalion, so that under-age, unfit, and untrained soldiers remained behind with the reserve battalion. From its beginning the 29th Battalion carried on the tradition of using pre-fixed serial numbers to distinguish its soldiers, although it would appear that men transferred in from the other battalions were allowed to keep their original numbers. Hopefully when these men were fit again they would be returned to their original unit, while men from the 29th Battalion would be transferred to any of the service battalions and keep their 29th Battalion regimental number.

That was the theory behind the formation of the battalion but in reality it was not allowed to work that way as many 29th Battalion men were transferred to other battalions of the Northumberland Fusiliers or away to other regiments altogether.

The first commanding officer of the 29th (Reserve) Battalion was Lieutenant Colonel V M Stockley, formerly the commanding officer of the 21st Battalion. By the end of July he had many officers under his command, many of them with previous service as other ranks in other service battalions of the Northumberland Fusiliers, or from other regiments. These officers also remained with the battalion until a vacancy occurred in one of the parent battalions, or they were sent to another unit.

The 29th Battalion remained at Alnwick throughout the remainder of 1915, carrying out a training programme that was peculiar to depot battalions, where new recruits were turned into trained soldiers fit to join service battalions.

Unfortunately a large number of unfit men had been dumped into the 29th Battalion when 102 Brigade left Alnwick and it continued to be so whilst 102 Brigade was based on Salisbury Plain. As an example of the sort of unfit men the battalion was receiving, 21/299 Private John William Scott, who had enlisted on 7 November 1914, was discharged from the 29th (Reserve) Battalion on 15 September with multiple hipomata. Medical examinations found many of the men from the other Tyneside Scottish battalions were of B1 category i.e. fit for service abroad, (but not for general service) in Garrison or Provisional units. Fortunately the formation of the 1st and 2nd Garrison Battalions[2] helped ease the growing problem and many of these B1 men were eventually transferred to these two battalions.

The transfer of these men brought a further problem in the fact that huge gaps appeared in the strength returns of the 29th Battalion which were not being filled by volunteer recruitment. For the first time since the formation of the Tyneside Scottish Brigade the media was used as an advertising platform and a specific group of men were aimed at for enlistment. These men were the Derby Scheme[3] men who, under the scheme organized by Lord Derby, had voluntarily registered for enlistment and who were to be called up in specific groupings.

Derby Scheme men were in fact being earmarked as replacements for the Territorial Force, but the Tyneside Scottish recruiting Committee used an advertisement which asked Derby men who expected to be called up to ask if

they could be placed in the Tyneside Scottish Brigade. The advertisement appeared in local newspapers in October and November 1915, although the first batch of Derby recruits were not expected to be called up until January 1916.

An unusual feature of both the 29th and 30th (Reserve) Battalions was the large number of men recruited from the West Riding of Yorkshire, especially from the Huddersfield district. Sadly not enough information is available at present to determine when and where they enlisted, and how they came to be serving in the Northumberland Fusiliers. From those records that have survived it has been possible to learn that they began to enlist in late 1915 and enlistments continued until mid-1916. It is almost certain that no advertising campaign was conducted in the West Riding by the Tyneside Scottish and Irish recruiting committees, so why these men ended up in the Northumberland Fusiliers is uncertain. One theory is that they were originally recruited for a local service battalion that did not reach the required numbers and were offered the Northumberland battalions as an alternative.

Towards the end of January 1915 the 29th Battalion prepared to move to Deerbolt Camp near Barnard Castle, County Durham, and an advance party left Alnwick on 21 January, 1916, arriving at Barnard Castle in the afternoon. Two days later, on Sunday 23 January 1916 a large detachment of Tyneside Scottish from 102 Brigade in Warminster arrived in Barnard Castle to join the reserve battalion. These were the surplus men of the four service battalions who had not proceeded overseas to France. They had been sent north to join the reserve battalion so that they could act as reinforcements at a later date. The remainder of the 29th Battalion moved from Alnwick on 26 January, 1916, headed by the Battalion Band, (which at this stage had no Pipers) to join the advance party.

The battalion was billeted in Barnard Castle and joined the 20th (Reserve) Brigade, whereas the other battalions of the Brigade, 30th and 31st (Reserve) Battalions Northumberland Fusiliers and 21st and 23rd (Reserve) Battalions Durham Light Infantry were based in Catterick. Collectively they recruited and trained, then drafted men for their respective battalions, which were already serving in France.

In April 1916 a second move took place for the 29th Battalion, when the whole of the 20th (Reserve) Brigade was moved to Hornsea on the Yorkshire Coast. Sadly information on the Battalion's time at Hornsea is very scant, but it is almost certain that they were part of the coastal defence network then in operation.

While at Hornsea the War Office saw it could increase the drafting capabilities of the reserve battalions by creating further reserve battalions. The 29th Battalion was duplicated and a 33rd (Reserve) Battalion (Tyneside Scottish) was formed. The idea seems to have been that the 29th

Above: Newspaper advertisment run by the Tyneside Scottish recruiting Committee which asked Derby men, who expected to be called up, to ask if they could be placed in the Tyneside Scottish Brigade.

Far left: 29/178 Private W A Leighton, 29th Battalion in January 1916.

Above: Unidentified members of the 29th Reserve Battalion.

Battalion would feed the 20th and 21st Battalions and the 33rd Battalion would supply its men to the 22nd and 23rd Battalions. Strangely, though, not many men have been found with 33/ regimental numbers.

This system would only last for a short time before the War Office introduced further changes. By the end of July 1916 casualties on the Western Front had become staggering and the cry for reinforcements outstripped what the reserve battalions could supply. By pooling the reserve forces in each command the War Office hoped this would offset the clamour by some regiments who required large numbers of reinforcements.

All regimental reserve battalions would lose their identity and become numbered battalions of the Training Reserve[4].

The Training Reserve Battalions within the Reserve Brigades absorbed some regimental reserve battalions and by this system reinforcements could now be sent where and when required.

By this means local units were diluted with men from outside the original recruiting area, and the identity between the Tyneside Scottish Brigade and its reserve units was lost.

On 1 September 1916 the 20th (Reserve) Brigade absorbed the 33rd Battalion and the 29th (Reserve) Battalion was renumbered as the 84th Training Reserve Battalion. From this date the affiliation between the 29th Battalion and the Tyneside Scottish Brigade ceased to exist. The officers, and NCOs and training staff continued to wear their own regimental insignia, but the 84th Training Reserve Battalion recruits would wear a peaked service cap instead of a Glengarry. The first cap badge worn was a brass General Service button with the royal coat of arms, backed by a piece of red cloth. Also worn was a 20th (Reserve) Brigade patch worn on the upper arm. Four colours were worn: white, green, red and blue, the white being worn by 29th Battalion and the 84th Training Reserve Battalion. Further changes took place to the Training Reserve in 1918, but these changes fall outside the history of the Tyneside Scottish.

The Pipes and Drums

Pipe Bands have traditionally formed part of Scottish regiments and the Tyneside Scottish were no exception to this rule, seeking to include pipers within its organization from the beginning. During the initial raising in September 1914, Munro Strachan of Wallsend was enlisted as Pipe Major, but with the War Office turning down recognition of the Tyneside Scottish no further effort was made to recruit other pipers.

After the visit of Lord Haldane to Newcastle in October 1914 and the official recognition of the Tyneside Scottish, local civilian pipe bands, such as The Northumberland Veteran Pipe Band, The Hebburn Pipe Band, The Caledonian Pipe Band and The Sunderland Pipe Band, were used at recruiting meetings to entice potential recruits to come

forward and enlist. Whether or not members of these civilian pipe bands came forward and enlisted is unknown. What is certain is that pipers were enlisted in the early days, many with previous military experience and eventually each battalion would have their own Pipes and Drums.

Despite lack of Government funding for clothing and equipment enough money was raised by public subscription to ensure that the Scottish piping tradition was not disgraced by these fine pipe bands.

Family connections were strong within the bands, for instance the 20th Battalion Pipes and Drums had as members, a father, John (Jock) Wilson and his two sons John junior and James, as well as Mrs Wilson's brother, Garnet Wolsley Fyffe. Owing to previous military service in 2/Scottish Rifles as a regular and time in the Territorials with 6/Royal Scots, Jock Wilson was elected Pipe Major and his son John became a Sergeant Piper. James, not to be outdone, became the Drum Major. Both Jock and John were loaned to the Tyneside Irish to assist with their pipe band, but only John returned to the Tyneside Scottish, where he took up the vacant post of Pipe Major, while his father became Pipe Major of the 24th Battalion (1st Tyneside Irish).

James Wilson did not remain with the 20th Battalion either, as he took up the post of Drum Major with the 22nd Battalion prior to going overseas, replacing the youngest Drum Major in the British Army, eighteen year-old Leonard Godber of Grantham, Lincolnshire. James Wilson was later posted to 10/Highland Light Infantry, but eventually returned to the 22nd Battalion later in the war.

Pipe Major John Wilson appears to have been an accomplished composer of Pipe Music, having composed the Battalion march past, which he simply entitled 'The 1st Battalion Tyneside Scottish March Past'. The adopted charging tune used on 1 July 1916 was 'The Haughs of Cromdale'.

The pipers of the 20th Battalion were distinguished by the wearing of a black and white checked plaid and kilt known as the Northumbrian or Shepherds' tartan. The hose tops were black and white diamonds, while the pipe bag cover and pipe ribbons were of Gordon tartan. Pipers of all the Tyneside Scottish bands wore Blackcock feathers behind the cap badges of the Glengarry. The Pipes and Drums of the 20th Battalion were quartered in St Michael's, Church of England School, in Headlam Street, Byker. John Sproat, then just five year old, recalled, how his class accompanied by their teacher, Miss Anne McFadd, would line up and watch as the Pipes and Drums marched up and down the playground playing the stirring tunes of glory that had played many Scottish regiments into battle.

In the 21st Battalion there was a similar feeling of it being a family affair; Munro Strachan took up the post of Pipe Major with another family member,

John Strachan, serving as a Piper. Munro Strachan was another Pipe Major who composed his battalion's march past, 'The 2nd Battalion Tyneside Scottish March Past'. The Plaid and kilt of the 21st Battalion was Campbell of Loudon tartan, as was the pipe bag, ribbons and hose tops.

Sadly very little is known about the Pipes and Drums of the 22nd Battalion, apart from Drum Major Leonard Godber previously mentioned, who came from a well known family of drummers and musicians who had served in the Lincolnshire Regiment. Unfortunately neither his regimental number nor any further details of his career have come to light.

Even less is known about the 23rd Battalion Pipes and Drums, although, the plaid, kilt, pipe bag, banners and hose tops were the same as the 21st Battalion, i.e. Campbell of Loudon tartan.

In late 1916, under the direction of Brigadier General Ternan, it was suggested that a Brigade tartan be introduced for wear by all four battalions. Once the battalion commanding officers agreed to this, a tartan, later known as 'Sandbag tartan' owing to its distinctive colouring, was submitted and selected. Since the bulk of the Brigade's piping equipment was lost at La Boisselle on 1 July 1916 the matter arose as to who would pay for new equipment and uniforms. Because these were paid for originally by public subscription, they could not be replaced at public expense. Eventually twenty-five sets of new pipes and outfits were supplied and paid for by the Cowan Fund.

Although in the early days a fife and drum existed in the 29th (Reserve) Battalion (Tyneside Scottish) there were no pipes and drums. This was not remedied until July 1916 when J R Hall, Honorary secretary of the Tyneside Scottish Committee, made an appeal for sponsors to help raise funds to equip a pipe and drum band for the

battalion. This was done by a newspaper appeal on 8 July 1916, when the costs were said to be £150 and that Colonel Hay, Colonel Hopkins, Sir Thomas Oliver and Mr Angus Watson had all offered ten pounds each.

Sadly no sooner had the money been raised and the band fitted out, than the 29th Battalion disappeared into the Training Reserve. Fortunately the band continued as the Pipes and Drums of the 84th Training Reserve Battalion and this band also wore the black and white check known as Northumbrian or Shepherds' Plaid. Owing to differences in dyes it is possible that this plaid may have been a dark chocolate and white check, as an example of this has been noted as a backing to a cap badge.

The story of the pipers and their leading the Brigade into battle on 1 July has already been told in Chapter Six. The casualties among these unarmed musicians were extensive as at least eleven pipers were killed in action or died of

Above: Regimental Pipe and Drums of one of the Tyneside Scottish Battalions.

Below: Young Drummers and Buglers of the 29th Reserve Battalion Tyneside Scottish Battalions.

wounds most of them on 1 July, 1916, and a further four at least are known to have been wounded at some stage during the war.

On the Somme battlefield in later days pieces of the original bagpipes were recovered, in one case the identity of the piper who had played the pipes was confirmed. An article on the recovery of the remains of a set of pipes appeared in the *Illustrated Chronicle* in August 1916, under the headings, 'Interesting Battle Relic – Newcastle Bagpipe remnants found at La Boisselle'.

'On 7 July a captain of the Royal Field Artillery was passing over what had been the point of the enemy's salient at La Boisselle. In the mass of debris he came upon some bagpipes. The drones had been beaten to pieces and the ribbons fell to fragments at a touch. There were signs of human remains at the spot. There was no means of recognizing the colours of the ribbons attached to the pipes, but a lieutenant was with the captain at the time, and he picked up the only fragment of the pipes that was intact. This fragment bore a small silver plate with the inscription, "Presented to the Tyneside Scottish by members of the Union Club, (per F E Forster) 1914".

It occurred to the captain that the relic should be returned to the splendid battalion that once owned it.'

Five members of the Union Club, Newcastle, in response to an appeal by the wife of the commanding officer of the battalion, had presented the set of pipes and Mr Forster was unaware that the inscription had been added to the pipes. The parents of 22/781 Piper Edward Grieves identified the remnants of the pipes as the pipes used by their son.

Other pieces of pipes were recovered by 23/546 CQMS Robert Muter of Bedlington Colliery, and although they had a silver inscribed mount, the piper who played them was never identified. The pipes of 21/558 Piper George Griffiths were also recovered and displayed for many years in a Tynemouth hotel, eventually they were presented to S (Tyneside Scottish) Battery of 439 (Tyne) Light Anti Aircraft Regiment, Royal Artillery(T.A.) in 1959.

The pipers also wore Dirks and these were numbered. Dirk Number 8 was found on the Somme battlefield and after the war was given to Grenfell Arnot, the son of Captain Arnot, by Mr J R Hall.

1. These companies were numbered 5th (Depot) and 6th (Depot) Companies before being lettered E and F Companies
2. See Chapter Four, 1st Garrison Battalion formed August 1915, 2nd Garrison Battalion formed October 1915.
3. The Derby Scheme was created in early 1915.
4. Army Council Instruction 1528 dated 6 August, 1916, brought the Training Reserve into existence on 1 September, 1916. It would appear that the Balmoral was not issued to the 29th Battalion.

Far left: Piper G Davison.

Below: Corporal Scoper Pipes and Drums.

Epilogue

ON 31 OCTOBER 1998 a gentleman from Colchester, Mr Drage, was walking near the Lochnagar Crater, on the flat ground at the far side beyond the rim, when he noticed something that looked like an army boot sticking out of the ground. He mentioned this to the owner of 'Le Tommy' Café in Pozières, Mr D Zanardi, who in turn informed the Commonwealth War Graves Commission Senior Head Gardener. It was noted that no human remains were visible above ground and it would therefore be appropriate to leave the waterlogged site unattended, until such time as an exhumation team could be organised to investigate the ground.

Upon a report being made to the Gendarmarie in Albert, approval to remove any remains was obtained, and an exhumation took place with all the items recovered being transported to the War Graves Commission mortuary at Beaurains.

One complete human skeleton – with skull damage – one pair of boots, over 100 rounds of ammunition, remains of a Short Lee Enfield rifle with bayonet and wire cutter attachment, rifle oil bottle, pieces of unidentifiable equipment, gasmask eye pieces, two water bottles (one British and one Canadian), pair of scissors, safety pin, food tin, two pocket knives, a pipe stem, shaving mirror, a hallmarked silver pen holder, 23 buttons and various buckles and webbing strap ends.

Two further items were also found which were to prove by far the most significant: a shoulder title with the words TYNESIDE 3 SCOTTISH; a folding cut throat razor with the owner's name and army number carved into the handle 'G Nugent 1306'.

Because of the possibility of a positive identification of the remains, responsibility passed from the Commonwealth War Graves Commission to the Ministry of Defence (Section PS4[Army] Casualty/ Compassionate Coordination), and attempts to trace relatives were initiated.

Because of the destruction of service records during the Second World War London Blitz, immediate identification was made more difficult. However, the Ministry of Defence department PS4 learned that *Tyneside Scottish* was being prepared and contacted John Sheen at Durham through the Barnsley-based publisher.

He was invited to London and was able to confirm, through nominal roles compiled for inclusion in this book, that a Private George Nugent, Army number 22/1306, Machine Gun section of C Company, 22nd Battalion, Northumberland Fusiliers (3rd Tyneside Scottish) was listed missing after the opening attack at the Battle of the Somme, 1 July 1916. The same day that the mine at Lochnagar was blown and the Tyneside Scottish advanced across that ground. The soldier's home address in 1914 had been 38 Franklin Street, Newcastle and he had enlisted 12 January 1915.

This Tyneside Scot will now be laid to rest after guarding Lochnagar Crater for the past eighty-two years.

Above: Machine gunners of the Tyneside Scottish Brigade at Alnwick 1915. This group includes men from four battalions of the Tyneside Scottish. Somewhere amongst the men of this group is George Nugent.

Below: Items recovered along with the remains of George Nugent at the Lochnagar Crater; they include: rifle with bayonet and wire cutter, shaving mirror, rifle oil bottle, scissors, two pocket knives, buttons, shoulder title, silver pen holder and cut throat razor – along with owner's name and number.
Reproduced by permission of the Ministry of Defence.

Gallantry Awards

Above: Lieutenant Norman Batey Pigg DSO, MC and two Bars.

Above: Second Lieutenant Robert Brewis Stephenson MC. He served for three years with the Northumberland Hussars before being commissioned into the 4th Territorial Battalion. He was posted to C Company of the 22nd Battalion where he won the Military Cross 15 September 1917. Wounded the following month he died 23 November 1917.

The Distinguished Service Order

Acklom Spencer Lieutenant Colonel, Highland Light Infantry, Commanding 22nd Bn LG 1/1/17
Bar 3/6/17

Algie William Lieutenant 23rd Bn LG 26/3/17
For conspicuous gallantry and devotion to duty during a raid on the enemyís trenches. He led the assaulting party with great dash and inf;icted many casualties on the enemy. He himself shot eight of the enemy with his revover, later, he skillfully withdrew his party under very heavy fire and assisted to bring in the wounded.
(He was recommended for the Victoria Cross for this action.)

Farquhar William Alexander LG 1/1/18

Macintosh Stanley Hugh Major LG 1/1/17

Mark Alan William Dobson Second Lieutenant LG 17/9/17
For conspicuous gallantry and devotion to duty in holding an extremly important point on the left of our line for twenty four hours, with his platoon repeatedly beating off determined counter attacks. After his party had been relieved the position was recaptured by the enemy, where upon he moved up again on his own initiative and drove them out a second time, regaining the whole of the lost ground. He led his men with the utmost dash and fearlessness through a heavy hostile barrage, setting a magnificent example by his own personal gallantry.

Pigg Norman Batey MC Lieutenant LG 8/3/19
For most conspicuous gallantry and initiative during the operations east of Solesmes, from 23 to 26 October 1918. He commanded a company which made three assaults during the operations. On one occassion he pushed forward with a small party, and captured a machine gun which had been causing casualties. Later he observed an enemy field battery, which he at once charged and routed the gunners. His fine acts of gallantry undoubtedly saved the battalion many casualties.

Porch Cecil Porch Lieutenant Colonel 23rd Bn LG 26/3/17
For able leading while in command of a raiding party. The success of the raid was largely due to his most careful work in preparing the details of the scheme and his own determined leading. Later, although wounded he continued to direct operations, and personally superintended the removal of the wounded under heavy fire.
Bar L G 18/7/17
He led his battalion with the greatest gallantry and determination. He personally superintended the cutting of the enemy wire under continuous machine gun and rifle fire. He set a very fine example of coolness and courage throughout.

Studd Francis Cyril Rupert, Lieutenant Colonel 22nd Bn

Whitehead Hector Fraser, Lieutenant 23rd Bn LG 1/1/18
Bar LG 18/7/18
By his gallantry, energy and marked ability he was able to keep his battalion in a high state of offensive spirit. Later, when his men were really tired after ten days continuous fighting and marching his splendid example encouraged them top hold on, even counter-attack under heavy artillery and machine gun fire.

Air Force Cross

Algie William DSO Lieutenant 23rd Bn attached Royal Flying Corps, For night flying operations over London.

Croix de Geurre (Belgian)
Legion of Honour (French)

Hunter Albert Richmond 23rd Bn

The Military Cross

Alexander.Ultrick. 22nd Bn Captain LG 2/12/1918
(Won att 10th Bn in Italy)
For conspicuous gallantry and able leadership in charge of a raiding party. He led his men through the gap in the enemy wire and assisted in bombing and clearing dug outs and capturing and killing many of the enemy. Before the raid took place here reconnoitred the assembly position and the enemy wire both by day and night.

Allen. Arnold Morley. 22nd Bn Major LG 18/7/1917.
Bar LG 16/8/1917
For conspicuous gallantry and devotion to duty. He led the company with great skill and determination. On reaching the final objective his example and energy under heavy fire greatly assisted in the task of consolidation.
Bar: For conspicuous gallantry and devotion to duty. He led his platoon with great courage and determination. By his skill repulsing continual hostile counter attacks, and, at a critical moment, defeating a violent hostile bombing attack which was seriously threatening our flank. He set a splendid example to all ranks.

Babbitt. Monte. 22nd Bn. 2Lt Major LG 4/10/1919
For conspicuous gallantry and devotion to duty near Bermerain on 24 October 1918, while leading his platoon into action under very heavy artillery and machine gun fire. At a critical stage in the advance he collected the elements of two companies, reconnoitered the enemies position, and then led his men forward to the final objective, capturing many prisoners.

Baty. Reginald Elphinstone. 21st Bn 2Lt LG 26/4/1917
For conspicuous gallantry and devotion to duty in leading a raiding party. Although seriously wounded, he continued to lead his men, and entered the enemy,s trench. He has previously done fine work.

Becke. A H 2Lt 20th Bn LG 8/3/19 (Att 9th Bn).

Begg. Alexander James Bartlett LG 3/6/17 20th Bn
Kings Birthday Honour award.

Blenkinsop. William. 21st Bn. 2Lt LG 16/9/1918
For conspicuous gallantry and devotion to duty. During the night, shortly afier he had taken over a post, the enemy attacked and outflanked the position. Cut off from his support, and with the enemy in his post and behind it, he collected what men he could and attacked the enemy, driving them Out of the post. His prompt action and gallant leading caused conflision in the enemy ranks, and they withdrew on the approach of a counter attack.

Boughton. Jack Leonard. 20th Bn. Lt. LG 17/1/17
For conspicuous gallantry and devotion to duty when in charge of brigade carrying parties. For seven nights in succession he led them through intense shelling, and in spite of casualties, he kept the front line troops supplied with rations and water under most trying conditions.

Broatch. Percy. 2Lt LG 7/3/1918 23rd Bn
For conspicuous gallantry and devotion to duty. He led his men to attack and got into action on the final objective in a very short time. Although half his men became; casualties he kept his mortars in action and supplied with ammunition until relieved three days later. It was only owing to his brilliant leadership and cheerful example that the mortars were kept in action.

Brough. Peter Hillary Lloyd Temp/Lt 20th Bn att 4th Bn LG 4/10/19
On 26 October 1918, at the capture of Engel Fontaine, he displayed conspicuous gallantry and leadership of a platoon. He succeeded in outflanking the village and cutting off the enemy's retreat, with the result that nearly 500 prisoners were captured. He did splendid work.

Brown. George Arthur. Lt. LG 7/3/1 918 22Bn

For For conspicuous gallantry and devotion to duty. When in charge of a carrying party. He made three journeys to the captured position with ammunition and R.E. material through a heavy barrage, during one of which four men were killed near him and several. others wounded.

Browning. Reginald Arthur 2Lt. LG 13/2/17 20Bn.

He led a successful raid against the enemy's trenches with great courage and skill. He set a splendid example throughout.

Carswell. James. Lt. LG 1/1/19 (23Bn att lst Bn)

For conspicuous gallantry and devotion to duty. In a hostile attack this officerwas in command of the right front company, which at one time had one of its platoon. completely surrounded. He collected what men he could of his support platoon, and the battalion, and led a counter attack, which was completely successful in routing the enemy, and resulted in the capture of forty prisoners. His prompt action gave the enemy no time to exploit their initial success.

Cook-Watson. Sydney Cameron 20Bn (att Light TMB) LG 22/9/16

For conspicuous gallantry. He dug in two trench guns in no-mans-land between our own and the enemy trenches, and remained with them for many hours, firing over 200 shells into the hostile trenches. He was under heavy shell and machine gun fire the whole time, and was several times buried.

Common. John Edward 2Lt LG 26/3/17 23fln

For conspicuous gallantry and devotion to duty. He led a raiding party with great dash, entered the hostile trenches and himself shot two enemy. He was severely wounded. He has on many previous occasions done fine work.

Daggett.Cedric Ilunton. Lt. LG 1/1/1917 21Bn New Year's Honour award.

Davies. Harold Haydin. 2Lt LG 7/3/1918 21Bn

For conspicuous gallantry and devotion to duty when in command of his company after the company commander had been wounded. Though the only other officer was killedand three bombing parties suffered heavy casualties, he held onto his position, and on supports coming up, went forward to the final objective.

Dodd. Urwin Hunter. Lt. LG 4/10/1919 (29Bn att 2Bn)

On 18 October 1918, near Le Cateau railway station, he commanded two companies in the successful attack on the triangle and railway east of the station. By his leading and skill he took the objective, including several machine gun posts, with slight casualties. He started his attack in the dark and with no previous knowledge of the ground. throughout the day he set a fine example by his coolness and courage.

Falcy. Humphrey Ned. 2Lt LG 21/12/1916 23Bn

For conspicuous gallantry in action. He led a raid against the enemy with great courage and skill. Later, he successfully withdrew his party, and himself carried a wounded man across 'No mans land' under heavy fire.

Fletcher. Leonard. MM. LG3/6/1918. Bar: LG 16/9/1918 23Bn

MC: Kings Birthday Honour award.

Bar: For conspicuous gallantry and devotion to duty during six days' fighting. This officer made a number of reconnaissance's under shell, machine gun and rifle fire bringing in information of the greatest value. His coolness and courage under adverse circumstances were a fine example to all his men.

Gibson. Wesley Milum. 2Lt LG 4/6/1917 Bar 18/7/17 20Bn

MC: Kings Birthday Honour award.

Bar: For conspicuous gallantry and devotion to duty. During the advance he showed great courage and coolness in rallying and encouraging his men under heavy fire. His personal example and disregard for danger largely contributed to the reaching of the final objective.

Gorrill. D.G.S. Lt. LG 16/9/1918 22Bn

For conspicuous gallantry and devotion to duty. when the enemy broke through on hi right he formed a defensive flank with his company. By rifle fire and grenade work checked the enemy's advance, and later got onto the parapet and bombed the enemy unil they were only a few yards off. He showed great courage and tenacity,

Heron. Thomas Emanuel. Capt. LG 26/3/1917. Bar LG July 1917 23Bn

For conspicuous gallantry and devotion to duty during a raid on the enemy's trench Although wounded, he continued to command his men for 35 minutes in the enemy's trenches, until the signal was given to withdraw. He displayed great courage and determination throughout. Bar: For conspicuous gallantry and devotion to duty. He led his company with skill and courage. Later, although wounded, he continued to lead his men and consolidated the captured position. He set a splendid example throughout.

Hodson. John 21/II2I RSM LG 22/9/1916 21Bn

For conspicuous gallantry and devotion to duty during an attack. After all the officers had fallen he led the men to the first line of enemy trenches, and, although wounded, continued to struggle on until he fell exhausted from loss of blood.

Housby. Robert Percival. Lt. 9/1/18 (23Bn att RFC)

For conspicuous gallantry and devotion to duty as observer. Having successfully bombed a station behind the enemy lines, he took control of the machine on his pilot fainting from a bullet wound in his arm. He managed to keep the machine level, and flew it until his pilot recovered. shortly afterwards the latter again lost consciousess, and this officer took control once more, managing to land the machine under very difficult circumstances well behind our lines. This officer has always shown a fine ample of courage and skill in the night bombing raids in which he was taking part.

Howard. Harry 2Lt LG 6/4/18   (29Bn att R.FC)

As observer, having successfully bombed a station behind enemy lines, he took control of the machine on his pilot fainting from a bullet wound in the arm. He managed to keep the machine level and flew it until his pilot recovered. Shortly afterwards the latter again lost consciousness, and this officer took control once more, managing to land the machine under very difficult circumstances well behind our lines. This officer has always shown a fine example of courage and skill in the many night bombing raids in which he has taken part.

Hughes. John Price 2Lt LG 16/9/1918 23Bn

For conspicuous gallantry and devotion to duty. He handled his platoon very skillfully during long and heavy bombardments, and rendered valuable assistance to his company commander in offering stubborn resistance and inflicting heavy casualties on the attacking forces. By his personal disregard of danger he set a fine example to a men.

Hunter. Albert Richmond. Lt. LG 3/6/1919 23Bn

Kings Birthday Honour Award.

Kerr. Albert Edward. Cap. LG. 22/9/16 20Bn

In an assault on enemy trenches, when, although seriously wounded, unable to move and exposed to heavy fire, he refused assistance and continued to encourage his men to advance.

Kerridge. Sydney Charles. 2Lt. LG 26/3/17 23Bn

During a raid on the enemy trenches, he systematically cleared the whole of the trench allotted to him, bombing the dugouts and killing the occupants. He set a splendid example to his men throughout the operation.

Lambert A. 2Lt LG 5/5/19 23Bn

Levin. Carl Norton 2Lt. LG 1/1/18 21Bn New Years Honour Award.

Lindsay. David Cranston. 2Lt 16/8/1917 22Bn

For conspicuous gallantry and devotion to duty. At a critical moment. after an enemy counter attack, when his men were badly shaken, he walked forward across the open to ascertain the enemy's dispositions. The information which he thus gained at personal enabled him to plan and lead a completely successful counter attack upon the enemy.

Logan Cyril. Lt. LG 3/6/1919 21Bn

Kings Birthday Honour award.

Lucas. William Henry Owen. Lt. LG 2/1919 23Bn

At Villers Guislaw on 29 September 1918, this officers company made two separate mopping up advances through the village, securing three officers and 107 other ranks as prisoners. It was largely due to his organisation that the operation was so successful in face of the most determined opposition, the enemy holding the village in great strength.

MacNaught. Eric Norman Cap. LG 3/2/17 20Bn

He led a successful raid against the enemy's trenches with great courage and skill. He set a splendid example throughout.

MacRae. George Arthur. Lt. LG 7/3/1918 22Bn

For conspicuous gallantry and devotion to duty during an attack,

Above: Second Lieutenant Reginald Baty prior to the award of his Military Cross at Buckingham Palace. He won the decoration for his part in the trench raid on the night of 7/8 March 1917, when, although he was wounded he successfully bombed some enemy dugouts.

Above: Captain H S Matthews 23rd Battalion, awarded the MC a Second Lieutenant 22 September 1916, for his actions on 1 July 1916. He was promoted to Captain 22 February 1918.

Above: Rev. Father Joseph McHardy, MC Tyneside Scottish Brigade RC Padre.

getting two Stokes mortars and a large carrying party to his objectives under intense fire. Finding that the mortars on his flank had failed to come up, he took one of the mortars to cover this flank. He continued in charge for three days and observed the fire with great courage, inflicting severe losses on the enemy.

Mark. Alan William Dobson. Capt. DSO 21Bn
MC LG 1/1/1917.
Bar: LG 10/10/1917.
2nd Bar: LG 16/9/1918
MC: New Years Honour Award.
Bar: For conspicuous gallantry and devotion to duty in leading two companies in a frontal attack, gaining his objective, and holding it under heavy shell fire.
2nd Bar: For conspicuous gallantry and devotion to duty. This officer formed no less than ten defensive flanks when the enemy had broken into the division on his right. Each line of these he held to the last minute, and then successfully withdrew to another position. His initiative and cheerfulness inspired all ranks with confidence.

Marshall. John Matthew. 2Lt LG 7/11/1918 22Bn
For conspicuous gallantry in a raid. He dashed into an enemy post, shot 8 of them and bombed a machine gun. He was then blown up by the explosion of a shell and had t be carried back. He behaved with splendid courage and determination.

Mathieson. Duncan. Cap. LG 1/1/17 20Bn
New Years Honour Award.

Matthews. Sydney Herbert. Capt. LG 2/9/1916 23Bn
For conspicuous gallantry in leading his men to the enemy's second line trenches and holding on for three days, under heavy shell and machine gun fire, in order to consolidate position.

McHardy. Joseph. Rev Father, Army Chaplins Department, Brigade RC Padre. LG 1/1/1917

McKeand. Alexander Brodie. 2Lt LG 18/7/1917 20Bn
For conspicuous gallantry and devotion to duty. He performed most valuable work whilst in charge of battalion carrying parties. He frequently took long journeys in his effort to secure water for the troops. His pluck and determination under heavy fire greatly assisted with the final consolidation.

Melvin. Frederick Christie. Temp/Lt 20th Bn att 9th Bn LG 4/10/19
He led his platoon with great gallantry and determination. In the attack on 24 October 1918 against the village of Bermerain, strongly held by machine guns. He cleared his portion and, pushing on for about a mile, with only the remnants of his platoon, dug in on the final objective, although his left flank was entirely unprotected. He set a very fine example of determined leadership to all about him.

Metcalfe. George. Capt. LG 11/1/1919 23Bn
For conspicuous gallantry and devotion to duty. In an attack near a farm this officer handled his company in a masterly manner, overcoming a strong point, and reaching his objective with very few casualties. He captured forty prisoners and six machine guns.

Milburn. Frank. Capt. LG 12/12/1918 23Bn
For conspicuous gallantry and devotion to duty. He commanded two companies in the crossing of an important river with skill and determination, and repelled a strong counter attack. Finally, having received a most painful wound, he handed over his company and returned to battalion headquarters, where he gave a full account of the situation before having his wounds attended to. He set a fine example of gallantry and endurance.

Milley. Stewart. Lt. LG 26/3/1917 23Bn
For conspicuous gallantry in action. He bombed two dug outs, killing three of the enemy, and rescued a wounded officer from the enemy front line. Later, he single handed, drove back a party of the enemy and rescued several men under heavy fire.

Morris. Arthur Agustus 2Lt LG 18/7/1917 23rd Bn
He patrolled for several hundred yards beyond the final objective and sent back most valuable information. This patrol was carried out under heavy artillery barrage.

Moyes. Edgar William. 2Lt LG 18/3/1918 22Bn
For conspicuous gallantry and devotion when in charge of a carrying party. When a brigade dump was set on fire by hostile shelling and the ammunition and bombs were exploding, he set to work and pulled some detonated Stokes' bombs out of danger, and shoveling earth on the

remainder extinguished the fire. This was carried out under heavy shelling.

Nelson. George Spoors. Lt. LG 22/9/1916 23Bn
For conspicuous gallantry before and during an assault on an enemy position. On reaching the hostile wire he found some men of another battalion, who had preceded him, he led them forward through the wire until only two or three remained unwounded. later he assisted in carrying in the wounded under heavy fire.

Orange Alfred. MM. 2Lt LG /2/1919 22Bn
For conspicuous gallantry and ability near Gazirin, on 2 September 1918, when in charge of a fighting patrol sent out to establish a post in the enemy's lines. He had reached his objective when 20 of the enemy, led by an officer, came down the trench. he shot the officer and a man behind him with his revolver, and, during a sharp fight with bombs, another enemy party attacked from the rear. Finding himself outnumbered, he fought his way through with his patrol, and successfully regained his lines, without a casualty, after killing and wounding several of the enemy and obtaining valuable information. He did fine work.

Pattullo. George Simpson. Lt. LG 7/6/16 2lBn

Peacock. Basil. 2Lt LG 7/3/1918 22Bn
For conspicuous gallantry and devotion to duty in charge of a wiring party, getting 5 men to work under heavy machine gun fire within ten minutes of the objective being reached, and completing the wiring in time to defeat several counter attacks.

Peterkin W. CSM LG 30/1/20 23Bn

Piegrove. Joseph Charles. Lt. LG 21/12/1916 22Bn
For conspicuous gallantry in action. He led a raid against the enemy's trenches with great courage and determination. He has on many previous occasions done fine work.

Pigg. Norman Batey. Lt. DSO 2lBn
LG 10/1/1917. Bar: LG 16/9/1918.2nd Bar: LG 16/9/1918
MC: For conspicuous gallantry in action. He led a successful raid against the enemy's inches with great courage and determination. He was severely wounded.
Bar: For conspicuous gallantry and devotion to duty during an enemy attack. For two days under repeated heavy bombardment and in face of massed attacks he held his men cleverly together, and rendered great assistance to his battalion commander. He did fine work.
2nd Bar: For conspicuous gallantry and devotion to duty. By his fine example of leadership and courage he encouraged his men to successfully repulse three heavy enemy attacks. Later, when the enemy drove back the line on his left, he quickly threw out a defensive flank enabling the remainder of his force to take up a new position in the rear. His rapid grasp of the situation considerably impeded the enemy's advance.

Robson. William Henry. Lt. LG 18/7/1917 22Bn
For conspicuous gallantry and devotion to duty. He advanced with a small party under intense machine gun fire, and captured and consolidated a position in front of the main attack, which had been held up. He held this post, repelling counter attack for twenty-four hours, when he was ordered to withdraw.

Rotherford. Robson Wilson. Lt. LG 22Bn Lg 27/7/16
For conspicuous gallantry. In spite of heavy casualties in his bombing party, he himself being bruised by shrapnel, he made most determined attacks on the enemy till the remainder of his bombers had been knocked out. Two days later he made an important reconnasance under machine gun fire.

Scaife. Arthur Lewis. 2Lt LG 2/12/18 (23Bn Won 12/13Bn)
As battalion intelligence officer he made an important reconnaissance, penetrating a great depth into the enemy lines, and bringing back valuable information. Subsequently; when the battalion was held up by a close range machine gun fire, he worked to a flank with a Lewis gun, and materially assisted to dislodge the enemy. In doing this he was hit on four separate occasions by enemy bullets. His courage and determination were conspicuous to all ranks.

Scott. Duncan. 2Lt LG 1/1/1918 23Bn New Year's Honour Award

Sim. Alexander. Capt. LG 15/10/1918 20Bn
For conspicuous gallantry and devotion to duty during an enemy attack. When ordered to form a defensive flank with his company, he led them through a heavy barrage to a position which he had had no chance of reconnoitering, and occupied it. It was largely due to his prompt

initiative and determination that a critical situation was saved.

Simpson. Henry Jackson. 2Lt LG 15/2/1919 23Bn
For conspicuous gallantry and devotion to duty during recent operations. On October 4th, near Billy - Barcleau, he led his platoon splendidly and captured a machine gun and its team in La Beau Marsis. He then pushed on and took the dynamite factory, and, still advancing, established a forward post at the bridge of the Canal. Losing several men here from heavy trench mortar and machine gun fire, he, with greet coolness and ability, succeeded in withdrawing his command to safety, getting in all the wounded He did fine work.

Spink. Henry Mawkinson. 2Lt LG 7/3/1918 23Bn
For conspicuous gallantry and devotion to duty. Although buried on three occasions enemy shells, he continued to carry out his work of consolidating a captured trench until wounded in the head and rendered unconscious.

Stephenson. Jonathan. Lt. LG 16/8/1917. Bar: LG 30/7/1919 20Bn (Bar won att 2Bn)
MC: For conspicuous gallantry and devotion to duty. He led his company to its objective with great initiative and courage, bombing the enemy trench and securing it against counter attacks by his skillful direction of rifle and Lewis gun fire.
Bar: For conspicuous gallantry and skill in operations north of Gouy on October 5th, 1918. This officer in the attack on Prospect Hill led his platoon with great dash to its objective, capturing 36 prisoners and two machine guns. He succeeded by skillful leadership in holding his objective against the enemy and throughout the operations showed great courage and a fine example of coolness under extremely heavy enemy fire.

Stephenson. Robert Brewis. 2Lt LG 7/3/1918 22Bn
For conspicuous gallantry and devotion to duty in leading his men to the attack. As soon as the objective was reached he pushed forward with his platoon, harassing the enemy as they retired, and inflicting heavy casualties. He afterwards, on his own initiative, organised two bombing posts and beat off a counter attack.

Viner. Frank Hillridge. 2Lt LG 16/9/1918 Bar: LG 11/1/1919 23Bn
For conspicuous gallantry and devotion to duty. During five days fighting this officer by his cheerfulness and initiative maintained a fine fighting spirit in his platoon, helping them to hold their section of the line against repeated attacks. Then is company commander was wounded he took command arid continued his good work until he as sent to hospital through illness.
Bar: He led his platoon forward in an attack with great gallantry under intense machine gun fire. He brought his men across 400 yards of open ground, and reached the objective, though his platoon was then reduced to ten man. He himself was severely wounded, but remained at his post. It was mainly due to his personal courage and fine example of leadership that he got his men so far in spite of the heavy casualties.

Wadge. John Robert. 22/1653 RSM LG 19/8/16 22Bn
For conspicuous gallantry during a heavy bombardment. He went out under heavy shell fire and dug out the Battalion signalers who were buried in a shelter.

Walker. Charles Hainmond. 2Lt LG 16/9/1918 2OBn
For conspicuous gallantry and devotion to duty. Then his company was being surround and fired on by machine guns by the enemy, who had crawled up to the wire, he killed 20 of them and was instrumental in the capture of two machine guns. He led his platoon 40 yards to a position, which he held for six hours. Later, when his platoon was subjected to another heavy attack, he held the fire of his men till the enemy were close on them, and then caused the enemy heavy casualties and broke up the attack. He showed fine courage.

Waller. Herbert William. 21Bn LG 10/1/17

Ward. Dennis Edwin. Lt. LG 16/9/1918 2OBn
For conspicuous gallantry and devotion to duty. Whilst the enemy was delivering a violent attack and the situation on the left flank was obscure, this officer took out a reconnoitering patrol, and for an hour and a half, under very heavy fire, kept the enemy movements under observation, and sent back valuable messages. He continued his work until seriously wounded in the leg later in the evening.

Watson. John. 2Lt LG 26/3/1917 23Bn
For conspicuous gallantry and devotion to duty during a raid on the enemy's trenches. although wounded in two places, he continued to lead and encourage his men until he fainted from loss of blood close to the enemy's wire.

Waugh. Thomas Hall.   22Bn. LG 10/1/17.

Whillis. Bertrand Percy. Capt. LG 1/1/18 20Bn New Year's Honour Award.

White. Cecil Hayhoe. 2Lt LG 18/3/1918 23Bn
For conspicuous gallantry and devotion to duty in leading his platoon in an attack. He penetrated the hostile defenses, but was severely wounded in the thigh. In spite of this he sent back a runner giving a report of the situation, and instructed the stretcher bearers to take him to company headquarters to report.

Wilmot. Ben. Lt. LG 25/11/1916 20Bn
For conspicuous gallantry in action. He led a daring raid against the enemy's trenches, 30 to 40 of the enemy were killed, and he himself accounted for two with his revolver.

Woodhead. Alfred. 2Lt LG 16/8/1917 20Bn
For conspicuous gallantry and devotion to duty. He held a shell hole for 24 hours against two enemy machine guns, keeping them from firing upon the troops on his flank, who would otherwise not have been able to maintain their position. He drove off a part who attempted to capture him, and eventually got back to our lines with only two men alive of the seven with whom he had started.

Others known to have won MC
Citation & Gazette date yet to be traced.

Acklom. Spencer. Lt-Col 22nd Bn. DSO+bar

Anderson. Kenneth Noel. Captain & Adjutant Seaforths att 23rd Bn

Curry. William P. Captain 20th Bn.

McCluskey. Arthur William. 2/Lieutenant 21st Bn

Moorwood. Thomas Hedley. 2/Lieutenant 23rd Bn

Thomson. John. 2/Lieutenant 20th Bn

Tilsley. Richard F. 2/Lieutenant 23rd Bn

Mentioned in Despatches
Lieutenant Colonel **Spencer Acklom** 21st Bn, Captain **J H Adams** 21st Bn, Lieutenant **William Algie** 23rd Bn, Lieutenant **Peter H L Brough** 20th att 4th Bn, A/Lieutenant Colonel **George Charlton** 23rd Bn, Captain **John M Charlton** 21st Bn, Captain **Thomas B Coull** 23rd Bn, Second Lieutenant **H V Crees** 22nd Bn, Lieutenant & Quartermaster **T V Foster** 22nd Bn, Second Lieutenant **John R Freeman** 32nd att 23rd Bn, Second Lieutenant **J Glencross** 22nd Bn, Second Lieutenant **George H Graham** 21st Bn, Second Lieutenant **Lawrence V Grice** 21st Bn, Second Lieutenant **Charles E Hardy** 22nd Bn, Captain **Arthur P Ker** 20th Bn, Lieutenant & Quartermaster **William J Lock** 21st Bn, Second Lieutenant **Cressy R Longhurst** 23rd Bn, Captain **Stanley H Macintosh** 23rd Bn, Second Lieutenant **Alan W D Mark** 21st Bn, Second Lieutenant **George Metcalfe** 23rd Bn, Second Lieutenant **Arthur A Morris** 23rd Bn, Lieutenant **A D M Napier** 21st Bn, Second Lieutenant **A E Neill** 22nd Bn, Captain Norman **B Pigg** 21st Bn, Lieutenant Colonel **Cecil P Porch** 23rd Bn, Captain **Edward J Smith** 22nd Bn, Second Lieutenant **William H Thompson** 23rd Bn, Second Lieutenant **John Thomson** 22nd Bn, Second Lieutenant **Emerson Turnbull** 20th Bn, Lieutenant **Hector F Whitehead** 23rd Bn, Second Lieutenant **Alfred G Young** 20th Bn.

The Distinguished Conduct Medal

23/689 Corporal **T W Allinson** LG 26/1/18
For conspicuous gallantry and devotion to duty when on patrol. He accompanied his officer on a difficult reconnaissance, and when the latter was severely wounded, and lying under fire, he went back and sheltered him with his body at great personal risk, remaining with him until it was possible to move him to a place of safety. No praise can be to great for this splendid act of devotion.

22/754 Bugler **J Blake** LG 22/9/16
For conspicuous gallantry when employed as a stretcher bearer. On entering a captured dug-out he discovered, with out being observed himself, four of the enemy. Borrowing a wounded Officer's revolver, he returned. On the enemy showing fight he shot one man, the remainder surrendered.

11874 Corporal **A E Collins** MM 23rd BN LG 30/1/20 No citation given.

23/822 Sergeant **C A Cowans** LG 3/10/18

For conspicuous gallantry during an enemy attack. He collected and assumed command of a body of men, and with a Lewis gun inflicted many casualties on the advancing enemy. Although ill and in an exhausted condition, he remained with his men until ordered to withdraw. He set a fine example of coolness and devotion to duty.

37972 Private E Craghill 23rd BN LG 26/3/17
For conspicuous gallantry and devotion to duty. He showed great initiative in collecting and leading his party after his officer and NCO had become casualties. Later, although wounded, he remained at his post and continued to encourage his men.

22/264 Private G Curry LG 6/2/18
For conspicuous gallantry and devotion to duty as a company runner, carrying messages, each time successfully, through a hostile barrage. When a shell fell in a trench, burying four men, he got on top of the parapet and under heavy machine gun fire dug them out.

22/980 CSM J Duffy LG 18/7/17
For conspicuous gallantry and devotion to duty. He led the company with great courage and skill. He was instrumental in capturing several enemy officers in their headquarters. Throughout he displayed the utmost coolness and initiative under heavy fire.

20/1563 Corporal T Easton LG 9/7/17
For conspicuous gallantry and devotion to duty. The lever came off one of the shells and started the fuse action. He picked up the shell, carried it down the trench and threw it over the parapet.

20/1038 Corporal C Felce LG 28/3/18
For conspicuous gallantry and devotion to duty. The conduct of the NCO during the operations was most conspicuous. When in charge of a bombing section he entered the enemy trench, and at once attacked, single handed a hostile bombing post, killing or putting to flight the whole garrison. In accordance with the plan he formed a bombing block in an enemy communication trench, from which he and his section repulsed bombing attacks for seven hours. Later, though the hostile infantry attacked in force and dislodged our garrison, he remained at his post until his own bombs and also those captured from the enemy had been thrown, and was the last man to leave the trench.

87453 CSM W G Gadsby 22nd BN LG 10/1/20
On 3 October 1918, near Billy-Berclau, the right flank was harassed by an enemy machine gun. CSM Gadsby first tried to seize the gun, but, being unsuccessful, he tried to bomb the gun from the other side of the embankment. He organised a small bombing party and, covered by a Lewis gun rushed the machine gun direct, capturing the gun and crew of eleven. Later, he performed most useful patrol work under constant fire, and set a very fine example of courage and determination.

22/1410 Sergeant J T Glendinning LG 18/7/17
For conspicuous gallantry and devotion to duty. He led his men with great dash and courage. He captured forty prisoners single handed and at great personal risk.

23/613 Sergeant T Halligan LG 21/10/18
For conspicuous gallantry and devotion to duty as CSM. He rendered invaluable assistance and under intense shell fire his coolness and courage did much to instil confidence into his men at times of great danger.

38102 CSM Acting RSM A S Harle 23rd BN LG 21/10/18
For conspicuous gallantry and devotion to duty during many months continuous service with the battalion, and also as acting RSM. During the fighting he rendered invaluable assistance, both in the attack and during consolidation. On one occasion he was largely responsible for leading his company out of newly won trenches under a heavy barrage and preventing heavy casualties.
Bar 30/1/20 No citation given.

41181 Private J W Harrison 23rd BN LG 3/9/18
For conspicuous gallantry and devotion to duty while in charge of a Lewis gun team. He repeatedly, under heavy fire, rushed his gun forward to within 100 yards of the advancing enemy and held up parties of them, thereby checking the advance and inflicting considerable casualties.

21/993 CSM R C Henderson LG 6/2/18
For conspicuous gallantry and devotion to duty in an attack. He tookcommand of a platoon when its officer was a casualty, and led the mento their objective. During consolidation of the captured position hedid splendid work in directing the operations under very difficult conditions and heavy fire.

21/236 Private W S Holland LG 10/1/17
For conspicuous gallantry in action. He displayed great courage and determination during a raid on the enemy's trenches. Later, he rescued a wounded officer under heavy fire.

21/377 Sergeant A F Jackson LG 13/2/17
For conspicuous gallantry in action. He organised the bomb supply and himself assisted in a bombing attack, setting a splendid example to the men under him.
Bar 26/3/17 For conspicuous gallantry and devotion to duty during a raid on the enemy's trenches. Although wounded, he continued to assist in repelling the enemy counter attacks and safeguarding the rear of the advance party in the enemy second line. He set a splendid example throughout.

38596 Lance Corporal H H Jagger MM 20th BN LG 16/8/17
For conspicuous gallantry and devotion to duty. He attacked an enemy machine gun single handed which was inflicting severe casualties on his company at a range of 100 yards, shot the gunner, and destroyed the breech action with another bullet, though heavily bombed at close range all the time. Immediately afterwards he fell seriously wounded in the head, having shown magnificent self sacrifice and disregard for his personal safety in the interests of his company.

21283 Sergeant F S Lazenby 22nd BN LG 11/3/20
Near Cambrin on 6 September 1918 he displayed the utmost courage and devotion to duty in charge of a Lewis gun team. When his platoon was held up by machine gun fire, he went forward and silenced the enemy, enabling his platoon to get forward and reach its objective.

20/825 Corporal J W Liddle LG 20/10/16
For conspicuous gallantry. When the enemy exploded a mine and attacked with bombs he rushed up with two boxes of bombs and for some time held a sap single handed.

38306 RSM A M Marr 22nd BN LG 21/10/18
For conspicuous gallantry and devotion to duty both in the line and during periods of training. He showed a splendid example, sometimes under the most adverse conditions and did much to maintain the spirit of the men by his personal courage under fire.

23/1124 CSM L Moore LG 26/3/17
For conspicuous gallantry and devotion to duty. He rendered most valuable services during a raid in the enemy's trenches and later brought in several wounded men under heavy fire.

21/840 CSM E J Patterson LG 19/9/16
For conspicuous gallantry when leading a bombing attack on the enemy, and for repulsing repeated counter attacks by the enemy during a considerable period.

20/614 Corporal J E Philipson LG 22/9/16
For conspicuous bravery and devotion to duty. Though wounded in four places he made gallant efforts to get a gun forward.
CSM Bar 17/4/19 For conspicuous gallantry and leadership near Marquion on 27 September 1918, in charge of the right flank of the company, which he directed with skill and dash. On 2 October after the capture of the railway, he crossed the embankment and carried rations and water to the forward platoon, repeating this on the four following days.

38116 Lance Sergeant E Russell 23rd BN LG 21/12/16
For conspicuous gallantry in action. He led a section of a raiding party with great courage and skill. He successfully carried out his orders and later dressed a wounded man under very heavy fire.

21/345 Private W Simpson LG 17/4/18
For conspicuous gallantry and devotion to duty as a signaller. He frequently restored communication under heavy fire and did excellent work during two engagements. He always showed magnificent courage and determination.

37469 Sergeant W H Thompson 20th BN LG 16/8/17
For conspicuous gallantry and devotion to duty. Under heavy rifle fire he put a hostile machine gun out of action and killed the men with rifle grenades, which he fired from No-Man's-Land. He afterwards assisted his platoon commander to bomb and clear an enemy trench, and throughout the whole action his energy and coolness set a splendid example to the men.

360008 CSM C Tinsley 22nd BN LG 11/3/20
During the advance from La Bassee to Tournai from 17 September to 11 November 1918 he displayed the utmost courage and devotion to

duty on several occasions. At Berclau from 3 to 6 October his company was in a very exposed position, and was frequently subjected to heavy machine gun fire, his company commander being killed.

23/1364 CSM E J Watson LG 26/3/17
For conspicuous gallantry and devotion to duty. He succeeded in bringing back several wounded men under very heavy fire. He has previously done fine work.

The Military Medal

21/16	L/Cpl	**Alcock E**
44107	Pte	**Allen E** 21st Bn
23/691	Sgt	**Alsop T**
14404	Pte	**Archbold W** 22nd Bn
87640	Pte	**Arnott J** 22nd Bn
60469	Pte	**Aspden H** 23rd Bn
47494	Pte	**Aspinall F** 23rd Bn
23/854	Pte	**Athey J**
20/157	Pte	**Bagnall J**
23/444	Cpl	**Bakewell H** and Bar
58379	Pte	**Barker C F** 23rd Bn
	Sgt	**Barton Jack** 23rd Bn with 254 Tun Comp.
23/1415	Sgt	**Bates W**
23/965	Pte	**Bell A A**
23/49	Pte	**Bell R**
37266	Pte	**Bennett T** 21st Bn
22/919	Pte	**Blyth A**
15220	Pte	**Boyle P** 20th Bn
22/366	Cpl	**Burns J**
21/766	Lsgt	**Bradley I**
20/310	Cpl	**Bradley T B**
38716	Pte	**Brown A** 22nd Bn
22/1599	Cpl	**Brown J**
23/1416	Pte	**Brown J**
37310	Sgt	**Brown R** and Bar 20th Bn
21/123	Sgt	**Cain W**
21/781	Lcpl	**Calvert R W**
22/339	Pte	**Cameron G**
20/30	Sgt	**Campbell J T**
23/976	Lcpl	**Carr T**
21/1336	Cpl	**Chapelhow G**
23/624	Lsgt	**Christmas W H** and Bar
37334	Cpl	**Clayton A** 23rd Bn
29/488	Pte	**Cock T**
20/390	Pte	**Collins R**
22/855	Pte	**Cook W**
35503	Cpl	**Cooper F** 22nd Bn
23/822	Sgt	**Cowans C A**
23/1228	Pte	**Crisfield W T**
21/1161	Sgt	**Crowe J A**
22/1708	Pte	**Cryle R**
20/1250	Pte	**Currie A**
29/79	Lcpl	**Davidson W** 20th Bn
21/927	Lcpl	**Davison A**
23/1106	Lsgt	**Davison R**
22/429	Cpl	**Day W**
23/1141	Pte	**Defty R** with Durham Light Inf.
205524	Pte	**Dingwall A** 22nd Bn
20/743	Pte	**Ditchburn**
20/1619	Pte	**Dixon W**
22/1191	Pte	**Dugdale J**
40688	A/Lcpl	**Dunn E V** formerly West Rid.Regt
20/394	Sgt	**Dunn T**
21/998	Pte	**Easton J**
23/1241	Sgt	**Edwards J**
21/1043	Pte	**Emery W**
37235	Sgt	**Estell W**
22/1670	Cpl	**Fairholme J**
20/1038	Cpl	**Felce C** DCM
21/1269	Pte	**Ferguson G**
20/765	Pte	**Ferguson J**
20/1284	Pte	**Felton J**
29/291	Pte	**Fisher T**
18/1065	Pte	**Fletcher R** 23rd Bn
22/1430	Pte	**Forsyth R**
37341	Pte	**Gibson F H** 20th Bn
23/849	Pte	**Gibson S**
20/9	Sgt	**Goodall D**

21/929	Pte	**Graham M**
21/782	Sgt	**Gray J** and Bar
37281	Cpl	**Gray J** and Bar 20th Bn
38691	Pte	**Haigh E** and Bar 22nd Bn
38619	Pte	**Hall T** 20th Bn
21/1049	Sgt	**Hamblin J** with 9th Bn
23/312	Sgt	**Harding J**
39004	Pte	**Harker G** 21st Bn
22/1206	Pte	**Harrison R**
20/801	Pte	**Hay G** and Bar
20/176	Sgt	**Hay J N**
37323	Pte	**Hay R** 20th Bn
21/1602	Pte	**Hayes J T** and Bar
37435	Sgt	**Hendry W** 20th Bn
20/1626	Pte	**Hepple T**
22/100	Sgt	**Heslop J T**
21/654	Pte	**Hills J**
22/749	Pte	**Hindmarsh G**
22/896	Pte	**Horsley J**
31893	Pte	**Hunt L** 21st Bn
23/245	Pte	**Hunter J**
21/817	Lcpl	**Jackson A**
20/184	Pte	**Jackson H**
31428	Lcpl	**Jackson W L** 22nd Bn
20/186	Sgt	**Jacques W**
38596	Pte	**Jagger H H** 20th Bn
22/430	Pte	**Johnson C B**
22/568	Pte	**Johnson G**
20/190	Pte	**Johnson J T** and Bar
20/573	Pte	**Joisce P**
22/485	Cpl	**Kempster J T**
22/713	Lcpl	**Kennedy G** with 1st Bn
20/1440	Pte	**Killip G**
20/423	Sgt	**Kirk G A**
22/596	Sgt	**Laing J**
20/1469	Cpl	**Lamb E** with 1st Bn
20/1321	Sgt	**Lamb V**
20/1319	Lcpl	**Laverick J G**
22/1223	Lcpl	**Lawson W**
20/1075	Pte	**Leatham J E**
20/823	Pte	**Ledger A F**
22/114	Pte	**Legg J** with 9th Bn
23/461	Pte	**Leonard E** with 13th Bn
10/19641	Pte	**Lillie T** 23rd Bn
23/974	Pte	**Lowes T** with 1st Bn
204559	Pte	**Lowson W** 22nd Bn
27123	Pte	**Lunness W** 23rd Bn
22/905	Lcpl	**Luke T**
22/1027	Sgt	**Malcolm J**
35534	Pte	**Mathewson H R** 21st Bn
23/678	Pte	**Mattison C**
22/1227	Pte	**McAndrew W**
22/216	Sgt	**McCourt J**
22273	A/Cpl	**McGuinness W** 22nd Bn
23/44	Lcpl	**McLachlan W R**
22/314	Sgt	**Middlemiss W A**
23/611	Pte	**Millican T**
23/1339	Lcpl	**Mitchell W**
21/1566	Pte	**Morgan F**
20/1099	Sgt	**Musgrove W J**
23/80	Cpl	**Mould J**
22/126	Lcpl	**Neale G** and Bar
37304	Cpl	**Nesbit F** 20th Bn
21/1709	Pte	**Nichol C** with Durham LI
20/1648	Pte	**Octon R R**
21/525	Pte	**Ord J R** with KOYLI
23/136	Lcpl	**Ord N**
19004	Pte	**Palmer J F** 21st Bn
21/288	Sgt	**Palmer J R**
22/587	Pte	**Parker J**
22/867	Pte	**Patrick J** with 1st Bn
22/1381	Pte	**Patterson E**
22/1556	Pte	**Patterson T W**
37506	A/Cpl	**Peacock T** 20th Bn
360039	Pte	**Peacy A** 22nd Bn
47717	Cpl	**Petruce P** 22nd Bn
38127	Lcpl	**Philips J E** Piper 23rd Bn
23/64	Pte	**Porter H D** with 9th Bn

Below: 23/1416 Private John Brown of North Seaton, awarded the Military Medal whilst serving with 102 Light Trench Mortar Battery. He was wounded and discharged in 1918.

Above: 20/394 Sergeant Thomas Dunn, 27 Kingsley Place, Newcastle, was awarded the Military Medal July 1917 and was discharged in September 1918.

22/1057	Sgt	**Poulton T**
21/860	Pte	**Preece C**
6439	Pte	**Price J** 22nd Bn
38569	Pte	**Pye R** 20th Bn
242896	Sgt	**Ratcliffe J** 22nd Bn
35477	Pte	**Reay J M** 20th Bn
23/66	Sgt	**Redshaw F W**
22/1759	Lcpl	**Renfree T**
21/1304	Sgt	**Renner J R**
22/487	Sgt	**Riddell G**
21/912	Pte	**Riley P**
21/965	Lcpl	**Rivett S**
266104	Pte	**Robson A** 22nd Bn
20/896	Sgt	**Robson W**
23/1639	Pte	**Rolfe A S**
23/759	Cpl	**Routledge A**
21/1270	Pte	**Sancaster G M** with 9th Bn
21/911	Pte	**Sanderson C J** with 22nd Bn
16355	A/Cpl	**Sandy W** 22nd Bn
21/903	A/Sgt	**Scott J**
242002	Pte	**Scott R R** 22nd Bn
23/1525	Sgt	**Scott W**
23/462	Pte	**Shanks G W**
23/1074	Pte	**Simpson A**
20/904	Pte	**Sims J** and Two Bars
21/1702	Sgt	**Slater T**
315443	Pte	**Stafford T** 20th Bn
23/265	Pte	**Stanger W M**
20/346	Pte	**Stewart J**
23/1370	Sgt	**Straker W A**
22/342	Lsgt	**Stuttard H**
38730	Lcpl	**Styan T** 22nd Bn
20/1525	Pte	**Taylor G H** Piper
21/226	Cpl	**Teague J**
200818	Pte	**Thirtle J** 22nd Bn
87505	Cpl	**Thomas W** 22nd Bn
23/513	Lcpl	**Thompson G A** with 20th Bn
37469	Sgt	**Thompson W H** 20th Bn
22/94	Sgt	**Todd T**
23/459	Pte	**Turnbull R** with 9th Bn
23/432	Pte	**Turnbull W**
38117	Sgt	**Tweedie D S** 23rd Bn
40746	Pte	**Waite A V** 23rd Bn
20/684	Pte	**Walker W**
38054	Lcpl	**Walker W** 23rd Bn
20/689	Pte	**Wardlaw R H** with 8th Bn
40863	Pte	**Waterworth E** 23rd Bn
21/593	Pte	**Watson J**
23/629	Pte	**Watson S S**
37480	Pte	**Waugh I** 20th Bn
21/565	Lsgt	**Wear R D**
23/415	Pte	**Wearmouth I** and Bar
22/66	Sgt	**Weetman J A**
37974	Pte	**Wenlock W** 23rd Bn
22/1683	Pte	**Wilkinson A W**
240629	Sgt	**Wilkinson T** 22nd Bn
21/642	Lcpl	**Williams J W**
39228	Sgt	**Williams S** 20th Bn
20/958	Pte	**Willis G E**
22/1287	Sgt	**Willis W**
23/514	A/Sgt	**Wilson H**
20/290	Sgt	**Wilson J** Piper
23/1308	Cpl	**Young M**
23/1217	Pte	**Young W**

FOREIGN DECORATIONS

CROIX DE GEURRE (Belgium)
22/1492	Pte	**Kenney J**
22/216	Sgt	**McCourt J** MM

CROIX DE GEURRE (France)
22/1670	Cpl	**Fairholm J** MM

MEDAL MILITAIRE (France)
20/1321	Sgt	**Lamb V** with 1st Bn
39228	Sgt	**Williams S** MM 20th Bn

23/1217	Cpl	**Young W**

BRONZE MEDAL FOR VALOUR (Italy)
21/549	Lcpl	**Cowan G E** DCM with 11th Bn
20/1563	Cpl	**Easton T** DCM

CROSS OF ST GEORGE 4th Class (Russia)
23/678	Pte	**Mattison C** MM

MERITORIOUS SERVICE MEDAL
31973	CSM	**Driscoll B** 22nd Bn
22/314	Sgt	**Middlemiss W A** MM
21/1702	Sgt	**Slater T** MM
22/48	CQMS	**Taylor J C**
22/629	CQMS	**Taylor W H**
21/1107	RQMS	**Todd H A** with 14th Bn
23/415	Pte	**Watson H H**

MENTION IN DESPATCHES

21/612	Cpl	**Angus J**
23/289	Sgt	**Beldon J R**
38592	Lcpl	**Blackmore W** 20th BN
37310	Sgt	**Brown R** MM & Bar 20th BN
23/1587	Sgt	**Byford G**
22/1191	Lcpl	**Dugdale J**
23/672	CQMS	**Doman W T**
20/1563	Sgt	**Easton T** DCM
20/9	Sgt	**Goodall D**
264001	RSM	**Grice J** 22nd BN
20/412	Pte	**Hamilton R**
20/176	Sgt	**Hay J N**
21/763	Pte	**Hedley W**
21/993	CSM	**Henderson R C** DCM
22/956	Pte	**Hethrington J W** with 2nd BN
22/1102	Sgt	**Johnson R E**
22/216	Sgt	**McCourt J** MM twice*
23/45	RSM	**Morgan W G**
59287	Pte	**Nichols P** 22nd BN
22/688	RQMS	**Parker W**
23/1231	Sgt	**Richardson A F**
20/638	Sgt	**Robson I**
22/889	Sgt	**Robson J**
20/896	Sgt	**Robson W**
22/94	Cpl	**Todd T T**
23/39	Sgt	**Turnbull W**
21/881	Lcpl	**Winter R** with 10th Bn

34TH DIVISIONAL CARDS OF HONOUR

20/21	Sgt	**Bestford G**
20116	Pte	**Dransfield** 23rd Bn
3375	Pte	**Howes** 23rd Bn
21/1566	Pte	**Morgan F** MM
315443	Pte	**Stafford T** MM 20th Bn
20/687	Cpl	**Walton T**

Appendix I

SOME PHYSICAL DEFECTS MET WITH IN THE RAISING OF AN ARMY

By

Sir Thomas Oliver MD Glasg, FRCP Lond.

Hon Colonel 20th (Tyneside Scottish) Northumberland Fusiliers

Above: Sir Thomas Oliver MD Glasg, FRCP Lond.Hon Colonel 20th (Tyneside Scottish) Northumberland Fusiliers

THE PRESENT CRISIS has given some of us the opportunity of coming into direct contact with large numbers of men drawn from various social grades and forms of human activity eager to join the ranks and serve their country. As it is more than likely that many men will yet be required for the army my remarks are not altogether uncalled for. As regards recruiting Newcastle and Tyneside have done well.

Between 40,000 and 50,000 men have been given to the Navy and the Army from this district alone. Until the end of December the Northumberland miners had alone contributed 12,059 men; 31.1 per cent of the men in this district between the ages of 18 and 38 have enlisted.

My own experience of the subjects later to be dealt with has been gained during the raising of the Tyneside Scottish Brigade. With the assistance of a local committee we succeeded in raising four battalions each of 1100 men, in the short space of 22 days. The recruits have been drawn mostly from artisan and labouring classes.

Only a few men have been clerks or shop assistants. Most of them have worked in shipyards, iron works and coal-mines. When Lord Kitchener invited us to raise one battalion of Tyneside Scottish he gave permission for men to be taken up to the age of 45 instead of 38. At the time, this extension of the age-period was a concession of some assistance to us in getting men, who were seasoned and looked at life more seriously than those of younger years Unless however, careful discrimination is made it is a question whether such a concession is an unmixed benefit. Local industries and their effects upon men must be considered. Many of the industries of Tyneside make heavy demands upon the physique and enduring powers of the men. They differ from the textile industries and some of the occupations of large towns, in so far as they stimulate development in early manhood they are hard and somewhat exhausting; they tend to cause premature decay, or at least unfitness to undertake hard muscular work in any other direction than that for which their daily work of 20 to 25 years has trained them. These men can go on doing their ordinary work after the age of 45 quite well, but is another thing to take them to another kind of work which makes new and engrossing demands upon them, since much of the elasticity of their tissues is gone, and with it the readiness to adapt themselves to other conditions of life and labour.

The number of men thus rejected as unfit for military purposes is considerable. It is 30 per cent. It was therefore with knowledge of these facts, based upon experience, that I concurred with General Ternan, Brigadier of the Tyneside Scottish, when he suggested that for men about to be enlisted for foreign service it would be better to make the maximum age 38 instead of 45. One of the advantages of having older men in a battalion is that in the billets they exercise an influence for good upon the younger men. They steady their juniors but in long distance marching 17-20 miles twice a week and in regular systematic drill the seniors are more apt to break down. Much of the breakdown would be avoided if the training was gradual and not so accelerated. I cannot be too insistent upon this point.

The disparaging remarks I have made in regard to age and fitness only apply to men who have been exposed to hard physical work, for there are many men who either at, or immediately beyond the age of 45 are just as good physically as, and who can probably endure more than men of 25, but they have been drawn from work which has not caused such severe physical strain as the occupations I have referred to. This applies for example to the men of the 'Scottish Horse' (Lord Tullibardine's) and to 'Lovat's Scouts,'who have been drawn mostly from the agricultural classes. The extended age limit, therefore, is a concession to be made use of in the case of well preserved men whose occupations have not aged them, also where men are required for home defence, and who in this country could probably be transported without great difficulty.

It is interesting to see how the previous occupation of the men has helped them as soldiers. Joiners, carpenters and builders' labourers have been most useful to the brigade in preparing the ground and in erecting the huts in Alnwick Park. Miners, for example have shown themselves to be extremely capable of making trenches. Military training however, soon finds out the weak spots in a man's body, and this leads me to speak especially of coal-miners who as a class suffer much from fractures of bone in close proximity to their joints. Miners who have followed their vocation for many years, working for the greater part of the shift in a stooping position become weak in the knees. They suffer very frequently, too from displaced cartilage of the knee joint. Dr E Napier Burnett found that the feet of middle-aged colliers 40 to 45 years of age readily gave way during military training owing to pain and thickening of the metatarso-phalangeal joint of the great toe.

Complaints are numerous all over the country as to the manner in which the medical examination of recruits has been made. There is not the least doubt that the examinations have not been so systematically and carefully carried out as they ought to have been. This may partly have been owing to the great rush of recruits, but allowing for this there have been such glaring physical defects and deformities overlooked by the doctors that clearly only the most cursory medical examination could have been made. There is no excuse for examiners having passed men total blind in one eye from cataract, men who have lost the index finger of the right hand, who have lost two fingers of the left hand or two toes, who have hernia, haemorrhoids, large and readily varicose veins, who are flat footed, or who are the subjects of advanced heart or lung disease. Here is an illustration.

A private, aged 30, who had been training in the south of England, consulted me as he had been discharged from the army as being physically unfit. The man could hardly walk across the floor of my consulting room without experiencing great dyspnoea. His feet and legs were swollen. On exposing the chest the apex of the heart could be readily seen and felt beating 2 inches below and external to the left nipple. On auscultation a loud rough systolic murmur could be heard which the merest tyro in medicine could have detected. The cardiac murmur must have been there at the date of examination for within four weeks after joining his battalion this man had made his first route march of 14 miles with a 20 minute break mid-way. On that occasion it took him all his time to walk into the camp. Shortness of breath developed the same evening or during the next day, and in five days afterwards he was discharged as unfit for military service. This case does not stand by any means alone in other instances the men had not been stripped sufficiently, otherwise paralysed shoulders and paralysed muscles of arms and forearms would be detected.

The number of men who have been allowed to pass into the army with flat feet and hammer toes is almost incredible.

The object of my remarks is as much as anything to draw the attention of medical examiners to the necessity of exercising greater than many of them have been doing. Apart from the expense, it lightens the work of future administration. Carelessness on the part of medical examiners has been evident in such a large number of instances that by permitting physically defective men to be attested, fed, uniformed and drilled, who are obliged to be discharged a few days or weeks after attestation, considerable expense has been incurred to the country, disappointment caused to the rejected men and through them returning home dissatisfied further recruitment has been made more difficult. It is estimated that the attestation along with the bonus, the clothing, feeding and subsequent discharge of those unfit for military service has cost the country nearly £2,000,000.

As regards the state of the teeth of recruits, the War Office has made valuable concessions. Bad teeth are so frequently met with among working men that it was clear unless something was done in regard thereto many men otherwise physically fit were being lost to their countryís service. Free dental treatment at dental hospitals was a step in the right direction. So far as the Tyneside Scottish battalions are concerned, the arrangement with the hospital worked satisfactorily. The work at the hospital was restricted at first to the extraction, with or without local anaesthesia as the patient preferred, and to fillings. Dentures were subsequently allowed, but these were only given to men of good character and of good physique, men who were likely to appreciate the gift. One drawback to supplying artificial teeth is that if a man at the front is dissatisfied or has a grievance he may throw his dentures away, and, pleading inability to masticate food, he may, when he can ill be spared have to be sent home.

The importance of testing the eyesight goes without saying, and yet in regard to this there have been several instances of men having been attested with very grave visual defects. Very interesting information has been gained in Newcastle in regard to this subject of eyesight. A large number of our recruits have been drawn from the mining population. It is difficult to give the percentage, but in some of the miners form 60 to 70 percent of the men. We were hardly prepared for the large number of cases of nystagmus which developed in the men after they had been in billets for several days or a few weeks. Sometimes the nystagmus has been the most pronounced type. There is nothing to indicate that the oscillatory condition of the eyeballs was always present at the primary medical condition examination. It might have developed as the men passed longer time in the daylight than their work previously allowed them. This however, cannot be the explanation otherwise nystagmus would ere this have developed during minersí strikes. So pronounced has been the nystagmus in some of the men, and so deficient their power of vision, that serious accidents have arisen. Many of the men who are the subjects of it have great difficulty in seeing clearly at the time daylight passes in to twilight. In one instance a recruit walked into a plate-glass window of a shop. He did not know that he had reached the window. Where nysagmus has been well developed none of the men improved rapidly enough under observation and treatment to be retained; they had therefore, to be dismissed. Where the defect was slight some of the men have been kept for lower forms of administrative work. Nystagmus is a disqualification for military service. The subjects of it cannot even undertake the ordinary physical drills since the rapid movements required, including those of rotation of head and body aggravate any nystagmus that maybe present. Since in many of the men who are affected with it in the right eye is worse than the left, the men can only shoot from the left shoulder. Without expressing an opinion as to the disability of associating such men in the trenches and elsewhere with those who fire from the right shoulder, a far more serious aspect of the question relates to sentry duty. As already stated, it is just as evening approaches, when the daylight is fading, that the vision of these men is worst. A sentinel on duty thus affected might, therefore, not through carelessness but disease, endanger not only the lives of the men of a whole battalion but wreck the chances of our troops at a critical moment through not observing the approach of the enemy. I am led to believe that the high percentage of nystagmus met with among North Country coal miners does not equally prevail in those drawn from other parts of the country.

Albuminuria has been found in a small percentage of otherwise apparently healthy recruits after hard physical drill and long route marching.

The small amount of venereal disease among the men of the Tyneside Scottish battalions has been a cause of congratulation. Dr N Maclay, who as civil surgeon was in charge for a time of one of the battalions, informs me that it has not been more than one to two per cent. A similar remark applies to crime. It is only right to say considering the fact that in Newcastle and district we had a few months ago upwards of 100,000 soldiers suddenly implanted in our midst, that the amount of crime has been extremely small.

As regards inoculation for Typhoid fever, the Tyneside Scottish raised no difficulty. Some of the battalions were done to a man without any dissent. At one stage of the proceedings it was thought the preventive measure ran the risk of receiving a check as one of the men died shortly after the inoculation, but fortunately, although the civil medical practitioner who had attended the patient gave a certificate that death was due to (1) typhoid inoculation, (2) pneumonia and heart failure, the necropsy revealed heart disease of long standing, chronic pleurisy, and an alcoholic liver.

Appendix II

NOMINAL ROLL OF OFFICERS WHO SERVED WITH THE TYNESIDE SCOTTISH BRIGADE

Number on Roll **695**; Killed or Died of Wounds **151**; known Wounded, Gassed, Sick **168**:
Total known casualties **319** (45.8 per cent)

SURNAME	FORENAMES	BN	RANK	DECORATION	WOUNDED	KILLED DIE	MEMORIAL/C	REMARKS
Acklom	Spencer	22	Mjr 22/5/16	DSO+Bar,MC.Mid 13/11/1		21/02/18	Arras Memorial	Age 44. From HLI, 2nd in CO 22Bn from 22/5/16. Became CO 2/7/16 on Death of Lt-Col Elphinstone.
Adams	JH	21	2/Lt 21/12/14	Mid 9/4/17				Arrives 21Bn 17/7/16 as A/Cap. Seniority backdated
Adamson	Charles Young	23	Hon-Lt 21/12/14			17/09/18	Karasouli Military Cemetery, Greece	Qm 23Bn 21/12/14 to 15/3/15. To 29Bn 24/9/15 as Qm then 87 TRB. Killed with 8Bn RSF in Salonica
Ainsworth	FR	22	2/Lt 28/11/17					Joins for duty 22/4/18. Posted from battalion 18/5/18
Alexander	Thomas	23	2/Lt 26/4/17					To 8Bn 1918. Relinquished commission on completion of service 9/12/20
Alexander	Utrick	22	2/Lt 6/1/15	MC				22Bn To 29Bn 3/9/15. MC won 10th Bn Italy.Relinquished commission due to ill-health caused by wounds 18/6/20
Algie	William	23	2/Lt 28/6/16	DSO,AFC,Mid 9/4/17 +1				Formerly Cpl 4th Dragoon Guards. To RFC (Flying Officer-Observer) 21/4/17
Allen	Arnold Morley	22	2/Lt 23/7/15	MC+Bar	15/4/18			To 22Bn gaz 3/8/16. Relinquished commission 14/9/20
Ambler	John James	20	2/Lt 27/8/17					
Amos	Herbert Hutton	22	2/Lt 10/12/14		22/6/16			Wounded by own gas 22/6/16. To 85 TRB 14/12/16. Relinquished commission on completion of service 1/9/21
Anderson	CS	22	2/Lt 30/5/15		21/3/18			Relinquished commission to resume medical studies 19/5/18
Anderson	HW	23	2/Lt 27/8/17					From Bn March 1918. Relinquished commission on completion of service 2/3/19
Anderson	Kenneth Arthur Noel	23	2/Lt 20/9/11	MC	1/7/16			From Seaforth Highlanders. Adjutant 24/12/15-4/7/16. Returns to Seaforth Highlanders 1/10/16
Anderson	Thomas Alexander	23	Cap 27/2/15	1914 Aisine.				Formally L/Sgt 4919 Scots Gds. Enlisted 27/6/03. Arrested drunk 7/3/16. Courts martial 20/3/16 (Repremanded). Dismiss
Andrew	John James	20	2Lt 13/2/17			29/04/17	Etaples Military Cemetery	Age 22. Formally L/Cpl A&SH
Angus	MS	22	Cap 22/4/18					Joined for duty 22/4/18 from ASC
Applegarth	JG	22	2/Lt 31/10/17					Joined for duty 16/1/18. Transferred to base depot B.E.F. 17/6/18
Arkle	Norman Armitage	20	2Lt 18/12/14			01/07/16	Thiepval Memorial	Age 21.
Armatage	Robert	21	2Lt 1/3/17			06/07/17	Aubigny Communal Cemetery Exten	Age 25
Armstrong	Harold	21	2Lt 2/6/16			14/11/16	Thiepval Memorial	28Bn to 21Bn gaz 21/7/16
Arnott	Spencer Lumsden	23	2Lt 24/11/14					OC of 'C' Co 22/12/14. 'E' Co 10/3/15-24/7/15. 23Bn to 29Bn 3/9/15. To 2nd Garrison Bn 2/10/15
Arthur	Alexander	21	2Lt 1/8/17	MC,MM		01/10/18	Bucquoy Road Cemetery	Formally Pte 1730. To 25Bn (2nd Tyneside Irish 1918). MC won att 2/7 Liverpool Regt.
Ashley	Claude	22	2Lt 20/7/15			01/07/16	Thiepval Memorial	15Bn to 22nd gaz 1/8/16
Ashworth	Fred	23	2Lt 13/2/17			10/04/17	Haute-Avesnes British Cemetery	Age 20. Formally L/Cpl Grenadier Guards
Atkinson	George William	22	2/Lt 3/12/14		1/7/16			Posted from battalion 18/5/18. Relinquished commission on completion of service 1/9/21
Audus	Stanley Newlove	29	2/Lt 10/11/15					Relinquished Commission 31/5/16
Babbitt	Monte	22	2/Lt 30/5/17	MC				Relinquished commission on completion of service 15/4/19
Baccus	Fred	23	2/Lt 27/6/17					24Bn to 23Bn 1918. Relinquished commission due to ill-health 1/6/19
Bacon	GD	22	2Lt 26/2/18					
Bailey	FA	23	2/Lt 31/10/17					
Baillie	George	21	2Lt 16/4/17			05/06/17	Arras Memorial	Formally L/Cpl Scots Guards
Bainbridge	Thomas Emery	21	2Lt 23/10/15			09/04/17	Roclincourt Valley Cemetery	29Bn to 21Bn gaz 3/8/16. Temp att 20Bn 7-13/11/16
Baldwin	PJ	20	2Lt 31/10/17		12/4/18			20Bn to 22Bn 1918
Banks	William Stephen	20	2Lt 26/4/17					To 20Bn 21/9/17. From Bn March 1918. Relinquished commission on completion of service 9/4/19
Bateson	WV	22	2Lt 28/11/17					Joins for duty 22/4/18. Posted from battalion 18/5/18
Baty	Reginald Elphinstone	21	2/Lt 19/9/16	MC				Formerly corporal NF. Reported for duty 19/9/16. MC won for raid on enemy position 7/3/17. Transferred to RFC 1918
Baynes	Vernon	21	2Lt 21/6/16		1/7/16			Formally Cpl 3709 28Bn London Regt. To 84th TRB 1/9/16 as A/Lt. To 14th Bn 10/1/17. To 27Bn 21/12/17. Later 24th Bn. R
Beales	George Ninian	22	2Lt 26/9/17			21/03/18	Arras Memorial	3rd(R)Bn (att'd) 22Bn. Also att'd 20Bn
Beardsall	Wilfred Charles	22	2/Lt 7/1/15		1/7/16			Relinquished commission due to wounds 7/2/18
Beaton	PF	21	2Lt 21/10/15		7/6/17			Com 5Bn. Att 21Bn from 3(R)Bn 1917
Beaumont	Reginald Clare	22	2Lt 16/11/14		6/17			To Reg Bn 8/11/17
Beck	JE	21	2Lt 1/8/17					21Bn to 23Bn 1918
Becke	AH	20	2Lt 1/8/17	MC				To 9Bn 1918 where won MC
Begg	Alexander James Bartlet	22	2Lt 30/7/15	MC	17/9/16	21/03/18	Arras Memorial	Age 21. 23 to 29Bn 1/11/15. To 22Bn gaz 3/8/16. To TRB 4/5/17. To 22Bn from Labour Corps 3/9/17.
Bell	EW	20	2Lt 26/4/17					
Bell	Fredrick Vincent	21	2Lt 1/2/15					To General List of Officers
Bell	Percy Reay	21	2Lt 12/2/15					
Bell	WS	21	2Lt 26/4/17					To 12Bn 1918
Bentley	C	23	2Lt 28/11/17					To MGC
Bibby	David Houghton	22	2Lt 18/11/14		1/7/16,21/3/1	13/04/18	Ploegsteert Memorial, Belgium	Temp Att 21Bn 12/6/16-7/9/16. Rejoins from hospital 1/4/18
Bickerton	Percy	20	2Lt 29/12/14					To MGC 22/11/15
Binet	Francis	21	2Lt 20/1/16		1/7/16			29Bn to 21Bn gaz 3/8/16 on probation.Confirmed in rank 6/9/16. To 85th TRB 5/4/17. Relinquished commission due to woun
Binns	Clement Stanley	21	2Lt 5/5/15			01/07/16	Thiepval Memorial	
Birkett	Arnold Miles	20	2/Lt 23/6/16		28/4/17			29Bn to 33Bn 23/6/16. To 20Bn gaz 11/11/16. To Reg Bn 27/1/18. Labour Corps 4/1/19
Black	John Gavin	20	2/Lt 26/4/17		9/9/17			Reg Bn to 20Bn 1917. 20Bn to 22Bn 22/4/18. To England sick 21/11/18
Black	RE	20	2/Lt 6/7/16					7Bn to 20Bn Oct 1916. Returns to 7Bn June 1917
Blackford	LL	20	2Lt 28/3/17					3rd(R) att 20Bn 1918
Blackford	LL	20	2Lt 28/3/17					From 3(R)Bn att 20Bn 1917

Blair-Imrie	HF	21	Lt-Col		28/7/16			CO 21Bn 13/7/16-28/7/16. To 23 CCS. Relinquished command wounded 28/7/16
Bleasdale	JW	21	2/Lt 26/4/17					Reg Bn att 21Bn 1918
Blenkin	Fred	22	2/Lt 26/5/16					From Artists Rifles O.T.C. From 31Bn to 28Bn gaz 24/8/16. Joned 22Bn 17/11/16
Blenkinsop	William	21	2/Lt 1/8/17	MC				To Reg Bn (SEP) 1918
Bloomfield	RG	20	2/Lt 27/6/17		11/9/17			3(R)Bn att 20Bn 1917
Bolton	Henry Albert	23	2Lt 14/12/14			01/07/16	Thiepval Memorial	Age 22.
Bonner	WG	22	2Lt 1/5/18					Joined for duty 5/10/18
Borland	G McP	20	2/Lt 27/6/17					3(R)Bn att 20Bn 1918
Borradale	JF	21	2/Lt 1/3/17					Com 4Bn . Att 21Bn from 1Bn 1917
Boughton	Jack Leonard	20	2/Lt 1/8/17	MC	29/12/17			3rd(R) att 20Bn 1918. Relinquished commission 1/4/20
Bourne	Warren James	21	2/Lt 13/1/15		1/7/16			25Bn to 30Bn 10/1/16. Joins 21Bn for duty 14/3/16
Bowkett	Edmund Farmaner	21	2/Lt 3/7/15					21Bn to 29Bn 3/9/15. TMB Officer June 1916
Bowman	WL	23	2/Lt 31/10/17					
Bowmer	John Simpson	21	2/Lt 31/10/17	MC				Formally L/Cpl 16/359. To 25Bn where MC won
Bowran	John Morgan	23	2/Lt 25/10/16					Com Reg Bn (att)
Boyd	W	23	2/Lt 31/10/17					
Bradnum	Arthur	22	2/Lt 26/4/17		26/8/17			Relinquished commission on completion of service 1/9/21
Bramwell	George Heron	29	2/Lt 19/10/15					29Bn then 84TRB 1/9/16
Broatch	Percy	23	2/Lt 3/6/16	MC				From Innes of Court OTC to 32nd Bn. To 23Bn gaz 24/8/16. Employed Ministry of munitions 1918
Brough	Peter Hillary Lloyd	20	2/Lt 16/5/15	MiD 9/4/17,31/3/19				27Bn to 30Bn 22/10/15.24Bn gaz 3/8/16. 20Bn 14/10/17. 23Bn (Apr)1918. Brigade Intelligence Officer. Relinquished commi
Brounger	William Henry Prescott	22	2Lt 5/8/16			09/04/17	Roclincourt Valley Cemetery	29Bn to 22Bn joined for duty 21/9/16
Brown	George Arthur	22	2/Lt 23/2/17	MC				A/Cap 13/11/17-21/11/17. Relinquished commission 14/9/20
Brown	HC	20	2/Lt 1/8/17					From Bn March 1918Relinquished commision 11/10/19 on completion of service
Brown	JC	21	2/Lt 1/8/17					From Bn (Sep) 1918
Brown	William	21	2/Lt 16/2/15					21Bn to 29Bn 3/9/15. 33Bn 1/6/16. 22Bn 2/7/16 as Lt 2/7/16
Brown	William Barrowclough	20	2/Lt 12/11/14					20Bn to 29Bn 18/12/15. From Bn 1/9/16
Brown	Sutherland	22	2/Lt 4/12/14					To 29Bn 3/9/16. To 16Bn 22/6/16
Browning	Reginald Arthur	20	2Lt 23/11/15	MC		10/04/17	Haute-Avesnes British Cemetery	From 15Bn to 20Bn gaz 24/8/16
Bryson	John	21	2Lt 26/4/17			14/10/17	Solferino Farm Cemetery, Belgium	Fatally wounded when Redan camp bombed by German Gotha bombers.
Buck	George Cecil	22	2/Lt 14/11/14					To 29Bn 3/9/15. Relinquished commission 10/5/16
Buckley	HH	23	2/Lt 1/8/17	DCM	16/10/17			Relinquished commision due to wounds 29/10/18
Bull	H	21	2/Lt 31/10/17					To 25th Bn
Bulman	CR	21	2/Lt 19/3/16		5/6/16			Formerly L/Cpl in Hampshire Regt. Relinquished commission due to wounds 21/8/17
Burge	Montague	23	Mjr 9/11/15			01/07/16	Thiepval Memorial	Formerlly 3rd Hussars. From reserve of Officers List to 23Bn as 2nd in Command 9/11/15
Burman	J	20	2/Lt 26/4/17		31/8/17			To Reg Bn MAR 1918
Burn	James	23	2Lt 1/8/17			17/10/17	Cement House Cem	Killed by shelling at Kortebeck farm
Burt	GA	22	2/Lt 20/12/15		9/4/17			6Bn to 1Bn. To 22Bn (att) 10/10/16. Returns to 6Bn 1917, Relinquished commission due to ill-health 30/5/18
Burt	W	20	2/Lt 31/10/17					Relinquished commision due to ill-health 16/6/18
Busbridge	GG	22	Lt 23/3/16					3rd(R) att 22Bn 1918. Posted from Bn 18/5/18
Buscke	George Hamilton	21	2/Lt 8/3/15					To MGC 22/11/15
Bushridge	GS	22	Lt					Joined for duty 22/4/18
Calder	E	21	2/Lt 1/8/17					To 25Bn 1918
Calkin	John Ernest	22	2Lt 26/5/16		9/4/17	09/04/17	Roclincourt Valley Cemetery	Artists Rifles O.T.C. From 32nd Bn to 22Bn 24/8/16
Calvert	FW	22	2Lt1/5/18					Joined for duty 3/10/18
Campbell	Colin	21	2/Lt 5/2/15		1/7/16			To ASC 10/3/16. Relinquished commission on completion of service 6/3/20
Campbell	Ian Stuart	23	2Lt 14/12/14			30/06/16	Thiepval Memorial	Age 21. Enlisted 16Bn Aug 1914.Seen lying in no Man's land. Uncofirmed report buried near Albert
Campbell	John Charles	23	Cap					First CO of 23Bn from 27/11/14 until 1/9/15. From 5th Bttln Royal Irish Regt
Campbell	RTO	22	2Lt 30/1/18					Joined for duty 3/10/18
Carr	Alfred Ernest	22	2/Lt 18/11/14					To 29Bn 3/9/15. From Bn 1/9/16. Draft conducting Officer 5/5/17
Carr	R	23	2/Lt 27/4/17		14/10/17			Relinquished commision due to ill-health 31/8/18
Carson	B	22	2Lt					Joined for duty 22/4/18
Carswell	James	23	2/Lt 1/3/17	MC				Reg Bn to 23Bn 1918. MC won 1st Bn
Carter	Arthur Earnest	22	2/Lt 26/5/16					From Artists Rifles O.T.C. From 31Bn to 22Bn gaz 24/8/16. Rejoins 24/11/18. Relinquished commission on completion of s
Casse	JB	21	2/Lt 31/10/17					To Reg Bn (Sep) 1918
Catling	EWC	29	2/Lt 24/7/15					To 29Bn from South Staffs. Regt. 10/5/16. From Bn 1/9/16. Relinquished commission (wounds) 28/2/17. Re-employed RFC eq
Catto	William Basil	23	2Lt 3/11/15			11/09/16	Erquinghem-Lys Churchyard Extensi	Age 21. Enlisted London Scottish shortly after outbreak of war. Temp att 21Bn 11/6/16-
Chalmers	John Cyril	20	2Lt 19/9/16	MM		15/10/16	Erquinghem-Lys Churchyard Extensi	Age 24. Formerly Co.Sgt.Mjr with the Cameron Highlanders.
Chapman	John William	20	2/Lt 26/4/17		9/9/17			Formally Pte 12193 'B' Co 9Bn NF. From Bn (March) 1918
Charlton	George	23	2/Lt 23/11/14	Mid 7/11/17				A/Lt-col 23Bn 2/11/17-28/1/18 when confirmed as CO 23Bn. Relinquished commission on completion of service 3/4/19
Charlton	John Macfarlan	21	2Lt 11/11/14	Mid 13/11/17		01/07/16	Thiepval Memorial	B 1/7/1891.Uppingham Cadet corps, N'land Yeo Oct 14.21Bn Div HQ Transport Officer.Brother Hugh kia 7th Bn 24/6/16.
Charlton	Thomas	20	2/Lt 26/4/17		9/9/17			To Reg Bn (Mar) 1918
Clark	GL	22	CAP 26/4/18					Joined for duty 25/6/18
Clarke	FP	20	2/Lt 27/8/17	DCM, C.D.G				Formally Pte 16/1112 16Bn NF(Commercials)
Close	HDS	23	2/Lt 26/4/17					To Labour Corps 3/7/17
Coates	Frederick Noel	22	2Lt 18/9/15		3/4/17	04/04/17	Faubourg D'Amiens Cemetery, Arras	Age 23. 16Bn to 31Bn 5/2/16. 22Bn 24/8/16.
Cocks	BA	21	2/Lt 28/3/17					Joined for duty from 24/27Bn 8/17 after term in hospital
Cogan	CTS	22	Cap 17/12/14					Joined 22Bn froM 18Bn 19/3/18
Cole	WRT	20	2/Lt 12/12/17					Reg Bn att 20Bn 1918
Coleman	Arthur	20	2Lt 14/6/15			01/07/16	Thiepval Memorial	Age 24.Commisioned 14/6/15 in 27th Bn. To 30th Bn 27/12/15.To 20Bn 22/6/16.
Collings	John Lawrence	23	2/Lt 18/3/15					Relinquished commission on nomination to RMC 23/1/17
Collings	William Norman	23	2Lt 19/5/15			06/10/18	Prospect Hill Cemetery	To 2Bn 2/12/17.
Common	John Edward	23	2/Lt 14/6/15	MC	11/4/17			From 15Bn to 23Bn gaz 3/8/16. From Bn 1917. 52Bn 1920. Relinquished commission 8/8/20
Connolly	Thomas Philip	20	2/Lt 7/6/15		1/7/16			Commissioned 7/6/15 in 27th Bn. To 30th Bn 13/1/16. To 20Bn 22/6/16. From Bn 19/3/18. 51Bn 1920
Constable	C	20	2/Lt 31/10/17					20Bn to 22Bn 1918
Constantine	Frank Iveson	22	2Lt 31/10/17			20/08/18	Bagneax British Cemetary, Gezainco	Age 23.
Cook	A	21	2/Lt 26/4/17		11/9/17			
Cook	AL	23	Cap 21/6/17					10th Bn to 23Bn 6/4/18. Relinquished commission on completion of service 1/9/21.
Cook	Edward Brown	20	2/Lt 8/10/15					Commissioned in 29Bn. To 20th gaz 3/8/16. To 80TRB 13/12/16 as A/Lt.
Cook-Watson	Sydney Cameron	20	2/Lt 26/4/15	MC	1/7/16.6/17			Enlisted Lanc Hussars on outbreak of war.TMB Officer 30/5/16. To 88TRB 20/10/17. Relinquished commission on completion
Cooper	Charles Richard	22	2/Lt 26/5/16		17/11/17			From Artists Rifles O.T.C. to 31Bn. Joins 22Bn for duty 28/10/16. Relinquished commission 19/4/20
Cope	George Edward	20	2Lt 5/4/15			01/07/16	Thiepval Memorial	Age 18.
Corke	Guy Harold	22	2Lt 9/1/15			17/09/16	Delville Wood, Longeval	15Bn (att) 22Bn
Corlett	Cyril Norman	21	2/Lt 2/6/16		9/4/17			Innes of Court OTC to 28Bn Joins 21Bn for duty 17/10/16. Relinquished commission due to wounds 16/1/18
Cosgrove	Albert Bruce	22	2Lt 9/4/15			31/05/16	Franvillers Communal Cemetery	Age 24.
Coull	Thomson Bankhead	20	Lt 9/11/14	Mid 13/11/17				20Bn to 23Bn as Cap 13/3/15. OC 'E' Co 24/7/15. From Bn 1917. Relinquished commission on completion of service 2/2/21.
Court	GR	22	2Lt 1/5/18					Joined for duty 3/10/18
Cowan	Douglas	20	2/Lt 1/8/17					To 53Bn (YS) NF 1918
Coward	S	21	2/Lt 29/12/15					6Bn att 21Bn joined for duty 10/10/16. Temp att 20Bn 7-13/11/16. To 6Bn 1917
Cowden	WA	22	2/Lt 26/4/17		11/19/17			
Cowley	Cecil	23	Lt 13/5/16	MC				Joined for duty 18/7/16 from 25th Bn. Enlisted 24Bn. Relinquished commission due to ill-health 15/9/18
Cowper	Leonard Harris	20	2Lt 3/6/16			07/11/16	Trois Arbres Cemetery, Steenwerck	From Artists Rifles OTC to 32nd Bn. To 20th from 32nd Bn 14/9/16
Cox	Edward Richard	23	2/Lt 7/7/16		3/17			Cadet Commissioned 7/7/16 on probation. To 23Bn gaz 17/10/16. relinquished commission due to ill-health 11/5/18.
Coxon	William Basil	23	2/Lt 19/12/16					26Bn to 23Bn 1918
Coyne	Patrick Sterling	23	2/Lt 23/6/16					Innes of Court OTC to 32Bn. To 23Bn gaz 18/9/16. To Labour Corps 28/11/17
Crabbe	Charles Henry	21	2/Lt 6/1/16					On probation 6/1/16 29Bn. Joines 21Bn for duty 17/7/16. Confirmed in rank 6/10/16. Relinquished commission on completi
Cree	James Fleming	22	2Lt 20/1/18			03/09/18	Sally-Labourne Communal Cemetery	Age 23. OTU to 3rd(R)Bn. (att) 22Bn 25/6/18. KIA on daylight patrol.
Crees	HV	22	2/Lt 26/4/17	Mid 5/7/19				Transferred to base depot B.E.F. 17/6/18. Relinquished commission on completion of service 16/10/19
Creighton	G	22	2Lt 30/1/18					Joined for duty 25/6/18 from 3(R)
Crichton	Thomas Smith	20	2/Lt 7/5/15					20Bn To 29Bn 7/1/16. From 29Bn to 18Bn 22/6/16
Cubey	Joseph Berkeley	23	2Lt 14/12/14			01/07/16	Ovillers Military Cemetery	Age 32. 'A' Company CO. Killed by machine gun bulletts before he had advanced 100yrds.
Curd	Christopher Walter	20	2/Lt 1/1/16					Cadet on probation. To 20Bn gaz 24/8/16. A/Cap 13/9/16 to 11/10/16 as Company CO. Confirmed in rank 6/10/16. to comman
Curdle	Thomas William	21	2/Lt 20/1/16					84th TRB 1/9/16 as A/Lt
Curry	AC	21	2Lt					Joins for duty 16/12/16
Curry	Arthur Vincent	21	2/Lt 10/11/14		1/7/16,6/17,7/4/17			Concussion wound from shelling 7/4/17. Brother Cap W.P. Curry.
Curry	William Parkinson	20	Lt 9/11/14	MC	3/6/16			To 80TRB 20/4/17. From Bn 1/11/17. Relinquished commission due to wounds 10/4/19. Brother Cap A.V. Curry.
Curson	V	22	2/Lt 28/11/17					Posted from battalion 18/5/18
Daggett	Cedric Hunton	21	2Lt 20/3/15	MC		11/02/17	Ploegsteert Memorial	Age 27. Originall enlisted 9Bn. 21Bn To 29Bn 3/9/15. To 23Bn gaz 1/7/16. Temp att 21Bn 11/6/16-
Davidson	Norman	22	2/Lt 1/3/17					Joined for duty 10/1/18
Davidson	Roland Cooper	20	Lt 23/12/14			01/07/16	Thiepval Memorial	Age 25. Enlisted Duke of Wellington's Regt 1914
Davies	AF	22	CAP 24/2/18					Joined for duty 24/6/18 from 1Bn P.O.W. Regt.
Davies	David Robert	21	2/Lt 15/12/15		1/7/16			29Bn to 21Bn gaz 17/10/16. From Bn 22/2/18. Relinquished commission due to wounds 16/1/19
Davies	Harold Haydin	21	2/Lt 26/4/17	MC				21Bn to 23Bn 1918. MC won 21Bn for operations 8-11/9/17. relinquished commission on completion of service 6/4/19
Davies	Robert William Marengwyı	22	2Lt 3/4/15		31/5/16(Acci	06/04/17	Bois-Carre British Cemetery, Thelus	16Bn to 28Bn 3/9/16. To 31Bn 14/12/15. To 22Bn gaz 17/10/16. To RFC 13/3/17 59 SQDN
Davis	AM	20	Cap 23/7/15					Reg Bn att 20Bn 1918
Davis	FT	21	2/Lt 1/8/17					To 14Bn 1918
Davis	William	22	2/Lt 18/11/14					To MGC 18/11/16
Davison		22	2Lt					Joined for duty 24/11/18
Dawson-Scott	Cecil Edward	22	2/Lt 26/5/16		9/4/17			From Artists Rifles O.T.C. to 32nd Bn. To 22Bn 24/8/16. Relinquished commission due to ill-health 29/9/17

Dear	HF	21	2/Lt 26/4/17					
Deas	H	20	2/Lt 1/8/17					To Reg Bn (May) 1918
Decham	P	22	2/Lt 30/5/17					Joins for duty 19/9/17. To England sick 13/1/18
Deuchar	Elliot Gordon	22	2/Lt 18/11/14					Relinquished commission due to ill-health 2/12/17
Dinicott	A	23	2Lt		29/4/17			
Dobson	Harold Percy	20	2Lt 6/1/16			16/10/17	Clement House Cemetery, Langemar	On probation 6/1/16-6/9/16.To 20Bn gaz 3/8/16.
Dodd	HF	21	2/Lt 30/5/17					To 12Bn 1918. Relinquished commisson on completion of service 1/3/19
Dodd	Urwin Hunter	29	2/Lt 19/10/15	MC				29Bn to 33Bn 23/6/16. To 2Bn gax 20/10/16. MC with 2Bn. Relinquished commission on completion of service 1/9/21.
Dodds	William Henry	28	2Lt 25/10/15			06/11/16	Ration Farm Mil.Cem.	From 28Bn to 20Bn gaz 24/8/16
Dodds	WM	23	Lt 10/6/16		29/4/17			To 23Bn 6/4/17. A/Cap 17/10/18
Donaghy	WCP	21	2/Lt 2/416		9/4/17,14/10/17			Joined 21Bn for duty 22/1/17 from 102 MGCo.
Donaldson	John	20	2Lt 21/4/15			01/07/16	Thiepval Memorial	Age 28.
Dorricott	A	23	2/Lt 13/2/17					Formally L/Cpl R.Highlanders. From Bn 1918
Dorward	W	22	2/Lt 28/11/17					Joins for duty 22/4/18
Dougal	Robert Joseph	23	2Lt 15/12/14			01/07/16	Thiepval Memorial	Age 21. 23Bn to 29Bn 8/8/15. To 21Bn 22/6/16.
Douglas	JNT	23	2/Lt 26/9/16					A/Cap 20/11/17
Dower	A	21	2/Lt 13/2/17		7/6/17			Formally Cpl A&SH
Dowse	Thomas William	21	Lt.			07/09/16		RE, Brigade Signals Officer 1916. Joins 21Bn for duty 14/2/17
Dunn	Frederick Oswald	23	2Lt 12/1/15			19/03/16	Erquinghem-Lys Churchyard Extensi	Age 26. Brigade bombing officer.
Dunn	Malcolm	22	2Lt 1/8/17			09/04/18	Strand Military Cemetery, Ploegsteert	Joins for duty 2/10/17
Earl	JB	22	2Lt 1/5/18					Joined for duty 7/10/18
Edgley	JHJ	22	2/Lt 27/6/17					
Egan	JF	22	2/Lt 28/11/17		28/4/18			3rd(R) att 22Bn joins for duty 22/4/18. Relinquished commission 22/4/20
Egan	SF	23	2/Lt 28/3/17					
Elias	Hewell James	21	2Lt 7/2/17			05/06/17	Arras Road Cemetery	Age 20. Formally Pte London Regt.
Elles	Walter Lionel	28	2/Lt 1/11/15					from 28Bn to 29Bn March 1916. To 20Bn gaz 3/8/16. Relinquished commission due to ill-health 16/1/17.
Elliott	Stanley James	20	2/Lt 7/1/15					To 29Bn 7/1/16. From Bn 1/9/16. Relinquished commission due to ill-health 26/1/17
Ellis	EB	22	2/Lt 7/4/17		9/4/17			Formally R. Scots. Fus. Relinquished commission on completion of service 3/6/19
Ellis	Jack	23	2/Lt 24/12/15					From 15Bn to 23Bn gaz 3/8/16.Joins 23Bn for duty 10/10/18. relinquished commission on completion of service 14/2/19
Ellis	RW	20	2/Lt 26/3/17					Formally L/Cpl 16/707 16th Bn. Resigned commission on appointment to RAF 1/6/18
Elphinstone	Arthur Percy Archibald	22	Lt-Col 16/12/14			01/07/16	Thiepval Memorial	First CO of 22Bn. Retired Indian Army 1/9/1911. 1st Commissioned 6/2/1884.
Eve	Ray Montague	22	2/Lt 26/5/16					From Artists Rifles O.T.C
Fairley	WM	20	2/Lt 1/8/17					Reg Bn att 20Bn 1918
Falcy	Humphrey Ned	23	2Lt 2/6/16	MC		21/11/16	Erquinghem-Lys Churchyard Extensi	Age 20. 32Bn to 23Bn gaz 14/9/16. Battalion inteligence officer
Farquhar	William Alexander	20	2Lt 18/4/1900	DSO				From RSF (Mjr).Took Command 20Bn 2/7/16 on death of Lt-Col Sillery arrives 6/7/16. Returns to RSF June 1918.
Faulder	John Harvey	22	2/Lt 17/8/15		24/8/16,9/4/17			28Bn to 31Bn 14/12/15. Joined 22Bn for duty 8/16. 22Bn.Adj 27/7/17-30/11/17. Relinquished commission on completion of
Fawley	P	22	2/Lt 26/6/17	DCM				To 19Bn 1918. Relinquished commission on completion of service 1/9/21
Fenn	AM	20	2/Lt 3/4/15		6/17			16Bn to 31Bn 14/12/15. Joined 20Bn for duty 17/8/16. From Bn 27/1/18. Then Kings African Rifles.
Fentum	Clarence George	22	2/Lt 26/5/16		5/9/16,9/4/17			Artists Rifles O.T.C. to 31Bn. To 22Bn 24/8/16. Labour Corps 6/7/17. Relinquished commission 31/1/20
Firth	C	23	2/Lt 28/11/17		6/17			
Fletcher	Leonard	23	2/Lt 30/5/17	MC+Bar,MM				Formally Pte 18/1065 18Bn N'land Fus.Relinquished commission on completion of service 1/9/21.
Fletcher	William Arthur	20	2/Lt 1/3/17					To Reg Bn (Mar) 1918. Labour Corps 30/8/18
Forcer	Fred	21	2/Lt 23/2/15		30/6/16			Evacuated from trenches wounded 30/6/16. Relinquished commission on completion of service 1/9/21.
Forster	John Percival	22	Lt 18/11/14			01/07/16	Thiepval Memorial	
Foster	TV	20	Hon-Lt 14/7/17	Mid 5/7/19				QM 20Bn 14/7/17-13/1/17.To 22Bn as QM 14/1/17
Fraser	JK	21	Lt 6/2/16					7Bn to 21Bn joines for duty 10/10/16. Att 34Div HQ as temp ADC to Div Gen 26/10/16. Returns to Bn 11/1/17. To 25Bn as
Freeman	John Roland	32	2Lt 2/6/16	Mid 9/4/17	11/2/17	12/02/17	Bailleul Communal Cemetary Extensi	Innes of Court OTC to 32nd Bn. To 23Bn gaz 24/8/16
Friend	Joshua	20	2Lt 26/4/17			09/09/17	Hargicourt British Cemetery	Killed due to shelling.
Fryer	James Whaley	22	2Lt 15/12/14			01/07/16	Thiepval Memorial	15Bn to 22Bn 7/4/15.
Furse	William Henry	21	2Lt 23/9/15		2/6/16	01/07/16	Bapaume Post Military Cemetery	Age 25. Formally L/Sgt 399 1st Birmingham City Bn. Shell shock 2/6/16
Futers	Norman Ratcliffe	20	2Lt 29/11/15			27/09/18	Lowrie Cemetery, Havrincourt	Com (R)Bn. Special Reserve att 16Bn (att 11bn 19/10/17) joined for duty 20Bn 11/17
Gallen	D	21	2/Lt 1/8/17					To 25Bn 1918. Relinquished commission on completion of service 22/1/19
Gallon	RD	22	2/Lt 31/10/17		21/3/18			Joined for duty 16/1/18. Relinquished commission due to wounds 10/10/18
Gardner	Charles James H.	21	Mjr 26/10/14					From Reserve of Officers. Mjr 6th Yorkshire Rgt 26/10/14. To 21Bn 15/3/15 as 2nd CO. To Northern Commannd as Dep. Asst
Gaskin	Robert Bertram		2Lt			09/09/17	Hargicourt British Cemetery	
Gerrard	W	23	2/Lt 28/11/17					
Gibson	Arthur Douglas	22	2Lt 7/4/15		19/6/16	09/04/17	Bailleul Road East Cemetery	Joins for duty 31/5/16. To hospital wounded by British gas 19/6/16. Re-joins 4/3/17
Gibson	GM	22	2Lt 30/1/18					Joined for duty 25/6/18 from 3(R)Bn. Reported missing 5/9/18
Gibson	Harold Kenneth	22	2/Lt 7/1/15					To RFC 29/5/16
Gibson	James Hurst	21	2/Lt 17/11/14		1/7/16			Wounded 1/7/16. Returns to 21Bn 10/6/17
Gibson	Wesley Milum	20	2/Lt 7/10/15	MC+Bar				29Bn to 20Bn AUG 1916. To Reg Bn 27/1/18. Resigned commission due to wounds 17/4/18
Gilling	JE	20	2/Lt 1/8/17					3(R)Bn att 20Bn 1918
Glencross	J	22	2/Lt 26/11/15	MBE.Mid 8/11/18				Joins 22Bn on attachment from 5Bn 10/10/16. Returns 5Bn 1917
Goater	Horace Benjamin	20	Cap 5/11/14					To 29Bn 3/9/15. To 2nd (Home Service)Bn West Yorks Regt. 10/4/16
Goldthorpe	John Richard	32	2/Lt 15/1/16					OTC to 32Bn 15/1/16. To 23Bn. To Labour Corps 5/7/17
Gorrill	Douglas Gordon Sheldon	22	2/Lt 26/4/17	MC				Formally Pte 16/1344. To 22Bn 21/9/17
Gracie	John Tweddell	20	Cap 10/11/14		1/7/16.8/16			2nd in Command 1917-18. A/Lt-Col 21Bn 24/7/17-27-7-17. A/Lt-Col 20Bn 24/9/17-19/10/17. Relinquished Comm' 27/10/20
Graham	Edwin	20	Lt 26/10/14		1/7/16			To 29Bn 3/9/15. Returned to 20Bn as QM 26/2/16. Relinquished commission due to wounds 5/6/17
Graham	George Herbert	21	2/Lt 19/9/16	Mid 7/11/17				Formerlly Pte in N'Fus. Joins for duty 19/9/16. Temp att 20Bn 7-13/11/16. From Bn August 1918. To 23Bn 1919
Graham	H	29	2/Lt 14/6/15					To 29Bn 12/4/16. 84TRB 1/9/16. From Bn 17/8/17
Grant	JEM	22	2/Lt 27/6/17		20/4/18			
Grant	John Housman	22	2/Lt 26/4/17					
Greener	AS	20	2/Lt 1/7/15					1Bn att 20Bn 1918
Greer	Joseph	20	2/Lt 6/1/16		1/7/16			29Bn to 20Bn gaz 3/8/16 on probation. Confirmed in rank 6/9/16. Relinquished commission due to wounds 15/4/19
Gregg	Alfred Edwin	20	2/Lt 10/11/14					20Bn to 29Bn 3/9/15. From 29 1/9/16. Relinquished commission 23/10/20
Grice	Lawrence Victor	21	2Lt 8/11/15	Mid 9/4/17	20/8/16	13/04/18	Ploegsteert Memotial, Belgium	Joins 21Bn for duty 15/11/17
Grice	MM	23	2/Lt 31/5/15					Com 7Bn. Att 23Bn from 2Bn 1917
Grimwood	Arthur	29	2/Lt 6/1/16					On probation 6/1/16. 29Bn to 33Bn 23/6/16. 84TRB 1/9/16
Gross	LF	20	2/Lt 27/8/17					To Reg Bn (Mar) 1918
Gunn	Hugh	22	Cap 1/4/15					To 29Bn 3/9/15.
Haggerty	John Joseph	22	2Lt 7/10/15			11/09/16	Erquinghem-Lys Churchyard Extensi	Age 18. 29Bn to 22Bn gaz 3/8/16
Hall	James	29	2/Lt 23/9/15					To MGC 1/9/16
Hall	John McRobb	21	2Lt 13/1/15			01/07/16	Thiepval Memorial	
Hall	Percy George	23	2Lt 26/3/15			30/06/16	Albert Communal Cemetary Extensio	Age 23. Att to 26th Bn.CO 11platoon 'C' Company.Son of J.R.Hall of TS Committee.
Hall	William Brown	22	2Lt 7/4/15			25/08/18	Daours Communal Cemetary Extensi	From DUOTC. To ACC Jan 1916. Fatally wounded with 24Bn London Regt.
Hamilton	Thomas Cressy	23	2/Lt 21/12/14					Temp Insp of Works 29/4/17
Hammond	Kenneth Lowton Charles	23	2Lt 28/3/17			22/03/18	Arras Memorial	Reg Bn att 23Bn 1918
Hannah	WC	23	2/Lt 27/4/17		14/10/17			
Hannington	Henry	23	2/Lt 26/4/17					
Hardwick	CW	22	Lt					Joined for duty 12/5/18. Posted from Bn 18/5/18
Hardy	Charles Edwin	22	2Lt 7/7/16	Mid		13/04/18	Ploegsteert Memotial, Belgium	Formally Pte 12196 'B' Co Bn NF. Joined 22Bn for duty 21/9/16
Hardy	Frederick	21	2Lt 27/6/17			09/09/17	Hargicourt British Cemetery	Age 35. Formally Pte 13220 'B' Co 9Bn. 3rd(R)Bn att 21Bn
Hardy	H	22	Lt 17/8/17		16/4/18			From 13Bn Royal Irish Rifles
Harland	E	22	Lt 22/12/17		13/4/18			Innes of Court OTC to 22Bn, joins for duty 7/1/18
Harms	William	21	2Lt 2/6/16			04/03/17	Berles New British Cemetery	Innes of Court OTC to 28Bn. To 21Bn gaz 24/8/16. To 59 SQDN RFC
Harrison	John George	21	Lt 4/1/15		2/6/16			
Harvey	A	23	Lt 1/12/16					To 23Bn from 1st Garrison Bn 7/10/17. Adj 23/3/18.
Harvey	Duncan	23	2/Lt 27/4/17					
Hawes	Ernest Harrington	23	2Lt 19/5/15			05/06/17	Arras Memorial	Age 26. To 29Bn 1/11/15. To 20Bn Sep 1916
Hay	Henry Thomas Horatio	29	Lt-Col 10/2/16					Commissioned 23/8/1884. Retired Indian Army 24/8/11 (Lt-Col).Took over as CO of 29Bn from Col Stockley. Vacates comman
Head	Albert Everset	20	2Lt 10/11/14			01/07/16	Gordon Dump Cemetery	Age 22. Enlisted in Tyneside territorial Bn on outbreak.
Henderson	EC	21	2/Lt 1/3/17		7/6/17			Com 6Bn. Att 21Bn 1917
Henderson	James Percy	21	2Lt			11/09/17	Thiepval Memorial	Age 31. Joins for duty 8/17
Hendrie	Harry George	21	2/Lt 12/9/15					21Bn to 33Bn 1/6/16. 84TRB 1/9/16. From Bn 11/4/17
Heneker	Frederick Christian	20	2Lt 28/11/1894			01/07/16	Ovillers Military Cem.	Age 43.2nd in Com 20Bn. Took over as CO of 21Bn on 30/6/16 when Col Stuart wounded. Formerlly 2Bn Leinster Regt.
Henry	Norman Cecil	22	2/Lt 26/4/17					
Hepworth	S	23	2/Lt 24/10/15					5Bn att 23Bn 1918
Herdman	FF	21	2/Lt 26/4/17		8/17			Relinquished commission due to ill-health caused by wounds 14/2/19
Heron	Thomas Emmanuel	23	2/Lt 19/12/14	MC+Bar	4/17,6/17			23Bn to 33Bn 1/6/16. To 23Bn 2/7/16. A/Mjr & 2nd in command 6/4/18. Relinquished commission due to wounds 15/7/19
Herries	William Mills	22	2/Lt 4/1/15					2nd in Command NOV 1917. CO Base Depot Harve 8/11/17
Hersey	H	21	2/Lt 1/8/17					To 14Bn 1918
Hewitson	John	23	2Lt 26/4/17			11/11/17	Guemappe British Cemetery	Age 33.
Hill	RC	23	2/Lt 3/11/15					3(R)Bn. Serves 1Bn 4/17. att 23Bn 1918
Hill	William Leonard	21	2/Lt 12/11/14					From 21Bn 21/7/15
Hillary	A	20	2/Lt 31/10/17					From Reg Bn to 20Bn Jan 1918
Hindle	J	23	2/Lt 28/11/17	MM				To 23Bn (x/x/18)
Hoard	Henry Herbert Hoare	21	2Lt 27/6/17			09/09/17	Jeancourt Communal Cemetery Exter	OCU to 3rd(R)Bn (att) 21Bn
Hobson	George Hubert	29	2/Lt 5/8/16					84th TRB 1/9/16 as A/Lt

Hodge	MB	22	2/Lt 31/10/17		13/4/18			Joined for duty 12/1/18
Hodge	MB	22	2Lt 31/7/17					Joined for duty 24/11/18
Holloway	Leonard	28	2Lt 26/5/16			09/04/17	Arras Memorial	From Artists Rifles OTC to 28Bn as temp 2/Lt 26/5/16.To 20th gaz 24/8/1616.Age 30.
Holmes	Frederick Charles Victor	32	2/Lt 26/5/16					Artists Rifles OTC to 32nd Bn. . To 23Bn gaz 24/8/16. Relinquished commission due to wounds 15/7/19
Hopkins	Charles Harry Innes	20	Lt-Col 26/10/14					b. 1858. Retired Scottish rifles 29/3/1899. Founder member of TS recruiting comittee. First CO of 20Bn. Relinquished c
Hopwood	Leonard Ernest William	20	2/Lt 26/4/17		31/8/17			Relinquished commission on completion of service 14/2/19
Horne	David Douglas	20	Cap 6/11/14			01/07/16	Thiepval Memorial	To 29Bn 18/12/15. To 21Bn
Houghton	WL	21	2/Lt 27/6/17					Joined 21Bn for duty 8/17
Housby	Robert Percival	23	2/Lt 28/3/17	MC				Relinquished commission on completion of service 30/11/20
Howard	Harry	29	2/Lt 20/1/16	MC				To 21Bn (attached) 22/10/16. 6/9/16.Bombing Officer. MC won RFC. Parents received telegram stating Kia 1/7/16
Howells	John Lancastle	21	2/Lt 1/3/17					To 21Bn
Howie	OW	23	2/Lt 28/11/17					
Howson	JH	20	2/Lt 1/8/17					To 9Bn 1918
Hughes	John Price	23	2/Lt 31/10/17	MC				
Hughff	RG	21	Lt 18/12/14					To 29Bn 3/9/15. Adjutant 23/11/15. To 33Bn 1/6/16. RFC 13/3/17
Hughs	J	21	2/Lt 26/4/17		11/9/17			
Hull	MR	20	2/Lt 22/11/16					From Reg Bn. Relinquished commission on completion of service 23/10/20
Hunt	JW	21	2/Lt 31/10/17					To 21Bn. To 14Bn 1918. 51Bn 1920
Hunter	Albert Richmond	23	2Lt 28/4/15	MC	30/3/16	11/02/19	Terlincthun British Cemetery, Wimill	Age 31. Wounded March 1916 when bullet hit cigarette case in pocket deflecting path
Hunter	GR	20	2/Lt 19/4/17		31/8/17			Reg Bn att 20Bn 1917
Hunter	JK	23	2/Lt 26/4/17					Employed Air Ministry 1918. Relinquished commission on completion of service 21/12/20
Irvine	William Magnus	23	2/Lt 28/3/17					
Jamieson	HG	20	2/Lt 31/10/17					To 9Bn 1918. Relinquished commission on completion of service 13/3/20
Jamieson	John	23	2Lt 4/3/17	DCM		29/04/18	Arras Memorial	Age 40. Formally Sgt Cameron Highlanders
Jansen	JT	22	Lt.Col 4/11/17					Cmmd 22Bn 4/18 from 7Bn KOYLI
Jarman	Andrew Hatch	20	2Lt 10/6/15			01/07/16	Ovillers Military Cem.	Age 34.
Jefferson	GR	23	2/Lt 27/4/17					
Jeffreys	Alexander Harry	20	2Lt 7/12/14			06/11/16	Ration Farm Military Cemetery.	Age 20.19Bn to 20Bn as A/Cap 4/8/16 as company CO. Volunteered on outbreak of war
Jennings	Alfred George McIvor	21	2/Lt 25/1/17	MC	31/8/17			Formally Cpl 10/722 Wellington Inf. Regt. NZ. Embarked for Egypt 3/12/14. Att 27Bn 1917. to 21Bn (Jan) 1918. To RAF 19
Jobson	Richard Henry Thorburn	22	Cap 21/11/14					22Bn Adj 21/11/14-15/6/15. 29Bn 11/12/15, 2nd in Com 22/5/16. 21Bn 17/10/16 as 2iC. Area Commandant Vermond 10/7/17.
Johnson	HL	21	2/Lt 31/10/17					To 12Bn 1918
Johnstone	John Murray	20	2/Lt 2/11/16					28Bn to 29Bn March 1916. To 20Bn 18/9/16. To 18Bn April 1918. Relinquished commission on completion of service 1/9/21
Joicey	Clive Monague	21	Lt		5/16	05/06/17	Browns Copse Cemetery, Roeux.	Com 4Bn. Att 21Bn when KiA
Jones	EC	21	2/Lt 30/5/17					To 12Bn 1918
Keen	HHE	29	2/Lt 24/12/15					To 29th 11/4/16. 84TRB 1/9/16. .
Keenan	George	22	2/Lt 26/4/17					From Labour Corps 26/9/17. Joins for duty 27/11/17. To England sick 19/1/18
Kell	AE	22	2/Lt 1/8/17					Formaly Cpl 19/720 19Bn. Joins for duty 2/10/17. Evacuated England wounded 9/11/17. Posted 19Bn 13/11/17.
Kelly	Oscar Raphael	20	2/Lt 2/6/16				15+29+33Bn ????	From Inns of Court OTC. To RFC 20/1/17 as Flying Officer.
Kent	Gordon	21	2/Lt 16/12/15					29Bn to 21Bn gaz 3/8/16. Relinquished command due to ill-health 9/5/17
Ker	Arthur Preston	20	Lt 10/11/14	Mid 31/1+7/11/17,1/1/1				Brigade Transport Officer. To Labour Corps 7/3/18
Kerr	Albert Edward	20	Lt 5/3/15	MC	1/7/16			20Bn Adj 10/6/15 to 1/7/16. To transport workers Bn 14/9/17. Relinquished commission 28/10/20
Kerridge	Sydney Charles	23	2/Lt 20/1/16	MC	6/17			Probation 20/1/16-6/9/16. 15Bn to 23Bn gaz 3/8/16. to 7th TRB 19/9/17
Kidd	Ernest Day	21	2/Lt 3/7/15		4/6/16			To MGC 6/11/16
Kindleysides	Charles Frederick	22	2Lt 1/5/18			04/10/18	Houchin British Cemetery	Joined for duty 27/6/18 from Army Cyclist corps
King	Soloman	21	2Lt 14/11/15			13/10/16	Erquinghem-Lys Churchyard Extensi	Age 23. 21Bn to 23Bn Sep 1916
Kinrade	Edward	22	2/Lt 31/10/17					Joined for duty 10/1/18
Kirk	LP	20	2/Lt 26/4/17					Relinquished commission due to ill-health 7/3/19
Kirkup		22	2Lt					Joins 22Bn for duty 8/16
Knott	Robert Cecil	20	2Lt 24/12/14			14/08/16	Guillemont Road Cemetery	21yrs. Enlisted 19Bn. 28Bn 4/2/16. To 20Bn date
Knox	Arthur Victor	21	2Lt			06/06/17	Arras Memorial	Joins 21Bn for duty 2/5/17
Laing	Dudley Ogilvie	22	Lt 14/11/14			01/07/16	Thiepval Memorial	Age 26. Younger brother of Cap Gerald Laing.
Laing	Gerald Ogilvie	20	Lt 3/11/14			05/06/17	Arras Memorial	Age 30. Elder brother of Cap Dudley Laing.
Laing	J	22	2/Lt 27/6/17		8/9/17			
Laing	John	21	Cap 11/2/15					Late of 7th Bn. 21st Bn to 29Bn 3/9/15. CO 'D' Co 19/1/15. Relinquishd commission 16/7/17
Lakeman	John Pearse	20	2Lt 22/11/16			20/04/17	Etaples Military cemetery	Age 19. Att from Reg Bn gaz 9/3/17
Lamb	James William	29	2/Lt 8/10/15					Commissioned 29Bn. From 29Bn to 22Bn gaz 17/10/16.From (S)Bn to Reg Bn 25/3/18
Lamb	Walter	22	2Lt 18/11/14			01/07/16	Thiepval Memorial	Age 26. Son of Warkwarth councillor
Lambert	A	23	2/Lt 1/8/17	MC				
Lambert	Arthur William	29	2/Lt 7/7/16					84 TRB 1/9/16 as A/Lt. Relinquished commission on completion of service 1/9/21
Lambert	WGC	22	2/Lt 8/12/14		1/7/16			15Bn to 22Bn 5/7/15. Relinquished commission due to wounds 3/8/18
Last	William Thorndyke Owen	21	2/Lt 28/3/17		8/17			Relinquished commision due to ill-health contractedd on active service 11/5/18
Lauder	James Alexander	22	Hon-Lt 5/8/15					22Bn QM 5/8/15. To 33Bn as QM 23/6/16. 84TRB QM 1/9/16
Leah	AC	20	2/Lt 31/10/17		21/3/18			20Bn to 22Bn 1918
Leathard	Lancelot F	20	2/Lt 31/10/17					Formally sgt 23/1432 23Bn NF. 20Bn to 23Bn 1918. Relinquished commission on completion of service 24/5/19
Leech	JWC	23	2/Lt 12/12/14	MC	1/7/16			13Bn to 23Bn 7/6/15. Relinquished commission on completion of service 1/9/21
Levin	Charles Norton	21	2Lt 26/4/15	MC		21/03/18	Pozieres Memorial	Originally enlisted 'B' Co 9Bn. Attached to 102 Trench Mortar Battery replacing Cap Bowkett. A/Cap when killed
Lewis	Francis Ball		Mjr 25/1/15					Relinquished commission 29/5/15.
Lewis	William Griffith	22	2/Lt 8/3/15					Posted back to England 1/4/18
Lewis	WT	23	2/Lt 27/4/17					
Liddell	Arthur Richard	23	2/Lt 26/5/16					From Artists Rifles OTC to 32nd Bn. To 23Bn gaz 24/8/16. Relinquished commission on completion of service 1/9/21
Lindsay	David Cranston	22	2/Lt 7/4/17	MC				Formally Cpl Cameron Highlanders. Joines for duty 7/4/17
Linford	HJ	20	2/Lt 31/10/18					26th Bn to 20Bn 3/2/18
Lingard	GR	20	2/Lt 1/8/17					3rd(R) att 20Bn 1918
Lingwood	Clement Robert	21	2/Lt 25/9/15					29Bn to 21Bn gaz 3/8/16. To 12Bn A/Cap 10/11/17. Relinquished commission on completion of service 1/9/21
Lingwood	Edward Charles	21	2/Lt 18/4/15		7/6/17			21Bn to 33Bn 23/6/16. To 16Bn 1/9/16. Relinquished commission on completion of service 6/2/19
Linsay	J	23	2/Lt 1/8/17					
Lion	Guy Osbourne	22	2/Lt 8/3/15					
Lloyd	EP	21	Bt-Mjr 1/1/16					CO 21Bn from Col Stuart 1917. To Lincolnshire Regt. 24/7/17
Loadman	LW	22	2/Lt 31/10/17		13/4/18			3rd(R) att 22Bn joined for duty 13/1/18
Lock	CC	21	2/Lt 28/3/17					3rd(R) att 21Bn joined for duty 10/6/17
Lock	William James	21	Hon-Lt 10/11/14	Mid 8/12/18				21Bn QM 10/11/14 to 10/11/17. To 12Bn 10/11/17
Logan	Andrew	21	2/Lt 26/4/17		11/9/17			3rd(R) att 21Bn 1918. Relinquished commission 9/8/20
Logan	Cyril	20	2/Lt 27/8/17	MC	11/9/17			To 18Bn 1918. 13Bn R. Innis Fus 1919
Lomax	Joseph Albert	21	2/Lt 28/3/17		8/17			Joins for duty 10/6/17. To MGC.
Longhurst	Cressy Roy	23	2Lt 14/12/14	Mid 13/11/16		08/03/18	Longbenton Cemetary	D.U.O.T.C. 2nd i/C 1/8/16. Killed when his motorcycle collided with a Tramcar during snowstorm in Newcastle whilst att
Lucas	William Henry Owen	23	2/Lt 16/8/15	MC				15Bn to 23Bn gaz 3/8/16
Lunn	Herbert Charles		Lt 8/2/15					To Local reserve 10/1/16
Lupton	HR	22	CAP 1/6/16	MC	8/10/18			Joined for duty 23/6/18 from 8Bn P.O.W Regt.
Lyle	William	23	Lt-Col 24/10/15			01/07/16	Bapaume Post Military Cemetary	Age 40. Replaced Captian Campbell as CO of 23Bn 24/10/15 from 3Bn Spec Res lancs Fus.1st Com 5/5/1900.Retired 13/6/191
Lynn-grant	CJ	22	2Lt 19/2/17					From 3(R) Garrison Bn R.I.R.
Macarthur	James	21	2/Lt 23/11/15					To 2nd Australian Tunnelling Company 5/12/16
Macdonald	Hugh	22	2Lt.			05/06/17	Arras Memorial	Age 24.
MacDonald	John	22	2Lt 18/11/15		1/7/16	21/11/16	Fodderty Old Churchyard, Ross & C	Shown in Lists as From 29Bn to 22Bn gaz 3/8/16 .
MacDonald	K	22	2Lt 1/7/17					Joined 22Bn 7/4/17 for duty from 1Bn
MacDonald	Roderick	23	2Lt 27/4/15			01/07/16	Thiepval memorial	
MacDonald	Simon	23	2Lt 26/1/15			01/07/16	Cerissy-Gailly French National Cemetary	
Macintosh	Charles John	23	2/Lt 1/1/16					23Bn to 29Bn 3/3/16. To 20Bn gaz 18/9/16. From Bn 27/1/18 att'd Army Records Office. Relinquished commission on comple
Macintosh	Stanley Hugh	23	Cap 21/12/14	DSO.Mid 13/11	1/7/16			Became 2nd in Command 2/7/16 until DEC 1916. From Bn 22/2/17. Relinquished commission on completion of service 23/3/19
MacIntyre	Thomas	21	2/Lt 11/11/14					21Bn to 29Bn 3/9/15. To 16Bn 16/6/16
Mackay	John Frederick	21	Cap 20/5/08	VC				From A & SH as 2nd CO 2nd TS 2/8/15. To HLI 28/8/16
Mackintosh	Charles John	23	2/Lt 1/1/16					To 29Bn 1/2/16. To 20Bn gaz 18/9/16
MacNaught	Eric Norman	20	2/Lt	MC				7Bn TF to 20Bn as temp Captain 6/8/16. Returns to 7Bn (Junw) 1917
MacNeil	Robert Archibald	21	2Lt 4/3/17			09/04/17	Roclincourt Valley Cemetery	Age 24. Formally Sgt A&SH. Joins for duty 4/3/17 on promotion. Killed in second line of German Trenches at Rochlincour
Macpherson	AG	21						Joins 21Bn for duty 5/10/16. To 14Bn 22/2/18
MacPherson	George Angus	21	2/Lt 1/1/16					To 33Bn 23/6/16. To regular Bn attached gaz 20/10/16
MacRae	GA	22	2/Lt 29/6/16	MC				Formerly Private in Scottish Rifles.On probation.
Makepeace	Ivor William	20	2/Lt 23/4/15					To 29Bn 3/9/15. To 18Bn 22/6/16. Relinquished commission on completion of service 1/9/21
Mark	Alan William Dobson	21	2/Lt 21/11/14	DSO,MC+2BA	1/7/16,13/4/18			21Bn to 84TRB 1/9/16. To 22Bn 19/2/17. Resigned commission on completion of service 16/4/19
Marrs	Lionel Geldart	21	2/Lt 11/7/15					21Bn to 29Bn 1/11/15. 84TRB 1/9/16
Marrs	Wallace	21	Lt 7/11/14	MC				Brigade Staff Captain Aug 1915. Later invalided home and replaced by Cap W.H.Wallace. Relinquished commission on compl
Marshall	John Marshall	22	2/Lt 31/10/17	MC				Joined for duty 13/1/18. Transferred to base depot B.E.F. 17/6/18
Martin	Joseph Johnson	29	2/Lt 21/12/15					84th TRB 1/9/16
Martindale	AC	22	2Lt 27/6/17					From 11Bn
Mason	George William Steel	22	2/Lt 25/3/15		1/7/16			Joins for duty 26/4/16. Relinquished commission on completion of service 1/9/21
Mason	Vernon	20	2Lt 31/10/17			01/04/18	Erquinghem-Lys Churchyard Extensi	Att 9Bn
Mather	Oswald Harvey	20	Cap 15/12/14		1/7/16			Led 4th wave of 1st July attack. From Bn 4/5/17 on appointment to Indian Army
Mathew	Ernest George	23	2/Lt 17/8/15					23Bn to 29Bn 1/11/15. To 33Bn 23/6/16. To 16Bn 17/11/16. Relinquished commission due to ill-health 11/5/18
Mathieson	Duncan	20	Lt 3/11/14	MC	1/7/16			Led 3rd wave of 1st July attack. Relinquished commission due to ill-health caused by wounds 23/2/19

Matthews	Sydney Herbert	23	2/Lt 5/3/15	MC				To 29Bn 1/11/15. To 21Bn 8/7/16. To 23Bn 22/2/18. Relinquished commission on completion of service 1/9/21
Maughan	HS	22	2/Lt 26/4/17					3rd(R) att 22Bn 1918. Cmd Depot Jul 1918. Relinquished commission 1/4/20
Mawston	E	22	2Lt 1/5/18					Joined for duty 3/10/18. Relinquished commission on completion of service 26/1/20
Mayer	WG	22	2Lt 28/5/17					Joined for duty 20/6/18 from ACC
McClay	John	20	Lt 3/11/14		2/16			To 22Bn as Cap 13/3/15. Attached to regular army 29/8/16.
McClintock	Edward Elsmere	20	Cap 9/11/14					Original member of Scottish recruiting committee. Transferred to General List 23/11/15
McCluskey	Arthur William	21	2/Lt 16/12/14	MC				D.U.O.T.C. MC won 1/7/16. To 14Bn 22/2/18
McCluskey	FJ	20	2/Lt 13/2/17					Formally Sgt HLI. To Indian Army 27/5/18.Relinquished commission 21/5/20
McHardy	Joseph	Bde	RAChD att	MC				Brigade Roman Catholic Padre.
McIntosh	William	22	2Lt 8/12/14		1/7/16	06/07/16	St. Sever Cemetery, Rouen	Age 28. Enlisted as private.
McIntosh	WJ	23	2/Lt 3/11/15					From 15Bn to 23Bn gaz 3/8/16. To 80TRB 13/12/16. From Bn 27/11/17. Relinquished commission due to ill-health 2/2/18
McKeand	Alexander Brodie	20	2/Lt 7/4/17	MC				Formally L/Cpl R.Highlanders. To 16Bn 24/2/19
McLay	Archibald	23	2/Lt 14/12/14		8/2/16			Resigns commission in 23Bn 18/10/15 due to ill-health. Re-commissoned in 29Bn 29/11/15. 84TRB 1/9/16. To 22Bn
McLean	GA	21	2/Lt 3/7/16		11/9/17			Formally Pte 19th Canadian Inf. Brig.
McQueen	Gordon	23	2/Lt 22/12/14		6/17			23Bn to 33Bn 23/6/16. To 23Bn 3/7/16 as Lt. From Bn 20/4/18. Relinquished commission on completion of service 1/9/21
McSorley	Frederick Wiliam	20	2Lt 12/2/17			05/04/17	Faubourg D'Amiens Cemetery, Arras	Age 33. Reg Bn att 20Bn 1918
Meadows	Robert Stephenson	23	2/Lt 6/3/15		1/7/16			To 83rd TRB 16/4/17
Melrose	Robert Graham	21	2/Lt 25/1/15		5/6/16			84th Training Reserve Battalion 17/10/16 as A/Lt.
Menzies	Harry	23	2Lt 7/4/17			29/04/17	Arras Memorial	Age 21. Enlisted 1914 Gordon Highlanders . Formally Col.Sgt.
Metcalfe	George	23	2/Lt 12/7/15	MC,Mid 7/11/1	29/4/17			15Bn to 23Bn gaz 3/8/16. Relinquished commission on completion of service 12/11/19
Middleton	Alan Edwin	20	2/Lt 7/4/15					A/Cap 1/8/16. Commanding Depot 1918. Relinquished commission 2/11/20
Milburn	Frank	23	2/Lt 14/12/14	MC				23Bn to 29Bn 27/11/15. To Labour Corps 1/9/16. 12/13Bn 15/7/18. Relinquished commission on completion of service 25/2/
Miller	JR	20	2/Lt 27/8/17					Relinquished commission on completion of service 1/9/21
Miller	JS	20	Lt 7/1/15					& Adjutant.20Bn to 29Bn 3/9/15. To MGC 22/22/15
Miller	W	20	2/Lt 15/7/15					15Bn to 20Bn gaz 24/8/16. A/Cap 31/8/17-1/11/17 as Company CO. Relinquished commission due to wounds 2/11/19
Milley	Stewart	23	2/Lt 28/6/16	MC	6/6/17			Formerly L/Cpl A & SH. Relinquished commission on completion of service 25/3/20.
Mills	William John	20	2Lt 26/4/17				Esquelbecq Military Cemetery	Age 23. Resigned commission on appointment to RAF 14/6/18. Died of Wounds 4/9/18 att 20Sqn RAF
Mitchell	GO	20	2/Lt 1/3/17		6/9/18			86TRB 1/11/17. Relinquished commission on completion of service 14/2/19
Moffett	John Enslie	22	2Lt					
Mole	Arthur Henry Wilson	22	2/Lt 17/12/15					Joins 22Bn from 28Bn for duty 31/5/16. Hospital sick 15/2/17. Relinquished commission due to ill-health caused by woun
Molineux	Ernest	Bde	RAChD att					Brigade Padre took over from Father McHardy April 1917.
Mont		22	2Lt					
Moore	Frederick Gordon	22	2/Lt 28/3/17		13/4/18			A/Cap 25/10/17-21/3/18
Moore	W	22	2Lt 6/2/18					
Moore	William Bewicke	22	2/Lt 28/3/17		21/3/18			Formally Pte 16/60 16Bn N'Fus. To R.I.F 29/11/18
Moorwood	James Colin	23	2/Lt 19/4/15					To 83rd TRB 16/4/17
Moorwood	Thomas Hedley	23	2/Lt 23/9/15	MC				
Morris	Arthur Augustus	23	2/Lt 22/1/16	MC				On probation. From 15Bn to 23Bn gaz 3/8/16. relinquished commission 10/11/20
Mowbray	William Moffatt	22	2Lt 29/5/18					Joined for duty 3/10/18
Moyes	Edgar Willaim	22	2/Lt 26/4/17	MC				Relinquished commission on completion of service 24/9/19
Murray	John William Ernest	21	2/Lt 21/11/14		26/6/16			Formally Scottish Horse. Brigade machine gun officer 19/6/15. Took over as temporary CO 21Bn 8/11/17-19/11/17. To HQ X
Mustard	Robert Willaim	21	2Lt 1/8/17			31/03/18	Pozieres Memorial	To 12/13Bn 1918
Napier	ADM	21	Lt	MiD 9/4/17				17Bn to 21Bn 2/2/15. Temp CO 4/7/17-13/7/16. To Labour Corps 14/4/17
Napier	John Chatt	23	2/Lt 1/3/17					Com 4Bn . Att 23Bn from 3(R)Bn 1917
Neeves	Horace Hunter	23	2/Lt 1/1/16	DSO,MC+Bar,Mid 7/11/17			DSO+MC won with 27th Bn	15-27Bn gaz 3/8/16.A/Cap 1/8/16.24Bn 14/10/17.A/Mjr 25/9/17.Mjr 14/10/17 26th Bn.A/Lt-Col 5/4/18.23Bn 21/3/18
Neill	AE	22	2/Lt 31/10/17	Mid 8/11/18				Joined for duty 13/1/18
Nelson	George Spoors	23	2/Lt 14/12/14	MC				23Bn Adj 4/7/16. To MGC 1918
Nicholls	F. Charles A.	23	Lt 19/12/14					To Reg Bn 3/9/16
Nicholson	JH	22	2/Lt 30/5/17		17/10/17			Joined 22Bn for Duty 27/7/17
Nisbett	RL	22	2/Lt 12/9/17					Joins 22Bn for duty from 3(R)Bn 27/11/17. Posted missing 13/4/18
Niven	Allan Graham	21	Cap 18/11/14		28/6/16	01/07/16	Thepval Memorial	Age 38. Returns to Bn 30/6 from hospital
Nixon	Fredrick	20	2/Lt 28/4/15		13/4/18			To 22nd Bn on disbandment of 20th Bn 3/2/18
Nixon	William	20	Cap 1/12/14			01/07/16	Thiepval Memorial	Age 32. Led 1st wave (4,8,9,14 platoons) in 1st July attack
Noble	JW	20	2/Lt 1/8/17					Relinquished commission due to wounds 26/2/19
Noble	Thomas Gibson	20	Cap 26/10/14			01/07/16	Thiepval Memorial	Age 28. 'A' Company CO. Led 2nd wave (3,7,11,16 platoons) in 1st July attack.
Noonan	Eric William	22	2/Lt 6/1/16	MC	1/7/16			On probation 6/1/16. To 22Bn gaz 3/8/16. Cofirmed in rank 6/9/16. To N'Land Vol. Regt. 11/6/18 as Adj.
Norris	Paul Buzzard	22	Mjr 12/12/06					Formerly 2nd Bn DCLI. 2CO 22Bn Feb 1915-Aug 1916. CO 21Bn 26/9-24/12/16. To England 24/7/17
Norris	RH	20	2/Lt 30/5/17					3(R)Bn to 20Bn 1917
Oliver	Fredrick George	22	2/Lt 27/6/17					
Oliver	John	23	Lt 26/3/15		1/7/16			To 29Bn 8/8/15. Returned to 23rd 2/7/16. From Bn 23/2/17. Relinquished commission due to wounds 6/2/18.
Oliver	CG	23	2/Lt 1/8/17					
Orange	Alfred	22	2/Lt 18/12/17	MC,MM	17/9/18			Att 22Bn 25/6/18
Parkin	W	22	2Lt 1/5/18					Joined for duty 3/10/18
Parslow	AJ	21	2/Lt 3/10/16					On probation. Formerly L/Cpl London Regt. T.F. From Bn 3/4/18
Patterson	John Hylton	23	2Lt 16/12/14			01/07/16	Thiepval Memorial	Age 22. 23Bn to 29Bn 8/8/15. To 23Bn June 1916.
Pattullo	George Simpson	21	2/Lt 11/8/16	MC				Formerly Sgt DLI. Ass to Brigade Staff Captain. 21Bn to 23Bn 22/2/18. Relinquished commission on completion of service
Peacock	Basil	22	2/Lt 26/4/17	MC				3rd(R) att 22Bn 1918
Peacock	GA	20	2/Lt 31/10/17					
Pearson	Robert	22	2/Lt 31/10/17					Joins fron duty 13/1/18. Transferred to base depot B.E.F 17/6/18
Peckston	Cuthbert L	21	2/Lt 26/3/17					Joins for duty 10/6/17.
Peters	David Bertram	20	2/Lt 25/4/15					20Bn to 29Bn 3/9/15. To 33Bn 23/6/16. From Bn 1/9/16
Peters	Norman	22	2/Lt 27/4/15		1/7/16			Joins for duty 31/5/16
Petrie	John Fenton	29	2/Lt 30/9/15					29Bn to 33Bn 23/6/16. 13Bn 17/10/16. Relinquished commission due to ill-health 8/3/19
Philip	David Carswell	23	2Lt 7/4/17			29/04/17	Arras Memorial	Formally Sgt R.Scots
Phillips	JH	21	Cap					Joins for duty 17/6/16
Phillips	Russell	23	2/Lt 14/12/14					Trench Motar Battery 102/1 from Feb to Jul 1916 when invalided home. To Tyne Electrical Engineers 1/5/17
Piegrome	Joseph Charles	22	2/Lt 5/6/15	MC	1/7/16			Joins for duty 31/5/16. Temp attached 21Bn 12/6-7/9/16. relinquished commission on completion of service 1/3/21.
Pigg	Norman Batey	21	2/Lt 11/11/15	DSO,MC+2Bar	3/17			29Bn to 21Bn 3/8/16. To 23Bn A/Cap 19/4/18. Relinquished commission 12/3/20
Pinkney	Robert Bruce Taylor	20	2/Lt 5/11/14					To 29Bn 3/9/15. To Tyne Electrical Engineers
Pinnington	Victor	21	2Lt 15/2/15			05/11/16	Ploegsteert Memotial, Belgium	Age 26. Enlisted N'land Hussars. 21Bn to 33Bn 23/6/16. To 23Bn gaz 17/10/16
Pitkethley	WB	20	2/Lt 31/10/17					26th Bn to 20Bn 3/2/18
Pollett	Lionel Williams	28	2/Lt 22/4/16		7/4/17			From I of Ct OTC to 28Bn. To 20Bn gaz 24/8/16. Found severely wounded in Aid Post in German 3rd line 9/4/17. From Bn
Porch	Cecil Porch	23	Lt-Col 2/7/16	DSO+2Bars,M	11/4/17,6/6/17			CO 23Bn 1918. DSO with 18Bn. Ceases to command Bn 4/5/19.
Potter	RD	21	2/Lt 1/8/17					To 25Bn 1918. Relinquished commission on completion of service 14/2/19
Potts	John	22	2/Lt 27/6/17					Relinquished commission due to wounds 16/10/18
Prankerd	Rowland John	22	2/Lt 19/5/15					Disappears from list JAN 1916
Prest	Stuart Osborne	20	2/Lt 12/7/15					To Labour Corps 6/3/18
Prior	P	20	2/Lt 1/3/17					Relinquished commission on completion of service 1/9/21
Pritchard	Henry Reginald	23	2/Lt 28/3/17		1/7/16			From Bn 7/4/18. att Royal Irish Regt. 1919
Pullein	TH	21	2/Lt 1/8/17					To 25Bn 1918
Punshon	JW	22	2Lt 28/11/17		5/9/18(Gas)			Joined for duty 20/6/18 from ACC
Purdy	George Robert	22	2/Lt 20/11/14		1/7/16			Relinquished commission 8/11/16 due to wounds received 1/7/16
Purnell	Edward Kelly	23	Mjr 22/2/15					(Cap 11/1/1902) 9Bn Lancs Fus to 23Bn 22/2/15. 2nd in Command from May until invalided by medical board 24/10/15
Purnell	GH	21	2Lt					Joins 21Bn from 101 Brigade HQ 5/12/16
Purnell	Stanley George Hardy	21	2Lt 10/1/16			05/06/17	Arras Memorial	On Probation. Ex-OTC. From 29th to 21st gaz 18/9/16
Raimes	Leslie Robinson	21	2Lt 7/12/14		1/6/16	01/07/16	Thiepval Memorial	Chatered accountant. Enlisted N'land Hussars. Wounded 1/6, rejoined unit 2 days prior to 1st July attack.
Rainbow	Arthur Lloyd	20	Cap					
Ramsey	CO	21	2/Lt 31/10/17					'A' Co CO. To 12Bn 1918
Ramsey	William Marshall	21	2/Lt 24/4/15	MC	30/4/17			16Bn to 31Bn 5/2/16. Joins 21Bn for duty 17/7/16. From Bn 1918
Rand	Charles Herbert Sidney	21	2Lt 28/3/17		11/9/17	18/09/18	Gouzeaucourt New British Cemetery	Age 29. Joins 21Bn for duty 10/6/17
Redder	Sydney de	21	2/Lt 6/1/15		1/7/16			25Bn to 30th Bn 4/1/16. Joins 21Bn for duty 14/3/16. Relinquished commission due to wounds 22/8/17.
Redpath	GE	21	2/Lt 1/8/17					To Reg Bn (Sep) 1918
Reeves	RWD	21	Cap					Joins for duty 17/6/16
Reid	R	22	2/Lt 23/2/17		9/4/17			Formally Cpl R. Scots. Joins 22Bn for duty 23/2/17
Renshaw	WA	21	2/Lt 1/8/17					To 25Bn 1918. Resigned commission on transfer to RAF 14/9/18. Relinquished commission 12/3/20
Rice	VHM	22	2Lt 27/3/18					Joined for duty 3/10/18
Richards	J	21	2/Lt 27/6/17					To Reg Bn 1918
Richards	William Norman	20	2/Lt 12/6/15					20Bn to 29Bn 7/1/16. To 33Bn 1/6/16. From Bn gaz 20/10/16
Richardson	John	23	2Lt 28/3/17			09/09/17	Hargicourt British Cemetery	3rd(R)Bn (att) 23Bn
Richardson	Norman Henry	20	2/Lt 27/12/15					29Bn to 20Bn gaz 3/8/16
Richardson	TWT	21	2/Lt 31/10/17					
Richley	Norman	22	2/Lt 12/8/15					22Bn to 29Bn 1/11/15. Dismissed the service by order of General Courts Martial 26/6/16
Ridley	JF	20	2/Lt 22/11/16		7/4/17			From Bn (Mar) 1918
Ridley	Sydney Graham	22	2/Lt 6/1/16		9/4/17			On probation 6/1/16. 29Bn to 22Bn 1/9/16
Roberts	Victor Cyril	23	2/Lt 20/8/15					23Bn to 29Bn 1/11/15. To 19Bn 22/6/16
Robertson	George	21	2Lt 12/11/14			01/07/16	Thiepval Memorial	Age 24. Adjutant 28/2/16.
Robinson	Arthur Albert	21	2/Lt 14/12/14					21Bn to 29Bn 3/9/15. To MGC 22/11/15. Rejoins 21Bn for duty 5/10/16
Robinson	G	22	2/Lt 31/10/17					

Robinson	J	22	2Lt					
Robson	Charles John	21	2/Lt 1/8/17					Joins 21Bn for duty 16/11/17 from 24/27Bn. To 22Bn 15/9/18
Robson	James Muir	22	2/Lt 2/6/15		26/8/16			Employed Agricultural Company 13/3/17. TRB 13/7/17
Robson	JC	23	2/Lt 31/10/17					26Bn to 23Bn 3/2/18. Relinquished commission due to wounds 11/2/19
Robson	Marshall	22	2/Lt 15/1/16					On probation. 32Bn to 22Bn 14/9/16. Special employment 15/11/17
Robson	William Henry	22	2/Lt 27/3/15	MC	1/7/16,26/4/17			To 84 TRB
Roddis	Frederick Archibald Nortor	23	2/Lt 26/4/17					27Bn to 23Bn. Relinquished commission on completion of service 14/2/19
Rodger	JC	20	2/Lt 31/10/18					26th Bn to 20Bn 3/2/18
Rodgers	ET	23	2/Lt 27/4/17					
Rodgers	FC	20	2/Lt 31/10/18					26th Bn to 20Bn 3/2/18. Relinquished commission due to wounds 11/2/19
Rogers	DA	22	2/Lt 27/6/17					3rd(R) att 22Bn 1918. Posted missing 20/10/17
Roscoe	Edgar	22	2/Lt 4/12/14		24/8/16			
Ross	George Munro	20	2Lt 8/4/15			01/07/16	Thiepval Memorial	Age 24. To A.C.C. 3/11/15. Attached 20Bn and 01/07/16
Ross	Percy Arthur	20	2/Lt 20/4/15					20Bn to 29Bn 7/1/16.
Rotherford	Robson Wilson	22	Lt 13/11/14	MC				Qm 22Bn 13/11/14-23/3/15. To HQ unit 22/11/17
Rough	WE	20	2/Lt 30/5/17					To 18Bn 1918
Routledge	W	23	2/Lt 31/10/17					
Rowell	Thomas	20	2/Lt 21/10/15					29Bn to 20th joins for duty 29/8/16. From Bn 27/1/18
Russell	WF	20	2/Lt 18/4/15					26Bn to 30Bn 4/11/15. To 20th 22/6/16. To 84TRB 1/9/16
Rutherford	Francis Ronald	21	2/Lt 13/2/17		8/17			Formally WOII Cameron Highlanders (No 13736), RSM RE(No 147104). 'C' Co CO 1917. Joined 21Bn for duty 14/2/17. From Bn
Ryle	E	22	2/Lt 27/6/17		8/9/17			
Sanby	William Worthington	20	2Lt 27/4/15			01/07/16	Thiepval Memorial	Age 21.Native of Stratford-On-Avon. Formally Pte 764 1st Birmingham City Bn
Sandeman	Gilbert Wall	28	2/Lt 8/12/15					28Bn to 20Bn gaz 24/8/16. From Bn 1918
Satchwell	Percy Henry	22	2/Lt 7/4/15					22Bn to 29Bn 3/9/15. To 33Bn 1/6/16. 84TRB 1/9/16 as Lt. & Adj. To Reg Bn 8/11/17. Relinquished commission due to wou
Scaife	Arthur Lewis	23	2/Lt 28/3/17	MC	6/6/17,20/10/17			To 12Bn Aug 1918. MC won 12/13th Bn. Relinquished commission on completion of service 1/9/21
Scarfe	CV	20	2/Lt 1/8/17					To Reg Bn (Mar) 1918
Scarff	G	22	Cap 18/5/18					Formally draft conducting officer
Scattergood	Tom Victor	21	2Lt 6/1/17			06/06/17	Duisans British Cemetery	Age 30. Formally Pte London Regt. Joins 21Bn for duty 6/1/17
Schooling	GR	20	2/Lt 26/4/17					To 18Bn on disbandment 1918. Resigned commission on appointment to RAF 26/11/18
Scott	Duncan	23	2/Lt 26/9/16	MC				
Scott	Earnest Arthur	21	Cap 28/12/14					21Bn to 29Bn 3/9/15. 2ic MAR to 23/6/16. To 33Bn 23/6/16.84TRB 1/9/16. Reg Bn 16/12/17.Resigned 10/11/20
Scott	HJ	23	2/Lt 1/3/17					Com 5Bn. Att 23Bn from 1Bn 1917
Scott	John	22	2/Lt 19/4/15					From Bn 8/11/17. Relinquished commission due to wounds 20/7/18
Sears	H	20	2/Lt 22/11/16					Reg Bn to 20Bn gaz 9/3/17. From Bn March 1918. Relinquished commission on completion of service 11/2/19
Selby	Marmaduke Frederick Lan[g]	20	2/Lt 27/1/16					On probation. 15Bn to 20Bn 14/9/16. A/Cap 1/1/17-6/7/17. From Bn 27/1/18
Shapley	Alfred Edwin	23	2Lt 6/1/15			01/07/16	Thiepval Memorial	Age 28. Served 6Bn. Joined Manchester Bn of Royal Fusiliers at outbreak of war.
Shield	J	23	2/Lt 1/8/17					
Sibbit	Henry	22	Lt 18/11/14		8/2/16	01/07/16	Thiepval Memorial	Age 27.
Siddall	A	20	2/Lt 21/9/15					To 29Bn 17/4/16. To 20Bn 18/9/16. To RFC as baloon officer 4/7/17
Signey	James Arnott	21	2/Lt 26/4/17					24/27Bn to 21Bn joins for duty 8/17. Formally brigade signals officer. PoW commandant 20/5/19
Silk	Rw	20	2/Lt 31/10/17					
Sillery	Charles Cecil Archibald	20	Mjr 24/10/14			01/07/16	Bapaume Post Mil. Cem	Age 54.Retired Indian Army 10/7/1907. 2nd in CO 1st TS 24/10/14. Took over as CO from Col Hopkins.
Sim	Alexander	20	2/Lt 9/6/15	MC				20Bn to 33Bn 1/6/16. 84TRB 1/9/16. To 10Bn 19/2/17. Relinquished commission on completion of service 13/1/19
Sim	George Stephen	23	2/Lt 27/6/17					24Bn to 23Bn 1918
Simms	JBP	20	2/Lt 1/8/17					3(R)Bn att 20Bn 1918
Simpson	David James Harcourt	21	2/Lt 17/11/14		2/4/16			Evacuated to England suffering shell-shock 28/4/17
Simpson	Henry Jackson	23	2/Lt 28/3/17	MC				MC won att 22Bn
Simpson	William Kingsbury	22	2Lt 5/8/16			05/06/17	Faubourg-D'Amiens Cemetery, Arras	Age 24. Formally L/Cpl PS-3202 R.Fus. 29Bn 5/8/16 to 22Bn joined for duty 21/9/16
Skene	Thomas Hamilton	22	Lt 5/7/15					To 22Bn 20/9/16. Evacuated to England sick 11/10/16. Rejoined 7/12/16 as transport officee. Relinquished commission du
Skinner	Samuel Stephenson	23	Hon-Lt 12/7/15					Quarter-master of 23Bn 12/7/15 to 11/3/16 when relinquished commission.
Slaughter	Edward William	23	2/Lt 28/3/17		22/10/17			Joins 23Bn for duty 22/9/17
Smith	Arthur Henry	22	2/Lt 20/9/15					29Bn to 22Bn 22/6/16. 84TRB 17/10/16. Re-joines 11/1/17
Smith	Edward John	22	Cap	Mid x2		05/10/18	Cambrin Military Cemetery	Age 29. General List att 22Bn 24/6/18
Smith	John Adams	28	2Lt 2/6/16	MC	7/1/17	28/04/17	Etaples Military Cemetery	Age 21. Innes of Court OTC to 28Bn. To 20Bn Aug 1916
Smith	Norman McNeill	21	2Lt 7/3/15			01/07/16	Thiepval Memorial	Age 21.
Smith	Patrick	23	2/Lt 23/7/15					23Bn to 29Bn 1/11/15. To 20Bn 2/7/16. From Bn 27/1/18
Smith	Percy Campbell	20	2/Lt 24/4/16		6/17			From Bn 27/1/18. Resigned commission under duty to Ministry of Shipping 17/11/18
Smith	Sydney	23	2/Lt 14/12/14					23Bn to 29Bn 3/9/15. To MGC 1/1/16
Smith	Vivian	21	2/Lt 16/12/14		5/6/17			To RFC 27/3/17 as Observer (Flying Officer)
Smith	Frederick John	23	2/Lt 11/10/15					23Bn to 29Bn 1/11/15. 84TRB 1/9/16
Snailham	JJ	21	2/Lt 2/7/16					Relinquished commisson on completion of service 22/2/19
Spearing	TEA	21	2/Lt 19/3/16		1/7/16			Relinquished commission due to wounds 19/5/18
Spink	Henry Mawkinson	23	2/Lt 26/9/16	MC				To Officer cadet Bn 1918. Relinquished commission on completion of service 1/9/21
Spoors	W	23	2/Lt 31/10/17					Employed School of aeronautics 1918
Stancer	John William	23	2Lt 31/10/17			17/04/18	Longuenesse Souvenir Cemetery, St.	Age 24.
Stanley	Harry Clarke	23	2/Lt 26/4/17					Employed ministry of Labour 1918
Steel	JR	21	2Lt 28/11/17					Joins for duty 15/11/17
Stephenson	Jonathan	20	2/Lt 7/7/16	MC~Bar	31/8/17			To 2Bn 1918. Relinquished commission on completion of service 1/9/21
Stephenson	Robert Brewis	22	2Lt 1/3/17	MC	20/10/17	23/10/17	Dozingham Military Cemetery, Belgi	Com 4Bn. Att 22Bn from 3(R)Bn joining for duty 2/5/17.'C' Company
Stevens	HN	22	2/Lt 29/11/15					To 29th 12/4/16. To 22Bn 8/16. To RAF 28/10/18
Stobbs	TH	22	2/Lt 30/5/17		17/11/17			Formally Cpl 19/273 19Bn N'Fus. To UK for commission 24/12/16. Joined 22Bn for duty 27/7/17. Relinquished commission d
Stockley	Vesey Mangles	21	Bt-Col 6/11/14					Retired Indian Army (Bt-col)12/6/12. To 29Bn 16/7/15 as Commanding Officer until 5/1/16
Stone	Frank William	29	2/Lt 6/1/16					On probation 6/1/16. 84TRB 1/9/16
Stuart	Alexander Percy Dunbar C.	20	Lt-Col 16/7/15		30/6+1/7/16			Retired Indian Army (Lt-Col)8/12/13.2nd in Command 1st TS from 2/15 until 16/7/15 when took command 2nd TS. Shell Shoc
Studd	Francis Cyril Rupert	22	Lt-Col 10/2/17	DSO		13/04/18	Ploegsteert Memorial, Belgium	Joined 22Bn from E.Kent R. 4/4/18
Tall	Edgar	23	2/Lt 7/3/15					To MGC 22/11/15
Tanner	Arthur Edward	29	2/Lt 6/1/16		4/17			On probation. Ex OTC. 29Bn to 33Bn 1/6/16. To 16Bn 1/9/16
Tate	George	22	Cap 16/12/14					To 29Bn 3/9/15
Taylor	Archibald Cameron	23	2Lt 13/2/17			29/04/17	Arras Memorial	Age 31. Formally Sgt HLI
Taylor	Benjamin Stone	22	2/Lt 29/10/15					29th to 22Bn joins for duty 31/8/16 and 22/4/18
Taylor	John Robert	21	2/Lt 5/3/15					25Bn to 30Bn 13/1/16. To 24/27Bn (date). Joins 21Bn for duty 8/17 from Bernes area commandant. To 14Bn
Taylor	TH	21	2/Lt 1/8/17					Relinquished commission on completion of service 9/2/19
Telford	Hilton Roberts	21	2Lt 30/1/15		8/9/17	09/09/17	Tincourt New British Cemetary	Age 23. Enlisted N'land Hussars Yeo. Aug 1914 as Pte 607. 21Bn Transport Officer. 80th TRB 13/12/16-13/2/17. To 21Bn 1
Ternan	Trevor		Bde	CB CMG DSO				Brigade Commander from formation until April 1917.
Terry	Arthur Octavius	23	Lt 22/2/15					To 29Bn 8/8/15. To 23rd 11/3/16 as QM replacing Lt. Skinner
Thirlaway	William	20	Lt 10/11/14					To 29Bn 2/11/15. Relinquished commission 11/4/16
Thom	Robert Jamieson	29	2/Lt 23/10/15					84th TRB 1/9/16
Thompson	Alan N	23	2/Lt 31/10/17					Brother of Stuart N.
Thompson	GL	21	Mjr		11/9/17			Joins 21Bn for duty 11/8/17 as 2nd in Command. Relinquished commission 31/3/20
Thompson	John Colin	21	2/Lt 26/4/17					Joins 21Bn for duty 3/8/17
Thompson	Stuart N	23	2/Lt 31/10/17					Joins 23Bn for duty 8/17. Brother of Alan N.
Thompson	William Harold	23	2/Lt 14/12/14	Mid 9/4/17				23Bn to 33Bn 23/6/16. 84TRB 1/9/16. To 23Bn (date)
Thomson	John	20	2/Lt 24/2/17	MC,Mid 1/1/18	7/4/17			Formally Sgt R.Scots Fus. A/Cap 29/8/17. Relinquished commission on completion of service 25/12/18
Thomson	N H T		Bde					Brigade Commander from April 1917, late Seaforth Highlanders.
Tilsley	Richard Frank	23	2/Lt 27/4/17	MC				Relinquished commission due to ill-health 2/7/19
Todd	John George	23	Cap 21/12/14			01/07/16	Bapaume Post Military Cemetery	Age 33. Cap DLI rifle Vols 1907. Enlisted Public Schools Bn,R.F Aug1914.
Travers	William	21	2/Lt 11/1/15		5/6/16			From Bn (att) 26/11/17. Relinquished commission due to wounds 19/2/18
Trigg	Charles Thomas	22	2/Lt 1/4/15		1/7/16			Originally enlisted 'B' Co 9Bn. From Bn (att) 8/11/17. Relinquished commission due to wounds 13/3/18
Trobridge	FG	20	Cap 1/12/14					34th Divisional Staff Officer 19/3/16 (Brigade Mjr)
Tucker	Lionel Louis Clerici	20	2Lt 24/4/15			01/07/16	Thiepval Memorial	Age 21.
Tullis	William	22	2Lt 29/11/05			01/07/16	Thiepval Memorial	From Royal Scots. Fus. as Adjutant 22Bn 14/12/15.
Turnbull	Emerson	20	2/Lt 11/11/14	Mid 6/19	1/7/16			Brigade HQ Staff Officer. A/Mjr 26/4/17-7/5/18. Lt-Col 22/8/18-7/10/18. Relinquished commission on completion service
Turnbull	SA	21	2/Lt 1/8/17					To Reg Bn 1918
Turner	J	23	2/Lt 1/8/17					
Tyson	William Henry Herbert	23	2/Lt 26/4/17					To 8Bn 1918
Tytler	William Boyd	23	2Lt 14/12/14			01/07/16	Thiepval Memorial	Commissioned in 23Bn.
Varley	S	20	2/Lt 16/4/17					3(R)Bn to 20Bn 1917
Venus	Frederick Arthur	20	2Lt 23/12/15			01/07/16	Ovillers Military Cemetery	Age 21. 29Bn to 20Bn
Viner	Frank Hillidge	23	2Lt 31/10/17	MC		12/09/18	Ecoust-St Mein British Cemetery	Died of wounds att 2/7/ K.Liverpool.R.
Walker	Charles Hammond	20	2/Lt 31/10/17	MC				MC won att 2/7th Bn Liverpool Regt. Relinquished commission due to ill-health caused by wounds 20/10/18
Waller	Herbert William	21	2Lt 11/2/15	MC		10/04/17	St. Catherine British Cemetary	Age 29. Replaced Captain Marrs as Brigade Staff Captain 29/9/16
Ward	Dennit Edwin	20	2/Lt 23/12/15	MC				15th to 20Bn. A/Cap 1/1/18. To 23Bn 1918. Relinquished commission on completion of service 2/2/19
Ward	John Inkster	21	2/Lt 15/12/15					29Bn To 21Bn 1/9/16. Evacuated to England sick 26/9/16. Relinquished commission due to ill-health 22/12/17
Ward	Thomas	23	Lt 6/1/15			11/06/16	Becourt Military Cemetery	To 29Bn 3/9/15. Temp rank of CAP 6/3/16 to 16/5/16 whilst Brigade Signalling Officer.
Watson	CN	22	2/Lt 28/11/17					Joins for duty 22/4/18. Transferred to base depot B.E.F. 17/6/18
Watson	James Laverick	23	2Lt 22/11/16			29/04/17	Arras Memorial	
Watson	John	23	2/Lt 28/6/16	MC	11/4/17,20/10/17			Formally Sgt N'Fus. Relinquished commission on completion of service 1/9/21
Watts	A	29	2/Lt 14/8/15					To 29Bn from Lincolnshire Regt. 26/4/16. Later Training reserve battalion

Surname	First name(s)	Age	Rank/Date	Medal	Date1	Death date	Cemetery/Memorial	Notes
Watts	Clive	29	2/Lt 14/9/15					Enlisted 14/9/15. To (S) Bn 22/6/16.
Watts	Hubert	22	2/Lt 19/5/15					To 29th 3/9/15. Transferred from Reserve 22/6/16
Waugh	Thomas Hall	22	2/Lt 18/3/15	MC		06/06/17	Faubourg-D'Amiens Cemetery, Arras	Age 28.
Wells	Arthur Scott	21	2Lt 18/12/14			26/09/16	Thiepval Memorial	21Bn to 33Bn 23/6/16. To 8Bn 1/9/16
Whalen	J	22	2Lt 1/5/18					Joined for duty 3/10/18
Whillis	Bertrand Percy	20	2/Lt 22/4/15	MC				20Bn to 29Bn 7/1/16. To 33Bn 1/6/16. To 20Bn as Lt 2/7/16 & Adj. To MGC (Adj) 6/5/17
Whitaker	John Clemson	22	2/Lt 9/4/15					To 29Bn 1/11/15. To 31Bn 12/2/16. To 23Bn AUG 1916 gaz 1/7/16. To RE 19/5/17
White	Bernard Charles de Boisma	20	2Lt 22/12/14			01/07/16	Thiepval Memorial	Age 29. 11th Yorks & Lancs To 20Bn 19/7/15.
White	Cecil Hayhoe	23	2Lt	MC		24/09/17	Bray Military Cemetery	
White	Ernest Harry Stobart	20	Lt 10/11/14		4/10			20Bn evacuated to England wounded 24/4/16. Joins 21Bn for duty 7/11/16 as 'C' Co CO. Relinquished commission on comple
White	Stewart Alexander	21	Lt 16/11/14			03/07/16	Thiepval Memorial	Adjutant 3/2/15 until 28/2/16.
White	Nathan	29	2Lt 10/1/16			01/07/16	Thiepval Memorial	Age 30. 29Bn to 21Bn June 1916.
Whitehead	Hector Fraser	23	Lt 22/12/14	DSO+Bar,Mid 1/7/16				Formally Lovats Scouts. To 5Bn E.Lancs 2/7/16. Relinquished commission on appointment to Territorial Force as Lt-Col 1
Whitlock	Tom Oliver	22	2Lt			24/08/16	Erquinghem-Lys Churchyard Extensi	Age 20. Joined for duty 17/8/16. Killed when shell landed on officers mess
Whittaker	Henry Dodd	23	2/Lt 14/12/14		1/7/16			To Yorkshire Regt. 14/11/16. Returns 11/1/17. To 17th (Home service)Bn Yorkshire Regt. 28/6/18
Whittaker	William Gaylard	23	2Lt 1/8/17			22/10/17	Tyne Cot Memorial, Belgium	OCU to 3rd(R)Bn (att) 23Bn
Wightman	GH	22	2/Lt 28/11/17					
Wilding	E	22	2Lt					
Wilkins	R	20	2/Lt 1/3/17					
Wilkins	Roland	22	2/Lt 1/3/17					
Williams	Brinley Jenkyn	29	2/Lt 13/9/15			20/05/16	Vieille-Chapelle New Military Cemet	From 29Bn 22/6/16 to 19Bn (gaz 22/6/16)
Williams	Godfrey Howell	22	Lt 16/11/14		1/7/16			From Bn 2/9/16. Relinquished commission due to wounds 8/1/18
Williams	HO	23	2/Lt 31/10/17					
Williams	John Collingwood	21	2/Lt 14/11/14					To Machine Gun Corps 1/1/16
Williams	Leslie	23	2Lt 12/5/15			01/07/16	Serre Road Cemetery No 2.	
Williams	Reginald Firniston	28	2/Lt 22/4/16					Innes of Court OTC to 28Bn. 28th to 20Bn. A/Cap 20/3/17-11/7/17 as company CO. From Bn 27/1/18
Williams	T	21	2/Lt 26/4/17					A/Cap 6/10/17. Civil employment 1918
Willmott	Stanley John	23	2/Lt 26/5/16					Artists Rifles OTC. 32nd Bn to 23Bn gaz 24/8/16
Wilmot	Ben	20	2Lt 25/9/15	MC		06/06/17	Arras Memorial	Age 21. A/Cap when KIA. MC won for action on 12/10/16. 15Bn to 20Bn gaz 24/8/16
Wilson	Herbert John	23	2/Lt 27/4/17					
Wilson	James Boyd	28	2/Lt 2/11/15			18/10/18	Maurois Communal Cemetery	28Bn to 33Bn 23/6/16. To 2Bn 1/9/16
Winfield	AG	20	2/Lt 26/4/17					
Wood	Norman Leslie	20	2/Lt 25/10/16		6/17			Com Reg Bn. To 20Bn 14/10/17. From Bn April 1918. Relinquished commission on completion of service 6/3/19
Woodcock	Leonard Albert	28	2Lt 2/6/16		9/4/17	11/04/17	Aubigney Communal cemetary exten	Innes of Court OTC to 28Bn. Joins 21Bn for duty 27/8/16
Woodhead	Alfred	20	2/Lt 17/4/17	MC	6/17			Formally Sgt. Reg Bn. Promoted for service in th field to 20Bn 17/4/17. Retired 5/3/19
Woodman	Frank Millican	23	2/Lt 26/7/15					23Bn to 29Bn 1/11/15. To 21Bn 2/7/16. Rejoins 2/12/16 from hospital. To 23Bn 27/4/18
Woods	Harold Ernest	29	2/Lt 30/12/15					From 29Bn to 9th Bn gaz 3/8/16. DoW 1/5/17 PoW
Wright	George Edward	23	2Lt 28/5/17					From ASC
Wright	W	20	2/Lt 26/9/17					3rd(R) att 20Bn 1918
Wynn-Mackenzie	Stanley Charles William	20	Hon-Lt 26/10/14					Quarter Master.
Wynn-Parry	Percy	22	2/Lt 12/11/15					Relinquished Commission 14/3/16
Youll	GB	23	2/Lt 1/3/17					Com 4Bn . Att 23Bn from 3(R)Bn 1917
Young	Alfred George	20	2/Lt 11/11/14	Mid 13/11/16	1/7/16			From Bn 23/2/17. Relinquished commission due to wounds 17/10/17
Young	Arthur Lloyd	20	2/Lt 9/11/14		1/7/16			A/Cap 15/2/17 to 24/2/17 as Company CO. Relinquished commission on completion of service 2/2/21
Young	Matthew	22	2/Lt 7/12/14					Disappears from list JULY 1916
Young	Percy Chaston	23	2/Lt 14/9/17		4/17			From Bn 30/9/17. Relinquished commission due to ill-health caused by wounds 14/2/19
Young	W	22	2Lt 18/12/17					Joined for duty 25/6/18 from 1Bn
Younger	JW	22	2/Lt 18/11/16					Transferred to base depot B.E.F 17/6/18

Appendix III

NOMINAL ROLL OF OTHER RANKS 20th NF (1st Tyneside Scottish)

Number on Roll **1365**; Killed or Died of Wounds **419**; Wounded **388**, Gassed, Sick etc **226**:
Total known casualties **1053** (77.1 per cent)
Not traced 354

NAME	INITIALS	RANK	BA	NUMB	CC	ADDRESS	TOWN_VILL	ENLISTI	DISCHA	CAUSE_DIS	WOUNDED	BURIED	TRANSFER	ADD
ADAMS	Peter	LSGT	20	/213		GARDEN HOUSE	MITFORD				1/7/16		TO 25th BN.	
ADAMSON	Robt	BGLF	20	/1207	C		GATESHEAD		1/8/18		9/3/16,16/11/16	RETHEL FRENCH CEM	TO 14th BN(A COY).	SHELLSHOCK
AISBETT	JohnT	PTE	20	/215	A						21/3/16		TO SCOTTISH RIFLES.	GSW NECK, SCOT RIF No 30741.
AITCHISON	R H D	SGT	20	/18			CHURNSIDE		9/3/19		1/7/16		TO KING'S OWN YORKSHIRE LI, CLASS Z RESERVE	KOYLI No 33603.
ALEXANDER	Gibsn	PTE	20	/702						MISSING 21/3/18			TO 12/13th, 22nd(B COY) BNS, CLASS Z RESERVE.	
ALLAN	Wm A	PTE	20	/1212	E	23 BYKER BUILDINGS	NEWCASTLE	9/1/15					TO 2nd GARRISON BN, CLASS Z RESERVE.	LABOURER AWOL 4/2/15, 1-6/3/15, DESERTED 5/6/15.
ALLAN	Wm Ed	PTE	20	/1667			FOREST HALL	26/6/15	24/4/18	GSW	1/7/16		TO 3rd BN.	
ALSOP	Jas W	PTE	20	/981			HECKLINGTON			KR para 392			TO 1st GARRISON, 26th BNS.	
ANDERSON	Edwd	PTE	20	/1573		31 LANGLEY STREET	FENCEHOUSES			28/12/16	1/7/16	RATION FARM CEM		AWOL 7-8/3/15, SHRAPNEL WND HEAD
ANDERSON	Rich	LCPL	20	/703	D						5/4/16			
ANDERSON	Thos	PTE	20	/494		PIKE STREET	PONTOP						TO 1st GARRISON BN, CLASS Z RESERVE.	
ANDERSON	Wm	PTE	20	/19			BYKER		10/8/17		1/7/16		TO KING'S OWN YORKSHIRE LI.	KOYLI No 33796.
ANDREWS	Wm Hn	PTE	20	/1213	E		WREKENTON	4/1/15	29/6/16	SICK			TO 1st GARRISON BN, 2nd BN.	FROM DEPOT COY TO B COY 25/2/15.LAB CORPS No 383865.
ANGLEY	Wm	PTE	20	/1214	E	EIGHTON BANKS	SUNDERLAND	5/1/15			1/7/16	THIEPVAL MEM	TO LABOUR CORPS, ROYAL FUSILIERS(43rd BN).	AGE 34, BORN THORNABY, FROM E COY TO A COY 19/6/15.
ANGUS	John	LCPL	20	/1508	A		SUNDERLAND	20/2/15			1/7/16		TO 16th, 2nd BNS.	BATH WAR HOSP 11/7/16.
ANNETT	JohnA	PTE	20	/131		20 BLYTH STREET	NEWCASTLE					THIEPVAL MEM		
ANNETT	Wm Ml	PTE	20	/130	A		NEWCASTLE				1/7/16	THIEPVAL MEM		
APPLEBY	Geo	PTE	20	/1512		20 VICTORIA TERRACE	OLD PENSHAW						TO 2nd GARRISON BN, CLASS Z RESEWRVE.	
APPLEBY	Henry	PTE	20	/1511		20 VICTORIA TERR	OLD PENSHAW						TO 2nd GARRISON BN, CLASS Z RESEWRVE.	
APPLEBY	JohnH	DRV	20	/1681	C	HIGH STREET	AMBLE						TO 25th, 19TH BNS.	MACHINE GUN DRIVER TO TI AT SUTTON VENY.
ARCHER	R	PTE	20	/367	A									AWOL 29/3/15.
ARKLE	ChasF	PTE	20	/1588	D	BANK TOP COTTAGE	EARSDON				1/7/16	THIEPVAL MEM		AGE 29, AWOL 6-7/10/15.
ARMITAGE	T H	PTE	20	/495	C					10/4/15 UNFIT				
ARMOUR	Jas	PTE	20	/81		8 EAST VIEW AVENUE	CRAMLINGTON						TO LABOUR CORPS(12 POW COY).	101 AMB TRAIN, 18 GHOSP 3/7 GSW R THIGH HSHIP 5/7/16.
ARMSTRONG	Andrw	PTE	20	/368		11 HAWTHORN TERRA	WALBOTTLE	16/10/14			1/7/16		TO 23rd, 16th BNS.	
ARMSTRONG	Chris	PTE	20	/1688		20 ELLISON VILLA'S	GATESHEAD						TO 1st GARRISON BN, CLASS Z RESERVE.	AWOL 20/2/15 TO 1/3/15, 2/4/15 TO 12/4/15 ALNWICK
ARMSTRONG	Edwd	PTE	20	/1219	E	46 ANNFIELD PLACE	ANNFIELD PLAIN	12/1/15	19/5/15	KR para 392				AGE 20 BORN CORSTORPHINE MIDLOTHIAN, 5'7", 152Lbs,39 Ch
ARMSTRONG	James	PTE	20	/132	E	265 HIGH STREET	WALLSEND			KR para 392			TO MUNITIONS.	AWOL 28/2/15 TO 2/3/15. MARRIED NO CHILDREN, NOT O/SEAS
ARMSTRONG	John	PTE	20	/291		377 WESTGATE ROAD	NEWCASTLE	27/10/14	13/4/15	EYESIGHT			TO DEPOT.	
ARMSTRONG	Mich	PTE	20	/1216	B		JARROW	5/1/15			1/7/16		TO CHESHIRE REGT(9th BN).	DESERTED 14/6/15 LABOURER AGE 29, FROM DEPOT COY 25/2
ARMSTRONG	Othel	PTE	20	/216	C		SWALWELL				1/7/16		TO 26th, 1/7th, 12/13th BNS, CLASS Z RESERVE.	AWOL 14-15/2/15.
ARMSTRONG	Rich	PTE	20	/1215	B		EYEMOUTH			30/1/16		Y FARM CEM		AWOL 6-7/10/14, SHOT THROUGH THE HEAD ON SENTRY DUTY
ARMSTRONG	Rob M	SGT	20	/212	E					KR para 392			TO DURHAM LIGHT INFANTRY, TRAINING RESERV; TO WEST YORKSHIRE REGT.	PROMOTED SGT 15/1/15 ACTING CSM E COY UNTIL 16/2/15. W YORKS No 46377.
ARMSTRONG	Robt	PTE	20	/1680							1/7/16		TO 2nd GARRISON BN, CLASS Z RESERVE.	
ARNSBY	Lio S	LCPL	20	/133	A									AWOL 5-8/2/15, FINED 7/- FOR ABSENCE 16/2/15.
ARTHUR	Du M	SGT	20	/134			BARROW			16/10/17	JULY 16	CEMENT HOUSE CEM LANGEMARCK		GSW LEG
ASHWORTH	Wm	PTE	20	/705	B		EARSDON				1/7/16	THIEPVAL MEM		BORN DURHAM.
ASKEW	Wm I	PTE	20	/135		16 STEPHEN STREET	HARTFORD	16/10/14			1/7/16			AGE 19, AWOL 6-8/2/15.
ATHERTON	Geo	PTE	20	/136	C		LIEGH LANCS			5/6/17	1/7/16	ARRAS MEM		101 AMB TRAIN, 3/7 18 GHOSP GSW L LEG HSHIP 5/7/16.
ATHERTON	Jos	PTE	20	/984			SEATON DELAVAL			5/6/17	1/7/16	ARRAS MEM	TO 21st BN(C COY).	AWOL 12-16/2/15,TRG RES No TR/5/59092.
ATHEY	Ralph	PTE	20	/496	C		NEWCASTLE			KR para 392	1/7/16		TO TRAINING RESERVE BN.	BORN HARTON.
ATKINSON	EdwdJ	PTE	20	/369	D		FELLING				1/7/16	THIEPVAL MEM		
ATKINSON	G	PTE	20	/138	A					10/4/15 UNFIT				
ATKINSON	Thos	PTE	20	/88			CHOPPINGTON			3/6/16		ALBERT COM CEM EXT	TO 18th, 12/13th BNS, CLASS Z RESERVE.	18 GHOSP 6/7 GSW R LEG TO BASE DEPOT 20/7/16.
AYNSLEY	Jos	SGT	20	/497	D		BEDLINGTON				1/7/16		TO 3rd BN.	3rd NTHN GHOSP SHEFFIELD 8/7/16.
AYNSLEY	Robt	LCPL	20	/985			SOUTH SHIELDS	14/11/14	30/10/17	GSW	1/7/16		TO 22nd BN, EAST YORKSHIRE REGT(1st BN).	E YORKS No 50645.
AYRE	Geo	PTE	20	/156						KR para 392			TO 2nd GARRISON BN.	
BABE	John	PTE	20	/297	C		RYTON			24/9/17		PLUMSTEAD CEM CAF		DID NOT SERVE OVERSEAS
BAGNALL	J	PTE	20	/498	C					10/4/15 UNFIT				
BAGNALL	John	PTE	20	/157		34 DUNNS TERRACE	NEWCASTLE	28/10/14	7/12/18	SICK	1/7/16		TO 26th, 22nd BNS.	
BAGNALL	Joshu	LCPL	20	/217			WINLATON	29/10/14	4/5/17	WOUNDS	1/7/16		TO DEPOT.	AGE 39, DESERTED 21/6/15.
BAIN	David	PTE	20	/218		16 BACK GLEN STREE	HARRINGTON	29/10/14						
BAIRD	Wm	PTE	20	/1542	D		NEWCASTLE				1/7/16	THIEPVAL MEM		AWOL 14-16/2/15.
BAITES	Geo	PTE	20	/708	D		ASHINGTON				1/7/16	THIEPVAL MEM		MINER AGE 42, DESERTED 14/6/15.
BAKER	Rob L	PTE	20	/298			SOUTH CHURCH	30/10/14						

BAKER	Wm	PTE	20 / 987	B		SOUTH SHIELDS						TO DURHAM LI.	AWOL 6-7/10/15, DLI No 46528.
BALL	Fos A	PTE	20 / 159	C		JARROW				10/3/16	THIEPVAL MEM		SHRAPNEL WOUND THUMB & FORFINGER 3/16. AGE 35.
BALL	J	PTE	20 /1227	E				12/2/15	UNFIT				
BALMER	JohnR	PTE	20 / 160		4 BURNT HOUSES	GREENSIDE	28/10/14	4/1/17	19/6/17		GREENSIDE ST JOHN	TO DEPOT.	AGE 39.
BAMBOROUGH	Robt	PTE	20 / 219	C	31 NICHOLSON TERRA	FOREST HALL	29/10/14	26/7/17	SICK			TO 23rd, 25th, 3rd BNS.	AWOL 12-16/2/15.
BARNES	J	PTE	20 / 499	D				10/4/15	UNFIT				
BARNES	Nathn	LCPL	20 / 141	C		HARTON COLLIERY			1/7/16	1/7/16	THIEPVAL MEM		PTE AWOL 7-9/2/15.
BARNES	ThosR	SGT	20 / 140		7 ST MARYS TERRACE	RYTON			13/7/16	1/7/16	ST SEVER CEM ROUEN		BORN NORTH SHIELDS AGE 41.
BARNES	Wm	LSGT	20 / 992		74 ASTLEY ROAD	SEATON DELAVAL						TO 22nd BN, CLASS Z RESERVE.	CSM.
BARNFATHER	Nich	PTE	20 / 993		10 SECOND ROW	CHOPPINGTON			18/8/18		CHOPPINGTON ST PAUL CHYD		AGE 45.
BARRON	Wm	SGT	20 / 707		9 CLAREMONT TERRA	PELTON						TO 23rd BN, CLASS Z RESERVE.	
BARROW	Thos	PTE	20 /1224	C		JARROW			23/2/16		SAILLY SUR LYS CANADIAN CEM		FROM DEPOT COY TO C COY 25/2/15, DIED AT 26TH FIELD AME
BATES	Alf	PTE	20 /1416	A	42 ROSE AVENUE	OXHILL	13/1/15					TO LABOUR CORPS.	LAB CORPS No 581302, FROM DEPOT COY TO A COY 25/2/15.
BATEY	Thos	PTE	20 / 300	A		NEWBURN				31/8/16, SSHOCK DEC 16.		TO LABOUR CORPS.	LAB CORPS No 476657, STRETCHER BEARER 1/7/15.
BATEY	ThosS	PTE	20 / 371	D		RYTON			9/4/17	1/7/16	ROCLINCOURT VALLE	TO 25th BN.	OFF RATION STRENGTH 7-13/2/15.18GHOSP GSW L LEG HSHIF
BATLEY	Chas	LSGT	20 / 994		63 MORTIMER STREET	HARTFORD EAST	2/11/14	31/3/19	KR para 392	1/7/16		TO 3rd, 53rd(YS)BN, ARMY RES CLASS P.	
BAYCROFT	JohnA	PTE	20 /1689	A		NEWBURN			1/7/16		THIEPVAL MEM		
BEASTON	Jas	PTE	20 / 372			WIDDRINGTON COL			1/7/16		THIEPVAL MEM		BORN SUNDERLAND.
BEECH	Sam	PTE	20 / 373				31/10/14	2/11/18	GSW			TO 22nd BN.	AGE 42.
BELL	C P	PTE	20 / 220					1/2/15	KR para 392				
BELL	Geo	SGT	20 /1230	A	18 PARMETER STREE	SOUTHMOOR			2/9/18		BANCOURT BRIT CEM	TO 22nd BN, EAST YORKSHIRE REGT(1st BN).	E YORKS No 42567.BORN BURNHOPE,FROM DEP COY TO A CC
BELL	Geo R	PTE	20 /1415	C	WILKINSONS BLDGS B	BEDLINGTON						TO 16th, 22nd BNS, CLASS Z RESERVE.	FROM DEPOT COY TO C COY 25/2/15.HOSP WEST DIDSBURY 2
BELL	Geo W	SGT	20 / 20									TO 18th, 22nd BNS, CLASS Z RESERVE.	
BELL	Her J	PTE	20 / 996	B		CHOPWELL			1/7/16		THIEPVAL MEM		BORN BRAMPTON CUMBERLAND.
BELL	John	PTE	20 / 374				31/10/14	21/8/17	SICK			TO 3rd BN.	
BELL	John	PTE	20 /1187	B								TO 18th BN, CLASS Z RESERVE.	AWOL 6-7/2/15, 6-7/10/15.
BELL	Jos	PTE	20 /1488			NEWCASTLE	12/2/15						MINER, DES 29/5/15 REJOINED 29/6/15, DES 20/7/15 AGE 33.
BELL	Jos	PTE	20 / 161				28/10/14	13/7/17	SICK			TO DEPOT.	
BELL	Jos E	BGLF	20 / 502			GATESHEAD			1/7/16		OVILLERS MIL CEM		POSTED TO DEPOT COY 5/3/15.
BELL	Marm	PTE	20 / 503			WALLSEND				1/7/16		TO LABOUR CORPS.	LAB CORPS No 425097.
BELL	Rob H	PTE	20 / 997	B	7 MINERS COTTAGES	WEST ALLOTMENT			1/7/16		THIEPVAL MEM		AGE 27
BELL	Thos	PTE	20 /1541			GATESHEAD	14/5/15						LABOURER AGE 38, DESERTED 15/5/15.
BELL	ThosC	PTE	20 / 164	A		WHICKHAM			1/7/16		THIEPVAL MEM		BORN GATESHEAD.
BELL	W	BGLF	20 / 303									TO 16th BN.	POSTED TO DEPOT COY 5/3/15
BELL	WaltM	PTE	20 / 302		CHURCH COTTAGE	WHICKHAM			3/9/15		WHICKHAM ST MARY'S CHCH YD		
BENNETT	Jas F	PTE	20 / 304	A		WESTERHOPE			1/7/16		THIEPVAL MEM		BORN SEATON BURN, 48 HRS DETENTION 3/12/15 FOR AWOL.
BENNETT	Jos	PTE	20 /1544				12/5/15	29/5/18	THROMBOSIS			TO 1st GARRISON BN, ARMY RES CLASS P.	
BENNETT	Lionl	LCPL	20 / 142			WINLATON			21/8/17		HAGRICOURT MIL CEM		AGE 25.
BENNETT	Wm H	LSGT	20 / 89			GATESHEAD	27/10/14	2/8/17	GSW	1/7/16		TO DEPOT.	
BENNS	Jos L	PTE	20 /1233	C		ASHINGTON			1/7/16		THIEPVAL MEM		FROM DEPOT COY TO C COY 25/2/15, BORN CAISTOR NORFOL
BENSON	Ralph	PTE	20 / 998	B		BARDON MILL			1/7/16		OVILLERS		BORN HALTWHISTLE, AWOL 6-8/2/15.
BENSON	Thos	LCPL	20 / 305	A		BARDON MILL	30/10/14	17/2/17	WOUNDS	1/7/16			
BESTFORD	Geo	SGT	20 / 21			GATESHEAD				1/7/16		COMMISSIONED 31/10/17 25th BN.	CARD OF HONOUR.
BESTFORD	Jos	LCPL	20 /1220		3 FRONT STREET	SHERBURN						TO 2nd GARRISON BN, CLASS Z RESERVE.	
BEWICK	Tempt	PTE	20 / 999	B	176 COMMERCIAL RO/	BYKER			1/7/16		THIEPVAL MEM		BN MG SECTION.
BICKLE	RichO	PTE	20 /1417	C		SEAHAM HARBOU	14/1/15	10/1/18	GSW			TO DEPOT.	STRETCHER BEARER 1/7/15.
BIGGS	Adam	PTE	20 / 306			WESTERHOPE			1/7/16		THIEPVAL MEM		BORN NETTLESWORTH.
BINGHAM	John	PTE	20 / 143	A	STRATHMORE TERRA	ROWLANDS GILL			1/7/16	1/7/16	THIEPVAL MEM		BORN BERWICK AGE 31.
BIRD	J	PTE	20 /1465	E									AWOL 20-23/2/15.
BLACK	Jas A	LCPL	20 / 709			ASHINGTON	3/11/14	18/1/18	WOUNDS	1/7/16		TO DEPOT.	3 CCS 2/7/16 EVAC 2/7/16, AGE 23.
BLACK	Lew Y	SGT	20 / 307			WALLSEND			1/7/16		THIEPVAL MEM		BORN JARROW
BLACKBURN	ThosD	PTE	20 / 162	A	7 RAILWAY TERR SUN	GATESHEAD			1/7/16		BAPAUME POST		BORN SCOTSWOOD AGE 33.
BLACKLOCK	T W	PTE	20 /1221	C		BURRADON				4/10/16		TO LABOUR CORPS.	FROM DEPOT COY TO C COY 25/2/15.LAB CORPS No 648271.
BLADES	Geo	PTE	20 /1234	B	9 COMMERCIAL STREI	BROWNEY COLLIERY						TO LABOUR CORPS.	FROM DEPOT COY TO B COY 25/2/15, LAB CORPS No 396917.
BLAIR	Geo	PTE	20 /1713						KR para 392			TO 2nd GARRISON BN.	
BLAIR	Jas C	PTE	20 / 23	A	9 OYSTERSHELL LANE	NEWCASTLE		10/4/15	UNFIT				AWOL 7-8/2/15.
BLAND	Jhn W	PTE	20 / 24	C									AWOL 7-8/2/15, 29/11/15-1/12/15.
BLENKINSOP	Mark	PTE	20 /1590		8 HIGH LANE ROW	HEBBURN COLL	31/5/15	14/10/16	GSW	1/7/16		TO DEPOT.	
BLYTHE	Thos	PTE	20 /1463	E			13/1/15						AWOL 27/2-4/3/15.
BOAG	JohnH	LCPL	20 / 163			NEWCASTLE	28/10/14	13/7/17	WOUNDS	1/7/16		TO 3rd BN.	REGIMENTAL POLICE 31/1/15.
BOGEY	A	PTE	20 /1236	D		SUNDERLAND				1/7/16			FROM DEPOT COY TO D COY 25/2/15, NAME SPELT BOGIE.
BOLLAND	John	PTE	20 /1190	B	18 BACK ROW	CULLERCOATES			1/7/16		THIEPVAL MEM		BORN CAMBOIS, AGE 32, AWOL 6-8/2/15.
BOLTON	Wm S	LCPL	20 /1000	A		ALNWICK			1/7/16		THIEPVAL MEM		
BOND	Wm	PTE	20 / 25	C	185 DOLPHIN STREET	NEWCASTLE	26/10/14	18/4/17	WOUNDS	1/7/16		TO DEPOT.	SERVED IN COLDM GDS BOER WAR.
BONE	RobtB	LCPL	20 / 221		29 CHIRTON STREET	BYKER	29/10/14	9/4/17	GSW	1/7/16		TO DEPOT.	
BONE	Wm	LCPL	20 / 309	A		ALNWICK			1/7/16	1/7/16	OVILLERS MIL CEM		IN 3 PLATOON.
BOSTON	Russl	PTE	20 /1232	C		NEWCASTLE			1/7/16		THIEPVAL MEM		FROM DEPOT COY TO C COY 25/2/15.
BOWDEN	G	PTE	20 / 711			WALLSEND				1/7/16			
BOWMAN	Geo	PTE	20 / 144	A	141 HOLYSTONE CRES	NORTH HEATON					NOWSHERA MIL CEM I	TO DURHAM LI(1st BN). DLI No 52347.	AWOL 14-15/2/15. AGE 43 BORN PENRITH DIED OF ENTERIC.
BOWRING	Corn	PTE	20 / 224		11 SPECULATION PLA(	GRANGE VILLA				1/7/16		TO 16th, 9th, 12th, 12/13th BNS, CLASS Z RESERVE.	FROM ALDERSLEY EDGE MANCHESTER.
BOYCE	Ern A	PIPR	20 / 223	A	182 DONCASTER ROAI	NEWCASTLE			1/7/16		THIEPVAL		BORN LEYTON ESSEX AGE 21.
BOYD	JohnT	PTE	20 /1222			CHESTER LE ST	12/1/15	19/4/18	GSW	1/7/16			AGE 42.
BOYD	MarkA	PTE	20 / 712	B	35 SMITH STREET	WHEATLEY HILL				12/6/16		TO 22nd BN, ATTACHED 102nd BDE HQ, CLASS Z R	BRUISED FACE SHELL SHOCK, AWOL 13-14/2/15.
BRADFORD	Ral S	PTE	20 /1545	C		ANNITSFORD			1/7/16		THIEPVAL MEM		FROM E COY TO C COY 19/6/15, AWOL 29-30/11/15.
BRADLEY	ThosB	LCPL	20 / 310	A	29 CHARLES STREET	DINNINGTON			10/4/18	2/9/16,13/10/16	NIEUPORT MEM	TO 10th, 22nd BNS.	WND DURING TRENCH RAID 13/10/16, STRETCHER BEARER 1/.
BRADY	Jas	PTE	20 /1560				14/5/15	4/2/17	SICK			TO DEPOT.	AGE 38, FROM E COY TO D COY 19/6/15.
BRAIN	Dick	PTE	20 / 375									TO 2nd GARRISON BN, CLASS Z RESERVE.	
BRANKSTONE	Arth	CPL	20 /1561	D	213 ELLESMERE ROAD	NEWCASTLE			1/7/16		THIEPVAL MEM		AGE 33, FROM E COY TO D COY 19/6/15,16 PLATOON, AWOL 7/
BREWIS		PTE	20	A									
BRIARS	Wm Wn	PTE	20 / 376			BLACKHILL	31/10/14	21/8/17	WOUNDS	1/7/16		TO 84th TRAINING RESERVE BN.	AGE 25.
BRIGGS	Clemt	PTE	20 /1464	C			13/1/15					TO 34th DIV CYC COY.	
BRIGGS	John	LCPL	20 /1235	B		NEW DELAVAL				23/6/16		TO 14th, 24th, 24/27th, 8th, 1/7th BNS, CLASS Z RESE	FROM DEPOT COY TO B COY 25/2/15, REVERTED TO PTE 16/5/
BROATCH	Wm	PTE	20 /1001	B		NEWCASTLE			1/7/16		THIEPVAL MEM		AWOL 6-7/2/15.
BRODIE	Rich	PTE	20 /1225		16 BRICKGARTH	HETTON LE HOLE						TO 1st GARRISON BN, CLASS Z RESERVE.	
BROWN	Adam	PTE	20 /1589		35 SMITH STREET	WHEATLEY HILL				4/6/16		TO 22nd BN, CLASS Z RESERVE.	GSW ARM
BROWN	Adam	PTE	20 /1004			ACKLINGTON				1/7/16		TO CLASS Z RESERVE.	AWOL 6-7/2/15, 3 CCS 2/7/16 EVAC 2/7/16.
BROWN	E	LCPL	20 / 311	C									REDUCED TO PTE FOR ABSENCE 16/2/15.
BROWN	J G	PTE	20 / 505			FOREST HALL				3/4/16, 1/7/16		TO LABOUR CORPS.	WND NECK 4/16, 18 GHOSP 6/7 GSW LEG HSHIP CALAIS 6/7/16
BROWN	Jas	PTE	20 / 508		57 MORTIMER STREET	HARTFORD COLLIE			1/7/16	1/7/16	BOULOGNE EASTERN		
BROWN	Jas	PTE	20 / 26	B		GLASGOW			1/7/16		THIEPVAL MEM	TO 23rd, 20th BNS.	
BROWN	Jas B	PTE	20 / 146		58 WINGROVE GARDE	NEWCASTLE	28/10/14	27/2/17	NEPHRITIS			TO DEPOT.	
BROWN	Jas H	LSGT	20 / 225									TO LABOUR CORPS.	LAB CORPS No 518916.
BROWN	John	PTE	20 /1481	D		NORTH SHIELDS	8/2/15		1/7/16		THIEPVAL MEM		BORN TYNEMOUTH, TOS DEPOT COY 11/2/15.
BROWN	John	PTE	20 /1574		35 HAMPDEN STREET	GATESHEAD			KR para 392			TO 1st GARRISON BN.	
BROWN	JohnR	PTE	20 / 91	C		NEWCASTLE	27/10/14	4/10/16	VDH	1/7/16		TO DEPOT.	AWOL 7-8/3/15.
BROWN	M	PTE	20 / 506	D				9/2/15	KR para 392				
BROWN	Mich	PTE	20 / 507	D		FELLING	1/11/14	4/11/16	WOUNDS	1/7/16		TO DEPOT.	AWOL 27/3/15.
BROWN	Robt	PTE	20 / 377			FOREST HALL	31/10/14	1/3/19	KR para 392	1/7/16			
BROWN	Robt	PTE	20 / 145	A			28/10/14	16/11/16	NEPHRITIS			TO ARMY RESERVE CLASS W.	AGE 38, AWOL 10-16/2/15.
BROWN	Wm	PTE	20 /1575		119 PINE STREET	GATESHEAD			5/11/17		WANCOURT		
BROWNSWORI	John	PTE	20 /1486			EASINGTON LANE			KR para 392	1/7/16			
BRUCE	Chas	PTE	20 / 27	A		NEWCASTLE				1/7/16		TO 23rd BN.	AWOL 28/3/15, 2nd SOUTHERN GHOSP BRISTOL 7/16.
BRUCE	Thos	PTE	20 / 226			SEATON DELAVAL				1/7/16		TO DURHAM LIGHT INFANTRY, TRAINING RESERVI	TRG RES No TR/5/64645.
BRUCE	Wm C	PTE	20 / 147			FELLING	28/10/14	8/9/17	WOUNDS	1/7/16		TO 3rd BN.	AGE 23.
BRUNTON	A F	PTE	20 / 28									TO MUNITIONS(ARMSTRONG WHITWORTH & CO).	
BUGLASS	John	CPL	20 /1197	B		BERWICK			1/7/16		THIEPVAL MEM		
BULMER	John	PTE	20 /1644			FENCEHOUSES	16/6/15			DEC 16.		TO 1st BN, WEST YORKS REGT(2nd&12th), DORSET	DESERTED 26/8/15, AWOL 2/1/16, AGE 21.
BURLEY	John	PTE	20 /1654			RUTHERGLEN			3/3/17	27/2/17	HARBARCQ CEM		
BURN	Wm	LCPL	20 / 378			WALLSEND						TO 23rd BN, CLASS Z RESERVE.	
BURNHAM	T	PTE	20 / 379	D				10/4/15	UNFIT				AWOL 7-8/3/15.
BURNS	Rich	PTE	20 / 148				28/10/14	1/2/19	KR para 392xvia			TO ARMY RESERVE CLASS P.	
BURTON	ThosE	PTE	20 /1668			NEWCASTLE			1/7/16		THIEPVAL MEM	TO 22nd BN(A COY), 20th BN.	BORN GATESHEAD.

BUTTERS	JohnK	PTE	20 / 313		37 DOCKWRAY SQUAF	NORTH SHIELDS				12/6/16	5/6/16	ETRETAT CHCH YD FRANCE		DIED AT No 1GHOSP,GSW FACE.BORN RENNINGTON AGE 28.
CALDER	Edwd	SGT	20 / 509		21 BEECH GROVE WE:	RYTON	2/11/14	31/7/17	COMMISSIC		1/7/16		COMMISSIONED 25th BN(1/8/17), TO 12/13th BN.	LCPL 13/3/15, CPL 9/6/16, SGT 13/7/16.
CAMERON	Alex	PTE	20 /1670						KR para 392				TO 1st GARRISON BN.	
CAMERON	J W	LCPL	20 / 714	D										AWOL 12-14/2/15.
CAMPBELL	J	PTE	20 / 29	D										REGIMENTAL POLICE 31/1/15.
CAMPBELL	JohnT	SGT	20 / 30		58 GROSEVNOR GARD	NEWCASTLE							COMMISSIONED WEST YORKSHIRE REGT(4th BN).	COMM 29/5/18.
CAMPBELL	Jos	SGT	20 / 715	B		NEWCASTLE				1/7/16	1/7/16	OVILLERS MIL CEM		BORN BEDLINGTON.
CAMPBELL	Ralph	PTE	20 / 716	D		BEDLINGTON				1/7/16		THIEPVAL MEM		BORN AMBLE, AWOL 7-8/3/15.
CAPE	John	PTE	20 / 380		WINGROVE VILLA	ROWLANDS GILL				3/6/16		ALBERT COM CEM EXT		KILLED BY SHELLFIRE, BORN WHITEHAVEN.
CARLIN	Denn	PTE	20 /1240	E			5/1/15	15/12/17	SICK				TO 3rd BN.	AGE 46, AWOL 6-8/2/15.
CARLTON	Jos	PTE	20 / 31	A									TO 18th BN, ROYAL FUSILIERS(24th BN).	AWOL 7-8/3/15. 20 9/1/16-3/7/18, 18 4/7/18-28/8/18.
CARR	JohnG	PTE	20 /1238			BEAMISH				15/6/16	15/6/16	ALBERT COM CEM EXT		KILLED BY RIFLE GRENADE, L ARM, BACK, HEAD.
CARR	Jos	SGT	20 / 717										TO 18th BN, CLASS Z RESERVE.	
CARR	Thos	PTE	20 /1421			SEAHAM HARBOUR				3/7/16		WARLOY BAILLON COM CEM		BORN CHESTER MOOR.
CARR	W	PTE	20 / 510			BEDLINGTON					1/7/16		to 25th BN, ROYAL FUSILIERS(24th BN).	20 9/1/16-4/7/16, 25 8/1/17-28/8/18, 24 RFUS 29/8/18-8/10/18
CARRUTHERS	John	PTE	20 / 227	A			29/10/14	10/4/15	UNFIT					DID NOT SERVE OVERSEAS.
CARRUTHERS	Thos	PTE	20 / 512		65 SHANKHOUSE TERI	CRAMLINGTON							TO 1st GARRISON BN, CLASS Z RESERVE.	
CARTER	Rob P	PTE	20 / 514			NEWCASTLE	1/11/14	3/6/18	GSW		1/7/16		TO DEPOT.	AGE 34.
CARTWRIGHT	A	PTE	20 /1266	E										AWOL 21-22/2/15.
CARTWRIGHT	Normn	PTE	20 /1260	C		SOUTHWICK				1/7/16		OVILLERS MIL CEM		FROM DEPOT COY TO C COY 25/2/15, FROM BORN HETTON LE
CASSIDY	Wm	PTE	20 /1008			W CRAMLINGTON	3/11/14	11/7/17	GSW		1/7/16		TO 3rd BN.	
CASSON	Thos	LCPL	20 / 719			HIRST	3/11/14	3/4/17	WOUNDS				TO 22nd BN, DEPOT.	DESERTED 21/6/15,MINER AGE 29,5'7",3 CCS 2/7/16 EVAC 2/7/1
CAVANAGH	John	PTE	20 / 381	A	CARRS ROW BELLS CI	SCOTSWOOD				1/7/16		THIEPVAL MEM		AGE 19, AWOL 29/3/15.
CHAMBERS	Edwd	PTE	20 /1259	E	37 NICHOLSON STREE	RYHOPE							TO 1st GARRISON BN, CLASS Z RESERVE.	FROM E COY TO A COY 19/6/15,AVL 57 NICHOLSON ST MONKH
CHAMBERS	H	PTE	20 /1252	C									TO ARMY SERVICE CORPS REMOUNTS.	FROM DEPOT COY TO C COY 25/2/15.ASC ORMSKIRK 19/7/15.
CHAMBERS	HenRL	PTE	20 / 382	C	81 EAST NORFOLK STI	NORTH SHIELDS				1/7/16		THIEPVAL MEM		
CHAPPELOW	J	PTE	20 /1239	E										AWOL 1-3/2/15, FROM DEPOT COY TO D COY 25/2/15.
CHARLETON	Thos	PTE	20 /1645			WHITLEY BAY				1/7/16		THIEPVAL MEM		BORN ELSDON.
CHARLTON	G	PTE	20 /1010	B										AWOL 6-7/10/15.
CHARLTON	New E	PTE	20 /1257	A									TO 26th BN, COUNTY OF LONDON REGT(1/16th BN)	26th 17/6/17-22/10/17,LONDON REGT 27/3/18-17/12/18,AWOL 3/1
CHARLTON	W	PTE	20 /1593		15 RAILWAY ROAD	NORTH SEATON					1/7/16			
CHARLTON	Wm	PTE	20 / 92	C									TO 1st GARRISON BN, 26th, 1/4th BNS.	AWOL 6-7/2/15.
CHILTON	Robt	PTE	20 /1241	C	MOORLAND COTTAGE	BEDLINGTON STN				1/7/16		THIEPVAL MEM		FROM DEPOT COY TO C COY 25/2/15, BORN BEDLINGTON AGE
CHIPCHASE	Geo E	PTE	20 / 722	B		GATESHEAD				1/7/16		OVILLERS MIL CEM		BORN DURHAM AGE 38.
CHIPCHASE	John	PTE	20 / 93			GATESHEAD	27/10/14	11/10/17	WOUNDS		1/7/16		TO 23rd BN.	AGE 42.
CHRISP	Geo	PTE	20 /1255			SEATON DELAVAL				1/7/16	JULY 16	THIEPVAL MEM		BORN NEW DELAVAL, CONTUSED ARM SHELL EXPLOSION.
CHRISP	John	LCPL	20 / 723			ACKLINGTON				1/7/16		THIEPVAL MEM		BORN ALNWICK
CHRISP	Osw W	PTE	20 / 383			NEWCASTLE			KR para 392		1/7/16		TO DURHAM LIGHT INFANTRY, TRAINING RESERVI	TRG RES No 41605.
CHRISTOPHEF	Robt	PTE	20 /1547	D		MURTON COLLIERY				1/7/16		THIEPVAL MEM		BORN HUTTON HENRY.
CHURCHILL	Robsn	LCPL	20 /1011	B	22 HARTBURN TERR	SEATON DELAVAL				18/6/16	15/6/16	HEILLY STATION		AWOL 7-8/3/15, DIED AT 36CCS, WND L ARM, AGE 27.
CLARK	ChasH	PTE	20 /1014		6 COACH LANE	DINNINGTON								
CLARK	ChasW	PTE	20 /1242	E		SUNDERLAND			KR para 392				ATTACHED DURHAM LI(13th BN).	FROM E COY TO A COY 19/6/15.
CLARK	D	PTE	20 / 725	B										CO's GROOM RETURNED TO COMPANY 31/1/15, AWOL 6-9/2/15
CLARK	Hen G	PTE	20 /1012	B	FREEHOLD TERRACE	GUIDE POST				1/7/16		THIEPVAL MEM		BORN ROTHBURY AGE 38.
CLARK	J	PTE	20 / 94	A										AWOL 7-8/2/15.
CLARK	MattL	SGT	20 / 384	D	42 CUTHBERT STREET	MARLEY HILL				1/7/16		THIEPVAL MEM		BORN TOW LAW.
CLARK	Peter	PTE	20 /1261	E	29 WARKSWORTH CRI	NEWBURN							CLASS Z RESERVE.	FROM E COY TO A COY 19/6/15.
CLARK	Thos	PTE	20 /1420		FOX STREET	DAWDON							TO 1st GARRISON BN, CLASS Z RESERVE.	
CLARK	W	PTE	20 /1013	D				20/4/15	KR para 392					
CLARK		PTE	20 / 515	C									TO 34th DIV CYC COY.	
CLARKE	Jos T	PTE	20 / 385	C		FOREST HALL				1/7/16		THIEPVAL MEM		BORN WEETSLADE NTHBLD, AWOL 6-9/2/15.
CLARKSON	A	PTE	20 /1244	E										AWOL 6-8/2/15.
CLASPER	Matt	PTE	20 /1546	C	42 WELLINGTON STRE	SOUTH SHIELDS				1/7/16		THIEPVAL MEM		FROM E COY TO C COY 19/6/15, AGE 26.
CLAY	Wm	PTE	20 /1591	A	3 SMITH PLACE	NORTH SHIELDS				1/7/16		THIEPVAL MEM		BORN TYNEMOUTH.
CLEWES	JohnG	PTE	20 / 386	B		WALBOTTLE							TO 25th, 1/4th BNS, CLASS Z RESERVE.	NEW NUMBER 204567, DESERTED 24/12/18.
CLIFF	J	PTE	20 /1243	A		NEWCASTLE	6/1/15	30/7/17	KR para 392		OCTOBER 16		TO 34th DIV CYC COY, 24th BN, DEPOT.	FROM DEPOT COY TO A COY 25/2/15, TYNESIDE IRISH No 24/1

CLOUGH	Barth	PTE	20 / 387	A	2 HUNTERS SQUARE	WREKENTON								AWOL 7-8/3/15.
CLOUGH	Matt	PTE	20 / 516				31/10/14	16/8/17	GSW		4/6/16		TO 84th TRAINING RESERVE BN.	CONTUSED BACK & SHELL SHOCK
COATES	ChasE	PTE	20											AWOL 20/7/15, AGE 20.
COATES	ChasF	PTE	20 / 33	C		ST ANDREWS	26/10/14			1/7/16		THIEPVAL MEM	DCM 11/4/15 56 DAYS YORK DETENTION BKS.	AWOL 6-10/2/15, LABOURER AGE 33, DESERTED 7/6/15.
COATES	Wm	PTE	20 /1254	C							1/7/16		TO 9th, 1/5th BNS, CLASS Z RESERVE.	FROM DEPOT COY TO C COY 25/2/15.
COCHRANE	W	PTE	20 /1657			NORTH SHIELDS					1/7/16			
COCKBURN	Robt	SGT	20 / 724	D		BEDLINGTON				1/7/16		THIEPVAL MEM		BORN BLYTH.
COCKRANE	Jas E	PTE	20 / 517	C			1/11/14	27/2/18	VARICOUS VEINS				TO ARMY RESERVE CLASS P.	AGE 36, STRETCHER BEARER 1/7/15.
COLDWELL	Henry	PTE	20 / 727	B			3/11/14	13/4/15	SICK					AGE 41, DIS ON ORDERS 10/4/15.
COLLINS	F	PTE	20 /1419	E										AWOL 12-15/2/15.
COLLINS	G W	PTE	20 /1289	D										OFF RATION STRENGTH 14-20/2/15.
COLLINS	Geo	PTE	20 / 728										TO ROYAL INNISKILLING FUSILIERS(6th BN).	R INNIS FUS No 21526.
COLLINS	Jas	PTE	20 / 229	C		WALLSEND				1/7/16		THIEPVAL MEM		BORN WORKSOP NOTTS.
COLLINS	Rich	PTE	20 / 390	D	RYTON PARK COTTAG	RYTON							TO 2/7th BN, CLASS Z RESERVE.	STRETCHER BEARER 1/7/15.
COLLINS	Robt	PTE	20 /1015	B									TO 2nd GARRISON BN, CLASS Z RESERVE.	AWOL 6-7/2/15.
COLLINS	S	CPL	20 / 518	D									TO 34th DIV CYC COY.	
CONNELLY	P	PTE	20 / 519	C				10/4/15	UNFIT					AWOL 6-9/2/15.
CONNEY	Robt	PTE	20 /1248	B									TO 19th BN, CLASS Z RESERVE.	FROM DEPOT COY TO B COY 25/2/15, NAME SPELT COURNEY.
CONNOR	Thos	PTE	20 /1256				12/1/15							
CONROY	J	PTE	20 / 524			GOSFORTH					1/7/16			
COOK	Geo	PTE	20 / 729	B		WILLINGTON	3/11/14	19/2/18	GSW		1/7/16		TO 3rd BN.	STRETCHER BEARER 1/7/15
COOK	T	PTE	20 / 520			NEWCASTLE					1/7/16			
COOMBE	Jas H	PTE	20 / 522	C		CRAMLINGTON				1/7/16		OVILLERS MIL CEM		
COPELAND	A	CSGT	20 /1535	C									FROM 11th BN, 16/4/15.	
CORBETT	Geo	PTE	20 /1527	C		GATESHEAD				1/7/16		THIEPVAL MEM		
CORKIN	John	PTE	20 /1246	B		SOUTH SHIELDS				1/7/16		OVILLERS MIL CEM		AWOL 1/2/15 FROM E COY, FROM DEPOT COY TO B COY 25/2/1
COTTER	Wm J	PTE	20 /1704				17/7/15	5/9/17	KR para 392				TO 84th TRAINING RESERVE BN.	DID NOT SERVE OVERSEAS.
COTTERELL	Henry	PTE	20 /1247	A		WEST SLEEKBURN				1/7/16		THIEPVAL MEM		BORN BEDLINGTON, FROM E COY TO A COY 19/6/15.
COTTERILL	Archi	PTE	20 /1699			ALNWICK				9/10/17		TYNE COT MEM	TO YORKSHIRE REGT(6th BN).	YORKS REGT No 33686.
COTTIER	Telfd	PTE	20 /1615						KR para 392		1/7/16			
COTTRELL	Jas	PTE	20 /1245	E		CHOPPINGTON	5/1/15	16/10/17	KR para 392		1/7/16		TO 22nD, 10th BNS, DEPOT.	FROM E COY TO A COY 19/6/15.
COUCH	J	PTE	20 /1016	B				1/2/15	KR para 392					
COULEY	Frank	LCPL	20 / 95	C		NEWCASTLE				1/7/16		OVILLERS MIL CEM		
COULSON	Wm	PTE	20 / 391	C	8 DELAVAL ROAD	FOREST HALL				1/7/16		THIEPVAL MEM		BORN GATESHEAD AGE 32.
COWAN	A	PTE	20 / 388					2/2/15	KR para 392					
COWAN	Dug	PTE	20 / 165	A	45 GRANGE RD	JARROW							TO 18th, 22nd BNS.	AWOL 7-8/3/15.
COWELL	John	PTE	20 / 293	C	45 CROSS ROW	CRAMLINGTON				12/12/15		SEATON VALLEY CEM		DIED ISOLATION HOSP OLD SARUM, BORN SEDGEFIELD, AGE
COWEN	Rob A	PTE	20 / 732			BEDLINGTON STN					1/7/16		TO 16th, 12/13th(D COY), CLASS Z RESERVE.	REPORTED MISSING 27-29/5/18.
COWIE	C	PTE	20 / 731					1/2/15	KR para 392					
COWIE	Jas	LCPL	20 / 730	B		NEWCASTLE				1/7/16		THIEPVAL MEM		REAL NAME CRAWLEY.
CRABTREE	J T	PTE	20 / 392		6 CLYDE STREET	CHOPWELL					1/7/16		TO ARMY ORDNANCE CORPS.	AOC No O39194.
CRACKET	Thos	PTE	20 / 733	D	3 FOURTH ROW	CHOPPINGTON				1/7/16	1/7/16	THIEPVAL MEM		STRETCHER BEARER 1/7/15
CRANNEY	Jos	PTE	20 /1253	C		SWALWELL					1/7/16		TO 20th, 23rd BNS, ROYAL FUSILIERS(24th BN).	FROM DEPOT COY TO C COY 25/2/15.FRANCE 20-5/7/16.
CRANSON	Geo W	PTE	20 / 393	C		NORTH SHIELDS				1/7/16	1/7/16	THIEPVAL MEM		BORN GATESHEAD
CRAWFORD	J	PTE	20 /1251	B										FROM DEPOT COY TO B COY 25/2/15.
CROOK	H	PTE	20 /1017	D				10/4/15	UNFIT					
CROOKS	S	PTE	20 /1612								MARCH 16			
CROSBY	Arthu	CPL	20 / 34											
CROSBY	Edwd	PTE	20 /1018	B		SEATON DELAVAL				1/7/16		THIEPVAL MEM		BORN NEWCASTLE, AWOL 7-8/3/15.
CROSBY	Rob J	PTE	20 / 525	C		CRAMLINGTON				1/7/16		THIEPVAL MEM		BORN BEDLINGTON.
CROSTON	Jos	PTE	20 / 526										TO 2nd GARRISON BN, CLASS Z RESERVE.	
CROZIER	Robt	PTE	20 /1019	B		GATESHEAD				1/7/16		THIEPVAL MEM	TO 34th DIV CYC COY, 20th BN.	MG SECTION, BORN GATESHEAD AGE 21.
CRUDDAS	Ambr	PTE	20 /1656	A		CHOPWELL				1/7/16		THIEPVAL MEM		BORN BEAMISH.
CRYLE	W	PTE	20 / 394			NEWCASTLE					1/7/16		TO DURHAM LIGHT INFANTRY, TRAINING RESERVI	TRG RES No TR/5/66982.
CUMMINGS	T M M	PTE	20 / 36	B	22 RICHARDSON TERF	USWORTH							TO 84th TRAINING RESERVE BN.	POSTED FROM B TO E COY 31/1/15, CQMS TRG RES No TR/5/5
CUNNINGHAM	Mich	PTE	20 /1020	D	83 MORTIMER STREET	HARTFORD COLL				1/7/16		THIEPVAL MEM		BORN BLYTH AGE 46, AWOL 7-9/2/15.

CURRAN	Wm	PTE	20 /1258				12/1/15	26/2/15	FLAT FEET					DID NOT SERVE OVERSEAS.
CURRIE	Alex	PTE	20 /1250										TO SCOTTISH RIFLES(18th BN).	SCO RIF No 55576.
CURRY	JohnT	PTE	20 / 149			FOREST HALL	28/10/14	5/1/18	WOUNDS		1/7/16		TO 85th TRAINING RESERVE BN.	AGE 28, BATH WAR HOSP 11/7/16.
CUSHNIE	Wm	CPL	20 / 38		27 MARY STREET	NEWCASTLE							TO 21st BN, DURHAM LI(13th BN).	DLI No 46056.
CUSWORTH	Fred	PTE	20 / 39		96 SHORTRIDGE TERF	NEWCASTLE								POW.
DAGLISH	Geo	LCPL	20 /1576		POTTERY ROW	NORTH HYLTON							TO 22nd BN(PIONEER SECTION).	
DALE	Rich	CSM	20 / 8	A	60 ALGERNON RD	NEWCASTLE				1/7/16		OVILLERS MIL CEM	EX NEWCASTLE POLICEMAN.	BORN KILLEVAN Co MONAGHAN, AGE 25.
DALLEY	J H	PTE	20 / 736	B				2/2/15	KR para 392					
DARRAGH	J	PTE	20 / 96	C										AWOL 29/11-1/12/15.
DART	John	PTE	20 /1263			SEAHAM HARBOU	6/1/15	9/8/18	GSW		1/7/16		TO 3rd BN.	
DAVIDSON	G	PTE	20 /1023			CHOPPINGTON COL					1/7/16			
DAVIDSON	JohnW	CPL	20 / 737	C	64 JUBILEE TERRACE	ANNITSFORD				1/7/16		THIEPVAL MEM		BORN PONTELAND AGE 23, STRETCHER BEARER 1/7/15.
DAVIDSON	Jos	PTE	20 / 231	C		MARYPORT				1/7/16	1/7/16	OVILLERS MIL CEM		BORN COCKERMOUTH, AWOL 28/2/15-7/8/15.
DAVIDSON	R	PTE	20 /1021											REGIMENTAL BUTCHER 31/1/15.
DAVIDSON	Robt	PIPR	20 /1594	B	112 HEDLEY STREET	SOUTH SHIELDS				1/7/16		THIEPVAL MEM		BORN ABERDEEN
DAVIDSON	Thos	CPL	20 / 315	A	62 CLAREMONT AVENI	GATESHEAD							TO 2nd GARRISON BN, CLASS Z RESERVE.	STRETCHER BEARER 1/7/15.
DAVIDSON		LCPL	20 / 530	C									TO 34th DIV CYC COY.	SIGNAL COURSE AT ALNWICK 11/4/15.
DAVIES	Wm	PTE	20 / 739	D		HIRST				12/7/16		BOULOGNE EASTERN	TO 34th DIV CYC COY, 20th BN.	BORN WIGTON CUMB, DAVIS IN WGR.
DAVIS	G	PTE	20 / 529	C				10/4/15	UNFIT					AWOL 13-16/2/15.
DAVISON	G	PTE	20 / 741								1/7/16			
DAVISON	Geo	PTE	20 /1424	E			12/1/15							AWOL 1-2/2/15. LCPL AWOL 12-13/2/15.
DAVISON	Rich	PTE	20 / 740	A		HEBBURN				1/7/16		THIEPVAL MEM		BORN JARROW
DAVISON	Rich	LCPL	20 / 742	B	31 DENE GARDENS	LEMINGTON				1/7/16		THIEPVAL MEM		AWOL 6-7/10/15, AGE 29 BORN NEWCASTLE.
DAVISON	Thos	CPL	20 /1423	A		SEAHAM HARBOUR							TO 22nd BN.	FROM DEPOT COY TO A COY 25/2/15, AWOL 7-8/3/15.
DAWSON	ChasR	PTE	20 /1270	C	5 SHOP ROW	PHILADELPHIA				1/7/16		THIEPVAL MEM		BORN NEW HERRINGTON,FROM DEPOT COY TO C COY 25/2/1
DAWSON	Thos	PTE	20 /1274										TO 2nd GARRISON BN, CLASS Z RESERVE.	
DENNIS	G	PTE	20 / 69	C				10/4/15	UNFIT					
DENT	Wm M	PTE	20 /1510	B		SPENNYMOOR				1/7/16		THIEPVAL MEM		
DEVINE	Ed A	SGT	20 /1679										COMMISSIONED.	
DEVLIN	Peter	PTE	20 / 531	B		NEWCASTLE				1/71/16		THIEPVAL MEM		BORN WORKINGTON, AWOL 8-9/2/15.
DEVONS	Edwd	PTE	20 / 66	C		EASINGTON	23/10/14							BRICKMAKER DESTD 5/6/15. AGE 42.CPL REVERTED TO PTE 6/
DEWSON	G	PTE	20 /1043	B										AWOL 6-7/10/15.No PROBABLY /1033!
DICK	Jas	PTE	20 /1268		16 FOX STREET	SEAHAM							TO 2nd GARRISON BN, CLASS Z RESERVE.	
DICKSON	Frcs	SGT	20 / 150	C		GATESHEAD				1/7/16		OVILLERS MIL CEM		BORN WARDLEY Co DURHAM,REGIMENTAL POLICE 31/1/15.
DICKSON	Jas	PTE	20 / 533	D		BEDLINGTON							TO 16th, 1/4th, 11th BNS.	AWOL 7-8/3/15.
DITCHBURN	Robt	PTE	20 / 743		8 MARKS ROW	AMBLE					27/2/17		TO 8th, 1/5th BNS, CLASS Z RESERVE.	
DIXON	Edwd	CPL	20 /1595		BREWERY YARD	NEWBIGGIN			KR para 392		1/7/16		TO DURHAM LIGHT INFANTRY, TRAINING RES BN.	TRG RES No TR/5/58176.
DIXON	Frank	PTE	20 / 395	C									TO 2nd GARRISON BN, CLASS Z RESERVE.	AWOL 12-16/2/15.
DIXON	Geo T	PTE	20 / 151			NEWCASTLE					1/7/16			3 CCS 2/7/16 EVAC 2/7/16.
DIXON	JohnW	PTE	20 /1025	D	10 CROSS ROAD	W CRAMLINGTON				1/7/16		OVILLERS MIL CEM		BORN LOW FELL, AGE 25.
DIXON	P	DRV	20 / 534	D									TO 25th BN.	MACHINE GUN DRIVER TO TI AT SUTTON VENY.
DIXON	Robt	PTE	20 / 744			BEDLINGTON				1/7/16		THIEPVAL MEM		BORN BLYTH.
DIXON	W	LCPL	20 /1619	B	1 DOVE COTTAGES	OLD HARTLEY				1/7/16		OVILLERS MIL CEM		BORN OLD HARTLEY.
DIXON	Wm	PTE	20 / 233	A		GATESHEAD				1/7/16		THIEPVAL MEM		
DOBINSON	Robt	PTE	20 /1026	B	17 THE FOLD	MONKSEATON				1/7/16		OVILLERS MIL CEM		BORN TYNEMOUTH AGE 39.
DODDS	T W	PTE	20 /1027	D		CRAMLINGTON					1/7/16			REPEATEDLY AWOL 1915, TRIED BY FGCM ARMENTIERES 11/3
DODDS	W	PTE	20 / 535	C									TO LABOUR CORPS.	AWOL 29/11/15-2/12/15.
DOLPHIN	Chris	LCPL	20 /1264	E		ESH	5/1/15			9/9/17		THIEPVAL MEM		BORN WHITTON PARK
DONALD	John	PTE	20 / 745										TO 2nd GARRISON BN, CLAS Z RESERVE.	
DONALD	ThosC	PTE	20 /1028	D			2/11/14	22/?/16	KR para 392					PROMOTED TO SGT 6/3/15.DID NOT SERVE O/SEAS.
DONALD	Wm A	PTE	20 / 167						KR para 392				TO 2nd GARRISON BN.	
DONALDSON	David	PTE	20 / 234											
DONALDSON	T	PTE	20 /1265	E										AWOL 3-5/2/15, 25-26/3/15.
DONEY	W H A	PTE	20 / 536	C		CRAMLINGTON				1/7/16		THIEPVAL MEM		BORN NEWCASTLE.
DOOLEY	D	PTE	20 / 41	C				9/2/15	KR para 392					
DORMAND	Geo D	PTE	20 /1029		9 MILL STREET	CHIRTON				1/7/16		THIEPVAL MEM		BORN CRAMLINGTON AGE 21.
DORMAND	Henry	PTE	20 /1617		24 CROSS ROW	W CRAMLINGTON	7/6/15	31/7/17	GSW		1/7/16			AGE 29.
DOUGHERTY	W	SGT	20 / 168		8 GUNN STREET	DUNSTON					1/7/16			
DOUGLAS	A	PTE	20 / 746		HENRY STREET	GOSFORTH					1/7/16			
DOUGLAS	Geo	PTE	20 / 748			BEDLINGTON				28/4/17		ARRAS MEM		
DOUGLAS	H	PTE	20 / 98	C										AWOL 6-8/2/15.
DOUGLAS	J	PTE	20 / 316	A				10/4/15	UNFIT					AWOL 7-8/2/15
DOUGLAS	Jas	PTE	20 /1193				2/11/14	30/11/14	KR para 392				TO DEPOT.	DID NOT SERVE OVERSEAS
DOUGLAS	Rob W	PTE	20 / 97		MIDDLE ROW	WALBOTTLE					1/7/16			
DOUGLAS	Robt	SIG	20 / 747		15 SUGLEY STREET	SUGLEY							TO 22nd BN, ROYAL FUSILIERS(24th BN).	FRANCE 20 9/1/16-2/2/18, 22 3/2/18-28/8/18, 24RF -7/1/19.
DOUGLAS	Selby	PTE	20 /1031	B									TO 2nd GARRISON BN, CLASS Z RESERVE.	AWOL 6-7/2/15.
DOUGLAS	Snowd	PTE	20 /1030				4/11/14	31/10/16	GSW		31/3/16		TO ARMY RESERVE CLASS P.	GSW L LEG, AGE 27.
DOUGLAS	Thos	LCPL	20 / 537			CAVERTON MILL				1/7/16		THIEPVAL MEM		BORN ROXBOROUGH
DOUGLAS	Wm F	PTE	20 /1032	B		ACKLINGTON				1/7/16		THIEPVAL MEM		BORN AMBLE, AWOL 6-7/2/15.
DOVER	Ralph	PTE	20 /1271	C		STANLEY				1/7/16	1/7/16	THIEPVAL MEM		FROM DEPOT COY TO C COY 25/2/15,BORN BRANDON.AWOL 7
DOW	M	PTE	20 /1521	A									TO 34th DIV CYC COY.	FROM E COY TO A COY 19/6/15.
DOWIE	Andrw	PTE	20 / 750	D	19 THIRD STREET	NETHERTON COLL				1/7/16		THIEPVAL MEM		BORN MONKWEARMOUTH.
DOWNIE	Jas	PIPR	20 / 154	A		GLASGOW				1/7/16		THIEPVAL MEM		
DOWSON	W	PTE	20 /1616		62 NEW ELVET	DURHAM CITY					1/7/16			TRIED BY FGCM STRIKING AN OFFICER ARMENTIERES 7/4/16.
DRAKE		PTE	20	A										
DREW	Wm	PTE	20 /1425	E			8/1/15							DESERTER 25/1/15.
DRIVER	ThosW	PTE	20 / 751	B	4 BELMONT COTTAGE	WESTERHOPE				1/7/16		THIEPVAL MEM		BORN FELLING, AWOL 28-29/3/15, 6-8/10/15.
DUFF	J N	PTE	20 / 235		57 SANDY LANE	EIGHTON BANKS					1/7/16			
DUFFY	Jas	PTE	20 / 752										TO 24/27th, 1/6th BNS, LABOUR CORPS, CLAS Z RESERVE.	
DUFFY	T	PTE	20 / 753	B										AWOL 13-14/2/15, 6-7/10/15.
DUKE	ChasM	SGT	20 / 42			NEWCASTLE				21/3/18		ARRAS MEM	TO 23rd, 22nd BNS.	
DUNBAR	J	PTE	20 /1275	E										AWOL 30/1/15-2/2/15.
DUNN	J	PTE	20 / 754	B										AWOL 28-29/3/15.
DUNN	Thos	SGT	20 / 396		27 KINGSLEY PLACE	NEWCASTLE	31/10/14	16/9/18	GSW				TO 4th(RES) BN.	
DUNSMORE		BGLF	20 /1211	D									TO 34th DIV CYC COY.	
DUNWOODIE	Alex	LCPL	20 /1646	B	PRIMROSE HILL	BOLDON COLLIERY				1/7/16		THIEPVAL MEM		BORN BELFAST AGE 36.
DUNWOODIE	Matt	PTE	20 /1618	B	MOUNT PLEASANT	HEXAM					1/7/16		TO 23rd BN.	AWOL 6-7/10/15. GSW L SHLDR 18 GHOSP 3/7 TO HSHIP 6/7/16.
DURNING	Jas	LCPL	20 / 317			RYTON ON TYNE					3/6/16		TO CHESHIRE REGT(9th BN).	WND L THIGH, CHESHIRE No 52324.
EASTON	Alf	PTE	20 /1564	D	36 SALISBURY STREE	COWPEN QUAY	15/5/15			1/7/16		THIEPVAL MEM		FROM E COY TO D COY 19/6/15.
EASTON	John	PTE	20 /1562	D	26 COWPEN SQUARE	COWPEN QUAY	15/5/15	18/2/17	SICK		1/7/16		TO 3rd BN.	FROM E COY TO D COY 19/6/15.
EASTON	Thos	SGT	20 /1563	D	79 SALISBURY STREE	COWPEN QUAY	15/5/15						TO 22nd, 17th BNS.	FROM E COY TO D COY 19/6/15.
EDGAR	Wm	PTE	20 /1034	B		ROWLANDS GILL				1/7/16		THIEPVAL MEM		BORN CONSETT.
EDWARDS	ChasR	PTE	20 /1489	E	3 WOOD ROW	EDMONDSLEY	15/2/15	31/3/19	KR para 392				TO 1st BN, ARMY RESERVE CLASS P.	FROM E COY TO A COY 19/6/15.9 PLEASANT ST 1918.
EDWARDS	Geo D	CPL	20 / 755			WHEATLEY HILL					1/7/16		TO ROYAL FLYING CORPS.	
ELLIOTT	Isa E	PTE	20 / 538	C	1 PLESSEY STREET	CRAMLINGTON	31/10/14	9/2/15	KR para 392					AGE 22,5'7", 121Lbs FAIR COMP,GREY EYES,L BROWN HAIR.
ELLIOTT	Jas	PTE	20 / 756	B		PLASHETTS				1/7/16		OVILLERS MIL CEM		
ELLIOTT	Jas H	PTE	20 /1426	A		SOUTHMOOR				1/7/16		THIEPVAL MEM		BORN CARLISLE,FROM DEPOT COY - A COY 25/2/15.AWOL 28-2
ELLIOTT	Roger	PTE	20 / 397	C			31/10/14	9/2/15	KR para 392					
ELLIOTT	ThosG	PTE	20 /1701			CHATHILL					JULY 16	THIEPVAL MEM	TO DURHAM LI(12th BN). DLI No 45898.	BORN LUCKER,AGE 26, REP MISSING 1/7/16.
ELLIS	Jos	PTE	20 /1658		6 ROSEBERRY TERRA	GATESHEAD	23/9/15						TO 2nd GARRISON BN.	
ELLISON	JohnW	PTE	20 / 539	C		W CRAMLINGTON				1/7/16		THIEPVAL MEM		BORN HEXAM
ELLISON	Thos	PTE	20 / 540		64 HASTINGS STREET	CRAMLINGTON							TO 1st GARRISON BN.	
ELSENDER	Rob E	PTE	20 / 398				31/10/14	22/5/18	INDEGESTI		1/7/16		TO 23rd BN.	
ELTRINGHAM	J	PTE	20 / 758	B										COY COOK 31/1/15.
ENGLISH	Robt	PTE	20 / 399			DINNINGTON COL	31/10/14	10/3/17	WOUNDS		1/7/16			
ENGLISH	Thos	PTE	20 /1035										TO 2nd GARRISON BN.	
ERRINGTON	Wm T	PTE	20 / 400	A	7 NEAL TERRACE	TANTOBIE				1/7/16		THIEPVAL MEM		BORN ANNFIELD PLAIN AGE 20.
EWING	G	PTE	20 /1037	B				10/4/15	UNFIT					
FAIR	Fred	PTE	20 /1577		11 WEAR STREET	HENDON				1/6/15		BISHOPWEARMOUTH		AGE 38 DIED AT HOME.
FAIRWEATHER	John	PTE	20 / 759	D		WALLSEND				1/7/16		THIEPVAL MEM		BORN NEWTYLE FORFAR. IN 14 PLATOON.
FALCONAR	T	PTE	20 /1276	D										AWOL 7-8/3/15.
FARRAR	Herbt	PTE	20 / 837			JARROW	2/11/14	22/8/17	WOUNDS		1/7/16		TO 84th TRAINING RESERVE BN.	AGE 37.

FARRELL	Frank	PTE	20 /1490		6 MAKENDON STREET	HEBBURN	12/2/15	14/9/16	SICK			TO DEPOT.	
FARROW	Geo W	PTE	20 / 760			CHOPWELL	3/11/14	8/8/17	FRACTUREI	1/7/16		TO DEPOT.	
FAWCETT	Wm	PTE	20 /1428	E	15 BEDE BURN ROAD	JARROW						TO DURHAM LI(15th BN).	FROM E COY TO A COY 19/6/15, DLI No 46610.
FAWDON	Geo R	PTE	20 /1671	B	10 UNION STREET	MORPETH			1/7/16		THIEPVAL MEM		AWOL 7-8/3/15, AGE 36 BORN BEDLINGTON.
FEARON	Jas	PTE	20 / 761				3/11/14	9/4/18	SICK			TO ARMY RESERVE CLASS P.	
FEARON	Sam	LCPL	20 / 980		HIGH GREENSIDE	RYTON				12/6/16		TO CHESHIRE REGT(9th BN).	L LEG, SHOCK, CHESHIRE No 52325.
FEARON	Wm	PTE	20 / 401		47 MILTON STREET	RYTON						TO 1st GARRISON BN.	
FELCE	Chas	CPL	20 /1038										AWOL 7/6/15.
FELLOWS	Jn Wm	PIPR	20 /1585	D	29 WEARDALE AVE	WALKER			1/7/16		THIEPVAL MEM		AGE 21.
FELTON	John	PTE	20 /1284	D		WARDLEY COLL	12/1/15	3/5/18	GSW	1/7/16			FROM DEPOT COY TO D COY 25/2/15.
FENWICK	David	LCPL	20 / 762	D		BEDLINGTON						TO 1st, 22nd, 1/4th, 11th BNS.	AWOL 6-7/2/15, PROMOTED TO CSM.
FERGUSON	Alex	PTE	20 / 763	C		WILLINGTON QUAY			1/7/16		THIEPVAL MEM		BORN KILWINNING AYRSHIRE.
FERGUSON	ChasW	PTE	20 / 43			NEWCASTLE			5/6/16	3/6/16	HEILLY STATION		DIED AT 36 CCS, WND CHEST,HEAD,LEGS,THIGHS,KNEE,LOSS
FERGUSON	Jas	PTE	20 / 765	B		BURNHOPE						TO 22nd, 14th BNS.	STRETCHER BEARER 1/7/15,AWOL 25-27/1/15, 6-7/10/15, SGT.
FERGUSON	Jos	PTE	20 / 764			NEWCASTLE	3/10/14	23/3/17	WOUNDS	3/8/16, DEC 16.		TO DEPOT.	
FINDLAY	Jas	PTE	20 / 766	B		TYNE DOCK			1/7/16		THIEPVAL MEM		BORN GLASGOW.
FISHER	J	PTE	20 / 767	B		NEWCASTLE							COY COOK 31/1/15, AWOL 7-8/3/15, 6-7/10/15.
FITZPATRICK	J	PTE	20 / 768	B									COY COOK 31/1/15
FLETCHER	Alf	PTE	20 /1565	D	17 WEAR STREET	CHOPWELL			1/7/16		THIEPVAL MEM		FROM E COY TO D COY 19/6/15.
FLINN	R	PTE	20 / 236			WINLATON				1/7/16			NORTH EVINGTON HOSP LEICESTER 11/7/16.
FLOCKHART	Wm	PTE	20 / 770	D		BEDLINGTON			1/7/16		THIEPVAL MEM		
FLOOD	Thos	PTE	20 /1430	C	75 ALBERT STREET	GRANGE VILLA						TO 8th,21st,22nd,4th(R)BNS, KO YORKS LI(5th BN).	FROM DEPOT COY TO C COY 25/2/15.
FLOYD	R	PTE	20 / 70	C				9/2/15	KR para 392				
FOLEY	B	PTE	20 /1283	E				12/2/15	UNFIT				
FORBES	JohN	PTE	20 /1039			SEATON DELAVAL			1/7/16		ALBERT COM CEM EXT		BORN FETTERCAIRN KINCARDINSHIRE.
FOREMAN	R	PTE	20 / 542	D				10/4/15	UNFIT				
FORREST	Chas	PTE	20 /1621		11 ALLAN ROAD	NEWBIGGIN B SEA			30/11/16		RATION FARM CEM		AGE 34, BORN BRAMPTON CUMBERLAND.
FORRESTER	J	PTE	20 /1040	B									AWOL 6-7/10/15.
FORSTER	John	PTE	20 / 543		OFFICE ROW	HARTFORD COLL			14/5/16		ETAPLES MIL CEM		AGE 52 BORN EARSDON.
FORSTER	T	PTE	20 / 771	B				9/2/15	UNFIT				
FORSTER	Wm	PTE	20 /1429	C	44 DOCTOR STREET	NEW SEAHAM			1/7/16	4/6/16	THIEPVAL MEM		SHRAPNEL WND BACK, BORN JESMOND.
FOSTER	Andrw	PTE	20 / 772						KR para 392			TO 2nd GARRISON BN.	
FOSTER	Dav W	BGLF	20 / 44		2 PERKINS STREET	SCOTSWOOD			15/6/18	1/4/16	LOOS MEM	TO 1st BN.	GSW L ARM & ABDOMEN, POSTED TO DEPOT COY 5/3/15.AGE
FOSTER	Hen W	PTE	20 /1427	C			14/1/15						FROM DEPOT COY TO C COY 25/2/15, AWOL 7-8/3/15.
FOSTER	Jas	PTE	20 /1279	C		CAMBOIS					ALBERT 12/6/16		FROM DEPOT COY TO C COY 25/2/15.
FOSTER	John	PTE	20 /1277	B	9 MICHAELS VILLA	GRANGE VILLA						TO 2nd GARRISON BN, CLASS Z RESERVE.	FROM DEPOT COY TO B COY 25/2/15.
FOSTER	Wrigh	PTE	20 /1278									TO 2nd GARRISON BN, CLASS Z RESERVE.	
FRANCE	Peter	PTE	20 / 45									TO 18th, 22nd BNS.	
FRASER	A	PTE	20 / 773	D									OFF RATION STRENGTH 7-13/2/15.
FRASER	John	PTE	20 /1659				21/6/15	22/4/16	KR para 392			TO DEPOT.	DID NOT SERVE OVERSEAS.
FRASER	Wm Hn	CSM	20 /1043			MILLOM			1/7/16		THIEPVAL MEM		BORN MILLOM CUMBERLAND.
FRAZER	Sam	SGT	20 /1280	B			8/11/14	17/11/17	GSW			TO 10th BN.	DEPOT COY TO B COY 25/2/15,AWOL 6-7/10 REVERTED PTE 9/1
FRAZER	Wm	SGT	20 / 545							MARCH 16			
FRENCH	Sept	PTE	20 / 774	D	597 WELBECK STREET	JARROW			28/4/17		ARRAS MEM	TO 9th, 24th BNS.	AWOL 6-8/10/15.
FYFE	Gar W	LCPL	20 / 237			SHIREMOOR			1/7/16		OVILLERS MIL CEM		PIPER BORN EDINBURGH, AGE 36.
GAINSBORO	G	PTE	20 / 403	A									AWOL 7-8/2/15.
GALLAGHER	J	PTE	20 / 546	C				10/4/15	UNFIT				
GALLAGHER	Jas	PTE	20 / 776		4 BURNS ROAD	GATESHEAD	3/11/14	8/8/17	GSW	1/7/16		TO 3rd BN.	
GALLON	ClavG	PTE	20 / 170	A	27 BRUSSELS STREET	GATESHEAD						TO 22nd BN.	AWOL 12-16/2/15.
GARBUTT	Robt	PTE	20 / 777	D		WILLINGTON QUA	3/10/14		1/7/16		THIEPVAL MEM		AWOL 7-9/2/15,LABOURER DESERTED 28/6/15, AGE 31.BORN W
GARDNER	RobtE	PTE	20 / 775									TO RIFLE BRIGADE(DEPOT), 1/5th LONDON REGT.	RIFLE BDE No 45162.
GARGIN	F	PTE	20 / 405	C									AWOL 29/11-1/12/15.
GARR	Burnp	PTE	20 / 319	A	105 FRAMWELLGATE	DURHAM CITY						TO 2nd GARRISON BN, CLASS Z RESERVE.	COY COOK 31/1/15, ALSO ON AVL 899 SCOTSWOOD ROAD.
GASCOIGNE	Jonth	PTE	20 / 547	A	349 STATION ROAD	WALLSEND			1/7/16		THIEPVAL MEM		AGE 44, BORN LESSARA STAFFS.
GAYNOR	Miltn	PTE	20 / 778	D	20 MAY AVENUE	RYTON				1/7/16		TO CLASS Z RESERVE.	TO 18 GHOSP 3/7 GSW R THIGH, TO HSHIP 9/7/16.
GEORGE	JohnR	PTE	20 /1497	E	44 CAMDEN STREET	NORTH SHIELDS	12/2/15			1/7/16		TO 25th, 1/5th BNS.	FROM E COY TO A COY 19/6/15, RENUMBERED 243151.
GIBBONS	D	PTE	20 /1623			TYNEMOUTH				1/7/16		TO 84th TRAINING RESERVE BN.	
GIBLIN	Geo	PTE	20 / 779	D								TO 18th, 22nd BN, CLASS Z RESERVE.	COY COOK 31/1/15, AWOL 6-8/10/15.
GIBSON	Andrw	PTE	20 / 780				2/11/14	28/12/17	GSW			TO DEPOT.	
GIBSON	JohnT	PTE	20 / 46	C	60 BK NAPIER STREET	TYNE DOCK		#	1/7/16	3/6/16	THIEPVAL MEM		SHELL SHOCK 3/6/16, AGE 20, MACHINE GUN SECTION.
GIBSON	Robt	PTE	20 /1044	B	9 ROCKWOOD TERRA(	RYTON	4/11/14	31/3/19	KR para 392	1/7/16		TO 36th BN, ARMY RESERVE CLASS P.	COY COOK 31/1/15
GIBSON	Sam	PTE	20 / 781	D		CHOPPINGTON			1/7/16	1/7/16	OVILLERS MIL CEM		BORN TANFIELD LEA.
GILBERT	Mart	PTE	20 / 47	A								TO 23rd BN, DURHAM LI(15th BN).	POSTED FROM A TO E COY 31/1/15, DLI No 46640.
GILBERT	Robt	PTE	20 /1432	A	22 MITCHELL STREET	OXHILL						TO 10th, 12/13th BNS, CLASS Z RESERVE.	FROM DEPOT COY TO A COY 25/2/15.
GILBERT	T	PTE	20 / 782					2/2/15	KR para 392				
GILCHRIST	Jos	PTE	20 /1433	E	12 HEWORTH VIEW	NEWCASTLE			1/7/16	1/7/16	THIEPVAL MEM		AWOL 25/3/15, AGE 35, TRANSFERRED TO A COY.
GILL	J	PTE	20 / 99	C				10/4/15	UNFIT				
GILL	John	PTE	20 /1292		SPICE CAKE ROW	SEGHILL	11/1/15					TO 2nd GARRISON BN, CLASS Z RESERVE.	
GILLESPIE	JohnT	PTE	20 /1046			NEWBURN			1/7/16		THIEPVAL MEM		AGE 21 BORN RYTON.
GILLIGAN	C	LCPL	20 /1047	B									AWOL 6-7/10/15.
GILLIS	H	PTE	20 / 549			DUDLEY				1/7/16			
GILMORE	Thos	PTE	20 /1048				4/11/14	28/10/17	SICK			TO 1st GARRISON BN.	
GITTINS	Harry	WOII	20 /1286									COMMISSIONED 29/5/18 KINGS SHROPSHIRE LI.	
GLAISTER	John	LCPL	20 /1049	B		NORTH SHIELDS			1/7/16		THIEPVAL MEM		
GLAZZARD	Jas T	PTE	20 / 550		SPICE CAKE ROW	SEGHILL						TO 2nd GARRISON BN, CLASS Z RESERVE.	
GLENTON	Thos	PTE	20 / 551	D		BEDLINGTON			1/7/16		THIEPVAL MEM		
GODSMARK	John	PTE	20 / 785	A		CHOPPINGTON			1/7/16		THIEPVAL MEM		BORN ESTON MINES NORTH YORKS.
GOLDIE	Jas	PTE	20 /1566	D	8 BOYD TERRACE	WESTERHOPE			5/6/17		ARRAS MEM		FROM E COY TO D COY 19/6/15, BORN STAKEFORD AGE 19.
GOLIGHTLY	Geo E	PTE	20 / 320	A	418 SUNDERLAND RO/	GATESHEAD			1/7/16		THIEPVAL MEM		AWOL 28/3/15, AGE 20
GOODALL	David	SGT	20 / 9	B	4 BADEN POWELL ST	GATESHEAD				1/7/16			REGIMENTAL POLICE 31/1/15. R VICTORIA HOSP NETLEY 11/7/
GOODWILL	Jos	PTE	20 /1050	B	251 YARD ROW	NETHERTON COLL			1/7/16		THIEPVAL MEM		AGE 35 BORN NEWTON ON THE MOOR.
GORDON	John	PTE	20 / 100		46 DONNISON STREET	WHICKHAM	27/10/14	9/8/18	GSW			TO 1st BN.	AGE 46.
GORDON	Robt	PTE	20 /1622		17 RAILWAY ROW	CRAMLINGTON				1/7/16		TO 16th, 23rd, 1/4th BNS, CLASS Z RESERVE.	PRISONER OF WAR 1/4th BN.
GORDON	Thos	PTE	20 / 786	D		NEWCASTLE			1/7/16		OVILLERS MIL CEM		BORN HOBSON COLLIERY.
GOUNDRY	James	PTE	20 / 787	B								TO 18th BN, CLASS Z RESERVE.	OFF RATION STRENGTH 1-7/2/15.
GOWLAND	J	PTE	20 /1287	E									FROM E COY TO A COY 19/6/15.
GRAHAM	J T	PTE	20 /1291		9a GALLERY ROW	SEAHAM							
GRAHAM	John	SGT	20 / 789		79 NEWGATE STREET	NEWCASTLE				1/7/16		TO 9th BN, CLASS Z RESERVE.	
GRAHAM	JohnJ	PTE	20 / 790			RYTON			1/7/16				BORN HEATHERY CLEUGH Co DURHAM
GRAHAM	ThosW	PTE	20 /1294	A	3 STAVORDALE STREI	DAWDON	13/1/15	25/10/18	AMPUTATEI	3/6/16		TO DEPOT.	FROM DEPOT COY TO A COY 25/2/15, AWOL 7-8/3/15, AGE 25.
GRAHAM	Wm	PTE	20 / 6	C		RYTON			1/7/16		THIEPVAL MEM		BORN FRIMLEY HAMPSHIRE.
GRANT	AlexM	PTE	20 / 321		3 CHARLIE STREET	RYTON						TO 19th, 22nd BNS, CLASS Z RESERVE.	
GRANT	J	SGT	20 / 101			NEWCASTLE				1/7/16			SGT SIGNAL COURSE ALNWICK 11/4/15.
GRANT	J	PTE	20 /1475	C									FROM DEPOT COY TO C COY 25/2/15.
GRANT	Wm H	SGT	20 / 791			NORTH SHIELDS			1/7/16		THIEPVAL MEM		
GRAY	James	PTE	20 / 552			BEDLINGTON			2/7/16		MILLENCOURT COM CEM EXT		AGE 34.
GRAY	John	PTE	20 / 553	C		NEWCASTLE			KR para 392	1/7/16		TO DURHAM LIGHT INFANTRY, TRAINING RES BN.	AWOL 13-16/2/15. TRG RES No TR/5/41598.
GRAY	John	LCPL	20 /1624	D	11 CUMBERLAND TERI	HENDON			1/7/16		THIEPVAL MEM		AWOL 6-7/10/15. BORN SOUTHWICK.
GRAY	RobtO	SGT	20 / 102		20 DERWENT ST WES'	BENWELL	27/10/14	26/1/15	KR para 392				DID NOT SERVE O/SEAS.
GREEN	C S	PTE	20 /1434	A									FROM DEPOT COY TO A COY 25/2/15.
GREEN	Chas	PTE	20 / 406	D		RYTON			1/4/16	22/3/16	ETAPLES MIL CEM		GSW HEAD
GREEN	Geo	PTE	20 /1288	D		DAWDON			15/6/16		ALBERT 16/6/16		FROM DEPOT COY TO D COY 25/2/15,AWOL 7-8/3/15, SHRAPNE
GREEN	Robt	PTE	20 / 407				27/10/14	26/1/15	DEAFNESS				DID NOT SERVE OVERSEAS
GREEN	Wm	PTE	20 /1289									TO 2nd GARRISON BN, CLASS Z RESERVE.	
GREENWELL	JOHN	CPL	20 / 792						24/10/18		VIS-EN-ARTOIS MEM	COMMISSIONED 30/1/18 TO 12/13th BN.	
GREENWOOD	John	PTE	20 /1293	E		SUNDERLAND	11/1/15	22/2/17	WOUNDS	1/7/16		TO DEPOT.	AWOL 6-8/2/15.
GRINDLE	JohnT	PTE	20 / 408	C		NORTH SHIELDS			1/7/16		THIEPVAL MEM		AWOL 6-8/2/15, BORN WEST PELTON, MACHINE GUN SECTION
GUIRE	T H	PTE	20 / 10	C				10/4/15	UNFIT				
GUY	Cyr D	PTE	20 / 409	A		BIRMINGHAM			1/7/16	1/7/16	OVILLERS MIL CEM		BORN OLDBURY WORCESTER.
HADDON	C J	LCPL	20 / 322			EAST DULWICH				1/7/16			
HAIR	Jermh	PTE	20 / 410			RYTON			30/11/16		RATION FARM MIL CEM		BORN SUNDERLAND.
HAKIN	Jas W	LCPL	20 / 556	C	59 MORTIMOR STREE'	HARTFORD EAST			KR para 392			TO 2nd GARRISON BN.	AWOL 14-16/2/15.

HALDANE	James	PTE	20 /1305	E			12/1/15	12/10/17	SICK				TO 1st GARRISON, 2nd, 3rd BNS.	AWOL 6-8/2/15, 7-8/3/15,AGE 41,E COY TO B COY 19/6/15.
HALE	Alex	PTE	20 / 557	D	20 DOCTOR TERRACE	BEDLINGTON				1/7/16		THIEPVAL MEM		AGE 19, MACHINE GUN SECTION.
HALEY	T	PTE	20 /1466	E										FROM E COY TO B COY 19/6/15.
HALKETT	James	LCPL	20 / 171	A		DUNDEE				11/7/16	1/7/16	DUNDEE WESTERN METROPOLIS CEM		OFF RATION STRENGTH 1-7/2/15, AGE 50.
HALL	Geo	PTE	20 / 238		3 POND COTTAGES	RYTON				11/8/17	1/7/16	ADINKERKE MIL CEM	TO 16th BN.	AGE 23.
HALL	Geo J	SGT	20 / 558				2/11/14	18/3/19	KR para 392				TO 22nd BN.	
HALL	James	PTE	20 / 172		2 ORMSTON STREET	HARTFORD	28/10/14	23/10/17	WOUNDS		1/7/16		TO DEPOT.	AGE 43.
HALL	James	PTE	20 / 793			BEDLINGTON	2/11/14	31/10/16	GSW		1/7/16		TO DEPOT.	
HALL	Jesse	PTE	20 /1052	B		EIGHTON BANKS	4/11/14						TO CLASS Z RESERVE.	MINER AGE 34, AWOL 2-9/2/15, DESERTED 12/6/15.
HALL	JohnT	PTE	20 / 173	A	17 HARRIET STREET	NEWCASTLE	28/10/14							AWOL 6-10/2/15
HALL	M	PTE	20 / 411	D									TO ROYAL ENGINEERS TUNNELLING DEPOT 13/10/15.	
HALL	RobtW	PTE	20 / 559	B			2/11/14	10/4/15	DEFORMED TOES					AWOL 7-8/3/15.DID NOT SERVE O/SEAS.
HALL	Wm	PTE	20 / 239			FOREST HALL	29/10/14	22/11/17	GSW				TO DEPOT.	
HALLAM	James	LCPL	20 /1053			NEWCASTLE	4/11/14	22/4/17	WOUNDS		1/7/16		80th TRAINING RESERVE BN.	AGE 28.
HALLIDAY	Robt	PTE	20 / 796	B		ASHINGTON					1/7/16		TO 21st, 1st BNS, CLASS Z RESERVE.	AWOL 2-9/2/15.
HAMILTON	Henry	CPL	20 /1054	D		CRAMLINGTON				1/7/16		THIEPVAL MEM		AWOL 6-8/10/15, IN 13 PLATOON.
HAMILTON	John	PTE	20 / 240		27 CRANK ROW	WEST MOOR					1/7/16		TO 22nd BN, CLASS Z RESERVE.	
HAMILTON	R	PTE	20 / 412											
HAMPTON	Thos	LCPL	20 / 560			NEWCASTLE				18/6/16		ALBERT 19/6/16		
HANCOCK	J S	PTE	20 / 413					2/2/15	KR para 392					
HANKIN	JohnW	PTE	20 / 49	C			26/10/14	25/10/17	SICK					AGE 42, AWOL 29/11-2/12/15, 10 DAYS FP 2 FOR AWOL 3/12/15.
HANNAH	T	PTE	20 /1308	E										DESERTER 24/1/15.
HANRATTY	Jas	PTE	20 / 104	C	21 PARK LANE	GATESHEAD				7/7/16		FLAT IRON COPSE CEM		IN 9 PLATOON.
HANRATTY	Thos	PTE	20 / 798	B		BURNHOPEFIELD				1/7/16		THIEPVAL MEM		
HARDIE	E	CPL	20 / 174					1/2/15	KR para 392					
HARDIE	Rich	LSGT	20 / 175		119 SYCAMORE STREI	NEWCASTLE					1/7/16			REGIMENTAL POLICE 31/1/15.
HARDIE	Wm	PTE	20 /1297	E		WEST SLEEKBURN				1/7/16		THIEPVAL MEM		BORN STAKEFORD, FROM DEPOT COY TO A COY 19/6/15.
HARDMAN	James	PTE	20 / 561				31/10/14	31/3/19	KR para 392				TO ARMY RESERVE CLASS P.	
HARDY	Edwd	PTE	20 /1056			WILLINGTON QUAY							TO CLASS Z RESERVE.	3rd SCOTTISH GEN HOSP GLASGOW 11/7/16.
HARDY	Wm O	LCPL	20 / 241		6 JOHN STREET	EARSDON							TO 22nd BN, CLASS Z RESERVE.	
HARLAND	Wm	PTE	20 /1625		5 RIVER STREET	NEWCASTLE							TO 2nd GARRISON BN, CLASS Z RESERVE.	
HARLOW	J	PTE	20 / 242	C										AWOL 7-8/2/15.
HAROLD	John	PTE	20 / 563	C			31/10/14	10/4/15	UNFIT					NAME POSSIBLY HERALD, DID NOT SERVE O/SEAS.
HARRIOT	J	PTE	20 /1326	B										FROM DEPOT COY TO B COY 25/2/15 PT 2 ORDER 53/4 25/2/15.
HARRIS	James	PTE	20 /1513	E		GATESHEAD				1/7/16		THIEPVAL MEM		BORN PONTYPOOL WALES, FROM E COY TO B COY 19/6/15.
HARRIS	Wm G	PTE	20 /1596		86 ELDON STREET	NORTH SHIELDS							TO 2nd GARRISON BN, CLASS Z RESERVE.	
HARRISON	Anthy	PTE	20 / 323	A	65 HAIG STREET	DUNSTON				1/7/16		THIEPVAL MEM		AGE 39 BORN LANCHESTER.
HARRISON	Robt	PTE	20 / 800		3 CLARENCE STREET	TANFIELD							TO 23rd BN, CLASS Z RESERVE.	AWOL 7/2/15-11/2/15, 120 HRS DETENTION.
HART	A	PTE	20 / 324					1/2/15	KR para 392					
HARVEY	Geo R	PTE	20 /1504	Depo		SUNDERLAND	20/2/15			1/7/16		THIEPVAL MEM		FROM E COY TO A COY 19/6/15.
HASTIE	Jas P	PTE	20 /1436	E		GATESHEAD					3/6/16		TO 23rd BN, TO CLASS Z RESERVE.	FROM E COY TO B COY 19/6/15, WND THIGHS, LEG & ARM.
HAVELOCK	JohnW	PTE	20 / 243						KR para 392					
HAY	Geo	PTE	20 / 801			BEDLINGTON				17/4/18	1/7/16	WIMEREUX COM CEM	TO 9th BN.	AGE 31.
HAY	Jos N	SGT	20 / 176		12 MELDON STREET	NEWCASTLE							TO 22nd BN.	
HAYES	Geo R	PTE	20 /1598		BEADLINGS COTTAGE	DUDLEY					6/11/16		TO 8th, 1/7th BNS, CLASS Z RESERVE.	
HAYES	J	PTE	20 / 562	D				10/4/15	UNFIT					AWOL 7-8/3/15, 7 DAYS FP2 MISCONDUCT 30/3/15.
HEADS	Geo	PTE	20 / 244		41 LONGRIGG	SWALWELL	29/10/14	1/10/18	WOUNDS		1/7/16		TO LABOUR CORPS.	LAB CORPS No 285248.
HEDLEY	Jos	PTE	20 /1505	Depo			21/2/15	12/9/16	SICK				TO DEPOT.	FROM E COY TO A COY 19/6/15.
HEDLEY	Jos	PTE	20 / 802			BACKWORTH	3/11/14	26/7/17	GSW		1/7/16		TO 3rd BN.	
HEENEY	Thos	PTE	20 / 105		39 BUCKINGHAM STRE	NEWCASTLE	27/10/14	31/10/18	GSW		1/7/16		TO 12th, 21st, 10th, 3rd BNS.	AGE 33,BEAUFORT WAR HOSP BRISTOL 8/7/16.
HEMSLEY	J	PTE	20 /1304	E										AWOL 1-3/2/15.
HENDERSON	Alb J	PTE	20 / 564	D		BEDLINGTON				1/7/16		THIEPVAL MEM		
HENDERSON	H	CSGT	20 /1536	A									FROM 11th BN, 16/4/15.	
HENDERSON	James	PTE	20 / 565	D		GOSFORTH				1/7/16		KNIGHTSBRIDGE CEM		BORN EDINBURGH.
HENDERSON	James	PTE	20 /1057	D		HORTON	2/10/14			1/7/16		THIEPVAL MEM		MINER AGE 40, DESERTED 28/6/15, IN 15 PLATOON.
HENDY	W	PTE	20 / 567	C				9/2/15	KR para 392					
HENRY	J	PTE	20 /1647			NEWCASTLE					JULY 16		TO MUNITIONS(DOXFORD & SONS).	
HEPPELL	Wm R	PTE	20 / 177		13 JAMES STREET	BLAYDON				24/3/18	1/7/16	DELSAUX FARM CEM I	TO CHESHIRE REGT(9th BN).	CHESHIRE REGT No 52329. AGE 38.
HEPPLE	David	PTE	20 / 246		16 PINE STREET	THROCKLEY							TO 9th BN.	
HEPPLE	Thos	PTE	20 /1626	B	18 BEACH STREET	THROCKLEY	3/6/15	31/3/19	KR para 392				TO ARMY RESERVE CLASS P	AWOL 6-8/10/15.
HERON	Ern H	PTE	20 /1298	B	2 LAMBERT TERR	TYNE DOCK				1/7/16		THIEPVAL MEM		AGE 24, FROM DEPOT COY TO B COY 25/2/15.
HERRON	JohnT	PTE	20 / 414	B	26 JESMOND TERR	WHITLEY BAY				5/6/17	6/8/16, DEC 16.	ARRAS MEM	TO 23rd BN.	
HESLIN	Thos	PTE	20 / 803	B		BURNHOPEFIELD				15/6/16		ALBERT 16/6/16		AWOL 6-8/2/15, 6-7/10/14, BORN MOTHERWELL.
HESLOP	John	PTE	20 / 325	A		ANNFIELD PLAIN				1/7/16		THIEPVAL MEM		AGE 22 BORN DURHAM.
HESLOP	JohnT	PTE	20 /1578	B	42 GARDNER STREET	NORTH SHIELDS				1/7/16		THIEPVAL MEM		AGE 22.
HEWITT	J	PTE	20 /1058	D				10/4/15	UNFIT					
HEWITT	Jas H	PTE	20 /1579		49 STEVENSON STREI	WESTOE				19/5/18		DENAIN COM CEM	TO 23rd BN(A COY).	
HIGGINS	James	PTE	20 /1060				22/10/14	11/4/17					TO 84th TRAINING RESERVE BN.	AWOL 2/4/15
HIGHMOOR	Robt	PTE	20 / 568			CRAWCROOK	2/11/14	26/10/17	SICK		1/7/16		TO 3rd BN.	AGE 32.
HILLS	JohnW	PTE	20 /1299	C		ASHINGTON							TO 22nd BN, CLASS Z RESERVE.	FROM DEPOT COY TO C COY 25/2/15.
HIND	Robt	PTE	20 / 804		51 MAPLE STREET	HIRST				6/4/16	31/3/16	HAZEBROUCK COM CEM		AGE 48, SHRAPNEL WOUND R TEMPLE.
HINDHAUGH	Geo H	PTE	20 / 569	D		BEDLINGTON				1/7/16		THIEPVAL MEM	TO 26th BN.	AGE 19, POSTING TO 26th BN CANCELLED.
HIRST	J G	PTE	20 / 415			RYTON					1/7/16			
HODGSON	J C	PTE	20 /1437			WASHINGTON					1/7/16			3 CCS 2/7/16 EVAC 2/7/16.
HOGG	Herbt	PTE	20 /1061										TO 22nd BN, CLASS Z RESERVE.	
HOGG	John	PTE	20 /1301	D		SUNDERLAND				1/7/16		OVILLERS MIL CEM		FROM DEPOT COY TO D COY 25/2/15.
HOGG	Rich	PTE	20 / 248	C		RYTON				1/7/16		THIEPVAL MEM		STRETCHER BEARER 1/7/15, BORN BROWNEY COLLIERY.
HOGG	T	PTE	20 / 806			WALKERGATE					1/7/16			
HOGG	ThosE	SGT	20 / 805			NORTH SHIELDS				12/7/16		THIEPVAL MEM		BORN BLYTH
HOLDER	ThosM	PTE	20 /1302				15/1/15	22/8/16	WOUNDS				TO 29th BN.	
HOLLAND	John	LCPL	20 / 72	C		HARTFORD COLL					1/7/16		TO CHESHIRE REGT(9th BN).	SGTS MESS WAITER 31/1/15,STRETCHER BEARER 1/7/15.
HOLMES	Robt	PTE	20 / 326	A	11 MOSS SIDE	WREKETON				1/7/16		OVILLERS MIL CEM		AGE 36.
HOLMES	S	BGLR	20 / 807											POSTED TO DEPOT COY 5/3/15
HOLMES	Thos	PTE	20 /1467				14/1/15							
HOME	J	PTE	20 / 73	C										AWOL 29-30/11/15.
HOPE	Chas	CPL	20 / 106		27 HUTT STREET	BENSHAM	27/10/14	3/12/18	KR para 392				TO LABOUR CORPS(284 A E COY + 595 HS COY).	SERVED RN 1887-90+DLI 1893-1906.LAB CORPS No 369553.
HOPE	G	PTE	20 /1062	B				10/4/15	UNFIT					AWOL 6-7/2/15.
HOPKINS	Edwd	PTE	20 / 178			NEWCASTLE				1/7/16		OVILLERS MIL CEM		BORN ORMSKIRK LANCS
HOPPER	Andrw	SGT	20 / 4	C			22/10/14	10/4/15	UNFIT					SERGEANTS MESS CATERER 31/1/15, POSTED TO DEPOT COY
HOPPER	Thos	PTE	20 /1528				18/3/15	29/6/15	INNEFFICIENT					DID NOT SERVE O/SEAS.
HOPPS	Thos	PTE	20 /1480	D		BISHOP AUKLAND				1/7/16		OVILLERS MIL CEM		
HOWARD	Matt	PTE	20 / 51	A									ATTACHED 34th DIV HQ 22/10/15, TO LABOUR CORPS.	
HOWEY	H	PTE	20 / 417					1/2/15	KR para 392					
HOWEY	James	PTE	20 / 179	A	20 SOUTH ROW	PELTON FELL				1/7/16		THIEPVAL MEM		AGE 34
HUDSON	G W	PTE	20 /1381	B										AWOL 6-8/2/15. SUSPECT CLERICAL ERROR WITH No.
HUMBLE	B	PTE	20 / 249					1/2/15	KR para 392					
HUNTER	Arth	PTE	20 /1468	A	15 LOW CHAPEL ROW	BIDDICK	13/1/15				MISSING 21/3/18		TO 22nd BN(C COY), CLASS Z RESERVE.	FROM DEPOT COY TO A COY 25/2/15.
HUNTER	Geo E	CPL	20 /1627	C	NORTH OPENS	OLD HARTLEY				5/6/17		ARRAS MEM		AGE 21.
HUNTER	JohnR	PTE	20 /1307	C		SEAHAM COLLIERY				1/7/16		THIEPVAL MEM		BORN SEAHAM HARBOUR, FROM DEPOT COY TO C COY 25/2/1
HUNTER	N	CSM	20 / 11											POSTED TO DEPOT COY 5/3/15.
HUNTER	Wm	PTE	20 / 418	D	7 OLD COLLIERY ROW	BEDLINGTON				1/7/16		SERRE ROAD No 2 CEM		AWOL 6-7/10/15, AGE 38 BORN BENTON.
HUSBAND	Thos	PTE	20 /1303										TO 1st GARRISON BN, CLASS Z RESERVE.	
HUTCHESON	Geo	PTE	20 / 250										TO 22nd BN, CLASS Z RESERVE.	
HUTCHINSON	S A	BGLR	20 / 52											POSTED TO DEPOT COY 5/3/15.
HUTCHINSON	Thos	PTE	20 / 251	A		WREKETON				1/7/16		THIEPVAL MEM		BORN STAFFORD.
HUTCHINSON	Thos	PTE	20 /1517		62 SALISBURY STREE	NEWCASTLE							TO 2nd GARRISON BN, CLASS Z RESERVE.	
HUTTON	Wm	PTE	20 /1064			DUDLEY	2/11/14	20/11/17	SICK		1/7/16		TO DEPOT.	AGE 44
INGHAM	Jas	PTE	20 /1673	C		MORPETH				1/7/16		THIEPVAL MEM		BORN BURNLEY.
INGLIS	Wm	PIPR	20 /1485	C		ALNWICK	16/2/15				1/7/16			
IRVING	Geo	PTE	20 / 353		6 EDNA TERR DENTON	NEWCASTLE							TO 12/13th, 23rd BNS, CLASS Z RESERVE.	
IRVING	Hen J	PTE	20 / 181	A	GREENSIDE	RYTON			KR para 392		31/8/16			OFF RATION STRENGTH 1-7/2/15.
IRVING	J	PTE	20 / 252	A				9/2/15	KR para 392					

IRVING	John	PTE	20 / 808									TO 2nd GARRISON BN, CLASS Z RESERVE.	
JACK	Alex	PTE	20 / 809			DUNDEE	3/11/14	22/8/17	WOUNDS	1/7/16		TO DEPOT.	
JACKSON	Edw H	PTE	20 /1311			SEAHAM HARBOUR			1/7/16		THIEPVAL MEM		
JACKSON	G	PTE	20 /1524	E		EDMONDSLEY				1/7/16		TO LABOUR CORPS.	FROM E COY TO B COY 19/6/15.
JACKSON	Geo	SGT	20 / 810	D		BEDLINGTON STN			1/7/16		THIEPVAL MEM		
JACKSON	Herbt	PTE	20 / 184	C	107 ST CUTHBERTS RI	GATESHEAD						TO 22nd BN.	AWOL 28/3/15.
JACKSON	Jos	PTE	20 / 185	A		NEWCASTLE			1/7/16		THIEPVAL MEM		BORN FARNWORTH LANCS.
JACKSON	PhilD	PTE	20 /1066	B								TO 2nd GARRISON BN.	AWOL 13-14/2/15.
JACKSON	Wm	PTE	20 / 182									TO 22nd BN.	
JACKSON	Wm	PTE	20 / 183				28/10/14	21/3/18	SICK			TO 1st GARRISON BN.	AGE 43.
JACQUES	Wm	LCPL	20 / 186			NEWCASTLE			27/4/17	13/10/16	ARRAS MEM		WND DURING TRENCH RAID 13/10/16, BORN CRAMLINGTON.
JAMESON	Jos	PTE	20 /1532				1/3/15	2/7/16	DISEASED ARTERY			TO 33rd BN.	DISCHARGED ON BATTALION PART 2 ORDERS 17/11/15.
JEFFERSON	Chris	PTE	20 / 811	D	1 NEW SOUTH ROW	BEDLINGTON COLL			1/7/16		THIEPVAL MEM		
JEFFERSON	Wm	PTE	20 /1309	D		SOUTHMOOR	5/1/15	25/4/17	WOUNDS	1/7/16		TO DEPOT.	FROM DEPOT COY TO D COY 25/2/15.
JENKINS	Geo	PTE	20 / 71	C			24/10/14	2/7/16	SICK			TO 33rd BN.	AWOL 6-9/2/15.
JEWELS	T	PTE	20 /1070			NORTH SHIELDS				1/7/16			
JOBE	Thos	PTE	20 / 107	C	34 SALISBURY STREET	BYKER			1/7/16	1/7/16	THIEPVAL MEM		AWOL 7-10/2/15, 29/11-1/12/15, AGE 39.
JOBLING	Jhn	PTE	20 / 812	A	195 CUTHBERT STREE	HEBBURN COLLIE	3/11/14	2/4/19	KR para 392			TO 22nd BN, DEPOT.	MASTER COOK 31/1/15, PROMOTED CPL 18/1/15, SGT.
JOBSON	Jos	LCPL	20 /1550	E		SOUTH SHIELDS			KR para 392	1/7/16			FROM E COY TO C COY 19/6/15.
JOHNSON	Frank	PTE	20 /1071	D		BARRINGTON			1/7/16		OVILLERS MIL CEM		AGE 42.
JOHNSON	Geo R	PTE	20 / 189		68 0AK STREET	GATESHEAD	28/10/14	4/10/18	GSW	1/7/16		TO DEPOT.	
JOHNSON	Gilbt	PTE	20 /1438	A		SEAHAM HARBOU	14/1/15	13/10/17	GSW	1/7/16		TO 16th BN, DEPOT.	FROM DEPOT COY TO A COY 25/2/15, AWOL 7-8/3/15.
JOHNSON	Isaac	PTE	20 /1310	D	3 MELBURY STREET	DAWDON			1/7/16		THIEPVAL MEM		AGE 19, FROM DEPOT COY TO D COY 25/2/15, IN 13 PLATOON.
JOHNSON	JohnT	PTE	20 / 190	A	3 LANDSDALE HOUSES	GREENSIDE			27/10/18		TEZZE BRIT CEM ITAL	TO 23rd, 11th BNS.	BORN RYTON, AGE 25.
JOHNSON	Thos	PTE	20 / 187	A	9 WEST WOOD ROW	LANCHESTER				NOV 16		TO 18th, 14th BNS.	AWOL 27-28/3/15.
JOHNSON	Wm F	PTE	20 /1599	C	9 WEST STREET	NORTH SEATON			1/7/16		THIEPVAL MEM		
JOHNSTON	Peter	DRMI	20 / 814	A		WALLSEND			1/7/16		THIEPVAL MEM		BORN GOVAN, IN 3 PLATOON.
JOHNSTON	R W	PTE	20 /1682			ACKLINGTON				1/7/16			
JOHNSTON	Wm B	PTE	20 / 191	C								TO MUNITIONS(ARMSTRONG WHITWORTH & CO).	AWOL 7-10/2/15, 19/7/15.
JOHNSTONE	John	PTE	20 / 815			CHOPPINGTON	2/11/14	16/11/16	GSW ABDO	1/7/16		TO ARMY RESERVE CLASS P.	AGE 22.
JOHNSTONE	John	SGT	20 / 192			WALLSEND			1/7/16		THIEPVAL MEM		
JOHNSTONE	John	PTE	20 / 194				28/10/14	2/2/15	KR para 392				DID NOT SERVE O/SEAS
JOISCE	Geo R	PTE	20 / 572	C	HARTFORD ROAD	BEDLINGTON			1/7/16	4/6/16	OVILLERS MIL CEM		SHRAPNEL WND BACK
JOISCE	P	PTE	20 / 573			BEDLINGTON				4/6/16			SHRAPNEL WND SIDE & RIBS
JONES	Franc	CPL	20 / 574	A				2/3/19				TO 18th BN, YORK & LANCASTER REGT(2/4th BN).	POSTED FROM A TO E COY 31/1/15.
JONES	J W	PTE	20 / 989			WILLINGTON QUAY				4/6/16, 1/7/16.			BRUISED SCAPULA
JONES	James	PTE	20 /1068	B		ACKLINGTON			13/7/16	1/7/16	TOTTENHAM & WOOD GREEN CEM		BORN AMBLE, AGE 22, AWOL 6-7/2/15.
JORDAN	JohnB	PTE	20 / 575	D		BEDLINGTON			1/7/16		THIEPVAL MEM		BORN LONGFRAMLINGTON.
KAY	Thos	PTE	20 /1315	A								TO 8th, 22nd, 12/13th BNS, CLASS Z RESERVE.	FROM DEPOT COY TO A COY 25/2/15, AWOL 7-8/3/15.
KEATING	C	CPL	20 / 85			NEWBURN ON TYNE				AUGUST 16			
KEENAN	Thos	PTE	20 / 354				30/10/14	2/9/17	SICK			TO 1st GARRISON BN, 2nd BN.	
KEEPIN	C	PTE	20 / 576	B				10/4/15	UNFIT				AWOL 6-8/2/15, 86HRS DETENTION.
KELL	GEO	PTE	20 / 817	D	12 COUNCIL HOUSES	SHERBURN HILL			1/7/16		THIEPVAL MEM		BORN SHERBURN.
KELLET		PTE	20	A									
KELLY	R	CPL	20 / 577			DUDLEY NTHBLD				1/7/16			
KERR	Jas	PTE	20 /1685	B		ACKLINGTON			1/7/16		OVILLERS MIL CEM		BORN BROOMHILL AGE 21.
KERR	T	PTE	20 / 818									TO MUNITIONS.	
KEW	J	PTE	20 /1314	C									FROM DEPOT COY TO C COY 25/2/15.
KILGOUR	Jas	PTE	20 / 579	C		CRAMLINGTON			1/7/16		THIEPVAL MEM		BORN BLYTH.
KILLIP	Geo W	PTE	20 /1440	A	13 TRENT STREET	CHOPWELL						TO CLASS Z RESERVE.	FROM DEPOT COY TO A COY 25/2/15.
KILPATRICK	Hen J	LCPL	20 / 420			POMEROY Co TYRO			28/4/17	1/7/16	ARRAS MEM	TO 25th BN.	BORN MAMORE Co TYRONE, AGE 38.
KING	Geo	PTE	20 /1500	E	9 MONK STREET	SUNDERLAND	15/2/15		1/7/16		THIEPVAL MEM		FROM E COY TO B COY 19/6/15, AGE 46.
KING	J	PTE	20 / 421	C								TO MUNITIONS(ARMSTRONG WHITWORTH & CO).	
KING	Jas	PTE	20 /1539			WARETON NTHBLD						TO 2nd GARRISON BN, CLASS Z RESERVE.	
KING	W	PTE	20 / 109	A		SUNDERLAND				MISSING 1/7/16.			
KINGHORN	Geo	PTE	20 / 819	D	6 PIONEER TERRACE	BEDLINGTON STN			1/7/16		THIEPVAL MEM		STRETCHER BEARER 1/7/15, AGE 39.
KINGHORN	Thos	PTE	20 / 820		13 PUDDLERS ROW	BEDLINGTON			15/4/17	1/7/16	DUISSANS BRIT CEM	TO 1st BN.	AGE 36.
KIRBY	Robt	PTE	20 /1439	D			14/1/15	26/10/17	GSW	29/1/16		TO 84th TRAINING RESERVE BN.	AWOL 7-8/3/15, SLIGHT WND R BUTTOCK, AGE 40.
KIRK	Geo A	SGT	20 / 423		51 TAVISTOCK ROAD	NEWCASTLE						TO 19th(Y COY), 18th BNS, CLASS Z RESERVE.	
KITCHEN	Steph	PTE	20 / 424		FARM ACRES COTTAG	DUNSTON				1/7/16		TO 85 TRAINING RESERVE BN, ROYAL DEFENCE C	TR/5/343869.FRANCE 9/1/16-6/7/16, RDC No 75924.
KNOTTS	Har B	PTE	20 / 425		20 COWAN TERRACE	WINLATON				JULY 16		TO 20th, 22nd, R FUSILIERS(24th BN).	20, 9/1/16-10/6/16, 20 19/11/16-2/2/18, 22 3/2/18-28/8/18
KNOX	Jas W	PTE	20 /1312	E					KR para 392			TO DURHAM LIGT INFANTRY, TRAINING RESERVE	AWOL 7-8/2/15.FROM DEPOT COY TO D COY 25/2/15,AWOL 7-8/
KNOX	Robt	PTE	20 /1313				5/1/15	28/4/19	KR para 392			TO 1st GARRISON BN.	
KNOX	W	PTE	20 / 831	A				20/4/15	KR para 392				
LACKENBY	Wm H	CPL	20 / 355	A	160 BOLAM STREET	BYKER			1/7/16		THIEPVAL MEM		AGE 40.
LAIDLAW	John	SGT	20 / 253	A	28 BERKELEY STREET	JARROW		16/2/15	MUNITIONS				DIS CANCELLED 13/2/15, ORDERLY ROOM SGT, RETURNED TC
LAIDLER	Geo	PTE	20 /1324	E	THE BARRACKS	HOLMSIDE						TO 1st GARRISON BN, 2nd BN. ENTERED SALONIK/	FROM DEPOT COY TO A COY 25/2/15, AWOL 7-8/3/15 LAIDLAW?
LAMB	E	PTE	20 /1469	E									FROM E COY TO B COY 19/6/15.
LAMB	Isaac	PTE	20 / 581			BEDLINGTON	1/11/14	11/7/17	GSW	1/7/16		TO DEPOT.	MIL HOSP BOSCOMBE HANTS 7/16, AGE 34.
LAMB	Leon	LCPL	20 / 580	C		GOSFORTH			1/7/16		THIEPVAL MEM		BORN SUNDERLAND.
LAMB	Vince	SGT	20 /1321									TO 1st, 1st GARRISON BNS, CLASS Z RESERVE.	
LAMBERT	Arth	PTE	20 /1628				3/6/15	21/6/17	SICK				
LANCASTER	JohnT	PTE	20 /1663			WEST MOOR				1/7/16		TO DURHAM LI(11th BN).	DLI No 46275.
LAND	Geo E	LCPL	20 / 426			NEWBIGGIN			1/7/16		ALBERT COM CEM		BORN BISHOP AUKLAND.
LANDRETH	Jos	PTE	20 / 427	A	11 EARSDON SQUARE	EARSDON						TO 2nd GARRISON BN, CLASS Z RESERVE.	COY COOK 31/1/15.
LANG	Robt	PTE	20 / 428	A		MORPETH			1/7/16		THIEPVAL MEM		BORN ROXBOROUGH.
LARKIN	T	PTE	20 / 356	A				10/4/15	UNFIT				
LAUGHLIN	Jas C	PTE	20 / 195	C			28/10/15	19/12/17	SICK				AWOL 3-6/2/15, AGE 51 ON DISCHARGE.
LAVERICK	JohnG	PTE	20 /1319	B								TO 18th, 1st BNS, CLASS Z RESERVE.	FROM DEPOT COY TO B COY 25/2/15, 6-7/10/15.SGT.
LAVERICK	Mark	PTE	20 /1072	D		W CRAMLINGTON			1/7/16		THIEPVAL MEM		
LAWS	Isaac	PTE	20 /1491	A	17 ELM STREET	HEBBURN			1/7/16		THIEPVAL MEM		
LAWS	John	PTE	20 /1074	B		HEBBURN			1/7/16		THIEPVAL MEM		BORN FELLING.
LAWSON	J J W	PTE	20 /1317	B		BEDLINGTON			1/7/16		THIEPVAL MEM		FROM DEPOT COY TO B COY 25/2/15.
LAWSON	John	PTE	20 /1318	B		BURRADON COLL				1/7/16		TO 8th, 1/7th BNS, CLASS Z RESERVE.	FROM DEPOT COY TO B COY 25/2/15.
LAX	JohnG	PTE	20 /1316	C		WEST SLEEKBURI	15/1/15	15/3/18	GSW	1/7/16		TO ARMY RESERVE CLASS P.	FROM DEPOT COY TO C COY 25/2/15, 3 CCS 2/7/16 EVAC 2/7/16
LAY	Thos	PTE	20 /1442				14/1/15	19/5/15	KR para 392			TO DEPOT.	
LAYBOURN	Thos	PTE	20 /1443	E		WHICKHAM			1/7/16		THIEPVAL MEM		AWOL 13-14/2/15, FROM E COY TO B COY 19/6/15.
LEATHAM	JohnE	PTE	20 /1075	B	25 LAUREL TERRACE	HOLYWELL	4/11/14	1/4/19	KR para 392			ATTACHED 102nd LIGHT TRENCH MORTAR BATTEI	AWOL 6-7/10/15.
LEATHERD	T	CPL	20 / 429		1 CHARLIE STREET	RYTON						TO 3rd BN.	
LEDGER	AlexF	PTE	20 / 823		8 NEALE TERRACE	TANTOBIE	16/10/14			1/7/16, JUNE 17.		TO 21st, 23rd BNS, ROYAL FUSILIERS(24th BN).	FRANCE 20 9/1/16-1/1/17,21 18/6/17-2/2/18,23 3/2/18-28/8/18
LEIGHTON	A	PTE	20 /1470	B								TO ROYAL ENGINEERS TUNNELLING DEPOT 13/10.	FROM E COY TO B COY 19/6/15.
LEWIS	Wm	PTE	20 /1320	E		NORTH SHIELDS						TO 8th BN, CLASS Z RESERVE.	AWOL 8/3/15, FROM E COY TO B COY 19/6/15.
LIDDELL	ChasS	PTE	20 /1076	B	18 THE LEAZES	THROCKLEY			9/4/17		ROCLINCOURT VALLEY CEM		AWOL 12-14/2/15, BORN NEWBURN AGE 20.
LIDDELL	Robt	PTE	20 / 110	C		GATESHEAD	27/10/14	31/12/17	SICK	1/7/16		TO 16th, 3rd BNS.	AWOL 29/11-1/12/15, AGE 32.
LIDDLE	J W	CPL	20 / 825	B		ROWLANDS GILL				JUNE 16, JULY 16, 11/12/1			PTE AWOL 6-7/2/15, PROMOTED SGT.
LIDDLE	Wm	CPL	20 / 430	C		BLAYDON			1/7/16	4/6/16	THIEPVAL MEM		SHELL SHOCK 6/16, BORN RYTON.
LILLEY	JohnJ	PTE	20 / 431	D	94 MOWBRAY STREET	HEATON			1/7/16	4/6/16	THIEPVAL MEM		BORN GATESHEAD, AGE 29.
LILLEY	Robt	PTE	20 /1600	C	6 COOPERATIVE TERF	WEST ALLOTMENT			1/7/16		THIEPVAL MEM		BORN MORPETH AGE 40.
LINDSLEY	C R	LCPL	20 /1323	E									AWOL 15-16/2/16.
LIPPEAT	Wm	PTE	20		17 COALY HILL TERR	WALBOTTLE							
LITTLE	Thos	PTE	20 /1718		26 TRAFALGAR STREE	NEWCASTLE						TO 2nd GARRISON BN, CLASS Z RESERVE.	
LOCKHART	R	PIPR	20 / 13			NEWCASTLE				MARCH 16			
LODGE	Fred	PTE	20 / 588			SOUTH GOSFORT	2/11/14	16/7/17	WOUNDS	1/7/16		TO DEPOT.	
LOGAN	Cyril	SGT	20 /1077	E								TO 18th BN, COMMISSIONED 27/6/17.	ACTING CSM E COY 16/2/15.
LOGAN	JohnW	LCPL	20 / 432				31/10/14	5/5/17	SICK			TO DEPOT.	AGE 41, RENUMBERED 259376.
LORD	Alf C	LCPL	20 / 433		18 ENID STREET	DINNINGTON			14/9/18		LOOS MEM	TO 22nd BN.	BORN BROOMSIDE DURHAM.
LORD	Geo H	PTE	20 / 434			NEWCASTLE			1/7/16		THIEPVAL MEM		BORN BROOMSIDE DURHAM.
LORD	Robt	PTE	20 / 435		96 BEAUMONT TERR	DENTON NEWCASTLE						TO CLASS Z RESERVE.	PRISONER OF WAR.
LOTHIAN	James	PTE	20 / 828	B	11 CORPORATION YAF	MORPETH	16/10/14		1/7/16		THIEPVAL MEM		AWOL 6-7/2/15, BORN ALNWICK.
LOWDEN	Henry	PTE	20 /1078	D		SHOTTON							AWOL 12-14/2/15, 27-29/3/15, DESERTED 28/6/15, MINER.
LOWDEN		PTE	20 / 590	C								TO 34th DIV CYC COY.	
LOWDON	J T H	PTE	20 / 436		9 SHIBDEN STREET	BLAYDON				1/7/16		TO 16th, 12/13th, 8th BNS.	

LOWERSON	JohnR	PTE	20 /1567	D	7 COTTAGES ROAD	DAWDON				1/7/16		THIEPVAL MEM		FROM E COY TO D COY 19/6/15.
LOWES	Thos	PTE	20 /1660			FOREST HALL	19/6/15	26/2/18	GSW		1/7/16		TO ARMY RESERVE CLASS P.	
LOWES	Wm	PTE	20 / 437	C		NORTH SHIELDS				1/7/16		THIEPVAL MEM		BORN THORNABY.
LUKE	Jos	PTE	20 / 829	B			3/11/14	10/4/15	UNFIT					AGE 43, DID NOT SERVE O/SEAS.
LUMSDEN	R	PTE	20 / 830	D				20/4/15	KR para 392					
LYNN	James	PTE	20 /1503	E	271 BACK ASKEW RD	GATESHEAD	17/2/15	10/6/18	WOUNDS		1/7/16		TO DEPOT.	FROM E COY TO B COY 19/6/15.
LYNN	M	PTE	20 /1653											
MACANALLY	Felix	PTE	20 / 255		62 BENTON WAY	WALLSEND	29/10/14	21/8/18	SICK				TO 3rd BN.	AGE 45.
MacDONALD	JohnA	PTE	20 /1343	A		EDMONDSLEY				1/7/16		THIEPVAL MEM		FROM DEPOT COY TO A COY 25/2/15, BORN USHAW MOOR, AL
MacDONALD	M	PTE	20 / 260	C				10/4/15	UNFIT					
MacDONALD	W A B	CQM:	20 / 257			ALNWICK			KR para 392		1/7/16		TO 1st BN, DURHAM LIGHT INFANTRY, TRAINING R	TRG RES BN TR/5/58163.
MACKAY	Hectr	PTE	20 / 53				26/10/14	26/7/15	HEART DISEASE					DID NOT SERVE O/SEAS.
MACKENZIE	Herbt	PTE	20 /1333	C		WIMBLEDON	11/1/15			1/7/16		THIEPVAL MEM		FROM DEPOT COY TO C COY 25/2/15, TRF D COY.
MACKENZIE	Wm	PTE	20 /1090				4/11/14	3/5/15	CYSTITUS					DID NOT SERVE O/SEAS.
MACKERETH	Garvn	SGT	20 / 258			GATESHEAD					1/7/16		TO ROYAL DEFENCE CORPS.	FRANCE 9/1/16-7/7/16,BEAUFORT HOSP BRISTOL 8/7/16.
MacLAREN	Robt	PTE	20 /1569	D	20 JOHN STREET	CULLERCOATES				1/7/16		THIEPVAL MEM		FROM E COY TO D COY 19/6/15, BORN DUNDEE.
MADDISON	J	PTE	20 / 197			NEWCASTLE					1/7/16			
MADDISON	J G	PTE	20 /1089	B	30 LOW FRIARSIDE	ROWLANDS GILL								AWOL 6-7/10/15.
MAIR	A	PTE	20 / 836	C										AWOL 6-9/2/15.
MAKEPEACE	Jos	PTE	20 /1631				7/6/15	23/8/18	SICK				TO ARMY RESERVE CLASS W	AGE 42.
MAKIN	Ben J	PTE	20 / 265			WALLSEND	19/10/14	2/2/15	KR para 392					
MALCOLM	Adam	PTE	20 /1334	E	14 QUARRY SQUARE	TANTOBIE	11/1/15				1/7/16		TO 25th, 8th BN(BN HQ), CLASS Z RESERVE.	AWOL 31/1-2/2/15, E COY TO B COY 19/6/15, AWOL 6-7/10/15.
MARLAND	John	CPL	20 /1337				12/11/14	17/12/17	SICK					AGE 33.
MARLEY	ThosG	PTE	20 /1629		29 LANE END	W CRAMLINGTON				1/7/16		OVILLERS MIL CEM		BORN CRAMLINGTON
MARR	Alf L	PTE	20 /1683								15/6/16		TO CLASS Z RESERVE.	SHRAPNEL L LEG
MARSHALL	W	PTE	20 / 593	C				9/2/15	KR para 392					
MARSHALL	Wm	LCPL	20 / 360			PELTON				26/4/17		PELTON CEMETERY		AGE 23
MARTIN	Jos	PTE	20 / 845	C		BEDLINGTON	2/11/14			1/7/16		OVILLERS MIL CEM		BORN GATESHEAD AGE 25, MINER DESERTED 12/6/15, 5'7".
MARTIN	Owen	PTE	20 /1087			NORTH SHIELDS				1/7/16		THIEPVAL MEM		BORN WHITBY NORTH YORKS.
MASON	Geo	PTE	20 /1178										TO 2nd GARRISON BN, CLASS Z RESERVE.	
MASON	John	PTE	20 / 198	C									TO 1st GARRISON BN, CLASS Z RESERVE.	AWOL 7-8/2/15.
MASON	Rob W	PTE	20 / 442	B		SEATON DELAVAL		2/2/15		1/7/16		THIEPVAL MEM		BORN KILLINGWORTH, DISCHARGE ON 2/2/15 KR para 392 CAN
MATHER	Edwd	PTE	20 / 361		EAST HOUSES	NETHERTON				6/7/16		ST SEVER CEM ROUEN		BORN MORPETH AGE 28.
MATTINSON	John	PTE	20 / 111		18 BAYLEY STREET	NEWCASTLE	27/10/14	1/2/19	KR para 392				TO 2nd GARRISON BN, ARMY RESERVE CLASS P.	
MAVIN	Anthy	PTE	20 / 595	C		BEDLINGTON				1/7/16		THIEPVAL MEM		
MAVIN	J W	PTE	20 / 596	D							29/1/16			SLIGHT WND EAR, REJOINED.
MAVIN	Wm	PTE	20 / 594			NEWCASTLE			KR para 392		29/12/16			
MAXEY	H R	PTE	20 /1479	B			29/1/15							
MAXWELL	Thos	PTE	20 / 847			CHOPPINGTON				3/10/18	1/7/16	TEMPLEUX LE GUERA	TO ROYAL INNISKILLING FUSILIERS(6th BN).	BORN GOSFORTH,3rd SCOTTISH GHOSP 11/7/16,RIFUS No 215
MAYES	J	PTE	20 / 848	D									TO 34th DIV CYC COY.	AWOL 6-7/2/15.
McALLISTER	Alex	PTE	20 / 591	D	73 BROADSHEATH TEI	SOUTHWICK				31/1/18	DECEMBER 16	GIAVERA CEM ITALY	TO 11th, 1st, 10th BNS	AWOL 7-8/3/15, AGE 41 BORN KILMARNOCK.
McALLISTER	J A	PTE	20 /1447	E										AWOL 1/2/15, AWOL 6-9/2/15.
McANALLY	Felix	PTE	20 / 255	C			29/10/14	21/8/18					TO 3rd BN.	COY COOK 31/1/15, AGE 45.
McARDLE	Robt	PTE	20 /1327	E		SUNDERLAND				1/7/16		THIEPVAL MEM		FROM E COY TO B COY 19/6/15.
McARTHUR	Alex	PTE	20 / 439	C		NORTH SHIELDS				9/4/17		BAILLUEL RD EAST CEM		COY COOK 31/1/15, BOORN CALDERCRUISE LANARK.
McCABE	Edwd	PTE	20 / 357	D	54 JOHN STREET	HEBBURN NEWTOWN					1/7/16		TO CLASS Z RESERVE.	84HRS DETENTION ABSENT 20-29/3/15, PRISONER OF WAR.
McCABE	J	PTE	20 /1079			BEDLINGTON					1/7/16			
McCARTNEY	JohnM	PTE	20 / 196			NEWCASTLE					1/7/16		TO 22nd BN.	
McDONALD	Chas	PTE	20 /1487				1/12/14	27/10/17	SICK				TO 1st GARRISON, 2nd BNS, ARMY RESERVE CLAS	AGE 38.
McDONALD	John	PTE	20 / 358	A	8 BOYD TERRACE	WESTERHOPE	30/10/14			9/4/17		ROCLINCOURT MIL CEM		BORN EDINBURGH, DRUNK & DISORDERLY ASSAULTED POLIC
McDONALD	JohnA	PTE	20 /1081	B	109 MILL LANE	NEWCASTLE				1/7/16		THIEPVAL MEM		AWOL 7-9/2/15, 31/5/15. AGE 24.
McDONALD	Rodrk	CQM:	20 / 14		18 HOOD STREET	GATESHEAD							TO 18th, 23rd BNS.	
McDONALD	T	PTE	20 / 839											
McDONALD	Thos	PTE	20 / 359		8 BOYD TERRACE	WESTERHOPE	30/10/14	21/8/17	WOUNDS		1/7/16		TO 80th TRAINING RESERVE BN.	AGE 22.
McDONALD	Wm	CPL	20 / 256		HUNTS BLDGS	PELTON				10/4/18		NIEUPORT MEM	TO 22nd BN(A COY).	AGE 34.
McGARRIGLE	Wm	PTE	20 /1448	E		SEATON DELAVAL				9/3/16		X FARM CEM		AWOL 7-9/2/15, 21-22/2/15, FROM E COY TO C COY 19/6/15.
McGEARY	JohnW	PTE	20 / 440	A	11 MOOR ROW	WIDDRINGTON							TO 2nd GARRISON BN, CLASS Z RESERVE.	AWOL 27-28/3/15.
McGINLEY	J	LCPL	20 / 199	C										AWOL 6-8/2/15.
McGINTY	Mich	DRMI	20 /1666	B							24/8/16			AWOL 6-7/10/14, DESERTED 18/1/19.
McGOWAN	Alex	PTE	20 /1341	E		NEWCASTLE				1/7/16		THIEPVAL MEM		AWOL 7-8/2/15, FROM E COY TO C COY 19/6/15.
McGREGOR	Frn A	PTE	20 /1082	B	111 DEWALDEN PLACI	PEGSWOOD COLL				1/7/16		THIEPVAL MEM		AGE 37 BORN ROTHBURY.
McGURK	J	PTE	20 / 841	D									TO 34th DIV CYC COY.	
McHUGH	Frank	PTE	20 / 263			CONSETT				27/4/17		ROEUX BRIT CEM		
McINTYRE	F	PTE	20 /1104	A				9/2/15	KR para 392					
McKENZIE	Dan	PTE	20 /1339	B		TOW LAW	12/1/15	8/8/17	GSW		1/7/16,DEC 16			AWOL 6-7/10/15, IN BN WAR DIARY AS KIA.
McLACHLAN	Don	PTE	20 / 441		9 WILSON STREET	MONKWEARMOUT	31/10/14							HOLDER UP, DESERTED 12/7/15 AGE 35, 5'8".BORN ARGYLL.
McLEAN	Chas	PIPR	20 / 840	A					KR para 392		1/7/16			AWOL 1-2/2/15, 4/6/15.
McLEAN	James	PTE	20 / 262			NEWCASTLE					1/7/16			AWOL 7-8/2/15, 26/5/15.
McLEAN	James	PTE	20 /1690		3 HENDERSON STREE	AMBLE							TO 2nd GARRISON BN, CLASS Z RESERVE.	
McLEAN	Raybn	PTE	20 /1328			BEDLINGTON					1/7/16			AWOL 17/7/15
McLEOD	Stewt	PTE	20 /1209			DUNDEE	10/11/14							DRILLER DESERTED 4/7/15 AGE 26, 5'3".
McNALLY	W	PTE	20 /1529	E										FROM E COY TO B COY 19/6/15.
McNEAL	J	PTE	20 / 844	B	6 FELL ROW	LANCHESTER							TO CHESHIRE REGT(9th BN).	STRETCHER BEARER 1/7/15,AWOL 23-26/1/15, CHESHIRE No 52
McNEAL	Thos	PTE	20 / 843	B		BURNHOPE				3/6/16		ALBERT COM CEM EXT		STRETCHER BEARER 1/7/15,AWOL 23-26/1/15,WND SHELLFIRE
McNEAL	Wm	PTE	20 / 842	B	6 FELL ROW	LANCHESTER							TO CLASS Z RESERVE.	STRETCHER BEARER 1/7/15,AWOL 23-26/1/15, 6-8/10/15.
McNEILL	J S	CPL	20 /1331	C										FROM DEPOT COY TO C COY 25/2/15.
McPHERSON	Robt	CPL	20 / 112		22 RIPON STREET	GATESHEAD	15/10/14						TO 18th, 8th BNS	ACTING ORDERLEY ROOM SGT 5/3/15, RQMS.
McPHILIPS	J	PTE	20 /1084			FOREST HALL					1/7/16			
McQUEEN	J		20 / 592		19 SEAHAM STREET	SEAHAM								
McTEAR	Jas	PTE	20 /1643	C		LIVERPOOL				1/7/16		THIEPVAL MEM		MACHINE GUN SECTION.
McTIER	Geo	PTE	20 /1085				4/11/14	16/8/17	WOUNDS		1/7/16		TO 3rd BN.	
MERRYWEATH	Wm	PTE	20 /1088	D		NEWCASTLE				3/4/16		X FARM CEM		AWOL 6-7/2/15, 7-8/3/15.
MIDDLEMISS	A	PTE	20 /1586								1/7/16			
MIDDLETON	G	PTE	20 /1092	B										REGIMENTAL POST ORDERLEY 31/1/15.
MILBURN	Wm R	CPL	20 / 364		EDGES GREEN	MELKRIDGE							TO 22nd BN, CLASS Z RESERVE.	
MILLER	E W	PTE	20 /1095	B										AWOL 2-9/2/15.
MILLER	Frc H	PTE	20 / 597	C		ASHINGTON	31/10/14	30/10/17	WOUNDS		1/7/16		TO 3rd BN.	SGTS MESS COOK 31/1/15,AGE 31,R VICTORIA HOSP NETLEY
MILLER	J	PTE	20 / 270	A										AWOL14-15/2/15.
MILLER	Jacob	PTE	20 /1580	B		NEW YORK NTHBLD				21/10/17		BARD COTTAGE CEM BOEZINGE		AWOL 6/10/15, BORN NEW DELAVAL.
MILLER	JohnG	PTE	20 / 443	A	57 BACK STREET	WINLATON							TO 1st GARRISON BN, CLASS Z RESERVE.	AWOL 7-8/3/15.
MILLER	Robt	PTE	20 /1604		BRUNSWICK STREET	NEWCASTLE	31/5/15	1/3/18	INSANITY				TO DEPOT.	AGE 39, TRIED BY FGCM STEENBECQUE 12/2/16, 84 DAYS FP N
MILLER	T	PTE	20 /1446	E										AWOL 9-11/2/15, 16-17/2/15.
MILLER	Tom H	CPL	20 /1330			BEDLINGTON	5/1/15	1/4/19	KR para 392		1/7/16		TO ARMY RESERVE CLASS P	
MILLICAN	Geo	LCPL	20 / 850										TO 18th, 14th BNS, CLASS Z RESERVE.	
MILLICAN	Jos	PTE	20 /1329			WEST SLEEKBURI	5/1/15	27/2/18	GSW		1/7/16		TO ARMY RESERVE CLASS P	AGE 21.
MILLION	Thos	LCPL	20 / 851	D		CHOPPINGTON					13/3/16 MIS 1/7/16		TO CLASS Z RESERVE.	SHRAPNEL WND R HAND, PRISONER OF WAR.
MILNE	James	PTE	20 /1602				31/5/15	9/9/16					TO 29th BN.	
MILNE	Wm	PTE	20 /1509	Depo			22/2/15							FROM E COY TO B COY 19/6/15.
MINTO	ArchE	PTE	20 /1332	E	31 RIVER STREET	NEWCASTLE	12/1/15			1/7/16		THIEPVAL MEM	TO & FROM 23rd BN.	AWOL 9/2/15, POSTED TO D COY, AGE 30.
MITCHELL	Andrw	PTE	20 / 598	A		GATESHEAD				1/7/16		THIEPVAL MEM		AGE 35 BORN EDINBURGH
MITCHELL	Edwd	PTE	20 /1206										TO 22nd BN, CLASS Z RESERVE.	
MITCHELL	J	PTE	20 / 327					2/2/15	KR para 392					
MITCHELL	J P	PTE	20 /1096	B										AWOL 7-9/2/15.
MITCHELL	Robt	PTE	20 / 853	B		WILLINGTON QUAY				1/7/16		THIEPVAL MEM		AWOL 6-7/10/15.
MITCHELL	Robt	PTE	20 / 852		HOPGARTH	CHESTER LE ST							TO 2nd GARRISON BN, CLASS Z RESERVE.	
MITCHINSON	Alex	PTE	20 /1097			ACKLINGTON				12/6/16		ALBERT COM CEM EXT		AGE 42 BORN NEWCASTLE
MOONEY	James	PTE	20 / 1			ELSWICK				1/7/16		THIEPVAL MEM		
MOONEY	Wm	PTE	20 /1445		2 HILLTHORN TERR	USWORTH	14/1/15	18/3/19	KR para 392				TO 2nd GARRISON BN.	ORIGINALLY ATTESTED FOR THE TYNESIDE IRISH.
MOORE	G	PTE	20 / 854			BEDLINGTON					1/7/16			
MOORE	John	PTE	20 /1205										TO 2nd GARRISON BN, CLASS Z RESERVE.	
MORAN	F	PTE	20 / 272			BURNHOPEFIELD					1/7/16			
MORGAN	Matt	PTE	20 / 599	D		NEWCASTLE				2/7/16		THIEPVAL MEM		BORN TYNEMOUTH.

MORGAN	T	PTE	20 / 294			ANNITSFORD				1/7/16			
MORGAN		PTE	20 / 855	D								TO 34th DIV CYC COY.	
MORRIN	James	PTE	20 / 114		31 TULLOCH STREET	NEWCASTLE	15/1/14		10/4/17		AUBIGNY COM CEM EXT		AGE 23, BATH WAR HOSP 11/7/16.
MORRIS	Chas	PTE	20 /1098				3/11/14	5/1/17	SICK			TO 2nd GARRISON BN, DEPOT.	
MORTON	G G	PTE	20 / 445	C									AWOL 6-9/2/15.
MORTON	Wm B	SGT	20 /1340		55 SPELTER WKS RD	GRANGETOWN SUND			18/9/17		HAGRICOURT MIL CEM		
MOSES	Edwd	PTE	20 /1338					3/4/19	UNFIT			TO 18th BN, YORK & LANCASTER REGT(2/4th BN).	Y & L No 57705.
MOWAT	JohnM	PTE	20 / 328	A	8 NORTHUMBERLAND	BACKWORTH						TO 18th, 3rd BNS, CLASS Z RESERVE.	POSTED FROM A TO E COY 31/1/15.
MUCKLE	J W	PTE	20 / 329	C				10/4/15	UNFIT				AWOL 12-16/2/15.
MUDD	Edwd	PTE	20 / 446	A		BEDALE			30/11/17		FIFTEEN RAVINE CEM	TO 34th DIV CYC COY, III CORPS CYCLIST BN.	ACC No 9471.
MUIR	RobtT	PTE	20 /1100			PERCY MAIN	4/11/14	28/7/17	GSW	1/7/16			NORTH EVINGTON HOSP LEICESTER 8/7/16.
MULLEN	Mich	CPL	20 / 296	C		GATESHEAD			3/4/16		X FARM CEM		AWOL 22-24/3/15, GSW ABDOMEN & LUNGS.
MUNCASTER	Jos	PTE	20 /1568	D	50 CANTERBURY STRI	SOUTH SHIELDS				1/7/16			FROM E COY TO D COY 19/6/15.
MUNN	Wm	PTE	20 /1102		217 WILLIAM STREET	HEBBURN COLL						TO 2nd GARRISON BN, CLASS Z RESERVE.	
MUNNOCH	J	PTE	20 /1530	E									FROM E COY TO B COY 19/6/15.
MUNRO	Her P	PTE	20 / 330										
MUNRO	John	PTE	20										ON PHOTOS WITH PTE KITCHEN.
MUNRO	K	PTE	20 / 273	D									CO's GROOM 31/1/15 VICE 725 PTE CLARK.
MUNRO	Thos	PTE	20 / 115	A	80 KING EDWARD STR	GATESHEAD	15/10/14		1/7/16		THIEPVAL MEM		SERVANT TO Lt McCLAY 31/1/15, AGE 38 BORN EDINBURGH.
MURPHY	Hugh	PTE	20 / 331	A		NEWCASTLE			1/7/16		SERRE RD No 2 CEM		
MURRAY	J	PTE	20 /1103	B									AWOL 28-30/3/15.
MURRAY	James	PTE	20 / 856	B		ACKLINGTON	2/11/14	28/1/18	WOUNDS	1/7/16			AWOL 6-7/2/15, AGE 32.
MURRAY	John	PTE	20 /1105		LONG ROW	SOUTH HAWKSLEY						TO 1st GARRISON BN, CLASS Z RESERVE.	AWOL 28/7/15, AGE 45.
MURRAY	Wm	PTE	20 / 185			ALSTON CUMB			15/12/17				
MUSGROVE	Wm J	LCPL	20 /1099	A	12 CHARLES STREET	EARSDON							REGIMENTAL BUTCHER 31/1/15, SGT.
MUSTARD	JohnJ	PTE	20 / 332		31 JAMES STREET	BLAYDON						TO 23rd BN, CLASS Z RESERVE.	
NASBY	Jas T	PTE	20 /1344	C		MARLEY HILL			1/7/16		OVILLERS MIL CEM		FROM DEPOT COY TO C COY 25/2/15, AGE 20.
NEAL	Sam	PTE	20 / 857	D		CHOPPINGTON			1/7/16		THIEPVAL MEM		BORN BEDLINGTON.
NELSON	Isaac	PTE	20 /1449		19 RED ROW	OXHILL						TO 2nd GARRISON BN, CLASS Z RESERVE.	
NESBIT	F	PTE	20 /1184	B									168HRS DETENTION 1/2/15, MISCONDUCT, AWOL 6-7/10/15.
NEWTON	Anth	PTE	20 /1450	C		SEAHAM HARBOUR			1/7/16		THIEPVAL MEM		
NICHOL	Jas	PTE	20 /1506	De	75 PALMERSTON STRI	SOUTH SHIELDS	20/2/15		1/7/16		THIEPVAL MEM		FROM E COY TO C COY 19/6/15.
NICHOLSON	Chris	LCPL	20 /1107	B		NEWBURN			1/7/16		THIEPVAL MEM		BORN BRAMPTON CUMB.
NICHOLSON	John	PTE	20 / 858		24 EAST TERRACE	BOOMERSUND	5/11/14	1/4/19	GSW	27/4/17 SEVERE R THIGH		TO DEPOT, ALNWICK, CATTERICK, DUBLIN, ROYAL	AGE 19, FRANCE 20 9/1/16-27/4/17.RDC No 72012.
NICHOLSON	Jos	PTE	20 /1106	B		EARSDON			1/7/16		THIEPVAL MEM		BORN BROOMHILL.
NICHOLSON	Wm	PTE	20 / 447	A				14/12/18				TO KINGS OWN YORSHIRE LI.	STRETCHER BEARER 1/7/16, KOYLI No 48305.
NISBET	John	PTE	20 /1708	C		LESBURY			1/7/16		THIEPVAL MEM		IN 11 PLATOON.
NIXON	Sam P	PTE	20 /1581		32 MIKE STREET	SOUTH SHIELDS			18/4/18		TYNE COT MEM	TO 26th, 21st, 12/13th(HQ) BNS.	
NIXON	ThosN	PTE	20 / 448				31/10/14	23/2/15	SICK				DID NOT SERVE O/SEAS
NOBLE	Andrw	CPL	20 /1108			NEWCSATLE				1/7/16		TO CLASS Z RESERVE.	
NOBLE	Mark	PTE	20 / 449	A								TO 22nd BN, ROYAL FUSILIERS(24th BN).	OFF RATION STRENGTH 7-13/2/15.R FUS No GS/93146.
NOBLE	Wm s	PTE	20 /1531	E	GREENHILL	MURTON COLL			5/6/17	10/3/16, 1/7/16.	ARRAS MEM		FROM E COY TO B COY 19/6/15, GSW R LEG.
NOON	John	PTE	20 / 444			WALLSEND			5/6/18	7/10/16	ETAPLES MIL CEM	TO 22nd BN.	AGE 46 BORN EDINBURGH.
OAKLEY	Solmn	PTE	20 /1345	C		NETHERTON COLL				1/7/16		TO CLASS Z RESERVE.	FROM DEPOT COY TO C COY 25/2/15.
O'BRIEN	EdwdJ	PTE	20 / 201		7 KYO LANE	OXHILL		2/2/15	KR para 392	4/6/16,1/7/16.		TO 1st, 23rd BNS.	DISC CANCELLED,AWOL 7-8/3/15, WND THIGH & LEG 1/7/16.
OCTON	Robsn	PTE	20 /1648									TO CLASS Z RESERVE.	
O'DONNELL	JohnW	PTE	20 / 274									TO 22nd BN, EAST YORKSHIRE REGT(1st BN), CLA!	E YORKS No 50673.
O'KEEFE	J	LCPL	20 / 859	D									FINED 7/- AND REDUCED TO PTE FOR ABSENCE 16/2/15.
OLIVER	Rich	PTE	20 / 861	B	13 DENE ROW	MEDOMSLEY	3/11/14	31/3/19	KR para 392	23/6/16, 1/7/16.		TO 23rd BN, DEPOT.	AWOL 6-7/10/15.
OLIVER	Wm Aw	PTE	20 / 860			BEDLINGTON	2/11/14	25/8/17	WOUNDS	1/7/16		TO 85th TRAINING RESERVE BN.	AWOL 14/2/15, 6-7/10/15, 3 CCS 2/7/16 EVAC 2/7/16.
O'NEILL	JohnT	PTE	20 / 450	C		NORTH SHIELDS			1/7/16		THIEPVAL MEM		BORN THORNABY N/YORKS, AWOL 7-8/2/15.
O'NEILL	T W	PTE	20 / 862							1/7/16			
ORD	Humph	PTE	20 /1109	B		BURNHOPEFIELD			15/6/16		ALBERT 16/6/16		BORN WHICKHAM, AWOL 14-15/2/15.
ORD	Rober	LSGT	20 / 570	D		HOBSON						FROM 20th BN TO TYNESIDE IRISH.	
ORNSBY		PTE	20	A									
ORNSBY		LSGT	20	A									
ORR	David	SGT	20 / 863	D		WHITEHAVEN			5/6/17		ARRAS MEM		
OSBOURNE	G W	DRMI	20 /1181			BUCKWORTH CAMBS				1/7/16			
OSBOURNE	Sam M	PTE	20 /1111			HIRST			KR para 392	1/7/16			
PALMER	Jas W	LCPL	20 / 864			NETHERTON COLL			28/4/17	1/7/16	ARRAS MEM	TO 27th BN.	BORN NEWCASTLE AGE 30.
PALMER	Jos	PTE	20 / 602			BACKWORTH			1/7/16	7/4/16	THIEPVAL MEM		BORN SEGHILL, GSW SHOULDER & HAND 7/4.
PARKER	Robt	PTE	20 /1347	E	3 ROBERT STREET	SEAHAM HARBOUR			1/7/16	JULY 16	THIEPVAL MEM		FROM E COY TO C COY 19/6/15, BORN CASTLE EDEN AGE 24.
PARKES	Thos	PTE	20 / 451									TO 2nd GARRISON BN, CLASS Z RESERVE.	
PARKIN	Wm	WOII	20 / 57									COMMISSIONED NORTHBLD FUS 1/5/18.	
PARNELL	Wm J	PTE	20 / 603	A		NEWCASTLE			21/11/16		ST JOHN'S WESTGATE & ELSWICK		BORN CRAGHEAD AGE 34 DIED OF PHITHISIS.
PATE	Wm	PTE	20 /1451	E	212 COLSTON STREET	NEWCASTLE						TO 1/7th, 26th BNS, CLASS Z RESERVE.	AWOL 7-8/2/15, FROM E COY TO C COY 19/6/15, AWOL 23/8/15.
PATERSON	W	LCPL	20 / 452					1/2/15	KR para 392				
PATTERSON	Alex	LCPL	20 / 604		81 VICTORIA ROAD	GATESHEAD			6/6/16	4/6/16	HEILLY STATION CEM		DIED AT 36 CCS SHRAPNEL WOUND SPINE.
PATTERSON	W	PTE	20 / 84	C				10/4/15	UNFIT				
PATTERSON	Wm	PTE	20 /1582		47 TATHAM STREET	SUNDERLAND				MARCH 1916		TO 21st BN, DURHAM LI(13th BN).	DLI No 46031.
PATTISON	Arth	PTE	20 / 605	D		NEWCASTLE			1/7/16		THIEPVAL MEM		BORN WINLATON.
PATTISON	F J	PTE	20 / 275	A				9/2/15	KR para 392				
PATTISON	Wm	PTE	20 / 607			BEDLINGTON			20/7/16	1/7/16	BEDLINGTON ST CUTHBERTS CH YD		BORN BLYTH.
PATTISON	Wm R	PTE	20 /1346	C	21 WATERGATE	CAMBOIS			1/7/16		THIEPVAL MEM		FROM DEPOT COY TO C COY 25/2/15, AGE 24 BORN BLYTH.
PAXTON	JohnR	PTE	20 / 609	D		NEWCASTLE			13/4/18	29/1/16	ETAPLES MIL CEM	TO 9th BN.	SLIGHT LEG WOUND, REJOINED.
PEAK	ChasJ	PTE	20 / 865									TO ROYAL DEFENCE CORPS.	FRANCE 10/1/16-13/9/17. RDC No 81972.
PEARCEY	ThosJ	PTE	20 / 611	D		BEDLINGTON	31/10/14	7/8/17	SHELLSHO(	1/7/16		TO 84th TRAINING RESERVE BN.	AWOL 6-7/10/14, AGE 29.
PEARCY	Jos	PTE	20 / 610	C		SEGHILL			1/7/16	4/6/16	THIEPVAL MEM		SHRAPNEL WND SIDE
PEARSE	D	PTE	20 /1113	D				9/2/15	KR para 392				
PEARSON	Ambro	PTE	20 /1551	E						1/7/16			FROM E COY TO C COY 19/6/15.
PEARSON	Henry	PTE	20 /1352	E		SEAHAM HARBOUR			1/7/16		THIEPVAL MEM		FROM E COY TO C COY 19/6/15, BORN SOUTHWICK.
PEARSON	James	CPL	20 /1200				1/11/14	2/3/18	SICK			TO DEPOT.	AGE 29.
PEEL	H	PTE	20 / 866	D				10/4/15	UNFIT				
PEGG	Robt	PTE	20 /1112		9 MILL STREET CHIRT(	NORTH SHIELDS			22/11/17	1/7/16	ETAPLES MIL CEM	TO 25th, 1/5th BNS.	BORN WEST PELTON,AGE 36, RENUMBERED 243182.
PEGGIE	Geo	PTE	20 / 454		2 LOW ROW	PERCY MAIN							
PELLOW	John	PTE	20 / 612	C		CRAMLINGTON			1/7/16		THIEPVAL MEM		AGE 31.
PELLOW	Rich	PTE	20 / 613		53 HASTINGS STREET	CRAMLINGTON						TO 2nd GARRISON BN.	
PENALUNA	J	PTE	20 / 867	B				2/2/15	KR para 392				
PENDLETON	Dan	PTE	20 / 334	A									AWOL 7-8/2/15.
PENDLETON	Henry	PTE	20 / 335	A		ANNFIELD PLAIN			1/7/16		THIEPVAL MEM		AWOL 7-8/2/15, BORN SOUTH SHIELDS.
PENNY	James	PTE	20 / 868				3/11/14	21/9/16	DEBILITY			TO 2nd WORKS COMPANY NORTHBLD FUS.	AGE 55.
PERKINS	T W	PTE	20 / 455	B				10/4/15	UNFIT				POSTED TO DEPOT COY 5/3/15.
PHILIPSON	Jas E	CPL	20 / 614	C						1/7/16		TO 8th BN, CLASS Z RESERVE.	
PHILIPSON	W	PTE	20 / 870	D								TO 34th DIV CYC COY.	
PHILLIPS	Wm G	PTE	20 / 117			TEAMS				1/7/16			
PIERCY	G	PTE	20 /1114	B				10/4/15	UNFIT				
PIKE	Henry	LCPL	20 / 871			GATESHEAD			KR para 392	1/7/16		TO 14th, 10th BNS.	
PILKINGTON	Geo W	PTE	20 / 615	B		ALNWICK			1/71/6		THIEPVAL MEM	TO 23rd BN.	AWOL 6-8/2/15.
PLEASANTS	Thos	PTE	20 / 336				13/10/14	4/8/16	SICK			TO 1st GARRISON BN, DEPOT.	AGE 39.
POND	FredW	PTE	20 / 118	A	201 PARKES STREET	BYKER			18/11/17		BYKER & HEATON CEI	TO 10th BN(D COY).	AWOL 6-8/2/15, AGE 21, BORN TRIMDON, TO C COY.
PORTEOUS	W	PTE	20 /1348	D									FROM DEPOT COY TO D COY 25/2/15.
PORTER	J	PTE	20 / 456	A									OFF RATION STRENGTH 1-7/2/15.
PORTER	Robt	SGT	20 / 457	C		SWALWELL			1/7/16		THIEPVAL MEM		BORN GATESHEAD.
PORTER	Sam	RQM!	20 / 276				29/10/14	31/12/17	SICK			TO 2nd GARRISON BN, 3rd BN.	AGE 38.
PORTLOCK	Wm	PTE	20 /1606	D	5 SWAN HOPE	SUNDERLAND						TO 26th BN	
POTTS	A	PTE	20 / 86	C									AWOL 6-8/2/15.
PRESTON	Simon	PTE	20 /1351	E		SEAHAM HARBOUR			1/7/16		THIEPVAL MEM		FROM E COY TO C COY 19/6/15, BORN TRIMDON.
PRICE	Jerem	PTE	20 / 873	D	19d BURDON STREET	HESELDENE				1/7/16			AWOL 6-7/2/15.
PRICE	MichN	PTE	20 /1203	D	OLD PIT	RYTON	3/12/14	1/4/19	KR para 392			TO ARMY RESERVE CLASS P.	STRETCHER BEARER 1/7/15.
PRICE	Walt	PTE	20 / 74	C								TO 1st GARRISON BN, CLASS Z RESERVE.	AWOL 28/3/15.
PRIOR	Denn	PTE	20 /1642	D		LESBURY			1/7/16		THIEPVAL MEM		BORN FELLING AGE 30.
PROCTOR	Fred	PTE	20 /1115			CHESTER LE ST			1/7/16		THIEPVAL MEM		

PROCTOR	Vince	PTE	20 /1116	D		CHOPPINGTON				1/7/16		TO CHESHIRE REGT(9th BN).	AWOL 6-7/2/15.
PROCTOR	W	PTE	20 /1202			WINLATON				1/7/16			
PROUD	J E	PTE	20 / 116	D		NEWCASTLE							
PROUD	Jos	PTE	20 / 460		6 SIMPSON TERRACE	NORTH WALBOTTLE				1/7/16		TO 23rd BN.	SCOTTISH RED CROSS HOSP GLASGOW 7/16.
PROUDLOCK	G	PTE	20 / 620	C									AWOL 29/11/15-1/12/15.
PROWSE	Geo L	PTE	20 /1507	Depo			20/2/15					TO 2nd GARRISON BN, CLASS Z RESERVE.	
PRUDHOE	RobtW	PTE	20 / 461		14 BLAYDON BURN	WINLATON				MISSING 21/3/18		TO 22nd BN(A COY).	
PRUDHOE	Wm E	SGT	20 / 59			BLAYDON	26/10/14	31/1/19	KR para 392	1/7/16			
PURDY	G W	PTE	20 /1350	D								TO 34th DIV CYC COY, 24th BN.	FROM DEPOT COY TO D COY 25/2/15, TYNESIDE IRISH No 24/1
PURVIS	A	LCPL	20 / 462					1/2/15	KR para 392				
PURVIS	Jas N	PTE	20 /1349		25 HOLLY STREET	MEDOMSLEY						TO 2nd GARRISON BN, CLASS Z RESERVE.	
PYLE	R	PTE	20 /1552	E									FROM E COY TO C COY 19/6/15.
RAFFLE	G	PTE	20 / 874	B				2/2/15	KR para 392				
RAIN	Albt	PTE	20 /1461	D		SEAHAM COLL	12/1/15	7/1/18	WOUNDS	1/7/16		TO 3rd BN.	FROM DEPOT COY TO D COY 25/2/15,NTH EVINGTON HOSP 11.
RAINE	Hall	PTE	20 /1117			DURHAM			2/4/16		SAILLY SUR LYS CAN	ATTACHED 181 TUNNELLING COY RE.	AGE 39.
RAINEY	P	ASGT	20 / 465	C		NORTH SHIELDS				1/7/16			PTE AWOL 7-8/2/15.
RAISBECK	Wm A	PTE	20 / 875		5 QUATRE BRAS	HEXAM		17/4/19				TO KINGS OWN YORKSHIRE LI, HOME DEFENCE L	KOYLI No 48310, LCPL
RAMSAY	Wm	PTE	20 /1119			CRAMLINGTON	3/11/14	1/3/18	WOUNDS	1/7/16		TO ARMY RESERVE CLASS P.	HOSP BOSCOMBE HANTS 7/16.
RAY	John	PTE	20 /1482	E	186 STEPHENSON RO	TYNEMOUTH	8/2/15						TOS DEPOT COY 11/2/15, FROM E COY TO C COY 19/6/15.
RAY	Wm	PTE	20 / 878	B		NEWCASTLE			1/7/16		THIEPVAL MEM		
RAYNE	John	PTE	20 / 202	A			28/10/14	16/3/18	SICK				AGE 46.48HRS DETENTION 3/12/15 FOR AWOL.
REAY	John	PTE	20 /1676			NEWCASTLE				1/7/16			R VICTORIA HOSP NETLEY 11/7/16, DESERTED 23/1/18.
REDMAN	W	CSGT	20 /1537	D								FROM 11th BN, 16/4/15.	
REED	Alex	PTE	20										AWOL 23/3/15.
REED	E	PTE	20 / 623	A				10/4/15	UNFIT				
REED	Edwd	PTE	20 /1369		33 AUSTRALIA STREE	SEAHAM						TO 22nd BN, CLASS Z RESERVE.	
REED	Geo W	PTE	20 / 464	A				7/2/19				TO 18th BN, YORK&LANCS(2/4th BN), Z RES.	Y&L No 57696, AWOL 28-29/3/15.
REED	Rich	PTE	20 /1523	D	5 CANDLISH STREET	SEAHAM		8/10/19		21/3/16		TO 22nd BN, YORK & LANCASTER REGT(2/4th BN).	GSW L SHOULDER, Y&L No 57659.
REED	Sept	PTE	20 /1361	C	5 CANDLISH STREET	SEAHAM			21/3/18	10/3/16, 4/6/16	ARRAS MEM	TO 23rd BN(C COY).	SHELLSHOCK JULY AUG OCT 1916.
REID	FitzC	PTE	20 /1636										
REILING	G	PTE	20 /1441	C									FROM DEPOT COY TO C COY 25/2/15, STRETCHER BEARER 1/
RENTON	James	PTE	20 / 880	B		USHAW MOOR			1/7/16		THIEPVAL MEM		AWOL 6-7/10/15, BORN SELKIRK FIFE.
REYNOLDS	Henry	PTE	20 /1364			SEAHAM HARBOU	12/1/15	16/2/18	GSW	1/7/16		TO DEPOT.	
RICHARDS	Henry	PTE	20 /1633	D		HASWELL PLOUGH			1/7/16		THIEPVAL MEM		BORN WINGATE.
RICHARDSON	G	PTE	20 / 625							1/7/16			
RICHARDSON	G	PTE	20 / 626	C				10/4/15	UNFIT				
RICHARDSON	Geo	PTE	20 / 624				31/10/14	3/4/18	GSW	1/7/16		TO ARMY RESERVE CLASS P.	
RICHARDSON	JohnW	PTE	20 / 883	D		BEDLINGTON			1/7/16		THIEPVAL MEM		
RICHARDSON	R	PTE	20 /1693				22/6/15						DESERTED ON THE WAY TO JOIN BATTALION.
RICHARDSON	Ralph	SGT	20 / 882									TO RIFLE BRIGADE(DEPOT), 1/5th LONDON REGT.	RIFLE BRIGADE No 45185.
RICHARDSON	RobtJ	PTE	20 / 277			SHIREMOOR	31/10/14	11/3/18	WOUNDS			TO ARMY RESERVE CLASS P.	AGE 27.
RICHARDSON	Thos	PTE	20 /1355	A	40 FOX STREET	DAWDON COLL			1/7/16		THIEPVAL MEM		BORN USWORTH AGE 46.
RICHARDSON	Wm	PTE	20 /1553	D		NEWCASTLE			1/7/16		THIEPVAL MEM		
RICHARDSON	Wm A	PTE	20 /1675			HIGH FOTHERLEY						TO 2nd GARRISON BN, CLASS Z RESERVE.	
RICKEARD	Wm Hy	PTE	20 / 628		20 HIGH PIT ROAD	CRAMLINGTON			12/7/16		BOULOGNE EASTERN CEM		AGE 22.
RIDDELL	James	CPL	20 / 884	B	91 NORTHBOURNE ST	GATESHEAD			1/7/16		THIEPVAL MEM		BORN MORPETH.
RIDDELL	Jos	SGT	20 / 629			BEDLINGTON			1/7/16		THIEPVAL MEM		AGE 22.
RIDGE	J	PTE	20 /1126	D								TO ROYAL ENGINEERS TUNNELLING DEPOT 13/10/15.	
RIDLEY	Thos	PTE	20 / 468	D		RYTON	31/10/14	14/12/17	SICK			TO DEPOT.	STRETCHER BEARER 1/7/15, LCPL
RIDLEY	Wm	PTE	20 / 630			BEDLINGTON			4/7/16		DAOURS COM CEM EXT		AGE 23
RIGBY	Walt	PTE	20 / 75	C		SEGHILL			KR para 392			TO DURHAM LIGHT INFANTRY, TRAINING RESERV	OFF RATION STREGTH 7-13/2/15.TRG RES No TR/5/58182.
RIPLEY	Jos	PTE	20 / 119	A	8 ETHEL TERRACE	HIGH SPEN			1/7/16		THIEPVAL MEM		OFF RATION STRENGTH 14-20/2/15, AGE 34 BORN WINLATON.
RISEBOROUGH	Robtw	LCPL	20 / 631	C		CRAMLINGTON	31/10/14	11/10/17	WOUNDS	11/6/16		TO 3rd BN.	WNDS FACE & L LEG, AWOL 14/2/15, AGE 26.
RITCHIE	James	PTE	20 /1354	B		ARBROATH			1/7/16		THIEPVAL MEM		FROM DEPOT COY TO B COY 25/2/15.AWOL 6-7/10/15.
RITCHIE	Thos	PTE	20 /1649									TO CLASS Z RESERVE.	
ROBERTS	Jas R	SGT	20 / 886		8 NORTH TERRACE	WIDEOPEN	3/11/14	13/10/17	WOUNDS	1/7/16		TO DEPOT	AGE 27.
ROBERTSON	Alex	PTE	20 / 889		12 SCOTT STREET	HARTFORD			3/10/18	1/7/16	HIGHLAND CEM LE CA	TO ROYAL INNISKILLING FUSILIERS(6th BN,C COY)	BORN GOSFORTH,AGE 30, R INNIS FUS No 21583.
ROBERTSON	Donld	PTE	20 / 632	B		SWALWELL			1/7/16		OVILLERS MIL CEM		AWOL 6-7/10/15, BORN PELTON FELL
ROBERTSON	James	PTE	20 / 76									TO 2nd GARRISON BN.	
ROBERTSON	JohnR	PTE	20 / 887		8 NORTH TERRACE	WIDEOPEN	3/11/14	15/3/18	RHEUMATISM			TO DEPOT	AGE 48.
ROBINSON	Edwd	PTE	20 / 891									TO 9th, 11th BNS, CLASS Z RESERVE.	DESERTED 30/4/18
ROBINSON	James	PTE	20 / 633	C		CRAMLINGTON			1/7/16		OVILLERS MIL CEM		AWOL 7-8/2/15.
ROBINSON	John	PTE	20 / 635		15 HIGH PIT ROAD	CRAMLINGTON						TO 2nd GARRISON BN, CLASS Z RESERVE.	
ROBINSON	JohnT	PTE	20 / 634	B	84 VICTORIA TERRACE	BEDLINGTON			1/7/16		THIEPVAL MEM		AWOL 6-8/10/15, AGE 27.
ROBINSON	Ralph	PTE	20 / 890	B	40 SEYMORE STREET	WINGATE			7/6/17	11/12/16, 5/1/17	DUISANS MIL CEM		AWOL 13-14/2/15, AGE 37 BORN EASINGTON.
ROBINSON	Robt	PTE	20 /1362	D			12/1/15					TO 34th DIV CYC COY.	FROM DEPOT COY TO D COY 25/2/15.
ROBSON	Carr	PTE	20 /1127			SEATON DELAVAL				1/7/16		TO ROYAL DEFENCE CORPS.	FRANCE 9/1/16-7/7/16, BEAUFORT WAR HOSP BRISTOL 8/7/16.
ROBSON	Chas	SGT	20 / 637	C		BEDLINGTON			1/7/16		OVILLERS MIL CEM		BORN COANWOOD AGE 29.
ROBSON	Geo	CPL	20 /1363	D		SEAHAM HARBOUR			5/6/17		ARRAS MEM		FROM DEPOT COY TO D COY 25/2/15, AWOL 7-8/3/15, BORN TR
ROBSON	Geo F	LCPL	20 /1554	C					9/3/16		X FARM CEM		FROM E COY TO C COY 19/6/15.
ROBSON	Herbt	PTE	20 / 639			HALTWHISTLE	2/11/14	13/4/15	KR para 392			SERVED WITH 4th NF TF PRE WAR.	CHRONIC DYSPEPSIA,ABSENCE OF TEETH,LOSING FLESH,UNA
ROBSON	Isaac	SGT	20 / 638							MISS 20-23/3/18		TO 23rd BN(B COY).	
ROBSON	J	PTE	20 /1365							1/7/16			
ROBSON	Jos	LCPL	20 /1635									TO 25th, 1/7th BNS, CLASS Z RESERVE.	RENUMBERED 292103.
ROBSON	Matt	PTE	20 /1367	E	STAGSHAW BANK GAT	CORBRIDGE	12/1/15	19/5/15	KR para 392			TO 23rd BN? ALL DOCS STAMPED 4th TS.	AGE 28, 6'0",39 CHEST.
ROBSON	R	PTE	20 /1368			MORPETH				1/7/16			
ROBSON	S	PTE	20 /1514	E									FROM E COY TO C COY 19/6/15.
ROBSON	Steph	PTE	20 /1356	E	19 EAST STREET	SUNDERLAND	5/1/15	19/5/15	KR para 392				AGE 20, AWOL 2/4/15-7/4/15, 5'9",35 CHEST.
ROBSON	Thos	PTE	20 / 469	D	60 STATION ROAD	EASINGTON COLL			1/7/16		THIEPVAL MEM		BORN KILLINGWORTH AGE 19.
ROBSON	Thos	PTE	20 /1357	D	6 ELGIN STREET	SUNDERLAND	5/1/15	19/5/15	DEFECTIVE TEETH			RECALLED TO ROYAL DEFENCE CORPS(8th BN).	HULL 18/12/17, AGE 36YRS 10MNTHS,5'6",34 CHEST, BOILERM
ROBSON	Thos	PTE	20 /1404	D	FRONT ST SCOTLAND	CHOPPINGTON	11/1/15	6/4/15	KR para 392				MINER AGE 20, FROM DEPOT COY TO D COY 25/2/15.
ROBSON	Thpsn	BGLF	20 / 350			SCOTSWOOD				1/7/16		TO 24th, 25th BNS, KO YORKS LI(2/4th BN).	POSTED TO DEPOT COY 5/3/15, KOYLI No 63326.
ROBSON	Wm	SGT	20 / 896			GOSFORTH	3/11/14	14/12/17	GSW	1/7/16		TO DEPOT.	
ROBSON	Wm	LCPL	20 / 894		3 CHARLOTTE STREET	SOUTHMOOR	3/11/14	1/54/19	KR para 392	6/11/16		TO 10th, 9th BNS, ARMY RESERVE CLASS P.	
ROBSON	Wm	LCPL	20 / 893	D		CHOPPINGTON			1/7/16		THIEPVAL MEM		
ROBSON	Wm	PTE	20 / 640		GRANGES BUILDINGS	BEDLINGTON	1/11/14	24/11/14	KR para 392			SERVED 3YRS TERRITORIALS.	AGE 29 BORN BIRTLEY.
ROBSON	Wm J	PTE	20 / 636	C		CRAMLINGTON	31/10/14	16/5/17	GSW	1/7/16		TO DEPOT.	AWOL 14/2/15, PROMOTED LCPL
ROBSON	Wm Jn	PTE	20 /1210			NEWCASTLE	3/10/14						MACHINE MINDER, DESERTED 28/6/15 AGE 40, 5'3".
ROBSON		PTE	20 / 895	B								TO 34th DIV CYC COY.	
ROCHE	Frank	LCPL	20 / 5	C	69 HOWICK CRESENT	NEWCASTLE	22/10/14	4/10/16	WOUNDS	1/7/16, DEC 16.		TO DEPOT.	AWOL 13-16/2/15, 168 HRS DETENTION 26/7/15.
ROCHESTER	Frank	PTE	20 /1583		75 TYNE ROAD	GATESHEAD	22/5/15	16/12/16	GSW			TO DEPOT.	
ROCKS	Peter	PTE	20 / 641			NETHERTON COLL	1/11/14	10/2/17	WOUNDS			TO DEPOT.	
RODDA	JohnH	SGT	20 /1128	D	5 GRIEVES ROW	DUDLEY			1/7/16		THIEPVAL MEM		AGE 26.
ROGERSON	J	PTE	20 / 471	C				10/4/15	UNFIT				
ROGERSON	T	PTE	20 /1498			NEWCASTLE				4/6/16,1/7/16.		FROM DURHAM LI(12th BN) 18/2/15.	SHELL SHOCK
RONALDSON	Geo	PTE	20 /1359	C		WEST SLEEKBURN				JULY 16		TO 1st, 1/4th BNS, CLASS Z RESERVE.	FROM DEPOT COY TO C COY 25/2/15.
ROSCOE	John	PTE	20 / 77	C	4 LANE ROW	WEST CRAMLINGTON						TO ROYAL ENGINEERS TUNNELLING DEPOT 13/10/15.	
ROSE	Alex	PTE	20 /1360	E								TO 2nd GARRISON BN.	AWOL 12-14/6/15.
ROSS	Jos	CSM	20 / 643									TO 12/13th, 1/4th BNS, CLASS Z RESERVE.	
ROSS	RobtJ	PTE	20 /1709		39 HEDGEHOPE TERR	EAST CHEVINGTON						TO 2nd GARRISON BN, CLASS Z RESERVE.	
ROUTLEDGE	Alf	PTE	20 /1370	C	25 RIDLEY STREET	BLYTH	21/1/15	21/2/19	KR para 392	1/7/16		TO 24th, 23rd BNS, ARMY RESERVE CLASS P.	FROM DEPOT COY TO C COY 25/2/15.
ROUTLEDGE	Henry	PTE	20 / 644		2 MINERS HOMES	BEDLINGTON			1/7/16		THIEPVAL MEM		AGE 34.
ROXBOROUGH	Rich	PTE	20 /1634		50 BELVEDERE STREE	NEWCASTLE							EDMONTON HOSPITAL LONDON OCT 16.
RUBY	A	PTE	20 / 645	C				9/2/15	KR para 392				
RUDD		PTE	20										
RUSSELL	John	LCPL	20 / 472	A		SEATON BURN			1/7/16		OVILLERS MIL CEM		
RUSSELL	Matt	PTE	20 / 646	D		RYTON			1/7/16		THIEPVAL MEM		AGE 40 BORN DURHAM.
RYLE	Wm	PTE	20 /1130		4 DIANA STREET	NEWCASTLE						TO 2nd GARRISON BN, CLASS Z RESERVE.	DISTRICT COURT MARTIAL 1/4/15.
SALT	J	PTE	20 /1376	D									FROM DEPOT COY TO D COY 25/2/15
SAMPLE	Rich	PTE	20 /1143	B		WINLATON	4/11/14	25/10/17	WOUNDS	1/7/16		TO 3rd BN.	AWOL 6-7/10/15, AGE 43.
SAMPSON	Edwd	PTE	20 /1147									TO 1st, 12/13th BNS, CLASS Z RESERVE.	
SAMSON	Jas R	PTE	20 /1607		72 TYNE STREET	NORTH SHIELDS				16/6/16			GSW HAND

SANDERSON	Rob S	PTE	20 /1707					20/3/19				TO 22nd BN, WEST YORKSHIRE REGT(2nd BN), CL/	W YORKS No 40997.
SANDERSON	Robt	PTE	20 / 648									TO 12th BN, CLASS Z RESERVE.	
SANDERSON	Robt	PTE	20 / 278			LEADGATE	29/10/14	8/9/16	HEART DISEASE			TO DEPOT.	
SANDERSON	RobtW	PTE	20 /1372	E		SUNDERLAND							AWOL 20-22/2/15, POSTED TO A COY SUPPOSEDLY KILLED.
SANDS	Robt	PTE	20 / 337				30/10/14	31/3/19	KR para 392			TO ARMY RESERVE CLASS P.	
SCANLAN	James	PTE	20 / 473			FOREST HALL	31/10/14	24/3/17	WOUNDS	1/7/16		TO DEPOT.	3rd SOUTHERN G HOSP OXFORD 12/7/16.
SCOTT	E	PIPR	20							1/7/16			
SCOTT	J	PTE	20 /1144	D									AWOL 6-8/10/15
SCOTT	T	PTE	20 /1476	E									AWOL 21-22/2/15.
SCOTT	ThosP	CPL	20 / 339	D		NEWCASTLE			1/7/16		THIEPVAL MEM		BORN SOUTH SHIELDS.
SCOTT	ThosW	PTE	20 /1149	B		ACKLINGTON			1/7/16		OVILLERS MIL CEM		AWOL 6-7/2/15, BORN HULL.
SCOTT	Wm A	CPL	20 /1148				4/11/14	6/3/18	GSW			TO DEPOT	AGE 25.
SCURR	Ernst	PTE	20 /1138									TO ROYAL ENGINEERS(278 FLD COY), GLOSTERSI	RE No 153013, GLOSTER No 53207.
SEATH	David	SGT	20 / 340	B	25 STOCKTON TERRA(	GRANGETOWN			1/7/16		THIEPVAL MEM		AGE 36 BORN LINTZFORD Co DURHAM.
SHADFORTH	JohnW	PTE	20 / 899			BEDLINGTON	2/11/14	20/11/17	GSW	1/7/16		TO DEPOT.	AWOL 6-8/10/15, AGE 31.
SHAW	A	PTE	20 /1452	E	WHITE LEES	ROWLANDS GILL						TO 18th, 8th BNS, CLASS Z RESERVE.	AWOL 6-8/2/15, FROM DEPOT COY TO A COY 25/2/15.
SHAW	J	PTE	20 /1371	D									6 WEEKS H LABOUR AT WESTBURY P/SESSIONS 20/10/15.
SHEARDOWN	Geo	PTE	20 / 474			NORTH SHIELDS	31/10/14	31/10/17	SICK	1/7/16		TO DEPOT.	AGE 39.
SHEPHERD RA	Jas	CSM	20 /1199	B	21 MOSELEY STREET	NEWCASTLE	17/10/14						POSTED FROM B TO E COY 31/1/15.
SHERWOOD	ChasH	PTE	20 /1386	E	1 CHURCH STREET	FENCEHOUSES				1/7/16		TO 23rd, 24th, 12/13th, 22nd BNS, CLASS Z RESERVI	AWOL 2-4/2/15, FROM DEPOT COY TO A COY 25/2/15.
SHIELD	Wm	PTE	20 /1137	B		SOUTHMOOR	4/11/14	13/4/18	GSW	1/7/16		TO ARMY RESERVE CLASS P.	AWOL 6-8/2/15, AGE 40.
SHORT	A	CSM	20 /1534	D								FROM 10th BN 5/3/15.	
SHORT	H	PTE	20 /1587			ASHINGTON				1/7/16			
SHORT	John	PTE	20 / 902			SCOTLANDGATE	2/11/14	27/2/18	GSW	1/7/16		TO ARMY RESERVE CLASS P.	
SHORT	RichG	PTE	20 /1570	D	237 SIMONSIDE TERR/	NEWCASTLE			KR para 392				FROM E COY TO D COY 19/6/15.
SIMMISTER	Fred	PTE	20 / 341			DINNINGTON				1/7/16		TO 23rd, 22nd, 9th BNS, CLASS Z RESERVE.	
SIMPSON	John	PTE	20 /1462	E			13/1/15						AWOL 1-3/2/15.
SIMPSON	T	PTE	20 / 906			SWALWELL				1/7/16			
SIMPSON	T H	PTE	20 /1383										DID NOT SERVE O/SEAS.
SIMPSON	Thos	PTE	20 /1382	E		RYHOPE			1/7/16		THIEPVAL MEM		FROM E COY TO C COY 19/6/15, AGE 24.
SIMS	Jos	PTE	20 / 904	A	44 COACH LANE	DINNINGTON	2/11/14	28/9/18	GSW			TO DEPOT.	STRETCHER BEARER 1/7/15, AGE 25, REAL NAME JOS SUIER.
SIMS	Robt	PTE	20 / 905	A		DUDLEY	2/11/14	31/3/19	KR para 392	1/7/16		TO ARMY RESERVE CLASS P.	STRETCHER BEARER 1/7/15
SINCLAIR	James	PTE	20 / 650			FORRES MORAYSHI			10/7/16		ST SEVER CEM ROUEN		AGE 41.
SINCLAIR	JohnJ	PTE	20 /1472		5 SIXTH STREET	SHOTTON			KR para 392			TO 2nd GARRISON BN.	
SINCLAIR	JohnJ	PTE	20 /1373	E	26 PEEL STREET	SOUTH SHIELDS			27/10/19		HARTON ST PETERS		AWOL 6-9/2/15, FROM E COY TO C COY 19/6/15, AGE 32.
SINCLAIR	JohnS	PTE	20 /1141		5a STRATHMORE TERI	ROWLANDS GILL						TO 2nd GARRISON BN(A COY), CLASS Z RESERVE.	
SKEDGE	Jas C	PTE	20 /1153	B	11 MORTIMORE TERR	HOLYWELL						TO 2nd GARRISON BN, CLASS Z RESERVE.	AWOL 13-14/2/15.
SKEOCH	Robt	PTE	20 / 907			BIRTLEY				1/7/16		TO 21st, 8th BNS, CLASS Z RESERVE.	
SLASOR	T	PTE	20 / 908	B									AWOL 6-7/10/15.
SLEE	Robt	SGT	20 / 476		14 CLYDE STREET	CHOPWELL			28/4/17		ARRAS MEM	TO 25th BN.	BORN CONISTON AGE 36.
SMEATON		PTE	20 / 651	C								TO 34th DIV CYC COY.	
SMILES	Tom P	PTE	20 /1131			PRESTON COLL				1/7/16		TO 22nd BN, CLASS Z RESERVE.	
SMITH	Frank	PTE	20 / 342		29 RIPON STREET	GATESHEAD						TO 2nd GARRISON BN, CLASS Z RESERVE.	
SMITH	J B	PTE	20 /1384	E									AWOL 24/1/15-2/2/15.
SMITH	J G	PTE	20 / 343	A				10/4/15	UNFIT				
SMITH	James	PTE	20 /1559		13 HOTSPUR STREET	ALNWICK						TO 1st GARRISON BN, CLASS Z RESERVE.	
SMITH	John	PTE	20 / 204				28/10/14	22/8/16	DEBILITY			TO 33rd BN.	AGE 48, DID NOT SERVE O/SEAS.
SMITH	Jos	PTE	20 / 652	D	15 TRINITY STREET	SOUTHWICK			10/3/16		X FARM CEM		AGE 32 BORN MONKWEARMOUTH.
SMITH	Jos W	PTE	20 / 910									TO ROYAL DEFENCE CORPS.	FRANCE 9/1/16-6/6/17. RDC No 65402.
SNAITH	M	PTE	20 / 653					2/2/15	KR para 392				
SNOWDON	Geo	PTE	20 / 123		3 BLANFORD STREET	NEWCASTLE						TO 22nd BN.	
SOUTHERN	CornR	SGT	20 / 914		42 ELSDON TERRACE	PERCY MAIN			21/9/17		TYNE COT MEM	TO DURHAM LI(20th BN). DLI No 44140.	
SOUTHERN	John	PTE	20 / 915									TO CLASS Z RESERVE.	AWOL 6-8/10/15.
SOUTHERN	Wm	LCPL	20 / 913	C	13 VICTORIA TERRACE	BEDLINGTON COLL			1/7/16		THIEPVAL MEM		POSTED FROM D TO C COY 10/2/15, AGE 20.
SPENCE	Robt	PTE	20 /1650			BLACKHILL	15/5/15						LABOURER, DESERTED 12/3/15, AGE 31, 5'9".
SPENCE	Thos	DRMI	20 /1180	B		NEWCASTLE			1/7/16		THIEPVAL MEM		BORN BACKWORTH.
SPICER	Geo A	PTE	20 / 654	B		WESTERHOPE	2/11/14	30/4/17	SICK	1/7/16		TO ARMY RESERVE CLASS W.	AWOL 6-8/2/15, 6-8/10/14, AGE 29.
SPINKS	Jos A	CPL	20 / 283	A	DYKE HEADS	GREENSIDE RYTON			1/7/16	31/3/16	THIEPVAL MEM		SHRAPNEL WOUND R SHOULDER, REJOINED, AGE 28, BORN D
SPRIGLEY	J		20 / 475		15 ROCKWOOD GDNS	CHOPWELL							
STAGG	Wm Wd	PTE	20 /1133	B		NORTH SHIELDS	4/11/14	28/12/17	DEBILITY	1/7/16		TO 3rd BN.	AWOL 8-9/2/15, AGE 34.
STARFORD	Wm	PTE	20 / 916	B		WHEATLEY HILL			1/7/16		THIEPVAL MEM		
STARK	JohnM	PTE	20 / 917			NEWCASTLE	2/11/14	6/7/17	UNFIT	1/7/16		TO ARMY RESERVE CLASS P.	AGE 42.
STARK	W	PTE	20 / 655	C				9/2/15	KR para 392				
STEEL	Geo	PTE	20 /1380	A		HETTON DOWNS	11/1/15	29/8/17	WOUNDS			TO 84th TRAINING RESERVE BN.	FROM DEPOT COY TO A COY 25/2/15, AWOL 7-8/3/15.
STEEL	Jas H	LCPL	20 / 657			NORTH WALBOTTLE						TO ROYAL INNISKILLING FUSILIERS(6th BN).	R INNIS FUS No 21594.
STEPHENS	J E	PTE	20 / 658	E				20/4/15	KR para 392				
STEPHENS		PIPR	20							1/7/16			
STEPHENSON	F	PTE	20 / 345			CRAMLINGTON				1/7/16			
STEPHENSON	JohnM	PTE	20 / 918	D		BEDLINGTON			1/7/16		THIEPVAL MEM		BORN BOOTLE CHESHIRE.
STEPHENSON	Jos	PTE	20 / 659			CRAMLINGTON				1/7/16		TO 21st, 8th BNS, CLASS Z RESERVE.	
STEPHENSON	Thos	PTE	20 / 919	B		GREENSIDE			1/7/16		THIEPVAL MEM		AGE 21.
STEVENS	Edwin	SGT	20 / 344	A		WESTERHOPE			1/7/16		THIEPVAL MEM		AGE 29 BORN MILLOM CUMBERLAND.
STEVENS	S	PTE	20 /1142	B		ASHINGTON				1/7/16			AWOL 6-8/2/15.
STEVENSON	J	PTE	20 /1186	B									AWOL 6-7/2/15, 6-7/10/15.
STEWART	John	SIG	20 / 346				30/10/14	25/10/17	SICK			TO 3rd BN.	AGE 31.
STEWART	Langl	LCPL	20 / 921	D	20 NEW SOUTH ROW	BEDLINGTON			1/7/16		OVILLERS MIL CEM		MACHINE GUN SECTION, AGE 20.
STEWART	Robt	PTE	20 / 660			BEDLINGTON			KR para 392	1/7/16			RENUMBERED 90587.
STEWART	Wm	PTE	20 /1385	E	1 CAMDEN TERRACE	NORTH SHIELDS			20/9/17		TYNE COT MEM	TO 10th BN.	FROM E COY TO C COY 19/6/15, AGE 30 BORN SOUTH SHIELDS
STIVEN	Harry	PTE	20 / 205	A		EDINBURGH			5/6/17		ARRAS MEM		
STOBBS	Wm	PTE	20 /1140		101 GAINSBOROUGH S	NEWCASTLE						TO 3rd BN.	
STOCKDALE	J	PTE	20 / 922			MORPETH				1/7/16			
STODDART	Albt	PTE	20 / 661	D	3 GORDON TERRACE	BEDLINGTON			1/7/16		THIEPVAL MEM		
STODDART	T	PTE	20 /1519									TO MUNITIONS(CAMMELL LAIRD BIRKENHEAD).	
STOKOE	Henry	CPL	20 / 16	C	KNOWESGATE BOTHY	KIRKWHELPINGTON			1/7/16		THIEPVAL MEM		AGE 28.
STOVES	John	PTE	20 /1453	D		SEAHAM COLL			1/7/16		THIEPVAL MEM		
STOVES	Mich	PTE	20 /1454									TO 18th BN, CLASS Z RESERVE.	
STRACHAN	Chas	PTE	20										AWOL 12/7/15.
STRAKER	James	LCPL	20 / 923			BEDLINGTON	2/11/14	3/5/18	GSW			TO 3rd BN.	AGE 26.
STRAUGHAN	Wm	PTE	20 / 124	C	247 SHIPLEY STREET	BYKER			9/3/16		ERQUIMGHEM LYS CH YD EXT		BORN JESMOND, DIED AT 104 FIELD AMBULANCE.
STRAUGHAN	Wm	PTE	20 / 125		124 SHIPLEY STREET	BYKER	27/10/14	18/12/17	GSW			TO 85th TRAINING RESERVE BN..	AGE 22,1st SCOTTISH GHOSP ABERDEEN 8/7/16.
STRINGER	David	LCPL	20 /1134	C	30 KILLINGWORTH LA	BARKWORTH			1/7/16		THIEPVAL MEM		AWOL 13-15/2/15, AGE 33 BORN BURNLEY.
STRONG	T	PTE	20 /1151										SERVANT TO LIEUT A W KERR.
STUART	James	PTE	20 / 663	A		NEWCASTLE			1/7/16		THIEPVAL MEM		BORN NORTH BROADFORD Co CORK.
STUART	Robt	PTE	20 / 924									TO CHESHIRE REGT(9th BN).	CHESHIRE REGT No 52333.
STUBBS	Jacob	PTE	20 / 61		22 WEST STREET	WHICKHAM						TO 2nd GARRISON BN, CLASS Z RESERVE.	
STURROCK	J	PTE	20 /1139	B								TO LABOUR CORPS.	AWOL 7-8/3/15, 6-7/10/15.
STURROCK	R	DRV	20 / 347	A								TO 25th BN.	
SUMBY	John	PTE	20 /1375	E		SUNDERLAND			10/8/16		CABERET ROUGE MIL CEM		AWOL 1-3/2/15,DEPOT COY TO B COY 25/2/15,DESERTED 3/4/15
SUMMERS	Geo	PTE	20 / 927	B	1 HEDGEHOPE TERR	E CHEVINGTON						TO 1st GARRISON BN, CLASS Z RESERVE.	SICK FURLOUGH 15/5/15-9/6/15, INITIAL J ON ORDERS, E IN AVI
SURMAN	C	PTE	20 / 348	A				1/2/15	KR para 392				
SUTCH	Jos	PTE	20 /1378	D		LANCHESTER			1/7/16		THIEPVAL MEM		
SUTHERLAND	G	PTE	20 / 928	D								TO 34th DIV CYC COY, 24th BN.	TYNESIDE IRISH No 24/1720.
SWANN	T W	PTE	20 /1477	A									FROM DEPOT COY TO A COY 25/2/15.
SWATTON	Geo	CPL	20 /1494			SEAHAM HARBOU	15/2/15	28/3/19	KR para 392	1/7/16,13/10/16		TO ARMY RESERVE CLASS P.	WND DURING TRENCH RAID 13/10/16
SWEENEY	J	PTE	20 /1518	E		STAITHES YORKS				1/7/16			FROM E COY TO C COY 19/6/15.
TAILOR	James	CSGT	20 / 668									TO 18th, 22nd, 12/13th BNS, CLASS Z RESERVE.	TAYLOR ON MR.
TAIT	Alex	PTE	20 / 285	C	42 BACK DURHAM ST	NEWCASTLE			1/7/16		THIEPVAL MEM		AGE 38 BORN KELSO.
TAIT	John	PTE	20 / 930						KR para 392				
TAIT	John	PTE	20 /1392	E	19 GROSVENOR STRE	GATESHEAD						TO 18th BN, CLASS Z RESERVE.	AWOL 26/2-3/3/15, 11/8/15, 26/5/15, AGE 28.
TAIT	Robt	LSGT	20 / 667	C		HARTFORD COLL			1/7/16		THIEPVAL MEM		BORN CRAMLINGTON.
TAIT	Robt	CPL	20 /1717			FELTON	2/9/15	11/3/19	KR para 392	MISSING 21/3/18		TO 1st BN, 22nd BN(B COY).	
TAIT	RobtC	PTE	20 / 929	B		BLACKHILL			1/7/16		THIEPVAL MEM		BORN EMBLETON

TAIT	Steph	PTE	20 / 666	D	75 FRONT STREET	BEBSIDE			1/7/16		THIEPVAL MEM		AGE 24.
TANSEY	James	LCPL	20 / 931	B		SUNDERLAND	3/11/14	24/1/19	1/1/20		BISHOPWEARMOUTH	TO DEPOT.	AWOL 6-7/10/15.
TATTERS	T	PTE	20 / 932	D								TO ROYAL ENGINEERS TUNNELLING DEPOT 13/10/15.	
TAYLOR	Alf	PTE	20 / 349	A	183 CONYERS ROAD	NEWCASTLE						TO 2nd GARRISON BN, CLASS Z RESERVE.	COY COOK 31/1/15.
TAYLOR	EmanJ	CPL	20 / 933	B		MORPETH			1/7/16		THIEPVAL MEM		BORN TYNEMOUTH.
TAYLOR	Geo H	PIPR	20 /1525									FROM 16th BN 17/3/15, TO 22nd BN, CLASS Z RESERVE.	
TAYLOR	Geo V	SGT	20 /1156		10 FRONT STREET	LINTZ COLLIERY						TO CLASS Z RESERVE.	
TAYLOR	J	PTE	20 /1166	A		NORTH SHIELDS				1/7/16			
TAYLOR	James	SGT	20 / 706	D		SOUTH SHIELDS			1/7/16		THIEPVAL MEM		BORN TYNEMOUTH AGE 25.
TAYLOR	JohnT	PTE	20 /1393	MGS		SEAHAM COLLIERY			20/2/16		RUE-DU-BOIS CEM FLEURBAIX		GSW NECK, FROM DEPOT COY TO A COY 25/2/15.
TAYLOR	Lewis	PTE	20 / 669			NEWCASTLE			1/7/16		THIEPVAL MEM		BORN LEITH.
TEASDALE	James	PTE	20 / 78			NEWBURN			1/7/16		OVILLERS MIL CEM		BORN GATESHEAD.
TEASDALE	N	PTE	20 / 929										AWOL 6-8/2/15 POSSIBLY THIS SHOULD BE /1157.
TEASDALE	Peter	PTE	20 /1155	B		SWALWELL			1/7/16		THIEPVAL MEM		BORN CROOK, AWOL 6-7/10/15. POSTED TO A COY.
TEMPERLEY	ThosW	PTE	20 / 935		104 NEWBURN LANE	NEWBURN	3/11/14	22/5/19	KR para 392	1/7/16		TO DEPOT.	
TENNANT	Jos	PTE	20 / 126		2 WEST LANE	CHESTER LE ST						TO LABOUR CORPS(452 AGRI COY), GORDON HIGI	AWOL 7-8/2/15. LAB CORPS No 552320.
TERRELL	Rich	PTE	20 / 670			SHANKHOUSE	31/10/14	14/1/18	WOUNDS	1/7/16		TO 85th TRAINING RESERVE BN.	AGE 29.
TETLEY	Mark	PTE	20 / 79		12 QUARRY ROAD	CRAMLINGTON			22/3/18		ARRAS MEM	TO 9th BN.	BORN WAKEFIELD AGE 32.
THIRKLE	T	PTE	20 /1387	E									AWOL 6-8/2/15, 15-16/2/15.
THISTLE	JohnJ	SGT	20 / 480									TO 23rd BN.	SIGNALS SERGEANT.
THOMPSON	E	CPL	20 /1192			BEDLINGTON STAT				1/7/16			
THOMPSON	Edwd	PTE	20 / 671	B		GOSFORTH	2/11/14	8/3/18	SICK	1/7/16		TO ARMY RESERVE CLASS P.	STRETCHER BEARER 1/7/15,AWOL 6-7/10/15.BATH WAR HOSP
THOMPSON	Edwd	PTE	20 / 481							MISSING 21/3/18		TO 22nd BN(A COY).	
THOMPSON	Frank	PTE	20 /1608		26 PORTLAND ROAD	SHIELDFIELD			13/12/17	1/7/16	WANCOURT BRIT CEM	TO LABOUR CORPS(231 DIVISIONAL EMP COY).	LAB CORPS No 223489.
THOMPSON	G	PTE	20 /1389	E									FROM E COY TO C COY 19/6/15.
THOMPSON	Hen D	BGLF	20 / 939	D	3 KINGS ROAD	BEDLINGTON			1/7/16		THIEPVAL MEM		BORN GATESHEAD AGE 24.
THOMPSON	J	PTE	20 /1319									TO DURHAM LI(13th BN).	TRANSFERRED ON 31/1/15.NUMBER REALLOCATED TO LAVER
THOMPSON	James	PTE	20 / 937			FOREST HALL			7/7/16		BOULOGNE EASTERN CEM		BORN BEDLINGTON AGE 39, AWOL 13/9/15.
THOMPSON	John	PTE	20 / 206	A	180 KENDAL STREET	NEWCASTLE						TO DEPOT.	AWOL 7-9/2/15.
THOMPSON	Jos	PTE	20 / 673	C	2 PARADISE STREET	CRAMLINGTON			1/7/16		OVILLERS MIL CEM		BORN LONGBENTON AGE 33.
THOMPSON	Robt	PTE	20 / 940	D		CHOPPINGTON			1/7/16		OVILLERS MIL CEM		BORN WARDEN LAW.
THOMPSON	RobtM	PTE	20 / 938	B	21 BLUE BELL ROW	W CRAMLINGTON			1/7/16		THIEPVAL MEM		AGE 30 BORN NEWCASTLE, AWOL 7-8/3/15, 6-7/10/15.
THOMPSON	W	PTE	20 /1540	D								TO 26th BN	
THOMSON	Wm	PTE	20 /1154	B		GLASGOW				1/7/16		TO 16th, 12th, 12/13th BNS, CLASS Z RESERVE.	OFF RATION STRENGTH 14-20/2/15.
THORBURN	Thos	PTE	20 /1677	B		NEWCASTLE			1/7/16		THIEPVAL MEM		BORN LONGTOWN CUMBERLAND.
TIESDELL	Normn	PTE	20 /1157			HOWDON			4/4/16		X FARM CEM		GSW HEAD, ACCIDENTALLY KILLED.
TIFFIN	Geo E	PTE	20 /1684			CHATHILL				1/7/16		TO 25th, 1/5th BNS, CLASS Z RESERVE.	ALLOTTED NEW No 243193
TILLEY	Jos W	PTE	20 /1167			DUDLEY			31/12/17	1/7/16	BUCQOUY RD CEM	TO 16th, 22nd BNS.	BORN HIGH SPEN.
TINGLE	H	PTE	20 / 675	A				10/4/15	UNFIT				
TINLIN	J A	PTE	20 /1664			CHATHILL				1/7/16			
TIPPINS	Wm	LCPL	20 / 87	C		NEWBURN				1/7/16			AWOL 28/3/15.
TODD	Henry	LCPL	20 /1696			ANNITSFORD	21/10/14	30/4/17	GSW BOTH	1/7/16		FROM SOMERSET LI(8th BN) 23/7/15, TO 84th TRGB	3 CCS 2/7/16 EVAC 2/7/16.
TODD	R	PTE	20 /1158	B									AWOL 6-7/3/15.
TODD	Wm	PTE	20 /1165		7 BARRAS ROW	SEGHILL			1/7/16		THIEPVAL MEM		BORN SEGHILL AGE 42.
TOLSON	T	PTE	20 /1159			LANCHESTER				1/7/16			
TOMS	Jas	LCPL	20 / 676			CRAMLINGTON				1/7/16		TO DURHAM LIGHT INFANTRY, TRAINING RESERVI	3 CCS 2/7/16 EVAC 2/7/16. TRG RES No 59104.
TORRENCE	W	LCPL	20 / 942			NEWCASTLE				1/7/16			
TROTTER	Edwd	PTE	20 /1160	B					KR para 392	1/7/16			AWOL 6-8/2/15.
TUCK	Rob W	PTE	20 /1394	D	66 SWINEBANK COTTA	DAWDON			23/2/19	21/3/16	NEW SEAHAM CH YD	TO 2nd GARRISON BN.	GSW L SHOULDER
TUCKER	Steph	PTE	20 / 943	D				3/12/17				TO KINGS OWN YORKSHIRE LI.	COY COOK 31/1/15.
TUDOR	Wm	PTE	20 / 207									TO 23rd BN.	
TULLY	JohnT	PTE	20 /1522	B	COQUET STREET	AMBLE						FROM RFA(96 BDE) 17/3/15,TO 2nd GARRISON BN,	RFA No 63951.
TUOHEY	Geo W	PTE	20 / 944	B			3/11/14	22/8/16	SICK			TO 33rd BN.	OFF RATION STRENGTH 14-20/2/15, DID NOT SERVE O/SEAS.
TURNBULL	Frncs	PTE	20 / 80	B								TO 18th, ROYAL FUSILIERS(24th BN).	AWOL 7-8/3/15. 20 9/1/16-3/7/18, 18 4/7/18-28/8/18
TURNBULL	Thos	SGT	20 / 127	C	3 QUALITY ROW	BYKER						TO 3rd BN.	
TURNER	Andrw	LCPL	20 / 287					18/2/19				TO 18th BN, YORK&LANCASTER REGT(2/4th BN)Z R	Y & L No 57706.
TURNER	ChasN	SGT	20 /1161			OVINGHAM			1/7/16		THIEPVAL MEM	TO 21st BN.	AGE 26.
TURNER	G W	PTE	20 /1555	C									AWOL 29/11/15-1/12/15.
TURNER	James	PTE	20 /1163	B	REAYS BLDGS	HARTON VILLAGE			1/7/16		THIEPVAL MEM		BORN TWEEDMOUTH AGE 31.
TURNER	T	PTE	20 /1390					20/4/15	MISCONDUCT				
TURNER	T	PTE	20 /1162	B									AWOL 6-7/2/15. 84HRS DETENTION 3/12/15 FOR AWOL.
TURNER	Wm G	PTE	20 /1191									TO 18th, 22nd BNS.	
TURNER	Wm T	PTE	20 / 677				31/10/14	30/10/17	SICK			TO 3rd BN.	AGE 45.
TWEDDLE	Wm	PTE	20 / 678	C		HARTFORD COLL						TO 18th BN, LABOUR CORPS(20th LAB COY).	AWOL 7-9/2/15.
TWEEDY	Drydn	PTE	20 /1496	E	25 WEST END	OLD HARTLEY						TO CLASS Z RESERVE.	FROM E COY TO C COY 19/6/15.
UPPERTON	Henry	LCPL	20 /1456	A			14/1/15	6/3/18	GSW	1/7/16		TO DEPOT.	FROM DEPOT COY TO A COY 25/2/15, AWOL 8/3/15.
URQUHART	D	PTE	20 /1168	B				10/4/15	UNFIT				
URWIN	Jas	PTE	20 /1395	D		STANLEY				1/7/16		TO 25th, 1/7th BNS.	FROM DEPOT COY TO D COY 25/2/15, RENUMBERED 293331.
URWIN	Jos	PTE	20 /1501				17/2/15						
VEITCH	Geo	PTE	20 /1686		172 NORTH ROW	CRAMLINGTON						TO 21st, 11th, 2nd BNS, CLASS Z RESERVE.	
VENT	Jas R	PTE	20 /1516	E	24 STRAUGHAM STRE	NEWCASTLE	26/1/15	25/1/18	SICK				FROM E COY TO C COY 19/6/15, AGE 23.
VICKERS	JohnW	PTE	20 / 208			FAIRFIELD DUR	28/10/14	28/8/16	KR para 392			TO 29th BN.	MINER DESERTED 5/6/15, DESCRIPTION IN POL GAZ.NOT O/SE
WADE	Geo H	PTE	20 / 679	C		WALLSEND			1/7/16		THIEPVAL MEM		BORN BISHOP AUKLAND.
WADE	JohnG	PTE	20 /1691		ALBERT HOUSE	AMBLE			12/6/19	1/7/16	AMBLE WEST CEMETE	TO 9th, 22nd BNS, CLASS Z RESERVE.	
WAINWRIGHT	A	PTE	20 / 680	C	13 CLAYTON STREET	DUDLEY NTHBLD			1/7/16		THIEPVAL MEM	TO 34th DIV CYC COY, 24th BN.	ACC No 9465, TI No 24/1718, BORN LONGBENTON, AWOL 6-8/2/
WAKE	Fred	PTE	20 /1526	E									FROM E COY TO C COY 19/6/15, VOL AID HOSP CHELTENHAM :
WAKE	Robt	PTE	20 / 681	A			2/11/14	9/2/15	ANKLE INJURY				DID NOT SERV E O/SEAS.
WAKE	ThosW	PTE	20 /1412	A		EDMONDSLEY			1/7/16		THIEPVAL MEM		FROM DEPOT COY TO A COY 25/2/15, BORN LANCHESTER AGE
WAKENSHAW	M	PTE	20 / 288	A									COY COOK 31/1/15.
WALKDEN	J	PTE	20 / 682	C									COY COOK 31/1/15
WALKER	Geo	PTE	20 / 483	B		BENWELL				1/7/16		TO 16th, 24th, 24/27th, 9th BNS.	AWOL 6-7/10/15.
WALKER	Joshu	PTE	20 / 945				3/11/14	22/9/17	SICK			TO DEPOT.	AGE 41.
WALKER	R R	PTE	20 /1170			NORTH SHIELDS				1/7/16			
WALKER	Robt	PTE	20 / 947	D								TO 18th BN, CLASS Z RESERVE.	AWOL 5-14/6/15.
WALKER	Wm	PTE	20 / 684		37 COMMERCIAL STRE	WILLINGTON			1/7/16	4/6/16	OVILLERS MIL CEM		SHRAPNEL WND HIP, AGE 40 BORN CATHERINE AYRSHIRE
WALLACE	Alf	PTE	20 /1174	B	14 DERWENT STREET	CHOPWELL				4/6/16		TO 19th, 25th, 22nd BNS.	AWOL 6-7/10/15. GSW EYE
WALLACE	Wm	PTE	20 /1557	E					KR para 392				FROM E COY TO C COY 19/6/15.
WALTERS	T	PTE	20 / 946	C								TO ROYAL ENGINEERS TUNNELLING DEPOT 13/10.	AWOL 7-8/2/15.
WALTERS	Thos	PTE	20 / 686	B			29/10/14	10/4/15	UNFIT				SWB GIVES DATE OF DISCHARGE AS 13/5/16.NOT O/SEAS.
WALTON	AlbtE	PTE	20 / 688			NEWBURN			3/8/16		CABERET ROUGE MIL CEM		BORN PRUDHOE AGE 39.
WALTON	Robt	LCPL	20 /1556	E	125 AUDLY ROAD	GOSFORTH			1/7/16		THIEPVAL MEM		FROM E COY TO C COY 19/6/15, BORN COANWOOD NTHBLD A
WALTON	Thos	CPL	20 / 687	B		WESTERHOPE			KR para 392	1/7/16			
WARD	Peter	PTE	20 / 209									TO 1st GARRISON BN, CLASS Z RESERVE.	
WARDELL	E	PTE	20 /1460	E									AWOL 15-16/2/15.
WARDLAW	Rob H	PTE	20 / 689			CLYDEBROOK						TO 23rd, 24th, 24/27th, 23rd, 8th BNS, CLASS Z RESERVE.	
WARDLOW	Geo	PTE	20 /1571	D	35 FORTH STREET	CHOPWELL			1/7/16		THIEPVAL MEM		FROM E COY TO D COY 19/6/15, BORN IRTHINGTON CUMBERL
WATERS	Lawr	LCPL	20 / 484	A	9 THE POPLARS	SOUTHWICK			1/7/16		THIEPVAL MEM		AWOL 7-8/3/15, AGE 30, SIGNALLER.
WATSON	Dav W	PTE	20 /1410	D		SEAHAM HARBOU	9/1/15	30/10/17	SICK	1/7/16		TO 3rd BN.	FROM DEPOT COY TO D COY 25/2/15, AGE 31.
WATSON	F	PTE	20 /1397	D									FROM DEPOT COY TO D COY 25/2/15.
WATSON	F T	SGT	20 /1538	B								FROM 11th BN, 16/4/15.	APPOINTED CSM B COY 16/4/15.
WATSON	G A	PTE	20 /1414	A									FROM DEPOT COY TO A COY 25/2/15.
WATSON	J	PTE	20 /1173					1/2/15	KR para 392				
WATSON	James	PTE	20 / 486			WEST ALLOTMEN	31/10/14	8/6/17	KR paras 39	1/7/16		TO DEPOT.	GROOM TO MAJOR NOBLE, HOSP WHALLEY CHESHIRE 7/7/16.
WATSON	John	PTE	20 /1176		33 CONDERCUM STRE	NEWCASTLE						TO 2nd GARRISON BN, CLASS Z RESERVE.	
WATSON	Jos	PTE	20 / 691				2/11/14	15/7/15	DEAFNESS				DID NOT SERVE O/SEAS.
WATSON	Jos	PTE	20 /1172	A		SWALWELL			../../17				AWOL 31/7/15, REPORTED DIED APRIL 1917.
WATSON	Martn	PTE	20 /1610	D	17 GARDEN TERRACE	EARSDON			1/7/16		THIEPVAL MEM		AGE 35.
WATSON	N V	BGLF	20 / 482										POSTED TO DEPOT COY 5/3/15.
WATSON	W	PTE	20 / 685	C									AWOL 29/11/15-1/12/15.
WATSON	Wm	PTE	20 / 128	D			27/10/14	10/7/18	SICK			TO 2nd GARRISON BN, DEPOT.	COY COOK 31/1/15, AGE 39.
WATTS	Robt	LCPL	20 /1169	B	5 PALMER STREET	WALLSEND	4/11/14	2/3/17	WOUNDS	1/7/16		TO DEPOT.	AWOL 6-8/10/15.
WAUGH	Jos W	PTE	20 / 694						KR para 392			TO 24th, 24/27th BNS.	

Surname	Forename	Rank	No	Coy	Address	Place	Date1	Date2	Cause	Death	Memorial/Cemetery	Transfer	Remarks
WAUGH	Ralph	PTE	20/693			W CRAMLINGTON	31/10/14	15/8/17	GSW	1/7/16		TO 3rd BN.	PRISONER OF WAR, AGE 28.
WAUGH	ThosW	SGT	20/695	C	51 HASTINGS STREET	CRAMLINGTON	31/10/14	28/1/19	GSW	1/7/16		TO DEPOT.	3 CCS 2/7/16 EVAC 2/7/16.
WEAR	J	LCPL	20/696										
WEARS	Jn Wm	PTE	20/1407	E	128 BRICKGARTH	HETTON LE HOLE						TO 2nd GARRISON BN, CLASS Z RESERVE.	FROM E COY TO C COY 19/6/15.
WEATHERHEA	Jas J	PTE	20/1719									FROM 19th BN, TO 14th, ROYAL FUSILIERS(24th BN) 19th BN No 19/1349.20 9/1/16-19/4/17, 14 18/7/18-28/8/18	
WEATHERHEA	RichJ	PTE	20/1398	E		GATESHEAD				1/7/16	THIEPVAL MEM		AWOL 3-4/2/15, 6-8/10/15, POSTED TO B COY, BORN LOW FELL.
WEBB	R	PTE	20/951	B								TO MUNITIONS(ARMSTRONG WHITWORTH & CO).	AGE 43.
WEDDLE	Hen M	CQMS	20/63	C	32 MARINE APPROACH	SOUTH SHIELDS						TO 3rd BN.	AGE 39, LSGT TRIED BY FGCM 20/1/16 REDUCED TO PTE.
WEIGHILL	Jos W	PTE	20/952				3/11/14	15/11/17	GSW				FROM E COY TO D COY 19/6/15, BORN COMMONDALE YORKS.
WELBURY	John	PTE	20/1572	D		WHITTON PARK				1/7/16	THIEPVAL MEM		
WELCH	T	PTE	20/697	A					10/4/15	UNFIT			FROM DEPOT COY TO A COY 25/2/15, BORN CHESTER LE STRI
WELLS	Henry	PTE	20/1474	A		FATFIELD				1/7/16	THIEPVAL MEM	TO ROYAL ENGINEERS TUNNELLING DEPOT 13/10/15.	
WELSH	J	PTE	20/953	D								TO 26th BN, LABOUR CORPS.	18 GHOSP 3/7 GSW L FOOT TO HSHIP 6/7/16.
WELSH	Wm	PTE	20/1406	D								TO 23rd BN.	AWOL 14-15/2/15.
WEST	Jos H	LSGT	20/954	D		NORTH SHIELDS	2/11/14	31/3/19	KR para 392	1/7/16			
WESTGARTH	J	PTE	20/699	B						1/7/16		FROM SOMERSET LI(8th BN) 23/7/15.	
WHEATON	Albt	PTE	20/1695	D		E CRAMLINGTON				1/7/16		FROM SOMERSET LI(8th BN) 23/7/15.	BORN CRAMLINGTON, SLI No 16691.
WHEATON	Jas	PTE	20/1694	D		SEATON DELAVAL				1/7/16	THIEPVAL MEM	TO DURHAM LIGHT INFANTRY, TRAINING RESERVI	TRG RES BN No TR/5/59077.
WHEATSON	Sam	PTE	20/1175			BROOMPARK COLL				1/7/16		TO ARMY RESERVE CLASS P.	AGE 44.
WHITE	Andrw	PTE	20/210			GATESHEAD	28/10/14	31/8/17	WOUNDS			TO DEPOT.	SHRAPNEL WND BUTTOCKS 3 CCS 2/7/16 EVAC 2/7/16.
WHITE	Chas	PTE	20/835			SEATON DELAVAL	31/10/14	16/8/17	WOUNDS	3/4/16, 1/7/16.		TO 3rd BN.	SHELL SHOCK, AGE 24.
WHITE	Harld	PTE	20/700			CRAMLINGTON	31/10/14	16/6/17	WOUNDS	3/6/16, 1/7/16			AWOL 21-23/2/15, 6-8/3/15.
WHITEHEAD	J	PTE	20/1459	E									
WHITFIELD	Thos	PTE	20/1458									TO 2nd GARRISON BN, CLASS Z RESERVE.	
WHITTAKER	W	PTE	20/1399	E									AWOL 1/2/15. 10/4/15.
WHYTE	Wm	PTE	20/955			ABERDEEN				1/7/16			DESERTED 16/1/17
WIDDRINGTON	M	PTE	20/1411	B		NEWCASTLE				1/7/16			FROM DEPOT COY TO B COY 25/2/15.
WIGGINS	L	BGLF	20/352					1/2/15	KR para 392			TO 24th, 21st BNS, ARMY RESERVE CLASS P.	AWOL 7-8/3/15.
WIGHT	JohnM	BGLF	20/956	D		BEDLINGTON	31/10/14	26/2/19	KR para 392	1/7/16		TO 2nd GARRISON BN, CLASS Z RESERVE.	
WILKES	Thos	PTE	20/487									TO 2nd GARRISON BN, CLASS Z RESERVE.	
WILKINSON	James	PTE	20/834										BORN STANHOPE AGE 40.
WILKINSON	John	PTE	20/488	D	37 COMMERCIAL STRE	WILLINGTON Co DUR				1/7/16	OVILLERS MIL CEM		BORN SEDGEFIELD AGE 41.
WILLIAMSON	Ernst	RQMS	20/1652		THE BUNGALOWS	HEWORTH				1/7/16	THIEPVAL MEM		FROM E COY TO C COY 19/6/15.
WILLIAMSON	John	PTE	20/1473	E		HORDEN COLL				13/6/16		TO 23rd, 12/13th, 18th BNS, CLASS Z RESERVE.	MINER DESERTED 14/6/15 AGE 23, 5'4".
WILLIAMSON	Matt	PTE	20/1584			BEDLINGTON	20/5/15						STRETCHER BEARER 1/7/15, AGE 30.
WILLIS	Geo E	PTE	20/958	D	5 LISHMAN TERR	CHOPWELL	2/11/14	5/6/18	GAS POISONING			TO 3rd BN.	AGE 43 BORN SEAHAM HARBOUR.
WILLISON	JohnT	PTE	20/489	D		FOREST HALL				1/7/16	THIEPVAL MEM		
WILSON	G	PTE	20/1687			ACKLINGTON				1/7/16		TO LABOUR CORPS.	AWOL 6-8/2/15, 12-16/2/15, 168 HRS DETENTION 7/- FINE.
WILSON	Geo	PTE	20/211	A								TO 18th, 22nd BNS.	
WILSON	Geo	PTE	20/1401									TO 2nd GARRISON BN, CLASS Z RESERVE.	
WILSON	Jas F	DrMj	20/289	C		BACKWORTH			16/11/15	UNFIT		REJOINED HIGHLAND LI(10th BN), TO 22nd BN, CLASS Z RESERVE.	PROMOTED CPL 29/10/14 Pt 2 ORDER 11/2/15, PIPE MAJOR.
WILSON	John	SGT	20/290			FOREST HALL	29/10/14	3/3/19	KR para 392			TO 2nd GARRISON BN, CLASS Z RESERVE.	
WILSON	Jos	PTE	20/490										AWOL 30-31/1/15, 20-22/2/15.
WILSON	R	PTE	20/838	E				20/4/15	KR para 392			TO MUNITIONS(ARMSTRONG WHITWORTH & CO).	
WILSON	T F	PTE	20/960										AWOL 1/2/15, 7-8/2/15.
WILSON	W	PTE	20/1402	E									BORN FENCEHOUSES AGE 24.
WILSON	Wm	PTE	20/1509	A	8 PROSPECT STREET	BIRTLEY				1/7/16	OVILLERS MIL CEM		FROM DEPOT COY TO B COY 25/2/15.
WILSON	Wm	PTE	20/1400	B								TO 2nd GARRISON BN, CLASS Z RESERVE.	SHRAPNEL WND BACK
WOOD	E	LCPL	20/961			NEWCASTLE				4/6/16, 1/7/16			
WOOD	J	PTE	20/832	C				2/2/15	KR para 392				BORN WINDY NOOK.
WOOD	Thos	PTE	20/129	C		GATESHEAD				1/7/16	THIEPVAL MEM		AWOL 28-29/3/15
WOODCOCK	R	PTE	20/64	A									
WOODHOUSE	Matt	PTE	20/962									TO 9th BN, CLASS Z RESERVE.	
WOODMASS	Stewt	PTE	20/1638		74 POPLAR STREET	ASHINGTON				23/7/16	PIETA MIL CEM MALTA	TO 1st GARRISON BN.	
WOODS		PTE	20/963	C								TO 34th DIV CYC COY.	
WOOLSEY	Geo	CQMS	20/1478		2 BATH PLACE	ILFRACOMBE				10/8/18	GLOUCESTER CEMETERY		AGE 53.
WOOTON	John	PTE	20/1408	D			9/1/15	1/10/17	WOUNDS			TO DEPOT.	FROM DEPOT COY TO D COY 25/2/15, AGE 38.
WRAITH	James	PTE	20/1413	E					KR para 392				AWOL 7-8/2/14, INITIAL W ON ORDERS, JAMES ON MR.
WRAY	Sam H	PTE	20/1152	B	15 STEPHENSON TERI	WALBOTTLE				1/7/16		TO 16th, 9th BNS, CLASS Z RESERVE.	AWOL 6-7/10/15.
WRIGHT	Andw	PTE	20/1520				16/2/15						ORIGINALLY ALLOTED 20/1498, ALLOTED TO T ROGERSON.
WRIGHT	Chas	PTE	20/1499				16/2/15						
WRIGHT	Hy Tl	PTE	20/1171		4 BOIUNDARY ROAD	CRAMLINGTON				1/7/16		TO 8th BN, DEPOT, CLASS Z RESERVE.	
WRIGHT	Jos R	PTE	20/1457	C	31 WEST STREET	GRANGE VILLA						TO 1st GARRISON BN, 7th, 14th BNS, CLASS Z RES	ON AVL URPETH PAPER MILL, FROM DEPOT COY TO C COY 25
WRIGHT	Mark	PTE	20/1403	D		DAWDON	5/1/15	4/5/18	GSW	1/7/16		FROM DEPOT COY TO D COY 25/2/15, AGE 31.	
WRIGHT	Thos	PTE	20/										AWOL 4/7/15.
WYLE	Ralph	PTE	20/1651	A		NORTH SHIELDS				1/7/16	THIEPVAL MEM		BORN TYNEMOUTH.
WYLIE	John	PTE	20/1692					6/3/19				TO 18th BN, YORK&LANCASTER REGT(2/4th BN) Z I Y & L No 57710.	
WYNN	H	PTE	20/1405	E									FROM E COY TO C COY 19/6/15.
YELLOW	J	BGLF	20/967										DESERTED 19/2/15
YOULL	Geo	PTE	20/1558	E		SOUTH SHIELDS	../5/15			1/7/16	THIEPVAL MEM		FROM E COY TO D COY 19/6/15, AWOL 6-7/10/15.
YOUNG	G	PTE	20/971	C					10/4/15	UNFIT			
YOUNG	Geo	PTE	20/978			ACKLINGTON	2/11/14	16/8/17	GSW	1/7/16		TO DEPOT.	
YOUNG	J	SGT	20/974			BEDLINGTON				1/7/16			
YOUNG	J	CPL	20/1201	D								TO 26th BN	
YOUNG	Jas	PTE	20/491	A		SHOTTON COLL			6/6/16	5/6/16	ALBERT FRENCH NAT CEM		GSW THIGH, BORN NEW BRANCEPETH, 48 HRS DETENTION 3/
YOUNG	John	LCPL	20/973			NEWCASTLE				1/7/16	THIEPVAL MEM	TO DEPOT.	AWOL 6-7/10/15.
YOUNG	John	Drmr	20/968	B			2/11/14	25/1/19	KR para 392			TO 1st GARRISON BN, CLASS Z RESERVE.	
YOUNG	John	PTE	20/833				3/11/14	1/2/15	KR para 392				DID NOT SERVE O/SEAS.
YOUNG	Matt	PTE	20/969									TO CHESHIRE REGT(9th BN).	CHESHIRE No 52336.
YOUNG	Stan	PTE	20/1639		93 CHESTNUT AVE	HIRST				1/7/16		TO ARMY RESERVE CLASS P.	
YOUNG	Wm	PTE	20/1611		78 DUNSTON STREET	HEBBURN	31/5/15	21/2/18	GSW	1/7/16			3 CCS 2/7/16, EVAC 2/7/16.
YOUNGER	JohnH		20/1177										
YOUNGS	C G	PTE	20/65	C									AWOL 6-8/2/15.

Appendix IV

NOMINAL ROLL OF OTHER RANKS 21st NF (2nd Tyneside Scottish)

Number on Roll **1049**; Killed or Died of Wounds **356**; Wounded **330**, Gassed, Sick etc **166**:

Total known casualties **852** (81.2 per cent)

Not traced 688

NAME	INITIAL	RANK	BA	NUMB	CO	ADDRESS	TOWN_VILL	ENLISTED	DISCHARGE	CAUSE_DIS	WOUNDED	BURIED	TRANSFER	ADD
ABALSOM	Matt	PTE	21	/1182			HARTFORD				1/7/16			BORN BEDLINGTON.
AGGETT	Alb E	PTE	21	/ 27	A	46 PERCY STREET	TYNEMOUTH				1/7/16	THIEPVAL MEM		
AIR	John	PTE	21	/ 995	C					MISS 21/3/18		THIEPVAL MEM		BORN STONEHOUSE DEVON.
AITHISON	Syd G	LCPL	21	/ 555	D		BLACKHILL				28/6/16	BECOURT MIL CEM	TO 23rd BN(D COY), CLASS Z RESERVE.	AGE 20, BN HQ RUNNER.
ALLAN	Fredk	LCPL	21	/1559		4 WILLIAM STREET	TUNSTALL	27/2/15	31/3/19	KRpara 392			TO 2nd GARRISON BN, ARMY RESERVE CLASS P.	BORN GATESHEAD, IN MACHINE GUN SECTION.
ALLAN	Geo	PTE	21	/ 398									TO DURHAM LIGHT INFANTRY, TRAINING RESERVE BN.	TRG RES No TR/5/59117.
ALLCOCK	JohnW	PTE	21	/1285		28 FRONT STREET	LOW MOORSLEY				12/10/16	RATION FARM MIL CEM		BORN SOUTH SHIELDS AGE 21.
ANDERSON	Robt	PTE	21	/ 392		14 DARLINGTON STREET	WHEATLEY HILL						TO 2nd GARRISON BN, CLASS Z RESERVE.	ALLISON IN AVL.
ANDERSON	Syd	PTE	21	/1028				12/11/14	23/10/17	WOUNDS			TO DEPOT.	
ANDERTON	Geo	PTE	21	/ 960			BARRINGTON COLL				9/6/16	HEILLY STATION CEM.		BORN MORPETH AGE 20.
ANGUS	Jas	PTE	21	/ 612			ASHINGTON				1/7/16	THIEPVAL MEM		BORN BLYTH.
ANGUS	Robt	PTE	21	/1644				30/6/15	14/6/16	SICK			TO 29th BN.	DID NOT SERVE OVERSEAS.
APPLEBY	Thos	PTE	21	/ 118			SEATON BURN				KRpara 392		TO 23rd BN.	
APPLETON	Geo	SGT	21	/1576		40 BRUNSWICK STREET	SOUTH SHIELDS		20/3/18	13/3/16		ARRAS MEM	TO 23rd BN(A COY).	AWOL 17-19/7/15, 29/11-3/1/16, DESERTED 13/12/15.
ARCHBOLD	Rich	PTE	21	/ 800									TO 22nd BN, ROYAL FUSILIERS(24th BN)	FRANCE 21 10/1/16-2/2/18, 22 2/2/18-28/8/18, 24RF -11/11/18
ARCHIBALD	Rich	PTE	21	/ 249			NEWCASTLE			SEPT 16				
ARKEL	Wm	PTE	21	/ 438		5 BRUCE STREET	SEATON BURN				1/7/16	THIEPVAL MEM		AGE 22.
ARMSTRONG	Adam	PTE	21	/1101	C		GATESHEAD				1/7/16	THIEPVAL MEM		BORN EDINBURGH AGE 19.
ARMSTRONG	JohnH	PTE	21	/ 540		12 SOUTH STREET	GATESHEAD	11/11/14	5/3/19	KRpara 392			TO ARMY RESERVE CLASS P.	
ARMSTRONG	Thos	PTE	21	/ 402			WHEATLEY HILL				27/3/18	LONDON CEM NEUVILLE	TO 23rd BN(B COY).	
ARMSTRONG	Thos	PTE	21	/ 784	A		WHEATLEY HILL				1/7/16	SSHOCK AUG THIEPVAL MEM		BORN NEWCASTLE
ARNOT	ThosH	PTE	21	/ 490	A	68 COOKSON STREET	NEWCASTLE				1/7/16	MISS NOV 16 THIEPVAL MEM		BORN THORNLEY.
ARREL	Wm	PTE	21	/ 438			SEATON BURN				1/7/16	THIEPVAL MEM		AGE 37 BORN YORK.
ASKWITH	C J	PTE	21	/ 896			CROOK				1/7/16	THIEPVAL MEM		AGE 22 BORN NEWCASTLE.
ATKINS	JohnW	PTE	21	/1370	A	83 PHILIP STREET	HEBBURN				1/7/16	MISS NOV 16 THIEPVAL MEM	TO 23rd BN(B COY 6 PLTN).	
ATKINSON	Isaac	PTE	21	/ 144			FELLING				4/6/17	POINT-DU-JOUR MIL CEM		BORN THORNLEY AGE 40.
AULD	Thos	PTE	21	/ 963	C		BEDLINGTON			MISS 21/3/18			TO 23rd BN(A COY), ATTACHED LTMB, CLASS Z RESERV AGE 24.	
AYRE	Thos	PTE	21	/1314			SEAHAM HARBOUR		8/10/18	SEPT 16		MARCOING BRIT CEM	TO 1st, 16th, 19th, 12/13th BNS.	
BAGE	Chris	PTE	21	/1411	D								TO 24th, 8th BNS, CLASS Z RESERVE.	
BAGGOTT	Rich	PTE	21	/ 913			WINLATON	12/11/14	5/3/18	SICK	JULY+SEPT 16		TO 11th BN, DEPOT.	AGE 36.
BAGNALL	Jos	PTE	21	/1718		23 DIBLEY STREET	NEWCASTLE	19/8/15	27/8/18	KRpara 392			TO 9th BN, DEPOT.	AGE 30.
BAILES	Thos	PTE	21	/1521		86 CHARLES STREET	BOLDON COLLIERY						TO 1st GARRISON BN, CLASS Z RESERVE.	
BAILEY	Jos	PTE	21	/ 661	D		BEDLINGTON				1/7/16	THIEPVAL MEM		AGE 39, BORN EAST RAINTON.
BAILEY	Mitch	PTE	21	/1715			ASHINGTON	23/8/15	20/8/17	WOUNDS			TO 23rd BN, 84th TRAINING RESERVE BN.	AGE 23.
BAILEY	Wm	PTE	21	/ 971			NEWSHAM				8/7/16	HEILLY STATION CEM		BORN BEDLINGTON AGE 36.
BAKER	Frank	PTE	21	/ 415			CHOPPINGTON				1/7/16	THIEPVAL MEM		BORN BLYTH
BAKER	ThosL	SGT	21	/ 255		BACK ROW	WHICKHAM					SSHOCK AUG 16	TO MACHINE GUN SCHOOL, 14th BN.	
BARBER	Dav H	PTE	21	/1710									TO 2nd GARRISON BN, DURHAM LIGHT INFANTRY(1st BN)	DLI No 52342.
BARBER	Jos	CPL	21	/ 196			NORTH SHIELDS	5/11/14	31/12/17	GSW			TO DEPOT.	AGE 31.
BARCLAY	JohnA	PTE	21	/1026	D	8 CARRICK STREET	SOUTH BYKER				1/7/16	THIEPVAL MEM		AGE 34.
BARDWELL	Sam	PTE	21	/1323									ATT 181 TUNN COY RE, TO 25th, 12/13th BNS, CLASS Z RESERVE.	
BARNES	JohnW	PTE	21	/ 258		27 COQUET STREET	CHOPWELL				10/7/16	ETAPLES MIL CEM		AGE 43 BORN BISHOP AUKLAND.
BARNETT	RobtC	PTE	21	/1278		22a SCHOOL STREET	SEAHAM						TO 3rd BN(G COY), CLASS Z RESERVE.	
BARNFATHER	Geo	PTE	21	/ 876	B	24 NORTH VIEW	HOLYWELL	11/11/14			MISSING JUNE 16		TO CLASS Z RESERVE.	BOMBER TAKEN PRISONER JUNE 1916.
BARRAS	Ben	CPL	21	/ 57	A					1/4/16			TO CHESHIRE REGT(9th BN).	CHESHIRE REGT No 52317.
BARRAS	Thos	PTE	21	/1611		13 LAYGATE LANE	SOUTH SHIELDS		17/12/15			HARTON ST PETERS	TO 2nd GARRISON BN.	DIED IN RAILWAY ACCIDENT.
BARRASS	Sam	PTE	21	/ 891									TO 2nd GARRISON BN, CLASS Z RESERVE.	
BARREN	JohnG	PTE	21	/1207			SUNDERLAND	4/1/15	11/2/18	GSW	OCT 16		TO DEPOT.	AGE 29.
BARRON	JohnG	SGT	21	/ 410		38 HARVEY STREET	NEW BRANCEPETH						TO 23rd BN.	REJECTED BY TYNESIDE IRISH, TOO SMALL.
BARTLETT	Thos	PTE	21	/ 293	B		BEBSIDE FURNACE				1/7/16	THIEPVAL MEM		BORN LINCOLN.
BARTON	Wm	LCPL	21	/1174		31 CASTLEREAGH STREET	NEW SILKSWORTH				9/4/17	ST CATHERINES CEM		
BATCHELOR	ChasH	PTE	21	/ 806			CHOPPINGTON				25/4/17	ARRAS MEM	TO 26th, 27th BNS.	AGE 38 BORN BIRMINGHAM.
BATCHELOR	Wm F	LCPL	21	/ 338			CHOPPINGTON				23/9/17	HAGRICOURT BRIT MIL C ATTACHED 102nd LIGHT TRENCH MORTAR BATTERY.		AGE 27.
BATTY	T	PTE	21	/ 729										BN TRANSPORT SECTION.
BEADNELL	Robt	PTE	21	/1291			HETTON LE HOLE				8/10/17	SEPT 16 ST SEVER CEM ROUEN	TO 26th BN.	BORN LOW MOORSLEY.
BEADNELL	Wm	PTE	21	/1281									TO 23rd BN, CLASS Z RESERVE.	
BEAVIS	JohnW	PTE	21	/ 158	B								TO 25th, 11th BNS.	
BECKWITH	Thos	PTE	21	/ 386		92 ARIEL STREET	HIRST	17/10/14	23/7/19		NOV 16		TO 3rd, 1/5th BNS, YORK & LANCASTER REGT(1/4th BN).	SERVANT TO Lt R E BATY JAN 1917, COMPANY FOOTBALLER Y & L No 58243.
BELL	James	PTE	21	/1353			WALLSEND				1/7/16	THIEPVAL MEM	TO 23rd BN.	BORN GATESHEAD.
BELL	James	PTE	21	/ 901									TO CLASS Z RESERVE.	

BELL	John	PTE	21 / 902			HIRST				JULY 16, 26/12/16 20th BN		TO 1st GARRISON, 20th, 24th, 1st, 22nd BNS, CLASS Z RESERVE.	
BELL	John	LCPL	21 / 466	C		GATESHEAD			1/7/16	MISS NOV 16	THIEPVAL MEM		
BELL	JohnJ	PTE	21 /1711			HARTFORD COLL			KRpara 392	AUG 16			
BELL	JohnW	PTE	21 / 935			GUIDE POST				NOV 16		TO 1st BN, CLASS Z RESERVE.	
BELL	Jos W	PTE	21 / 659			BEDLINGTON	9/11/14	17/9/19	KRpara 392			TO 12/13th, 1st BNS, DEPOT.	
BELL	Robt	SGT	21 / 535			HIRST				NOV 16		TO 12th BN.	
BELL	Thos	SGT	21 / 285		11 BALKWELL AVE	PERCY MAIN			1/7/16		THIEPVAL MEM		BORN NORTH SHIELDS AGE 38.
BELL	Thos	PTE	21 /1400			NEWCASTLE			15/2/15		STELLA ST CUTHBERTS		
BENNETT	Archi	PTE	21 / 624										
BERESFORD	Geo	CPL	21 / 908		6 THIRD ROW	ASHINGTON			3/5/17	AUG 16	ARRAS MEM	TO 16th, 1st BNS.	AGE 25, NORTH EVINGTON HOSP LEICESTER 11/7/16.
BERRIMAN	Wm	PTE	21 /1273		29 LYON STREET	HETTON LE HOLE						TO CLASS Z RESERVE.	
BERTRAM	Geo W	PTE	21 / 51		9 CRONE STREET	EARSDON						TO 23rd BN.	
BERTRAM	JohnW	PTE	21 /1614			TYNEMOUTH	1/6/15					TO 22nd, 1st, 12/13th BNS, CLASS Z RESERVE.	GARDENER, DESERTED 12/7/15, AGE 23, 5'7".
BEST	Ralph	PTE	21 /1730		251 BELFORD STREET	NORTH SHIELDS	11/8/15	26/6/18	SICK			TO DEPOT.	AGE 22.
BEST	Robt	PTE	21 /1616		2 RAMSAY STREET	CHOPWELL				DEC 16		TO 23rd BN.	
BEST	Thos	PTE	21 /1362	C	22 UNION TERRACE	SHIELDFIELD			1/7/16		THIEPVAL MEM		AGE 25.
BILCLOUGH	Robt	LCPL	21 / 246				7/11/14	22/10/17	GSW			TO 1st BN, DEPOT.	
BILLINGHURST	John	PTE	21 /1175		32 GEORGE STREET	TUNSTALL	31/12/14	1/4/19	KRpara 392			TO ARMY RESERVE CLASS P.	
BILLS	Wm	PTE	21 /1725										
BIRD	Jos	PTE	21 / 827									TO 22nd BN, ROYAL FUSILIERS(24th BN).	FRANCE 21 10/1/16-15/4/18, 22 16/4/18-28/8/18, 24RF - 8/1/19
BLACK	Isaac	LCPL	21 / 334			CHOPPINGTON			5/6/17		ARRAS MEM		BORN ALNWICK
BLACKETT	Mich	PTE	21 / 257			BYKER			10/10/17	AUG 16	UNCOMMEMORATED	TO 20th, 10th BNS.	
BLACKLIDGE	Jos	PTE	21 / 381		105 BENSON ROAD	NEWCASTLE						TO 19th(C COY), 23rd BNS.	
BLAND	Thos	PTE	21 / 457	C		BURRADON	9/11/14	20/8/17	GSW	JULY 16		TO DEPOT.	
BODDY	Thos	PTE	21 / 133		18 GRACE STREET	SOUTH SHIELDS	6/11/14	9/3/17	6/11/18		HARTON ST PETER	TO DEPOT.	DIED OF HEART DISEASE.
BOLAM	John	PTE	21 / 301			NORTH SHIELDS			14/10/17		TYNE COT MEM	TO 23rd BN.	BORN DURHAM CITY.
BOLL	JohnW	PTE	21 /1482									TO 14th BN, CLASS Z RESERVE.	
BOLTON	Robt	CPL	21 / 575	C	FRONT STREET	NEWBIGGIN / SEA				SEPT 16		TO 27th, 12/13th BNS.	AGE 21, PRISONER OF WAR.
BOND	JohnT	PTE	21 /1274			HETTON LE HOLE	9/1/15	27/2/18	GSW	JULY 16		TO ARMY RESERVE CLASS W 16/11/16, TO CLASS P.	AGE 25.
BOND	Pat	PTE	21 /1467		44 ELLISON ST WEST	GATESHEAD	18/1/15					TO 1st BN, CLASS Z RESERVE.	AWOL 16/7/15, 24/12/15, AGE 30.
BONE	ThosF	PTE	21 / 925			CRAMLINGTON	10/11/14	1/8/17	GSW	DEC 16		TO DEPOT.	
BOOTH	RobtH	CPL	21 /1298			SEAHAM HARBOU	22/12/14	1/4/19	KRpara 392	JULY 16		TO 18th, 11th BNS, ARMY RESERVE CLASS P.	
BOSOMWORTH	Rolnd	PTE	21 /1737									TO 20th BN, DURHAM LIGHT INFANTRY(13th BN).	DLI No 45946.
BOURKE	Mich	PTE	21 /1448	D	87 BRUNSWICK STREET	SOUTH SHIELDS			1/7/16		THIEPVAL MEM	TO 1st GARRISON BN, 26th BN.	ROURKE IN PAPERS
BRADLEY	Dan	CPL	21 / 942			BEDLINGTON	11/11/14	12/10/17	SICK	JULY 16			AGE 29.
BRADLEY	Isaac	SGT	21 / 766		8 HARRINGTON STREET	WALLSEND			9/4/17	OCT 16	ARRAS MEM		AGE 25 BORN BIRMINGHAM.
BREEN	Wm	PTE	21 /1622									TO 1st GARRISON BN, CLASS Z RESERVE.	
BREW	JohnW	PTE	21 /1201		23 HENDON STREET	SUNDERLAND			29/6/18	NOV 16	BISHOPWEARMOUTH	TO 25th BN.	AGE 44, DESERTED 1/10/15.
BRIAN	Edw G	PTE	21 / 990	C								TO 14th BN, ROYAL FUSILIERS(24th BN).	AGE 19, BN HQ RUNNER.FRANCE 21 10/1/16-3/7/18, 14-28/8/18
BRIDGES	FredW	PTE	21 /1361	A	106 BROMLEY ROAD	HORFIELD BRISTL			1/7/16		OVILLERS MIL CEM		AGE 23 BORN WEST HARTLEPOOL.
BRIGGS	JohnH	SGT	21 / 859	A		WATERHOUSES			17/2/16		RUE-DU-BOIS CEM FLEURBAIX		
BRIGHT	J G	PTE	21										AWOL 23/12/15.
BROOKSBANK	John	PTE	21 /1443		38 FRONT STREET	NORTH SHIELDS	18/1/15	1/4/19	KRpara 392			TO 2nd GARRISON BN, ARMY RESERVE CLASS P.	
BROTHERICK	Robt	PTE	21 / 93			BEDLINGTON	6/11/14	29/8/17	WOUNDS	OCT 16		TO 80th TRAINING RESERVE BN.	
BROWN	Chas	PTE	21 /1514									TO 2nd GARRISON BN, CLASS Z RESERVE.	
BROWN	ChasE	PTE	21 / 59			COCKERMOUTH			1/7/16		THIEPVAL MEM		BORN BIRTLEY.
BROWN	Geo	PTE	21 / 351									TO 25th, 1st BNS.	
BROWN	Geo H	PTE	21 / 635			GATESHEAD	9/11/14	10/5/18	GSW	SEPT 16		TO ARMY RESERVE CLASS P.	AWOL 24/12/15, AGE 42.
BROWN	Geo R	CPL	21 / 41									TO 23rd BN, KINGS OWN YORKSHIRE LI(5th BN).	
BROWN	John	PTE	21 / 668			BEDLINGTON	30/11/14	26/2/18	GSW	AUG 16		TO ARMY RESERVE CLASS P.	AGE 33.
BROWN	Jos	SGT	21 / 43	A	1 JUBILEE TERRACE	SEATON DELAVAL			1/7/16		GORDON DUMP		AGE 34 BORN NEWCASTLE.
BROWN	Wm	PTE	21 /1581	D		SEAHAM HARBOUR			1/7/16		THIEPVAL MEM		BORN LEAMSIDE
BROWNLESS	Thos	PTE	21 / 311			THORNLEY	7/11/14	30/4/17	GSW FACE	OCT 16		TO 84th TRAINING RESERVE BN.	AGE 35, VOL AID HOSP CHELTENHAM 8/7/16.
BUCKHAM	Robt	PTE	21 / 797		65 FRONT STREET	BEBSIDE			28/9/16		RATION FARM MIL CEM		AGE 27.
BUGLASS	Geo	PTE	21 / 572			CAMBOIS	7/11/14	5/3/18	SICK	SEPT 16		TO DEPOT.	AGE 36.
BULLOCK	Fred	PTE	21 / 464			BURRADON	9/11/14	5/10/16	GSW	OCT 16		TO DEPOT.	AGE 23, 3CCS 2/7/16 EVAC 2/7/16 WND ABDOMEN.
BUNCE	Thos	PTE	21 / 826			NEWCASTLE	11/11/14	30/10/17	WOUNDS	AUG 16		TO DEPOT.	AGE 29, 2nd STHN GHOSP BRISTOL 8/7/16.
BUNTING	Henry	PTE	21 /1218			SEAHAM HARBOU	2/1/15	12/1/17	WOUNDS	SEPT 16		TO 23rd BN, 84th TRAINING RESERVE BN.	
BURKE	Pat	PTE	21 /1079			CAMPERDOWN	12/11/14	1/1/18	GSW	OCT 16		TO DEPOT.	LCPL AGE 42.
BURN	JohnR	PTE	21 / 779						KRpara 392				
BURNETT	Geo W	PTE	21 /1318		TAILORS ARMS YARD	ALNWICK						TO LABOUR CORPS.	
BURNEY	Thos	PTE	21 /1649				31/7/15	9/9/16	KRpara 392			TO 29th BN.	DID NOT SERVE OVERSEAS.
BURNS	John	PTE	21 /1409				18/1/15	1/4/19	KRpara 392	JULY 16		TO ARMY RESERVE CLASS P.	
BURTON	Andrw	CSM	21 /1089			NEWCASTLE				SEPT 16		TO 14th, 12/13th BNS, CLASS Z RESERVE.	
BURTON	Geo E	PTE	21 / 369	D		DURHAM CITY	7/11/14	11/4/18	SICK	OCT 16		TO 3rd BN.	
CABE	James	PTE	21 /1596			NEWCASTLE			1/7/16		THIEPVAL MEM	TO 23rd BN.	
CADE	David	PTE	21 / 554		31 MEDOMSLEY ROAD	CONSETT				SEPT 16		TO 16th, 22nd, 19th, 9th BNS.	
CAIN	Wm	SGT	21 / 123			BLYTH				SEPT 16		TO 1st BN, COMMISSIONED 3rd BN 11/9/18.	
CAINE	Jas J	PTE	21 /1015	C	1 DURHAM ROAD	BENEFIELDSIDE						TO 14th BN.	
CAIRNS	John	PTE	21 /1195		3 IRONSIDE STREET	HOUGHTON LE SP	4/1/15	17/9/19	KRpara 392	OCT 16		TO 16th BN.	
CALVERT	David	PTE	21 /1380		12 HORNEY TERRACE	EASINGTON LANE			4/7/16	OCT 16	MEAULTE MIL CEM		BORN HOUGHTON LE SPRING, AGE 39.
CALVERT	Frn D	LCPL	21 / 708			SOUTH BENWELL	9/11/14	2/11/17	GSW	OCT 16		TO DEPOT.	AGE 43, 3rd NTHN GHOSP SHEFFIELD 8/7/16.
CALVERT	RobtW	LCPL	21 / 781	A	18 BRUNELL STREET	GATESHEAD			1/7/16		THIEPVAL MEM		BORN DURHAM.
CAMPBELL	Geo	PTE	21 / 996	C	160 CHILLINGHAM ROA	NEWCASTLE	9/11/14	24/9/19	KRpara 392				AGE 19 BN HQ RUNNER.
CAMPBELL	Jos D	LCPL	21 / 893		65 HYDE TERRACE	GATESHEAD	12/11/14	9/2/15	KRpara 392				DID NOT SERVE OVERSEAS.
CANNON	John	CSM	21 / 839			STIRLING			KRpara 392	OCT 16		COMMISSIONED 3rd BN.	
CARDIGAN	Geo	PTE	21 / 665		2 BANKWELL LANE	GATESHEAD						TO 2nd GARRISON BN, CLASS Z RESERVE.	
CAREY	Peter	PTE	21 / 39				5/11/14	24/7/18	GSW			TO DEPOT.	AGE 27.
CARNABY	Wm T	PTE	21 / 688				7/11/14	31/3/19	KRpara 392			TO 23rd BN, ARMY RESERVE CLASS P.	
CARNEGIE	James	PIPR	21 /1228		4 BURN AVE	FOREST HALL				NOV 16		TO 22nd BN, ROYAL FUSILIERS(24th BN).	FRANCE 22 10/1/16-30/8/18, 24 RF-16/11/18, RFUS No GS/9312
CARR	Henry	PTE	21 /1085			BURNHOPEFIELD	12/11/14	22/3/17	WOUNDS	SEPT 16		TO DEPOT.	
CARR	John	PTE	21 / 16		110 ST GEORGES TERR	GATESHEAD	5/11/14	13/2/15	KRpara 392				BORN BERWICK AGE 25 35 CHST FRSH COMPLX BLUE EYES
CARR	JohnS	SGT	21 / 10				12/11/14	1/8/17	GSW			TO 3rd BN.	MAY BE SAME MAN ERROR IN NUMBER.
CARR	JohnS	SGT	21 /1084			SOUTH BENWELL			KRpara 392	OCT 16			MAY BE SAME MAN ERROR IN NUMBER.
CARR	Robt	SGT	21 /1036									TO 12/13th BN, CLASS Z RESERVE.	
CARRICK	Thos	PTE	21 /1508			HEBBURN	19/1/15	16/2/18	GSW	JULY+OCT 16		TO 3rd BN.	AGE 38
CARRICK	Wm	PTE	21 /1507			HEBBURN			17/10/17	NOV 16	CEMENT HOUSE CEM LANGEMARCK		BORN HASWELL.
CARTER	Henry	PTE	21 /1515			NEWCASTLE	21/1/15	1/1/18	WOUNDS	JULY+OCT+NOV 16		TO 3rd BN.	AGE 26.
CASE	PeteS	PTE	21 / 503		19 FRONT ST MILBURN	NORTH SHIELDS			23/4/17		ARRAS MEM	TO 9th BN(C COY).	AGE 21, REPORTED MISSING JULY 16.
CHADWICK	Enoch	PTE	21 / 926		207 SYCAMORE STREE	HIRST	12/11/14	31/3/19	KRpara 392			TO ARMY RESERVE CLASS P.	
CHADWICK	James	PTE	21 / 139			NEWCASTLE			1/7/16		THIEPVAL MEM		BORN MANCHESTER.
CHAMBERS	Mich	SGT	21 /1442			GATESHEAD			11/9/17	NOV 16	THIEPVAL MEM		BORN USWORTH
CHAPELHOW	Geo	CPL	21 /1336	C		MEALSGATE			1/7/16		THIEPVAL MEM		AGE 28, BORN HARRASMOOR CUMBERLAND.
CHAPMAN	Arth	PTE	21 / 928		24 FIFTH ROW	ASHINGTON	12/11/14	11/2/17	GSW	JULY 16		TO 3rd BN.	AGE 27.
CHAPMAN	Job	PTE	21 /1254			GREAT LUMLEY			19/10/16		BAILLEUL COM CEM EXT		BORN SHINEY ROW
CHARLTON	Arth	PTE	21 /1345									TO 23rd BN, KINGS OWN YORKSHIRE LI(5th BN).	
CHARLTON	Edwd	PTE	23 / 169		LOW ROW NORTH	ACKLINGTON	4/11/14	17/11/14	MED UNFIT				MINER AGE 28, 5'6", 36 CHEST, DARK COMPLX, BLUE EYES,
CHARLTON	Geo	PTE	21 /1283		15 RAILWAY ROW	NORTH SEATON						TO 14th BN, ATTACHED 17th CORPS SCHOOL, CLASS Z RESERVE.	
CHARLTON	Geo R	PTE	21 /1402		515 SCOTSWOOD ROA	NEWCASTLE	14/1/15	31/3/19	KRpara 392			TO 25th BN(A COY), ARMY RESERVE CLASS P.	
CHARLTON	Jos F	SGT	21 / 580		16 JOHN STREET	NEWCASTLE	10/11/14	23/12/16	WOUNDS	SEPT 16		TO DEPOT.	AGE 42.
CHARLTON	Ralph	PTE	21 / 343		16 ROUTLEDGES BLDG	BARRINGTON			1/7/16		THIEPVAL MEM		AGE 17 BORN BEDLINGTON.
CHARTERS	Hen J	PTE	21 / 864			PELTON FELL	11/11/14	31/3/19	KRpara 392			TO ARMY RESERVE CLASS P.	
CHATER	ThosW	CPL	21 / 243	B		CRAMLINGTON			1/7/16		THIEPVAL MEM	TO 22nd BN(B COY).	BORN BIRMINGHAM, AGE40.
CHEYNE	John	PTE	21 /1176									TO 1st GARRISON BN, CLASS Z RESERVE.	
CHILDS	Henry	PTE	21 / 694									TO 23rd BN, ROYAL FUSILIERS(24th BN).	R FUSILIERS No G/93160.
CLARK	James	PTE	21 /1045	D	57 GLADSTOE STREET	COWPEN QUAY			1/7/16		THIEPVAL MEM		AGE 30 BORN NEWCASTLE.
CLARK	Jas W	PTE	21 /1280		54 BLIND LANE	TUNSTALL						TO 2nd GARRISON BN, CLASS Z RESERVE.	
CLARK	Thos	PTE	21 /1052	D		NEWCASTLE			1/7/16		THIEPVAL MEM		BORN ABERDEEN
CLARK	W	LCPL	21 /1188										PIPER.
CLARK	Wm	PTE	21 / 511			NORTH SHIELDS			7/7/16		WIMEREUX COM CEM EXT		AGE 29.
CLARK	Wm	PTE	21 /1598	D		WALKER			1/7/16		THIEPVAL MEM		BORN JARROW
CLEGHORN	Jos	PTE	21 /1103		49 TYNESIDE TERRACE	NEWCASTLE						TO 25th, 1st, 12/13th BNS, CLASS Z RESERVE.	
CLEMENTS	Henry	PTE	21 / 380			BYKER				SSHOCK AUG 16		TO 12/13th BN.	
CLENNAN	Wm	PTE	21 / 548	C		WESTERHOPE			6/3/20	JULY 16	HINDERWELL YORKS	TO 16th, 20th, 14th, 9th BNS.	AGE 35, WIFE LIVING HINDERWELL 1920.
COCKBURN	John	PTE	21 / 484			GOSFORTH				OCT 16		TO ROYAL INNISKILLING FUSILIERS(6th BN).	R INNIS FUS No 21525, R VIC HOSP NETLEY 11/7/16.
COCKBURN	Robt	PTE	21 / 64									TO 23rd BN, DURHAM LIGHT INFANTRY(15th BN).	DURHAM LI No 46577.
COCKERILL	Dan	PTE	21 /1663		143 DOLPHIN STREET	NEWCASTLE						TO CLASS Z RESERVE.	
COLE	Jos	CSM	21 /1019			NEWCASTLE				14/3/16, NOV 16		TO 13th, 20th, 23rd BNS, CLASS Z RESERVE.	
COLLINS	Geo T	PTE	21 / 604						KRpara 392			TO 12/13th, 1st BNS.	
COLLINWOOD	Jas R	CPL	21 /1696	D	32 MORTIMER STREET	HARTFORD COLL	16/8/15		5/6/17		ARRAS MEM		AGE 26, BORN BEDLINGTON, SPELT COLLINGWOOD ON MR.
COMRIE	Peter	PTE	21 /1040		10 GRAINGER STREET	COWPEN QUAY			30/3/17		WARLINCOURT HALTE CEM		AGE 46 BORN CRIEFF PERTHSHIRE.
CONWAY	Geo R	PTE	21 / 117	A		NORTH SHIELDS			5/6/17		CANADIAN CEM No2 NEUVILLE ST V		

COOK	Jacob	PTE	21 /1458	C		SEAHAM HARBOUR			9/4/17	NOV 16	ROCLINCOURT VALLEY CEM		AGE 35 BORN BLYTH.
COOK	Jas A	PTE	21 /1057						KRpara392			TO DURHAM LIGHT INFANTRY.	DLI No 78077.
COOK	ThosE	PTE	21 /1047		49 SALISBURY STREET	BLYTH			12/3/16		RATION FARM MIL CEM		AGE 30 BORN SUNDERLAND.
COOPER	Edwd	PTE	21 /1003				7/11/14	23/10/17					
COOPER	Geo	SGT	21 / 564			BLYTH			4/6/16		HEILLY STATION CEM		
CORKHILL	Jos	PTE	21 / 843		18 BIRKLEY STREET	WALLSEND						TO 23rd BN, CLASS Z RESERVE.	
CORNISH	Edwd	PTE	21 /1543			NEWCASTLE						TO CLASS Z RESERVE.	PRISONER OF WAR.
COULTER	Chas	PTE	21 /1727		SHEARLEGS ROAD	GATESHEAD				MISSING JUNE 16		TO CLASS Z RESERVE.	AGE 20, PRISONER OF WAR 1916.
COURTNEY	John	PTE	21 / 309				9/11/14	23/10/17	DEFORMED T			TO 84th TRAINING RESERVE BN.	AGE 45, DID NOT SERVE OVERSEAS.
COUTT	Wm	PTE	21 / 819			GATESHEAD			1/7/16		THIEPVAL MEM		AWOL 7/5/15.
COWAN	Geo E	LCPL	21 / 549										
COWAN	Wm	PTE	21 /1066			NEWCASTLE			7/7/16		WIMEREUX COM CEM EXT		AGE 20.
COWANS	Andrw	PTE	21 / 295			CHOPPINGTON				SEPT 16		TO 28th, 8th, 1st, 12/13th BNS.	AWOL 10/5/15.
COWELL	James	PTE	21 /1333			SUNDERLAND	13/1/15	28/2/17	WOUNDS	AUG 16		TO DEPOT.	
COWIE	JohnE	PTE	21 / 594		13 SMITH STREET	WHEATLEY HILL	10/11/14	7/1/18	WOUNDS	OCT 16		TO DEPOT.	AGE 24
COYNE	Mich	PTE	21 / 403	B	23 SALISBURY STREET	NEWCASTLE			1/7/16		THIEPVAL MEM		AGE 23.
CRACKETT	Hen B	PTE	21 / 954									TO 23rd BN, CLASS Z RESERVE.	
CRAGGS	John	PTE	21 / 760									TO 14th BN, ROYAL FUSILIERS(24th BN).	FRANCE 21 10/1/16-19/6/18, 14 20/6/18-28/8/18, 24RF-11/11/18
CRAIG	Robt	PTE	21 / 111	A	2 BROWNS BLDGS TYNI	NEWCASTLE						TO 34th DIV BASE DEPOT.	SERVANT TO Lt R E BATY 9/16 - 12/16.
CRAIG	Thos	PTE	21 /1193			SILKSWORTH COLI	2/1/15	22/8/17	SICK	JULY 16		TO 84th TRAINING RESERVE BN.	AGE 44.
CRAIGS	Luke	PTE	21 / 951									TO 1st GARRISON BN, CLASS Z RESERVE.	
CRAWFORD	G	PTE	21 /1284		10 ELEMORE LANE	HETTON LE HOLE				SEPT 16		TO 25th BN.	
CRAWFORD	James	LCPL	21 /1054	D		ASHINGTON			1/7/16		THIEPVAL MEM		
CRAWFORD	Thos	PTE	21 / 988			SOUTH NEWSHAM				SEPT 16		TO 23rd BN, CLASS Z RESERVE.	
CREE	Chris	PTE	21 /1568	C		COCKFIELD			2/2/16		SAILLY SUR LYS CANADIAN CEM		AGE 38 BORN EVENWOOD
CROSS	David	CPL	21 / 461	C	109 LANE ROW	WESTMOOR				1/7/16			BOMBER AGE 19, 34 CCS 2/7/16 EVAC 5/7/16, SHOWN AS 24th
CROSS	Edwd	LCPL	21 / 463		109 LANE ROW	WESTMOOR			25/6/16		KILLINGWORTH ST JOHN CH YD		AGE 24, BORN GATESHEAD
CROWE	Jas A	SGT	21 /1161			NORTH SHIELDS						TO 12/13th BN.	
CROWE	ThosW	PTE	21 /1317			SEAHAM COLL				AUG 16		TO 10th BN, CLASS Z RESERVE.	
CROYLE	JohnW	PTE	21 / 60			MORPETH			27/7/16	OCT 16	THIEPVAL MEM	ATTACHED KINGS OWN YORKSHIRE LI.	BORN BELFORD.
CRUICKSHANK	Geo	PTE	21 /1483			BOWNESS LANARKS			8/10/18		VIS-EN-ARTOIS MEM	TO 1/5th, 12/13th BNS.	
CUMMINGS	Alex	PTE	21 /1492			SUNDERLAND						TO 26th, 1/7th BNS, CLASS Z RESERVE.	
CUMMINGS	Alex	PTE	21 /1381			MURTON DUR	16/1/15	11/4/17	NEURATHE	JULY 16			
CUMMINGS	Jas R	PTE	21 / 638			WILLINGTON QUAY	1/12/14	18/7/17	SICK	JULY 16		TO DEPOT.	
CUNNINGHAM	JohnH	PTE	21 / 394		18 FRYER STREET	BURNOPFIELD				JULY 16		TO 9th BN.	
CURRAN	John	PTE	21 /1424			HOUGHTON LE SPR				OCT 16		TO DURHAM LI(11th BN).	DLI No 46185.
CURRY	John	PTE	21 / 498		37 COACH LANE	DINNINGTON COLL	10/11/14	27/3/19	KRpara 392			TO DEPOT.	
CURRY	Mich	PTE	21 /1634		51 WYLAM STREET	CRAGHEAD	28/4/15	15/3/18	WOUNDS			TO 3rd BN.	AGE 21.BROTHER JOHN 44063 2nd YORKS REGT.
CURRY	Mich	PTE	21 /1724		MECHANICS STREET	WEST CORNFORTH				NOV 16		TO 22nd, 8th BNS, CLASS Z RESERVE.	
CUTHBERT	John	PTE	21 / 805									TO 14th BN, CLASS Z RESERVE.	
CUTLER	W	PTE	21 / 937										TO 3CCS 2/7/16 EVAC 2/7/16 SHELLSHOCK.
CUTTER	RobtD	PTE	21 / 968									TO 9th BN, CLASS Z RESERVE.	
DAGG	Mart	PTE	21 /1183			SUNDERLAND	4/1/15	13/7/17	GSW	NOV 16		TO DEPOT.	AGE 32.
DAGLISH	Abner	PTE	21 /1561		7 STAVORDALE STREET	DAWDON			1/7/16		THIEPVAL MEM		BORN USWORTH AGE 20.
DAGLISH	Wm A	CSGT	21 / 854									TO 14th, 12/13th BNS, CLASS Z RESERVE.	
DALTON	GEO	PTE	21 /1657		69 DIANA STREET	NEWCASTLE			1/7/16		THIEPVAL MEM	TO 20th, 22nd BNS	AGE 18.
DAVIDSON	Fred	CPL	21 /1441		20 CORONATION TERR	ESH WINNING	18/1/15		9/4/18		NIEUPORT MEM	TO 18th, 25th(D COY) BNS.	AGE 26 BORN BENTON, 9 STATION VIEW ESH W 1914.
DAVIDSON	Geo Y	PTE	21 / 408			CHOPPINGTON			28/3/15		BEDLINGTON ST CUTHBERTS		
DAVIDSON	James	CPL	21 / 53									COMMISSIONED.	
DAVIDSON	John	PTE	21 / 50	A	4 WARK AVENUE	SHIREMOOR			1/7/16		THIEPVAL MEM		AGE 29 BORN PERCY MAIN.
DAVIDSON	Robt	PTE	21 /1573						KRpara 392			TO 1st GARRISON BN, 12/13th BNS.	
DAVIES	Rich	PTE	21 / 829		30 JOAN STREET	NEWCASTLE						TO 14th, 9th BNS, CLASS Z RESERVE.	
DAVIS	Geo H	PTE	21 /1209			CASTLETOWN			9/7/16		ST SEVER CEM ROUEN		BORN HOUGHTON LE SPRING
DAVIS	James	PTE	21 /1277			MIDDLESBROUGH			26/1/16		SEATON VALLEY CEM	TO 2nd GARRISON BN.	
DAVISON	Andrw	PTE	21 / 927		COCKHALL	EGLINGHAM	12/11/14	1/4/19	KRpara 392	SEPT 16		TO 22nd, 3rd, 53rd(YOUNG SOLDIER) BNS.	
DAVISON	Geo	PTE	21 / 159									TO 2nd GARRISON BN, CLASS Z RESERVE.	
DAVISON	James	PTE	21 / 42				5/11/14	22/10/17	SICK			TO DEPOT.	AGE 43.
DAVISON	JohnJ	PTE	21 /1712			NEWCASTLE				AUG 16		TO 23rd BN, CLASS Z RESERVE.	
DAVISON	JohnW	PTE	21 /1205									TO 2nd GARRISON BN, CLASS Z RESERVE.	
DAVISON	Jos	PTE	21 / 807				10/11/14	2/11/18	GSW			TO 23rd BN, DEPOT.	AGE 27.
DAWSON	Geo	PTE	21 /1287			CHOPPINGTON	8/1/15	6/3/18	GASSED	JULY 16		TO ARMY RESERVE CLASS P.	AGE 29.
DAWSON	Rob A	PTE	21 /1578				15/3/15	1/4/19	KRpara 392			TO 1st GARRISON BN.	
DAWSON	Robt	PTE	21 /1462			SUNNYSIDE			28/3/16		X FARM CEM		
DAWSON	Thos	CPL	21 / 803									TO 23rd, 1st BNS, CLASS Z RESERVE.	
DAY	Jas T	SGT	21 / 514			NEWCASTLE			1/7/16		THIEPVAL MEM		
DEMPSEY	JohnW	PTE	21 / 28									TO 1st GARRISON BN, CLASS Z RESERVE.	
DETCHEON	JohnT	PTE	21										AWOL 24/12/14
DEVINE	Edwd	PTE	21 / 692									TO 26th, 25th BNS, CLASS Z RESERVE.	
DEWAR	MattB	PTE	21 / 460		28 ASKEW ROAD EAST	GATESHEAD						TO 2nd GARRISON BN, CLASS Z RESERVE.	
DICKENSON	Wm	PTE	21 / 160				5/11/14	24/4/18	GSW			TO 3rd BN.	AGE 39.
DICKIE	Thos	LCPL	21 /1060			ASHINGTON	12/11/14	18/11/18	KRpara 392	SEPT 16		TO ARMY RESERVE CLASS W.	AGE 32.
DICKINSON	Thos	PTE	21 / 651			CHOPPINGTON	9/11/14	31/5/17	WOUNDS	SEPT 16		TO DEPOT.	
DICKSON	Thos	PTE	21 /1698		58 MORTIMER STREET	HARTFORD COLLIE	16/8/15					TO 1st GARRISON BN, CLASS Z RESERVE.	
DIXON	JohnR	PTE	21 /1005			COWPEN			5/6/17	SEPT 16	ARRAS MEM	TO 20th BN(B COY).	
DIXON	Rob E	PTE	21 / 546		164 WAGONMAN ROW	FOREST HALL			10/4/17		ROCLINCOURT MIL CEM		BORN WALKER AGE 23.
DIXON	Tom	PTE	21 / 684			BLYTH			5/6/17	AUG 16	ARRAS MEM	TO 23rd, 20th(A COY) BNS.	
DOCHERTY	Jas C	PTE	21 / 355		RIDGE TERRACE	BEDLINGTON			3/6/16		BECOURT MIL CEM		AGE 32.
DODD	JohnR	PTE	21 / 235									TO 2nd GARRISON BN, CLASS Z RESERVE.	
DODDS	Jas W	PTE	21 /1720		43 CANNON STREET	NEWCASTLE						TO 2nd GARRISON BN, CLASS Z RESERVE.	
DODDS	JohnT	SGT	21 / 58		139 BOTHAL TERRACE	PEGSWOOD	6/11/14	31/1/19	KRpara 392			TO 3rd BN, ARMY RESERVE CLASS P.	
DONALDSON	James	PTE	21 /1450		1 PAN YARD	SOUTH SHIELDS	18/1/15			22/3/16, SSHOCK AUG 16		TO 1/5th BN, CLASS Z RESERVE.	
DONKIN	Henry	SGT	21 / 985		104 DISRAELI STREET	BLYTH			1/7/16		BAPAUME POST		AGE 33.
DORWARD	Geo	PTE	21 /1342			SUNDERLAND			28/6/16		BECOURT MIL CEM		
DORWARD	Wall	PTE	21 /1343	D		SUNDERLAND			1/7/16		THIEPVAL MEM		
DOUGLAS	JohnG	PTE	21 /1127				14/11/14	31/12/17	SICK			TO 3rd BN.	AGE 50.
DOUGLAS	Jos	PTE	21 / 115	A		BYKER			1/7/16		THIEPVAL MEM		BORN GATESHEAD.
DOWDALL	Wm	PTE	21 / 507	B		SHIREMOOR			10/8/16		CABERET ROUGE MIL CEM		AGE 21, BORN NEWCASTLE.
DOWER	Alf	LCPL	21 /1061			ASHINGTON	12/11/14	24/8/17	GSW	SEPT 16		TO DEPOT.	
DOWSEY	Thos	CPL	21 /1250									TO 23rd BN, CLASS Z RESERVE.	
DOWSEY	Thos	CPL	21 /1580		29 BLACK HORSE TERR	PELTON						TO 23rd BN, CLASS Z RESERVE.	
DRIFFIELD	JohnW	CSGT	21 /1106			LONGRIDGE				OCT 16		COMMISSIONED, SERVED WITH KOYLI(1st GARR BN), LABOUR CORPS	
DRURY	Harry	CSM	21 / 485		29 MARKET STREET	ALNWICK				OCT 16		TO 16th BN, OFF CADET BN, COMMISSIONED BLACK WA	TO 3CCS 2/7/16 EVAC 2/7/16 WND UPPER ARM.
DUCE	T	PTE	21 / 599	C									AGE 46.
DUFFY	ArthJ	PTE	21 /1069									TO 23rd BN, KINGS OWN YORKSHIRE LI(5th BN).	
DUNBAR	James	PTE	21 / 809	A	105 JUBILEE TERRACE	BEDLINGTON STN			1/7/16		THIEPVAL MEM		AGE 27.
DUNBAR	John	PTE	21 /1679			BELFORD			1/7/16		THIEPVAL MEM	TO 22nd BN(B COY).	BORN NEWCASTLE
DUNN	Chas	CPL	21 / 182			MORPETH			17/2/16		RUE-DU-BOIS CEM FLEURBAIX		
DUNN	Jas	PTE	21 /1196			HETTON LE HOLE			1/7/16	OCT 16	THIEPVAL MEM		BORN WILLINGTON Co DURHAM
DUNN	Robt	PTE	21 /1325				13/1/15	21/4/16				TO 29th BN.	DID NOT SERVE OVERSEAS.
DUNN	Wm	PTE	21 /1192				31/12/14	3/2/16	KRpara 392			TO 2nd GARRISON BN.	DID NOT SERVE OVERSEAS
DUNWOODIE	John	PTE	21 / 200			NEW YORK NTHBLD			27/8/18		VIS-EN-ARTOIS MEM	TO KINGS OWN YORKSHIRE LI(5th BN).	KOYLI No 63125.
DUNWOODIE	Jos R	PTE	21 / 198									TO 2nd GARRISON BN, CLASS Z RESERVE.	
DYSON	Alf	PTE	21 /1480		3 BLAST ROW	WASHINGTON STN	19/1/15	11/11/17	WOUNDS	OCT 16		TO DEPOT.	
EARL	John	PTE	21 / 353		GLADSTONE TERRACE	BEDLINGTON			29/4/17	SSHOCK AUG	ST NICHOLAS CEM		AGE 35.
EARLE	Jas B	CSM	21 / 259			CRAMLINGTON				SEPT 16		COMMISSIONED	
EASTHAUGH	Edwd	PTE	21 /1615			CHESTER LE ST				SEPT 16		TO 14th, 9th, 19th BNS, CLASS Z RESERVE.	
EASTON	Andrw	PTE	21 / 571		33 HUNTER AVENUE	BLYTH			1/7/16		THIEPVAL MEM		BORN CORNHILL ON TWEED AGE 25.
EASTON	Jos	PTE	21 / 998	C								TO 23rd BN, DURHAM LI(15th BN).	AGE 19 SIGNALLER 11 PLATOON, DURHAM LI No 46643.
EASTON	Thos	PTE	21 /1000	C								TO 23rd BN, CLASS Z RESERVE.	AGE 19 SIGNALLER 11 PLATOON.
EDWARDS	John	PTE	21 / 45				4/11/14	16/3/17	TUBERCULOS			TO DEPOT.	
EDWARDS	Robt	PTE	21 /1348			DAWDON COLL	15/1/15	30/10/17	SICK	JULY 16		TO DEPOT.	AGE 42.
ELLIOTT	David	PTE	21 /1636		116 ROSYLEN STREET	HIRST						TO 2nd GARRISON BN, CLASS Z RESERVE.	
ELLIOTT	JohnS	ASGT	21 /1469									TO 2nd GARRISON BN, CLASS Z RESERVE.	
ELLIOTT	JohnW	ACPL	21 /1699		17 MORTIMOR STREET	HARTFORD COLLIE	16/8/15						
ELLIS	John	PTE	21 / 796			BEDLINGTON			13/8/16		THIEPVAL MEM		BORN CHOPPINGTON.
ELSDON	Sydny	PTE	21 /1437		19 CAROLINE STREET	BENWELL				SEPT 16		TO 27th, 16th BNS, CLASS Z RESERVE.	
EMERY	WM	PTE	21 /1043			NEW DELAVAL						TO 11th BN, CLASS Z RESERVE.	
EMMERSON	Wm	PTE	21 / 691			BLYTH	7/11/14	31/7/17	GSW	OCT 16		TO 3rd BN.	
ENGLISH	John	PTE	21 /1685		5 PITT STREET	NEWCASTLE			19/10/17		TYNE COT MEM		
ERRINGTON	Edmd	PTE	21 /1076		35 RENFORTH STREET	DUNSTON				OCT 16		TO 25th, 26th 9th, 1st, 22nd BNS, CLASSS Z RESERVE.	
ERRINGTON	Frank	CPL	21 / 6		53 WELLINGTON STREE	NEWCASTLE			10/1/17	NOV 16	OVILLIERS MIL CEM		BORN PALLION SUNDERLAND AGE 28.
ERROLL	Wm	ASGT	21 /1053			HIRST			1/7/16		THIEPVAL MEM		BORN PEGSWOOD.

FAIRCLOTH	AdamJ	PTE	21 / 147									TO 2nd GARRISON BN, CLASS Z RESERVE.	
FARMER	W	SGT	21 /1577										
FAWCETT	Fred	SGT	21 / 482			BURNHOPE COLLIERY				SHELL SHOCK		TO DURHAM LI.	HEWER BURNHOPE COLLIERY.
FAWCUS	Edwd	PTE	21 / 82		10 ALBION STREET	HEWORTH						TO 2nd GARRISON BN, CLASS Z RESERVE.	
FENWICK	Edwd	PTE	21 / 114			NEW YORK NTHBL	6/11/14	27/3/17	WOUNDS	AUG+OCT 16		TO 80th TRAINING RESERVE BN.	
FERGUS	ThosJ	PTE	21 /1367				16/1/15	22/8/16	SICK			TO 33rd BN.	DID NOT SERVE OVERSEAS.
FERGUSON	Geo	CPL	21 /1269			SPENNYMOOR	11/1/15	21/12/17	SICK			TO 3rd BN.	AGE 34.
FERGUSON	Sam M	PTE	21 / 895		NEWLANDS	WARETON						TO 3rd BN, CLASS Z RESERVE.	
FINN	John	PTE	21 /1302		4 LOVE STREET	BELMONT						TO 1st GARRISON BN, CLASS Z RESERVE.	
FIRMAN	ThosW		21 /1620		94 RAILWAY STREET	HEBBURN COLLIER						TO CLASS Z RESERVE.	
FISHER	Jas R	PTE	21 /1701		WEST FARM	CRAMLINGTON						TO 2nd GARRISON BN.	
FISK	JohnR	PTE	21 /1087	D		BURNHOPEFIELD			1/7/16		SERRE ROAD No 2 CEM		BORN LINTZ Co DURHAM.
FITZSIMMONS	Walkr	PTE	21 / 945	C		BEDLINGTON						TO 12/13th, 1st BNS, CLASS Z RESERVE.	AGE 32.
FLOCKHART	John	PTE	21 / 341			BEDLINGTON STN	7/11/14	23/8/17	SHELLSHC	NOV 16		TO 84th TRAINING RESERVE BN.	
FORBES	Geo	PTE	21 / 280									TO MACHINE GUN CORPS.	TO 3 CCS 2/7/16 EVAC 2/7/16, MGC No 182014.
FORD	Basil	CSM	21 / 368			WIDNES LANCS			21/8/18		VIS-EN-ARTOIS MEM	TO 14th, 12/13th BNS.	
FORD	GeoWn	SGT	21 / 539			SWALWELL				SEPT 16		TO 12th BN.	
FORREST	James	PTE	21 / 588			WALLSEND	10/11/14	31/3/19	KRpara 392	OCT 16		TO DEPOT.	
FOSTER	Frank	PTE	21 / 811	A		CHOPPINGTON			1/7/16		THIEPVAL MEM		BORN WARENTON NTHBLD.
FOSTER	Geo	PTE	21 /1421		7 COUNCIL STREET	HOUGHTON				MISSING JUNE 16.		TO CLASS Z RESERVE.	PRISONER OF WAR 1916.
FOWLER	R	PTE	21 /1407		40 CHURCH STREET	MURTON DUR				SEPT 16			
FOX	JohnE	PTE	21 / 519				11/11/14	2/3/17	WOUNDS	13/3/16		TO DEPOT.	
FOX	Thos	PTE	21 /1617		5 NEAL TERRACE	TANFIELD LEA						TO 1st GARRISON BN, CLASS Z RESERVE.	
FRAZER	Peter	PTE	21 / 494	C			16/11/14	5/3/19	KRpara 392			TO ARMY RESERVE CLASS P.	STRETCHER BEARER 11 PLATOON.
FULLER	Smt E	PTE	21 / 581		8 LEAD ROAD	RYTON				MISSING 21/3/18		TO 23rd BN(D COY).	
FURNESS	JohnT	PTE	21 /1013	C		STANLEY			1/7/16		THIEPVAL MEM		SNIPER 11 PLATOON, BORN WATERHOUSES AGE 35.
GATES	Thos	PTE	21 / 443	C		SEATON BURN			1/7/16		BAPAUME POST MIL CEM		BORN MILBOURNE NTHBLD.
GATISS	Henry	PTE	21 /1330			DIPTON			6/6/17	NOV 16	F D'AMIENS, ARRAS		
GAY	Phili	PTE	21 /1100			CULLERCOATES	12/11/14	12/10/17	WOUNDS	SEPT 16		TO 3rd BN.	AGE 28.
GEDGE	Wm A	PTE	21 / 70				4/11/14	31/1/19	KRpara 392			TO ARMY RESERVE CLASS P.	
GIBSON	All W	PTE	21 / 14		74 BEDE STREET	NEWCASTLE				OCT 16		TO 20th, 25th, 12/13th BNS.	
GIBSON	Geo	SGT	21 / 686			BLYTH			30/11/18	DEC 16	ETAPLES MIL CEM	TO 12/13th BN.	BORN MURTON Co DURHAM.
GIBSON	Henry	PTE	21 / 396			BURNHOPEFIELD	9/11/14	15/12/16		SSHOCK AUG 16		TO DEPOT.	
GIBSON	ThosW	PTE	21 / 790				10/11/14	6/11/19	KRpara 392			TO 23rd, 9th BNS, DEPOT.	
GIBSON	Wm	SGT	21 /1044									TO CLASS Z RESERVE.	
GILCHRIST	John	LCPL	21 / 614			ASHINGTON	10/11/14	7/3/19	KRpara 392			TO DEPOT.	
GILROY	John	PTE	21 / 230									TO 24th, 12/13th, 23rd BNS, KINGS OWN YORKSHIRE LI(5	KOYLI No 63152.
GLASGOW	Alex	PTE	21 / 62									TO 2nd GARRISON BN, CLASS Z RESERVE.	
GORDON	Andrw	PTE	21 /1120	C		JARROW			1/7/16		THIEPVAL MEM		AGE 36 IN 11 PLATOON.
GORDON	Thos	PTE	21 / 444			SEATON BURN	9/11/14	19/12/17	GSW	NOV+DEC 16		TO 3rd BN.	AGE 28.
GORDON	Wm	PTE	21										AWOL 12/2/15.
GORMAN	Fred	SGT	21 / 346				7/11/14	1/3/19	KRpara 392			TO ARMY RESERVE CLASS P.	
GOULD	Ben H	PTE	21 /1601			FERRYHILL				SEPT+DEC 16		TO 1st, 21st BNS, KINGS OWN YORKSHIRE LI(5th BN).	KOYLI No 63149.
GOWLAND	R	PTE	21 / 476			NORTH SHIELDS				MAR 16, SSHOCK DEC 16.			
GOWLAND	Ralph	PTE	21 / 303									TO ROYAL FUSILIERS(24th BN).	FRANCE 21 10/1/16-28/8/18, 24 RF-6/1/19, RFUS No GS/93131
GRAHAM	James	PTE	21 / 73		4 COOPERATIVE BLDGS	SEATON DELAVAL						TO 3rd BN.	
GRAHAM	Jos	PTE	21 / 4			BISHOP AUKLAND			1/7/16		THIEPVAL MEM		
GRAHAM	Jos	PTE	21 / 34			RYTON				SSHCK AUG+MISS NOV 16			
GRAHAM	Mark	PTE	21 / 929			GATESHEAD			1/7/16		OVILLERS MIL CEM		BORN TWEEDMOUTH.
GRAHAM	Robt	LSGT	21 / 919		16 ELM ST BENWELL	NEWCASTLE			5/6/17	JULY 16	ARRAS MEM	TO 22nd BN(C COY).	AGE 30.
GRAHAM	Robt	PTE	21 / 102				6/11/14	8/1/15	MEDICALLY				DID NOT SERVE OVERSEAS.
GRAY	A	PTE	21 /1463	C	BELTON BANK	LESBURY	18/1/15						MACHINE GUN SECTION 11 PLATOON, AGE 30.
GRAY	Albt	PTE	21 / 556			BELMONT DURHAM			5/6/16		BECOURT MIL CEM		
GRAY	James	PTE	21 / 278			BYKER			5/6/17	SEPT 16	ARRAS MEM		
GRAY	John	PTE	21 / 782		27 LIDDELL TERRACE	GATESHEAD						TO 8th BN, CLASS Z RESERVE.	CSM.
GRAY	John	PTE	21 / 536										
GRAY	JohnT	PTE	21 /1431			DENTON BURN			5/6/17		ARRAS MEM		
GRAY	Robt	PTE	21 / 350				8/11/14	10/4/15	KRpara 392				DID NOT SERVE OVERSEAS.
GREAVES	Frank	PTE	21 / 660			CHOPPINGTON	9/11/14	17/2/19	KRpara 392	OCT 16		TO DEPOT.	
GREEN	James	LCPL	21 / 568				9/11/14	11/10/17	GSW			TO 3rd BN.	
GREEN	James	PTE	21 /1058				11/11/14	9/1/15	KRpara 392				DID NOT SERVE OVERSEAS.
GREEN	Jos	SGT	21 / 242		43 STATION ROAD	CRAMLINGTON				JUNE 16			PRISONER OF WAR 1916, INTERNED IN HOLLAND 1918.
GREEN	Matt	PTE	21 /1039			MORPETH			3/7/17		ACHIET-LE-GRAND COM	TO 25th, 1/7th BNS.	RENUMBERED 292101.
GREENFELL	Rich	SGT	21 / 263			NEW WASHINGTON	7/11/14	29/10/17	WOUNDS			TO 3rd BN.	AGE 37.
GREENWELL	W A B	SGT	21 / 697							1/4/16		TO 12/13th BN, CLASS Z RESERVE.	
GREENWOOD	Ralph	PTE	21 /1382		21 FRANCIS STREET	SEAHAM HARBOUR				OCT 16		TO 24th, 8th BNS, CLASS Z RESERVE.	
GREGORY	Cuthb	PTE	21 / 677		3 NEW ROW	ISABELLA PIT			14/7/16	AUG 16	ETAPLES MIL CEM	TO 23rd BN.	AGE 27, 3 CCS 1/7/16 GSW FACE, EVAC 2/7/16.
GRICE	Jos	LCPL	21 /1435		3 WILLIAM STREET	HOUGHTON LE SP	18/1/15			NOV 16		TO 8th, 9th BNS, KINGS OWN YORKSHIRE LI(8th BN), Z RI	AWOL 11/10/15, KOYLI No 37797.
GRIERSON	James	SGT	21 / 825		THAMES STREET	CHOPWELL			9/4/18	SEPT 16	PLOEGSTEERT MEM	TO 25th BN(D COY).	SHOWN AS 25/825 ON MEM REGISTER.
GRIFFITHS	Geo L	PIPR	21 / 558		3 ALEXANDRA STREET	CONSETT						TO 23rd, 11th BNS, KINGS OWN YORKSHIRE LI(5th BN).	KOYLI No 63154.
GRIFFITHS	JohnE	DRMR	21 / 557		1 BLUE ROW	CROOKHALL						TO 23rd BN.	
GRIGGS	James	PTE	21 /1160			SOUTH SHIELDS				SEPT 16		TO CHESHIRE REGIMENT(9th BN).	CHESHIRE REGT No 52321.
GUTHRIE	James	PTE	21 /1197			NEWCASTLE			1/7/16		THIEPVAL MEM		
GUTHRIE	John	PTE	21 / 458			BURRADON	9/11/14	8/11/17	SICK			TO 1st BN, DEPOT.	AGE 30.
HALL	Ait S	PTE	21 /1202			SUNDERLAND			12/3/16		RATION FARM MIL CEM		
HALL	David	PTE	21 /1162			NORTH SHIELDS				OCT 16		TO 26th, 25th, 1/4th BNS, CLASS Z RESERVE.	ALLOTTED NEW No 204622.
HALL	Geo	PTE	21 / 456	C	7 CAMPERDOWN AVENU	BURRADON			4/6/16		BECOURT MIL CEM		BORN DURHAM AGE 42, IN 11 PLATOON.
HALL	Geo	LCPL	21 /1222	C	45 CLEVELAND AVENUE	NORTH SHIELDS			1/7/16		THIEPVAL MEM		AGE 19 BORN TYNEMOUTH.
HALL	John	PTE	21 /1279									TO 1st GARRISON BN, CLASS Z RESERVE.	
HALL	Jos	PTE	21 /1734		60 MONK STREET	GATESHEAD			3/7/16		ALBERT COM CEM EXT	TO 20th, 23rd BNS.	AGE 18.
HALL	Thos	PTE	21 /1444			USWORTH			1/7/16		THIEPVAL MEM		
HALL	Wm	PTE	21 / 373			SOUTHMOOR			3/6/16		BECOURT MIL CEM		BORN CHESTER LE STREET
HALLIDAY	Robt	SGT	21 / 833			SWALWELL				JULY 16		TO 16th, 22nd, 9th BNS, CLASS Z RESERVE.	
HALLIDAY	Wm G	PTE	21 /1385				18/1/15	20/12/17	GSW			TO DEPOT	AGE 44.
HAMBLIN	Jos	SGT	21 /1049									TO 9th, 25th BNS, CLASSZ RESERVE.	
HAMILTON	Andw	PTE	21 / 987		14 LAUREL STREET	WALLSEND			2/3/16		RUE-DU-BOIS FLEURBAI	ATT 181 TUNNELLING COY RE.	BORN ASHINGTON AGE 42.
HAMILTON	James	PTE	21 / 166		5 CROSS ROW	HAUXLEY						TO 23rd BN.	PRISONER OF WAR.
HAMILTON	JohnW	PTE	21 / 887									TO 14th BN, ROYAL FUSILIERS(24th BN).	FRANCE 21 10/1/16-3/7/18, 14 4/7/18-28/8/18 24RF-11/11/18
HARAM	Thos	PTE	21 /1520		129 CHARTER STREET	BOLDON COLLIERY	21/1/15			SEPT 16		TO 14th BN, CLASS Z RESERVE.	
HARBRON	Wm	PTE	21 /1290			LEITH			1/7/16		THIEPVAL MEM		
HARDING	Jos	LCPL	21 / 848		57 NICHOLSON STREET	MONKHESLEDON						TO 23rd, 19th(W COY) BNS, CLASS Z RESERVE.	
HARKER	JohnR	PTE	21 / 162									TO 2nd GARRISON BN, CLASS Z RESERVE.	
HARRALD	ChasE	PTE	21 /1522		2 YORK ROAD	SEAHAM HARBOUR	20/1/15	28/10/18	GSW	NOV 16		TO 10th, 23rd, 24th BNS.	AGE 21.
HARRIS	David	SGT	21 / 858				11/11/14	12/4/19	6/4/20		BYKER & HEATON CEM	TO DEPOT.	
HARRIS	JohnO	SGT	21 / 836		7 JULIET ST ELSWICK	NEWCASTLE			1/7/16		THIEPVAL MEM		BORN GREAT YARMOUTH AGE 29.
HARRIS	JohnW	PTE	21 /1563									TO 23rd BN, CLASS Z RESERVE.	
HARRISON	Ambr	PTE	21 / 141		77 WINDY KNOOK	GATESHEAD						TO 14th BN, ROYAL FUSILIERS(24th BN).	FRANCE 21 10/1/16-3/7/18, 14 4/7/18-28/8/18, 24RF-11/11/18.
HARRISON	ThosB	PTE	21 /1360	D		TYNEMOUTH			5/6/17		ARRAS MEM		
HARRISON	Wm	PTE	21 /1204			SEATON DELAVAL	4/1/15	13/9/17	WOUNDS	OCT 16		TO 84th TRAINING RESERVE BN.	AGE 41.
HART	Arth	PTE	21 /1355				16/1/15	27/9/17	GSW			TO DEPOT.	AGE 24.
HART	Jas H	PTE	21 / 576									TO 23rd BN.	
HART	JohnW	PTE	21 / 195			NEW YORK NTHBLD			29/7/17	24/2/16	MONT-HUON MIL CEM	TO KINGS OWN YORKSHIRE LI(1/4th BN).	AGE 28 BORN EARSDON, KOYLI No 203478.
HART	Wm	PTE	21 / 11		11 BLAGDON STREET	NEWCASTLE							
HARTLEY	JohnR	SGT	21 /1388			TYNEMOUTH			9/4/17		ARRAS MEM		
HAVELOCK	Rob E	PTE	21										AWOL 4/11/15.
HAW	RobtW	PTE	21 / 40	A	31 DENE STREET	NORTH SHIELDS			1/7/16		THIEPVAL MEM		AGE 24 BORN TYNEMOUTH.
HAY	Robt	PTE	21 /1565						KRpara 392			TO 1st GARRISON BN, 26th BN.	
HAYES	JohnT	PTE	21 /1602				29/3/15	25/1/18	SICK			TO 3rd BN.	AGE 33.
HEDLEY	Wilf	PTE	21 / 763									TO 23rd BN, CLASS Z RESERVE.	
HELSDON	JohnE	LCPL	21 / 698									TO 1st, 14th, 12/13th BNS, CLASS Z RESERVE.	
HENDERSON	Geo R	PTE	21 / 801									TO 23rd, 22nd BNS, CLASS Z RESERVE.	
HENDERSON	Geo W	LCPL	21 / 685	D		BLYTH	7/11/14	27/11/16	WOUNDS	OCT 16		TO DEPOT.	
HENDERSON	John	PTE	21 / 687									TO 14th BN, ROYAL FUSILIERS(24th BN).	FRANCE 21 10/1/16-9/5/18, 14 10/5/18-28/8/18, 24RF-11/11/18.
HENDERSON	JohnY	PTE	21 / 433	C		WINLATON			1/7/16		THIEPVAL MEM		BORN NEWCASTLE
HENDERSON	Jos M	PTE	21 / 427			GATESHEAD						TO 9th, 19th BNS.	
HENDERSON	RichT	PTE	21 / 506		48 MORPETH TERRACE	PERCY MAIN			13/4/17	JULY 16	ETAPLES MIL CEM	TO 16th, 22nd BNS.	BORN SUNDERLAND AGE 26.
HENDERSON	RobtC	CSM	21 / 993		3 TWEEDY STREET	COWPEN			17/10/18		COWPEN CEM BLYTH	TO 23rd BN.	BORN HETTON LE HOLE.
HENDERSON	T	PTE	21 / 977				7/11/14	24/10/17	KRpara 392			TO 33rd BN.	DID NOT SERVE OVERSEAS, No ALSO ALLOTTED TO B MOOF
HENDERSON	Wm J	LCPL	21 / 286		MIDDLE ENGINE	PERCY MAIN			28/4/17		LEICESTER WELFORD ROAD CEM		AGE 26.
HENDERSON	Wm J	CPL	21 / 54						KRpara 392				
HEPPLE	Peter	SGT	21 / 207			NORTH SHIELDS			5/6/17		ARRAS MEM		
HEPPLE	Thos	PTE	21 /1330		6 LAURIE STREET	THROCKLEY			18/8/15		NEWBURN ST MICHAEL CHYD		No ALSO ALLOCATED TO GATTISS, AGE 18.

HERBERT	C E	PTE	21 / 439			SEATON BURN					NOV 16			
HERBERT	Robt	PTE	21 / 437										TO 23rd BN, ROYAL FUSILIERS(24th BN).	FRANCE 10/1/16-2/2/18, 23 3/2/18-28/8/18, RFUS-28/9/18.
HERRON	Alex	PTE	21 /1004			BLYTH				2/6/17	OCT 16	BUCQOUY RD CEM FICHI	TO 14th BN.	AGE 37.
HERRON	John	PTE	21 / 765										TO 23rd BN, CLASS Z RESERVE.	
HERRON	Thos	PTE	21 /1117		12 TEES STREET	CHOPWELL							TO 23rd BN, CLASS Z RESERVE.	
HESLOP	Jos	LCPL	21 /1186			HIRST					SEPT 16		TO 23rd, 9th, 18th, CLASS Z RESERVE.	
HESLOP	MattB	PTE	21 / 530			WILLINGTON QUAY	10/11/14	6/3/18	GSW		SEPT 16		TO ARMY RESERVE CLASS P.	AGE 35.
HETHERINGTON	Thos	PTE	21 /1629		JUBILLEE COTTAGES	ALNWICK MOOR				2/7/16		PUNCHVILLERS BRIT CEM		AGE 19.DIED WHILST A PATIENT AT 3CCS
HETHERINGTON	Wills	PTE	21 /1460										TO 2nd GARRISON BN, CLASS Z RESERVE.	
HETHRINGTON	J	SGT	21 / 788	A							17/2/16			
HEWITT	Tim D	PTE	21 / 631										TO 8th BN.	
HIGGINSON	Thos	PTE	21 /1212			SUNDERLAND	2/1/15	31/3/19	KRpara 392		OCT 16		TO 26th BN, ARMY RESERVE CLASS P.	
HILLS	James	CPL	21 / 654										TO 23rd BN.	
HILLS	Robt	PTE	21 / 655										TO 14th BN, ROYAL FUSILIERS(24th BN).	FRANCE 21 10/1/16-3/7/18, 14 4/7/18-28/8/18 24RF-11/11/18
HILLS	Thos	PTE	21 / 656										TO ROYAL DEFENCE CORPS.	FRANCE 10/1/16-5/1/17.RDC No 65693.
HIND	John	PTE	21 / 263		7 COOPERATIVE TERR	BURNHOPEFIELD					SEPT 16		TO ROYAL INNISKILLING FUSILIERS(6th BN).	R INNIS FUS No 21550.
HINDMARSH	Geo C	SGT	21 /1012	C	8 TEMPEST TERRACE	STANLEY							TO 25th BN, CLASS Z RESERVE.	
HINDMARSH	James	PTE	21 / 835	A	65 OSWIN AVENUE	FOREST HALL				1/7/16		THIEPVAL MEM		BORN WEST MOOR AGE 34, IN 3 PLATOON.
HIRD	Lance	PTE	21 / 602		14 WOLMERHAUSEN ST	WHEATLEY HILL							TO 14th BN.	
HODSON	John	CSM	21 /1121		HAZEL COTTAGE	SUNNISIDE GATESHEAD				9/9/17	OCT 16	JEANCOURT COM CEM EXT		RSM,AGE 36, BORN GATESHEAD.
HOGG	JohnW	PTE	21 /1041			BLYTH	9/11/14	25/8/17	SICK		OCT 16		TO 85th TRAINING RESERVE BN.	
HOGG	RobtH	PTE	21 / 974	C			9/11/14	16/8/17	GSW		NOV 16		TO 84th TRAINING RESERVE BN.	AGE 32, IN 11 PLATOON.
HOLLAND	WaltS	LCPL	21 / 236			HETTON LE HOLE				10/3/17	NOV 16	CABERET ROUGE MIL CEM		AGE 21 BORN NEWCASTLE.
HOLLIDAY	John	PTE	21 / 812			HIRST				6/8/17	SEPT 16	OOSTTAVERNE WOOD C	TO CHESHIRE REGIMENT(9th BN).	CHESHIRE REGT No 52320, BORN FLIMBY CUMBERLAND.AGE
HOLMES	Geo	PTE	21 /1260	C		SEAHAM HARBOUR					SEPT 16		TO 8th, 14th BNS, ATTACHED LIGHT TRENCH MORTAR B	IN 11 PLATOON,21 AMBT 6/7, 18 GHOSP, HSHIP 9/7/16 AGE 34
HOLMES	Thos	PTE	21 /1423		20 GARDEN STREET	NEWBOTTLE							TO 1st GARRISON BN, CLASS Z RESERVE.	AGE 48, AWOL 3/9/15.
HOLMES	ThosH	LCPL	21 /1165		25 TALBOT STREET	MURTON DUR					SEPT 16		TO 16th, 22nd BNS, CLASS Z RESERVE.	
HOOD	Jas	PTE	21 / 245										TO EAST YORKSHIRE REGT.	E YORKS No 44988, DESERTED 5/11/18.
HOOD	John	PTE	21 /1590	D	30 BARLOW	BLAYDON				5/6/17		ARRAS MEM		
HOOD	Rich	PTE	21 /1662			SUNDERLAND				1/7/16		THIEPVAL MEM	TO 23rd BN(C COY).	AGE 22 BORN BERWICK.
HOOK	James	PTE	21 / 504			CROOK				5/6/16		HEILLY STATION CEM	TO 23rd BN.	BORN DURHAM, AWOL 20/6/15 IN COURT DURHAM.
HOPE	JohnT	PTE	21 /1252										TO 23rd BN, ROYAL FUSILIERS(24th BN).	FRANCE 21 11/1/16-2/2/18, 23 3/2/18-29/8/18, RF -14/11/18.
HORNBY	Henry	PTE	21 / 110										TO 2nd GARRISON BN, CLASS Z RESERVE.	
HORSFIELD	ChasG	PTE	21 /1562		221 GILLON STREET	CORNSAY								
HOWARTH	John	PTE	21 /1556		6 MAKENDON STREET	HEBBURN COLLIERY				2/9/18		VAULX HILL CEM	TO KINGS OWN YORKSHIRE LI(5th BN).	KOYLI No 63142. BORN BRYN LANCS.
HOWE	Art W	PTE	21 / 883				11/11/14	3/8/17	WOUNDS		SEPT 16		TO 3rd BN	AGE 36.
HOWE	John	PTE	21 / 390			WHEATLEY HILL	9/11/14	26/3/18	GSW		JULY 16		TO ARMY RESERVE CLASS P.	AGE 42
HOWE	Sam	PTE	21 /1668										TO 14th BN, CLASS Z RESERVE.	
HOWMAND	Jas J	PTE	21 /1137				12/11/14	18/1/18	WOUNDS				TO DEPOT.	AGE 37.
HUDSON	Nich	PTE	21 / 675	D		NORTH SEATON				1/7/16		THIEPVAL MEM		BORN CAMBOIS.
HUGHES	Henry	PTE	21 /1429	C	7 OGDEN STREET	SUNDERLAND	18/1/15						TO 14th, 23rd BNS, KINGS OWN YORKSHIRE LI(5th BN).	AGE 25, BOMBER 11 PLATOON, KOYLI No 63161.
HUGHFF	T	PTE	21 /1126		NEWCASTLE ROW	FRAM/GATE MOOR							TO KOYLI, WEST YORKS, DURHAM LI(COMMISSION 28th	COMMISSIONED 23/10/17.
HUNT	John	PTE	21 /1409						KRpara 392					
HUNTER	John	PTE	21 / 3			BACKWORTH				1/7/16		THIEPVAL MEM		
HUNTER	Thos	PTE	21 / 499			NEWCASTLE				1/7/16		THIEPVAL MEM		BORN GATESHEAD.
HUNTER	Wm	PTE	21 /1275		43 REGENT STREET	HETTON LE HOLE				27/5/18	AUG 16	SOISSONS MEM	TO 1/4th BN(D COY SIGNAL SECTION).	TO UNIVERSITY COLLEGE HOSP LONDON 5/7/16 GSW SHOUI
HUNTER	Wm	PTE	21 / 678			PEGSWOOD	9/11/14	25/5/17	PHYSICALL				TO DEPOT.	AGE 41.
HUNTER	Wsn R	PTE	21 /1328		SANDHILL ROW	OXHILL					SEPT 16		TO 18th BN, CLASS Z RESERVE.	
HUTCHINSON	AlexO	PTE	21 /1504			NEWCASTLE				5/6/17	JULY 16	ARRAS MEM	TO 16th, 22nd(C COY) BNS.	AWOL 28/10/15.
HUTCHINSON	Jos	PTE	21 / 862		WHITE HOUSE	HEWORTH					MISSING JUNE 16		TO CLASS Z RESERVE.	PRISONER OF WAR 1916.
HUTHART	N	PTE	21											
HYDE	James	PTE	21 /1625		2 CHAPEL ROW	CAMBOIS				1/7/16		THIEPVAL MEM	TO 23rd BN(C COY).	AGE 18 BORN CAMBOIS.
INNERD	Thos	PTE	21 /1677							17/6/16		KARACHI WAR MEM PAKI	TO 2nd GARRISON BN.	
IRVING	Jas J	PTE	21 / 224			SLAGGYFORD					MISSING JUNE 16			PRISONER OF WAR 1916.
IRWIN	Geo	PTE	21 / 264		2 CALADONIA STREET	WINLATON				21/3/18		ARRAS MEM	TO 23rd BN.	BORN RYTON
JACKSON	Arn F	SGT	21 / 377											
JACKSON	Arth	PTE	21 / 817			BLYTH				24/8/18		VIS-EN-ARTOIS MEM	TO DURHAM LI(15th BN).	DLI No 46643.
JACKSON	Jas G	PTE	21 / 872	B	3 ANNIE STREET	GATESHEAD					NOV 16		TO 3rd BN.	25 AMBT 5/7 18 GHOSP HSHIP 7/7/16 CONTUSION SPINAL MU
JACKSON	John	PTE	21 / 623		9 SUNDERLAND STREE	WHEATLEY HILL				7/7/18	MISSING JUNE	COLOGNE MIL CEM		BORN WINGATE, DIED WHILST A POW AGE 31.
JACKSON	Robt	PTE	21 / 959	C		BARRINGTON COLL					MISSING JUNE 16		TO CLASS Z RESERVE.	AGE 20 IN 11 PLATOON, PRISONER OF WAR 1916.
JACKSON	Wm	PTE	21 /1170				4/1/15	15/10/17	KRpara 392				TO DEPOT.	DID NOT SERVE OVERSEAS.
JAMIESON	Wm	PTE	21 / 789	A	29 PETERS ROAD	NEWCASTLE				1/7/16		OVILLERS MIL CEM		BORN BEDLINGTON COLLIERY AGE 27.
JARDINE	Wm	PTE	21 /1693		75 BATH LANE	NEWCASTLE	18/8/15	22/11/16	WOUNDS		OCT 16		TO DEPOT.	
JARVIS	James	PTE	21 / 777			NEWCASTLE				25/10/18		BERMAIN MIL CEM	TO 25th, 1st, 24/27th, 1/6th, 14th, 9th BNS.	BORN LONGTON LANCS.
JARVIS	Wm	PTE	21 /1030										TO 23rd BN, CLASS Z RESERVE.	
JAY	Robt	PTE	21 / 307		WILSONS BLDGS	MURTON NTHBLD			KR Para 39				TO 2nd GARRISON BN.	
JEFFERSON	Robt	PTE	21 / 918			NEWCASTLE	12/11/14	13/12/17	SHELLSHOCK				TO DEPOT.	TO 3 CCS 2/7/16 EVAC 2/7/16.
JEFFREY	John	PTE	21 /1215				2/1/15	31/7/17	SICK				TO 1st GARRISON BN, DEPOT.	
JENKINS	Henry	PTE	21 /1391		15 CASTLE STREET	HYLTON							TO 1st GARRISON BN, CLASS Z RESERVE.	
JOHNSON	Anthy	PTE	21 /1312	C		HASWELL PLOUGH					MISSING JUNE 16		TO CLASS Z RESERVE.	AGE 25 IN 11 PLATOON, PRISONER OF WAR 1916.
JOHNSON	ChasE	PTE	21 / 31				4/11/14	14/12/18	SICK				TO 25th BN, DEPOT.	SGT, AGE 25.
JOHNSON	Fred	PTE	21 /1080				10/11/14	1/8/18	GSW				TO DEPOT.	AGE 27.
JOHNSON	Geo W	PTE	21 /1072			BENWELL	12/11/14	10/10/17	WOUNDS		OCT 16		TO 85th TRAINING RESERVE BN.	
JOHNSON	James	PTE	21 / 914			ELSWICK				9/4/17	JULY 16	ARRAS MEM		
JOHNSON	James	PTE	21 /1104			NEWCASTLE				1/7/16		THIEPVAL MEM		BORN HEXAM.
JOHNSON	James	PTE	21 /1256	C	11 BK CLANNY STREET	SUNDERLAND				1/7/16		THIEPVAL MEM		AGE 32.
JOHNSON	James	PTE	21 / 315			CRAWCROOK	9/11/14	1/3/18	WOUNDS		SEPT 16		TO ARMY RESERVE CLASS W.	
JOHNSON	Matt	PTE	21 / 578		11 WEST ROW	COWPEN				31/4/18		MONS BEREEN CEM	TO 23rd BN(C COY).	DIED WHILST A POW. BORN HORTON.
JOHNSON	Robt	PTE	21 /1605	D	32 SPOOR TERRACE	SOUTH SHIELDS				13/3/16		SAILLY SUR LYS CAN CEM		AGE 17.
JOHNSTON	Geo W	PTE	21 / 808				10/11/14	26/8/16	KRpara 392				TO 29th BN.	DID NOT SERVE OVERSEAS.
JOHNSTON	Jos W	PTE	21 / 772			MARYPORT				1/7/16		THIEPVAL MEM		
JONES	JohnT	PTE	21 /1722		5 MILL STREET	DUNSTON	26/8/15	4/2/16	KRpara 392				TO 2nd GARRISON BN.	DID NOT SERVE OVERSEAS.
JONES	Wm H	PTE	21 / 388		30 ANNE STREET	WHEATLEY HILL							TO 2nd GARRISON BN, CLASS Z RESERVE.	
JORDAN	Jacob	PTE	21 /1699		1 SHOTTON STREET	HARTFORD	16/8/15							
JORDAN	James	PTE	21 /1697		1 SHOTTON STREET	HARTFORD	16/8/15	31/3/19	KRpara 392				TO 22nd BN, ARMY RESERVE CLASS P.	
JULIAN	A E	PTE	21 / 356								13/3/16			
KANE	Rob J	ACPL	21 /1643		14 RAVENSWORTH TER	BEDLINGTON				17/9/16		RATION FARM CEM		BORN HENSINGHAM CUMBERLAND.
KAY	Thos	PTE	21 / 481			PERCY MAIN				27/6/16		BECOURT MIL CEM		BORN DURHAM
KEMP	Henry	PTE	21 /1511		37 WALKER RD	NEWCASTLE	20/1/15			12/4/17	OCT 16	AUBIGNY COM CEM EXT		
KENNEDY	Art J	PTE	21 / 559			CRAGHEAD				20/4/18		NIEUPORT MEM	TO 23rd BN.	BORN LEADGATE.
KENT	John	PTE	21 /1609			BEARPARK	10/4/15	10/1/18	WOUNDS		SEPT 16			AGE 37.
KILPATRICK	Jn E	LCPL	21 / 921			BACKWORTH	11/11/14	28/6/17	KRpara 392		AUG 16		TO 22nd BN, DEPOT.	
KING	Frank	PTE	21 / 516				11/11/14	9/8/18	KRpara 392				TO 33rd BN.	DID NOT SERVE OVERSEAS.
KINSEY	Geo	PTE	21 /1420		30 JOHN STREET	BLAYDON							TO 1/7th BN, CLASS Z RESERVE.	
KIRBY	R	PTE	21			DAWDON COLL					FEB 16			
KIRK	Walt	PTE	21 / 664				9/11/14	31/10/18	KRpara 392				TO DEPOT.	
KIRKLAND	Robt	PTE	21 /1128						KRpara 392					
KIRKWOOD	Wm	PTE	21 / 131										TO 23rd BN.	
KNOTTS	Thos	PTE	21 / 886						KRpara 392				TO 1st GARRISON BN.	
LAMB	David	PTE	21 / 822	A		WHEATLEY HILL				1/7/16		THIEPVAL MEM		BORN EASINGTON LANE.
LAMBERT	Geo	PTE	21 /1272			HEXAM	11/1/15	26/7/17	GSW		OCT 16		TO 3rd BN.	2nd STHN GHOSP BRISTOL 8/7/16.
LANGTON	ThosE	PTE	21 /1255	D		RYHOPE				1/7/16		THIEPVAL MEM		BORN SOUTH HETTON.
LAUDERDALE	Edwd	PTE	21 / 538				10/11/14	8/4/18	SPINAL INJ				TO ARMY RESERVE CLASS P.	AGE 41.
LAVERICK	Wm	PTE	21 / 446			SEATON BURN					SEPT 16		TO 20th, 8tH, 1/7th BNS.	
LAVERTON	Fred	PTE	21 /1374			CONSETT			KRpara 392		JULY 16		TO UNKNOWN TERRITORIAL FORCE BN.	ALLOTTED NEW NUMBER 204174.
LAWSON	Geo	LCPL	21 / 68			WALKER				1/7/16	AUG 16	THIEPVAL MEM		BORN SEGHILL.
LAWTON	Wm S	PTE	21 / 904			NEWCASTLE	12/11/14	2/5/17	WOUNDS		SEPT 16		TO DEPOT.	
LAYBOURNE	Geo	PTE	21 /1647		HARTLEPOOL STREET	THORNLEY								
LEADBITTER	Chris	PTE	21 / 241		52 BENSHAM CRESENT	GATESHEAD			KRpara 392		SEPT 16		TO 23rd BN.	
LEADBITTER	Thos	PTE	21 / 185			NEW YORK NTHBL	5/11/14	19/12/17	SICK		SSHOCK AUG 16		TO 3rd BN.	AGE 32.
LEE	James	PTE	21 /1350	C		EASINGTON COLL				1/7/16		THIEPVAL MEM		BORN BARNARD CASTLE.
LEE	John	PTE	21 /1379						KRpara 392					
LEGENDER	Geo	LCPL	21 / 13		22 WESLEY STREET	NEWCASTLE								NAME SPELT DE GENDER IN AVL.
LIDDLE	Robns	PTE	21 / 879			HENDON				12/3/16		RATION FARM MIL CEM		
LIDDLE	Wm	CPL	21 / 573	C		SOUTH NEWSHAM				1/7/16		THIEPVAL MEM	ATTACHED 102nd LIGHT TRENCH MORTAR BATTERY.	AGE 19 IN 11 PLATOON.
LIEGHTLEY	Robt	LCPL	21 /1313	C		ACKLINGTON							TO 23rd, 24th, 24/27th BNS, CLASS Z RESERVE.	AGE 34 BOMBER 11 PLATOON.
LILLIE	JohnT	LCPL	21 / 126	A	38 COOPERATIVE TERR	NEW DELAVAL				1/7/16		THIEPVAL MEM		BORN HORTON AGE 25.
LISTER	Wm	PTE	21 /1468	D	31 CARON STREET	DAWDON				1/7/16		THIEPVAL MEM		BORN SUNDERLAND.
LITHERLAND	Thos	SGT	21 / 486			FENCEHOUSES	9/11/14	18/7/17	WOUNDS		OCT 16		TO DEPOT.	
LITTLE	Geo	PTE	21 /1055			ASHINGTON	13/11/14	1/4/19	KRpara 392		OCT 16		TO 1/6th, 19th BNS, ARMY RESERVE CLASS P.	
LITTLEJOHN	Henry	PTE	21 /1655			NEWCASTLE					OCT 16		TO 16th, 22nd, 24/27th, 9th BNS, CLASS Z RESERVE.	
LIVESAY	Thos	SGT	21 / 728			BISHOP AUKLAND	9/11/14	29/4/18	GSW				TO DEPOT.	AGE 38, BEAUFORT WAR HOSP BRISTOL 11/7/16.

LOAN	James	PTE	21 / 32				4/11/14	20/9/18	VDH			TO DEPOT.	AGE 23.
LOCKEY	Peter	PTE	21 / 69		7 MILBURN TERRACE	HOLYWELL			30/1/15		EARSDON ST ALBAN'S CH YD		BORN ALNWICK.
LOFTUS	Andrw	PTE	21 /1498									TO ROYAL DEFENCE CORPS.	FRANCE 10/1/16-3/7/16. RDC No 69692.
LOGAN	Wm	PTE	21 / 157			BARRINGTON			14/6/17		MENIN GATE MEM	TO KOYLI(1/4th BN), 13th, 8th BNS NTHBLD FUS.	BORN FELLING, KOYLI No 7107.
LONG	Harry	PTE	21 /1642			HIRST			17/10/17		CEMENT HOUSE CEM LA	TO 19th, 25th BNS.	
LONGSTAFF	Jos H	PTE	21 / 265		15 ALMA TERRACE	RYTON						TO 23rd BN.	
LOVEKIN	Thos	PTE	21 / 931									TO ROYAL INNISKILLING FUSILIERS(6th BN).	R INNIS FUS No 21562.
LOWES	Geo	LCPL	21 / 289			CHOPPINGTON			1/7/16		THIEPVAL MEM		BORN THROCKLEY.
LUKE	James	PTE	21 /1368			USWORTH	16/1/15	27/7/17	SICK	OCT 16		TO 26th, 3rd BNS.	
LYONS	John	SGT	21 / 680			GATESHEAD			12/8/16		ETAPLES MIL CEM		
LYONS	JohnR	PTE	21 /1138	D	2 NEW ROW	ISABELLA PIT			1/7/16		THIEPVAL MEM		BORN CROFTON AGE 23.
LYONS	ThosE	CPL	21 / 165				4/11/14	11/6/18	INJURIES			TO ARMY RESERVE CLASS P.	AGE 28.
MacDONALD	Wm	PTE	21 /1637									TO 14th BN, ROYAL FUSILIERS(24th BN).	FRANCE 21 10/1/16-3/7/18, 14 4/7/18-28/8/18, 24RF-9/1/19.
MacFARLANE	Jos A	PTE	21 / 487			NEWBIGGIN/SEA	10/11/14	30/4/18	GSW			TO DEPOT.	AGE 22.
MACKENZIE	ThosR	PTE	21 / 975	C		NEWSHAM				JULY 16		TO ROYAL DEFENCE CORPS	IN 11 PLATOON.FRANCE 10/1/16-16/6/16.RDC No 61166.
MACKIE	Thos	PTE	21 / 304										
MADDEN	John	PTE	21 /1356				18/1/15	3/7/16	KRpara 392			TO 1st GARRISON, 2nd BNS, DEPOT.	
MADDISON	Jos	LCPL	21 / 305			MONKSEATON						TO 14th, 9th BNS.	
MAHON	John	PTE	21 /1575									TO 1st GARRISON BN, CLASS Z RESERVE.	
MAIN	Alex	PTE	21 /1164			NORTH SHIELDS			1/7/16		CERISY GAILLY CEM		BORN TYNEMOUTH
MAIN	Wm	PTE	21 / 187									TO 14th, 17th BNS.	
MAIN	Wm H	LCPL	21 / 900			SEATON HIRST						TO CLASS Z RESERVE.	
MAITLAND	John	PTE	21 /1675		22 CARLIOL SQUARE	NEWCASTLE	12/8/15		KRpara 392			TO 23rd BN.	
MARLEY	Isaac	PTE	21 /1211	D	2 BARRON STREET CAS	SUNDERLAND			2/7/16		MEAULTE MIL CEM		AGE 44.
MARSDEN	Jos	PTE	21 /1427		8 GREGSTON TERR	SEAHAM COLLIERY						TO 23rd BN, CLASS Z RESERVE.	
MARSTON	Albt	PTE	21 / 471			GATESHEAD			23/3/18		ETAPLES MIL CEM		
MARTIN	Normn	PTE	23 / 103		42 COPELAND TERRACI	SHIELDFIELD	20/11/14	11/3/18	GSW L ARI	1/7/16		TO 85th TRG RES BN.	HOSP ROUEN, ORPINGTON MIL HOSP 7/16, REACHED GERM.
MASON	Edwd	PTE	21 / 962	C		BEDLINGTON			4/6/16		BECOURT MIL CEM		AGE 41 IN 11 PLATOON.
MATTHEWS	Wm	PTE	21 /1418			RYHOPE	16/1/15	21/5/17	WOUNDS	NOV 16		TO DEPOT.	
MAUGHAN	Edwd	LCPL	21 / 770		COPELAND LANE	WEST AUKLAND			12/3/16		RATION FARM CEM		
MAUGHAN	W	PTE	21 / 384	D		HIGH SPEN				SEPT 16			101 AMBT 3/7 TO 18 GHOSP HSHIP 9/7 WND LEG+R ARM AGE
MAXWELL	Alex	PTE	21 / 383			WALLSEND	9/11/14	11/5/17	WOUNDS			TO ARMY RESERVE CLASS W.	AGE 26.
McALLISTER	Andrw	PTE	21 /1261			DAWDON			18/10/17		TYNE COT MEM	ATTACHED 102nd LIGHT TRENCH MORTAR BATTERY.	BORN GRANGETOWN.
McARTHUR	JohnA	PTE	21 /1512		113 MAUGHAN STREET	NEWCASTLE			7/10/19		ST JOHNS WESTGATE &	TO 23rd BN, CLASS Z RESERVE.	AGE 37.
McARTHUR	Lesli	PTE	21 /1735			WHITLEY BAY			1/7/16		THIEPVAL MEM	TO 20th BN. *	
McCABE	James	PTE	21										AWOL 25/7/15.
McDONALD	Anthy	PTE	21 / 49	A		PERCY MAIN			1/7/16		THIEPVAL MEM		BORN NORTH SHIELDS, DESERTED 17/5/15.
McDONALD	Wm	CSM	21 /1570		32 SALTWELL PLACE	GATESHEAD	8/3/15	3/2/19	SICK	NOV 16		TO 3rd BN.	AGE 41.
McEVOY	Edwd	PTE	21 /1732				25/8/15	27/4/16	KRpara 392			TO 29th BN.	DID NOT SERVE OVERSEAS.
McGARRIGLE	Wm	PTE	21 / 792		33 ELLIOTT STREET	NEWSHAM			12/3/16		RATION FARM MIL CEM		AGE 29 BORN BLYTH.
McGARVIE	Wm	PTE	21 / 863		58 D STREET EAST	PELTON						TO 2nd, 14th BNS, CLASS Z RESERVE.	
McGEE	Robt	PTE	21 /1316			FENCEHOUSES			1/7/16		THIEPVAL MEM		BORN WEST RAINTON.
McGREGOR	Thos	CPL	21 / 643									TO 23rd BN.	
McGUIRE	John	PTE	21 /1068				12/11/14	1/3/19	KRpara 392			TO 12/13th BN, DEPOT.	
McGUIRE	Wm H	PTE	21 / 298									TO 1st GARRISON BN, CLASS Z RESERVE.	
McKENZIE	Wm D	CSM	21 / 882		800 SHIELDS ROAD	WALKERGATE			5/9/19		BYKER & HEATON CEM	TO 8th, 23rd BNS, CLASS Z RESERVE.	AGE 37.
McKEOWN	Hugh	PTE	21 / 701				7/11/14	8/10/18	SICK			TO DEPOT	AGE 32.
McKIE	JohnJ	PTE	21 / 852						KRpara 392				
McLEAN	James	PTE	21 / 425						11/9/17		THIEPVAL MEM		
McMURDO	J W C	PTE	21 /1567									TO 23rd BN, CLASS Z RESERVE.	
McNAB	John	PTE	21 / 55				6/11/14	22/12/17	GSW			TO DEPOT.	AGE 22.
McROY	David	PTE	21 /1478									TO 22nd, 1st, 12/13th BNS, CLASS Z RESERVE.	
McTARNEY	James	PTE	21 / 501									TO 23rd BN.	
MEIN	Robt	PTE	21 / 296				8/11/14	31/3/19	KRpara 392			TO 1st, 2nd, 14th BNS, ARMY RESERVE CLASS P.	
MEIR	Sam	PTE	21 /1459		50 HENRY STREET	SEAHAM HARBOUI	19/1/15	11/12/17	SICK			TO 3rd BN.	AGE 43.
MELVIN	Walt	PTE	21 / 633				7/11/14	28/10/18	GSW			TO 23rd, 1/4th BNS, DEPOT.	AGE 30.
MERTON	Wm	PTE	21 /1525		79 SUNDERLAND STREI	HOUGHTON	20/1/15			JUILY 16		TO 22nd, 20th, 10th BNS, CLASS Z RESERVE.	
MIDDLEMAS	James	PTE	21 /1489		CARVEY COTTAGE	COXGREEN	19/1/15		KRpara 392			TO 2nd BN.	
MIDDLETON	JohnR	PTE	21 / 570	C			9/11/14		SICK			TO 23rd, 22nd BNS.	AGE 24 PIONEER 11 PLATOON.
MIDDLETON	JohnW	PTE	21 / 290			BEDLINGTON			17/10/17		TYNE COT MEM		AWOL 3/1/16.
MILBURN	JohnP	SGT	21 /1014		32 SEA VIEW VILLAS	CRAMLINGTON			31/8/17		TINCOURT NEW BRIT CEM		BORN BLYTH AGE 40.
MILLER	Art N	PTE	21 /1166			SEAHAM HARBOUR				SEPT 16		TO CHESHIRE REGT(9th BN).	CHESHIRE REGT No 52315
MILLER	Frank	PTE	21 /1519		38 SUNNISIDE SOUTH	NEWBOTTLE			21/11/18		CAUDAY BRIT CEM	TO 22nd, 1st, 14th BNS.	
MILLER	James	PTE	21 / 152	A		WALLSEND			1/7/16		OVILLERS MIL CEM		
MILLER	John	PTE	21 / 973					11/1/19				TO KINGS OWN YORKSHIRE LI.	KOYLI No 68679.
MILLER	Wm	PTE	21 /1571									TO ROYAL DEFENCE CORPS.	FRANCE 10/1/16-4/7/16.RDC No 65387.
MILLIGAN	Thos	PTE	21 / 254		14 CHURCH ROAD	FERRYHILL			5/6/16		BECOURT MIL CEM		BORN DURHAM, AGE 30.
MILNE	JohnG	PTE	21 / 269		44 RABY STREET	GATESHEAD				MISSING AUG 16			PRISONER OF WAR 1916.
MITCHELL	James	PTE	21 / 933			STAKEFORD				SEPT 16, MISS 21/3/18		TO 1st, 20th, 22nd(C COY) BNS, CLASS Z RESERVE.	
MITCHELL	John	PTE	21 /1691	B	71 WORSLEY STREET	SWINTON MCHSTR			1/7/16		THIEPVAL MEM	TO 22nd BN.	BORN OLDHAM LANCS AGE 42.
MITCHINSON	A	PTE	21 /1093	C						MISSING 5/6/17			
MOAT	JohnW	PTE	21 / 894			GOSFORTH			1/7/16		THIEPVAL MEM		
MOFFATT	Hugh	PTE	21 /1513		20 WINNIFORD GARDEN	WALLSEND				MISSING 30/4/18		TO 23rd(C COY) BN.	
MOLE	John	PTE	21 / 515		93 SALTERS ROAD	GOSFORTH			27/6/16		BECOURT MIL CEM		
MOLLON	Henry	CQMS	21 / 92				6/11/14	27/11/16	SICK				MOLLON IN SWB LIST.
MOORE	Benj	PTE	21 / 997			SLEEKBURN	9/11/14	26/2/19	KRpara 392	SSHOCK AUG 16		TO ARMY RESERVE CLASS P.	
MOORE	Robt	PTE	21 /1372			CONSETT			KRpara 392				
MORALEE	Wm H	LCPL	21 / 371		3 THE GARTHS	LANCHESTER				SS AUG,WNDOCT16,M 21/3/18		TO 16th, 22nd(A COY) BNS.	ACTING CSM A COY 22nd BN.POW.HEWER BURNHOPE COLL
MORGAN	Fred	PTE	21 /1566		SAND PITTS COTTAGE	GROVE STURRY CANTERBURY			27/9/18		CHAPEL CORNER SAUCH	TO 18th, 8th BNS.	AGE 32, BORN MARGATE KENT.
MORGAN	RichH	PTE	21 /1038			BLYTH	7/11/14	29/5/17	WOUNDS	SEPT 16		TO NORTHERN COMMAND DEPOT.	
MORGAN	Steph	PTE	21 /1059			MORPETH			5/6/17		ARRAS MEM	TO 16th, 22nd BNS.	
MORRIS	Alex	PTE	21 / 991	C	21 GLOUCESTER STREI	NEW HARTLEY			1/7/16		THIEPVAL MEM		AGE 21 IN 10 PLATOON.
MORRISON	James	PTE	21 /1303			MARYPORT			14/3/16		RATION FARM CEM		REAL NAME JAMES MINSHAM.
MORTON	Wm	PTE	21 /1006		12 HIGH QUAY	BLYTH			25/6/16		BECOURT MIL CEM		AGE 25 BORN HEXAM.
MOSCROP	David	PTE	21 / 469	C	123 SALTWELL ROAD	GATESHEAD			1/7/16		THIEPVAL MEM		BORN BELLINGHAM, AGE 32.
MOSCROP	Geo	PTE	21 / 339							1/4/16		TO 1st, 24th, 24/27th, 23rd BNS.	
MOULE	C E	PTE	21 / 108		75 HAIG STREET	DUNSTON			22/12/17		WHICKHAM CEM	TO 22nd BN.	AGE 43.
MUIR	John	PTE	21 / 493			BENWELL	11/11/14	14/8/17	GSW	JULY 16		TO DEPOT.	
MURPHY	Mich	PTE	21 / 211			SHIREMOOR		14/12/18		JULY 16		TO KINGS OWN YORKSHIRE LI.	KOYLI No 48330.
MURPHY	Thos	PTE	21 / 291			BEDLINGTON	8/11/14	26/10/16	KRpara 392	DEC 16		TO DEPOT.	
MURPHY	Wm	LCPL	21 /1558			WHEATLEY HILL				NOV 16	DOCHY FARM NEW BRIT	TO ROYAL INNISKILLING FUSILIERS(8th BN).	R INNIS FUS No 21429, BORN CARLISLE.
MUSGROVE	Wm Ed	PTE	21 / 400		5 BEECHGROVE TERRA	CHOPWELL	9/11/14	3/12/18	GSW	JULY 16, MISS 21/3/18		TO 25th, 23rd, 22nd(C COY) BNS, DEPOT.	AGE 34, TO 3CCS 2/7/16 EVAC 2/7/16 WND BACK.
MYERS	Thos	PTE	21 /1258		7 RADCLIFFE STREET	BIRTLEY						TO 1st GARRISON BN, CLASS Z RESERVE.	
NAISBETT	Thos	PTE	21 /1486		8 SEYMOUR STREET	HORDEN	15/1/15	25/8/16	SHELLSHC	JULY 16		TO DEPOT.	
NASEBY	James	PTE	21 /1344										POSSIBLY 20/1344??
NASH	Henry	PTE	21 /1536			SEAHAM HARBOUI	20/1/15	17/12/17	GSW	AUG 16		TO DEPOT.	
NEEDHAM	Geo E	PTE	21 / 74			CRAMLINGTON	6/11/14	13/6/17	GSW	OCT 16		TO DEPOT.	AGE 25.
NELSON	James	PTE	21 /1051			BLYTH			26/6/16		HEILLY STATION CEM		
NELSON	Thos	PTE	21 /1419			CONSETT	18/1/15	22/8/17	WOUNDS	OCT 16		TO 84th TRAINING RESERVE BN.	AGE 39.
NESBITT	Geo	PTE	21 / 922			BEDLINGTON			19/10/17		TYNE COT MEM		
NEWTON	Al A	CPL	21 / 590			NEWCASTLE				SEPT 16			
NICHOL	Chas	PTE	21 /1709			WEST HARTLEPOOL			7/10/18		DOINET COM CEM EXT	TO DURHAM LI(13th BN).	DURHAM LI No 46042, AGE 20.
NICHOL	Chas	PTE	21 /1694		33 HUDSON STREET	NEWCASTLE	16/8/15						
NICHOL	David	PTE	21 /1289			NORTH SHIELDS				JULY 16			DESERTED 25/11/16
NICHOL	John	PTE	21 / 553			WHEATLEY HILL	11/11/14	14/2/17	GSW	AUG 16		TO 16th, 22nd BNS, DEPOT.	AGE 29.
NICHOL	Robt	PTE	21 / 636	D		BACKWORTH			1/7/16		THIEPVAL MEM		BORN NEWCASTLE.
NICHOLSON	James	PTE	21 / 669			BEDLINGTON			30/6/16		ST SEVER CEM ROUEN		BORN GATESHEAD
NICHOLSON	John	PTE	21 /1305		48 SOUTH ROW SUNNIS	FENCEHOUSES	13/1/15	4/2/19	MALARIA			TO BORDER REGT, LABOUR CORPS.	AGE 40, 112 DAYS DETENTION(STRIKING NCO) 6/7/15. POSTE
NICHOLSON	Rich	PTE	21 /1129	A		CHOPPINGTON			1/7/16	1/4/16	THIEPVAL MEM		BORN NEW ZEALAND.
NICHOLSON	Rob H	PTE	21 / 874	B					14/11/15		ST JOHNS WESTGATE NEWCASTLE		ACCIDENTALLY KILLED DURING TRAINING.
NICHOLSON	Thos	LCPL	21 / 217			FOREST HALL				OCT 16			
NICHOLSON	ThosW	LCPL	21 /1208		57 BRIGHT STREET	MONKWEARMOUTI	4/1/15	15/4/19		5/6/17		TO ROYAL DEFENCE CORPS.(STANHOPE POW CAMP).	FRANCE 10/1/16-12/6/17.RDC No 72961.BURNT DOCS
NICHOLSON	Wm	PTE	21 / 671			BEDLINGTON			2/7/16		ST SEVER CEM ROUEN		BORN GATESHEAD
NIGHTINGALE	Thos	PTE	21 / 885		2 FRONT ST PRESTON	NORTH SHIELDS			16/5/16	13/3/16	SAILLY SUR LYS CAN CEM		AGE 37.
NOBLE	Matt	PTE	21 / 47		6 TYNE VIEW	HOWDEN ON TYNE			12/7/16	SEPT 16	WALLSEND CHURCH BANK CEM		AGE 28 BORN BACKWORTH.
NOBLE	Wm	PTE	21 /1094		77 WALKER RD	BYKER			9/4/17	AUG 16	BAILLEUL RD EAST CEM	TO 16th, 22nd(C COY) BNS.	1st SCOTTISH GHOSP ABERDEEN 7/16, AGE 22 BORN WALLS
NOONE	Thos	PTE	21 / 399	C	5 BEECH GROVE	BLACKHALL MILL			9/7/16		BOULOGNE EASTERN CEM		AGE 30 BORN ROSSCOMMON IRELAND, IN 11 PLATOON.
NURSE	Jos	SGT	21 /1189		1 CHURCH ROAD	HETTON LE HOLE	20/1/15	10/8/19	KRpara 392			TO 12/13th, 23rd BNS, DEPOT.	
O'BRIAN	Andrw	PTE	21 / 695				16/11/14	21/4/16	KRpara 392			TO 29th BN.	DID NOT SERVE OVERSEAS.
O'CONNELL	Edwd	PTE	21 / 104		12 GARDEN ST BENWEL	NEWCASTLE						TO 2nd GARRISON BN, CLASS Z RESERVE.	BROTHER IN LAW OF 26/92 CPL PETER BARRETT.
OGDEN	FredA	PTE	21 / 474			JARROW	11/11/14	18/3/19	KRpara 392	NOV 16		TO DEPOT.	TO 18 G HOSP 2/7/16 EVAC HSHIP CALAIS 5/7 WND L LEG.
OLIVER	Jas A	PTE	21 /1703			NEWCASTLE			18/6/17		BAILLEUL RD EAST CEM		AWOL 27/10/15

OLIVER	John	PTE	21 / 333			CHOPPINGTON	7/11/14	16/7/17	GSW	OCT 16		TO DEPOT.	TO 3CCS 2/7/16 EVAC 2/7/16 WND LEGS.
ORD	JohnR	PTE	21 / 525		25 BOWES TERRACE	HOBSON			5/10/17		GODEWAERSVELDE BRI	TO KINGS OWN YORKSHIRE LI(9th BN).	AGE 38 BORN WHICKHAM.
ORD	Wm G	SGT	21 / 428			BURNOPFIELD				JULY 16		TO 1st BN.	
ORMISTON	Geo W	PTE	21 / 679			ISABELLA PIT			3/7/16		HEILLY STATION CEM		BORN BOSTON FENS LINCS.
OWENS	Edwd	PTE	21 / 824	A		WHEATLEY HILL			1/7/16		THIEPVAL MEM		BORN SEDGEFIELD.
OXENHAM	Rich	PTE	21 /1394	A	CASTLE ROW	SUNDERLAND			1/7/16	MISS NOV 16	THIEPVAL MEM		BORN HOUGHTON LE SPRING
OXLEY	JohnG	PTE	21 / 395			BURNOPFIELD			14/10/17		SOLFERINO FARM CEM		BORN NEWCASTLE
PALMER	JohnR	SGT	21 / 288				8/11/14	3/3/19	KRpara 392				
PARKER	Alf	PTE	21 / 534				11/11/14	23/10/17	SICK			TO ARMY RESERVE CLASS W.	DID NOT SERVE OVERSEAS.
PARKER	Geo	PTE	21 / 762			DUDLEY			26/10/17	AUG 16	TYNE COT MEM	TO 14th, 1st, 1/7th BNS.	BORN NEWCASTLE, AGE 34.
PARKER	JohnJ	LCPL	21 / 450							MISSING 11/4/18		TO 23rd, 25th BNS.	
PARKER	Jothn	PTE	21 / 611		2 LOCA STREET	DINNINGTON							
PARNABY	Alf	PTE	21 /1516				9/1/15	23/10/17	SICK			TO ARMY RESERVE CLASS W.	DID NOT SERVE OVERSEAS.
PASCOE	G	LCPL	21 /1214										P14 SWB LIST.
PATTEN	Wm	PTE	21 / 174			SOUTH SHIELDS	6/11/14	29/10/17	WOUNDS	JULY 16		TO 3rd BN.	AGE 41.
PATTERSON	Jas E	CSM	21 / 840		78 ROOSLEY AVENUE	GATESHEAD						ATTACHED BRITISH WEST INDIES REGT(9th BN), CLASS Z RESERVE.	
PATTIE	Thos	PTE	21 / 362									TO 14th BN, ROYAL FUSILIERS(24th BN).	FRANCE 21 10/1/16-3/7/18, 14 4/7/18-28/8/18, 24RF-11/11/18.
PATTIE	Wm	PTE	21 / 363									TO 14th BN, ROYAL FUSILIERS(24th BN).	FRANCE 21 10/1/16-3/7/18, 14 4/7/18-28/8/18, 24RF-11/11/18.
PATTISON	C T E	CPL	21 / 128			BLYTH							
PEACOCK	Rich	PTE	21 / 846		2 THIRD STREET	WHEATLEY HILL						TO 2nd GARRISON BN, CLASS Z RESERVE.	
PEARSON	JohnT	PTE	21 /1167			SEAHAM HARBOUR				SEPT 16		TO 1st, 23rd BNS, CLASS Z RESERVE.	TO 3CCS 2/7/16 EVAC 2/7/16 WND LEGS.
PEEL	Edwd	PTE	21 / 957	C		BARRINGTON				MISSING JUNE 16		TO CLASS Z RESERVE.	IN 11 PLATOON, PRISONER OF WAR 1916.
PENDRICK	James	PTE	21 / 335	C		CHOPPINGTON			1/7/16		THIEPVAL MEM		BORN NEWCASTLE, MACHINE GUN SECTION.
PETRIE	Geo C	PTE	21 / 316		86 ELSWICK EAST TERF	NEWCASTLE			16/6/16		HEILLY STATION CEM		AGE 26 BORN GATESHEAD.
PHAROAH	Jos	PTE	21 / 192				5/11/14	22/4/18	GSW			TO DEPOT.	AGE 31.
PHILIPSON	Mich	PTE	21 / 986	C		NEWSHAM			1/7/16		THIEPVAL MEM		AGE 34 BORN ELSDON, BOMBER 11 PLATOON.
PHILLIPS	Geo	PTE	21 /1065									TO 23rd, 10th BNS, CLASS Z RESERVE.	
PHILLIPS	James	PIPR	21 /1151		4 BURN AVE	FOREST HALL			1/7/16		THIEPVAL MEM		BORN NEWCASTLE AGE 41, STEP FATHER OF PIPER JAS CAI
PHILLIPS	John	PIPR	21										SON OF 21/1225.
PHILLIPS	JohnM	PIPR	21 /1225			SUNDERLAND			2/9/18	JULY 16	VIS-EN-ARTOIS MEM	TO KINGS OWN YORKSHIRE LI(5th BN).	BORN HEBBURN
PIGFORD	Robt	PTE	21 /1582		7 CHAPEL ROW	PENSHAW						TO 2nd GARRISON BN, CLASS Z RESERVE.	
PINE	Sam J	SGT	21 /1479		11 SOUTH JAMES ST	MURTON DUR	18/1/15	13/3/19	KRpara 392	OCT 16		TO ARMY RESERVE CLASS P.	
PINKERTON	Wm	PTE	21 / 562	C	28 LIME STREET	SOUTHMOOR			1/7/16		OVILLERS MIL CEM		AGE 21.
POOLEY	Edwd	CPL	21 / 212			NORTH SHIELDS			27/3/18	OCT 16	ARRAS MEM	TO 9th, 1st BNS.	BORN SUNDERLAND.
POTTS	Geo H	PTE	21 / 151				3/11/14	3/3/15	KRpara 392			TO DEPOT.	DID NOT SERVE OVERSEAS.
POTTS	Wm I	PTE	21 / 312		30 VIOLET ST BENWELL	NEWCASTLE			1/7/16		THIEPVAL MEM		AGE 42 BORN GATESHEAD.
POULTON	J J W	CPL	21 / 251			EAST STANLEY	7/11/14	24/8/17	GSW	JULY 16		TO DEPOT.	
PREECE	C	PTE	21 / 860										
PRICE	John	PTE	21 /1393	A	12 OSWALD TERRACE	CASTLETOWN			1/7/16		BAPAUME		BORN HANLEY STAFFS.
PRINCE	Dan	PTE	21 /1719			NEW BRANCEPETH	23/8/15	27/2/18	GSW	OCT 16		TO 23rd BN, ARMY RESERVE CLASS P.	AGE 38.
PRINGLE	Geo	PTE	21 /1007				9/11/14	31/3/19	KRpara 392			TO 23rd BN, ARMY RESERVE CLASS P.	
PRINGLE	Jos	ASGT	21 / 266										No ALSO ALLOTED TO J BARTRAM.
PRINGLE	Thos	PTE	21 / 813			BEDLINGTON			8/4/18	OCT 16	NIEUPORT MEM	TO 23rd BN.	
PROCTOR	Wm	PTE	21 / 404		12 OAK TERRACE	WINLATON							
PUNTER	Albt	CPL	21 /1315			ALNWICK			1/7/16		THIEPVAL MEM	TO 23rd BN.	
PURDY	JohnA	PTE	21 /1705		494 TIN STREET	CROOKHALL						TO 2nd GARRISON BN, CLASS Z RESERVE.	
PURDY	Jos	PTE	21 / 184									TO 2nd GARRISON BN.	
PURDY	Wm	PTE	21 /1092				10/11/14	1/4/19	KRpara 392			TO ARMY RESERVE CLASS P.	
RACE	Chas	PTE	21 /1497		36 JOHNSON TERR	USWORTH	19/1/15	27/4/17	WOUNDS	OCT 16		TO DEPOT.	
RACE	Geo	PTE	21 / 526			BURNHOPEFIELD	11/11/14	30/5/17	WOUNDS	OCT 16		TO DEPOT.	
RACE	Thos	PTE	21 /1496									TO DURHAM LIGHT INFANTRY, TRAINING RESERVE BN.	TRG RES No TR/5/59089.
RAILTON	Henry	PTE	21 / 672				9/11/14	7/4/16	KRpara 392			TO 1st GARRISON BN, DEPOT.	
RAMSAY	Wm	PTE	21 /1134		48 PILGRIM STREET	NEWCASTLE			3/11/18		RUESNES COM CEM	TO 23rd BN, KINGS OWN YORKSHIRE LI(5th BN).	KOYLI No 63206. BORN ALNWICK AGE 39.
RAMSBOTTOM	Albt	PTE	21 /1526		23 LAMBTON STREET	HOUGHTON LE SP	20/1/15	13/9/18	GSW			TO DEPOT.	AGE 23.
RAMSEY	Gordn	PTE	21 /1692									TO 11th BN, KOYLI(1/4th BN) 1st NF, SCOTTISH RIFLES(1	KOYLI No 7129, SCO RIF No 55639.
RANDLE	Alb E	SGT	21 / 909			ASHINGTON	12/11/14	31/3/19	KRpara 392			TO ARMY RESERVE CLASS P.	
RANKIN	John	PTE	21 / 306			SEATON DELAVAL				NOV 16		TO 25th, 1/4th, 19th(W COY) BNS, CLASS Z RESERVE.	BEAUFORT WAR HOSP BRISTOL 11/7/16, RENUMBERED 2045
READ	James	CSM	21 /1415		63 CORBRIDGE STREET	NEWCASTLE						TO 12th BN, 85th TRAINING RESERVE BN.	
REDPATH	Adam	PTE	21 / 861			NEWCASTLE			24/7/16		WARLOY BAILLON COM CEM		
REDPATH	Wm	PTE	21 /1077			NEWCASTLE			1/7/16		THIEPVAL MEM		
REED	Thos	PTE	21 / 441			SEATON BURN			28/4/17		ARRAS MEM	TO 20th, 25th BNS.	AGE 27.
REES	Ernst	CPL	21 /1033			BLYTH				MISSING JUNE 16		TO CLASS Z RESERVE.	PRISONER OF WAR 1916, INTERNED IN HOLLAND.
REMMER	Albt	PTE	21 /1179			SEAHAM			25/7/16	JULY 16	CHRISTCHURCH NEW SEAHAM CHYD		BORN CARLTON MINNIOTT N YORKS.
RENNER	JohnR	CSM	21 /1304			DOXFORD						TO CLASS Z RESERVE.	
RENTON	RobtN	PTE	21 /1288	D		SUNDERLAND			1/7/16		THIEPVAL MEM		IN 13 PLATOON.
REYNOLDS	John	PTE	21 / 666			BEDLINGTON			23/11/17		WANCOURT BRIT CEM	ATTACHED 102nd LIGHT TRENCH MORTAR BATTERY.	AGE 23.
RICHARDSON	Matt	PTE	21 / 219		NEW SQUARE	SEGHILL				MISSING JUNE 16			PRISONER OF WAR 1916.
RICHARDSON	Peter	PTE	21 / 653									TO 1/4th, 1st, 12/13th BNS.	
RIDDELL	JohnT	PTE	21 /1251			ASHINGTON	11/1/15	4/12/17	WOUNDS	NOV 16		TO 1st, 16th BNS.	AGE 21.
RIDGE	Thos	PTE	21 / 79	A		CHOPPINGTON			5/6/17		ARRAS MEM		BORN COCKERMOUTH.
RIDLEY	Henry	PTE	21 / 756		2 MORPETH TERRACE	PERCY MAIN			5/6/17	NOV 16	ARRAS MEM	TO 16th, 21st BNS.	BORN NORTH SHIELDS AGE 30.
RILEY	Edwd	PTE	21 /1286									TO DURHAM LIGHT INFANTRY, TRAINING RESERVE BN.	TRG RES No TR/5/58177.
RILEY	Pat	PTE	21 / 912									TO 23rd BN, CLASS Z RESERVE.	
RIVETT	Sid	LCPL	21 / 965			NEATISHEAD				SEPT 16		TO 23rd BN, ROYAL FUSILIERS(24th BN).	R FUS No GS/93162.
RIX	ChasH	PTE	21 / 89						KRpara392			TO DURHAM LIGHT INFANTRY.	DLI No 80323.
RIX	RobtE	PTE	21 / 90			CHOPPINGTON			27/6/16		HEILLY STATION CEM		BORN MORPETH.
RIX	Wm	CPL	21 / 87			STAKEFORD			KRpara 392	JULY 16		TO 10th BN.	
ROBE	Jas H	PTE	21 / 215			NORTH SHIELDS			KRpara 392	SSHOCK AUG 16, WND SEP 16		TO 11th, 26th BNS.	
ROBERTS	ChasS	PTE	21 /1689		66 WINSHIP STREET	NEWSHAM	18/8/15	2/7/16	UNFIT			TO 33rd BN.	DID NOT SERVE OVERSEAS.
ROBERTS	James	PTE	21 /1262				9/1/15	23/1/19				TO DEPOT	DID NOT SERVE OVERSEAS, AGE 36.
ROBERTS	ThosP	PTE	21 / 440			SEATON BURN			15/11/16		TROIS ARBRES MIL CEM		
ROBERTSON	AlexY	PTE	21 / 1				5/11/14	23/10/15	NEURASTHEN			TO 22nd BN.	DID NOT SERVE OVERSEAS.
ROBINSON	Abrah	PTE	21 /1390		4 MILBURN STREET	DAWDON			29/4/17	SEPT 16	BROWNS COPSE CEM	TO 23rd BN.	AGE 23.
ROBINSON	Chris	PTE	21 / 941			BEDLINGTON	11/11/14	17/4/17	WOUNDS	JULY 16		TO DEPOT.	
ROBINSON	Fred	LCPL	21 / 983			NEWCASTLE			14/4/16		RATION FARM MIL CEM		
ROBINSON	JohnE	PTE	21 /1347		MARY STREET	HETTON LYONS				JULY 16		TO 20th, 1st, 1/6th BNS.	CONTUSED BACK 4/6/16 WITH 20th BN.
ROBINSON	Wm	PTE	21 / 143	A		BLACKHILL			1/7/16		THIEPVAL MEM		IN 3 PLATOON, AGE 27.
ROBINSON	Wm	SGT	21 / 561		13 BELL TERRACE	KYO LAWS							
ROBSON	Geo	PTE	21 /1445		58 STAVORDALE STREE	DAWDON	19/1/15	28/2/18	SICK	NOV 16		TO ARMY RESERVE CLASS W 9/1/17, TO CLASS P.	AGE 41.
ROBSON	JeffC	PTE	21 /1118			NEWCASTLE		26/3/19		OCT 16		TO 9th, 1/5th BNS, YORK & LANCASTER REGT(1/4th BN), .	Y & L No 57759.
ROBSON	Jn Wm	SGT	21 / 231		5 SCOTLAND HEAD	WINLATON	6/11/14	18/11/14	KRpara 392			SERVED 2YRS 6 MNTHS IN DURHAM LI.	AGE 42, PROMOTED SGT 12/11/14.
ROBSON	JohnR	PTE	21 /1436	A		GATESHEAD			1/7/16		THIEPVAL MEM		BORN EASINGTON LANE
ROBSON	Rich	PTE	21 /1510		35 PENN STREET	NEWCASTLE				JULY 16		TO 14th BN, SUFFOLK REGIMENT(1st GARRISON BN).	
ROBSON	Stan	PTE	21 / 342	B	HURN'S BIULDINGS	CHOPPINGTON	7/11/14	2/2/15	KRpara 392				AGE 19, 150Lbs, 5'6", 35 CHEST.
ROBSON	ThosE	PTE	21 / 124		11 CARLTON STREET	BLYTH			26/8/18		ST HILAIRE CEM EXT	TO 9th, 23rd BNS, KINGS OWN YORKSHIRE LI(1/5th BN).	KOYLI No 63207.AGE 30.
ROBSON	Wm	PTE	21 /1540		12 ILCHESTER STREET	DAWDON						TO 1st GARRISON BN(A COY), CLASS Z RESERVE.	
RODGERS	JohnF	PTE	21 / 657									TO YORKSHIRE REGT(13th BN).	YORKS No 63456.
ROGERSON	Matt	PTE	21 / 589			NEWCASTLE	10/11/14	21/12/16	WOUNDS	OCT 16		TO DEPOT.	TO 3CCS 2/7/16 EVAC 2/7/16
ROGERSON	ThosW	LSGT	21 /1105			WHITLEY BAY			1/7/16		THIEPVAL MEM		BORN NEWCASTLE
ROLLINS	Wm	PTE	21 /1199		3 BYKER HILL SQUARE	NEWCASTLE						TO 14th, 9th BNS, CLASS Z RESERVE.	
ROPER	Wm	PTE	21 /1695		83 CROSS ROAD	CRAMLINGTON	16/8/15						
ROSE	Mich	PTE	21 /1680		3 SPENCERS BANK	SWALWELL	11/8/15		18/4/17		ST ALBANS CEM HERTS	TO DURHAM LI(13th BN).	DLI No 46006.
ROSS	Edwd	PTE	21 / 936			BYKER			21/10/17	SSHOCK AUG	TYNE COT MEM		
ROUTLEDGE	John	PTE	21 / 451			NEWCASTLE				NOV 16		TO COUNTY OF LONDON REGT(QUEENS WESTMINSTEF	IN FRANCE 11/1-10/7/16, 31/3-27/8/17, 27/3/18-8/2/19.
ROUTLEDGE	John	SGT	21 / 943						KRpara 392			TO 25th BN.	
ROUTLEDGE	Wm L	PTE	21 / 794			BLYTH	10/11/14		SHELLSHC	NOV 16		TO ARMY RESERVE CLASS W.	TO 3CCS 2/7/16 EVAC 2/7/16 WND LEGS.
ROWAN	JohnN	SGT	21 / 409		WESTERN HOTEL	DURHAM CITY			21/5/15		ST BEDES REDHILLS DURHAM		BORN DUNDEE AGE 46. ACCOUNT OF FUNERAL IN DURHAM
ROWE	Fr H	PTE	21 /1574									TO 1st GARRISON BN, CLASS Z RESERVE.	
ROWE	Wm J	PTE	21 /1152	D	8 WORTHYS COURT	NEWCASTLE			1/7/16	NOV 16	THIEPVAL MEM		AGE 29 BORN PENZANCE CORNWALL.
ROWELL	T	PTE	21 /1067		27 CANNON ST ELSWICI	NEWCASTLE			20/9/20		ST JOHNS WESTGATE &	TO LABOUR CORPS.	LAB CORPS No 582484, AGE 41.
RUDD	Geo F	PTE	21 / 976			BLYTH	9/11/14	30/3/18	WOUNDS	SEPT 16		TO ARMY RESERVE CLASS P.	AGE 23.
RUTHERFORD	Wm	SGT	21 /1432	C		NEWCASTLE			1/7/16		THIEPVAL MEM		
RUTHERFORD	Wm	PTE	21 / 2			EARSDON	5/11/14	20/12/17	SICK	DEC 16		TO DEPOT.	AGE 35.
RUTHERFORD	Wm	SGT	21 /1363					24/3/19				TO 23rd BN, KINGS OWN YORKSHIRE LI(5th BN).	KOYLI No 63208.
RUTTER	Geo C	PTE	21 / 956	C		BARRINGTON COLL				MISSING JUNE 16		TO CLASS Z RESERVE.	AGE 26, IN 11 PLATOON, PRISONER OF WAR 1916.
RYAN	James	PTE	21 /1229				1/1/15	15/4/18	GSW			TO 1st GARRISON BN.	AGE 45.
RYLE	Geo	PTE	21 / 421										
SADLER	Geo	SGT	21 / 606			NEWCASTLE				OCT 16		TO ROYAL INNISKILLING FUSILIERS(6th BN).	R INNIS FUS No 21587.
SAMSON	Henry	PTE	21 / 163			NORTH SHIELDS			KRpara 392	SSHOCK AUG 16		TO 12/13th, 25th, 8th BNS.	
SAMSON	JohnT	CPL	21 / 146			NORTH SHIELDS	5/11/14	1/2/19	KRpara 392	SEPT 16		TO ARMY RESERVE CLASS P.	
SANCASTER	Geo M	PTE	21 /1270		42 CROSS ROW	WEST MOOR			28/10/18		AWOINGT BRIT CEM	TO 16th, 22nd, 14th, 1/5th, 9th BNS.	BORN HEBBURN.
SANDERS	JohnW	SGT	21 / 629									TO KINGS OWN YORKSHIRE LI(5th BN).	KOYLI No 63219.

SANDERSON	Chas	PTE	21 / 676			TYNEDOCK	7/11/14		GSW	AUG 16		TO ARMY RESERVE CLASS P.	AGE 27, 2nd STHN GHOSP BRISTOL 8/7/16.
SANDERSON	ChasJ	CPL	21 / 911			BLYTH				NOV 16		TO 16th, 22nd BNS, CLASS Z RESERVE.	
SANDERSON	Thos	PTE	21 /1541	B		BIRTLEY			1/7/16	JULY 16	THIEPVAL MEM		
SAVAGE	John	PTE	21 /1484		41 TENTH STREET	HORDEN				SEPT 16		TO CHESHIRE REGIMENT(9th BN).	CHESHIRE REGT No 52313.
SAVAGE	Rich	PTE	21 /1485		41 TENTH STREET	HORDEN			5/6/17		ARRAS MEM		BORN SPENNYMOOR.
SCOTT	Alex	PIPR	21 /1150			GOSFORTH			KRpara392	JULY 16		TO DURHAM LIGHT INFANTRY, TRAINING RES BN.	TRG RES No TR/5/58172.
SCOTT	J W A	PTE	21 / 299				7/11/14	15/9/15	HIPOTAMA			TO 29th BN.	DID NOT SERVE OVERSEAS.
SCOTT	James	PTE	21 / 12			ASHINGTON		18/4/19		JULY 16		TO WEST RIDING REGT.	
SCOTT	James	SGT	21 / 903			NEWCASTLE				NOV 16		TO 22nd BN, CLASS Z RESERVE.	
SCOTT	Jas	PTE	21 / 100				4/11/14	27/12/17	GSW			TO 1st GARRISON BN, 19th, 27th BNS.	
SCOTT	Jas A	PTE	21 / 523			HEATON	11/11/14	17/10/16	WOUNDS	OCT 16		TO DEPOT.	
SCOTT	JohnT	PTE	21 / 783			NEWCASTLE			1/7/16		THIEPVAL MEM		AGE 40 BORN BRAMPTON CUMBERLAND.
SCOTT	Wilk	PTE	21 / 663		16 EDEN PLACE	BEAMISH			20/10/16		RATION FARM MIL CEM		AGE 19 BORN BEARPARK.
SCOTT	Wm	PTE	21 / 66	A	DODDS BLDGS	HOLYWELL			1/7/16		THIEPVAL MEM		BORN EARSDON AGE 39.
SCOTT	Wm	SGT	21 /1481	D	7 CHURCH STREET	BERWICK/TWEED				OCT 16		TO 25th, 11th BNS, CLASS Z RESERVE.	25 AMBT 5/7 18 GHOSP HSHIP 7/7/16 AGE 29 WND L LEG.
SCOTT	Wm A	PIPR	21 /1230			ELSWICK			1/7/16		THIEPVAL MEM		
SEARLE	Andrw	PTE	21 /1433	D	10 RYTON STREET	GATESHEAD				JULY 16		TO 36th BN, CLASS Z RESERVE.	BROTHER /1196 DLI.
SEAWARD	James	CPL	21 / 271			SOUTH GOSFORTH			28/6/17	JULY+SSHOCK AUG 16		TO 25th, 1/5th BNS.	BORN CHESTER LE STREET, ALLOTTED NEW No 243191.
SEYMOUR	Wm	PTE	21 / 890			BYKER			14/10/17	SEPT 16	SOLFERINO FARM CEM		
SHARP	Geo	PTE	21 / 364									TO 14th BN.	
SHARP	James	PTE	21 /1672		TOWER HOUSE	NEWCASTLE	12/8/15	14/6/16	KRpara 392			TO 29th BN.	DID NOT SERVE OVERSEAS.
SHAW	Harry	CPL	21 / 113			BLYTH	3/11/14	27/11/18	GSW	OCT 16		TO ARMY RESERVE CLASS W.	AGE 27.
SHELL	Edwd	PTE	21 /1451	C								TO ROYAL DEFENCE CORPS	IN 11 PLATOON, FRANCE 10/1/16-27/4/17.
SHEPHERD	John	PTE	21 /1216	B		CASTLETOWN			1/7/16		THIEPVAL MEM		BORN PENSHAW.
SHERRINGTON	John	PTE	21 / 37	A		BEBSIDE			1/7/16	MISS OCT 16	THIEPVAL MEM		BORN NORTH SHIELDS.
SHERRY	B	PTE	21 / 61							17/2/16			
SHIEL	Geo		21 / 201			WALLSEND	4/11/14	28/1/19	DEBILITY	SEPT 16		TO DEPOT.	
SHIEL	James		21 / 202			WALLSEND			1/7/16		THIEPVAL MEM		BORN GATESHEAD AGE 36.
SHORT	Edwd	PTE	21 / 646			BEDLINGTON				JULY 16		TO 10th, 20th, 8th, 1/7th BNS.	
SHORT	Geo	PTE	21 / 865				11/11/14	18/12/14	KRpara 392				DID NOT SERVE OVERSEAS.
SIMM	John	PTE	21 / 420			CHOPPINGTON	6/11/14	14/9/17	GSW			TO 3rd BN.	AGE 22.
SIMONS	EdwdM	LCPL	21 /1017	C		TEAMS			24/3/18	OCT 16	DENAIN COM CEM	TO 16th, 22nd(C COY) BNS.	AGE 40 BORN NEWCASTLE, IN 11 PLATOON.
SIMPSON	Grain	PTE	21 / 560		16 SHAFTO TERRACE	CRAGHEAD				SEPT 16			
SIMPSON	Robt	PTE	21 /1194		19 ROBINSON STREET	HOUGHTON LE SPR				SEPT 16		TO 9th, 25th BNS, CLASS Z RESERVE.	
SIMPSON	Wm	PTE	21 / 345									TO 23rd BN.	
SIMPSON	Wm	PTE	21 /1327				14/1/15	26/5/19	KRpara 392			TO DEPOT.	
SINCLAIR	Matt	PTE	21 /1217			SUNDERLAND	2/1/15						BLACKSMITH AGE 22, 5'5", DESERTED 24/4/15.
SKIPPER	Sam	PTE	21 / 510			NORTH SHIELDS			18/10/17		TYNE COT MEM		
SLATER	Thos	SGT	21 /1702									TO 9th BN, CLASS Z RESERVE.	
SLAUGHTER	JohnW	PTE	21 / 225			CHOPPINGTON			9/4/17		ARRAS MEM		AGE 20.
SLOAN	Wm	PTE	21 / 318				9/11/14	29/7/16	KR para392			TO DEPOT.	
SLOWE	Jos	PTE	21 /1454		48 NOBLE STREET	NEWCASTLE						TO 1st BN, CLASS Z RESERVE.	
SMILES	EdwdW	PTE	21 /1517		42 SOUTH MARKET STR	HETTON LE HOLE			9/10/17		TYNE COT MEM	TO KINGS OWN YORKSHIRE LI(1/4th BN).	KOYLI No 203487. AGE 31.
SMITH	Adam	PTE	21 /1490									TO ROYAL DEFENCE CORPS.	FRANCE 10/1/16-19/9/17.RDC No 72967
SMITH	David	PTE	21 / 552	C		BYKER			1/7/16	MISS OCT 16	THIEPVAL MEM		
SMITH	Edwd	PTE	21 / 907		16 EIGHTH ROW	ASHINGTON			8/9/18		VIS-EN-ARTOIS MEM	TO 1st, 2nd, 12/13th(A COY) BNS.	AGE 25 BORN SEGHILL.
SMITH	James	PTE	21 / 972			BLYTH			9/4/17	SEPT 16	BEAURAINES ROAD CEM	TO 1st BN.	
SMITH	James	PTE	21 /1564				7/3/15	10/6/18	SICK			TO DEPOT.	
SMITH	Jas	PTE	21 / 798									TO 25th, 1/7th BNS, CLASS Z RESERVE.	RENUMBERED 292098.
SMITH	Jon H	PTE	21 /1332			GRANGETOWN	13/1/15	16/5/17	WOUNDS	OCT 16		TO 3rd BN.	
SMITH	Jos	PTE	21 / 947			BEBSIDE	11/11/14	19/2/18	GSW	OCT 16		TO 3rd BN.	AGE 35
SMITH	Percy	PTE	21 / 617			PRUDHOE			21/2/16		PRUDHOE NEW CEM		MAY NOT BE TYNESIDE SCOTTISH No IN WGR 2617.
SMITH	R	PTE	21 / 149										P 25 SWB DID NOT SERVE OVERSEAS.
SMITH	Ralph	SGT	21 / 405		38 MALCOLM STREET	NEWCASTLE			25/3/18	SSHOCK AUG	ARRAS MEM	TO CHESHIRE REGIMENT(9th BN).	CHESHIRE REGT No 52318.
SMITH	RobtL	SGT	21 / 347		12 BRICK ROW	BEBSIDE FURNACE			5/6/17	JULY 16	ARRAS MEM		AGE 22.
SMITH	Thos	PTE	21 / 116		9 WALKERS BLDGS	SEATON BURN			1/7/16		THIEPVAL MEM		AGE 37 BORN TYNEMOUTH.
SMITH	Thos	PTE	21 / 418		40 RICHMOND STREET	NEWCASTLE							
SMITH	Wm	PTE	21 /1646	C	32 LESLIE ROW	ASHINGTON			1/7/16	MISS OCT 16	THIEPVAL MEM		AGE 23 BORN BAMBOROUGH, NOK RADCLIFFE LANCS.
SMITH	Wm A	PTE	21 / 776				11/11/14	10/4/15	SICK				DID NOT SERVBE OVERSEAS, AGE 41.
SMITHWHITE	John	PTE	21 /1627									TO 12/13th, 1st BNS, CLASS Z RESERVE.	
SNELL	James	PTE	21 /1337		41 WILLIAM STREET	TUNSTALL	13/1/15	9/4/19	KRpara 392			TO 8th BN, DEPOT.	
SNOWBALL	T	PTE	21 / 522	C									IN 11 PLATOON.
SNOWDON	Alb E	PTE	21 / 605	B		ASHINGTON				OCT 16		TO 18th, 23rd BNS.	SGT 25 AMBT 5/7 18 GHOSP HSHIP 9/7/16 AGE 35 WND L HAN
SNOWDON	JohnG	PTE	21 / 359			GATESHEAD				MISSING 27/5/18		TO 1st, 14th(A COY) BNS.	
SOULSBY	Robt	PTE	21 /1449		53 FRONT STREET	TYNE DOCK	18/1/15	7/2/19				TO 20th,21st,LAB CORPS(188 COY),14th BN,YORK&LANC	Y & L No 57692.
SPENCER	Robt	PTE	21 / 648				9/11/14	20/9/16	SICK			TO DEPOT.	
STALKER	Robt	PTE	21 / 91				6/11/14	13/5/18	GSW			TO 3rd BN.	AGE 26.
STANLEY	Arth	CQMS	21 /1088		29 HARTINGTON ST	NEWCASTLE				SEPT 16		TO 14th, 8th, 23rd BNS, CLASS Z RESERVE.	
STANLEY	John	PTE	21 / 845									TO 1st GARRISON BN, CLASS Z RESERVE.	
STEEL	Mark	PTE	21 / 832		45 FALMOUTH ROAD	HEATON	11/11/14		14/9/18		HEATON & BYKER CEM	TO DEPOT.	DIED OF PARALYSIS.
STEELE	Jos	PTE	21 /1544			ALLENDALE COTTS			1/7/16	MISS OCT 16	THIEPVAL MEM		
STEPHENSON	Dick	PTE	21 /1198				4/1/15	2/6/16	WOUNDS			TO DEPOT.	
STEPHENSON	Herbt	LCPL	21 /1707		17 ALLEN STREET	CHESTER LE ST			5/6/17	JULY 16	ARRAS MEM	TO 22nd BN(A COY).	BORN LANCHESTER AGE 28.
STEPHENSON	Jas S	PTE	21 / 20		45 APPLEBY STREET	NORTH SHIELDS			4/7/16		ST SEVER CEM ROUEN		AGE 21.
STEPHENSON	Rob T	PTE	21 / 422	C	20 PURVIS ROW	BEBSIDE FURNACE			1/7/16		THIEPVAL MEM		BORN SUNDERLAND AGE 26.
STEPHENSON	Wm	PTE	21 / 175	D									
STEPHENSON	Wm L	PTE	21 / 856									TO 26th BN.	DESERTED 25/5/18.
STEVENSON	Wm	PTE	21 / 775	D	95 BURDON STREET	GATESHEAD			1/7/16		THIEPVAL MEM		AGE 31.
STEWART	G	PTE	21 / 634	D		ACKLINGTON				MISSING 1/7/16			
STEWART	James	PTE	21 /1600				22/3/15	26/1/16	HEART DISO			TO 29th BN.	DID NOT SERVE OVERSEAS.
STEWART	John	PTE	21 /1099			MORPETH			3/7/16		LA NEUVILLE BRIT CEM		BORN BEDLINGTON
STEWART	Thos	PTE	21 /1487		28 NORTH TERRACE	BEDLINGTON	19/1/15					TO CLASS Z RESERVE.	
STOBBS	Jos	PTE	21 / 795			BEDLINGTON			2/1/16		HORTON ST MARY'S CH	TO 2nd GARRISON BN.	
STODDART	Wm	PTE	21 /1396			SEAHAM HARBOUR			10/4/18	OCT 16	NIEUPORT MEM	TO 22nd, 1/5th(A COY) BNS.	
STONACH	Henry	PTE	21 /1417			RYHOPE				SEPT 16		TO DURHAM LI.	3rd SCOTTISH GHOSP GLASGOW 11/7/16, DLI No 48407.
STONE	T	PTE	21 /1011	C									MACHINE GUN SECTION 11 PLATOON.
STONEMAN	Geo	PTE	21 / 300			NORTH SHIELDS						TO 22nd BN.	EMPLOYED AT SMITHS DOCK.
STOREY	Wm T	PTE	21 /1011			STANLEY			31/8/18			TO LONDON REGIMENT(1/5th BN).	LONDON REGT No 45216.
STOTT	ThosH	PTE	21 /1171				4/1/15	25/10/17	SICK			TO DEPOT.	AGE 39.
STOVES	John	PTE	21 / 512			NORTH SHIELDS				SEPT 16		TO 23rd BN.	
STRACHAN	John	PIPR	21 /1149		20 DIAMOND STREET	WALLSEND						TO 23rd BN, KINGS OWN YORKSHIRE LI(5th BN).	KOYLI No 63222.
STRACHAN	Munro	PMJR	21 /1147		20 DIAMOND STREET	WALLSEND							
STRAUGHAN	John	PTE	21										AWOL 10/10/15.
STUBBS	Chas	PTE	21 / 168									TO 14th BN, ROYAL FUSILIERS(24th BN).	FRANCE 21 10/1/16-3/7/18, 14 4/7/18-28/8/18, 24RF-28/9/18.
SUMMERBELL	Geo E	LCPL	21 / 982		27 NEW ROW	ISABELLA PIT			9/4/17		BAILLEUL ROAD EAST CEM		SIGNALLER AGE 20 BORN HORTON,
SUMMERS	Wm	PTE	21 /1301		1 WEST VIEW	OLD PENSHAW			27/10/20		PENSHAW ALL SAINTS C	TO 1st GARRISON BN.	DIED OF APPENDICITIS,BROTHER David 26/665 3rd TYNESIDE
SWAINSTON	ThosY	PTE	21 /1264		16 STRANGEWAYS ST	DAWDON						TO 1st GARRISON BN, CLASS Z RESERVE.	
SWAN	JohnT	PTE	21 / 689			BLYTH		16/1/19		OCT 16		TO 22nd BN, YORK & LANCASTER REGT(2/4th BN), CLAS	SPRINGBURN WOODSIDE HOSP GLASGOW 11/7/16, Y & L No
SWINDON	Geo U		21 /1687		37 ELSWICK STREET	GATESHEAD			22/10/17		GATESHEAD EAST CEM	TO DEPOT.	
SYKES	Wm	PTE	21 /1359					11/1/19				TO 11th BN, WEST YORKSHIRE REGT(2nd, 10th BNS ATT	WEST YORKS No 41006, CLASS Z RESERVE.
TABERNER	James	SGT	21 / 743									TO 11th, 12/13th BNS, CLASS Z RESERVE.	
TAIT	Robt	PTE	21 / 658			CHOPPINGTON	9/11/14	29/8/17	WOUNDS	JULY 16		TO DEPOT.	
TAIT	ThosW	PTE	21 / 67		11 WALLACE TERRACE	SEATON DELAVAL	5/11/14	31/3/19	KRpara 392	OCT 16		TO 37th BN, ARMY RESERVE CLASS P.	
TALBOT	James	PTE	21 / 916			CHOWDENE						TO 1st GARRISON BN, CLASS Z RESERVE.	
TANNER	Harry	PTE	21 /1097		91 BUCKINGHAM STREE	NEWCASTLE						TO CLASS Z RESERVE.	
TATE	Ralph	PTE	21 / 449	C								TO 8th BN.	AGE 33, IN 11 PLATOON, RQMS STOREMAN.
TAYLOR	Geo	LCPL	21 /1276			NEWCASTLE			5/6/16		BECOURT MIL CEM		BORN HARRINGTON CUMBERLAND.
TAYLOR	Geo W	PTE	21 /1031			BLYTH	7/11/14	10/4/18	SICK	SEPT 16		TO ARMY RESERVE CLASS P.	
TAYLOR	James	PTE	21 /1056				13/11/14	31/10/16	WOUND R	1/4/16		TO 84th TRAINING RESERVE BN.	AGE 40.
TAYLOR	John	PTE	21 /1493		23 EDWARD STREET	TUNSTALL						TO 23rd BN, CLASS Z RESERVE.	
TAYLOR	Wm H	SGT	21 / 595	D		LEEDS			1/7/16		THIEPVAL MEM		
TAYLOR	Wm M	CPL	21 /1403			NEWCASTLE	18/1/15	6/5/18	WOUNDS	JULY 16		TO ARMY RESERVE CLASS P.	AGE 32, VOL AID HOSP CHELTENHAM 8/7/16.
TEAGUE	John	CPL	21 / 226			WASHINGTON STN	6/11/14	25/4/18	SICK	SSHOCK AUG 16		TO 3rd BN.	
TELFORD	Andrw	PTE	21 /1505		167 CHARLES STREET	BOLDON COLLIERY			1/7/16		THIEPVAL MEM	TO 23rd BN(B COY).	AGE 38 BORN KIBBLESWORTH.
TERNENT	Rob H	LCPL	21 / 804			JESMOND	10/11/14	14/2/18	GSW	OCT 16		TO DEPOT.	AGE 36.
THEW	John	PTE	21 /1688									TO KINGS OWN YORKSHIRE LI(2/4th BN).	KOYLI No 63352.
THOMAS	James	LCPL	21 /1172		5 WYNYARD STREET	SILKSWORTH	31/12/14	12/4/17	SICK	SEPT 16		TO DEPOT.	
THOMPSON	Alan	CPL	21 /1081									TO 23rd BN, CLASS Z RESERVE.	
THOMPSON	Alex	PTE	21 / 370		29 THERESA STREET	STANLEY				SEPT 16		TO 9th BN, COMMISSIONED MACHINE GUN CORPS.	
THOMPSON	Alf G	SGT	21 / 105			EDINBURGH	6/11/14	1/2/19	KRpara 392			TO 21st, 24th, 21st BNS, ARMY RESERVE CLASS P.	
THOMPSON	Andrw	PTE	21 /1506			NORTH SHIELDS	18/1/15	25/10/17	SICK	NOV 16		TO 3rd BN.	AGE 33.
THOMPSON	Bernd	PTE	21 / 693			CRAMLINGTON	7/11/14	28/9/17	WOUNDS	SEPT 16		TO DEPOT.	AGE 27.

THOMPSON	FredW	SGT	21 / 462	C		KILLINGWORTH				JUL 16		TO 25th, 1st BNS.	IN 11 PLATOON, AGE 19.
THOMPSON	Geo	PTE	21 / 206		1 WALTON AVE PRESTC	NORTH SHIELDS			1/7/16		THIEPVAL MEM		AGE 39 BORN ASPATRIA CUMBERLAND.
THOMPSON	Geo	PTE	21 /1470		63 BURDON STREET	RYHOPE	16/1/15	29/8/17	WOUNDS	OCT 16		TO 85th TRAINING RESERVE BN.	
THOMPSON	Geo H	PTE	21 /1446				19/1/15	30/3/17	CHRON NEPH			TO DEPOT.	
THOMPSON	Geo N	PTE	21 / 961	C								TO 23rd, 9th BNS, CLASS Z RESERVE.	AGE 20 IN 11 PLATOON.
THOMPSON	John	PTE	21 /1422	A		BELFORD			1/7/16		THIEPVAL MEM		BORN NORTH LYHAM NTHBLD.
THOMPSON	Jos	PTE	21 /1180			SEAHAM HARBOUR			1/7/16		OVILLERS MIL CEM		BORN BLAYDON.
THOMPSON	Jos	CPL	21 /1653		14 NOBLE STREET	FELLING			18/5/18	SSHOCK AUG	LOOS MEM	TO DURHAM LI, 8th BN NF.	DURHAM LI No 48408.
THOMPSON	Jos	PTE	21 / 818									TO CHESHIRE REGIMENT(9th BN).	CHESHIRE REGT No 52322.
THOMPSON	Sam	PTE	21 /1157			NORTH SHIELDS			5/6/16		BECOURT MIL CEM		AGE 42 BORN TYNEMOUTH.
THOMPSON	Thos	SGT	21 / 167			ACKLINGTON			27/8/17		TINCOURT NEW BRIT CEM		BORN AMBLE.
TICKLE	W	PTE	21 /1503	C	20 WOODLAND TERRAC	NETTLESWORTH							AGE 33 IN 11 PLATOON ATTACHED BN TRANSPORT.
TINNION	John	PTE	21 /1686			GOSFORTH			1/7/16		THIEPVAL MEM	TO 23rd BN(B COY).	BORN PLUMBLAND CUMBERLAND.
TIPPLE	Arth	PTE	21 / 352			BEBSIDE FURNACE	8/11/14	10/7/17	WOUNDS	DEC 16		TO DEPOT.	AGE 22.
TODD	Henry	PTE	21 /1693			NEWCASTLE			KRpara 392				
TODD	HerbA	CQMS	21 /1107									TO 14th BN, CLASS Z RESERVE.	
TODD	JohnG	PTE	21 /1404			HOUGHTON LE SP			12/3/16		BREWERY ORCHARD CEM		
TOLSON	Jos B	PTE	21 / 88			BLAYDON			2/7/16	AUG 16	WARLOY BAILLON COM CEM		BORN CREWE CHESHIRE.
TOVEY	Fred	PTE	21 / 387									TO DURHAM LIGHT INFANTRY, TRAINING RESERVE BN.	TRG RES No TR/5/58184.
TRACEY	John	PTE	21 /1177			SEAHAM HARBOUR	2/1/15	1/4/19	KRpara 392	JULY 16		TO ARMY RESERVE CLASS P.	
TREMBLE	John	PTE	21 / 138									TO ROYAL DEFENCE CORPS.	FRANCE 10/1/16-20/2/17.RDC No 65709.
TREWICK	Matt	PTE	21 / 764	D		DUDLEY			1/7/16		THIEPVAL MEM		BORN LONGBENTON.
TROTTER	Alex	PTE	21 /1083		32 PONT STREET	NEWCASTLE				JULY 16		TO 1/7th, 14th, 1st BNS, CLASS Z RESERVE.	
TROTTER	JohnJ	PTE	21 /1608			SUNDERLAND				JULY 16		TO 23rd BN, KINGS OWN YORKSHIRE LI(5th & 2 GARR BN	KOYLI No 63202.
TROTTER	Thos	PTE	21 / 229			BYKER			1/7/16		THIEPVAL MEM	TO 20th BN(A COY).	
TULLY	Thos	PTE	21 /1452		96 DOCK STREET	SOUTH SHIELDS	16/1/15	9/5/18	GSW	MISSING JUNE 16		TO DEPOT.	
TULLY	Thos	LCPL	21 / 436			SEATON BURN				JULY 16		TO 16th, 22nd BNS.	
TURNBULL	David	PTE	21 / 857		8 THAMES STREET	CHOPWELL						TO 1st GARRISON BN, CLASS Z RESERVE	
TURNBULL	Henry	PTE	21 / 683	D		BLYTH			1/7/16		THIEPVAL MEM		BORN NORTH SHIELDS.
TURNBULL	Jas	PTE	21 / 136									TO 14th BN, ROYAL FUSILIERS(24th BN).	FRANCE 21 10/1/16-3/7/18, 14 4/7/18-28/8/18 24RF-11/11/18
TURNBULL	Jos	PTE	21 /1001			BLYTH			1/7/16		THIEPVAL MEM		
TURNBULL	Thos	PTE	21 / 121		7 SHORT ROW	ISABELLA PIT			5/5/17		ETAPLES MIL CEM	TO 24th BN.	AGE 42 BORN COWPEN.
TURNBULL	Wm H	PTE	21 / 244			BEDLINGTON	7/11/14	14/3/17	WOUNDS	JULY 16		TO DEPOT.	
TURNER	Geo H	PTE	21										AWOL 9/8/15.
TURNER	Jas L	PTE	21 /1271				9/1/15	8/12/17	SICK			TO 2nd GARRISON BN, DEPOT	AGE 47.
TURNER	Thos	PTE	21 / 814			NEWCASTLE	10/11/14	20/3/18	WOUNDS	JULY 16		TO DEPOT.	AGE 38.
TURNER	Wm E	LCPL	21 /1389		64 ANLABY ST	SHEFFIELD			1/7/16		THIEPVAL MEM		BORN GARSTON LANCS, DESERTED 1/10/15, AGE 39.
TWEDDALL	T L P	PTE	21 / 142	A		CONSETT			18/2/16	FEB 16	MERVILLE COM CEM		
TWEDDLE	Chas	PTE	21 / 690		29 DISRAELI STREET	COWPEN QUAY			12/4/17		ETAPLES MIL CEM		AGE 22 BORN BEBSIDE.
TWEDDLE	John	PTE	21 / 641		FLAT TOP ROW	SEGHILL						TO 1st GARRISON BN, CLASS Z RESERVE.	
TYERMAN	Wm	PTE	21 /1294			WHITBY				OCT+DEC 16		TO 16th, 22nd BNS, CLASS Z RESERVE.	
TYLDESLEY	Jos	PTE	21 / 815									TO 2nd GARRISON BN, CLASS Z RESERVE.	
URWIN	Robt	PTE	21 /1640									TO 25th, 1st BNS, CLASS Z RESERVE.	
WALKER	Dick	PTE	21 / 583	C		BLAYDON				JULY 16		TO 10th, 24/27th, 11th BNS.	AGE 29 IN 11 PLATOON.
WALKER	Fred	PTE	21 / 81										
WALKER	JohnW	PTE	21 / 35			BEBSIDE	4/11/14	3/9/17	SICK	OCT 16		TO DEPOT.	AGE 27.
WALKER	Percy	PTE	21 /1398		20 CAROLINE STREET	SEAHAM HARBOUR			4/6/16		BECOURT MIL CEM		AGE 30.
WALKER	Wm	PTE	21 / 518										
WALLACE	Alex	PTE	21 /1108			SUNDERLAND	7/11/14	27/7/17	SHELLSHC	OCT 16		TO 84th TRAINIING RESERVE BN.	AWOL 18/5/15.
WALLACE	Thos	CPL	21 / 15	A		NEWCASTLE			1/7/16		THIEPVAL MEM		
WALLIS	Robt	PTE	21 /1529									TO 14th BN, ROYAL FUSILIERS(24th BN).	FRANCE 21 10/1/16-3/7/18, 14 4/7/18-28/8/18 24RF-11/11/18
WALTER	RichH	PTE	21 /1320			DAWDON			1/7/16		THIEPVAL MEM		BORN DOVER KENT.
WALTON	Chas	SGT	21 / 365									TO DURHAM LIGHT INFANTRY, TRAINING RESERVE BN.	TRG RES No TR/5/58186.
WALTON	Geo	CPL	21 /1339				14/1/15	2/1/17	MYALGIA			TO 84th TRAINING RESERVE BN.	DID NOT SERVE OVERSEAS.
WALTON	Geo M	CPL	21 / 282		16 ELTRINGHAM STREE	BLACKHILL	9/11/14	3/3/19	KR para392			TO 3rd BN, DEPOT.	
WARD	Benj	PTE	21 /1136		1 MIDDLE ROW	MEDOMSLEY				MISSING 20-23/3/18		TO 23rd BN(BN HQ).	
WARD	Jas M	PTE	21 / 328			STOCKSFIELD	7/11/14	31/3/19	KRpara 392	SEPT 16		TO ARMY RESERVE CLASS P.	
WARD	Robt	PTE	21 /1308									TO CHESHIRE REGIMENT(9th BN).	CHESHIRE REGT No 52314.
WARD	Thos	PTE	21 / 520				11/11/14	29/8/18	GSW			TO DEPOT.	AGE 31.
WARDHAUGH	Alf	PTE	21 / 992		14 HESTER GARDENS	NEW HARTLEY			6/7/17	SEPT 16	HERMIES BRIT CEM	TO 18th, 1st BNS.	BORN BLYTH AGE 22.
WATERSTON	Jos	CPL	21 / 173		NORTH HAY LEAZES	ALLENDALE				SEPT 16		TO 3rd BN.	
WATSON	Bernd	PTE	21 / 505			NORTH SHIELDS						TO 20th, 18th, 14th BNS.	
WATSON	David	PTE	21 / 234	B		GATESHEAD	7/11/14	13/8/17	GSW	SEPT 16		TO DEPOT.	25 AMBT 5/7 18 GHOSP HSHIP 9/7/16 WND L LEG+R ANKLE AC
WATSON	Fr Rb	PTE	21 / 297			TYNEMOUTH			27/10/18	SSHOCK AUG	TEZZE BRIT CEM ITALY	TO 13th, 12/13th, 23rd, 10th BNS.	AGE 40.
WATSON	Geo	SGT	21 /1090				9/11/14	22/5/17	SICK			TO 84th TRAINING RESERVE BN.	AGE 41.
WATSON	Geo W	ACSM	21 /1604		22 CHURCH ST HEAD	DURHAM CITY			KRpara 392			TO 11th BN.	
WATSON	John	PTE	21 / 593		6 FORREST YARD	MORPETH	9/11/14		10/1/17		RATION FARM MIL CEM	TO 23rd BN.	BORN CASTLE EDEN AGE 26.
WATSON	John	PTE	21 /1405									TO ROYAL AIR FORCE.	
WATSON	Robt	PTE	21 /1547		23 MONUMENT TERRAC	USWORTH							
WATSON	Robt	PTE	21 / 491									TO 19th, 23rd, 12/13th BNS.	
WATSON	T	PTE	21 /1224			N WALBOTTLE	24/8/14						MINER AGE 29,5'6", DESERTED 24/4/15.
WATSON	Wm J	PTE	21 /1447		39 STAVORDALE STREE	DAWDON			1/7/16		BAPAUME POST		BORN KELLOE.
WATSON	Wm T	LCPL	21 / 344			CHOPPINGTON			9/9/17			TO 2nd GARRISON BN.	BORN BEDLINGTON
WAUGH	Frank	PTE	21 / 897			NEWCASTLE						TO 1st, 23rd, 14th, 19th BNS, CLASS Z RESERVE.	
WEALANDS	Alf	SGT	21 / 625				16/11/14	10/3/16	25/3/16		ST ANDREWS JESMOND	TO 29th BN.	DID NOT SERVE OVERSEAS.
WEAR	Abrhm	SGT	21 / 214		28 POST OFFICE LANE	PRESTON	5/11/14	21/10/18	19/2/20		TYNEMOUTH(PRESTON)	TO 14th BN, DEPOT.	AGE 36 BORN ASHINGTON.
WEAR	Rob D	LSGT	21 / 565			BLYTH			9/7/16		BOULOGNE BRIT CEM		AGE 26 BORN BACKWORTH.
WEATHERITT	Wm F	PTE	21 / 247			GATESHEAD	7/11/14						TAR MIXER AGE 33, 5'4", DESERTED 30/5/15.
WEATHERSTON	Robt	PTE	21 / 810		186 CHESTNUT STREET	HIRST			23/11/16		RATION FARM MIL CEM		AGE 36 BORN BOTHAL NTHBLD.
WEBSTER	Robt	PTE	21 / 740		10 CHURCH STREET	BACKWORTH			KRpara 392	JULY 16		TO 16th, 1st, 12/13th BNS.	TO 3 CCS 2/7/16 EVAC 2/7/16
WEDDELL	Thos	SGT	21 /1020	C		OVINGHAM			9/4/17		ARRAS MEM		
WELBURY	Wm S	PTE	21 / 332									TO 18th, 8th BNS.	
WELCH	Geo	PTE	21 / 253										
WELSH	John	CPL	21 / 939	C		FENCEHOUSES			5/6/16		BECOURT MIL CEM		AGE 38 BORN BISHOP AUKLAND, IN 11 PLATOON.
WHEATLEY	JohnA	PTE	21 /1156			NORTH SHIELDS			14/10/17		CEMENT HOUSE CEM LA	TO 26th BN.	BORN TYNEMOUTH.
WHITE	Luke	PTE	21 /1531		8 LOW POTTERS YARD	HOUGHTON LE SP	20/1/15	26/10/18	GSW			TO 3rd BN.	AGE 34.
WHITEMAN	Matt	PTE	21 /1583						KRpara 392			TO 2nd GARRISON BN.	
WHITTLE	Walt	CPL	21 / 702	D	5 SEA VIEW	BEBSIDE			4/4/16		RATION FARM MIL CEM		BORN NEWBIGGIN AGE 33.
WIGHAM	Chas	LCPL	21 /1545			ALLENDALE COTTS				JULY 16		TO 16th, 23rd, 9th BNS, CLASS Z RESERVE.	
WIGHAM	James	PTE	21 / 682			NEWSHAM			1/11/17		BLYTH COWPEN CEM		
WILKINSON	Geo	PTE	21 / 898			ASHINGTON						TO 1st, 21st, 24th BNS, CLASS Z RESERVE.	AWOL 1915.
WILKINSON	Geo	PTE	21 / 888				12/11/14	21/4/16	HEART DISE			TO 29th BN.	DID NOT SERVE OVERSEAS.
WILKINSON	James	LCPL	21 / 769	D	94 VICTORIA ROAD	GATESHEAD			1/7/16		THIEPVAL MEM		BORN BENWELL AGE 31.
WILKINSON	Jos	PTE	21										AGE 33 AWOL 10/7/15.
WILKINSON	Ralph	PTE	21 / 910			GATESHEAD			3/6/16		BECOURT MIL CEM		BORN HOUGHTON LE SPRING.
WILKINSON	Thos	CPL	21 / 222			DUDLEY	6/11/14		KRpara 392			TO ARMY RESERVE CLASS P.	
WILKINSON	ThosR	PTE	21 /1557		20 ASHFIELD ROAD	GOSFORTH						TO 23rd, 22nd, 26th, 10th BNS, CLASS Z RESERVE.	
WILLCOX	Sam	PTE	21 /1607		ROSE DALE COTTAGE	ALNWICK MOOR			1/7/16		THIEPVAL MEM		
WILLIAMS	JohnW	LCPL	21 / 642			WEST SLEEKBURN				OCT 16			
WILLIAMSON	Anthy	PTE	21 / 478				9/11/14	8/12/17	WOUNDS			TO 3rd BN.	AGE 26.
WILLIAMSON	Jas A	PTE	21 /1181			SEAHAM HARBOUR	31/12/14	27/2/18	GSW	OCT 16		TO ARMY RESERVE CLASS P	AGE 30.
WILLIAMSON	Robt	PTE	21 / 164									TO 14th BN, ROYAL FUSILIERS(24th BN).	FRANCE 21 10/1/16-3/7/18, 14 4/7/18-28/8/18, 24RF-11/11/18.
WILSON	Adam	CPL	21 /1613		7 HOWARD STREET	NEWCASTLE			9/4/18	OCT 16	NEIUPORT MEM	TO 16th, 1st, 22nd BNS.	AGE 27.
WILSON	Dix R	PTE	21 /1464		12 WOOD ROW	BEBSIDE	16/1/15					TO 16th BN, CLASS Z RESERVE.	
WILSON	Geo	PTE	21 / 821			FOREST HALL	11/11/14	26/11/17	GSW	SEPT 16		TO 16th, 22nd BNS, DEPOT.	AGE 36.
WILSON	James	PTE	21 / 65				7/11/14	3/8/17	SHELLSHOCK			TO DEPOT.	AGE 36 AWOL 24/12/15.
WILSON	JohnT	PTE	21 / 77									TO 25th BN.	
WILSON	Ralph	PTE	21 / 585									TO 2nd GARRISON BN, CLASS Z RESERVE.	
WILSON	Robt	PTE	21 / 964									TO 1st GARRISON BN, CLASS Z RESERVE.	
WILSON	Sam J	PTE	21 /1334	C	23 COAL BANK TER	HETTON LE HOLE			1/9/18	AUG 16	HAC CEM ECOUST ST ME	TO 1st BN.	AGE 20 BORN LEAMSIDE, IN 11 PLATOON OFFICERS ORDERL
WILSON	Thos	PTE	21 / 994			BLYTH	9/11/14	1/11/17	SICK	SSHOCK AUG 16		TO DEPOT.	AGE 27.
WIND	Alf J	PTE	21 / 193		HEDLEYS BLDGS	MURTON NTHBLD						TO 2nd GARRISON BN, CLASS Z RESERVE.	
WINTER	Robt	CPL	21 / 881			GATESHEAD				DEC 16		TO 10th BN, KINGS OWN YORKSHIRE LI(1/4th BN), CLASS	KOYLI No 7106.
WOLFENDALE	W	PTE	21 / 218										
WONNACOTT	James	PTE	21 / 647			BEDLINGTON			29/5/17	OCT 16	BAILLEUL COM EXT	TO 8th BN.	25 AMBT 5/7 18 GHOSP HSHIP 7/7 AGE 34, BORN OSWORTHY
WOOD	James	PTE	21										AWOL 3/1/16.
WRAY	Hen E	PTE	21 / 24				5/11/14	5/3/18	GAS POISON			TO 2nd BN, DEPOT.	AGE 46.
WRIGHT	John	PTE	21 /1098		117 ALBION ROW	BYKER			12/10/16		RATION FARM MIL CEM		AGE 26 BORN CHOPWELL.
WRIGHT	Sam D	PTE	21 / 791			BEDLINGTON STN			29/6/16		BECOURT MIL CEM		
WRIGHT	Wm	PTE	21 / 609		22 KIMBERLEY TERR	CRAGHEAD						TO 2nd GARRISON BN, CLASS Z RESERVE.	AWOL 5/7/15.
YEAMAN	Wm	PTE	21 / 508									TO 1st GARRISON BN, CLASS Z RESERVE.	
YORKE	Thos	PTE	21 / 744			FOREST HALL	9/11/14	30/12/16	KRpara 392	OCT 16		TO 20th, 29th BNS.	
YOUNG	Alex	PTE	21 / 204									TO 2nd GARRISON BN, CLASS Z RESERVE.	
YOUNG	Dan	PTE	21 / 563			BEBSIDE				JULY 16		TO 16th, 9th, 22nd, 1/5th BNS.	
YOUNG	Edwd	SGT	21 /1119									TO 14th BN, CLASS Z RESERVE.	
YOUNG	Geo	PTE	21 / 413			BYKER	7/11/14	5/10/17	GSW	JULY 16		TO DEPOT	AGE 26.
YOUNG	J	PTE	21 / 21										P 25 SWB LIST.
YOUNG	John	PTE	21 / 984	C		COWPEN			1/7/16		THIEPVAL MEM		AGE 40 IN 11 PLATOON.
YOUNG	ThosM	PTE	21 / 84									TO 14th BN, ROYAL FUSILIERS(24th BN).	FRANCE 21 10/1/16-3/7/18, 14 4/7/18-28/8/18 24RF-11/11/18
YOUNG	W	PTE	21 / 670										TO 3CCS 2/7/16 EVAC 2/7/16 SHELLSHOCK.
YOUNG	Wm	PTE	21 / 673	D		BEDLINGTON	9/11/14	25/10/17	WOUNDS			TO 84th TRAINING RESERVE BN.	101 AMBT TO 18 GHOSP 3/7/16 HSHIP 5/7, SSHOCK, AGE 38.
YOUNG	Wm H	SGT	21 / 899									TO 1st GARRISON BN, CLASS Z RESERVE.	

Appendix V

NOMINAL ROLL OF OTHER RANKS 22nd NF (3rd Tyneside Scottish)

Number on Roll **1089**; Killed or Died of Wounds **349**; Wounded **425**, Gassed, Sick etc **182**:
Total known casualties **956** (81.2 per cent)
Not traced 710

NAME	INITIALS	RANK	BAT	NUMB	CC	ADDRESS	TOWN_VILL	ENLISTED	DISCHAR	CAUSE_DIS	WOUNDED	BURIED	TRANSFER	ADD
ADAMS	JohnA	PTE	22	/1364		1 HUTS	NEWBIGGIN	11/1/15					TO 2nd GARRISON BN, CLASS Z RESERVE.	
ADAMS	Thos	PTE	22	/728									TO DURHAM LIGHT INFANTRY(18th, 19th BNS), CLASS Z F DLI No 78117.	
ADEY	Wm	SGT	22	/1151		14 FAIREY STREET	HETTON LE HOLE				AUGUST 16			
AITKEN	Wm	PTE	22	/218									TO EAST YORKSHIRE REGT(1st BN), CLASS Z RESERVE. E YORKS No 50767.	
ALCOCK	Edwd	PTE	22	/1152	B		SUNDERLAND			1/7/16	MISSING OCT 16	THIEPVAL MEM		
ALDER	Barth	PTE	22	/154			WALLSEND			30/6/16	WND & MISSING SEPT 16	THIEPVAL MEM		BORN SOUTH SHIELDS.
ALDERSON	Geo W	PTE	22	/1149			SEAHAM HARBOUR						TO 25th, 20th, 9th BNS, CLASS Z RESERVE.	
ALLAN	Jos	PTE	22	/394		1 WOOD STREET	BENFIELDSIDE							BORN HEDDON AGE 33.
ALLAN	Wm	PTE	22	/653		50 HIGH STREET	NEWBURN			17/6/17		ARRAS MEM		
ALLEN	Thos	PTE	22	/1680				29/4/15	13/3/19	KR para 392			TO DEPOT.	
ALLISON	D	PTE	22	/549									TO 2nd GARRISON BN, CLASS Z RESERVE.	
ALLISON	ThosW	CPL	22	/689										
ANDERSON	Hilyd	SGT	22	/322				17/11/14	1/4/19	KR para 392			TO ARMY RESERVE CLASS P.	
ANDERSON	James	PTE	22	/242		15 CANADA STREET	CHESTER LE ST	16/11/14	31/3/19	KR para 392			TO 2nd GARRISON BN.	
ANDERSON	John	PTE	22	/219		105 DAVIDSON STREET	GATESHEAD						TO 10th BN.	
ANDERSON	Rich	PTE	22	/1150		37 GARDEN STREET	SEAHAM HARBOUR			22/6/16		HEILLY STATION CEM		AGE 29.
ANGUS	Edwd	PTE	22	/110	C	31 STATION ROAD	CRAMLINGTON			30/6/16		THIEPVAL MEM		BORN NORTH SHIELDS AGE 32.
APPLEBY	JohnH	PTE	22	/1681			AMBLE							
APPLEBY	Rob B	PTE	22	/1120	C		EDMONDSLEY			1/7/16	JUNE 16, MISS OCT 16.	THIEPVAL MEM		BORN WATERHOUSES.
ARKLE	ThosD	PTE	22	/971			WIDDRINGTON COL	16/11/14	29/1/17	WOUNDS	AUGUST 16		TO DEPOT.	DID NOT SERVE OVERSEAS.
ARKLESS	Jos	CQMS	22	/1654				26/9/14	26/1/16	CHRONIC ECZMA			TO 29th BN.	
ARKLEY	ThosW	PTE	22	/835									TO 13th, 12/13th BNS, CLASS Z RESERVE.	
ARMES	Steph	LSGT	22	/1388		83 LONGNEWTON STRE	DAWDON						TO 2nd GARRISON BN, CLASS Z RESERVE.	
ARMSTRONG	Edwd	PTE	22	/1365			DIPTON			19/5/17		POINT DU JOUR MIL CE	TO 9th BN, ATTACHED MGC.	BORN KIBBLESWORTH.
ARMSTRONG	Geo	PTE	22	/96					6/2/19				TO YORK & LANCASTER REGT(2/4th BN).	Y&L No 57718.
ARMSTRONG	Henry	PTE	22	/203			GATESHEAD				SEPT 16			TRANSPORT SECTION.
ARMSTRONG	J W	PTE	22	/616										
ARMSTRONG	JohnN	PTE	22	/1561			MONKWEARMOUTH				AUGUST 16		TO 1st, 12/13th BNS, CLASS Z RES.	
ARMSTRONG	Peter	PTE	22	/42				14/11/14	22/10/17	DAH			TO DEPOT.	AGE 44, DID NOT SERVE OVERSEAS.
ARMSTRONG	ThosP	PTE	22	/521	B		NORTH SHIELDS			1/7/16	MISSING OCT 16	THIEPVAL MEM		BORN NEWCASTLE, MACHINE GUN SECTION.
ARMSTRONG	Wm	PTE	22	/1697		29 ALBION STREET	JARROW						TO 2nd GARRISON BN, CLASS Z RESERVE.	
ARNELL	JohnT	PTE	22	/60		DEE SQUARE	SOUTH FELLING						TO 1st GARRISON BN, CLASS Z RESERVE.	
ARTHURS	L J	PTE	22	/1534										MACHINE GUN SECTION.
ASHLEY	Jas W	CPL	22	/299			ANNITSFORD	17/11/14	12/10/17	WOUNDS	AUGUST 16		TO 3rd BN.	AGE 28.
ASHTON	Jas T	PTE	22	/672		6 STANLEY STREET	NEWBURN HALL						TO EAST YORKSHIRE REGT(1st BN), CLASS Z RESERVE. IN CCS 7/16. E YORKS No 50644.	
ATKINSON	Ben B	CPL	22	/14				12/11/14	26/11/17	GSW			TO 1st, 22nd BNS, DEPOT.	AGE 28.
ATKINSON	David	PTE	22	/435	D		BIRTLEY			1/7/16	MISSING OCT 16	OVILLERS MIL CEM		
ATKINSON	JohnT	LSGT	22	/13			SEATON HIRST			KR para 392	SEPT 16			
ATKINSON	Peter	PTE	22	/656			NORTH SHIELDS			30/6/16		THIEPVAL MEM		
ATKINSON	Wm G	PTE	22	/652			WINLATON			19/10/17	JULY 16, JULY 17.	TYNE COT MEM	TO 26th, 21st BNS.	
AUSTIN	Rob J	LCPL	22	/1097									TO CLASS Z RESERVE.	
AUTON	Walt	LSGT	22	/712		28 WEST END VILLAS	CROOK			9/2/16		BAILLEUL COM CEM EXT		DIED AT No 8 CCS, AGE 20.
AYTON	Jas W	PTE	22	/647				14/11/14	2/2/15	KR para 392				DID NOT SERVE OVERSEAS.
BAILEY	Thos	PTE	22	/235		3 WEST BURN	CRAWCROOK	16/11/14	26/2/17	SICK			TO 2nd BN, DEPOT.	STONEMAN STELLA COLLIERY.
BAIN	T		22	/1545		BEATRICE TERR	PENSHAW							
BAIRD	MattB	PTE	22	/850			SEAHAM HARBOUR			11/7/17		PHILOSOPHE BRIT CE	TO DURHAM LI(2nd BN).	DURHAM LI No 45993.
BAKER	Elij	PTE	22	/152		8 BERKLEY STREET	JARROW						TO 1st GARRISON BN, CLASS Z RESERVE.	
BALL	Steph	PTE	22	/514		47 BENTNICK STREET	NEWCASTLE			10/6/16		BECOURT MIL CEM		BORN SEATON BURN.
BAMFORD	HughB	PTE	22	/1367									TO 9th BN, CLASS Z RESERVE.	
BANKS	John		22	/170										
BARBER	Hen E	PTE	22	/1018	D		GREAT YARMOUTH			1/7/16		THIEPVAL MEM		BORN ROLLESBY NORFOLK.
BARKER	Alb E	PTE	22	/1717		32 OYSTERSHELL LANE	NEWCASTLE							DID NOT SERVE OVERSEAS.
BARKER	John	PTE	22	/1472	B	2 GARDEN PLACE	OLD PENSHAW	25/1/15	1/7/16		MISSING OCT 16	THIEPVAL MEM		BORN CHESTER LE STREET.
BARLOW	ThosN	PTE	22	/1386			MOSSTON LINCS			28/4/17		ST JOHN'S WESTGATE	TO DEPOT.	
BARNETT	T H	PTE	22	/579			GATESHEAD				NOV 17			
BARREN	Ernst	PTE	22	/1121		SHERBOURNE HSE FR/	DURHAM CITY			9/7/17	OCT 16		HENINEL COM CEM EX TO 25th , 1/7th BNS.	RENUMBERED 293330.AGE 21.
BARRON	Fred	PTE	22	/349									TO 13th BN, ROYAL DEFENCE CORPS.	RDC No 71996, FRANCE 22 10/1/16-14/2/17, 13 15/10/17-4/
BARRON	JohnW	PTE	22	/75		17 PLANTAGENET AVE	CHESTER LE ST			3/9/16	SEPT 16	DIPTON ST JOHN CH YD		BORN MINSTER ACRES AGE 47.
BARRON	Robsn	SGT	22	/102		14 HAWTHORNE TERR	MEDOMSLEY				AUGUST 16		TO 16th BN.	BROTHER IN DURHAM LI.
BATES	James	PTE	22	/913		15 FRANKLIN STREET	SOUTH SHIELDS			6/3/16		RATION FARM CEM		AGE 45.

BATTY	Thos	PTE	22 /1778					23/4/19				TO YORK & LANCASTER REGIMENT(2/4th BN), CLASS Z F	Y&L No 57713.
BAWN	Alf	PTE	22 /1154		PERCY TERRACE	ALNWICK						TO EAST YORKSHIRE REGT(1st BN), CLASS Z RESERVE.	EAST YORKS No 50777.
BAWN	Geo	PTE	22 /1156		49 CHESTNUT STREET	HIRST	9/1/15					TO 1st GARRISON BN, CLASS Z RESERVE.	
BEADLE	Walt	PTE	22 / 320									TO ROYAL FUSILIERS(24th BN).	FRANCE 22 10/1/16-28/8/18, 24RF-8/1/19, R FUS No GS/93
BEAZLEY	Fred	CPL	22 / 670			SWINDON WILTS			KR para 392	JULY 16			
BECK	James	PTE	22										AWOL 29/11/15.
BEDFORD	Arth	PTE	22 /1059			WALLSEND	13/11/14	16/7/18	MYALGIA	JULY 16		TO ARMY RESERVE CLASS W.	AGE 47.
BELL	Anthy	PTE	22 / 800		4 GORDON STREET	GATESHEAD							
BELL	Geo	CPL	22 / 504	A	17 DURHAM STREET	BLACKHILL			5/6/17		ARRAS MEM		GAS NCO AGE 23.
BELL	John	PTE	22 / 490	A		NEWCASTLE			14/3/17		FAUBOURG DE AMIENS	TO 20th, 25th BNS.	OPERATION 18 GHOSP 5/7 GSW LTHIGH SHIP 11/7/16 AG
BELL	JohnH	PTE	22 / 669			BOLDON COLLIERY			3/5/17	JULY 16	ARRAS MEM	TO 16th, 1st BNS.	AGE 37.
BELL	Jos R	PTE	22 / 497										
BELL	L	PTE	22 / 920			NEWCASTLE			3/5/19	AUGUST 16	EARSDON ST ALBAN C	TO LABOUR CORPS(285 AGRI COY).	TO 3CCS 2/7 EVAC 2/7 TO 4th STHRN GHOSP PLYMOUTH
BELL	Les	CPL	22 /1159		15a HAWTHORN TERRA	MEDOMSLEY			11/9/17	JULY 16	HAGRICOURT BRIT CEM		BORN DURHAM CITY.
BELL	Matt	PTE	22 / 17		RIVERSIDE COTTAGES	MORPETH			7/7/16		ABBEVILLE COM CEM		AGE 42.
BELL	Robt	PTE	22 / 668			BOLDON COLLIERY				OCT 16		TO 25th, 1/4th BNS, CLASS Z RESERVE.	
BELL	Robt	LCPL	22 /1157	A	20 WYLAM STREET	BOWBURN			1/7/16	MISSING OCT 16	THIEPVAL MEM		BORN STATION TOWN.
BELL	Thos	PTE	22 / 9				13/11/14	22/10/17	SICK			TO DEPOT.	AGE 46.
BELL	Wm	PTE	22 / 975									TO 1st GARRISON BN, CLASS Z RESERVE.	
BENNETT	W	PTE	22 / 289										
BERESFORD	Ste S	PTE	22 /1505									TO 25th , 1/7th BNS, CLASS Z RESERVE.	RENUMBERED 293328.
BERESFORD	Thos	PTE	22 / 444		YMCA BUILDINGS	MORPETH				JULY 16		TO DURHAM LI(11th BN).	AWOL 28/6/15, DURHAM LI No 46274.
BERRY	MattE	PTE	22 /1589			SEAHAM HARBOUR			2/9/16		RATION FARM CEM		BORN MURTON.
BESFORD	Geo	PTE	22 / 79			ASHINGTON			KR para 392	OCT 16		TO 25th, 1/7th BNS.	ALLOTTED NEW NUMBER 292099.
BEST	David	PTE	22 /1744		25 BELFORD TERRACE	NORTH SHIELDS			3/7/16		ALBERT COM CEM EXT		AGE 17.
BEST	James	PTE	22 / 847		28 CROSS ROW SOUTH	CHOPWELL	16/11/14	21/12/18	WOUNDS	JULY 18		TO DEPOT.	AGE 27.
BEWICK	Wm R	PTE	22 / 270			HOBSON Co DURHAM	14/11/14	27/3/18	SICK			TO ARMY RESERVE CLASS P.	DID NOT SERVE O/SEAS.
BEWLEY	EdwdT	PTE	22 / 464				14/11/14	21/1/15	CARTLIDGE				AGE 41, DID NOT SERVE OVERSEAS.
BEWLEY	Wm	PTE	22 / 681						KR para 392			TO 25th, 1/5th BNS.	ALLOTED NEW No 293333.
BILCLOUGH	Wm	LCPL	22 / 922	D	6 ALICE STREET	WINLATON			5/6/17		ARRAS MEM		AGE 22 IN MACHINE GUN SECTION.
BIRCHALL	Sam	PTE	22 / 617	A		BIRTLEY			1/7/16	MISSING OCT 16	THIEPVAL MEM		BORN ST HELEN'S LANCS.
BLACK	Dav J	PTE	22 / 513		204 HOPE STREET	JARROW						TO 1st GARRISON BN, CLASS Z RESERVE.	
BLACK	Geo	PTE	22 /1087									TO 1st GARRISON BN, CLASS Z RESERVE.	
BLACK	John	PTE	22 / 259									TO 23rd BN, ROYAL FUSILIERS(24th BN).	FRANCE 22 10/1/16-5/7/16, 23 19/1/17-30/8/18, 24RF-27/11/
BLACKETT	ThosS	PTE	22 / 385			BYKER	16/11/14	3/8/16	WOUNDS	JULY 16		TO DEPOT.	
BLAGBURN	Wm M	PTE	22 /1486		12 SIDNEY STREET	NORTH SHIELDS			8/6/20		TYNEMOUTH PRESTON	TO 2nd GARRISON BN.	AGE 46.
BLAIR	Matt	PTE	22 / 589		30 PORTBERRY STREE	SOUTH SHIELDS			29/3/16		RATION FARM MIL CEM		AGE 38 BORN NORTH SHIELDS.
BLAIR	Wm	PTE	22 / 611	TPT									
BLAKE	James	BGLR	22 / 754				16/11/14	19/4/18	SICK			TO 3rd BN.	AGE 20.
BLAKEY	J	PTE	22 /1546		6 OAK COTTAGES	SEAHAM HARBOUR	1/2/15						
BLAKEY	SeptJ	PTE	22 / 395			NEWCASTLE	16/11/14	14/3/17	WOUNDS	AUGUST 16		TO DEPOT.	AWOL 14/12/14.
BLANCH	H H E	PTE	22 /1160									TO 2nd GARRISON BN, CLASS Z RESERVE.	
BLAND	Geo	PTE	22 / 202		1 WALKERS BLDGS	SEATON BURN			11/10/17		NORTH GOSFORTH BU	TO DEPOT.	
BLAYLOCK	Frank	PTE	22 /1718		26 ELSWICK ROAD	NEWCASTLE	13/7/15	22/8/16	SICK			TO 33rd BN.	DID NOT SERVE OVERSEAS.
BLEMINGS	John	PTE	22 / 103	B	71 MEDOMSLEY ROAD	CONSETT			1/7/16	MISSING OCT 16	THIEPVAL MEM		AGE 31.
BLYTH	Alex	PTE	22 / 919									TO ROYAL FUSILIERS(24th BN).	FRANCE 22 10/1/16-28/8/18, 24RF-16/11/18. R FUS No GS/
BOAD	Robt	PTE	22 /1161	B	53 MOUNT STEWART S	DAWDON			1/7/16	MISSINGOCT 16	THIEPVAL MEM		AGE 19 BORN SOUTH HETTON.
BOOTH	Thos	PTE	22 / 623									TO ROYAL FUSILIERS(24th BN).	FRANCE 22 10/1/16-28/8/18, 24RF-14/9/18. RF No GS/9310
BOURNE	JohnT	SGT	22 /1444		106 MAPLE STREET	HIRST	6/1/15		15/4/17		ETAPLES MIL CEM		AGE 22 BORN ASHINGTON.
BOWDEN	Geo	PTE	22 /1335				5/1/15	20/7/16	WOUNDS			TO DEPOT.	
BOWEY	Jos	PTE	22 /1162		2 FREDERICK STREET	HEBBURN	9/1/15					TO 2nd GARRISON BN, CLASS Z RESERVE.	
BOWMAN	Wm R	CSM	22 /1062			BLYTH	10/11/14	14/2/17	WOUNDS	AUGUST 16		TO DEPOT.	NORTH EVINGTON HOSP LEICESTER 11/7/16.
BOX	Jos	CSM	22 / 741				18/11/14	6/9/18	SICK			TO DEPOT.	AGE 36.
BOYD	Alex	PIPR	22 / 751			NEWCASTLE				1/7/16			TO 3CCS 2/7/16 EVAC 2/7/16 GSW HAND.
BOYD	Frank	LSGT	22 / 726			WINLATON			29/8/17		TINCOURT NEW BRIT CEM		
BRADY	Edwd	PTE	22 /1578		19 GLADSTONE TERRA	OLD PENSHAW				AUGUST 16		TO CLASS Z RESERVE.	STRETCHER BEARER.
BRADY	Wm	PTE	22 /1726				14/7/15	31/3/19	KR para 392			TO ARMY RESERVE CLASS P.	AWOL 13/9/15.
BRAITHWAITE	Edmd	PTE	22 /1163		16 MILLFIELD LANE	WOODHORN				SSHOCK DEC 16		ATTACHED VII CORPS SCHOOL.	
BRAMWELL	FredW	PTE	22 /1690			NEWCASTLE	6/7/15	27/2/18	GSW	AUGUST 16		TO ARMY RESERVE CLASS P.	AWOL 24/9/15.
BRAMWELL	James	PTE	22 / 412		40 SHIELDS ROAD	NEWCASTLE							
BRANDER	Jos	PTE	22 / 642						KR para 392			TO DURHAM LIGHT INFANTRY.	DLI No 74888.
BREESE	John	PTE	22 /1085			WALKER			KR para 392	SEPT 16, JAN 18.			LCPL.
BRESLIN	Geo	PTE	22 /1086			WILLINGTON QUAY			24/10/18	JULY 16, NOV 16.	VIS-EN-ARTOIS MEM	TO 19th, 16th, 1/5th, 9th, 1st BNS.	
BREWER	Walt	PTE	22 / 441	C	89 SOUTH BENWELL RD	NEWCASTLE			1/7/16	MISSING OCT 16	THIEPVAL MEM		AGE 42
BREWIS	Robt	PTE	22 / 895			ALNWICK			1/7/16		THIEPVAL MEM		BORN BEDLINGTON
BRIDGES	Wm	PTE	22 /1415		4 THIRLEMERE STREET	NEWBIGGIN	11/1/15					TO 25th, 1/4th BNS, CLASS Z RESERVE.	ALLOTTED NEW No 204577.
BRIGGS	JohnT	PTE	22 / 552		32 TEES STREET	CHOPWELL			29/4/17	JULY 16	CRUMP TRENCH CEM	TO 27th, 23rd BNS.	AGE 32.
BRIGGS	Wm	PTE	22 /1340		21 MERSEY STREET	CHOPWELL	9/1/15					TO 3rd BN, CLASS Z RESERVE.	
BRITT	Wm	PTE	22										AWOL 13/11/15.
BRODIE	John	PTE	22 / 853		7 SHORTRIDGE TERRA	JESMOND			9/4/17		ST CATHERINE BRIT CEM		AGE 21.
BROOKS	Val	PTE	22										
BROOKS	Wm	CSGT	22 /1658				5/10/14	14/6/16	MEDICALLY UNFIT			TO 29th BN.	AGE 31.
BROWN	Albt	PTE	22 /1165									TO EAST YORKSHIRE REGT(1st BN), CLASS Z RESERVE.	E YORKS No 50653.
BROWN	Geo	PTE	22 / 806	D	43 JAMES STREET	BENWELL			1/7/16	MISSING OCT 16	THIEPVAL MEM		AGE 43, IN 13 PLATOON.
BROWN	Jas A	PTE	22 /1745			NORTH SHIELDS	21/7/15	15/6/17	SICK	MISSING OCT 16, NOT MISS			SADLER BY TRADE.
BROWN	Jas F	PTE	22 /1743		36 NORTHUMBERLAND	NORTH SHIELDS			1/7/16	MISSING OCT 16	THIEPVAL MEM		AGE 20.
BROWN	John	PTE	22 / 431	C	4 EAST SIDE OLD ROW	NORTH WALBOTTLE			1/7/16		THIEPVAL MEM		AGE 43 IN 11 PLATOON.
BROWN	John	CPL	22 /1599		SMITHS BLDGS	WINLATON				JAN 18, JULY 18.			
BROWN	JohnA	PTE	22 / 309	D	11 ALDWYN GARDENS	CONSETT			1/7/16	MISSING OCT 16	THIEPVAL MEM		
BROWN	Jos	PTE	22 /1007			ROWLANDS GILL			29/4/17	JULY 16	ATHIES COM CEM EXT	TO 16th, 23rd BNS.	
BROWN	Josh	PTE	22 /1698		103 NEW FIFTH STREET	HORDEN			30/8/16		NIEUPORT MEM		AGE 27 BORN PHILADELPHIA Co DURHAM.
BROWN	Matt	PTE	22 / 937			SOUTH SHIELDS			22/6/16		ALBERT COM CEM EXT		
BROWN	Thos	PTE	22 /1652			SOUTHWICK	16/4/15	20/3/18	GSW	AUGUST 16		TO 9th BN, DEPOT.	
BROWN	Wm	PTE	22 / 518		38 STRAKER STREET	TYNE DOCK	18/11/14		12/7/16	AUGUST 16	HARTON ST PETER'S CH YD		MINER DESERTED 14/6/15, DIED IN HOSP MANCHESTER.
BRUCE	Wm	PTE	22 / 974			BLYTH			1/7/16		THIEPVAL MEM		
BUCKHAM	Wm	PTE	22 / 551				21/11/14	20/12/17	SICK			TO 2nd GARRISON, 3rd BNS.	AGE 40.
BUGLASS	Ben	LCPL	22 / 74										
BULLER	Chas	PTE	22 /1166			HUNWICK			10/4/17			TO YORK & LANCASTER REGIMENT(8th BN).	Y&L No 34348.
BULTON	W	PTE	22			FATFIELD							HOSPITAL MARCH 16.
BURDON	Thos	PTE	22 / 194	D	50 THAMES STREET	SOUTH SHIELDS			1/7/16	MISSING OCT 16	SERRE ROAD No 2		AGE 28.
BURDUS	Cuthb	LCPL	22 /1491		14 BYRON TERRACE	SEAHAM				AUGUST 16		TO 11th, 1/7th BNS, CLASS Z RESERVE.	
BURN	Wm	PTE	22 / 495									TO EAST YORKSHIRE REGT(1st BN), CLASS Z RESERVE.	E YORKS No 50703.
BURNS	J	CPL	22 / 366			FELLING				AUGUST 16			
BURNS	James	SGT	22 / 931			WEST SLEEKBURN	10/11/14	31/3/19	KR para 392	OCT 16, NOV 17.		TO ARMY RESERVE CLASS P.	
BURNS	JohnG	PTE	22 / 972				16/11/14	21/4/15	SICK				AGE 39, DID NOT SERVE OVERSEAS.
BURROWS	Jas H	PTE	22 / 780		41 CLIFFORD TERRACE	CRAWCROOK			10/6/16		BECOURT MIL CEM		BORN RYTON AGE 25.
BURT	RobtA	PTE	22 /1167	C		ASHBY LEICESTER			5/6/17		ARRAS MEM		IN 9 PLATOON.
BURTON	Wm	PTE	22 / 541				21/11/14	19/4/17	KRpara392			TO 1st GARRISON BN, DEPOT.	
BURTON	Wm	PTE	22 / 527				21/11/14	19/4/17	KR para 392			TO DEPOT.	
BUSHBY	Wm	PTE	22 / 909					6/5/19				TO YORK & LANCASTER REGIMENT(2/4th BN), CLASS Z F	Y&L No 57620.
BUTTON	Wm	PTE	22 /1465				28/1/15	25/4/19	KR para 392			TO 23rd BN, DEPOT.	
BYGATE	ThosR	PTE	22 /1539		10 PALATINE VIEW	DURHAM CITY				MISSING 27/5/18		TO 1/4th BN(D COY).	
BYRON	Ernst	PTE	22 /1571		10 COOPER STREET	RYHOPE						TO 1st GARRISON BN, CLASS Z RESERVE.	
CAHILL	JasP	PTE	22 /1495		9 SOPHIA STREET	SEAHAM HARBOUR	1/2/15	10/1/17	WOUNDS			TO DEPOT.	
CAHILL	Jos	PTE	22 /1507									STILL SERVING 1921.	
CAIRNS	Pat	LCPL	22 / 473									TO 1st GARRISON BN, CLASS Z RESERVE.	
CAMERON	Geo	PTE	22 / 399	D	103 FRAMWELLGATE	DURHAM CITY				MISSING 21/3/18			
CAMERON	Walt	PTE	22 / 423									TO ROYAL DEFENCE CORPS.	RDC No 65598, FRANCE 22 10/1/16-8/7/16.
CAMERON	Wm	PTE	22 /1023	D		NAIRN SCOTLAND			1/7/16	MISSING OCT 16	THIEPVAL MEM		
CAMPBELL	Ed M	PTE	22 / 945			SOUTH SHIELDS			18/6/16	JUNE 16	HEILLY STATION CEM		
CAMPBELL	J	PTE	22 / 118										
CAMPBELL	James	PTE	22 /1169			BLYTH			22/6/16		HEILLY STATION CEM		
CAMPBELL	John	PTE	22 /1168		50 CAMDEN STREET	NORTH SHIELDS				AUGUST 16		TO 10th, 9th, 23rd BNS, CLASS Z RESERVE.	
CAMPBELL	Robt	PTE	22 /1685		15 KNOWE HEAD	TWEEDMOUTH			20/8/16		BERKS CEM EXT		AGE 40.
CARLING	Edwd	PTE	22 /1170	B	2 COTTAGES ROAD	DAWDON			1/7/16	MISSING OCT 16	THIEPVAL MEM		BORN BROOMSIDE DURHAM.
CARMICHAEL	Rich	PTE	22 /1739	C		SOUTH SHIELDS				JUNE 16, JUNE 17,MISS 21/		TO 26th BN, CLASS Z RESERVE.	
CARR	Edwd	PTE	22 / 432			DIPTON			27/5/18	NOV 16	SOISSONS MEM	TO 25th, 1/5th BNS.	BORN KIMBLESWORTH. RENUMBERED 243169.
CARR	Geo	PTE	22 / 619		6 PRUDHOE PLACE	NEWCASTLE							
CARR	H	SGT	22 / 977										
CARR	Peter	SGT	22 /1094	A		NEWSHAM			1/7/16	MISSING OCT 16	THIEPVAL MEM		BORN BLYTH.
CARR	Stan	PTE	22 /1082		11 HARLE STREET	GATESHEAD			KR para 392			TO 2nd GARRISON, 17th, 12/13th BNS.	
CARRUTHERS	F	PTE	22 / 480										TUNNELLING SECTION?

CARSON	Sam	PTE	22 / 662				24/11/14	2/2/15	UNFIT				TO DEPOT.	
CARVER	JohnW	PTE	22											AWOL 20/11/15
CAUSEWELL	Jos	PTE	22											AWOL 16/10/15
CAYGILL	Ralph	PTE	22 / 209			DURHAM CITY	16/11/14	3/1/18	WOUNDS		JUNE 16		TO 3rd BN.	AGE 48.
CHAMBERS	Jas R	PTE	22 / 768			CATCHGATE				9/4/17	JULY 16	ARRAS MEM	TO 16th BN.	BORN NEWCASTLE.
CHAPMAN	FredT	PTE	22 / 591		142 STEVENSON ROAD	SOUTH SHIELDS				29/3/16		BREWERY ORCHARD CEM		AGE 39.
CHARLTON	David	PTE	22											AWOL 5/12/15
CHARLTON	G	PTE	22 /1174	TPT									TO EAST YORKSHIRE REGT(1st BN), CLASS Z RESERVE.	EAST YORKS No 50768.
CHARLTON	Geo	PTE	22 / 415	C		BURNHOPEFIELD				1/7/16	MISSING OCT 16	THIEPVAL MEM		BORN MORPETH.
CHARLTON	Geo W	PTE	22 / 212											
CHARLTON	JohnE	SGT	22 / 877						KRpara392				TO DURHAM LIGHT INFANTRY, TRAINING RESERVE BN.	TRG RES No TR/5/58185.
CHESNEY	Robt	LCPL	22 /1175		56 WYNYARD STREET	DAWDON				5/7/16	AUGUST 16, DoW OCT 16	HEILLY STATION CEM		BORN SUNNYSIDE AGE 24.
CHISHOLM	Jasp	PTE	22 /1688			SEAHAM	16/7/15	12/2/18	GSW		NOV 16, DEC 17.		TO DEPOT.	AGE 27.
CHORLEY	Wm	PTE	22 / 266										TO 18th, 9th BNS.	
CHURCHILL	Jos A	LCPL	22 /1348										TO CLASS Z RESERVE.	
CLARENCE	EdwdP	TE	22 / 220		1 TYNE VIEW	BROMLEY								
CLARK	Archi	PTE	22 / 794	D	BANK TOP	THROCKLEY					MARCH 17, MISS 21/3/18		TO CLASS Z RESERVE.	
CLARK	Berrt	SGT	22 / 271	C	16 BRUNEL STREET	GATESHEAD				1/7/16	JULY 16, MISS NOV 16.	THIEPVAL MEM		BORN GRANTHAM LINCS.
CLARK	John	PTE	22 /1171			SUNDERLAND	4/1/15	1/4/19	KR para 392		MISSING OCT 16, NOT MISS		ATTACHED 102nd LIGHT TRENCH MORTAR BATTERY, A RES CLASS P	
CLARK	PhilM	LCPL	22 / 295			BEDLINGTON STN				1/7/16		THIEPVAL MEM		BORN BLYTH.
CLARK	Wm	PTE	22 / 408		13 HIGH ST WEST	GATESHEAD							TO 1st GARRISON BN.	
CLARK	Wm	SGT	22 / 879			STAKEFORD	17/11/14	9/7/17	GSW		JAN 17		TO DEPOT.	AGE 22.
CLARKE	Geo	PTE	22 /1421		42 CURTHBERT STREET	MARLEY HILL	9/1/15	10/8/17	GSW		AUGUST 16		TO DEPOT.	
CLARKSON	JohnT	PTE	22											AWOL 26/10/15
CLEARY	Wm	PTE	22 /1122		120 FRAMWELLGATE	DURHAM CITY							TO 2nd GARRISON BN.	ALSO ON AVL MISSION YARD NEW ELVET.
CLIMPSON	Cuth	PTE	22 /1172		7 LAMPTON STREET	BIDDICK							TO 1st GARRISON BN, CLASS Z RESERVE.	
CLISH	John	PTE	22 /1176		2 CAROLINE STREET	HETTON LE HOLE					SEPT 16		TO ROYAL DEFENCE CORPS(151 PROTECTION COY).	AWOL 15/7/15.
COCHRANE	Thos	PTE	22											AWOL 2/8/15, AGE 22.
COE	RobtW	PTE	22 /1420	C	56 THIRD ROW	ASHINGTON				1/7/16	MISSING OCT 16	THIEPVAL MEM		
COLE	Thos	PTE	22 / 583		6 MILTON ROW	OLD BENWELL				24/2/16		SAILLY SUR LYS CANADIAN CEM		AGE 34.
COLE	Wm	PTE	22 / 178			NEWCASTLE					AUGUST 16		TO 9th BN.	
COLEMAN	A F J	CPL	22 /1177			BLYTH					JULY 16, JAN 18.		TO 16th BN, CLASS Z RESERVE.	
CONDER	Geo	DRMR	22 / 860		23 ABBOTT STREET	GATESHEAD	23/11/14	30/10/17	WOUNDS		AUGUST 16		TO 3rd BN.	AGE 22.
CONLEY	Peter	PTE	22 /1558			MONKWEARMOUTH					MARCH 18			AWOL 9/8/15
CONNELL	James	PTE	22											AWOL 25/9/15
CONNELLY	James	PTE	22											DESERTED 20/3/15
CONROY	Wm	PTE	22 /1178			SEAHAM HARBOUR				30/5/16		ALBERT COM CEM EXT		BORN KELLOE.
COOK	RichH	PTE	22 /1592						KR para 392					
COOK	Wm	PTE	22 / 769			WEST RYTON				1/7/16	MAY 16, MISS OCT 16.	THIEPVAL MEM		
COOK	Wm	CPL	22 / 855		34 DOUBLE ROW BATES	SEATON DELAVAL				8/8/18		MAILLY WOOD CEM	TO EAST YORKSHIRE REGT(1st BN).	STRETCHER BEARER, E YORKS No 42578.AGE 33.
COOPER	Geo A	PTE	22 /1179		40 ETHEL STREET	SUNDERLAND	29/12/14				AUG 16,APR 18,REP MISS 29		TO 24th, 1st BNS, CLASS Z RESERVE.	
COPE	JohnW	PTE	22 /1180				4/1/15	6/11/17	SICK				TO 1st GARRISON BN, DEPOT.	AGE 41.
CORBRICK	John	PTE	22 / 331		5 D'ARCY STREET	TYNEDOCK	17/11/14	20/10/17	KR para 392					
CORBRICK	John	PTE	22 / 318		5 D'ARCY STREET	TYNEDOCK	17/11/14						TO 1st GARRISON BN, CLASS Z RESERVE.	
CORNER	Thos	PTE	22 / 138			TYNEDOCK	13/11/14							MINER AGE 24, DESERTED 8/3/15, 5'4". FELL IN THE TYNI
CORNISH	Thos	PTE	22 /1594		32 GARDEN PLACE	OLD PENSHAW	23/1/15	19/7/18	DEBILITY				TO 2nd GARRISON BN, DEPOT.	AGE 47.
COSSER	Edwd	LCPL	22 /1100		AKELD	WOOLER				12/8/18	SEPT 16	ETAPLES MIL CEM	TO CORPS OF MILITARY POLICE(ATT APM ETAPLES).	MIL POL No P/15490.AGE 43.
COWEN	JohnT	PTE	22 / 326			LANGLEY MOOR	17/11/14	11/10/17	WOUNDS		AUGUST 16		TO 3rd BN.	AGE 32.
COWIE	Geo	PTE	22 / 351						KR para 392				TO EAST YORKSHIRE REGT(1st BN).	E YORKS No 50666.
COWIE	James	PTE	22 / 730	B		NEWCASTLE				1/7/16	MISSING OCT 16	THIEPVAL MEM		IN 7 PLATOON.
COWLE	Wilf	PTE	22 /1011										TO 20th BN, EAST YORKSHIRE REGT(1st BN), CLASS Z RE	E YORKS No 50656.
CRAIG	Jos	PTE	22 /1631			JARROW				7/7/16		BOIS GUILLAUME COM CEM		BORN NORTH SHIELDS.
CRAIG	Jos	LCPL	22 /1425		212 HIGH STREET	HETTON LE HOLE							TO 2nd GARRISON BN, CLASS Z RESERVE.	
CRANE	Ste J	PTE	22 /1756		27 MILBOURNE TERRAC	HOLYWELL					NOV 17		TO 21st, 11th, 16th, 1/4th, 9th, 1st, 3rd BNS, CLASS Z RES.	
CRANSWICK	EdmdJ	PTE	22 /1487			SUNDERLAND				1/7/16	MISSING OCT 16	THIEPVAL MEM		BORN YORK.
CRAWFORD	Geo	PTE	22 /1181		10 ELEANOR LANE	EASINGTON LANE	6/1/15	27/2/18	KR para 392				TO 2nd GARRISON BN.	
CRELLIN	JohnW	PTE	22 /1017										TO EAST YORKSHIRE REGT(1st BN), CLASS Z RESERVE.	E YORKS No 50654.
CRISFIELD	Wm T	LCPL	22 /1228				31/12/14	8/4/18	GSW				TO DEPOT.	
CROSSTHWAIT	Fred	PTE	22 /1735										TO EAST YORKSHIRE REGT(1st BN), CLASS Z RESERVE.	E YORKS No 50655.
CRUICKSHANK	John	CPL	22 / 976			BLYTH	10/11/14	1/4/18	VDH		SEPT 16		TO DEPOT.	AGE 41.
CRUICKSHANK	RobtW	LCPL	22 / 590										TO 12/13th BN.	
CRYLE	Robt	PTE	22 /1708	C	23 BOWMAN STREET	NEWCASTLE				1/7/16	MISSING OCT 16	THIEPVAL MEM		AGE 18.
CULLERTON	Thos	PTE	22 /1496				1/2/15	2/9/17	DAH				TO DEPOT.	AGE 22.
CUNNINGHAM	J	PTE	22 / 965			SOUTH SHIELDS					NOV 16, JUNE 18.			
CURRY	Adam	PTE	22 / 386			WESTMOOR		9/2/19			AUGUST 16		TO YORK & LANCASTER REGIMENT(18th BN).	Y&L No 62386.
CURRY	Alex	PTE	22 /1564										TO ROYAL FUSILIERS(24th BN).	FRANCE 22 10/1/16-18/6/17, 22 28/11/17-28/8/18, 24RF-7/1/
CURRY	Geo	PTE	22 / 264			SOUTH SHIELDS				20/10/17		TYNE COT MEM		BORN DURHAM CITY.
CURRY	Luke	PTE	22 /1025		5 BILLY MILL LANE	CHIRTON	12/11/14	16/4/18	SICK				TO DEPOT.	AGE 35.
CURRY	Ralph	PTE	22 / 582	A		USWORTH	20/11/14	26/7/17	GSW		OCT 16		TO 3rd BN.	
CURRY	Rich	LCPL	22 / 185			PELTON FELL					AUGUST 16		TO 26th BN.	
CUTTER	Edwin	PTE	22 / 898	C		FELLING				1/7/16	MISSING OCT 16	THIEPVAL MEM		AGE 21.
CUTTER	Wm	PTE	22 / 437						KRpara392				TO DURHAM LIGHT INFANTRY, TRAINING RESERVE BN.	TRG RES No TR/5/41413.
DAGLISH	Chas	CPL	22 /1397		10 PERCY TERRACE	ANNFIELD PLAIN	8/1/15	31/3/19	KR para 392		AUGUST 16		TO ARMY RESERVE CLASS P.	
DAGLISH	Frn S	PTE	22 /1396				9/1/15	31/3/19	KR para 392				TO 23rd BN, ARMY RESERVE CLASS P.	
DALE	James	LCPL	22 / 911	A		TYNEMOUTH				1/7/16	MAY 16, MISS OCT 16	THIEPVAL MEM		BORN BERMONDSEY.
DALEY	J T	PTE	22 /1619		56 CHURCH STREET	BOLDON COLLIERY								
DALEY	Jos	PTE	22 / 593				20/11/14	22/10/17	SICK					AGE 43, DID NOT SERVE OVERSEAS.
DAVIDSON	Cuth	PTE	22 /1185								MISSING 21/3/18		TO CLASS Z RESERVE.	
DAVIDSON	JohnG	SGT	22 /1182			EASINGTON LANE	2/1/15	4/3/18	WOUNDS		AUGUST 16		TO DEPOT.	AGE 27.
DAVIES	Geo	CPL	22 /1186	B		SEAHAM HARBOUR				10/9/16		BAILLEUL COM CEM EXT		BORN BINCHESTER.
DAVIES	Wm H	PTE	22 / 413		6 TWEED STREET	CHOPWELL							TO 1st GARRISON BN, CLASS Z RESERVE.	ALSO ON AVL 10a BENFIELDSIDE RD BENFIELDSIDE.
DAVIS	James	PTE	22 /1763										TO 2nd GARRISON BN.	
DAVIS	Wm	LCPL	22 / 882		23 BELL VUE TERRACE	TYNEDOCK				25/6/16		HEILLY STATION CEM		AGE 27
DAVISON	John	CPL	22 /1098					23/10/17	KR para 392				TO 84th TRAINING RESERVE BN.	AGE 33.
DAVISON	Percy	PTE	22 /1720				14/7/15	31/3/19	KR para 392				TO ARMY RESERVE CLASS P.	AWOL 6/8/15
DAVISON	R	LSGT	22 /1106											
DAVISON	Rich	PTE	22 / 526		BOTHAL PARK	PEGSWOOD				27/9/18		ROYAULCOURT MIL CE	TO 14th, 1st BNS.	AGE 27.
DAVISON	Robt	PTE	22 / 348		15 WOOD ROW	NORTH SEATON							TO 1st GARRISON BN, CLASS Z RESERVE.	
DAVISON	Thos	PTE	22 /1117			ASHINGTON	4/1/15				OCT 16		TO 24th, 8th BNS, CLASS Z RESERVE.	MINER AGE 22, DESERTED 25/6/15, 5'5".
DAWSON	Thos	PTE	22 /1189		16 MOUNT STEWART S	SEAHAM COLLIERY		24/7/19					TO YORK & LANCASTER REGT(2/4th BN), CLASS Z RESEI	Y&L No 57628.
DAY	Wm	CPL	22 / 429		90 BLANFORD STREET	NEWCASTLE							TO 3rd BN.	
DEAS	Robt	LCPL	22 / 801										REENLISTED NORTHUMBERLAND HUSSARS 1/7/20.	
DELANEY	Edwd	PTE	22 / 789		36 MILITARY ROAD	SOUTH SHIELDS				17/2/16		RUE PETILLON MIL CEM		BORN TYNEDOCK, ACCIDENTALLY KILLED.
DENMEAD	Llewl	PTE	22 / 831			LESBURY				3/7/16		HEILLY STATION CEM		BORN EMBLETON.
DENNISON	JohnB	CPL	22 / 227			NORTH SHIELDS	18/11/14	27/10/17	KR para 392		OCT 16		TO 3rd BN.	AGE 27.
DERBY	Wm S	LCPL	22 / 848			HETTON LE HOLE				23/4/17		ARRAS MEM	TO 10th, 9th(B COY) BNS.	
DERBYSHIRE	Thos	PTE	22 / 3		97 BEDE STREET	SOUTH SHIELDS				4/7/16		PUCHEVILLERS BRIT CEM		BORN WEST HAM, DIED AT 44 CAS CLR STN AGE 31.
DICKENSON	Alf B	PTE	22 /1063			NEWCASTLE					AUGUST 16		TO DURHAM LI.	DURHAM LI No 46283.
DISBERRY	Wm	PTE	22 / 928			STOCKSFIELD				2/10/16		RATION FARM CEM		BORN SHOTLEY BRIDGE AGE 22.
DISTON	Henry	SGT	22 / 699		20 FIFE STREET	NEWCASTLE							TO 2nd GARRISON BN, CLASS Z RESERVE.	
DIXON	Chris	PTE	22 /1190	B		ASHINGTON				21/8/17		IN INDIA	TO 2nd GARRISON BN.	
DIXON	Jas	PTE	22 / 245			ASHINGTON				10/7/16	AUGUST 16	BOULOGNE EASTERN CEM		BORN BEDLINGTON.
DIXON	John	CPL	22 /1099	C	65 ROSALIND STREET	ASHINGTON				1/7/16	MISSING OCT 16	THIEPVAL MEM		BORN BLYTH AGE 41.
DIXON	JohnW	LCPL	22 / 941		207 TAYLOR STREET	SOUTH SHIELDS				8/6/17		ARRAS MEM	TO 16th, 22nd BNS.	AGE 23.
DIXON	Jos W	CPL	22 / 799			BEDLINGTON	16/11/14			9/4/17	AUGUST 16	BAILLEUL RD EAST CEM		HORSEMAN DESERTED 19/7/15, AGE 19, 5'5".
DIXON	Wm	CPL	22 / 595		THE AVENUE	CHESTER LE ST				5/6/17	AUGUST 16	ARRAS MEM	TO 16th, 22nd BNS.	BORN FELTON AGE 21.
DIXON	Wm	PTE	22 /1630			WALLSEND	13/11/14	21/8/17	GSW		AUGUST 16			AGE 24, ROYAL VICTORIA HOSP NETLEY 11/7/16.
DOBINSON	Geo	PTE	22 /1123		2 BRICK ROW	FRAMGATE MOOR				21/3/18		ARRAS MEM		COMPANY RUNNER AGE 21.
DOBSON	Mart	PTE	22 / 520	C		BEBSIDE FURNACE				1/7/16	MISSING OCT 16	THIEPVAL MEM		BORN BLYTH.
DOBSON	T G	LCPL	22 / 494											MACHINE GUN SECTION.
DODD	Geo	PTE	22 / 585	B		NEWCASTLE				1/7/16	MISSING OCT 16	THIEPVAL MEM		IN 7 PLATOON.
DODDS	Geo	PTE	22 / 229			WALLSEND					SEPT 16, DEC 16.		TO 12/13th BN.	
DONALD	G M	PTE	22			PENSHAW								
DONALD	Thos	PTE	22 / 234		95 ALBION STREET	NEWCASTLE							TO 2nd GARRISON BN , CLASS Z RESERVE.	
DONALDSON	Robt	PTE	22 / 934		14 ASHLEY ROAD	TYNEDOCK				20/3/16		SAILLY SUR LYS CANADIAN CEM		BORN SUNDERLAND AGE 22.
DONNELLY	Thos	PTE	22 /1569						KRpara392				TO DURHAM LIGHT INFANTRY, TRAINING RESERVE BN.	TRG RES No TR/5/58189.
DONNOLLY	Thos	PTE	22 /1569											AWOL 15/12/15.
DOUGLAS	Frncs	CPL	22 / 871			MORPETH				22/6/16		ALBERT COM CEM EXT		BORN ALNWICK.
DOUGLAS	JohnT	PTE	22 /1548		8 CHAPEL ROW	NEW PENSHAW	1/2/15						TO 1st GARRISON BN.	
DOVER	Jos	PTE	22 /1649				29/3/15	19/2/18	SICK				TO 1st GARRISON, 3rd BNS.	AGE 40.
DOW	Thos	CSM	22 /1103				17/12/14	31/1/16	TUBERCULOSIS				TO 2nd GARRISON BN.	DID NOT SERVE OVERSEAS.
DOWLING	John	PTE	22 /1503			FENCEHOUSES	25/1/15				SSHOCK DEC 16		TO CLASS Z RESERVE.	MINER BORN CUMBERLAND, DESERTED 28/6/15, AGE 24

DOWLING	Jos	PTE	22										AGE 25 AWOL 16/7/15.
DOWNS	Thos	LCPL	22 / 397	D	26 VINE STREET	GATESHEAD				1/7/16		TO ROYAL ENGINEERS(G&M COY).	XI PLN, COUNTY OF LONDON WAR HOSP EPSOM 7/16, R
DOWSON	Wm J	PTE	22 /1742			NORTH SHIELDS			22/6/16		HEILLY STATION CEM		
DRURIE	Jas E	CPL	22 / 936						KR para 392			TO DURHAM LIGHT INFANTRY, TRAINING RESERVE BN.	TRG RES No TR/5/59067.
DRYDEN	JohnT	PTE	22 /1471		19 MOUNT PLEASANT	OLD PENSHAW	25/1/15	12/10/18	SICK			TO 1st GARRISON BN.	AGE 47.
DRYSDALE	Law H	PTE	22 / 436						2/11/17		GAZA WAR CEM	TO NORTHAMPTONSHIRE REGT(1/4th BN).	AWOL 13/3/15, 19/7/15, NORTHANTS No 47035.
DUFFY	John	CSM	22 / 980			NEW DELAVAL				NOV 16		TO CLASS Z RESERVE.	ACTING RSM.
DUFFY	Mich	CPL	22 / 121				10/11/14	5/3/15	SICK				AGE 40.
DUGDALE	John	SGT	22 /1191			HORDEN			5/6/17		ARRAS MEM		BORN SOUTHWICK
DUNBAR	Wm	PTE	22										AWOL 19/11/15
DUNCAN	John	PTE	22 /1502		32 EAST STREET	SUNDERLAND	25/1/15		1/7/16		THIEPVAL MEM		
DUNN	Alex	LCPL	22 /1584	A		ASHINGTON			1/7/16	MISSING OCT16	THIEPVAL MEM		BORN GLASGOW
DUNN	Edwd	PTE	22 / 461			BEDLINGTON				MARCH 17			
DUNN	Geo	CPL	22 / 246			HIRST			19/9/18	AUGUST 16	VIS-EN-ARTOIS MEM	TO 1st BN.	BORN WIGTON CUMBERLAND.
DUNNING	Jas W	PTE	22 /1427		115 FRONT STREET	CROOKHALL				NOV 16		TO 16th BN, CLASS Z RESERVE.	
DURHAM	Geo S	PTE	22 / 139			SOUTH SHIELDS				JULY 16, SEPT 16.			
EDDY	Arth	PTE	22 / 715				14/11/14	23/10/15	KR para 392				DID NOT SERVE OVERSEAS
EDGAR	Ernst	PTE	22 /1423			NEWCASTLE			KR para 392	OCT 16			
EDGELL	Geo	PTE	22 / 648			NORTH CRASTER	13/11/14	28/3/18	SICK	AUGUST 16		TO ARMY RESERVE CLASS P.	AGE 23.
EDWARDS	J S W	PTE	22 /1330						KR para 392				
EGLINTINE	Alf P	PTE	22 / 134	B	39 JOHNSON STREET	SOUTH SHIELDS			1/7/16	MISSING OCT 16 GAZ	SERRE ROAD No 2.		AGE 19.
ELLIOTT	David	PTE	22 / 313									TO 2nd GARRISON BN, CLASS Z RESERVE.	AWOL 7/8/15.
ELLIOTT	JohnR	PTE	22 /1043			WHITLEY BAY			26/2/17		FABOURG DE AMIENS ARRAS		
ELLISON	A	PTE	23 / 377									TO LABOUR CORPS.	TO 3CCS 2/7/16 EVAC 2/7/16 WND LEGS.LAB CORPS No 4
ELLWOOD	Isaac	PTE	22 / 263										
ELSENDER	Robt	PTE	22 / 119			FOREST HALL	14/11/14	17/11/16	WOUNDS	JULY 16		TO DEPOT.	
ELSENDER	Wm	PTE	22 / 120										
EMBLETON	Albt	PTE	22 / 196					4/3/19	PHYSC UNFIT			TO YORK & LANCASTER REGT(2/4th BN).	Y&L No 57605.
EMBLETON	James	PTE	22 / 621		47 MELBOURNE STREE	NEWCASTLE						TO 8th, 18th BNS.	OFFICERS GROOM.
EMMERSON	John	PTE	22 / 757		14 ROBINSON STREET	SOUTH SHIELDS			1/5/17	JULY 16	AUBIGNY COM CEM	TO 20th, 26th BNS.	DIED OF GAS POISONING, AGE 24.
EMMERSON	JohnJ	PTE	22 / 101		4 HARTINGTON STREET	CONSETT			3/7/16		HEILLY STATION CEM		AGE 36.
ENGLISH	Alb G	PTE	22 /1193	C	12 CROWTREE TERRAC	SUNDERLAND			1/7/16	MISSING OCT 16 GAZ	THIEPVAL MEM		AGE 19.
ENGLISH	McG	SGT	22 /1194				10/1/15	29/10/17	GSW			TO 3rd BN.	AGE 23.
ERRINGTON	Cuth	PTE	22 / 933	B		SOUTH SHIELDS				JULY 16, MISS 21/3/18		TO CLASS Z RESERVE.	
ESPIE	Robt	CPL	22 / 923									TO CLASS Z RESERVE.	
EVANS	Edw W	PTE	22 / 387				17/11/14	5/7/18	SICK			TO ARMY RESERVE CLASS W.	AGE 43.
EYTON	Hugh	CPL	22 / 482				18/11/14	18/10/17	SICK			TO 1st GARRISON BN, DEPOT.	
FAIRBAIRN	CharT	PTE	22 /1604	C		SEAHAM HARBOUR			1/7/16	MISSING NOV 16	THIEPVAL MEM		BORN DURHAM CITY.
FAIRBRIDGE	Wm	PTE	22 /1489		3 LIVINGSTONE ROAD	SUNDERLAND	1/2/15		SICK				AGE 40.
FAIRBURN	Hen A	LCPL	22 /1195		6 FIFTH ST EAST	EASINGTON			23/10/18	SEPT 16		TO 1st BN.	BORN SOUTH SHIELDS.
FAIRHOLM	Jos	CPL	22 /1670		87 BEATRICE STREET	HIRST						ATTACHED 102nd LIGHT TRENCH MORTAR BATTERY.	
FAIRHOLME	Adam	PTE	22 /1092			NEWCASTLE	12/11/14	16/6/17	GAS POISONING	JULY 16		TO 3rd BN.	AGE 39.
FAIRLEY	W P F	PTE	22 / 777			NEWCASTLE	16/11/14	17/9/18	EPILEPSY	AUGUST 16		TO 10th, 18th, 19th BNS.	AGE 21.
FALCONER	Alex	CSM	22 /1078	C		NEWCASTLE			1/7/16	MISSING OCT 16	THIEPVAL MEM		BORN GLASGOW.
FALLON	Thos	PTE	22										AWOL 13/5/15.
FARRIMOND	JohnJ	PTE	22 / 406				17/11/14						MINER AGE 19, 5'4", DESERTED 25/6/15.
FARROW	Robt	PTE	22 / 914		THE FOUNDRY	CASTLE EDEN						TO CLASS Z RESERVE.	
FAULDER	ThosH	PTE	22 /1339	C		CHOPWELL			1/7/16	MISSING OCT 16	THIEPVAL MEM		AGE 21.
FELTON	Jos W	PTE	22 /1575		58 RESEVOIR STREET	WARDLEY COLL						TO 1st GARRISON BN, CLASS Z RESERVE.	
FELTON	Wm	PTE	22 / 486		21 RESEVOIR STREET	WARDLEY COLL			22/6/16		ALBERT COM CEM EXT		BORN BILLQUAY.
FENWICK	Jos	PTE	22 / 371	C		ANNFIELD PLAIN			1/7/16	MISSING OCT 16	OVILLERS MIL CEM		
FERGUSON	Jos	PTE	22 / 967					KRpara392				TO DURHAM LIGHT INFANTRY, TRAINING RESERVE BN.	TRG RES No TR/5/58190.
FERGUSON	Robt	PTE	22 / 179									TO 1st GARRISON BN, CLASS Z RESERVE.	
FERGUSON	Wm	PTE	22 / 942	B	15 TYRELL STREET	GATESHEAD			1/7/16	MISSING OCT 16	SERRE ROAD No 2		BORN SOUTH SHIELDS AGE 18.
FERRIDAY	Wm H	PTE	22 /1104									TO 2nd GARRISON BN, CLASS Z RESERVE.	AWOL 3/7, 10/8, 23/9, 13/10/15, MULTIPLE COURT APPEA
FINDLEY	Alex	PTE	22 /1079	A	HIGH MICKLEY	STOCKSFIELD			1/7/16	MISSING OCT 16	THIEPVAL MEM		BORN DISSINGTON CUMBERLAND AGE 38.
FINLAY	Ernst	PIPR	22 /1198		4 ILCHESTER STREET	DAWDON			22/6/16		THIEPVAL MEM		BORN HOUGHTON LE SPRING AGE 22.
FIRBANKS	James	PTE	22 / 70		38 BYKER PLACE	NEWCASTLE			1/7/16	MISSING DEC 16	THIEPVAL MEM	TO 23rd BN(C COY).	BORN GATESHEAD AGE 20.
FISHER	Ferg	PTE	22 / 492		61 OAK STREET	GATESHEAD						TO 1st GARRISON BN, CLASS Z RESERVE.	
FISHER	Geo W	PTE	22 /1377									TO SCOTTISH RIFLES(18th BN).	SCO RIF No 55583.
FOGGO	Steph	PTE	22 / 330			BYKER			21/7/16	AUG 16, DOW NOV 16.	BYKER & HEATON CEM		
FORBES	Thos	PTE	22 / 244			BURRADON			KR para 392	OCT 16		TO TERRITORIAL BN.	ALLOTED NEW No 267614.
FORRESTER	Robt	LCPL	22 / 846		15 SHORT ROW WEST	HIGH SPEN				AUGUST 16, DEC 17.		TO 8th, 23rd, 9th BNS, CLASS Z RESERVE.	
FORSTER	Chris	PTE	22 / 231		42 FRONT STREET	CHESTER LE ST						TO 2nd GARRISON BN, CLASS Z RESERVE.	
FORSTER	Dav W	PTE	22 / 44		2 PERKINS STREET	NEWCASTLE							
FORSTER	Geo	PTE	22 /1538	B		JARROW			1/7/16	MISSING OCT 16	THIEPVAL MEM		AGE 23, BORN TYNE DOCK.
FORSTER	Robt	PTE	22 / 874	C		RYTON			1/7/16	JULY 16, MISSING OCT 16	THIEPVAL MEM		
FORSYTH	R	PTE	22 /1430										
FOSTER	E	LCPL	22 / 356										
FOSTER	Thos	PTE	22 /1474	B		JARROW			1/7/16	MISSING OCT 16	THIEPVAL MEM		BORN TYNE DOCK AGE 23.
FOWLER	Geo	LCPL	22 /1350			BURNHOPEFIELD	6/1/15		10/9/16	MISSING FEB 17	NEIUPORT MEM		MINER BORN SUNDERLAND AGE 23, 5'7" DESERTED 10/
FOX	Jas B	PTE	22 / 612		18 MILITARY ROAD	SOUTH SHIELDS			19/2/16		MERVILLE		
FRASER	Jas M	PTE	22 / 144			CHOPPINGTON	12/11/14	11/12/17	GSW	JULY 16		TO DEPOT.	AGE 22.
FRASER	Jos	PTE	22 / 622	A	31 SOMERSET STREET	GATESHEAD				MISS OCT 16, N MIS WND FE			TRANSPORT SECTION.
FRAZER	Geo	LCPL	22 /1135	C	13 CORT STREET	BLACKHILL			1/7/16	MISSING OCT 16	CERISY GAILLY CEM		BORN CONSETT AGE 26.
FRENCH	Thos	SGT	22 / 823				18/11/14	7/8/19	KR para 392				
FURLONG	Chas	PTE	22 / 643										
GALES	Robt	PTE	22 /1727			CHESTER MOOR	15/7/15	25/1/17	WOUNDS	AUG 16		TO DEPOT.	
GARDINER	Geo	PTE	22 / 674		22 THAMES STREET	SUNDERLAND			12/6/15		BISHOPWEARMOUTH		BORN CULLEN SCOTLAND.
GASCOIGNE	Chris	PTE	22 / 986	C		ASHINGTON			1/7/16	MISSING OCT 16 GAZ	THIEPVAL MEM		BORN KILLINGWORTH.
GIBSON	James	PTE	22 / 554				21/11/14	18/8/17	GSW			TO 23rd, 20th BNS, DEPOT.	AGE 38.
GILLESPIE	Wm	PTE	22 / 364			HEBBURN	16/11/14	16/2/17	WOUNDS	JULY 16		TO 84th TRAINING RESERVE BN.	
GIRKING	Thos	PTE	22 / 563		20 THE PARADE	HARRATON							
GLEASE	John	PTE	22 / 546	TPT				7/2/19				TO YORK & LANCASTER REGT(2/4th BN).	Y&L No 57635.
GLENDINNING	Jos J	SGT	22 /1410		13 OAST ROAD	MICKLEY				SHELLSHOCK AUG 16		COMMISSIONED 2Lt 11/9/18.	
GODBER	Len	DMJR	22			GRANTHAM LINCS							
GOODALL	Wm	PTE	22 /1682				21/4/15	25/5/17	VDH			TO 1st GARRISON BN, DEPOT.	AGE 47.
GOODFELLOW	Wm N	PTE	22 /1678		PICKARDS YD CLAYPOI	ALNWICK				OCT 16		TO LEICESTERSHIRE REGT(13th BN), LABOUR CORPS(2(	TO 9th BN NF, CLASS Z RESERVE. LEIC No 35299.LAB No
GOTTS	Jas A	LCPL	22 / 155	B	43 MIDDLE ROW	SEATON DELAVAL			1/7/16	MISSING NOV 16 GAZ	THIEPVAL MEM		BORN EARSDON AGE 22.
GOUGH	Wm	LCPL	22 /1470		7 NELSON STREET	SOUTHWICK			9/4/17		BAILLEUL ROAD EAST CEM		BORN MANCHESTER.
GOURLEY	John	PTE	22 / 145			NORTH SHIELDS	16/11/14	2/3/18	GSW	SEPT 16		TO DEPOT.	
GRAHAM	A	PTE	22 / 478										MACHINE GUN SECTION.
GRAHAM	Geo	PTE	22 /1536		2 THIRD STREET	WHEATLEY HILL			9/4/17		ROCLINCOURT MIL CEM		BORN SOUTHWICK AGE 22.
GRAHAM	John	PTE	22 /1624						KR para 392			TO EAST YORKSHIRE REGT(1st BN).	E YORKS No 50769.
GRAHAM	Jos	PTE	22 / 282			WEST SLEEKBURN	10/11/14	28/2/19	KR para 392	JULY 16, JUNE 18.		TO ARMY RESERVE CLASS P.	
GRAHAM	Robt	LCPL	22 / 166									TO ROYAL INNISKILLING FUSILIERS(6th BN).	R INNIS FUS No 21539.
GRAHAM	Thos	LCPL	22 / 614			SOUTH SHIELDS				OCT 16		TO 9th, 23rd, 1/4th BNS.	
GRAINGER	Chas	PTE	22 / 657			BRADFORD			20/7/18			TO KINGS OWN YORKSHIRE LI(2/4th BN).	KOYLI No 42396. THIS MAN IS PROB 29/
GRANT	Thos	PTE	22 / 285			EAST JARROW				NOV 16		TO 19th BN.	
GRANT	WmEm	PTE	22 /1728			WHITLEY BAY	15/7/15	30/11/17	SICK	MARCH 17		TO DEPOT.	AGE 41.
GRAY	Jas H	PTE	22 / 615									TO DURHAM LIGHT INFANTRY(1/7th BN), CLASS Z RESEF	MACHINE GUN SECTION. DLI No 78087.
GREEN	Geo	PTE	22 /1582				5/1/15	2/1/18	WOUNDS			TO DEPOT.	BOMBER.
GREEN	Thos	CPL	22 / 307		97 ELM STREET	SOUTH MOOR			2/11/18	OCT 16	TERLINCTHUN BRIT CE	TO ROYAL FUSILIERS(24th BN).	R FUS No G/93094.
GREENHAIGH	Osw P	CQMS	22 / 809				16/11/14	11/5/18	NEURASTHENIA			TO 3rd BN.	AGE 24.
GREENWOOD	John	PTE	22 /1199		3 WYNYARD STREET								
GRIEVES	Edw R	PIPR	22 / 781		32 HEATON GROVE	HEATON			6/7/16		ETAPLES MIL CEM		BORN BLYTH AGE 18.
GRIFFITHS	Chas	PTE	22 /1389	B	84 LONGNEWTON STRE	DAWDON			1/7/16		THIEPVAL MEM		BORN HASWELL.
GRUNLAW	J	PTE	22 / 796										
GUDGEON	Wm	PTE	22 / 261			SOUTH SHIELDS				SEPT 16		TO ROYAL INNISKILLING FUSILIERS(6th BN).	R INNIS FUS No 21544.
GUNN	Phil	RQMS	22 / 984				3/11/18	13/3/18	5/4/18 VDH		ST ANDREWS JESMOND		
HAGGERTY	J E G	PTE	22 /1667		1 ARGYLE TERRACE	NEWBIGGIN							
HAIGH	James	SGT	22 / 11									TO 2nd GARRISON BN, CLASS Z RESERVE.	
HAILEY	Dan	PTE	22										AWOL 10/10/15.
HAKIN	Frank	PTE	22 /1032										
HAKIN	James	CPL	22 /1031			BLYTH	11/11/14	5/11/17	WOUNDS	NOV 16		TO DEPOT.	AGE 25.
HAKIN	John	PTE	22 / 970										
HALL	Alex	PTE	22 / 354										
HALLIBURTON	Wm	PTE	22 / 527				19/11/14	23/10/17	KR para 392				DID NOT SERVE OVERSEAS.
HALLIDAY	John	PTE	22 / 955									TO 19th BN, CLASS Z RESERVE.	
HAMILTON	J	PTE	22 / 524	D						MISSING 21/3/18			
HAMILTON	R	PTE	22 /1089			JARROW				AUGUST 16			R VICTORIA HOSP NETLEY 11/7/16
HARDY	James	CPL	22 /1669		WESTBOAT	HEXAM			5/6/17		ARRAS MEM		

HARDY	Luke	PTE	22	/1737		66 GRACE STREET	BYKER			29/3/16		ETAPLES MIL CEM		AGE 26 BORN STANLEY.
HARDY	Wm	LCPL	22	/1202			EASINGTON			29/12/16	JULY 16	RATION FARM MIL CEM	TO 16th BN.	BORN SOUTH SHIELDS, BEAUFORT WAR HOSP BRISTOL
HARKNESS	JohnT	PTE	22	/ 443			DURHAM CITY			2/9/18			TO YORK & LANCASTER REGT(1/4th BN).	Y&L No 57689.
HARME	ChasF	PTE	22	/ 86			SWALWELL			14/10/17		TYNE COT MEM	TO 10th BN.	BORN DURHAM CITY.
HARPER	RobtW	SGT	22	/ 87			NEWCASTLE	14/11/14	22/3/17	GSW	AUGUST 16		TO 85th TRAINING RESERVE BN.	AGE 29.
HARRIS	Geo C	PTE	22	/1091			JARROW						TO CLASS Z RESERVE.	
HARRIS	James	PTE	22	/1765				30/7/15		VDH			TO 2nd GARRISON BN.	
HARRIS	John	PTE	22	/1572		6 GIRVEN TERRACE	HETTON LYONS							QUATERMASTERS COOK.
HARRIS	John	PTE	22	/1766									TO 20th BN, DURHAM LI(13th BN).	DURHAM LI No 46016.
HARRIS	Robt	PTE	22	/ 731						KR para 392			TO 2nd GARRISON BN.	
HARRISON	Cairn	CPL	22	/1013			SHERRIFF HILL			5/6/17		ARRAS MEM	TO 20th BN(D COY).	
HARRISON	JohnJ	PTE	22	/ 548				17/11/14	27/8/17	DEAFNESS			TO 85th TRAINING RESERVE BN.	
HARRISON	Jos	PTE	22	/ 666		17 SOUTHEND TERRAC	GATESHEAD	21/11/14	26/11/18	GSW	SEPT 16		TO 27th, 16th, 19th BNS.	AGE 22.
HARRISON	Normn	CPL	22	/1206		9 STORE TERRACE	HETTON LE HOLE							
HART	Wm T	PTE	22	/1679		46 MILLING STREET	GATESHEAD	29/4/15	26/2/18	GSW	AUGUST 16		TO ARMY RESERVE CLASS P.	AGE 39.
HARVEY	Andrw	PTE	22	/1500		28 NORTH TERRACE	SEAHAM HARBOUR	1/2/15		17/12/16		SAILLY SUR LYS CANADIAN CEM		BORN GLASGOW AGE 19.
HAWES	Herbt	PTE	22	/1671		76 WOULDHAVE STREE	SOUTH SHIELDS	20/4/15		KR para 392	AUGUST 16			
HAWTHORN	Hen J	SGT	22	/ 779									COMMISSIONED 2nd Lt 1/5/18, ATTACHED R WARWICKSHIRE REGT.	
HAWXBY	JohnT	LCPL	22	/1296			WARDLEY COLL			17/10/17		TYNE COT MEM	TO 21st BN.	
HAYES	Percy	LCPL	22	/ 962	B	12 MAUD ROAD	LEMINGTON			1/7/16	MISSING DEC 16	THIEPVAL MEM		AGE 21.
HEDLEY	Geo	PTE	22	/ 376			NEWCASTLE	16/11/14	19/2/17	WOUNDS	AUGUST 16		TO DEPOT.	TO 3CCS 2/7/16 EVAC 2/7/16 WND BACK.
HEDLEY	Matt	PTE	22	/1369	B		SOUTHWICK			5/6/17		ARRAS MEM		
HEDLEY	Robt	PTE	22	/ 620			ASHINGTON			4/4/17	AUGUST 16, NOV 16.	AUBIGNY COM CEM		BORN BOLDON.
HENDERSON	Archi	PTE	22	/1677				19/4/15	23/11/17	SICK			TO 84th TRAINING RESERVE BN.	AGE 43, DID NOT SERVE OVERSEAS.
HENDERSON	Geo W	PTE	22	/ 92				14/11/14	19/12/17	SICK				AGE 40.
HENDERSON	JohnT	SGT	22	/ 465	C	11 KITCHENER STREET	GATESHEAD	13/11/14	28/8/17	GSW	AUGUST 16		TO DEPOT.	Lt FRYERS PLN SGT, 1/5 NORTHN G HOSP LEICSTER 7/1
HENDERSON	Jos	PTE	22	/ 88									TO 2nd GARRISON BN, CLASS Z RESERVE.	
HENDERSON	Mart	CPL	22	/ 250				15/11/14	26/8/17	SICK			TO 85th TRAINING RESERVE BN.	
HENDERSON	Wm	PTE	22	/ 73	B		FELLING			1/7/16	MISSING DEC 16	THIEPVAL MEM		BORN GLASGOW.
HENLEY	Jos	PTE	22	/ 344				17/11/14	17/7/17	SICK			TO 1st GARRISON BN, DEPOT.	AGE 44.
HENNESSEY	Edwd	PTE	22	/1124	C		ASHINGTON			1/7/16	MISSINGOCT 16	THIEPVAL MEM		
HENRY	James	PTE	22	/1647			NEWCASTLE				JULY 16		TO ROYAL INNISKILLING FUSILIERS(6th BN).	R INNIS FUS No 21549.
HEPPLE	John	PTE	22	/1607									TO 8th BN, CLASS Z RESERVE.	
HEPPLEWHITE	Wm	LCPL	22	/ 594									TO 23rd, 26th BNS.	MACHINE GUN SECTION.
HERMISTON	James	PTE	22	/ 472			NEWCASTLE	18/11/14	18/2/18	GSW	AUGUST 16		TO DEPOT.	AGE 31.
HESLOP	FranS	PTE	22	/ 267									TO 25th, 1/5th, 14th BNS, CLASS Z RESERVE.	ALLOTTED NEW No 243155.
HESLOP	Jos T	PTE	22	/ 100		1 AYNSLEY TERRACE	CONSETT				AUGUST 16		TO 1st, 14th BNS.	
HETHRINGTON	J W	PTE	22	/ 956			SOUTH SHIELDS				OCT 16		TO 2nd BN.	
HETHRINGTON	Normn	PTE	22	/1115				16/11/14	31/12/14	SICK				AGE 23 DID NOT SERVE OVERSEAS.
HEYWOOD	Thos	PTE	22	/ 20									TO 8th, 1/7th, 1st BNS, DURHAM LI(1/5th BN).	NEW No's 5707(8th),291822(1/7th),59357(1/5 DLI).
HILLS	Robt	PTE	22	/ 4			SEATON HIRST		19/3/19	KR para 392	AUGUST 16		TO 12th, 20th, 22nd BNS, YORK & LANCASTER REGT(2/4th	Y&L No 57641.
HINDMARSH	Geo	PTE	22	/ 749			BEBSIDE FURNACE			KR para392	SSHOCK DEC 16			
HINGLEY	Wm J	PTE	22	/1357		12 SWAN STREET WES'	EASINGTON LANE	6/1/15	26/10/17	GAS POISONING				AGE 45.
HIRST	Robt	PTE	22	/1039						26/8/16			TO EAST YORKSHIRE REGT(1st BN).	E YORKS No 50770.
HOBBS	Alf	PTE	22	/1618		115 BEDFORD STREET	NORTH SHIELDS			15/6/15		PRESTON CEM TYNEMOUTH		AGE 34, COMMITTED SUICIDE.
HOBBS	RobrP	PTE	22	/ 547			SOUTH SHIELDS	9/2/15	17/10/17	WOUNDS	AUGUST 16		TO DEPOT.	AGE 29.
HODGES	Robt	PTE	22	/1072			NEWCASTLE	13/11/14	12/3/18	GSW	OCT 16		TO ARMY RESERVE CLASS P.	AGE 31, SPRINGBURN WOODSIDE HOSP GLASGOW 11/7
HODGSON	G W	PTE	22	/ 51										
HOLDEN	EdwdO	LSGT	22	/ 844	D		WEST AUKLAND			1/7/16	MISSING OCT 16			
HOLLAND	Harry	PTE	22	/ 193									ATTACHED 102nd LIGHT TRENCH MORTAR BATTERY.	
HOLMES	Jas C	LCPL	22	/ 30			SEATON DELAVAL				AUGUST 16		TO 12/13th, 19th, 2nd BNS.	
HOLMES	Jas C	PTE	22	/ 80		20 LAUREL TERRACE	HOLYWELL						TO 12/13th BN.	DESERTER.
HOLT	Jos T	PTE	22	/1549		26 BACK CORNHILL RO/	SOUTHWICK	1/2/15					TO 2nd GARRISON BN, CLASS Z RESERVE.	
HOPE	Jos	PTE	22	/1329			HYLTON				AUGUST 18		TO 1st, 12/13th BNS, CLASS Z RESERVE.	
HOPE	Wm	SGT	22	/1398		3 TRAFALGAR ROW	BIDDICK						TO 25th BN, CLASS Z RESERVE.	
HORN	JohnH	PTE	22	/1073			CARLISLE			11/1/18		LONDON CEM NEUVILLE VITASSE		BORN SLAGGYFORD, ACCIDENTALLY KILLED.
HORSLEY	J	PTE	22	/ 896			SOUTH SHIELDS							
HOWARD	Wm	PTE	22	/ 851			NEW YORK NTHBLD	19/11/14	8/9/17	WOUNDS	NOV 16		TO 3rd BN.	AGE 36.
HOWE	John	PTE	22	/ 260			SOUTH SHIELDS	14/11/14	2/2/19	KR para 392	JAN 18		TO DEPOT.	
HOWELL	Wm	PTE	22	/1021			HEBBURN	16/11/14	20/12/17	GSW	OCT 16		TO 3rd BN.	AGE 39.
HOWES	Wm	PTE	22	/ 651		6 GLENSIDE TERRACE	PELTON FELL			22/6/16		HEILLY STATION CEM		AGE 18.
HOWEY	A	PTE	22	/ 890										
HOWEY	Chas	LCPL	22	/ 788	C	11 ISABELLA STREET	SOUTH SHIELDS			1/7/16	MISSING OCT 16	THIEPVAL MEM		BORN JARROW AGE 30.
HUDSON	Chas	LCPL	22	/ 625										
HUGHES	James	PTE	22	/ 679		3 CASTLE ST CHAPELT(	LEEDS	14/11/14	12/1/18	SICK	AUGUST 16		TO 24th(A COY), 3rd BNS.	AGE 22, ON A COY ROLL 24th BN IN IRISH HEROES.
HUGHES	John	PTE	22	/ 440	A		DUDLEY			1/7/16		THIEPVAL MEM		
HUGHFF	Thos	PTE	22	/1126		NEWCASTLE ROW	FRAM/GATE MOOR						TO KOYLI, WEST YORKS, DURHAM LI(28th BN) COMMISSI	COMMISSIONED 23/10/17, ENGINEMAN KIMBLESWORTH
HULL	J T	PTE	22	/ 906										DID NOT SERVE OVERSEAS.
HUME	John	PTE	22	/1125				4/1/15	29/11/15	KR para 392			TO 29th BN.	DID NOT SERVE OVERSEAS.
HUNTER	Arth		22	/1468		15 LOW CHAPEL ROW	BIDDICK							
HUNTER	David	PTE	22	/ 251				15/11/14	23/10/17	SICK			TO 84th TRAINING RESERVE BN.	DID NOT SERVE OVERSEAS.
HUNTER	R	LCPL	22	/ 676			NEWCASTLE				SEPT 16			PIONEER.
HURNEYMAN	David	SGT	22	/1211				4/1/15	7/11/17	SICK				AGE 32.
HUTCHINSON	Wm Ed	PTE	22											AWOL 24/9/15.
HYDE	Chas	PTE	22	/1675		13 ANDERSON STREET	SOUTH SHIELDS	20/4/15					TO CLASS Z RESERVE.	BOMBER.
INGHAM	Robt	SGT	22	/1071				13/11/14	27/10/17	GSW			TO 3rd BN.	AGE 24.
INNES	Robt	PTE	22	/1298		FRONT STREET	HUTTON HENRY			10/10/18		KIRKEE MEM	TO 2nd GARRISON BN.	BORN CASTLE EDEN.
IRVING	ChasA	PTE	22	/1438			SEAHAM HARBOUR			7/7/16		SEAHAM HARBOUR CEM		AGE 40 BORN HULL,DIED ROYAL VICTORIA HOSP NETLE
IRVING	Fred	PTE	22	/1609			SUNDERLAND	26/1/15	24/9/18	GSW	SSHOCK AUGUST 16.		TO 23rd, 12/13th BNS, DEPOT.	AGE 33, TO 3CCS 2/7/16 EVAC 2/7 WND UPPER ARM..
IRVING	ThosL	PTE	22	/1297		SHOP ROW	PLASHETTS	11/1/15	12/12/18	SICK			TO INFANTRY COMMAND DEPOT CATTERICK, DEPOT NF	AGE 42.
JACKSON	Jos T	PTE	22	/1451										
JACOBSON	James	LCPL	22	/ 581									TO ROYAL INNISKILLING FUSILIERS(6th BN).	R INNIS FUS No 21555.
JAMES	David	PTE	22	/1587									TO 1st GARRISON BN, CLASS Z RESERVE.	
JASPER	JohnG	PTE	22	/ 818			NORTH SHIELDS	18/11/14	26/10/17	WOUNDS	AUGUST 16		TO DEPOT.	AGE 27.
JASPER	RobtE	PTE	22	/ 108	C		NORTH SHIELDS			1/7/16	JULY 16, MISSING OCT 16	THIEPVAL MEM		
JEWITT	JohnG	PTE	22	/1674	A	10 HEWITT STREET	FELLING	20/4/15		1/7/16		THIEPVAL MEM		AGE 21.
JOBSON	John	PTE	22	/ 7	TPT				19/3/19				TO YORK & LANCASTER REGT(2/4th BN), CLASS Z RESE	Y&L No 57642.
JOHNSON	A	PTE	22	/ 180			NEWCASTLE	16/11/14	11/10/17	WOUNDS	AUGUST 16		TO DEPOT.	NORTH EVINGTON HOSP LEICESTER 7/16. AGE 42.
JOHNSON	ChasB	PTE	22	/ 430			FELLING			1/7/16		THIEPVAL MEM		BORN BERWICK.
JOHNSON	Geo	PTE	22	/ 568				23/11/14	10/10/17	SICK			TO 3rd BN.	OFFICERS SERVANT, AGE 46.
JOHNSON	Geo S	PTE	22	/ 990			ASHINGTON			13/7/16		ST GERMAIN CH YD MARSKE		AGE 30.
JOHNSON	Henry	PTE	22	/1215			SUNDERLAND			1/7/16		THIEPVAL MEM		
JOHNSON	Herbt	PTE	22	/ 457		12 EMMA STREET	BENFIELDSIDE							
JOHNSON	J	PTE	22	/ 157						9/7/18		BISHOPWEARMOUTH	TO 33rd BN.	
JOHNSON	James	PTE	22	/ 580		38 TYNDAL GARDENS	DUNSTON	21/11/14	4/3/19	KR para 392	MARCH 18		TO 23rd, 26th, 3rd BNS.	
JOHNSON	Rob E	PTE	22	/1102		1 HIGHFIELD TERRACE	USHAW MOOR		18/2/19				TO YORK & LANCASTER REGT(2/4th BN), CLASS Z RESE	Y&L No 57600, SGT.
JOHNSON	Robt	PTE	22	/ 991			BLYTH	11/11/14	26/10/17	GSW	OCT 16.		TO ARMY RESERVE CLASS W.	AGE 38.
JOHNSON	Thos	PTE	22	/ 795		BOTHAL	PEGSWOOD						TO CLASS Z RESERVE.	
JOHNSON	ThosL	SGT	22	/ 147		28 DRUMMOND TERRA(	NORTH SHIELDS			22/6/16		HEILLY STATION CEM		AGE 26 DIED OF GAS POISONING.
JOHNSON	Wm	PTE	22	/ 459	A	68 OLD FORD LANE	GATESHEAD				SSH DEC 16, MISS 21/3/18		TO 16th, 22nd BNS.	
JOHNSTON	Anthy	PTE	22	/ 41		SCHOOL HOUSE	SWALWELL			2/7/16		MEAULTE MIL CEM+THIEPVAL MEM		NAME SPELT JOHNSON ON TM.AGE 47.
JOHNSTON	Jos	PTE	22	/ 188		21a WEST ROAD	PRUDHOE			26/2/17		FAUBOURG DE AMIENS	TO 23rd BN.	BORN BROUGH BY SANDS WESTMORLAND AGE 47.
JOHNSTON	Sam	PTE	22											AWOL 7/12/15.
JOICE	James	PTE	22	/ 624				23/11/14	28/4/15	SICK				DID NOT SERVE OVERSEAS.
JOICEY	JohnE	PTE	22	/ 476		43 RHODES STREET	WALKER			8/7/16		BOULOGNE EASTERN CEM		BORN WINDY KNOOK AGE 31.
JOICEY	Wm	LSGT	22	/ 174			NEWCASTLE	16/11/14	20/1/19	GSW	AUGUST 16		TO DEPOT.	
JONES	Frank	SGT	22	/ 197			SEATON BURN	16/11/14	13/7/17	GSW	JULY 16		TO 3rd BN.	AGE 35.
JONES	FredJ	PTE	22	/1732	C	14 BARRAS COURT	GATESHEAD			30/6/16		THIEPVAL MEM		BORN BERMONDSEY MIDDLESEX.
JONES	Geo	PTE	22	/1024				12/11/14	11/12/17	SICK			TO 3rd BN.	REAL NAME Geo TONES, AGE 46.
JONES	Geo R	PTE	22	/1070			WEST SLEEKBURN	10/11/14	25/10/18	SICK	OCT 16		TO 10th, 9th, 20th BNS, NORTHERN COMMAND DEPOT CA	AGE 23.
JONES	John	LCPL	22	/1446		117 OLD ROW	STOCKLEY						TO CLASS Z RESERVE.	
JONES	John	PTE	22	/ 938			WORKINGTON	21/11/14						ENGINEER AGE 34, DESERTED 19/6/15, 5'4".
JORDAN	Peter	PTE	22	/1528			SUNDERLAND	25/1/15	17/9/17	WOUNDS	AUGUST 16		TO DEPOT.	AGE 47.
JORDAN	Roy G	PTE	22	/ 810									TO EAST YORKSHIRE REGT(1st BN), CLASS Z RESERVE.	EAST YORKS No 50798.
JUDD	Wm R	PTE	22	/1714				12/7/15	30/10/17	SICK			TO 3rd BN.	AGE 22, AWOL 4/9/15.
KAY	Robt	PTE	22	/1501		2 STAVORDALE STREE'	DAWDON	1/2/15	24/4/18	GSW			TO 11th, 3rd BNS.	AGE 22.
KAY	Wilf	PTE	22	/1128	C	9 LILY TERR DERWENT	MEDOMSLEY			1/7/16	MISSING OCT 16 GAZ	THIEPVAL MEM		AGE 23.
KEATING	Peter	PTE	22	/1753									TO 10th, 1/5th, 8th BNS, CLASS Z RESERVE.	
KEAVENY	Chas	PTE	22	/1537		TP OXCLOSE	COXHOE		10/3/19				TO YORK & LANCASTER REGT(2/4th BN), CLASS Z RESE	Y& L No 57646.
KEEPIN	Arth	CPL	22	/ 168			CORNSAY COLL			1/7/16		THIEPVAL MEM		
KEERS	James	SGT	22	/ 32		12 HEMMING STREET	RYHOPE							NAME KERR IN AVL, KEERS ON MR.
KEGG	Thos	PTE	22											AWOL 10/8/15, 26/9/15.

KEGG	Wm	PTE	22											AWOL 10/10/15.
KELLY	Jas H	SGT	22	/1403		1 LILYWHITE TERRACE	HETTON LE HOLE	6/1/15	1/4/19	KR para 392	JAN 18		TO 20th BN.	
KELLY	JohnL	PTE	22	/1542					KRpara392				TO DURHAM LIGHT INFANTRY, TRAINING RESERVE BN.	TRG RES No TR/5/41416.
KEMPSTER	Hor D	PTE	22	/1703			NORTH SHIELDS			1/7/16		THIEPVAL MEM		BORN TYNEMOUTH.
KEMPSTER	JohnT	CPL	22	/ 485	D						MISSING 21/3/18			
KENNEDY	Gabrl	PTE	22	/ 713		MOOR COTTAGES	HALTWHISTLE			KR para 392	JULY 16		TO 1st BN.	
KENNEDY	Thos	PTE	22	/1510				26/1/15	21/5/17	VDH			TO DEPOT.	
KENNY	John	PTE	22	/1492			SEAHAM HARBOUR	1/2/15	18/2/18	GSW	DEC 16, NOT WND FEB 17.		TO 3rd BN.	AGE 24.
KERRIGAN	Frncs	PTE	22	/1627			DURHAM CITY	24/2/15	25/3/18	SICK	JAN 18		TO 3rd BN.	AGE 39.
KILLORAN	Jas W	PTE	22	/ 930	D	20 RED ROW	WEST SLEEKBURN			1/7/16	MISSING OCT 16 GAZ	BECOURT MIL CEM		
KINNAIR	C P	PTE	22	/1299	A									FROM 101 AMBT TRN TO 18 GHOSP 3/7, No 6 CONV DEP(
KIRKHAM	Thos	PTE	22	/1764									TO DURHAM LI(13th BN), 27th, 24/27th 8th, 14th BNS NF, Z	DURHAM LI No 46018.
KIRKUP	Jos	SGT	22	/ 939						KR para 392			TO 2nd GARRISON BN.	
KIRKWOOD	James	CPL	22	/ 255			SOUTH SHIELDS	15/11/14	29/10/17	WOUNDS	OCT 16		TO 3rd BN.	AGE 43.
KIRTON	JohnS	PTE	22	/1517		16 HAWKES COTTAGES	GATESHEAD	1/2/15		KR para 392			TO 10th, 25th BNS.	
KIRTON	Mark	CPL	22	/ 228	A	194 WINDSOR AVENUE	BENSHAM G/HEAD			1/7/16	MISSING OCT 16 GAZ	THIEPVAL MEM		AGE 46 BORN LEEDS.
KITWOOD	John	PTE	22	/1705		9 SIDNEY STREET	NORTH SHIELDS	10/7/15	13/12/16	4/5/17		TYNEMOUTH PRESTON	TO DEPOT.	AGE 41.
KNOX	JohnT	PTE	22	/1218			ASHINGTON			KR para 392	OCT 16		TO 1/4th BN, ATT 257 TUNNELLING COY RE, 1/5th BN.	VOL AID HOSP CHELTENHAM 8/7/16, NEW No 204620.
LAFFERTY	Henry	PTE	22	/ 745									TO 8th BN, CLASS Z RESERVE.	
LAING	Jos	SGT	22	/ 596			SOUTH SHIELDS				AUGUST 16		COMMISSIONED 27/6/17.	
LAKE	Sam M	LSGT	22	/ 912			SOUTH SHIELDS			24/6/16		HEILLY STATION CEM		
LANAGAN	Jos	PTE	22	/1224		2 PILOT STREET	SEAHAM HARBOUR						TO LABOUR CORPS.	
LANE	Normn	PTE	22	/ 830	D		GOSFORTH			1/7/16	MISSING OCT 16	THIEPVAL MEM		
LASCELLES	Fred	PTE	22	/1700	A	49 FERRY ST	JARROW			1/7/16	MISSING OCT 16	THIEPVAL MEM		AGE 19.
LAUDER	Art G	PTE	22	/1768					1/4/19				TO YORK & LANCASTER REGT(2/4th BN), CLASS Z RESE	Y&L No 57648.
LAVERICK	RobtW	PTE	22	/1579			FENCEHOUSES			5/6/17		ARRAS MEM		BORN PENSHAW, BOMBER AWOL 27/8/15.
LAWS	Thos	CPL	22	/ 498		ST OSWALDS ROAD	HEBBURN COLLIER				AUGUST 16			
LAWSON	JohnG	PTE	22	/1220		10 GOSFORTH STREET	SUNDERLAND			1/7/16		THIEPVAL MEM		AGE 24.
LAWSON	Percy	PTE	22	/1222						KR para 392			ATTACHED 102nd LIGHT TRENCH MORTAR BATTERY.	
LAWSON	Thos	PTE	22	/ 865		3 EMMERSON ROAD	WOODHORN	23/11/14	31/3/19	KR para 392	OCT 16		TO 23rd BN, NORTHERN COMMAND DEPOT CATTERICK, ARMY RES P.	
LAWSON	Wm	SGT	22	/1223		52 MOUNT STEWART ST	SEAHAM HARBOUR				JAN 18		TO CLASS Z RESERVE.	
LEADBITTER	Albt	PTE	22	/1301									TO CLASS Z RESERVE.	
LEADBITTER	Geo H	SGT	22	/ 71			HAMSTERLEY COLL			12/4/17		AUBIGNY COM CEM EXT		BORN HAWKWELL NTHBLD.
LEDGER	Wm	PTE	22	/ 815	C		GATESHEAD			1/7/16	MISSING OCT 16	THIEPVAL MEM		BORN DIPTON.
LEE	Robt	CSM	22	/ 208		19 SHIBDEN ST	BLAYDON						TO 12/13th, 9th, 3rd BNS.	
LEGG	John	PTE	22	/ 114									ATTACHED 102nd LIGHT TRENCH MORTAR BATTERY, 9th BN.	
LEGG	Wm	PTE	22	/ 829			LONDON			4/7/16		HEILLY STATION CEM		AGE 42.
LENNOX	Henry	PTE	22	/1761			NEWCASTLE			5/6/17		ARRAS MEM		AGE 19.
LEWIS	James	PTE	22	/ 277		35 ROSEBERRY TERRA	CONSETT			27/9/18		GOUZEAUCOURT NEW	TO 23rd, 21st, 8th, 1st, 12/13th BNS.	BORN WEDENSBURY STAFFS.AGE 32.
LIDDELL	Ralph	PTE	22	/ 706	D		BLYTH			1/7/16	MISSING OCRT 16	THIEPVAL MEM		BORN BEADNELL, IN MACHINE GUN SECTION.
LIDDLE	Geo H	LCPL	22	/1300				8/1/15	21/5/17	SICK			TO 3rd BN.	
LIDDLE	Sam S	PTE	22	/1351		44 CLYDE STREET	SUNDERLAND						TO 26th BN, CLASS Z RESERVE.	
LILLEY	Wm	PTE	22	/1540		41 BURDEN STREET	RYHOPE							
LILLY	EdwdM	PTE	22	/ 718			SOUTH SHIELDS				NOV 16		TO 1st BN, CLASS Z RESERVE.	
LINDSLEY	Robt	SGT	22	/1302		26 HENRY STREET	HETTON LE HOLE	7/1/15	11/9/18	SICK	JULY 16, OCT 16.		TO DEPOT.	AGE 39.
LINER	Fred	PTE	22	/ 951			WEST JARROW	21/11/14	7/11/17	GSW	JULY 16		TO 20th, 25th BNS, DEPOT.	AGE 22, TO 3CCS 2/7/16 EVAC 2/7/16 GSW CHEST.
LITTLE	Jos H	PTE	22	/ 734			ASHINGTON				DEC 16		TO 11th BN, CLASS Z RESERVE.	
LIVESLEY	James	PTE	22	/1475		OLD PENSHAW VILLAGE	PENSHAW							
LIVINGSTONE	Alex	SGT	22	/ 19		9 LAMPORT STREET	HEBBURN QUAY							
LIVINGSTONE	Geo	PTE	22											AWOL 10/7/15
LOCKRANE	Mich	PTE	22	/ 210			SUNDERLAND			28/9/16		PLOEGSTEERT MEM	TO 21st BN.	AGE 19.
LOGAN	Thos	PTE	22	/1067		3 FRONT STREET	LEAMSIDE			26/10/17	JULY 16	TYNE COT MEM	TO 25th, 1/4th BNS.	BORN SILKSWORTH ALLOTTED NEW No 204615.AGE 28.
LONG	Alf J	SGT	22	/1129		16 COXONS ROW	EDMONDSLEY	4/1/15	1/4/19	KR para 392			TO ARMY RESERVE CLASS P.	
LONG	Sam	PTE	22	/ 77			BURNHOPEFIELD			9/4/17		BAILLEUL RD EAST CEM		AGE 39 BORM BELMONT LANCS.
LONGSTAFF	ThosR	LCPL	22	/ 849		VICTORIA HSE GREY ST	CROOK			30/3/16		RATION FARM MIL CEM		BORN BISHOP AUKLAND AGE 23.
LONSDALE	Robt	PTE	22	/1225		24 HILL STREET	SILKSWORTH COLL	5/1/15	31/3/19	KR para 392			TO ARMY RESERVE CLASS P.	
LOUGH	Thos	PTE	22	/1752									TO 2nd GARRISON BN, CLASS Z RESERVE.	
LOUTTET	Wm	LCPL	22	/ 907			EDINBURGH			19/10/17		TYNE COT MEM		BORN SUNDERLAND.
LOVELY	Geo	LCPL	22	/1747				26/8/15					TO 2nd GARRISON BN, CLASS Z RESERVE.	FORFIET MEDALS FOR FRAUDULENT ENLISTMENT.
LOWERSON	Thos	LCPL	22	/ 774		6 HIGH HOWLETT	PELTON FELL			1/7/16		THIEPVAL MEM	TO 23rd BN(A COY).	BORN MURTON, AGE 21.
LOWES	Jacob	PTE	22	/ 770			CORNSAY VILLAGE	16/11/14	15/2/17	ARTHRITIS			TO DEPOT.	
LOWREY	Thos	PTE	22	/1303						KR para 392			TO EAST YORKSHIRE REGT(1st BN).	E YORKS No 50766.
LOWRIE	Wm	CPL	22	/ 785	A	WEST STOBSWOOD	WIDDRINGTON			1/7/16	MISSING OCT 16	THIEPVAL MEM		BORN ALNHAM AGE 20.
LOWSON	Wm	PTE	22	/ 262	D						MISSING 21/3/18		TO CLASS Z RESERVE.	IN 15 PLATOON.
LUKE	Geo	PTE	22	/ 740		POST OFFICE	EMBLETON	19/11/14	19/8/18	GSW	AUGUST 16		TO 3rd BN.	AGE 23.
LUKE	Herbt	PTE	22	/ 739	B		LESBURY			1/7/16	MISSING OCT 16	THIEPVAL MEM		BORN EMBLETON AGE 26.
LUKE	Matt	PTE	22	/ 91		5 WALKER STREET	BOWBURN				OCT 16			
LUKE	Thos	PTE	22	/ 905		16 HARRAS BANK	BIRTLEY			2/9/18		BANCOURT BRIT CEM	TO EAST YORKSHIRE REGT(1st BN).	E YORKS No 50664.
LUMSDEN	Andrw	PTE	22	/ 297			CHOPPPINGTON	16/11/17	10/12/17	GSW	AUGUST 16		TO 3rd BN.	AGE 43.
LUNAM	Adam	PTE	22	/ 825			FELLING	21/12/14		22/6/16		ALBERT COM CEM EXT		MINER AGE 22, DESERTED 12/6/15, 5'1"
LUPTON	FredG	PTE	22	/ 836			LANCASTER LANCS			1/7/16		THIEPVAL MEM		AGE 27.
LYDDON	Thos	PTE	22											AWOL 4/12/15
LYNCH	Andrw	PTE	22	/ 501	B		NEWCASTLE			1/7/16	MISSING DEC 16	THIEPVAL MEM		
LYNCH	Thos	PTE	22											AWOL 1/9/15, 19/12/15.
MACAULEY	ArthM	PTE	22	/1666			JARROW	28/4/15	6/6/17	WOUNDS	AUGUST 16		TO DEPOT.	
MACK	James	LCPL	22	/ 899			SOUTH SHIELDS				OCT 16		TO 9th, 23rd BNS, CLASS Z RESERVE.	
MACKAY	ThosR	PTE	22	/ 737	B	177 SYCAMORE STREET	ASHINGTON			1/7/16	MISSING OCT 16	THIEPVAL MEM		AGE 24.
MACKENZIE	Dan T	PTE	22	/ 997			ASHINGTON	16/11/14	5/9/17	WOUNDS	AUGUST 16		TO 3rd BN.	AGE 31.
MACKENZIE	Sid A	PTE	22	/ 269			NEWCASTLE	14/11/14	28/7/17	GSW	AUGUST 16		TO 3rd BN.	
MACKINNON	T	PTE	22	/ 305										MACHINE GUN SECTION.
MacLENNAN	John	PTE	22	/ 287		26 STOWELL STREET	NEWCASTLE				JULY 16		TO 23rd, 20th BNS.	
MADDEN	Alf	LCPL	22	/1345	D		SUNDERLAND			1/7/16	MISSING DEC 16	THIEPVAL MEM		BORN BOLDON COLLIERY
MADDEN	Bernd	LCPL	22	/1230									TO CLASS Z RESERVE.	
MADDISON	Geo A	LCPL	22	/ 562			NEW WASHINGTON				JULY 16		TO TERRITORIAL BN.	ALLOTTED NEW No 267659.SEE ALSO JOHN & JOSEPH I
MADDISON	Jacob	PTE	22	/ 893	A		BLYTH	17/11/14	28/2/18	ARTHRITIS	MISS OCT 16, WND DEC 16		TO ARMY RESERVE CLASS P.	AGE 37.
MADDISON	Robt	PTE	22	/1422	B		SHINCLIFFE			1/7/16	MISSING OCT 16	THIEPVAL MEM		BORN WILLINGTON ON TYNE.
MAGEE	ThosF	PTE	22	/ 943		12 WENLOCK ROAD	TYNEDOCK			27/4/18	AUGUST 18	ARNEKE BRIT CEM	TO 12/13th BN.	BORN SOUTH SHIELDS, IN MACHINE GUN SECTION.
MAIN	Jas	PTE	22	/ 130									TO LABOUR CORPS.	TO 3CCS 2/7/16 EVAC 2/7/16 WND NECK.LAB CORPS No
MAITLAND	Geo W	PTE	22	/ 778									TO CLASS Z RESERVE.	MACHINE GUN SECTION.
MAKEPEACE	Wm	SGT	22	/ 944									TO 1st BN, CLASS Z RESERVE.	
MALCOLM	Alex	SGT	22	/ 586			NEWCASTLE			1/7/16		THIEPVAL MEM		BORN SOUTH SHIELDS.
MALCOLM	John	SGT	22	/1027		12 MIDDLE FRIARSIDE	BURNHOPEFIELD						TO 19th BN(Y COY), CLASS Z RESERVE.	PROMOTED CSM.
MALONE	John	SGT	22	/1684				25/9/14	30/3/16	SVC NOT REQ			TO 29th BN.	AGE 50.
MALONEY	Roger	PTE	22											AWOL 19/9/15.
MANEYLAWS	JohnA	CPL	22	/ 686			BLACKHILL				AUGUST 16			
MARCH	James	PTE	22	/ 273	C	28 MAPLE STREET	SOUTHMOOR			1/7/16	MISSING OCT16	THIEPVAL MEM		AGE 36, BROTHERS Jos & Thos IN TYNESIDE IRISH.
MARR	Chris	LCPL	22	/ 866			NEWCASTLE				JULY 16		TO ATT 102 LTMB, 16th, 23rd BNS, CLASS Z RESERVE.	TO 3CCS 2/7/16 EVAC 2/7/16 WND LEGS.
MARSDEN	James	PTE	22	/ 644									TO 1st GARRISON, 26th BNS.	
MARSH	Robt	PTE	22	/ 328		8 BIRTLEY TERRACE	BIRTLEY				AUGUST 16			
MARSHALL	C W	PTE	22	/1721		18 WEST END	OLD HARTLEY			21/4/16		OUR LADY CH YD DELAVAL		
MARSHALL	Robt	PTE	22	/ 659		9 PLESSEY VIEW	BLYTH			3/7/16		HEILLY STATION CEM		BORN HEDDON ON THE WALL AGE 34.
MASON	RobtW	PTE	22	/ 524	C		LESBURY			1/7/16	MISSING OCT 16	THIEPVAL MEM		AGE 21 BORN EMBLETON.
MASTERS	Wm	PTE	22	/1328				4/1/15	1/4/19	KR para 392			TO ARMY RESERVE CLASS P.	COOK.
MATTHEWS	Wm	PTE	22	/1231				1/5/15	6/11/17	DEAFNESS			TO DEPOT.	
MAYOR	Rich	PTE	22	/ 503						KR para 392			TO 1st GARRISON BN.	
McALL	ThosF	PTE	22	/1034		26 TYNE STREET	NORTH SHIELDS				AUGUST 16		TO 25th, 26th BNS, CLASS Z RESERVE.	ALLOTTED NEW No 243177.
McANDREW	Wm	PTE	22	/1227		9 BACK RAILWAY ST	SEAHAM						TOO EAST YORKSHIRE REGT(1st BN), CLASS Z RESERV	BATTALION RUNNER. E YORKS No 50638.
McANDREWS	James	PTE	22	/ 717		9 ACADEMY HILL	SOUTH SHIELDS			1/7/16		BECOURT MIL CEM		AGE 23.
McCAW	James	PTE	22	/1065	C		NEWCASTLE			1/7/16	MISSING OCT 16	THIEPVAL MEM		AGE 39
McCLETCHIE	Alex	PTE	22	/ 401				17/11/14	28/7/15	SICK				DID NOT SERVE OVERSEAS.
McCONNACHIE	John	PTE	22	/ 252			SOUTH SHIELDS			30/8/16		RATION FARM CEM	ATTACHED 102nd LIGHT TRENCH MORTAR BATTERY.	
McCOURT	James	SGT	22	/ 216		1 HARVEY STREET	HEBBURN COLL	16/11/18	15/7/18	SICK	AUGUST 18.		TO DEPOT.	AGE 37.
McDONALD	Cyril	PTE	22	/ 852			SOUTH SHIELDS				JULY 16, DEC 16.		TO 26th, 25th BNS, CLASS Z RESERVE.	
McDONALD	Geo	PTE	22	/1615				10/4/15	12/7/17	WOUNDS			TO 84th TRAINING RESERVE BN	
McDOUGAL	J H	PTE	22	/ 319			SOUTH SHIELDS				OCT 16			OFFICERS SERVANT
McEVOY	Pat	PTE	22	/1725			CHESTER LE ST	13/7/15	19/3/18	GSW	JULY 16		TO ARMY RESERVE CLASS P.	AGE 33.
McGEEVER	James	LCPL	22	/1541				1/2/15	24/11/16	SICK			TO 1st GARRISON BN, DEPOT.	
McGRATH	Edwd	LCPL	22	/1229			HETTON LE HOLE	4/1/15	2/10/16	DEAF	AUGUST 16		TO DEPOT.	
McGUINESS	James	PTE	22	/1755		202 CONYERS ROAD	BYKER			19/2/17	JULY 16	HEATON & BYKER CEM		AGE 40, DIED OF PNEUMONIA.
McINTYRE	John	PTE	22	/1454			JARROW	6/1/15	21/5/17	SICK	JAN 17		TO 3rd BN.	
McIVER	Thos	PTE	22	/ 363				10/11/14	3/1/18	SICK			TO 33rd BN.	AGE 50 DID NOT SERVE OVERSEAS.
McKENZIE	Jas	LCPL	22	/ 968	B		GOSFORTH			1/7/16	MISSING DEC 16	THIEPVAL MEM		

McKINLEY	M	PTE	22	/1719				13/7/15	5/9/16	KR para 392			TO 33rd BN.	DID NOT SERVE OVERSEAS.
McKNIGHT	JohnG	PTE	22	/537	B		SUNDERLAND			1/7/16	MISSING OCT 16	THIEPVAL MEM		
McMAHON	Geo D	PTE	22	/ 39		39 FORTH STREET	CHOPWELL						TO 1st GARRISON BN, CLASS Z RESERVE.	
McMILLAN	Sam	CPL	22	/ 628		108 WESTBOURNE AVE	GATESHEAD			5/6/17		ARRAS MEM		BORN AYR SCOTLAND.
McNALLY	Archi	PTE	22	/ 946	A		SOUTH SHIELDS			1/7/16	MISSING OCT 16	THIEPVAL MEM		
McPHERSON	Angus	LCPL	22	/ 142		15 2nd SINGLE ROW	NORTH SEATON			22/6/16		ALBERT COM CEM EXT		
McSPARRON	Thos	LCPL	22	/ 996			ASHINGTON			25/6/16		HEILLY STATION CEM		
McVINNIE	John	PTE	22	/1228		BEDLINGTONS BLDGS	OVINGTON				DEC 16		TO 10th BN, CLASS Z RESERVE.	
MEARNS	James	PTE	22	/ 761			SOUTH SHIELDS	14/11/14	31/3/19	KR para 392	OCT 16		TO DEPOT.	
MEINS	Andrw	PTE	22	/ 6	A		STAKEFORD			1/7/16	MISSING OCT 16	CERISY GAILLY CEM		BORN BEDLINGTON.
MESSER	Jas H	PTE	22	/1506			FENCEHOUSES			4/7/16		HEILLY STATION CEM		BORN HIGHER INCE CHESHIRE.
METCALFE	Matt	PTE	22	/1232	C		SUNDERLAND			1/7/16	MISSING OCT 16	THIEPVAL MEM		
MIDDLEMISS	WaltA	SGT	22	/ 314										MACHINE GUN SECTION.
MIDDLETON	James	PTE	22	/ 561				21/11/14	10/4/18	GSW			TO 3rd BN.	AGE 29.
MILBURN	Ernst	PTE	22	/1234	A		EASINGTON LANE			1/7/16	MISSING OCT 16	OVILLERS MIL CEM		BORN GUISBOROUGH.
MILBURN	JohnB	PTE	22											AWOL 2/2/15.
MILBURN	JohnT	PTE	22	/ 627			ASHINGTON				MISSING OCT 16, POW FEB 1			
MILBURN	Robt	SGT	22	/1235									TO EAST YORKSHIRE REGT(1st BN), CLASS Z RESERVE.	E YORKS No 50661.
MILLER	Gor C	PTE	22	/1466		54 BARRASFORD STRE	EAST HOWDEN				SEPT 16		TO 9th BN.	DESERTED 4/2/18.
MILLER	Hendn	PTE	22	/ 29									TO 2nd GARRISON BN, CLASS Z RESERVE.	
MILLER	James	PTE	22											AWOL 19/9, 27/10, 19/12/15.
MILLER	John	PTE	22	/1356	B		GLASGOW			1/7/16	MISSING DEC 16	THIEPVAL MEM		
MILLICAN	Geo	PTE	22	/1145			WEST SLEEKBURN	10/11/14	11/12/17	KR para 392	AUGUST 16		TO KINGS OWN YORKSHIRE LI(1st GARRISON BN).	NORTH EVINGTON HOSP LEICESTER 7/16.
MILNE	Geo	PTE	22											AWOL 12/9/17 - 26/9/15.
MITCHELL	James	CPL	22	/ 173	C		SEATON BURN			1/7/16	MISSING OCT 16	THIEPVAL MEM		BORN BEDLINGTON.
MITCHELL	JohnJ	PTE	22	/1060	D	CLARENCE STREET	SEATON SLUICE			1/7/16	MISSING DEC 16	THIEPVAL MEM		AGE 23 BORN BLYTH, IN 13 PLATOON.
MITCHELSON	Forst	PTE	22	/1799		35 EDWINS AVENUE	FOREST HALL					BRANDEHOEK MIL CEM	TO LABOUR CORPS(164 LABOUR COMPANY).	LAB CORPS No 386330, AGE 38.
MOFFAT	James	PTE	22	/ 445				16/11/15	30/1/19	GSW			TO DEPOT.	
MOODY	Frank	PTE	22	/1237				4/1/15	22/8/17	SICK			TO DEPOT.	AGE 40.
MOODY	R	SGT	22	/ 334										
MOODY	Sam	PTE	22	/ 604									TO EAST YORKSHIRE REGT(1st BN), CLASS Z RESERVE.	E YORKS No 50608. SHOEMAKER.
MORGAN	Geo	LCPL	22	/1238			WESTOE			13/4/18	SEPT 16	PLOEGSTEERT MEM	TO 1st BN.	TO 3CCS 2/7/16 EVAC 2/7/16 WND BACK, BORN SUNDERI
MORGAN	Jas E	PTE	22	/1707	C	10 CHAUCER STREET	GATESHEAD			24/8/16	OCT 16	ALL SAINTS NEWCASTLE		BORN NEWCASTLE AGE 18.
MORGAN	Sam	PTE	22	/ 303	C	8 MURTON ROW	PERCY MAIN			1/7/16	MISSING OCT 16	THIEPVAL MEM		AGE 33 BORN BLYTH
MORRELL	Geo	PTE	22	/ 505			SOUTH SHIELDS			7/7/16		ABBEVILLE COM CEM		DIED AT No 2 STATIONARY HOSP, AGE 36 BORN SUNDEI
MORRIS	John	PTE	22	/ 857									TO 1st GARRISON BN, CLASS Z RESERVE.	
MORRISON	Donld	PTE	22	/1769						KR para 392			TO DURHAM LIGHT INFANTRY, TRAINING RESERVE BN.	TRG RES No TR/5/58193.
MORSON	WaltE	PTE	22	/1583		5 ASHLEY TERRACE	CHESTER LE ST			15/6/16			TO 2nd GARRISON BN.	
MORTIMER	Thos	PTE	22	/ 558	B		GRANGEVILLA			1/7/16	MISSING OCT 16	THIEPVAL MEM		BORN DURHAM CITY.
MOUNSEY	Thos	PTE	22	/ 645		41 ANN STREET	GATESHEAD				JULY 16		TO 23rd, 26th, 1/7th BNS.	
MOY	Geo	PTE	22	/ 719									TO 1st, 14th, 1/7th BNS, CLASS Z RESERVE.	
MUERS	Wm	SGT	22	/ 995			CHOPPINGTON	16/11/14	11/10/17	GSW	AUGUST 16		TO 3rd BN.	AGE 35.
MUIR	Jas P	SGT	22	/1066									REENLISTED ROYAL AIR FORCE. SERVED MERCHANT N	BWAR & VIC MEDALS, MERCHANT MARINE, RAF LSGC, [
MULVEY	Chas	PTE	22	/1417					KRpara392				TO DURHAM LIGHT INFANTRY, TRAINING RESERVE BN.	TRG RES No TR/5/41533.
MUNRO	Alex	SGT	22	/1716			NEWCASTLE				JAN 17		TO CLASS Z RESERVE.	
MURPHY	James	PTE	22	/ 156		11 KING WILLIAM ST	GATESHEAD						TO 2nd GARRISON BN, DURHAM LI(1st BN).	DURHAM LI No 52327.
MURPHY	John	PTE	22	/ 682	D		CHOPWELL			1/7/16	MISSING DEC 16	THIEPVAL MEM		BORN GREENHEAD CUMBERLAND.
MURRAY	JohnG	PTE	22	/ 787				15/11/14	20/2/18	TRENCH FEET			TO 3rd BN.	
NAISBITT	Chas	PTE	22	/1241		67 BURTON STREET	RYHOPE	5/1/15	12/2/17	WOUNDS	AUG 16		TO DEPOT.	
NATTRASS	John	PTE	22	/1555		3 BRICKGARTH	EASINGTON LANE			10/6/16		BECOURT MIL CEM		BORN BILLQUAY.
NATTRASS	RobtS	PTE	22	/ 93	B	73 OAKWOOD ROAD	BLACKHILL			1/7/16	MISSING DEC 16 GAZ	THIEPVAL MEM		BORN ALSTON CUMBERLAND AGE 37.
NEALE	Geo	PTE	22	/ 126		112 BOWES STREET	BLYTH			30/8/16		NIEUPORT MEM	ATTACHED 102nd LIGHT TRENCH MORTAR BATTERY.	BORN BERWICK AGE 33.
NELSON	RobtW	LCPL	22	/ 539		108 SPENCER STREET	HEATON			22/6/16		ALBERT COM CEM EXT		AGE 29.
NESBIT	Arth	PTE	22	/1704		6 BEDFORD LANE	NORTH SHIELDS	10/7/15		KR para 392			TO 12/13th BN.	
NEWTON	E	PTE	22	/1440				11/1/15						MINER AGE 25 DESERTED 17/6/15,REJOINED 29/6/15, 5'4
NICHOLSON	David	CPL	22	/1410									TO EAST YORKSHIRE REGT(1st BN), CLASS Z RESERVE.	E YORKS No 50612
NICHOLSON	Geo	PTE	22	/ 81	B		BARROW/FURNESS			1/7/16		THIEPVAL MEM		IN 7 PLATOON.
NICHOLSON	Herbt	PTE	22	/1240	E	LITTLE EPPLETON FARI	EPPLETON	4/1/15	4/2/15	MED UNFIT				AGE 20, 5'5", 36 CHEST FRESH COMPLX BLUE EYES LT E
NICHOLSON	James	PTE	22	/1464	C		FATFIELD			1/7/16	MISSING DEC 16 GAZ	THIEPVAL MEM		BORN BEARPARK.
NIXON	JohnT	PTE	22	/1635		2 NIXONS BLDGS	DUDLEY			27/8/17		TINCOURT BRIT CEM		AGE 24.
NOBLE	Jos W	PTE	22	/1459	C		NEWCASTLE			1/7/16	MISSING DEC 16 GAZ	THIEPVAL MEM		BORN LEADGATE.
NUGENT	Geo	PTE	22	/1306	C	38 FRANKLIN STREET	NEWCASTLE	12/1/15		1/7/16	MISSING DEC 16	THIEPVAL MEM		MACHINE GUN SECTION(NOV 1st 16 RC LIST)
O'CONNELL	Thos	PTE	22	/1434				11/1/15	11/12/17	SICK			TO 2nd GARRISON, 3rd BNS.	AGE 37.
O'DONNELL	Jos	PTE	22	/1724		38 HENRY STREET	NEWCASTLE			5/6/17		ARRAS MEM	TO 21st BN(A COY).	AGE 32.
O'DONNELL	W	PTE	22	/1687									TO 25th, 1/5th BNS.	ALLOTTED NEW NUMBER 243168.
OGDEN	James	PTE	22	/1242		15 UNION STREET	SEAHAM HARBOUR			12/4/18		LA KREUZE MIL CEM	TO 1/4th BN.	BORN NEWBOTTLE AGE 26.
OLIVER	Jacob	SGT	22	/1058			RYTON	13/11/14	13/10/16	GSW L AXILLA	JULY 16		TO DEPOT.	
OLIVER	Thos	PTE	22	/ 564				21/11/14	13/4/18	SICK			TO ARMY RESERVE CLASS P.	AGE 33.
O'NEILL	James	PTE	22											AWOL 1/12/15 AGE 23.
O'NEILL	Ternc	PTE	22	/ 657									TO ROYAL INNISKILLING FUSILIERS(6th BN).	R INNIS FUS No 21573.
ORD	Jas E	PTE	22	/ 771										
ORMSTON	Wm	PTE	22	/ 808	C	5 CHAPEL HOUSES	BACKWORTH			1/7/16		THIEPVAL MEM		AGE 20 BORN EARSDON.
ORR	Her W	SGT	22	/ 458		6 HAWTHORN TERRACI	MEDOMSLEY	13/11/14	31/3/19	KR para 392	JULY 16, AUG 18.		TO ARMY RESERVE CLASS P.	
ORRICK	Wm	PTE	22	/1138				16/11/14	22/1/15	INEFFICIENT				
PAGE	John	CPL	22	/1000		14 HAWTHORN ROAD	ASHINGTON			9/4/17	1/7/16	ARRAS MEM		AGE 33.
PALMER	Andrw	PTE	22	/1665									TO 2nd GARRISON BN, CLASS Z RESERVE.	
PALMER	JohnJ		22	/ 72		72 RAVENSWORTH RO/	DUNSTON						TO 1/4th BN.	OFFICERS SERVANT.
PALMER	Wm	PTE	22	/1327	B		SEAHAM COLLIERY			1/7/16	MISSING DEC 16	THIEPVAL MEM		
PARK	JohnJ	PTE	22	/ 460				17/11/14	31/3/19	KR para 392			TO ARMY RESERVE CLASS P.	
PARK	Wm	PTE	22	/ 887			CARLISLE	17/11/14	27/5/17	WOUNDS	OCT 16		TO 80th TRAINING RESERVE BN.	AGE 37
PARKER	J	PTE	22	/ 587										
PARKER	Jos W	RQMS	22	/ 688									TO CLASS Z RESERVE.	
PARKIN	Jos	PTE	22	/1308				11/1/15	13/7/16	WOUNDS	MARCH 16		TO DEPOT.	
PATRICK	Fred	PTE	22											AWOL 21/2/15
PATRICK	JohnT	PTE	22	/ 867									TO 1st BN, CLASS Z RESERVE.	
PATTERSON	Edwd	PTE	22	/1381		BEADNELL	CHATHILL	5/1/15		14/4/18	JULY 16	NEIUPORT MEM		TO 3CCS 2/7/16 EVAC 2/7 WND UPPER ARM, BORN BEAD
PATTERSON	Robt	PTE	22	/1001			BLYTH			22/6/16		ALBERT COM CEM EXT		BORN WOOLER.
PATTERSON	Robt	PTE	22	/ 544		26 SOUTH STREET	PENSHAW			KR para 392			TO 2nd GARRISON BN.	
PATTERSON	Thos	CPL	22	/1556		2 HENRY STREET	SEAHAM HARBOUR			KR para 392	AUGUST 16		TO 12th, 1st BNS.	
PATTERSON	White	PTE	22	/ 10	TPT			12/11/14	11/10/17	SICK			TO 3rd BN.	
PATTINSON	Jacob	CSGT	22	/1136		SIDNEY HSE BELLVUE 1	CONSETT			15/10/19		CASTLESIDE ST JOHN (	TO CLASS Z RESERVE.	AGE 32.
PAUL	Thos	PTE	22											AWOL 9/6/15
PAULSEN	Wm J	PTE	22	/ 758	D	282 HS EDWARD ST	SOUTH SHIELDS			1/7/16		THIEPVAL MEM		IN 13 PLATOON AGE 24.
PAXTON	John	PTE	22	/1015									TO 1st GARRISON BN, CLASS Z RESERVE.	
PEACOCK	Alex	PTE	22	/ 720		47 BEWICK STREET	SOUTH SHIELDS			27/6/16		ALBERT COM CEM EXT		AGE 22.
PEACOCK	Geo	PTE	22	/1244									TO 2nd GARRISON BN, CLASS Z RESERVE.	
PEARCE	G	PTE	22	/ 607			MARSDEN				AUGUST 16			BOMBER
PEARCE	John	PTE	22	/1245		26 FRANKLIN STREET	JARROW			1/7/16		THIEPVAL MEM		AGE 33.
PEARSON	Alex	PTE	22	/ 237		CHAPEL COTTAGE	MICKLEY				AUGUST 16		TO 19th, 16th, 1/7th BNS.	TO 3CCS 2/7/16 EVAC 2/7/16 WND LEGS.
PEART	Robt	PTE	22	/1246		1 SWAN STREET	MONKWEARMOUTH	5/1/15	12/3/18	GSW	AUGUST 16		TO ARMY RESERVE CLASS P.	AGE 35.
PEDERSON	James	SGT	22	/1247									TO CLASS Z RESERVE.	
PEEL	Mart	PTE	22	/ 746			SOUTH SHIELDS				AUGUST 16		TO 25th, 1/5th BNS, CLASS Z RESERVE.	ALLOTTED NEW No 243167.
PENCOTT	Thos	PTE	22	/ 661	B		HEXAM			1/7/16	MISSING DEC 16	OVILLERS MIL CEM		BORN ASHINGTON.
PENDER	Thos	PTE	22	/ 881			NEWCASTLE			1/7/16		THIEPVAL MEM		BORN JETHOLME ROXBOROUGHSHIRE.
PHAROAH	Geo	PTE	22	/1012									TO DURHAM LIGHT INFANTRY, TRAINING RESERVE BN.	TRG RES No TR/5/127364
PHILLIPSON	Thos	PTE	22	/ 204		16 EMMAVILLE	WEST RYTON	16/11/14		12/7/16		HEILLY STATION CEM		BORN WESTGATE DURHAM.
PIGG	John	PTE	22	/ 335				17/11/14	22/11/18	GSW			TO DEPOT.	AGE 23.
PINDER	John	PTE	22	/ 776			SEATON BURN	16/11/14	14/3/18	GSW	OCT 16		TO ARMY RESERVE CLASS P.	AGE 36.
PORDUM	Ernst	LCPL	22	/1030			NEW HARTLEY			9/4/17		ROCLINCOURT VALLEY		
POSNETT	ChasH	CPL	22	/ 258			SOUTH SHIELDS	14/11/14	12/3/18	GSW	AUGUST 16		TO ARMY RESERVE CLASS P.	AGE 45.
POTTS	ThosW	PTE	22	/1248			MONKWEARMOUTH				AUGUST 16		TO 9th BN, CLASS Z RESERVE.	
POULTON	Thos	SGT	22	/1057		24 COACH LANE	DINNINGTON				JULY 16, 0CT 16.		TO EAST YORKSHIRE REGT(1st BN), CLASS Z RESERVE.	E YORKS No 50613.
PRATT	JohnF	CSM	22	/ 819			ASHINGTON				OCT 18			STILL SERVING 1920.
PRESTON	J A	PTE	22		C									IN 10 PLATOON.
PRESTON	John	PTE	22	/1093									TO 19th, 2nd BNS, CLASS Z RESERVE.	
PRESTON	Thos	PTE	22	/1493	A	7 WYNYARD STREET	DAWDON COLLIERY			5/6/17	MISSING DEC 16	SUNKEN ROAD CEM FAMPOUX		BORN TRIMDON
PRICE	M	PTE	22	/ 873	D						MISSING 21/3/18			
PRICE	Nelsn	CPL	22	/ 724				12/11/14	27/9/16	WOUNDS			TO DEPOT.	
PRITCHARD	Geo	PTE	22	/ 448			SOUTH SHIELDS				MISSING DEC 16			REPORTED PRISONER OF WAR FEB 17.
PROUD	Jos	LCPL	22	/1307			SHILDON			17/3/16		RATION FARM CEM		
PROUD	Matt	PTE	22	/ 302	C		NEW YORK NTHBLD			1/7/16	MISSING DEC 16	THIEPVAL MEM		BORN HALTWHISTLE.
PROUD	Sam	PTE	22	/ 214			NEWCASTLE			26/8/17	AUGUST 16	HAGRICOURT COM CEI	TO 16th, 22nd BNS.	BORN DENTON BURN.

Surname	Forename	Rank	Regt No	Coy	Address	Place	Dates	Cause	Service Dates	Memorial / Cemetery	Transfers	Remarks
PROUD	Thos	LCPL	22 /352		TPT		6/2/19				TO YORK & LANCASTER REGT(2/4th BN).	Y&L No 57712.
PROUDFOOT	Sid A	PTE	22 /540		13 ASTLEY ROAD	SEATON DELAVAL					TO 1st GARRISON BN, CLASS Z RESERVE.	
PROUDLOCK	Robt	PTE	22 /542	B		NEWCASTLE	1/7/16			THIEPVAL MEM		BORN OLD BANKGATE CUMBERLAND.
PROUDLOCK	Wm	PTE	22 /131								TO 2nd GARRISON BN.	
PURDY	ThosG	PTE	22 /249			ASHINGTON	14/11/14 3/2/19	KR para 392	NOV 16, MAR 18		TO ARMY RESERVE CLASS P.	
PURVIS	J H	PTE	22 /599			SOUTH SHIELDS			SSHOCK AUGUST 16			PIONEER.
QUINN	C	PTE	22 /1002			BLYTH			SEPT 16, MAR 17, OCT 18.		TO 30th BN, LABOUR CORPS.	UNITS SERVED WITH IN FRANCE UNCONFIRMED.!!
QUINN	Frncs	PTE	22 /1681		12 CONNAUGHT ROAD	JARROW			AUG 16, NOT WND DEC 16.		TO 23rd BN.	TAKEN POW 7/16 REPATRIATED
RAILTON	Thos	PTE	22 /1051			LANERCOST ABBEY	10/11/14 23/3/17	WOUNDS	AUGUST 16		TO DEPOT.	
RAITT	Robt	PTE	22 /817			ASHINGTON	17/4/17		AUGUST 16	HOLYBROOK MEM	TO 20th BN.	BORN WALKER. AWOL 6/10/15, DESERTED 31/10/16, DRC
RALPH	Geo	PTE	22 /960		11 COLSTON STREET	NEWCASTLE					TO 16th BN, CLASS Z RESERVE.	REPORTED PRISONER OF WAR FEB 17.
RAMSHAW	Thos	PTE	22 /346		21 BACK DENE TERRAC	NEWCASTLE	31/3/15 5/5/18	WOUNDS			TO 3rd BN.	MACHINE GUN SECTION AGE 28, AWOL 17/3/15, 30/4/15.
RATHBONE	Wm	PTE	22 /1612	D	7 WATERSIDE	SOUTH HYLTON	1/7/16		MISSING DEC 16	THIEPVAL MEM		
REAY	Clark	LCPL	22 /329		8 ST BEDES ROW	BIRTLEY			JULY 16		TO 19th, 21st, 23rd, 25th, 12/13th BNS.	
REAY	James	PTE	22 /1757			NEW DELAVAL			MARCH 17		TO 9th, 23rd BNS, CLASS Z RESERVE.	
REAY	JohnJ	PTE	22 /840									
REAY	Rich	PTE	22 /1311				8/1/15 24/9/18	SICK				RENUMBERED 54430, DIED?
REDSHAW	Robt	PTE	22 /456		ESLINGTON TERR	TEAM COLLIERY	14/11/14 11/11/18	KR para 392	AUGUST 16, JULY 18.		TO DEPOT.	SANITARY SECTION.
REED	David	PTE	22 /1387		16 HIGH ROW	WESTMOOR	6/1/15 10/8/16			BECOURT MIL CEM	TO DEPOT.	BORN FELLING.
REED	FredE	SGT	22 /310		30 WEST VIEW	MEDOMSLEY					TO 1st BN.	SIGNALLER.
REED	Rich	PTE	22 /1252		19 SCHOOL STREET	DAWDON	18/7/16		AUG 16, DoW NOV 16	SUNDERLAND MEREKNOLLS CEM		TO 3CCS 2/7 EVAC 2/7/16 WND ABDOMEN, BORN WHITE)
REILLY	Pat	PTE	22 /1250								TO 1st GARRISON BN, CLASS Z RESERVE.	
RENFREE	Thos	PTE	22 /1759			NEW DELAVAL		KR para 392	MARCH 18		TO DURHAM LIGHT INFANTRY, TRAINING RESERVE BN.	TRG RES No TR/5/58171.
RETALLECK	Geo E	PTE	22 /1254			SUNDERLAND		KRpara392	OCT 16			
RICE	RobtW	PTE	22 /158	C	24 LAMB ST	E CRAMLINGTON	1/7/16		MISSING NOV 16	THIEPVAL MEM	TO 2nd GARRISON BN.	BORN NEWCASTLE AGE 23.
RICE	ThosW	PTE	22 /105		219 DERWENT WATER I	GATESHEAD	22/6/16			ALBERT COM CEM EXT		BORN CONSETT AGE 35, DIED OF GAS POISONING.
RICHARDS	Art E	PTE	22 /1256			SUNDERLAND	6/1/15	KR para 392				RIVET HEATER AGE 28, DESERTED 28/6/15, 5'4".
RICHARDSON	Geo	PTE	22 /1426			SUNDERLAND	29/3/16			ERQUINGHEM LYS CH YD		
RICHARDSON	JohnC	PTE	22 /141			SOUTH SHIELDS	13/11/14 8/9/17	WOUNDS	AUGUST 16		TO 3rd BN.	
RICHARDSON	T P	PTE	22 /1576								TO 1st GARRISON BN, CLASS Z RESERVE.	
RICHARDSON	Thos	PTE	22 /1457			CAMBOIS	1/7/16			THIEPVAL MEM		
RICHES	Ben	PTE	22 /841	D								
RIDDLE	Geo	CPL	22 /487		21 MIDDLE FRIARSIDE	BURNHOPEFIELD	18/11/14 22/3/19	KR para 392			TO ARMY RESERVE CLASS P.	
RIDLEY	Jos L	PTE	22 /723		7 SHUTTLEWORTH ST	NEWCASTLE					TO 2nd GARRISON BN, CLASS Z RESERVE.	
RIDLEY	Thos	PTE	22 /161			SUNDERLAND			AUGUST 16		TO 9th BN.	
RILEY	Wm	PTE	22 /1003			NEWCASTLE	19/10/17		JULY 16, DEC 16.	DOZINGHEM MIL CEM		MACHINE GUN SECTION, AWOL 17/3/15, DESERTED 31/3.
RIPPON	Thos	SGT	22 /1040	C	21 UNION STREET	CORNSAY COLL	1/7/16		MISSING NOV 16	THIEPVAL MEM		BORN BRANDON AGE 30.
RISE	Geo T	CPL	22 /467		6 CUTHBERT STREET	HEBBURN QUAY						
RISEBOROUGH	Chas	PTE	22 /1259								TO CLASS Z RESERVE.	
RITSON	Roger	PTE	22 /1054			GATESHEAD	21/6/16			ALBERT COM CEM EXT		
RITSON	ThosH	PTE	22 /1053			SHOTTON COLL	13/11/14 17/11/16	SICK	JULY 16		TO DEPOT.	AGE 26.
ROBERT	John	LCPL	22 /452				15/11/14 8/6/17	WOUNDS			TO DEPOT.	AGE 27.
ROBERTSON	ChasD	PTE	22 /747								TO 1st GARRISON BN, CLASS Z RESERVE.	
ROBERTSON	James	PTE	22 /177				16/11/14 23/10/17	SICK			TO DEPOT.	AGE 46, DID NOT SERVE OVERSEAS.
ROBINSON	Geo	PTE	22									AWOL 4/10/15.
ROBINSON	James	PTE	22									AWOL 25/9/15.
ROBINSON	JohnA	PTE	22 /1518									
ROBLEY	Nev	PTE	22 /276			CONSETT	14/11/14 28/2/18	GSW	JULY 16		TO 2nd GARRISON BN, CLASS Z RESERVE.	
ROBSON	ChasW	PTE	22 /1681	HC	20 FREDERICK STREET	GATESHEAD			JULY 16		TO ARMY RESERVE CLASS P.	AGE 38.
ROBSON	Geo	PTE	22 /705		11 LADY'S WALK	SOUTH SHIELDS	14/11/14 6/3/15	KR para 392			TO CLASS Z RESERVE.	
ROBSON	J E	PTE	22 /247			HIRST			MARCH 16			AGE 37YRS 5MNTHS,5'3",107Lbs,36 CHEST.
ROBSON	Jn Js	SGT	22 / 52		282 BUDDLE ROAD	NEWCASTLE	14/11/14 31/1/19	KR para 392	AUGUST 16		TO COMMAND DEPOT ALNWICK(24/7/17), 3rd BN(23/10/17	HOSP SHIP ST GEORGE 5/7/16
ROBSON	John	PTE	22 /470		10 ST GEORGES TERR	WEST DENTON					TO 1st GARRISON BN, CLASS Z RESERVE.	
ROBSON	JohnH	PTE	22 /854		19 LICHFIELD ROAD	GATESHEAD	8/7/16			BOULOGNE EASTERN CEM		AGE 27.
ROBSON	Jos	SGT	22 /889		24 HENCOTES	HEXAM					TO CLASS Z RESERVE.	
ROBSON	Robt	PTE	22 /502								TO EAST YORKSHIRE REGT(1st BN), CLASS Z RESERVE.	E YORKS No 50707.
RODGERS	Isaac	PTE	22 /1689		17 LIVERPOOL STREET	NEWCASTLE			SEPT 16		TO DURHAM LI(12th BN).	DURHAM LI No 45877.
RODGERSON	Thos	PTE	22 /1424			ESH WINNING			OCT 16		TO 21st, 25th BNS	
ROLL	JohnF	PTE	22 /948					KR para 392			TO EAST YORKSHIRE REGT(1st BN).	E YORKS No 50736.
ROSS	AlbT	PTE	22 /1061				13/11/14 8/7/16	SICK			TO DEPOT.	
ROSS	Geo	PTE	22 /1260		4 CLYDE STREET	SUNDERLAND	5/1/15 2/2/16			ESTAIRES COM CEM		BORN KELSO AGE 32.
ROSS	Matt	PTE	22 /1261		178 CHURCH STREET	WALKER	5/1/15				TO CLASS Z RESERVE.	OFFICERS SERVANT.
RUDKIN	John	PTE	22 /1262		16 BK RAILWAY STREET	DAWDON					TO 2nd GARRISON BN, CLASS Z RESERVE.	
RUNCIMAN	JohnR	PTE	22 /411	D		GATESHEAD	1/7/16		MISSING NOV 16	THIEPVAL MEM		
RUSH	Robt	PTE	22 /1553		5 FREDERICK STREET	SEAHAM COLLIERY					TO 2nd GARRISON BN, CLASS Z RESERVE.	
RUSSELL	J W	PTE	22 /1573		15 EDEN TERRACE	WASHINGTON						
RUTHERFORD	Cuth	PTE	22 /566		14 ELIZABETH STREET	WHEATLEY HILL					TO 1st GARRISON BN, CLASS Z RESERVE.	
RUTHERFORD	ThosG	PTE	22 /565								TO 1st GARRISON BN, CLASS Z RESERVE.	
RUTLEY	Wm H	PTE	22 /1263		3 VICTORIA STREET	BLYTH	6/1/15 1/4/19	KR para 392			TO ARMY RESERVE CLASS P.	
RYLE	G	PTE	22 /421									
SAINT	Anthy	PTE	22 /477			BYKER	18/11/14 17/3/17	WOUNDS	AUGUST 16			
SANDERSON	Geo	PTE	22 /278				14/11/14 28/2/19	KR para 392			TO ARMYRESERVE CLASS P.	
SANDERSON	John	PTE	22 /1524	C	108 MAIN ST PARTON	WHITEHAVEN	1/7/16			THIEPVAL MEM		AGE 40.
SANDERSON	JohnW	PTE	22 /1483		13 SOULSBY STREET	BLYTH	6/1/15 22/7/18	GAS POISONING			TO DEPOT.	AGE 30.
SCOLLAN	John	PTE	22 /1581	A		SEAHAM HARBOUR	1/7/16		MISSING NOV 16	THIEPVAL MEM		BORN NEWCASTLE AGE 28.
SCOTT	Edwd	PTE	22 /1008	C		ASHINGTON	1/7/16		MISSING NOV 16	THIEPVAL MEM		
SCOTT	Harry	PTE	22 /531	D		BURNHOPEFIELD	1/7/16		MISSING NOV 16	THIEPVAL MEM		BORN DEARHAM CUMBERLAND.
SCOTT	Herbt	PTE	22 /1476			FATFIELD	4/7/16		JULY 16	HEILLY STATION CEM		BORN FELLING.
SCOTT	JohnC	PTE	22 /438	A		BYKER	1/7/16		MISSING NOV 16	OVILLERS MIL CEM		
SCOTT	Mich	PTE	22 /191				16/11/14 29/8/17	SICK			TO DEPOT.	AGE 34.
SCOTT	Wm	PTE	22 /1565	D	6 MOUNT PLEASANT	NEW PENSHAW	1/7/16		MISSING NOV 16	THIEPVAL MEM		AGE 31 BORN PHILADELPHIA USA.
SCOTT	Wm	PTE	22 /1488		11 BATH LANE	NEWCASTLE					TO 2nd GARRISON BN, CLASS Z RESERVE.	
SCOTT	Wm E	PTE	22 /1319		105 DENMARK STREET	NEWCASTLE					TO 1st GARRISON BN(A COY), CLASS Z RESERVE.	
SHARP	Geo	PTE	22 /1490			NORTH SHIELDS			AUG 16,MISS 29/4/17,POW D		TO 16th, 23rd(C COY) BNS, CLASS Z RESERVE.	
SHARPE	Sam	PTE	22 /1570			SOUTH SHIELDS			OCT 16		TO 1/6th BN, CLASS Z RESERVE.	
SHAW	JohnG	PTE	22 /1760			NORTH SEATON	11/10/16			WIMEREUX COM CEM		
SHAW	Jos	PTE	22 /378				18/11/14 6/12/17	WOUNDS				AGE 36.
SHAW	Thos	SGT	22 /1522								TO CLASS Z RESERVE.	
SHERMAN	Reubn	PTE	22 /883				17/11/14 14/6/16	KR para 392				DID NOT SERVE OVERSEAS
SHERMAN	Wm C	SGT	22 /343		40 VICTORIA TERRACE	WALLSEND	15/6/17		NOV 16	ETAPLES MIL CEM		AGE 38 BORN AUCHINARNE SCOTLAND.
SHERWOOD	Wm H	PTE	22 /410			ELSWICK	30/6/16			WARLOY BAILLON COM CEM		
SHIELD	John	PTE	22 /657				10/11/14 16/2/18	GSW			TO DEPOT.	AGE 24.
SHORT	Edwd	PTE	22 / 28		11 EMILY STREET	GATESHEAD	12/9/18			VIS-EN-ARTOIS MEM	TO YORK & LANCASTER REGT(2/4th BN).	Y&L No 57666.AGE 35 BORN HASWELL MOOR.
SILMEEN	Wm Mc	LCPL	22 /790			WARDLEY COLL	5/6/17			ARRAS MEM		BORN SOUTH SHIELDS.
SIMPSON	J	PTE	22 / 57			NEWCASTLE	14/11/14 4/9/18	GSW	DEC 16		TO 25th, 19th, 25th BNS.	
SIMPSON	JohnR	PTE	22 /484	D	788 SCOTSWOOD ROAD	NEWCASTLE	1/7/16		FEB 18 MISSING NOV 16	THIEVAL MEM		AGE 33.
SIMPSON	Jonth	CPL	22 /1267		6 MOOR VIEW	NEWBIGGIN / SEA	6/1/15		JULY 16		TO 1st, 16th, 17th, 12/13th BNS, CLASS Z RESERVE.	BORN SWALWELL AGE 38.
SIMPSON	R A	PTE	22 /143	HQ					AUGUST 16			
SIXSMITH	JohnJ	PTE	22 /1006								TO 1st, 9th BNS, CLASS Z RESERVE.	
SKELTON	Anthy	PTE	22 /236								TO 16th, 23rd BNS.	
SLAUGHTER	Wm	CPL	22 /762				14/11/14 31/3/19	KR para 392			TO DEPOT.	
SMAILS	Arth	PTE	22 /324		46 CHESTNUT STREET	ASHINGTON	21/3/18			ARRAS MEM	TO 23rd BN.	BORN ROTHBURY AGE 27.
SMALL	Thos	PTE	22 /904	C		CUPAR ANGUS	1/7/16		MISSING NOV 16	THIEPVAL MEM		
SMEATHAM	Fred	PTE	22 /763	D		SOUTH SHIELDS	1/7/16		MISSING NOV 16	THIEPVAL MEM		
SMEE	Archi	PTE	22									AWOL 27/3/15.
SMITH	Andrw	PTE	22 /1588			SOUTH SHIELDS	27/6/16			ALBERT COM CEM EXT		AWOL 22/7/15.
SMITH	E	LCPL	21 /638									TO 3CCS 2/7/16 EVAC 2/7/16 WND LEGS.
SMITH	Fred	PTE	22 /454								TO EAST YORKSHIRE REGT(1st BN), CLASS Z RESERVE.	E YORKS No 50740.
SMITH	FredE	CPL	22 /907			MORPETH			OCT 16		TO CLASS Z RESERVE.	
SMITH	Geo	PTE	22 /1605			STOCKSFIELD	1/7/16			THIEPVAL MEM		
SMITH	Herbt	PTE	22 /1662			GATESHEAD	28/4/15 18/5/17	VDH	SEPT 16		TO DEPOT.	BORN HEXAM
SMITH	J	PTE	22 /1270		GUNN BLD ADOLPHUS !	SEAHAM						
SMITH	Job	PTE	22 /1614	D		FENCEHOUSES	1/7/16		MISSING NOV 16	OVILLERS MIL CEM		BORN HATELEY HEATH NTHBLD.
SMITH	John	CPL	22 /1644								TO 23rd BN, EAST YORKSHIRE REGT(1st BN), CLASS Z R	E YORKS No 50742.
SMITH	JohnW	PTE	22 /1268			WEARMOUTH	25/11/19		MISSING NOV 16, POW FI	MEREKNOLLS CEM SUNDERLAND		
SMITH	Jos	PTE	22 /1004			BLYTH			SEPT 16		TO 27th, 18th, CLASS Z RESERVE.	
SMITH	Robt	PTE	22 /1710								TO 2nd GARRISON BN.	
SMITH	Thos	PTE	22 /1139	C	46 NORFOLK ROAD	BYKER	1/7/16		MISSING NOV 16	THIEPVAL MEM		MACHINE GUN SECTION AGE 19.
SMITH	Thos	PTE	22 /1380		35 WILFRED STREET	NEWCASTLE					TO 19th BN.	
SMITH	Wm	SGT	22 /1405			CROOK	1/12/17			ROCQUILNY EQUINT RI	TO DURHAM LI(20th BN).	DURHAM LI No 53737.
SMITH	Wm	PTE	22 /221			GOSFORTH	3/7/16			CORBIE COM CEM		AGE 32.
SMITH	Wm	PIPR	22 /1144	B		DAWDON COLLIERY	1/7/16			CERISY GAILLY CEM		

SMITHSON	Thos	PTE	22	/1269									TO 1st GARRISON BN, CLASS Z RESERVE.	
SOMERVILLE	Hugh	PTE	22	/1523	D	73 THIRD STREET	HORDEN			1/7/16	MISSING NOV 16	THIEPVAL MEM		BORN CARNWATH SCOTLAND.
SPEED	Geo	PTE	22	/1406			SOUTH HETTON	6/1/15	8/4/18	GSW	SEPT 16		TO DEPOT.	AGE 26.
SPITTAL	PeteH	PTE	22	/232			PERTH			18/10/17	JAN 17	TYNE COT MEM	TO 19th BN.	
SPOORS	Thos	PTE	22	/1515	B	27 HARRIOT STREET	NEWCASTLE	1/2/15		1/7/16	MISSING NOV 16	OVILLERS MIL CEM		
SPROAT	Bert	PTE	22	/240			CORNSAY VILLAGE						TO 2nd GARRISON BN, CLASSZ RESERVE.	
SPROAT	Edwd	PTE	22	/797			DURHAM CITY	16/11/14	3/7/17	GSW	JULY 16		TO DEPOT.	
SPROAT	James	PTE	22	/802			CORNSAY VILLAGE				JULY 16		TO 23rd, 24th, 26th, 25th, 8th BNS, CLASS Z RESERVE.	
STEELE	David	PIPR	22	/1439	C		PLASHETTS			1/7/16	MISSING NOV 16	THIEPVAL MEM		BORN DUMFRIES.
STENHOUSE	Wm	PTE	22	/803				16/11/14	19/1/17	SICK				
STEPHENS	J W	PIPR	22	/248					18/3/19		1/7/16		TO 11th BN, WEST YORKS(2nd), NF(22nd), Y&LANCASTEF	RENUMBERED 22/1730 ON REJOINING 22nd BN.
STEPHENS	J W	PTE	22	/1730					18/3/19				TO 11th BN, WEST YORKS(2nd), NF(22nd), Y&LANCASTEF	Y&L No 57665. ORIGINALLY 22/248
STEPHENSON	ChasE	PTE	22	/1740				17/7/15	21/9/15	INEFFICIENT			TO 29th BN.	AGE 29.
STEPHENSON	Robt	PTE	22	/532			SCOTSWOOD	19/11/14	18/1/18	SHELLSHOCK	JULY 16, SSHOCK DEC 16.		TO ARMY RESERVE CLASS W.	AGE 36, STEVENSON IN STGGAZ,
STEPHENSON	Robt	SGT	22	/636										
STEPHENSON	Wm	CPL	22	/1314			HETTON LE HOLE	7/1/15	13/6/18	WOUNDS	AUGUST 16, MARCH 18.		TO DEPOT.	AGE 25.
STERLING	Wm G	PTE	22	/516									TO 8th BN.	
STEWART	Henry	LCPL	22	/842			SLEEKBURN				JULY 16		COMMISSIONED, STILL SERVING 1920.	
STEWART	James	PTE	22	/1009				17/11/14	28/11/18	KR para 392			TO DEPOT.	DID NOT SERVE OVERSEAS.
STOBBART	Wm	PTE	22	/1626						19/1/16		PIETA MIL CEM MALTA	TO 1st GARRISON BN.	
STOCKTON	MattH	PTE	22	/1442			SEAHAM HARBOUR	11/1/15	7/3/18	WOUNDS	AUGUST 16		TO DEPOT.	AGE 44,ROYAL VICTORIA HOSP NETLEY 11/7/16.
STOKOE	Wm	SGT	22	/224		18 ST GEORGES TERR	NEWCASTLE				JULY 16			BORN PRUDHOE, DIED NEWCASTLE AGED 94 1978.
STONEHOUSE	Stan	PTE	22	/1484		5 ELEMORE LANE	HETTON LE HOLE	6/1/15	15/11/18	SICK				AGE 29.
STOREY	James	PTE	22	/1275			EASINGTON LANE	4/1/15	30/3/18	GSW	AUGUST 16		TO DEPOT.	AGE 23.
STOREY	John	PTE	22	/317			TYNEDOCK			27/10/18	SEPT 16	TEZZE MIL CEM ITALY	TO DURHAM LI(12th BN).	DURHAM LI No 45879.
STOREY	John	PTE	22	/1276				6/1/15	1/4/19	KR para392			TO ARMY RESERVE CLASS P.	
STOREY	Wm	PTE	22	/1456		2 BACK NORMANDY STI	MONKWEARMOUTH	23/1/15	16/3/18	DEAFNESS			TO 1st GARRISON BN.	AGE 47.
STRONG	Geo	PTE	22	/224		40 FRONT STREET	HOBSON COLLIERY				AUGUST 16			
STUTTARD	Herbt	SGT	22	/342		24 NORFOLK ROAD	NEWCASTLE	17/11/14	23/11/18	GSW	JULY 16, DEC 16, OCT 18.		TO 3rd BN.	AGE 38.
SUMMERS	Tom	PTE	22	/921			DUDLEY	17/11/14	16/3/18	GSW	JULY 16		TO ARMY RESERVE CLASS P.	AGE 21
SURTEES	Wm	LCPL	22	/869			CHESTER LE ST			9/3/16		ERQUINGHEM LYS CH YD		
SUTTON	Jas S	PTE	22	/362	D		NEWCASTLE			1/7/16	MISSING NOV 16	THIEPVAL MEM		BORN BRANDLING VILLAGE
SWAN	Wm	LCPL	22	/1272		3 PILOT TERRACE	SEAHAM HARBOUR			5/10/18		TEMPLEUX-LE-GUERAF	TO 2nd BN.	AGE 24.
SWANSON	Thos	PTE	22	/929						KR para 392				
SWIFT	James	PTE	22	/1277									TO 2nd GARRISON BN, CLASS Z RESERVE.	
TAIT	Thos	PTE	22											AWOL 10/3/15.
TATE	Harry	SGT	22	/1278			NORTH SHIELDS			26/8/16	AUGUST 16	ERQUINGHEM LYS CEM		BORN HOUGHTON LE SPRING.
TAYLOR	James	PTE	22	/1137				13/11/14	31/3/19	KR para 392			TO ARMY RESERVE CLASS P.	
TAYLOR	JohnC	CQMS	22	/ 48		128 CLAVERING AVENU	DUNSTON							
TAYLOR	JohnG	PTE	22	/107			NORTH SHIELDS	14/11/14	3/12/17	WOUNDS			TO DEPOT.	AGE 27.
TAYLOR	JohnH	PTE	22	/601										BOMBER
TAYLOR	MattF	PTE	22	/908	C	64 POPLAR ST HIRST	ASHINGTON			1/7/16	MISSING NOV 16	THIEPVAL MEM		BORN CRAMLINGTON AGE 21.
TAYLOR	MattH	PTE	22	/217		21 COMMERCIAL ROAD	NEWCASTLE	16/11/14	16/12/19	KR para 392			TO 2nd GARRISON BN, DEPOT.	
TAYLOR	Sam	PTE	22	/380				16/11/14	4/8/17	INJURIES			TO 85th TRAINING RESERVE BN.	
TAYLOR	Wm H	CQMS	22	/629										
TAYLOR	Wm T	LCPL	22	/750									TO ROYAL FUSILIERS(24th BN).	FRANCE 22 10/1/16-28/8/18, 24RF 29/8/18-18/9/18.
TENNANT	Ralph	PTE	22	/1352									TO 1st GARRISON BN, CLASS Z RESERVE.	
THIRWELL	John	PTE	22	/694		34 MEDOMSLEY ROAD	CONSETT						TO 1st, 16th, 1/6th, 3rd BNS, CLASS Z RESERVE.	SIGNALLER.
THOMPSON	Andrw	PTE	22	/813			SOUTH SHIELDS				MARCH 18		TO CLASS Z RESERVE.	
THOMPSON	Arth	LCPL	22	/1521		11 ROBINSON STREET	BLAYDON				NOV 16		TO 24th BN, CLASS Z RESERVE.	
THOMPSON	Fred	CPL	22	/1282		19 LYONS COLLIERY	HETTON LE HOLE			3/4/15		EASINGTON LANE CEM		AGE 22 DIED OF PNEUMONIA.
THOMPSON	Geo	LCPL	22	/744			SOUTH SHIELDS			22/6/16		ALBERT COM CEM EXT		AGE 28.
THOMPSON	Geo H	PTE	22	/474										
THOMPSON	James	LCPL	22	/1341	C		CHOPWELL			1/7/16	MISSING NOV 16	THIEPVAL MEM		BORN DUMFRIES.
THOMPSON	John	PTE	22	/1323	C		CHOPPINGTON			1/7/16	MISSING NOV 16	THIEPVAL MEM		
THOMPSON	John	PTE	22	/639			GATESHEAD	23/11/14	31/3/19	KR para 392	SEPT 16, FEB 18		TO ARMY RESERVE CLASS P.	
THOMPSON	Lesli	PTE	22	/ 33			CROSBY ON EDEN			10/6/16		BECOURT MIL CEM		BORN CARLISLE AGE 25.
THOMPSON	Thos	PTE	22	/1010			ASHINGTON	14/11/14	16/8/17	GSW	AUGUST 16		TO DEPOT.	
THOMPSON	Wm H	CPL	22	/820	A		NEWBURN			1/7/16		THIEPVAL MEM		BORN FIFE.
THORBURN	ThosA	PTE	22	/602									TO 2nd GARRISON BN, CLASS Z RESERVE.	MEDALS FORFEIT FOR THEFT.
THORNLEY	John	PTE	22	/316				17/11/14	11/7/18	SICK			TO DEPOT.	AGE 41.
THROWER	Albt	CPL	22	/807		103 COPELAND TERRA(	NEWCASTLE	16/11/14	3/7/18	WOUNDS	JUNE 18		TO DEPOT.	EMPLOYED AT HEATON STATION BY NER Co.
TILLEY	Geo	SGT	22	/1660				3/10/14	3/3/16	SICK			TO 29th BN.	AGE 47, DID NOT SERVE OVERSEAS.
TODD	John	PTE	22	/109				14/11/14	12/11/18	DAH			TO DEPOT.	AGE 41.
TODD	John	PTE	22	/1748			NORTH SHIELDS				AUGUST 16		TO 16th, 23rd BNS.	
TODD	Thos	ASGT	22	/ 94			CONSETT						COMMISSIONED	ACTING CSM.
TOOLEY	Geo	PTE	22	/963			BIRTLEY			22/6/16		HEILLY STATION CEM		BORN CHESTER LE STREET.
TREGASKIS	Rich	PTE	22	/722		GEORGE STREET	WHICKHAM						TO 1st GARRISON BN, CLASS Z RESERVE.	
TREMBLE	Arth	PTE	22	/534	B	10 HIGH GROVE	RYTON	20/11/14		1/7/16	MISSING NOV 16	THIEPVAL MEM		BORN NEWCASTLE AGE 34.HEWER STELLA COLLIERY.
TRENCH	Thos	CQMS	22	/405				17/11/14	11/1/19	SICK			TO 3rd BN.	AGE 48.
TROTTER	David	PTE	22	/918	D		USWORTH COLL			1/7/16	MISSING NOV 16	THIEPVAL MEM		BORN WILLINGTON.
TURNBULL	Geo	PTE	22	/426		6 CHURCH STREET	BIRTLEY	17/11/14	29/8/18	SICK	JULY 16		TO 9th BN.	
TURNBULL	Geo	PTE	22	/1321		19 KING GEORGES RD	WOODHORN						TO LABOUR CORPS(12 POW COY).	
TURNBULL	Henry	PTE	22	/333			DUDLEY			5/6/17		ARRAS MEM	TO 20th BN(A COY).	
TURNBULL	James	PTE	22	/721						KR para 392				
TURNBULL	Jas H	PTE	22	/949			WEST SLEEKBURN	17/11/14	2/9/18	KR para 392	NOV 16		TO DEPOT.	
TURNBULL	John	PTE	22	/1320	C	18 KING GEORGES RD	NEWBIGGIN / SEA			1/7/16	MISSING NOV 16	SERRE ROAD No 2		BORN WEST SLEEKBURN AGE 40.
TURNBULL	Rich	PTE	22	/786			ISABELLA PIT			31/7/16	JULY 16	BLYTH COWPEN CEM	TO 21st BN(A COY).	BORN COWPEN AGE 20.
TURNBULL	Wm	LCPL	22	/684		UPTON HSE OAKWOOD	BLACKHILL			5/6/17	NOV 16	ARRAS MEM		SNIPER AGE 30.
TURNER	Sam	PTE	22	/1047		72 ALGERNON ROAD	HEATON	13/11/14	15/10/17	25/10/19		BYKER & HEATON CEM	TO 2nd GARRISON BN, DEPOT.	AGE 37
URQHART	Alf L	PTE	22	/1284		5 SOUTH MOOR STREE	HENDON			9/4/17	AUGUST 16	ARRAS MEM	TO 16th, 23rd BNS.	AGE 27.
VALENTINE	JOhn	LCPL	22	/1046									TO 19th, 25th, 14th, 12/13th BNS, CLASS Z RESERVE.	
VASEY	Wm	PTE	22	/767									TO 1st BN, CLASS Z RESERVE.	
WADGE	JohnR	RSM	22	/1653			EDMONDSLEY			14/8/16	AUG 16, JAN 17(DoW)	GOSFORTH ST NICHOLAS CH YD		AGE 35 BORN WINGATE.
WALES	Edwd	SGT	22	/1325		254 SYCAMORE STREE	ASHINGTON			18/11/17	NOV 18	MONT HUON CEM LE TREPORT		BORN JARROW AGE 40.
WALKER	AlanA	PTE	22	/1623				16/1/15	1/4/19	KR para 392			TO ARMY RESERVE CLASS P.	
WALKER	Robt	PTE	22	/1651			GLASGOW	15/4/15						SHIPS COOK AGE 36, DESERTED 31/5/15, 5'6".
WALL	Robt	PTE	22	/845			CORNSAY VILLAGE						TO CLASS Z RESERVE.	
WALLACE	John	PTE	22	/1577	A		BOLDON COLLIERY				MISS NOV 16, OK FEB 17, F		TO 24th, 21st, 12/13th BNS	BOMBER.
WALLACE	Walt	PTE	22	/1045				13/11/14	1/10/18	VDH			TO 1st GARRISON BN.	
WALLS	JohnR	PTE	22	/1353			DAWDON COLLIERY				AUGUST 16		TO 16th, 1/6th BNS, CLASS Z RESERVE.	
WALLWORTH	JohnJ	PTE	22	/293			BEDLINGTON	16/11/14	12/4/18	GSW	OCT 16, JAN 18.		TO 3rd BN.	AGE 22.
WALTERS	Arnld	PTE	22	/1663				30/4/15	7/8/17	SICK			TO 3rd BN.	
WALTON	Thos	PTE	22	/ 97		13 WALTON TERRACE	MEDOMSLEY							
WARD	Wesly	PTE	22	/159			NORTH SHIELDS			17/6/17		VOORMEZEELE ENCLC	TO 10th BN.	
WARDLE	Edwd	PTE	22	/272		DURHAM STREET	SACRISTON				JAN 17			
WATERS	Robt	PTE	22											AWOL 9/6/15.
WATERS	Thos	LCPL	22	/ 34			WEST RYTON				AUGUST 16, MISS 31/3/18		TO 18th(W COY), 1st BNS.	
WATERS	Thos	PTE	22	/522			SOUTH SHIELDS				JULY 16		TO 16th, 23rd BNS.	
WATSON	Arch	PTE	22	/969			COWPEN			26/10/17			TO 1/4th BN.	
WATSON	Henry	PTE	22											AWOL 20/9/15
WATSON	John	PTE	22	/655									TO 25th , 1/7th BNS, CLASS Z RESERVE.	RENUMBERED 293327.
WATSON	JohnT	PTE	22	/106	B	67 MORRIS ST TEAMS	GATESHEAD			1/7/16	MISSING NOV 16	THIEPVAL MEM		AGE 37.
WATSON	JohnW	PTE	22	/1513				23/1/15	23/10/17	SICK			TO 84th TRAINING RESERVE BN.	DID NOT SERVE OVERSEAS.
WATSON	Robt	PTE	22	/538			NEWCASTLE	7/9/14	24/7/17	GSW	OCT 16		TO DEPOT.	
WATSON	Sept	PTE	22	/1650									TO CLASS Z RESERVE.	RENUMBERED 89747 NF.
WATSON	Thos	PTE	22	/755			WALKER				JAN 18		TO 23rd, 1/4th BNS, CLASS Z RESERVE.	
WAUGH	Adam	PTE	22	/483		18 SOUTH BENWELL RC	NEWCASTLE			2/5/18	JULY 16	LARCH WOOD(RAILWA'	TO WEST YORKSHIRE REGT(1/5th BN).	W YORKS No 27459, BORN RYTON AGE 33, AWOL 21/6/15
WAUGH	John	PTE	22	/468			NEWCASTLE			1/7/16	OCT 16	THIEPVAL MEM	TO 26th BN.	BORN WOODSIDE Co DURHAM.
WEDDERBURN	Wm	CPL	22	/ 82	HQ			14/11/14	27/2/17	GSW			TO DEPOT.	AGE 32.
WEDDLE	AlexT	CSM	22	/1036		28 ELLISON STREET	JARROW				AUGUST 16		TO CLASS Z RESERVE.	
WEETMAN	Hallo	SGT	22	/687									TO CLASS Z RESERVE.	
WEETMAN	JohnA	SGT	22	/ 66			SUNDERLAND				AUGUST 16		TO ROYAL FUSILIERS(24th BN).	FRANCE 22 10/1/16-28/8/18, 24RF-6/4/19. R FUS No GS/93
WELSH	John	PTE	22	/1706			NORTH SHIELDS	10/7/15	22/6/17	WOUNDS	JUNE 16		TO DEPOT.	
WEST	John	PTE	22											AWOL 16/12/15.
WESTGATE	Robt	PTE	22	/1617		212 LONGHIRST STREE	PEGSWOOD	29/1/15	31/3/19	KR para 392			TO 2nd GARRISON BN, ARMY RESERVE CLASS P.	
WHITE	Geo E	PTE	22	/947	A	14 REKENDYKE LANE	SOUTH SHIELDS			1/7/16		THIEPVAL MEM		AGE 22.
WHITE	Thos	PTE	22	/1372			EASINGTON LANE	6/1/15	28/12/17	GSW	MARCH 17		TO 3rd BN.	AGE 50.
WHITE	Wm Rb	PTE	22	/ 43				14/11/14	11/9/16	EMPHYSEMA			TO DEPOT.	
WHITFIELD	Jos	PTE	22	/390		13 STEPHENSON TERR	WALBOTTLE						TO 2nd GARRISON BN, CLASS Z RESERVE.	
WHITFIELD	Tho A	PTE	22	/176			CORNSAY VILLAGE							
WIDDOWFIELD	JohnW	PTE	22	/1399			HETTON LE HOLE	6/1/15	26/11/17	GSW	SEPT 16		TO DEPOT.	CPL AGE 22.

Surname	Forename	Rank	Bn	No.	Coy	Address	Place	Date 1	Date 2	Cause	Service	Cemetery/Mem	Transfer	Remarks
WIGHAM	Chas	PTE	22	/1545		19 MAPLE STREET	MEDOMSLEY							
WIGHTMAN	John	PTE	22	/700									TO CLASS Z RESERVE.	
WILDE	Ken J	PTE	22	/1324									TO 1st GARRISON BN, CLASS Z RESERVE.	
WILKES	Isiah	PTE	22											
WILKEY	Frank	PTE	22	/1762	A		NEWPORT MON			1/7/16	MISSING NOV 16.	THIEPVAL MEM		AWOL 26/11/15
WILKINSON	Alf W	PTE	22	/1683				3/4/15	3/5/18	GSW			TO 3rd BN.	BORN BRISTOL.
WILKINSON	Geo W	PTE	22	/133			SOUTH SHIELDS			30/7/16	AUGUST 16	BOULOGNE EASTERN CEM		AGE 22.
WILKINSON	J	PTE	22	/535	D	9 ROBINSON STREET	HOBSON COLLIERY				MISSING 21/3/18			
WILKINSON	JohnG	PTE	22	/1286		2 ALLISON YARD	NEWBIGGIN / SEA	6/1/15		1/6/16		HEILLY STATION CEM		BORN ASHINGTON AGE 26.
WILKINSON	ThosF	PTE	22	/417		LINTZ FORD	ROWLANDS GILL			8/7/16		BOULOGNE EASTERN CEM		BORN LANCHESTER, AGE 24.
WILLIAMS	JohnH	PTE	22	/1485									TO CLASS Z RESERVE.	
WILLIS	Chas	PTE	22											
WILLIS	James	SGT	22	/743			SOUTH SHIELDS	18/11/14	30/8/17	GSW	JULY 16		TO DEPOT.	AWOL 13/11/15
WILLIS	Wm	PTE	22	/1287	B		BLYTH			KR para 392	SEPT 16			TO 18 GHOSP 6/7/16, BASE DEPOT 7/7/16.
WILSON	A	PTE	22	/283		70 SOUTH ROW	NEW DELAVAL			7/1/16				AGE 25.
WILSON	Albt	SGT	22	/605			SOUTH SHIELDS				SEPT 16		TO DURHAM LI(12th BN).	
WILSON	Harld	CPL	22	/811		5 GREEN TERRACE	SUNDERLAND			10/6/16		BECOURT MIL CEM		DURHAM LI No 45878.
WILSON	J G	PTE	22	/603			SOUTH SHIELDS				NOV 18			AGE 21.
WILSON	John	PTE	22	/189		18 JOHN STREET	NEWFIELD							SECTION COMMANDER, LCPL
WILSON	Jos	PTE	22	/1288		137 SALEM STREET	JARROW						TO 1st GARRISON BN, CLASS Z RESERVE.	
WILSON	Ralph	PTE	22	/169		80 LIDDLE STREET	CORNSAY						TO CLASS Z RESERVE.	
WILSON	Robt	PTE	22	/1373		24 JANE STREET	HETTON LE HOLE	5/1/15	25/2/19	KR para 392			TO 11th BN.	
WILSON	Robt	PTE	22	/213		34 RAMSAY STREET	CHESTER LE ST						TO ARMY RESERVE CLASS P.	
WILSON	Robt	PTE	22	/570				21/11/14	5/9/16				TO 2nd GARRISON BN.	
WILSON	Robt	PTE	22	/1672	D		SOUTH SHIELDS			1/7/16	MISSING NOV 16	THIEPVAL MEM		DID NOT SERVE OVERSEAS.
WILSON	Thos	PTE	22	/1499		129 BILLEN STREET	SOUTH SHIELDS	30/1/15					TO 2nd GARRISON BN, CLASS Z RESERVE.	AGE 32 IN 13 PLATOON.
WINDAS	J W	LCPL	22	/314							MISSING 21/3/18			
WINTER	James	PTE	22	/1767									TO 2nd GARRISON BN, CLASS Z RESERVE.	
WOMACK	Sydny	PTE	22	/1709			HEXAM			1/10/16	DEC 16		TO YORK & LANCASTER REGT(8th BN).	Y&L No 34349.
WOMBWELL	Ben	PTE	22											AWOL 20/11/15
WOOD	Chas	PTE	22	/1443						KR para 392			TO 1st GARRISON BN.	
WOOD	Geo	PTE	22	/1285			SEAHAM HARBOUR			KR para 392	AUGUST 16		TO 23rd BN.	
WOOD	John	PTE	22	/1436	B		SEAHAM HARBOUR			1/7/16	MISSING NOV 16	THIEPVAL MEM		BORN BOLDON.
WOOD	John	PTE	22	/1691						KR para 392			TO DURHAM LIGHT INFANTRY, TRAINING RESERVE BN.	TRG RES No TR/5/59961.
WOODS	ChasE	PTE	22	/1634	C	23 REGINALD STREET	SUNDERLAND			1/7/16		THIEPVAL MEM		AGE 38.
WOODWARD	John	PTE	22	/1512		141 PARKER STREET	NEWCASTLE						TO 2nd GARRISON BN, CLASS Z RESERVE.	
WORMALD	Tennt	PTE	22	/1557		6 TOWNLEY STREET	ROWLANDS GILL			6/7/16		HEILLY STATION CEM		BORN CHARLESTOWN YORKS.
WRAITH	R J	PTE	22	/610			SOUTH SHIELDS				AUGUST 16			BOMBER
WRIGHT	ArthT	PTE	22	/631					7/2/19				TO YORK & LANCASTER REGT(2/4th BN), CLASS Z RESEI	Y&L No 57690.
WRIGHT	John	PTE	22	/241					KRpara392				TO DURHAM LIGHT INFANTRY, TRAINING RESERVE BN.	TRG RES No TR/5/58187.
WRIGHT	JohnT	PTE	22	/675	A		CHOPPINGTON			1/7/16	MISSING NOV 16	THIEPVAL MEM		BORN CAMBOIS.
WRIGHT	RobtR	PTE	22	/1437	C	9 STRANGWAY STREET	DAWDON			1/7/16	MISSING NOV 16	THIEPVAL MEM		BORN FELLING AGE 20.
WRIGHT	Wm	PTE	22	/135	A		SOUTH SHIELDS			1/7/16	MISSING NOV 16	THIEPVAL MEM		AWOL 29/3/15.
WYLAM	Wm	PTE	22	/952			CAMBOIS				JAN 18		TO 21st, 23rd, 1/5th BNS	
YARE	Robt	PMJR	22	/129				13/11/14	18/1/15	KR para 392				DID NOT SERVE OVERSEAS.
YARROW	Thos	PTE	22	/462			CHOPPINGTON	17/11/14	28/5/17	WOUNDS	AUG 16		TO DEPOT.	AWOL 8/7/15, To 3CCS 2/7/16 EVAC 2/7/16 SHELLSHOCK.
YARROW	Wm H	LCPL	22	/332			SOUTH SHIELDS	17/11/14	3/10/17	GSW	AUG 16		TO DEPOT.	AGE 33.
YELLOWLEY	Mark	PTE	22	/511		67 RICHARDSON STREET	SEATON HIRST			5/4/17		AUBIGNY COM CEM		AGE 35 BORN MORPETH.
YETTS	Geo L	PTE	22	/727									TO EAST YORKSHIRE REGT(1st BN), CLASS Z RESERVE.	E YORKS No 50705.
YOUERN	Arth	CPL	22	/1294	D		SUNDERLAND			1/7/16		THIEPVAL MEM		BORN MONKWEARMOUTH.
YOUNG	AlexH	SGT	22	/597		40 LAVENDER GARDEN	WEST JESMOND		1921	KR para 392	OCT 16, JAN 18, NOV 18.			RENUMBERED 4257352.
YOUNG	Geo	PTE	22											AWOL 1/12/15 IN COURT BLYTH AGE 20.
YOUNG	Jas W	PTE	22	/1428		75 HOUGHTON ROAD	HETTON LE HOLE						TO 2nd GARRISON BN, CLASS Z RESERVE.	
YOUNG	John	PTE	22	/1326	B		SEAHAM HARBOUR			3/7/16		THIEPVAL MEM		BORN GATESHEAD.
YOUNG	Thos	PTE	22	/418		28 WILLIAM STREET	LINTZ COLLIERY				SEPT 16			
YOUNG	ThosG	PTE	22	/1701			COWPEN				NOV 18		TO CLASS Z RESERVE.	

Appendix VI

NOMINAL ROLL OF OTHER RANKS 23rd NF (4th Tyneside Scottish)

Number on Roll **1060**; Killed or Died of Wounds **379**; Wounded **357**, Gassed, Sick etc **189**:
Total known casualties **925** (87.2 per cent)
Not traced 694

NAME	INITIALS	RANK	BAT	NUMB	CC	ADDRESS	TOWN_VILL	ENLISTE	DISCHAR	CAUSE_DIS	WOUNDED	BURIED	TRANSFER	ADD
ADAMS	Cal A	PTE	23	/1225									TO 2nd GARRISON BN, CLASS Z RESERVE. TO ARMY RESERVE CLASS P.	
AIMSBURY	Thos	PTE	23	/158				2/12/14	1/2/19	KR para 392			TO DEPOT.	AGE 21.
ALDERSON	Fred	PTE	23	/1414			ASHINGTON	31/7/15	16/11/16	GSW R LEG	JULY 16		TO 8th, 1st, 11th BNS., CLASS Z RESERVE.	IN 11 PLATOON.
ALDERSON	Fred	PTE	23	/1026	C		EASINGTON				NOV 16			
ALDRIDGE	Wm	PTE	23	/1137	C	32 FULWELL ROAD	SUNDERLAND	30/12/14		1/7/16	MISSING DEC 16	THIEPVAL MEM		
ALEXANDER	Robt	PTE	23	/170		47 BARLOW RD	BLAYDON			KR para 392			TO 2nd GARRISON BN.	
ALLAN	Harry	PTE	23	/683			ASHINGTON			27/5/18	AUGUST 16	MARFEUX BRIT CEM	TO 24th, 8th, 1/5th BNS.	DESERTED AUGUST 15, AWOL 6/11/15. IN 11 PLATOON.
ALLAN	John	CPL	23	/83	C		NEWCASTLE			1/7/16	NOV 16, WND+MISSING DEC	THIEPVAL MEM		
ALLAN	John	PTE	23	/565						FEB 16			TO 9th, 10th BNS.	
ALLAN	Mark	PTE	23	/366	A		FOREST HALL			30/6/16	MISSING AUGUST 16,	OVILLERS MIL CEM		
ALLCOCK	Wm	PTE	23	/1088		148 MARIAN STREET	GATESHEAD			KR para 392			TO 2nd GARRISON BN.	
ALLEN	Fred	PTE	23	/1503						KR para 392				
ALLISON	Robt	PTE	23	/308									TO 2nd GARRISON BN, CLASS Z RESERVE.	
ALLISON	ThosW	CPL	23	/689			CHOPPINGTON STN	15/12/14	31/3/19	KR para 392	SEPT 16, JAN 18.		TO ARMY RESERVE CLASS P.	
ALLSOP	Thos	SGT	23	/691			AMBLE			29/4/17		BROWNS COPSE CEM		AWOL 1915.
ANDERSON	Alex	PTE	23	/505	D		HIRST			1/7/16	MISSING DEC 16	THIEPVAL MEM		
ANDERSON	David	PTE	23	/489		98 EDMUND STREET	HEBBURN COLL						TO 1st GARRISON BN, CLASS Z RESERVE.	
ANDERSON	John	PTE	23	/1010			LEMINGTON				JULY 16		TO 11th, 9th BNS, CLASS Z RESERVE.	
ANDERSON	JohnG	PTE	23	/1178		8 DELAVAL TERRACE	BLYTH	30/12/14		1/7/16		OVILLERS MIL CEM		BORN BANCHORY SCOTLAND
ANDERSON	Messr	PTE	23	/335									TO CLASS Z RESERVE.	
ANDERSON	RobtW	PTE	23	/1603				31/7/15	22/8/16	SICK			TO 20th, 29th BNS	
ANDERSON	Thos	PTE	23	/923	D	5 PERCY PLACE	NEWCASTLE							DESERTED 29/4/15, AGE 21, 5'8", BROWN EYES BROWN H
ANDERSON	Vic	PTE	23	/1523			SOUTH SHIELDS	24/4/15					TO ARMY RESERVE CLASS P.	AGE 39.
ANDERSON	Wm	PTE	23	/1613				5/8/15	1/6/18	MYALGIA			SERVED SOUTH AFRICA ROYAL IRISH RIFLES	3 YEARS PENAL SERVITUDE FOR LARCENY 9/4/15.
ANDREWS	JohnG	SGT	23										TO CLASS Z RESERVE.	
ANNAKIN	Wilk	PTE	23	/861						1/7/16	NOV 16 WND+MISSING DEC	THIEPVAL MEM		AGE 37 BORN LUMLEY, RESIDED NETHERTON COLLIERY
APPLEBY	Henry	LCPL	23	/591	D	7 NEVADA STREET	GREENWICH LDON							DID NOT SERVE OVERSEAS.
APPLEBY	John	PTE	23	/1061				26/12/14	26/6/15	INEFFICIENT			TO DEPOT.	AGE 39.
APPLEBY	MattR	PTE	23	/1059				26/12/14	11/12/17	SICK		ETAPLES MIL CEM		BORN CRAMLINGTON.
APPLEBY	Ralph	PTE	23	/502			NEWBURN			12/7/16			TO CLASS Z RESERVE.	
ARMSTRONG	John	PTE	23	/275		50 ABBOTT STREET	GATESHEAD				MISSING JUNE 16, POW OCT		TO ARMY RESERVE CLASS P.	AGE 36.
ARMSTRONG	John	CPL	23	/1467			RUSHYFORD	27/2/15	22/6/18	WOUNDS	JULY 16		RE ENLISTED 7th NORTHUMBERLAND FUSILIERS	AGE 29, 5'6", 36 CHEST, MINER BORN 2/11/86.
ARMSTRONG	Jos H	PTE	23	/690	D	52 HOWARD ROW	NETHERTON COLL	16/11/14	27/2/15	KR para 392				AGE 45, 5'5", 36 CHEST, MARRIED 2 CHILDREN.
ARMSTRONG	Robt	PTE	23	/692		De 8 DOUBLE ROW	BARRINGTON COLL	15/12/14	24/4/15	KR para 392				MARBLE FINISHER, AGE 36YRS 11MNTHS, 5'5", 34 CHEST
ARMSTRONG	Robt	PTE	23	/311	C	11 GERTRUDE STREE	NEWCASTLE	26/11/14	18/2/15	KR para 392	NOV 16 WND+MISSING DEC	BAPAUME POST MIL CEM		AGE 19 BORN NEWCASTLE.
ARMSTRONG	RobtJ	CPL	23	/622	D					1/7/16		HEILLY STATION CEM		BORN RYHOPE.
ARMSTRONG	Thos	PTE	23	/ 2			SOUTH SHIELDS			27/5/16			TO DEPOT.	AGE 35.
ARMSTRONG	Thos	SGT	23	/ 27		1 DERWENT TERRACI	TANFIELD	24/11/14	6/8/16	GSW				BORN HASWELL AGE 35.
ARNOLD	John	PTE	23	/334	C	6 BOWES TERR	MARLEY HILL			1/7/16	MISSING DEC 16	THIEPVAL MEM	TO DEPOT.	
ARNOTT	James	PTE	23	/968				28/12/14	12/3/18	SICK			TO ARMY RESERVE CLASS P.	AGE 39.
ARNOTT	Perci	PTE	23	/651			ASHINGTON	9/12/14	18/12/17	WOUNDS	JULY 16		TO 3rd BN.	AGE 44.
ASHCROFT	Thos	PTE	23	/424			HIGH FELLING			26/3/18		ST PIERRE CEM AMIEN	TO LABOUR CORPS(200 LAB COY).	LAB CORPS No 118805.
ASKEW	Robt	PTE	23	/228			BLACKHILL	20/11/14	8/3/18	GSW	AUGUST 16		TO DEPOT.	AGE 32, TO 3CCS 2/7/16 EVAC 2/7/16 WND LEGS.
ASKEW		PTE	23	/225	C									11 PLATOON ATTACHED BN TRANSPORT SECTION.
ATHEY	John	PTE	23	/854	D		CHOPPINGTON				JULY 16		TO CLASS Z RESERVE.	BORN DURHAM CITY.
ATKINSON	Alex	PTE	23	/826	D		BLYTH			1/7/16	NOV 16, MISS DEC 16	THIEPVAL MEM		RENUMBERED 61129.
ATKINSON	Geo R	PTE	23	/592			SCOTLAND GATE			KR para 392	SEPT16			AGE 34 BORN METHERTON SCOTLAND.
ATKINSON	Jas W	PTE	23	/824	D		BEDLINGTON			1/7/16	MISSING DEC 16	THIEPVAL MEM		
ATKINSON	Walt	PTE	23	/805	D		BLYTH			1/7/16	MISSING DEC 16	THIEPVAL MEM		BN SPORTS ALNWICK.
AULD		PTE	23											TO CLASS Z RESERVE.	
BAINBRIDGE	James	SGT	23	/1133		23 BACK STABLES	HOWDON	29/12/14					TO 20th, 21st, 3rd BNS.	
BAINBRIDGE	John	PTE	23	/1191		4 PIT COTTAGES	HOWDON	29/12/14	10/10/17	GSW	AUGUST 16			BORN TYNEMOUTH.
BAKER	Jos S	PTE	23	/ 18	A		NORTH SHIELDS			1/7/16	MISSING DEC 16	THIEPVAL MEM		
BAKEWELL	Horce	CPL	23	/444	B		BLOXWICH STAFFS			29/4/17		ARRAS MEM		
BANKS	JohnE	PTE	23	/451			CHOPWELL	4/11/14	3/5/18	GSW	MARCH 17		TO ARMY RESERVE CLASS P.	VOLUNTARY AID HOSP CHELTENHAM 8/7/16.
BARBER	Jas	PTE	23	/1630			HARTFORD COLL			4/4/17	SEPT 16	ST NICHOLAS BRIT CE	TO 16th, 21st, 20th BNS.	
BARBER	J W	PTE	23	/1593			HEDDON / WALL				AUGUST 16			
BARKER	JohnR	PTE	23	/251										AGE 38.
BARKER	Jos	PTE	23	/1175				30/12/14	20/11/17	SICK			TO 10th BN.	AWOL 29/3/15.
BARNES	James	PTE	23											

BARNES	Jas	PTE	23	/1349						KR para 392			TO 1st GARRISON, 2nd BNS.	
BARNES	Nor W	PTE	23	/1632			CRAMLINGTON	9/8/15	11/8/17	GSW	AUGUST 16		TO 20th BN, ARMY RESERVE CLASS W.	
BARR	JohnF	LCPL	23	/1407		28 BACK HIGH ST WE:	SUNDERLAND			16/11/16	SSHOCK NOV 16	THIEPVAL MEM	TO CHESHIRE REGIMENT(9th BN).	CHESHIRE REGT No 52259. AGE 40.
BARTON	Adam	PTE	23	/1152		31 CASTELREAGH STI	TUNSTALL						TO KINGS OWN YORKSHIRE LI(5th BN).	KOYLI No 63096.
BARTON	Jack	SGT	23			31 CASTLEREAGH STI	TUNSTALL						TO ROYAL ENGINEERS(245 TUN COY).	RE No 133664.
BARTON	Wm Sn	PTE	23	/1149		31 CASTLEREAGH STI	TUNSTALL	28/12/14	24/2/19				TO ROYAL ENGINEERS.	RE No 132663, 10 AUSTRALIAN FLD AMB 4/6/18.
BARWICK	RobtE	PTE	23	/1325			HORDEN COLL			1/7/16	NOV 16, WND+MISSING DEC	THIEPVAL MEM		
BATE	Sam J	PTE	23	/ 946			CORNSAY COLL	21/12/14	21/4/17	WOUNDS	AUGUST 16		TO DEPOT.	
BATES	Gilb	SGT	23	/ 817	D		MORPETH			1/7/16	NOV 16, WND+MISS DEC 16	THIEPVAL MEM		
BATES	Wm	SGT	23	/1415		SPARROW HOUSE FA	SHEEPWASH						TO CLASS Z RESERVE.	
BAXTER	Bruce	PTE	23	/ 688	C						MISSING 21-23/3/18		TO CLASS Z RESERVE.	
BEAL	Thos	PTE	23	/ 902			NEWBIGGIN / SEA			20/4/18		OUTTERSTEENE COM CEM EXT		
BEATTIE	Alex	CPL	23	/ 145			HOUGHTON LE SP	3/12/14	8/4/17	WOUNDS	JULY 16		TO DEPOT.	AGE 30.
BELDON	JohnR	SGT	23	/ 289			BARRINGTON COLL				SSHOCK NOV 16, JUNE 17.			
BELL	Alb A	PTE	23	/ 965									TO CLASS Z RESERVE.	
BELL	JohnW	PTE	23	/ 399						11/9/15		ST ANDREWS JESMOND		AGE 42, COMMITTED SUICIDE.
BELL	R	CPL	23	/ 49										
BELL	Thos	SGT	23	/ 85		10 WEST VIEW	EARSDON	23/11/14	31/1/19	KR para 392	FEB 16		TO 8th BN, ARMY RESERVE CLASS P.	
BELL	Thos	PTE	23	/1377			SEAHAM COLLIERY				SEPT 16		TO DURHAM LI(15th BN).	DURHAM LI No 45580.
BENGALL	CuthR	PTE	23	/ 314		9 MARGARET ROAD	WHITLEY BAY							PRISONER OF WAR.
BENGALL	Thos	LCPL	23	/ 391			SHIREMOOR			10/4/18	APRIL 17	TROIS ARBRES CEM	TO 1/5th BN.	BORN EARSDON.
BENN	Mark	PTE	23	/ 156			NEWCASTLE	2/12/14	2/5/17	GSW L LEG				BEAUFORT WAR HOSP BRISTOL 11/7/16.
BENNETT	RichT	PTE	23	/ 50		2 WELL CLOSE	NORTH SHIELDS			26/2/17	AUGUST 16	FAUBOURG DE AMIENS ARRAS		AGE 24 BORN SHILDON, IN 10 SECTION 11 PLATOON.
BENNETT	Thos	PTE	23	/ 685									TO CHESHIRE REGIMENT(9th BN).	CHESHIRE REGT No 52260.
BENTLEY	Harry	SGT	23	/ 522	A		JARROW			1/7/16	MISSING DEC 16	THIEPVAL MEM		
BENTLEY	Jos	PTE	23	/ 4									TO 2nd GARRISON BN, CLASS Z RESERVE.	
BESFORD	John	PTE	23	/ 493		7 ELISABETH STREET	CRAMLINGTON							
BILTCLIFFE	LeonS	PTE	23	/ 508									TO 1st BN.	
BILTON	Geo	PTE	23	/ 332			WALKER	24/11/14	15/10/17	GSW	JULY 16		TO DEPOT.	AGE 38.
BIRCHALL	Peter	PTE	23	/1005									TO DURHAM LIGHT INFANTRY.	DLI No 74897.
BLACK	D J	PTE	23	/ 513		204 HOPE STREET	JARROW							
BLACKBIRD	Ralph	PTE	23	/ 211		JANE PIT	NEWBOTTLE	24/11/15	7/5/19	KR para 392			TO 1st GARRISON BN, ARMY RESERVE CLASS P.	
BLACKHALL	Wm H	PTE	23	/ 686		13 ST MARY STREET	MORPETH			21/1/17	AUGUST 16	MORPETH SS MARY &	TO 2nd GARRISON BN.	DROWNED, AGE 34.
BLAND	Henry	PTE	23	/ 443			WESTERHOPE			29/4/17	SEPT 16	BROWNS COPSE CEM	TO 27th, 23rd BNS.	BORN CONSETT.
BLANEY	Jos	PTE	23	/ 132										
BLAYLOCK	JohnW	PTE	23	/ 614		27 MILBURN TERRACI	CHOPPINGTON			3/7/16		DAUORS COM CEM EXT		AGE 22.
BLAYLOCK	Sam	PTE	23	/ 929		10 PARK TERR	IVESTON							
BLENKINSOP	Henry	SGT	23	/ 76										
BLENKINSOP	John	PTE	23	/1037	B		HENDON			1/7/16	MISSING DEC 16	THIEPVAL MEM		
BLENKINSOP	ThosJ	PTE	23	/1014			ANNFIELD PLAIN			29/5/16		MARCEUIL BRIT CEM	ATTACHED ROYAL ENGINEERS(181 TUNNELLINC	AGE 35.
BLOOMFIELD	Wm T	PTE	23	/ 696			NETHERTON COLL	15/12/14	18/5/17	WOUNDS	AUGUST 16		TO DEPOT.	AGE 42.1st STHN GEN HOSP BIRMINGHAM 25/7/16.
BRADLEY	Pat	PTE	23	/ 693		1 PARK ROW	FELLING			1/7/16	OCT 16, WND+MISSING DEC	THIEPVAL MEM	TO 26th BN.	
BRADLEY	Robt	LCPL	23	/ 955									TO 1st GARRISON BN, CLASS Z RESERVE.	
BRADY	Jos S	PTE	23	/ 403			NEWCASTLE			22/10/17	AUGUST 16	TYNE COT MEM	TO 9th, 20th BNS.	TO 3 CCS 2/7/16 EVAC 2/7 WND LEGS, BORN BEDLINGTOI
BRADY	RobtD	SGT	23	/1139	C	5 JOHNSON TERR	LOW PALLION	28/12/14	29/11/15	23/12/18		BISHOPWEARMOUTH	TO 29th BN.	DID NOT SERVE OVERSEAS, AGE 38.
BRAYSHER	Alf	PTE	23	/1113		103 FRAMWELLGATE	DURHAM CITY			KR para 392			TO 1st GARRISON BN.	AWOL 2/7/15.
BRODIE	F J	PTE	23	/ 135										DID NOT SERVE OVERSEAS.
BROOMFIELD	Olivr	PTE	23	/1567			BEBSIDE	19/7/15	4/1/18	WOUNDS	APRIL 17		TO DEPOT.	AGE 22.
BROWN	Anthy	PTE	23	/ 694			CHOPPINGTON				AUGUST 16		TO 14th BN, CLASS Z RESERVE.	
BROWN	Geo	SGT	23	/1409			WEST HARTLEPOOL				JULY 16		COMMISSIONED.	
BROWN	J	PTE	23	/ 909										TO 3CCS 2/7/16 EVAC 2/7/16 WND UPPER ARM.
BROWN	James	LCPL	23	/ 290		2 STATION ROAD	CRAMLINGTON						TO 2nd GARRISON BN, CLASS Z RESERVE.	
BROWN	Jas A	PTE	23	/1177		15 ERNEST STREET	PELTON						TO 1st, 12/13th BNS, CLASS Z RESERVE.	
BROWN	John	PTE	23	/ 695			BEDLIINGTON				AUGUST 16		TO 19th(Z COY), 1st, 16th, 1/6th BNS, CLASS Z RESERVE.	
BROWN	John	PTE	23	/1416		16 INSTITUTE ROW	NORTH SEATON	2/1/15	6/9/18	GSW	FEB 18		TO DEPOT.	
BROWN	John	SGT	23	/ 877									TO 25th BN, CLASS Z RESERVE.	
BROWN	John	PTE	23	/1107						KR para 392			TO DURHAM LIGHT INFANTRY, TRAINING RESER	TRG RES No TR/5/58188.
BROWN	Matt	PTE	23	/ 608			CHOPPINGTON			1/7/16	NOV 16, WND+MISSING DEC	THIEPVAL MEM		BORN NORTH SEATON.
BROWN	Thos	PTE	23	/ 139									TO KINGS OWN YORKSHIRE LI(5th BN).	KOYLI No 63099.
BROWN	Thos	PTE	23	/ 51	C		HEXAM			KR para 392	AUGUST 16		TO 25th, 1/5th BNS.	25 AMBT 5/7 18 GHOSP HSHIP 9/7/16 WND R LEG+FOOT
BROWN	Thos	PTE	23	/ 162				9/8/15	19/10/18	DEBILITY			TO ARMY RESERVE CLASS W.	
BROWN	Wm	PTE	23	/1262									POSSIBLY TRANSFERRED OR REENLISTED ROY.	DESERTED 26/10/17, MEDALS CLAIMED BY ADMIRALTY.
BROWN	Wm Ed	PTE	23	/1526		5 BOUNDARY ROW	SHANKHOUSE			26/9/15		PIETA MIL CEM MALTA	TO 1st GARRISON BN.	AGE 28 DIED OF DYSENTRY.
BROWN	Wm H	PTE	23	/ 455			NORTH SHIELDS	4/11/14	24/8/17	GSW	OCT 16		TO 20th BN, DEPOT.	
BRUNSKILL	Andrw	PTE	23	/ 316		37 GEORGE ROAD	NEWCASTLE				AUGUST 16		TO 11th BN, ATT ROYAL ENGINEERS(INLAND WATERWAYS TRANSPORT)	
BRYANT	Jos H	PTE	23	/1075			SOUTH SHIELDS			30/4/17	SEPT 16	DUISANS BRIT CEM	TO 16th BN.	AGE 30.
BRYSON	Geo	PTE	23	/ 960			BLYTH	24/12/14	13/1/19	SHELLSHOCK	SSHOCK AUGUST 16		TO 25th, 20th, 3rd BNS.	
BUGLASS	Dav W	PTE	23	/1192		13 ALEXANDER ROW	SEAHAM HARBOUR	30/12/14	23/10/17	SICK			TO 84th TRAINING RESERVE BN.	DID NOT SERVE OVERSEAS.
BUGLASS	Geo	PTE	23	/1195			SEAHAM HARBOUR			1/7/16	NOV 16, WND+MISSING DEC	THIEPVAL MEM		
BULLEN	Chas	CPL	23	/ 631			NETHERTON COLL	10/12/14	16/4/18	GSW	AUGUST 16		TO ARMY RESERVE CLASS P.	AGE 22.
BULMAN	Geo S	SGT	23	/ 161		14 SIMPSON STREET	STANLEY				MARCH 17		TO 11th BN.	
BULMAN	John	PTE	23	/ 269			GATESHEAD			17/10/17	JULY 16	TYNE COT MEM		SHOWN ON TCM AS 22/289.
BULMAN	JohnA	PTE	23	/1294		29 WINDERMERE TER	SOUTHMOOR			23/3/16		SOUTHMOOR ST GEORGE CH YD		AGE 26 BORN MEDOMSLEY.
BUNTING	Fred	CPL	23	/1487				9/12/14	23/10/17	KR para 392			TO DEPOT	
BUNTING	JohnE	SGT	23	/1144		PENTS YARD	DAWDON						TO 1st GARRISON BN, CLASS Z RESERVE.	
BURGE	Matt	PTE	23	/1172		TOYSTON TERRACE	NORTH BROOMHILL			29/4/17		BROWNS COPSE CEM		BORN AMBLE AGE 22.
BURGE	Wm H	PTE	23	/1355		41 EAST STREET	GATESHEAD			1/7/16		THIEPVAL MEM		AGE 34 BORN PLYMOUTH DEVON.
BURN	Jas H	SIG	23	/ 176				1/12/14	16/8/18	GSW			TO DEPOT.	AGE 23.
BURRELL	Wm	PTE	23	/ 840	D	5 SECOND ROW	CHOPPINGTON			1/7/16	NOV 16, WND+MISSING DEC	THIEPVAL MEM		AGE 26 BORN BACKWORTH.
BURTON	Geo	PTE	23	/ 376			WALLSEND			5/7/16	JULY 16	PUCHEVILLERS BRIT CEM		BORN HEXAM.
BURTON	Wm	PTE	23	/1155	B	1 INFANT STREET	SEAHAM HARBOUR			1/7/16	MISSING DEC 16	THIEPVAL MEM		AGE 40 BORN STOCKTON ON TEES.
BUTTERS	StanH	PTE	23	/1545			ASHINGTON			KR para 392	AUGUST 16		TO 25th, 1/7th BNS.	
BYERS	Rich	PTE	23	/ 499										
BYFORD	Geo	SGT	23	/1587			EGLINGHAM						TO 3rd BN, CLASS Z RESERVE.	
CAHILL	Pat	PTE	23	/1383		74 VICEROY STREET	SEAHAM HARBOUR	25/1/15	14/11/17	SICK			TO DEPOT.	AGE 42.
CALDER	Edwd	SGT	20	/ 509		21 BEECH GROVE WE	RYTON	2/11/14	31/7/17	COMMISSION	1/7/16		TO CADET SCHOOL 22/2/17, COMMISSIONED 25tl	LCPL 13/3/15, CPL 9/6/16, SGT 13/7/16.PAINTER BY TRADE
CAMERON	W	PTE	23	/1446			NEWCASTLE				NOV 17			
CAMMERON	Donld	PTE	23	/ 654	D		NETHERTON COLL			1/7/16	MISSING DEC 16	THIEPVAL MEM		BORN CORNIRLISH SCOTLAND.
CAMPBELL	Thos	PTE	23	/ 796			BOOMERSUND				JULY 16, MISSING 27/5/18		TO 1/5th, 1/6th(A COY) BNS, CLASS Z RESERVE.	
CAMSALL	Geo W	PTE	23	/1560				13/7/15	26/2/18	SICK			TO 3rd BN.	
CARDY	Wm T	PTE	23	/1020	B	32 CORNISH STREET	NEW SEAHAM			1/7/16	MISSING DEC 16	THIEPVAL MEM		AGE 38 BORN NEW HERRINGTON, IN 6 PLATOON.
CARLYON	Henry	CSM	23	/1084		11 KIMBERLEY TERR	CRAGHEAD			KR para 392	MISSING 21/3/18		TO 22nd BN.	
CARMICHAEL	Wm A	PTE	23											AWOL 11/1/15
CARNEY	Harry	PTE	23	/ 669			SUNDERLAND				SEPT 16		TO 16th, 1st BNS, CLASS Z RESERVE.	
CARR	AlbtE	PTE	23	/ 702		8 BENSON TERRACE	HEBBURN NEWTOWN			21/8/18	SEPT 16	QUEENS CEM BUCQOL	TO MANCHESTER REGIMENT(1/7th BN).	R VIC HOSP NETLEY 11/7/16, MANCHESTER REGT No 769
CARR	Andrw	PTE	23	/ 527				8/12/14	23/8/17	KR para 392			TO DEPOT	
CARR	J J	PTE	23	/1575							24/8/16		TO 20th BN.	AWOL FROM 20th BN 6-8/10/14.
CARR	John	PTE	23	/ 186										
CARR	Thos	PTE	23	/ 239		8 BENSON TERRACE	FELLING			29/5/18		MONS COMMUNAL CEM		
CARR	Wm	PTE	23	/ 231		4 BREWERY SQUARE	STANLEY	30/11/14	3/2/19	KR para 392	APRIL 17		TO ARMY RESERVE CLASS P.	
CARROLL	James	PTE	23	/ 179		84 BEATRICE STREET	ASHINGTON			12/7/17	SEPT 16	MENIN GATE MEM	TO 10th BN.	AGE 23.
CARROLL	James	PTE	23	/ 506		3 COACH ROAD	BEDLINGTON			1/7/16	NOV 16, WND+MISSING DEC	THIEPVAL MEM		AGE 20.
CARRUTHERS	Fred	SGT	23	/1513		2 PIONEER TERRACE	BEDLINGTON			30/1/19		BEDLINGTON ST CUTH	TO DEPOT.	
CARSON	Robt	PTE	23	/ 143		7 HEWORTH STREET	FELLING			1/7/16	OCT 16, MISSING DEC 16	THIEPVAL MEM		AGE 23.
CARSS	Wm	PTE	23	/ 86			LESBURY	23/11/14	15/5/18	GSW	NOV 16, SSHOCK FEB 17.		TO 11th BN, DEPOT.	AGE 27.
CARTLIDGE	John	PTE	23	/1044	C		SEAHAM HARBOUR			1/7/16	MISSING DEC 16	THIEPVAL MEM		
CASSON	Anthy	PTE	23	/ 701		39 STEPHENSON STR	WILLINGTON QUAY			11/11/19		WALLSEND CHURCH BANK CEM		AGE 48.
CAWSON	John	PTE	23	/ 804			SHERSTONE WILTS			19/8/15		JESMOND ST ANDREW'S		
CHADKIRK	RichH	PTE	23	/1079			BYKER				AUGUST 16			
CHAMBERS	James	PTE	23	/ 593			HIRST	9/12/14	25/8/17	WOUNDS	JULY 16		TO 3rd BN.	AGE 39.
CHAMBERS	Septi	PTE	23	/ 319			DALTON ON TYNE				AUGUST 16		TO 20th, 10th BNS.	TO 3CCS 2/7/16 EVAC 2/7/16 WND LEGS.
CHANCE	James	CPL	23	/ 324	C	19 HIGH STREET	BRANDON COLL			1/7/16	MISSING DEC 16	THIEPVAL MEM		BORN AMBELCOTE STAFFS
CHAPMAN	Frank	PTE	23	/ 936			CORNSAY COLL			17/6/17		HAMSTEELS ST JOHN (	TO 16th BN.	AGE 27.
CHAPMAN	G J	PTE	23	/1065			ELDON				AUGUST 16			
CHARLTON	Henry	PTE	23	/ 19			MONKSEATON	23/11/14	22/1/19		SEPT 16, MARCH 18.		TO 10th BN.	SEE WO364/668 DATES FOR F AMB, CCS, AND G HOSP +
CHARLTON	JohnE	PTE	23	/ 313	C	8 STREATLAM TERRA	SOUTH GOSFORTH			1/7/16	MISSING DEC 16	THIEPVAL MEM		AGE 21.
CHARLTON	Robt	PTE	23	/ 53			PRESTON COLL				SEPT 16			
CHERRY	Wm	PTE	23	/1637			HARTFORD COLL	12/8/15	20/8/17	WOUNDS	OCT 16		TO 21st BN, 84th TRAINING RESERVE BN.	
CHISHOLM	Thos	PTE	23	/ 87			ALNWICK				JULY 16		TO 16th, 1st, 26th, 25th BNS.	
CHRISTMAS	WaltH	LSGT	23	/ 624			BLYTH				SEPT 16		TO 1st BN.	TO 3 CCS 2/7/16 GSW LEGS EVAC 2/7/16.
CLARK	Jas W	PTE	23	/1585			ASHINGTON	22/7/15	27/2/18	GSW	SSHOCK AUGUST 16, OCT 16		TO ARMY RESERVE CLASS P.	AGE 37.
CLARK	Thos	LCPL	23	/ 976					30/5/19				TO KINGS OWN YORKSHIRE LI(5th BN).	KOYLI No 63082.

CLARK	Wm	PTE	23	/1564				18/7/15	27/12/18	AMPUTATION			TO DEPOT.	AGE 37.
CLARK	Wm C	CPL	23	/1277	A	17 GEORGE STREET	ASHINGTON			20/3/18	AUGUST 16	ARRAS MEM		BORN BLYTH AGE 22, IN 1 PLATOON.
CLARKE	John	PTE	23	/ 924		10 GLADSTONE TERR	USWORTH						TO 1st GARRISON BN, CLASS Z RESERVE.	
CLASPER	Simps	PTE	23	/1168		57 CHURCH STREET	SEAHAM HARBOUR	13/7/15	10/1/18	SICK	AUGUST 16		TO 85th TRAINING RESERVE BN.	AGE 42.
CLENNEL	Thos	PTE	23	/1615									TO CHESHIRE REGIMENT(9th BN).	CHESHIRE REGT No 52262.
CLOUGH	Geo	LCPL	23	/1371			ASHINGTON			29/6/16		THIEPVAL MEM		
COATES	Geo A	CQM:	23	/ 706									TO 1st, 29th BNS, CLASS Z RESERVE.	
COATES	Henry	CPL	23	/1143	B	35 CORNISH STREET	SEAHAM HARBOUR			1/7/16	MISSING DEC 16	THIEPVAL MEM		BORN SEAHAM COLLIERY.
COATES	Thos	PTE	23	/ 697		34 SHAMROCK STREE	HEBBURN NEWTOWN						TO 2nd GARRISON BN, CLASS Z RESERVE.	
COCHRANE	Chas	PTE	23	/1508									TO 25th, 1/7th BNS, CLASS Z RESERVE.	RENUMBERED 292102.
COCKING	JohnA	SGT	23	/ 847	D		BEDLINGTON	20/12/14	26/3/19	KR para 392	AUGUST 16		TO DEPOT.	
CODLING	Wm	CQM:	23	/1429			NEWCASTLE	15/10/14	27/11/16	WOUNDS	SEPT 16		TO DEPOT.	
COLE	JohnR	PTE	23	/1417			BLACKHILL	2/1/15	23/11/17	GSW	SEPT 16		TO DEPOT.	AGE 27.
COLTMAN	Dan	PTE	23	/1354		12 LENNOX STREET	MIDDLESBOROUGH			14/10/16		BAILLEUL COM CEM EXT		BORN GRANGEMOUTH SCOTLAND AGE 31.
COLTMAN	James	PTE	23	/1353									TO 1st GARRISON, 2nd BNS, CLASS Z RESERVE.	AWARDED 1914/15 STAR ENTERED SALONIKA 9/10/15.
COLWELL	Robt	PTE	23	/1511			NORTH SHIELDS	19/4/15						LABOURER AGE 19 DESERTED 1/5/15, 5'8", BROWN EYES
CONNELLY	James	PTE	23	/ 429	D		NEWCASTLE	4/12/14		1/7/16	MISSING DEC 16	THIEPVAL MEM		DESERTED 15/1/15, REJOINED 9/2/15, AWOL 1/6/15.
COOK	Henry	PTE	23	/1394				30/1/15	4/11/18	GSW			TO 11th, 24th, 20th, 18th BNS.	AGE 40.
COOPER	Geo	PTE	23	/ 486	C	12 PAINTERS HEUGH	NEWCASTLE			1/7/16	MISSING DEC 16	THIEPVAL MEM		AGE 43.
COOPER	Wm R	PTE	23	/1570		32 MIDDLE ROW	NEW DELAVAL			3/10/18	JULY 16	GUIZANCOURT FARM C	TO 20th BN, ROYAL INNISKILLING FUSILIERS(6th I	R INNIS FUS No 21529. LCPL.
CORBETT	Thos	PTE	23	/1635			HIRST			KR para 392	AUGUST 16			
COULSON	John	PTE	23	/ 97		29 WILLIAM STREET	CONSETT							
COULSON	Wm	PTE	23	/1091			SUNDERLAND			KR para 392	JULY 16		TO 16th BN.	
COWANS	CyrlA	SGT	23	/ 822			ASHINGTON				JULY 16, JUNE 17.			
COWELL	Geo	PTE	23	/1100			SEAHAM HARBOUR	28/12/14	22/8/17	GSW	AUGUST 16		TO DEPOT.	
COWEN	ThosH	PTE	23	/ 541		7 WHITLEY TERRACE	BEDLINGTON			20/2/16		RUE PETILLON MIL CEM		AGE 26 BORN MORPETH.
COWIE	Dav Y	PTE	23	/1122	D	WEST EDLINGTON	MORPETH	29/12/14					TO 2nd GARRISON BN, CLASS Z RESERVE.	AWOL 23/3/15.
COWING	Geo E	PTE	23	/1592			WEST RAINTON			7/6/17	AUGUST 16	DUISANS BRIT CEM	TO 22nd BN.	
COXON	Mich	PTE	23	/1205						KR para 392			TO DURHAM LIGHT INFANTRY, TRAINING RESER	TRG RES No TR/5/59132.
COXON	Oswld	PTE	23	/ 29			SOUTH SHIELDS			12/2/17		CITE BON JEAN BRITCEM		
COXON	Robt	PTE	23	/ 365	B		NEWCASTLE			1/7/16	MISSING DEC 16	THIEPVAL MEM		
CRAM	Wm	SGT	23	/ 795			BEDLINGTON			1/7/16	NOV 16, WND+MISSING DEC	THIEPVAL MEM		BORN SPENNYMOOR.
CRAWSHAW	Jos H	PTE	23	/ 30			TYNEMOUTH				AUGUST 16		TO 12th, 21st BNS.	TO 3CCS 2/7/16 EVAC 2/7/16, EMPLOYED BY SMITHS DOC
CRISFIELD	Wm T	LCPL	23	/1228				31/12/14	8/4/18	KR para 392			TO DEPOT.	
CROMARTY	Wm	PTE	23	/ 949		7 HIGH FRIARSIDE	BURNHOPEFIELD						TO 1st GARRISON BN, CLASS Z RESERVE.	
CROSLEY	Wm	PTE	23	/1624							MISSING 20-23/3/18		TO 21st BN, CLASS Z RESERVE.	CROSBEY IN MR.
CROSS	Herbt	PTE	23	/1046			SEAHAM HARBOUR			KR para 392				
CROW	RobtF	PTE	23	/ 77			SOUTH SHIELDS			1/7/16		THIEPVAL MEM		
CUDLIP	MartE	PTE	23	/ 492		6 PERCY STREET	CRAMLINGTON						TO KINGS OWN YORKSHIRE LI(5th BN).	KOYLI No 63122.
CUNNINGHAM	JohnW	PTE	23	/ 698	D	1 SECOND STREET	NETHERTON COLL			1/7/16	MISSING DEC 16	THIEPVAL MEM		AGE 18
CUNNINGHAM	Steph	PTE	23	/ 844						KR para 392			TO 1st GARRISON BN.	
CURRAN	Mich	LCPL	23	/1027				26/12/14	22/10/18	SICK			TO 2nd GARRISON BN, CLASS Z RESERVE.	AGE 49.
CURRAN	Thos	LCPL	23	/1016		25 FOX STREET	DAWDON						TO 2nd GARRISON BN, CLASS Z RESERVE.	
CURRY	David	PTE	23	/ 7		8 DACRE STREET	SOUTH SHIELDS			13/7/17		HAGRICOURT BRIT MIL CEM		
CURRY	Luke	SGT	23	/1125		46 COWPER STREET	GATESHEAD						TO CLASS Z RESERVE.	
CURRY	RobtD	LCPL	23	/ 705	D		ASHINGTON			1/7/16	MISSING DEC 16	THIEPVAL MEM		
CURRY	Thos	PTE	23	/ 580				9/12/14	2/4/18	GSW			TO 3rd BN.	TO 3CCS 2/7/16 EVAC 2/7/16 MULTIPLE WOUNDS.
CURRY	Wm	PTE	23	/1282			CHOPPINGTON			KR para 392	AUG 16, DEC 16, MARCH 18.		TO 1st, 9th BNS.	
CURTISS	Lionl	PTE	23	/1588				27/7/15	14/6/16	SICK			TO 29th BN.	
CUSKERAN	James	LCPL	23	/ 261				3/12/14	22/1/17	WOUNDS			TO DEPOT.	
CUTMORE	Geo	PTE	23	/ 935			CORNSAY COLL			20/10/17		TYNE COT MEM		
DAGG	Sam	PTE	23	/1017	B		SUNDERLAND			1/7/16	MISSING DEC 16	THIEPVAL MEM		
DAGLISH	Albt	CSM	23	/1369			ASHINGTON				AUGUST 16		TO ROYAL INNISKILLING FUSILIERS(6th BN).	NTH EVINGTON HOSP LEICESTER 7/16,RINNIS FUS No 21
DALEY	JohnW	PTE	23	/ 707		55 CHARLES STREET	BOLDON COLL			28/3/21		SOUTH SHIELDS WESTOE CEM		
DALEY	Robt	CPL	23	/1220	C		SOUTH SHIELDS			1/7/16	MISSING DEC 16	THIEPVAL MEM		BORN BURNHOPE.
DALZIEL	Jermi	PTE	23	/ 951									TO 1st GARRISON BN, CLASS Z RESERVE.	
DAVIDSON	Jos	PTE	23	/1573			NEW DELAVAL				AUGUST 16		TO 20th BN, MACHINE GUN CORPS.	
DAVIS	JohnT	PTE	23	/1292				2/1/15	16/2/18	GSW			TO 3rd BN.	AGE 29.
DAVIS	Reubn	PTE	23	/1204		19 BARRON STREET	HYLTON			KR para 392			TO 1st GARRISON BN.	
DAVIS	Thos	PTE	23											AWOL 23-25/6/15.
DAVISON	Raym	CPL	23	/1106			SUNDERLAND	29/12/14	28/2/18	GSW	OCT 16		TO 3rd BN.	AGE 30.
DAWSON	R	PTE	23	/ 912										TO 3 CCS 2/7/16 EVAC 2/7/16 WND HEAD.
DAWSON	Reubn	PTE	23	/1361	C		DAWDON COLL	31/12/14	2/7//17	GSW	MARCH 17			
DAWSON	Robt .	PTE	23	/ 712			NORTH SHIELDS	14/12/14	18/1/17	WOUNDS	AUGUST 16		TO DEPOT.	
DAWSON	Wm G	PTE	23	/1608	B	11 MONKSEATON TEF	SEATON HIRST			1/7/16	MISSING DEC 16	THIEPVAL MEM		AGE 31.
DEFTY	Robt	PTE	23	/1141		10 ADOLPHUS STREE	SEAHAM HARBOUR	29/12/14			NOV 16		TO DURHAM LI(12th BN).	DURHAM LI No 45880.
DELF	Fred	SGT	23	/ 88			WORSTEAD NORFK			9/6/18	OCT 16	PERNES BRIT CEM	TO 1st BN.	AGE 23 BORN NORTH WALDEN NORTHANTS.
DEMPSEY	Mich	PTE	23	/1480	A	14 BEAMISH ST	NEWCASTLE			1/7/16	MISSING DEC 16	THIEPVAL MEM		AGE 28, IN 4 PLATOON.
DENWOOD	Herbt	PTE	23	/ 549				7/12/14	24/10/17	SICK			TO DEPOT.	AGE 41 DID NOT SERVE OVERSEAS.
DEVENISH	Harry	PTE	23	/1012	D	10 HILL STREET	BIRTLEY							
DEWS	Geo W	SGT	23	/ 809			BURNHOPEFIELD			1/7/16	NOV 16, WND+MISS DEC 16	THIEPVAL MEM		BORN NORMANTON YORKS.
DICKIE	JohnN	PTE	23	/ 325										
DICKINSON	E	PTE	23	/ 55									TO 22nd BN(MACHINE GUN SECTION).	
DICKINSON	JohnH	PTE	23	/1447	A		HAMSTERLEY COLL			1/7/16	MISSING DEC 16	THIEPVAL MEM		BORN WINLATON.
DICKINSON	Wm	PTE	23	/ 141		23 HEWORTH STREET	FELLING			1/7/16	NOV 16, WND+MISSING DEC	THIEPVAL MEM		AGE 21.
DIMMOCK	Albt	PTE	23	/1431	A	12 ELTRINGHAM STRE	BLACKHILL			1/7/16	NOV 16, MISSING DEC 16	THIEPVAL MEM	TO 22nd BN.	AGE 24.
DIXON	Arth	PTE	23	/1326	A		HENDON			1/7/16	MISSING DEC 16	THIEPVAL MEM		
DIXON	JohnT	PTE	23	/1285	B		NETHERTON COLL			1/7/16	MISSING DEC 16	THIEPVAL MEM		BORN ALLENDALE.
DIXON	Robt	PTE	23	/1629			HARTFORD COLL	11/8/15	21/9/17	WOUNDS	NOV 16		TO 21st BN, DEPOT.	
DIXON	Thos	PTE	23	/ 398			CHOPPINGTON			29/6/16		THIEPVAL MEM		
DOBEY	Wm	PTE	23	/ 394			BOOMERSUND	2/12/14	3/11/17	GSW	AUGUST 16		TO 3rd BN.	AGE 23, DESERTED 28/2/17.
DOBIE	ThosW	SGT	23	/1280		10 FENWICKS BLDGS	SCOTLAND GATE			1/7/16		THIEPVAL MEM		BORN NEWCASTLE
DOBSON	Hugh	SGT	23	/1239		17 MIDDLE DOUBLE R	NORTH SEATON				SEPT 16		TO 11th, 1st, 53(YS) BNS, CLASS Z RESERVE.	2nd STHN GHOSP BRISTOL 8/7/16
DOBSON	Wm	PTE	23	/ 621	D		BEDLINGTON			23/3/18		ARRAS MEM		
DOCKERTY	John	LCPL	23	/ 578		SUN INN YARD	BEDLINGTON			11/2/17	NOV 16	NIEUPORT MEM		AGE 21.
DODD	Luke	PTE	23	/ 986			BEDLINGTON				AUGUST 16		TO 24/27th BNS, 25th BN, CLASS Z RESERVE.	
DODDS	Edwd	PTE	23											AWOL 8/4/15.
DODDS	John	PTE	23	/ 321			WALLSEND			1/7/16	NOV 16, WND+MISSING DEC	THIEPVAL MEM		BORN WALKER, PUPIL ROYAL GRAMMAR SCHOOL NEWC
DODDS	Robt	PTE	23	/ 708	D	3 MARSHES TERRACE	WEST SLEEKBURN			1/7/16	NOV 16,WND+MISSING DEC	THIEPVAL MEM		AGE 22.
DODDS	Wm	PTE	23	/ 714			CHOPPINGTON				NOV 16		TO 27th BN, ROYAL FLYING CORPS.	
DOMAN	Wm T	RQM:	23	/ 672						KR para 392				
DONEY	Ernst	PTE	23	/1628									TO 1st BN, DURHAM LI.	DURHAM LI No 59370.
DONNELLY	Pat	PTE	23	/ 350				28/10/14	22/10/17	SICK			TO 29th BN.	AGE 45 DID NOT SERVE OVERSEAS.
DONNELLY	Wm	PTE	23	/ 56		176 PILGRIM STREET	NEWCASTLE						TO 26th BN.	
DORAN	James	PTE	23	/1219	C	28 WELLS ROW	BOLDON	29/12/14		1/7/16	MISSING DEC 16	THIEPVAL MEM		
DOUGLAS	Peter	LCPL	23	/ 414									TO 1st, 12/13th BNS.	
DOUGLAS	Robt	PTE	23	/1030				26/12/14	19/11/17	SICK			TO DEPOT.	AGE 40.
DOUGLAS	Zach	SGT	23	/ 468										
DOWNING	Jas A	PTE	23	/1418		ALBERT TERRACE	SHOTTON COLL			KR para 392			TO 2nd GARRISON BN.	
DOWSON	Geo	PTE	23	/ 941		106 LIDDLE STREET	CORNSAY COLL						TO 11th BN, CLASS Z RESERVE.	
DOYLE	Jas H	LCPL	23	/1189						29/5/18			TO 1st BN, WEST YORKSHIRE REGT(2nd BN).	WEST YORKS No 41005.
DUCKWORTH	James	PTE	23	/1049			DAWDON			6/9/16		ADDOLRATTA MIL CEM	TO 1st GARRISON BN.	
DUGDALE	Jos	PTE	23	/ 57	A		NEWCASTLE			1/7/16	MISSING DEC 16	THIEPVAL MEM		
DUNBAR	Anthy	PTE	23	/1404		279 TIPPERARY ST	OUSTON			27/10/18	SEPT 16	TEZZE BRIT CEM ITALY	TO 11th BN.	BORN NEWCASTLE
DUNN	John	PTE	23	/ 713	D		CHOPPINGTON			1/7/16	MISSING DEC 16	THIEPVAL MEM		BORN BAMBURGH.
DUNN	Robt	PTE	23	/ 243			BEDLINGTON				AUGUST 16		TO 2nd BN.	
DUNN	Sam	PTE	23	/1438			HORDEN COLL			1/7/16	MISSING DEC 16	THIEPVAL MEM		BORN WEST CORNFORTH.
EARL	Wm R	PTE	23	/ 412				4/12/14	27/2/15	SICK				DID NOT SERVE OVERSEAS.
EARLE	Jos	PTE	23	/ 879	D		MORPETH			1/7/16	MISSING DEC 16	THIEPVAL MEM		BORN SEATON NTHBLD
EARLY	Thos	PTE	23	/1385						KR para 392			TO 2nd GARRISON BN.	
EASTON	JohnW	PTE	23	/ 258		25 NORTH TERRACE	BEDLINGTON			1/11/17	AUG 18	BEDLINGTON ST CUTHBERT'S		AGE 39.
EDWARDS	James	SGT	23	/1241		91 SECOND STREET	SHOTTON						TO CLASS Z RESERVE.	
EDWARDS	Wm	PTE	23	/1333		95 SECOND STREET	SHOTTON				SEPT 16		TO 16th, 1/4th BNS, CLASS Z RESERVE.	
ELLIOTT	Geo	LCPL	23	/1266	A		SEAHAM HARBOUR			21/3/18		ARRAS MEM		MACHINE GUN SECTION.
ELLIOTT	Geo	PTE	23	/ 717	D	3 OLD COLLIERY ROW	BEDLINGTON			29/4/17	AUGUST 16	BROWNS COPSE CEM		AGE 33.
ELLIOTT	Jas S	LCPL	23	/ 628		38 BOATHOUSE TERF	CAMBOIS			25/8/17	JULY 16	TINCOURT NEW BRIT C	TO 8th BN.	AGE 22.
ELLIOTT	Robt	PTE	23	/ 966						KR para 392			TO 2nd GARRISON BN.	
ELLIOTT	Wm	PTE	23	/1419									TO 12/13th, 1st BNS, CLASS Z RESERVE.	
ELLIS	Anthy	PTE	23	/ 157			NORTH SHIELDS			28/7/16	NOV 16	ST JOHNS WESTGATE & ELSWICK		DIED AT THE ROYAL VICTORIA HOSPITAL NETLEY.
ELSTOB	ThosB	PTE	23	/1073			SOUTH SHIELDS			9/6/16		HEILLY STATION CEM		
ELVIN	Jas E	PTE	23	/1115		31 THOMAS STREET	WALLSEND	30/12/14					TO CLASS Z RESERVE.	DESERTED 2/7/17
EMERY	John	PTE	23	/1247		49 THIRD STREET	SHOTTON			KR para 392			TO 2nd GARRISON BN.	

EWING	Alex	PTE	23 /1013				29/12/14	17/10/17	WOUNDS			TO 16th, 1st BNS.	
FAIL	David	PTE	23 / 226			BURNHOPEFIELD	1/12/14	4/4/17	WOUNDS	AUGUST 16		TO DEPOT.	
FAIRWEATHER	Chas	SGT	23 / 950	A		NORTH SHIELDS	23/12/14	29/10/17	GSW	JULY 16		TO DEPOT.	AGE 28.
FARIE	JohnC	PTE	23										AWOL 5/7/15
FARM	Andrw	PTE	23 /1118		HERALD OFFICE YARI	MORPETH	29/12/14			AUGUST 16		TO 16th BN, CLASS Z RESERVE.	
FARNISH	Sam	LCPL	23 /1185			SPRINGWELL	31/12/14	23/7/17	WOUNDS	MARCH 17		TO 85th TRAINING RESERVE BN.	AGE 22.
FENTON	Fred	SGT	23 / 295			LOW FELL	30/11/14	19/6/18	GSW	SEPT 16		TO DEPOT.	
FENWICK	Ephrm	CPL	23 / 31	A		SOUTH SHIELDS			1/7/16	NOV 16, WND+MISSING DEC	THIEPVAL MEM		
FENWICK	Geo	PTE	23 /1105		6 MARY STREET	TUNSTALL						TO 1st GARRISON BN, CLASS Z RESERVE.	
FENWICK	JohnE	PTE	23 / 649	D		ASHINGTON			1/7/16	MISSSING DEC 16	THIEPVAL MEM		
FERGUSON	Geo	PTE	23 / 852	D		NETHERTON			1/7/16	MISSING DEC 16	THIEPVAL MEM		
FERGUSON	Peter	PTE	23 / 90			NEWCASTLE	21/11/14	4/12/16	KR para 392	JULY 16		TO DEPOT.	
FERGUSON	Robt	PTE	23 /1290			NETHERTON COLL	3/1/15	9/7/17	GSW	JULY 16		TO DEPOT.	
FERRIER	JohnR	PTE	23 / 961		23 HIRST TERRACE	BEDLINGTON			1/7/16	MISSING DEC 16	THIEPVAL MEM		AGE 24.
FISHER	Thos	CQMS	23 /1380	D	103 THE AVENUE	HETTON LE HOLE	24/11/14	31/3/19	KR para 392	AUGUST 16		TO ARMY RESERVE CLASS P.	3rd NTHN GHOSP SHEFFIELD 8/7/16.
FITZGERALD	Pet H	PTE	23 / 627	D						MISSING 20-23/3/18			IN 16 PLATOON.
FITZSIMMONS	Dan	PTE	23 / 718		17 RAVENSWORTH TE	BEDLINGTON			21/7/18	JULY 16, OCT 16.	COLOGNE MIL CEM	TO 16th BN.	AGE 30 BORN DUBLIN, DIED WHILST POW.
FLECK	Geo	PTE	23 / 570	B	BUTCHER HILL	MATFEN			1/7/16	MISSSING DEC 16	THIEPVAL MEM		AGE 17.
FLOCKHART	James	PTE	23 / 518	D	TANKERVILLE YARD	BEDLINGTON			1/7/16	MISSSING DEC 16	OVILLERS MIL CEM		AGE 41.
FORD	James	PTE	23 / 303			GATESHEAD	28/12/14	12/10/16	WOUNDS	SEPT 16		TO DEPOT.	
FORREST	John	PTE	23 / 673	A	22 McADAM STREET	GATESHEAD			1/7/16	MISSSING DEC 16	THIEPVAL MEM		BORN NEWBURN.
FORSHAW	WM a	LCPL	23 / 447						KR para 392				
FORSTER	J W	PTE	23 / 58	A									EMPLOYED BY SMITHS DOCK Co.
FORSTER	John	PTE	23 / 988			BEDLINGTON	27/12/14	7/11/17	SICK	SEPT 16		TO 16th BN, DEPOT.	AGE 25.
FOSTER	Geo W	LCPL	23 / 200									TO 2nd GARRISON BN.	
FOX	Jas H	PTE	23 / 91	B	44 NEW ELVET	DURHAM CITY			1/7/16	NOV 16, WND+MISSSING DE	THIEPVAL MEM		AGE 19.
FRATER	Wm	PTE	23 / 719									TO 2nd GARRISON BN, CLASS Z RESERVE.	
FRAZER	Isaac	PTE	23 /1595			CHOPPINGTON			2/10/17	1/7/16(20TH) DEC 16(ATT C	OUTTERSTEENE COM (	TO 20th BN, CHESHIRE REGIMENT(9th BN).	BORN AMBLE.CHESHIRE REGT No 52323.
FREEMAN	Rich	PTE	23 / 583	D		ASHINGTON			1/7/16	MISSSING DEC 16	THIEPVAL MEM		BORN PLYMOUTH.
FRENCH	Bertr	PTE	23 / 995	B	70 BRUSSELS ST TEA	GATESHEAD			1/7/16	MISSING DEC 16	THIEPVAL MEM		AGE 21 BORN CHOPPINGTON.
FULCHER	Alf	PTE	23 /1403		11 FOURTH CROSS R	HASWELL PLOUGH			KR para 392				
FULCHER	JohnE	SGT	23 / 436						KR para 392			TO DURHAM LIGHT INFANTRY, TRAINING RESER	TRG RES No TR/5/59065.
FULLER	S E	PTE	23 / 581		8 LEAD ROAD	RYTON							
FULTON	Geo E	PTE	23 /1437				18/12/16	31/11/17	WOUNDS			TO DEPOT.	AGE 33.
GAIR	Oswld	PTE	23 /1281									TO DURHAM LI(15th BN).	DURHAM LI No 46591.
GALES	Thos	PTE	23 /1558	C		ASHINGTON			1/7/16	MISSING DEC 16	THIEPVAL MEM		BORN ALNWICK.
GALLON	JohnR	PTE	23 / 720		3 ROSE VILLAS	CHOPPINGTON			25/6/16		ALBERT COM CEM EXT		BORN BEDLINGTON.
GALLON	Wm	PTE	23 / 722	D		CHOPPINGTON			1/7/16	MISSING DEC 16	OVILLERS MIL CEM		BORN BEDLINGTON.
GAMBLE	Hen J	PTE	23 /1401	D	130 ARGYLE STREET	HEBBURN			1/7/16	MISSING DEC 16	THIEPVAL MEM		BORN SPRINGWELL IN 15 PLATOON.
GAMBLE	ThosW	PTE	23 /1400		12 FIRST STREET	HEBBURN COLL	1/2/15			OCT 16, FEB 18.		TO 16th, 23rd BNS, ROYAL DEFENCE CORPS.	FRANCE -4/7/16, BEAUFORT HOSP BRISTOL 8/7/16, RDC N
GAMBLES		PTE	23 / 553	C									IN 11 PLATOON.
GARDNER	David	PTE	23 / 660				13/12/14	6/11/18	SICK			TO 23rd, 2nd BNS, DEPOT.	AGE 42.
GELDER	Geo	PTE	23 /1134		50 DENT STREET	SUNDERLAND	28/12/14	3/1/17	WOUNDS	OCT 16		TO 20th BN.	
GIBLIN	Andrw	PTE	23 /1188				30/12/14	31/12/15	KR para 392			TO DEPOT.	DID NOT SERVE OVERSEAS.
GIBSON	Steph	PTE	23 / 849	D						MISSING 20-23/3/18		TO CLASS Z RESERVE.	
GILBRAITH	Robt	PTE	23 /1153	C	11 ADOLPHUS STREE	SEAHAM HARBOUR	29/12/14		1/7/16	MISSING DEC 16	THIEPVAL MEM		
GILLESPIE	Mich	PTE	23 /1146		8 STEWART STREET	TUNSTALL	25/12/14	31/3/19	KR para 392	AUGUST 16		TO ARMY RESERVE CLASS P.	
GILLIS	Edwd	PTE	23 / 894		62 HARVEY STREET	NEWCASTLE						TO 1st GARRISON BN, CLASS Z RESERVE.	AWOL 13/2/15.
GILMORE	Jn Wm	LCPL	23 /1554			BROOMHILL			8/5/18		TYNE COT MEM	TO CAMERONIANS(5/6th BN).	CAMERONIANS No 241883.
GIRENS	Wm	PTE	23 /1561				13/7/15	19/12/17	SICK			TO 3rd BN.	DID NOT SERVE OVERSEAS.
GLEDHILL	Harld	PTE	23 /1544			BOLDON	5/7/15	8/3/18	WOUNDS	3/6/16, JULY GAZ		TO 20th BN, ARMY RESERVE CLASS P.	BACK & LUNGS
GODFREY	Fred	PTE	23 / 220			NEWCASTLE				JULY 16, FEB 18.		TO 21st, 9th, 1/5th BNS.	
GODSMARK	Alf	PTE	23 / 723			MIDDLESBOROUGH			1/7/16	MISSING DEC 16	THIEPVAL MEM		
GOLDSBURY	Hugh	CPL	23 / 194	D	126 BEATRICE STREE	ASHINGTON			1/7/16	MISSING DEC 16	THIEPVAL MEM		AGE 33 BORN WALLSEND.
GOODALL	James	PTE	23 /1384		49 CALIFORNIA STREI	SEAHAM HARBOUR			1/7/16	NOV 16, WND+MISSING DEC	THIEPVAL MEM		
GORDON	James	PTE	23 / 355										
GORDON	John	PTE	23 / 380										
GOWLAND	Thos	PTE	23 / 370				27/11/14	28/4/16	KR para 392			TO 29th BN.	AWOL 10/4/15
GRAHAM	Alex	PTE	23 / 422		15 LYNWOOD AVENUI	NEWBIGGIN / SEA			23/2/17	WND+MISSING JULY 17	RUE PETILLON MIL CE	TO 20th BN.	AGE 22.
GRAHAM	Andrw	PTE	23 / 661	B		NEWCASTLE			1/7/16	MISSING DEC 16	THIEPVAL MEM		BORN CARLISLE.
GRAHAM	Dav G	PTE	23 / 794									TO ROYAL FUSILIERS(24th BN).	FRANCE 23 9/1/16-28/8/18, 24RF-30/9/18, R FUS No GS/931
GRAHAM	Hen O	PTE	23 / 575			HIRST				AUGUST 16			
GRAHAM	Jos	PTE	23 / 489	B	25 STANHOPE STREE	RYTON			1/7/16	MISSING DEC 16	THIEPVAL MEM		BORN BYERS GREEN AGE 34.
GRAHAM	Robt	PTE	23 / 969			SHIELDMOOR			1/7/16	MISSING NOV 16	THIEPVAL MEM	TO 22nd BN(A COY).	BORN WISHAW SCOTLAND.
GRAHAM	RobtH	PTE	23 / 59		15 CHIRTON GREEN	NORTH SHIELDS			26/6/16		ALBERT COM CEM EXT		AGE 32.
GRAHAM	T W	PTE	23 /1294			SEAHAM HARBOUR				3/6/16, JULY 16.		TO 20th BN.	SHOULD BE 20/
GRAHAM	Wm	PTE	23 /1443				19/2/15	28/8/17	SICK			TO DEPOT.	AGE 46.
GRAHAM	Wm	PTE	23 /1200		CARRS FARM	SOUTH HETTON COLL	30/12/14	22/3/17	GASSED			TO DEPOT.	
GRANT	Geo	PTE	23 / 980									TO 2nd GARRISON BN, CLASS Z RESERVE.	
GRANT	Jas C	PTE	23 /1534		276 MILBURN ROAD	SEATON HIRST			20/7/16	JULY 16	SEATON HIRST ST JOHN		BORN ANNFIELD PLAIN, R LEG AMPUTATED.
GRANT	Thos	CPL	23 / 180	A		NEWCASTLE			11/2/17		CITE BON JEAN MIL CEM		
GRAY	Geo	PTE	23 / 886		12 JUBILEE TERRACE	BEDLINGTON STN			7/7/16		HEILLY STATION CEM		AGE 35.
GRAY	JohnG	PTE	23 / 721		22 NORTH ROW	WEST SLEEKBURN			1/7/16		THIEPVAL MEM		AGE 18 BORN BEDLINGTON.
GREAVES	James	PTE	23 / 351						KR para 392			TO 1st GARRISON, 27th BNS.	
GREAVES	John	PTE	23 / 357				27/10/14	25/1/18	SICK			TO DEPOT.	AWOL 8/3/15, 10/4/15.
GREEN	Geo	PTE	23 / 538			NEWBIGGIN / SEA	7/12/14	24/2/17	19/12/17	SEPT 16	SEGHILL HOLY TRINITY	TO DEPOT.	AGE 46.
GREEN	Geo	PTE	23 /1160		50 BRICKGARTH	EASINGTON LANE	29/12/14		26/10/17	JULY 16	CEMENT HOUSE CEM L	TO 25th, 1/5th BNS.	RENUMBERED 243152, BORN NEW HERRINGTON.
GREEN	Jas	PTE	23 /1470									TO 2nd GARRISON BN, DURHAM LI(1st BN), CLAS	DLI No 52341.
GREEN	MarkF	CPL	23 / 982	D	18 VICERAGE TERR	BEDLINGTON			1/7/16		THIEPVAL MEM		BORN BARRINGTON CAMBS AGE 30.
GREEN	Robt	PTE	23 / 382				29/11/14	9/1/15	INEFFICIENT				DID NOT SERVE OVERSEAS.
GREENWOOD	Henry	PTE	23 / 602									TO ROYAL SUSSEX REGIMENT(11th BN).	ROYAL SUSSEX REGT No G/17282.
GREENWOOD	Walt	PTE	23										AWOL 5/8/15.
GRIEG	Holly	PTE	23 /1212			SUNDERLAND				POW DEC 17		CLASS Z RESERVE.	
GRIEVESON	Geo	PTE	23 / 724			CHOPPINGTON				AUGUST 16		TO 24/27th BN, CLASS Z RESERVE.	
GUY	Wm F	PTE	23 /1420			BURNHOPEFIELD				JULY 16			
HAILES	Thos	PTE	23 /1236		103 BLENHEIM STREE	NEWCASTLE				OCT 16		TO CLASS Z RESERVE.	
HALEY	James	SGT	23 /1529		34 WORSLEY STREET	NEWCASTLE			KR para 392			TO 2nd GARRISON BN.	
HALL	C	PTE	23 / 559		9 BIRCHAM STREET	SOUTHMOOR						TO 1st BN, CLASS Z RESERVE.	
HALL	John	PTE	23 /1221				1/1/15	1/4/19	KR para 392			TO ARMY RESERVE CLASS P.	
HALL	JohnC	SGT	23 / 952		CRUDDAS TERRACE	BELLINGHAM	28/12/14	19/2/19	KR para 392	AUGUST 16			PRISONER OF WAR.
HALL	Wm W	PTE	23 /1512		154 NILE STREET	GATESHEAD			9/5/17	JULY 16	THIEPVAL MEM	TO NOTTS & DERBY REGIMENT(15th BN X COY).	N&D No 80126, AGE 19.
HALLIGAN	Thos	SGT	23 / 613			CHOPPINGTON	10/12/14	31/3/19	KR para 392	JULY 16		TO ARMY RESERVE CLASS P.	
HALLIMAN	Thos	PTE	23 / 69	A		NORTH SHIELDS			1/7/16	NOV 16, WND+MISSING DEC	THIEPVAL MEM		BORN HOUGHTON LE SPRING
HAMILTON	Robt	PTE	23 /1626			HARTFORD		14/12/18		AUGUST 16		TO KINGS OWN YORKSHIRE LI	KOYLI No 48299.
HAMILTON	Thos	PTE	23 / 833			NETHERTON COLL	19/12/14	23/3/17	SICK	MARCH 17		TO 10th BN, DEPOT.	
HAND	John	PTE	23 / 989				8/5/15	31/10/17	GSW			TO 85th TRAINING RESERVE BN.	AGE 24.
HANN	James	PTE	23 / 989	B	2 MILLBANK TERRACI	BEDLINGTON			1/7/16	MISSING DEC 16	THIEPVAL MEM		
HARDING	Chas	PTE	23 / 244									TO KINGS OWN YORKSHIRE LI(5th BN)	KOYLI No 63166
HARDING	J	SGT	23 / 312									TO DURHAM LI(15th BN).	DURHAM LI No 46590.
HARDY	Jas W	PTE	23 / 193									TO ROYAL FUSILIERS(24th BN).	FRANCE 23 9/1/16-28/8/18, 24RF-6/1/19. R FUS No GS/9313
HARLE	James	PTE	23 / 727	B	2 SCHOOL ROW	BARRINGTON COLL	14/12/14		1/7/16	MISSING DEC 16	THIEPVAL MEM		MINER, AGE 35, 5'6", L BROWN HAIR, BLUE EYES.
HARM	Thos	LCPL	23 / 922	B		THROCKLEY			1/7/16	NOV 16, WND+MISSING DEC	THIEPVAL MEM		BORN WHICKHAM AGE 33.
HARMISON	Geo	PTE	23 /1279			AMBLE	2/1/15	9/10/16	WOUNDS	AUGUST 16		TO DEPOT.	
HARRIS	JohnG	CPL	23 / 846									TO CLASS Z RESERVE.	
HARRIS	Jos C	PTE	23 /1305			SCOTSWOOD				SEPT 16, JULY 17, FEB 18.		TO CLASS Z RESERVE.	
HARRISON	John	PTE	23 / 926			WESTGATE			7/2/16		SAILLY SUR LYS CANADIAN CEM		
HARVEY	RichJ	PTE	23 /1218		2 SOUTH VIEW	EAST SLEEKBURN			1/7/16		THIEPVAL MEM		AGE 20.
HARVEY	Wm	PTE	23 / 340		7 MILLER TERRACE	TUNSTALL							
HARVEY	Wm	PTE	23 / 547									TO KINGS OWN YORKSHIRE LI(5th BN)	KOYLI No 63157.
HAY	ThosR	PTE	23 / 255										
HAYES	Wm H	LCPL	23 / 816			NEWCASTLE	19/12/14	27/4/18	SICK	NOV 16		TO DEPOT.	AGE 36.
HEBRON	RobtW	PTE	23 /1008									TO KINGS OWN YORKSHIRE LI(5th BN)	KOYLI No 63164.
HECKLES	John	PTE	23 /1021			SEAHAM COLLIERY				AUGUST 16		TO DURHAM LI.	DURHAM LI No 48395.
HEDLEY	JohnT	PTE	23 / 525						KR para 392			TO 2nd GARRISON BN.	
HEDLEY	Robt	PTE	23 /1072			SOUTH SHIELDS	26/12/14	3/4/18	WOUNDS	SEPT 16		TO 1st BN, DEPOT.	AGE 36.
HEMSTED	John	PTE	23 / 964			BEDLINGTON COLL				NOV 16		TO DURHAM LI(15th BN).	DURHAM LI No 46639.
HENDERSON	Thos	PTE	23 / 288									TO 2nd GARRISON BN, CLASS Z RESERVE.	
HERON		PTE	23 / 169	C									IN 11 PLATOON.
HETHERINGTON	JohnW	PTE	23 / 862	D		CHOPPINGTON			1/7/16	MISSING DEC 16	OVILLERS MIL CEM		BORN CARLISLE CUMBERLAND.
HEWITSON	Chas	PTE	23 / 872			CONSETT			KR para 392	AUGUST 16			
HICKEY	JohnT	PTE	23										AWOL 3/5/15
HINDHAUGH	Jos R	PTE	23 / 372						KR para 392			TO DURHAM LIGHT INFANTRY, TRAINING RESER	TRG RES No TR/5/41428.

HIRD	Normn	PTE	23	/1067			HETTON LE HOLE	23/12/14	12/10/17	GSW	AUGUST 16		TO 3rd BN.	AGE 28.
HOBSON	Harld	CPL	23	/1636			NEWBIGGIN	9/8/15	31/12/17	WOUNDS			TO 3rd BN.	AGE 27.
HODGSON		PTE	23	/1094	C									12 SECTION ROLL BOOK.
HOGG	J	PTE	23	/ 286			NEWCASTLE				AUGUST 16		TO LABOUR CORPS.	TO 3CCS EVAC 2/7/16 WND CHEST,FACE.LAB CORPS 371
HOLLIDAY	Robt	CPL	23	/ 728		38 POLMAISE STREET	BLAYDON			5/4/16		BOULOGNE EASTERN CEM		BORN CARLISLE CUMBERLAND, AGE 22.
HOLMES	Jos	PTE	23	/ 214	B		BLAYDON			1/7/16	NOV 16, WND+MISSING DEC	OVILLERS MIL CEM		
HOLMES	Wm J	PTE	23											AWOL 10/4/15
HOLT	Frncs	CSM	23	/1435			SHINCLIFFE		20/12/19		DEC 16		TO KINGS OWN YORKSHIRE LI	KOYLI No 52867.
HOLYOAK	Jos	PTE	23	/1321	B		MONKWEARMOUTH			1/7/16	MISSING DEC 16	OVILLERS MIL CEM		
HOOD	J	PTE	23	/1695	C									IN 11 PLATOON.
HOOD	JohnH	SGT	23	/ 482	C		EARSDON			1/7/16	MISSING DEC 16	OVILLERS MIL CEM		BORN LONGBENTON, IN 12 PLATOON.
HOOPER	Geo	PTE	23	/1634						KR para 392			TO DURHAM LIGHT INFANTRY, TRAINING RESER	TRG RES No TR/5/58164.
HOPE	NeiMc	PTE	23	/ 647									TO 9th BN.	AWOL 20/3/15.
HOWETT	Henry	PTE	23	/ 235	C			1/12/14	4/12/17	WOUNDS			TO DEPOT.	AGE 24.
HUGGANS	Robt	PTE	23	/ 95		34 MARIAN STREET	GATESHEAD			28/7/16	OCT 16	SALTWELL CEM GATESHEAD		ROYAL VICTORIA HOSP NETLEY 11/7/16.
HUGHES	Wm	PTE	23	/1060				26/12/14	23/3/18	SICK			TO DEPOT.	AGE 40.
HUME	Robt	PTE	23	/1589			BERWICK	27/7/15	31/3/17	WOUNDS	JULY 16, SEPT 16.		TO 20th BN, DEPOT.	
HUME	Thos	PTE	23	/1119		422 LONGWELL TERR	PEGSWOOD COLL	29/12/14	25/10/18	GSW	AUGUST 16		TO ARMY RESERVE CLASS W.	
HUMES	John	PTE	23	/1097	C		SEAHAM	28/12/14		25/2/17		FAUBOURG DE AMIENS	TO 16th, 21st BNS.	IN 11 PLATOON AGE 32.
HUMPISH	John	PTE	23	/1063		5 LOMBARD STREET	SUNDERLAND			1/7/16	NOV 16, WND+MISSING DEC	THIEPVAL MEM		BORN SEAHAM HARBOUR.
HUNTER	J	PTE	23	/ 245			RIDING MILL				OCT 16			
HUNTER	Robt	LSGT	23	/1317		205 BOUNDARY ROAD	BYKER			7/6/17	FEB 16	ARRAS MEM	TO 9th BN.	AGE 31 BORN HEBBURN.
HUNTER	Robt	PTE	23	/ 573			NETHERTON COLL	9/12/14	13/9/17	WOUNDS	AUGUST 16		TO 3rd BN.	AGE 36, 3CCS 2/7/16 WND BACK.
HUNTER	Wm	LCPL	23	/ 615			SLEEKBURN			25/6/16		ALBERT COM CEM EXT		
HURRELL	Archi	PTE	23	/1343			CAMBOIS				APRIL 17		TO 25th, 20th BNS, CLASS Z RESERVE.	
HURST	Jas S	PTE	23	/ 439			NEWCASTLE	2/11/14	14/12/16	WOUNDS	OCT 16		TO DEPOT.	
HUTCHINSON	John	PTE	23	/ 663		79 CROSS STREET	NETTLESWORTH	14/12/14	21/6/18	PARALYSIS			TO DEPOT.	
HUTCHINSON	John	PTE	23	/ 48		32 CHARLES STREET	GATESHEAD						TO 14th BN.	
HYMERS	John	LCPL	23	/ 643	C	TILE ROW	PLASHETTS			1/7/16	MISSING DEC 16	THIEPVAL MEM		BORN LANGHOLME SCOTLAND AGE 31.
INCE	Robt	PTE	23	/ 190	D		WEST SLEEKBURN			1/7/16	MISSING DEC 16	THIEPVAL MEM		
INCE	Thos	PTE	23	/1375									TO 25th, 9th BNS, CLASS Z RESERVE.	
IRVING	Henry	PTE	23	/1450			SHIREMOOR	23/11/15	15/3/18	GSW	SEPT 16, NOV 17.		TO 3rd BN.	
IRVING	ThosF	PTE	23	/ 353			SOUTH SHIELDS				MISSING OCT 16.			
JACKSON	Geo	PTE	23	/1605			SOUTH SHIELDS			1/7/16		THIEPVAL MEM		
JACKSON	Jos T	PTE	23	/1451	A	58 BEAUMONT STREE	NEWCASTLE			1/7/16	MISSING DEC 16	THIEPVAL MEM		AGE 42, AWOL 16/4/15, 9/7/15, 1/8/15.
JACKSON	Robt	PTE	23	/ 934	D	28 LIDDLE STREET	CORNSAY COLL			1/7/16	MISSING DEC 16	THIEPVAL MEM		AGE 32.
JACKSON	Wm H	PTE	23	/ 395			COWPEN VILLAGE			9/4/17	SEPT 16	BAILLEUL ROAD EAST (	TO 20th BN.	
JAMES	John	PTE	23	/1537				5/7/15	17/10/18	SICK			TO 2nd GARRISON BN, DEPOT.	
JAMES	RobtW	LCPL	23	/ 893	C		DUNSTON	22/12/14		1/7/16	MISSING DEC 16	OVILLERS MIL CEM		BORN PONTELAND AGE 39 IN 11 PLATOON.
JAMES	Wm W	PTE	23	/1076			SOUTH SHIELDS				SEPT 16		TO 25th, 1/5th BNS, CLASS Z RESERVE.	RENUMBERED 243159.
JAMIESON	Robt	PTE	23	/ 247				18/11/14	10/12/17	SICK			TO 3rd BN.	
JAMIESON	Thos	PTE	23	/ 41				24/11/14	29/11/15	KR para 392			TO 29th BN.	
JARVIS	ChasW	PTE	23	/1002			NEWCASTLE			1/7/16	MISSING DEC 16	POZIERES MIL CEM		IN MACHINE GUN SECTION.
JEFFERSON	Sam	PTE	23	/ 183	D	10 SEVENTH AVE	SEATON HIRST			1/7/16	MISSING DEC 16	THIEPVAL MEM		AGE 20 BORN NORTH SEATON.
JEFFERSON	Wm	PTE	23	/1054		32 WEST WEAR STRE	SUNDERLAND			19/8/16	SEPT 16	ETAPLES MIL CEM		AGE 43.
JEFFREY	Alex	SGT	23	/ 668			BEDLINGTON STN			5/11/16		TROIS ARBRES CEM		BORN NETHERTON FORFAR.
JENKINS	Albt	CPL	23	/ 11	A		SOUTH SHIELDS			1/7/16	MISSING DEC 16	THIEPVAL MEM		BORN LANGLEY MOOR.
JENKINS	John	PTE	23				BYKER				FEB 16			
JENKINSON	John	LCPL	23	/ 206			WALKER			KR para 392	AUGUST 16.		TO 8th, 1/7th, 23rd BNS.	RENUMBERED 291825, AWOL 6/10/15.
JENKINSON	Walt	PTE	23											AWOL 28/12/15.
JOBSON	Ernst	PTE	23	/1167		26 BK SOUTH RAILWA	SEAHAM HARBOUR	28/12/14	3/10/17	WOUNDS	AUGUST 16		TO DEPOT.	
JOBSON	James	PTE	23	/ 397			CHOPPINGTON				AUGUST 16, APRIL 17.		TO 10th, 11th BNS, CLASS Z RESERVE.	DESERTED 16/4/17.
JOHNSON	Geo	PTE	23	/ 310			FELLING	30/11/14	27/6/17	GSW	APRIL 17		TO DEPOT.	AGE 41.
JOHNSON	James	PTE	23	/1159		35 SEAHAM STREET	SEAHAM HARBOUR			12/7/16		PUCHEVILLERS MIL CEM		AGE 20.
JOHNSON	JohnH	LCPL	23	/ 240		37 RAGLAN STREET	SOUTH SHIELDS			9/4/17	JULY 16, NOV 16.	ROCLINCOURT VALLEY	TO 1st, 20th BNS.	AGE 32
JOHNSON	JohnH	SIG	23	/ 730									TO CLASS Z RESERVE.	
JOHNSON	Jos	PTE	23	/ 144		34 DUNSTON ROAD	DUNSTON				SEPT 16		TO 16th BN.	
JOHNSON	PeteW	PTE	23	/1539		32 ARIEL STREET	ASHINGTON			1/7/16	NOV 16 WND+MISSING DEC	THIEPVAL MEM + SERRE RD No 2		BORN TWEEDMOUTH AGE 25.
JOHNSON	Wm	PTE	23	/ 640			BEDLINGTON				JULY 16			
JOHNSON	Wm E	PTE	23	/ 287				1/12/14	20/4/17	NEURASTHENIA			TO DEPOT.	
JOHNSTON	Wm	PTE	23	/1410		5 LONG STAIRS	NEWCASTLE				OCT 16		TO LABOUR CORPS.	
JOHNSTONE	Alex	PTE	23	/ 876	D	13 ENID STREET	HAZELRIGG COLL			1/7/16	MISSING DEC 16	THIEPVAL MEM		BORN GUIDE POST NTHBLD.
JONES	EdwdR	CPL	23	/1311			NEWCASTLE	4/1/15	1/4/19	KR para 392	SEPT 16		TO AEMY RESERVE CLASS P.	
JONES	Fred	PTE	23	/1332			HORDEN	31/12/14	27/2/18	GSW	JULY 16		TO ARMY RESERVE CLASS P.	
JONES	Isrea	SGT	23	/ 309	D			30/11/14	6/3/18	GSW			TO 3rd BN.	AGE 40.
JONES	Lou O	PTE	23	/ 430									TO 1st, 22nd BNS.	
JONES	Robt	PTE	23	/ 970			SUNDERLAND	28/12/14	12/7/18	GSW	OCT 16		TO ARMY RESERVE CLASS W.	
JONES	Wm	PTE	23	/1180			NEWCASTLE	30/12/14	10/4/18	20/9/19		ALL SAINTS NEWCASTL	TO DEPOT.	AWOL 28/4/15.
JORDAN	Edwd	PTE	23	/ 625			CHOPPINGTON	10/12/14	5/10/17	SICK	SEPT 16		TO 3rd BN.	
KANE	Henry	PTE	23	/ 159									TO 1st GARRISON BN, CLASS Z RESERVE.	
KEATING		PTE	23	/1752										GRENADIER 11 PLATOON.
KEEN	R	PTE	23	/1454	C		DALMELLINGTON				AUGUST 16			BORN BEDLINGTON, DESERTED 6/11/15.
KEENEY	Jos	PTE	23	/1411	D		ASHINGTON			1/7/16	MISSING DEC 16	THIEPVAL MEM		DID NOT SERVE OVERSEAS.
KELLY	John	PTE	23	/1089		1 FAIRLESS STREET		30/12/14	12/5/15	SICK				
KELLY	Sam	SGT	23	/ 945									TO DURHAM LI(12th, 15th BNS).	DURHAM LI No 46594.
KELLY	Thos	PTE	23	/1330	C		HENDON				JULY 16, MISSING 20/4/18		TO 16th, 12/13th BNS, CLASS Z RESERVE.	
KELTIE	Geo A	SGT	23	/1452	B		GATESHEAD			1/7/16	MISSING DEC 16	THIEPVAL MEM		BORN EDINBURGH.
KEMP	Frank	PTE	23	/ 96		11 HARTBURN TERRA	SEATON DELAVAL			26/2/17	DEC 16	FAUBOURG DE AMIENS ARRAS		BORN NORTH WALSHAM NORFOLK.
KENNEDY	Hugh	PTE	23	/ 62			SOUTH SHIELDS			KR para 392	AUGUST 16		TO 8th, 1/7th BNS.	TO 3CCS 2/7/16 EVAC 2/7/16, RENUMBERED 291820.
KERR	Wm	PTE	23	/ 555				8/12/14	9/4/18	DEBILITY			TO ARMY RESERVE CLASS P.	
KILGOUR	Wm	PTE	23	/ 35				23/11/14	31/1/19	KR para 392			TO ARMY RESERVE CLASS P.	
KIRKLEY	James	PTE	23	/1609	B	56 DOCK ST	TYNE DOCK			1/7/16	MISSING DEC 16	THIEPVAL MEM		AGE 27.
KIRKUP	Robt	PTE	23	/1269				14/1/15	20/12/17	SICK			TO 11th BN, DEPOT.	
KIRSOPP	Thos	LSGT	23	/ 327	A	14 ST GEORGES TERI	SCOTSWOOD			1/7/16	NOV 16, WND+MISSING DEC	THIEPVAL MEM		MINER, AGE 26.
KIRTON	RobtS	SGT	23	/1099	B		SOUTHWICK			1/7/16	MISSING DEC 16	THIEPVAL MEM		BORN HOUGHTON LE SPRING.
KNOX	Jas W	CSG1	23	/1436									TO 2nd GARRISON BN, CLASS Z RESERVE.	
KNOX	Nich	PTE	23	/ 639	D	5 KINGS ROAD	BEDLINGTON STN			1/7/16	MISSING DEC 16	THIEPVAL MEM		AGE 19.
LACKENBY	Robt	PTE	23	/1025						KR para 392			TO 2nd GARRISON BN.	
LAIDLER	Jos	LCPL	23	/1066	C		SUNDERLAND				APR 17, MISS 20-23/3/18		TO CLASS Z RESERVE.	
LAING	Wm	PTE	23	/ 42		82 COMMERCIAL ROA	JARROW						TO 1st, 14th BNS, ROYAL FUSILIERS(24th BN).	FR/CE 23 9/1/16-3/2/17, 1 1/6/17-18/4/18, 14 18/7/18-28/8/18
LASHBROOK	Fred	PTE	23	/ 732			CHESTER LE ST	15/12/14	1/1/18	GSW	SEPT 16		TO 3rd BN.	
LATTY	Wm G	PTE	23	/ 638	B	72 SOUTH ROAD	BEDLINGTON			1/7/16	NOV 16, WND+MISSING DEC	OVILLERS MIL CEM		AGE 19 IN 8 PLATOON.
LAUDER	Jas A	CQM:	23	/ 1									COMMISSIONED Lt & QM, TO 22nd BN.	JOINED BN DEC 1914.
LAUDER	JohnS	PTE	23	/1395	B		NORTH SHIELDS			1/7/16	MISSING DEC 16	THIEPVAL MEM		BORN TYNEMOUTH.
LAURIE	Geo	PTE	23	/1486			SEAHAM HARBOUR			8/10/16		THIEPVAL MEM	TO 21st BN, DURHAM LI(13th BN).	AWOL 6/2/15, 3/5/15, DURHAM LI No 46029.
LAWS	Anthy	PTE	23	/ 609			CHOPPINGTON			1/7/16		THIEPVAL MEM		
LAWS	Herbt	PTE	23	/ 375										
LAWSON	Ernst	PTE	23	/ 43	A		HEBBURN			1/7/16	MISSING DEC 16	THIEPVAL MEM		BORN JARROW.
LAWSON	John	PTE	23	/ 736		2 CORPORATION YAR	MORPETH			29/3/17		MORPETH SS MARY&J/	TO DEPOT.	AGE 26.
LAWSON	JohnH	CPL	23	/1392		6 FARM COTTAGES	SHOTTON COLL			14/12/18		ST GERMAIN AU MONT	TO 1st GARRISON BN.	
LEATHARD	Lance	SGT	23	/1432		12 CROSS ROW	BEDLINGTON						COMMISSIONED 2Lt 31/10/17 SERVED WITH SAME BN.	
LEE	Geo	PTE	23	/ 280			BEDLINGTON	28/11/14	5/1/17	WOUNDS	JULY 16		TO DEPOT.	
LEE	ThosH	PTE	23	/1121	C	6 PERCY COURT	MORPETH	29/12/14		1/7/16	MISSING DEC 16	THIEPVAL MEM		AGE 31 BORN LESBURY.
LEE	ThosJ	PTE	23	/ 37		35 JUBILEE TERR	HOLYWELL						TO 1st GARRISON BN, CLASS Z RESERVE.	
LEECE	JohnT	PTE	23	/ 552		9 HAYMARKET BLDGS	NEWCASTLE			6/3/16		X FARM CEM		
LEONARD	Edwd	PTE	23	/ 461									TO 12/13th, 9th, 1/5th BNS.	
LEONARD	Mart	PTE	23	/ 798				17/12/14	2/5/17	KR para 392			TO DEPOT	
LIDDEL	Jos	PTE	23	/1643				17/8/15	4/10/19	KR para 392	MISSING 25th BN 21-23/3/1		TO 25th BN(D COY).	
LIDDELL	Edwd	PTE	23	/ 268		20 DOROTHY STREET	HEBBURN NEWTOWN				AUGUST 16		TO KINGS OWN YORKSHIRE LI(5th BN).	KOYLI No 63088.
LIGHTFOOT	Wm	PTE	23	/ 10			STANLEY			1/7/16	NOV 16, WND+MISSING DEC	THIEPVAL MEM		BORN SILKSWORTH.
LIPPEATT	Geo	PTE	23	/ 733		MILLFIELD	NEWBURN			KR para 392	SEPT 16		TO 25th, 11th BNS.	
LISTER	Allan	SGT	23	/1468		4 BIRTLEY LANE	BIRTLEY			KR para 392			TO 2nd GARRISON BN.	
LITTLE	Alex	PTE	23	/ 501									TO 26th, 9th, 24/27th, 10th BNS.	
LLOYD	Robt	PTE	23	/ 12			SOUTH SHIELDS			4/7/16		HEILLY STATION COM CEM		
LOCKE	MattT	PTE	23	/ 842	D		CHOPPINGTON			1/7/16	MISSING DEC 16	THIEPVAL MEM		BORN UPINGTON NTHBLD.
LOGAN	James	SGT	23	/ 253									TO 2nd GARRISON BN, CLASS Z RESERVE.	
LOGAN	ThosH	PTE	23	/1006	C		CHOPPINGTON			1/7/16	MISSING DEC 16	THIEPVAL MEM		AGE 32 BORN BELFORD IRELAND.
LONG	Geo	PTE	23	/1313									TO DURHAM LI(15th BN).	DURHAM LI No 46593.
LONG	Mark	PTE	23	/1314	HQ						MISSING 21-23/3/18		TO CLASS Z RESERVE.	
LONGCAKE	Sam	PTE	23	/1350						KR para 392.			TO DURHAM LIGHT INFANTRY, TRAINING RESER	TRG RES No TR/5/41414.
LONGSTAFF	JohnG	PTE	23	/ 735		3 NOEL STREET	EAST STANLEY			9/4/16		ETAPLES MIL CEM		AGE 40 BORN DIPTON.
LOTHIAN	T	CPL	23	/ 904										DID NOT SERVE OVERSEAS.

LOUIS	Harry	SGT	23 /1082				30/12/14	2/5/18	MALARIA			TO 3rd BN.	AGE 51.
LOWES	Thos	PTE	23 / 974			BEDLINGTON				SEPT 16		TO 16th, 18th BNS.	
LOWTHER	Thos	PTE	23 / 540	D	16 LONG ROW	WIDDRINGTON			1/7/16	WND+MISSING DEC 16	THIEPVAL MEM+SERRE RD No 2		BORN EGREMONT CUMBERLAND.
LOWTON	Thos	PTE	23 /1145		8 GREEN STREET	SEAHAM						TO CLASS Z RESERVE.	
LUCAS	Wm T	CSM	23 /1466			LEEDS				SSHOCK OCT 16		TO ROYAL FLYING CORPS.	
LUGO	A	PTE	23 / 477			NORTH SHIELDS				SEPT 16		TO LABOUR CORPS.	TO 3CCS EVAC 2/7/16.LAB CORPS No 402123,LFUS No 49
LUKE	JohnG	PTE	23 / 937		85 LIDDLE STREET	CORNSAY COLL			2/4/17	SEPT 16	ST CATHERINE BRIT CE	TO 24th BN.	AGE 34.
MACKAY	Alex	PTE	23 / 569	B		MORPETH			1/7/16	MISSING DEC 16	THIEPVAL MEM		
MACKAY	JohnW	PTE	23 / 987	C	FOURTH ROW	CHOPPINGTON COL			1/7/16	MISSING DEC 16	THIEPVAL MEM		BORN SCOTLAND GATE NTHBLD.
MACKENZIE	Mich	PTE	23 / 636		250 YARD ROW	NETHERTON COLL			1/7/16	WND+MISSING DEC 16	THIEPVAL MEM		AGE 33.
MADDEN	Jos	SGT	23 /1208		12 WREATHQUAY RO	SUNDERLAND	29/12/14		10/6/18		BERLIN STAHNSDORF CEM		DIED WHILST POW.
MADDEN	Wm	LCPL	23 /1206		6 AMY STREET	SUNDERLAND	29/12/14	10/4/17	WOUNDS	SEPT 16		TO DEPOT.	
MADDISON	Wm	PTE	23 / 983									TO 2nd GARRISON BN, CLASS Z RESERVE.	
MADDOX		PTE	23										BN SPORTS ALNWICK.
MADHILL	Thos	PTE	23										AWOL 12/9/15.
MAIN	Alex	PTE	23 /1019	B		BLYTH			1/7/16	NOV 16, WND+MISSING DEC	THIEPVAL MEM		BORN ULGHAM PARK NTHBLD.
MAIN	Fred	PTE	23 /1559				13/7/15	27/2/18	ARTHRITIS			TO ARMY RESERVE CLASS P.	AGE 40.
MAITLAND	Geo	PTE	23 / 900			SEAHAM HARBOUR			1/3/17		AVESNES-LE-COMTE COM CEM		SEE James, Sam, Thos, Wm, BROTHERS.
MAITLAND	James	PTE	23 /1138		7 WILLIAM STREET	SEAHAM HARBOUR	28/12/14	20/5/18	GSW	JULY 16		TO DEPOT.	AGE 34.
MAITLAND	Sam	LCPL	23 / 898			SEAHAM COLLIERY	21/12/14	1/6/17	WOUNDS	DEC 16		TO DEPOT.	
MAITLAND	Thos	PTE	23 /1034			SEAHAM HARBOUR			1/7/16	NOV 16, WND+MISSING DEC	THIEPVAL MEM		BORN DURHAM CITY.
MAITLAND	Wm	PTE	23 / 897			SEAHAM COLLIERY	21/12/14	13/2/18	GSW	SEPT 16		TO DEPOT.	AGE 28.
MALCOLM	Peter	PTE	23 / 65									TO 1st GARRISON BN, CLASS Z RESERVE.	
MALLOWS	Jas L	LCPL	23 / 425				17/11/14	31/3/19	KR para 392			TO ARMY RESERVE CLASS P.	
MARCH	Henry	SGT	23 / 341			HOUGHTON NTHBLD							
MARKWELL	John	PTE	23 / 936										
MARLING	Wm R	LSGT	23 /1114	B	16 WAIT STREET	WALLSEND	30/12/14		1/7/16	MISSING DEC 16	THIEPVAL MEM		BORN JARROW.
MARSHALL	Robt	CSM	23 /1398	D		E CRAMLINGTON			KR para 392	AUGUST 16			
MARSHALL	Thos	PTE	23 / 418	C		BYKER	5/12/14		1/7/16	MISSING DEC 16	THIEPVAL MEM		AGE 38.
MARTIN	JohnJ	PTE	23 / 510		7 PITT STREET	CONSETT				AUGUST 16			
MARTIN	Normn	PTE	23 / 103		42 COPELAND TERRA	SHIELDFIELD	20/11/14	11/3/18	GSW	24/4/17		TO 85th TRAINING RESERVE BN, ARMY RESERV	MALTSMAN, AGE 38. 5'8" GSW L FOREARM
MARTIN	Thos	CSG1	23 /1238									COMMISSIONED.	
MASON	Geo	PTE	23 / 544			BEDLINGTON STN				SEPT 16		TO ROYAL INISKILLING FUSILIERS(6th BN)	R INNIS FUS No 21566.
MASON	John	PTE	23 / 979				27/12/14	26/12/17	SICK			TO DEPOT.	AGE 48.
MASON	JohnJ	PTE	23 / 967	A		JARROW			1/7/16	MISSING DEC 16	THIEPVAL MEM		
MASON	T H	PTE	23 / 209			GATESHEAD				AUGUST 16			
MATTHEWS	Reg	PTE	23 / 102	A	SOUTH CHURCH LANI	BISHOP AUKLAND				MISSING 20-23/3/18			
MATTISON	Cuthb	PTE	23 / 678										
MAVIN	John	PTE	23 /1551				13/7/15	16/3/18	GSW			TO DEPOT.	AGE 22.
MAW	Ralph	PTE	23 /1199									TO CLASS Z RESERVE.	
MAYES	Wm	PTE	23 / 739									TO CLASS Z RESERVE.	
McANDREW	Phil	PTE	23 / 744		2 GIBSON STREET	AMBLE			12/7/17		HAGRICOURT BRIT CEM		BORN BALLINA IRELAND
McCABE	Albt	PTE	23 / 884	D	HOWARD TERR BANK	BEDLINGTON			1/7/16	MISSING DEC 16	THIEPVAL MEM		BORN ASHINGTON.
McCARTHY	Harld	PTE	23 / 962			NETHERTON COLL			1/7/16		THIEPVAL MEM		BORN BERKELEY GLOUCESTERSHIRE.
McCARTHY	James	PTE	23 / 859			NEWBIGGIN			19/10/17		TYNE COT MEM		BORN ROTHBURY.
McCLACHLAN	Wm R	LCPL	23 / 44									TO DURHAM LI(15th BN).	DURHAM LI No 46581.
McCLAN	Pat	PTE	23 / 907			NORTH SHIELDS	22/12/14	2/8/18	GSW	MARCH 18		TO DEPOT.	AGE 44.
McCLOUD	Thos	PTE	23 /1274			AMBLE	2/1/15	5/10/17	WOUNDS	AUGUST 16		TO DEPOT.	
McCOWLIFFE	F	PTE	23 / 236			BURNHOPE COLL				AUGUST 16			HEWER BURNHOPE COLLIERY.
McCULLY	ThosB	PTE	23 / 320										
McDONALD	Alast	SGT	23 /1530			SOUTH UIST				OCT 16		TO CLASS Z RESERVE.	
McDONALD	Ken C	PTE	23 / 388			HEBBURN	25/11/14	8/4/17	GSW ELBOW	OCT 16		TO 20th BN, ARMY RESERVE CLASS W.	AGE 39.
McDOUGAL	JohnA	PTE	23 / 100		31 SCOTT STREET	AMBLE			27/8/15		HEDON RD CEM HULL	TO 29th BN.	BORN EMBLETON.
McFARLAND	RobtW	PTE	23 /1488									TO KINGS OWN YORKSHIRE LI(5th BN).	KOYLI No 63189.
McGARRIGLE	Robt	PTE	23 / 38									TO DURHAM LI(15th BN).	DURHAM LI No 46625.
McGEE	Luke	PTE	23 / 393			ASHINGTON			31/7/16		DANTZIG ALLEY BRIT CEM		BORN CHOPPINGTON.
McGILL	James	PTE	23 /1382	C		SUNDERLAND			1/7/16	MISSING DEC 16	OVILLERS MIL CEM		AGE 40.
McKAY	JohnNW	SGT	23 / 293			NEWCASTLE				JULY 16		TO DURHAM LI(15th BN).	TO 3CCS 2/7/16 EVAC 2/7/16, DURHAM LI No 46516.
McKEITH	JohnF	PTE	23 /1340			SEAHAM HARBOUR			7/6/16		ALBERT COM CEM EXT		BORN SOUTH SHIELDS.
McKIE	Wm	LCPL	23 /1363			GREENOCK				SEPT 16		TO 11th, 1st, 10th BNS.	2nd STHN GHOSP BRISTOL 8/7/16, STILL SERVING 21/12/2
McNALLY	John	PTE	23 / 742	D	2 BLACKSMITHS ROW	BARRINGTON COLL	15/12/14	15/2/15	KR para 392				AGE 32, 5'6", 37 CHEST, MINER
McTAVISH		DMJF	23	B									BN SPORTS ALNWICK
METCALFE	Andrw	PTE	23 / 533		6 WEAR TERRACE	WASHINGTON			KR para 392			TO 1st GARRISON BN.	
MIDDLEMISS	John	PTE	23 / 857		6 MELROSE TERR	BEDLINGTON STN			5/3/17	AUGUST 16	FAUBOURG DE AMIENS	TO 20th BN.	AGE 31.
MIDDLETON	Robt	PTE	23 /1163		TURNBANK COTTAGE	DAWDON	25/12/14	31/3/19	KR para 392	AUGUST 16		TO ARMY RESERVE CLASS P.	
MILBURN	RobtW	PTE	23 /1434	B	40 ALBION STREET	JARROW			27/2/17		AUBIGNY COM CEM		AGE 18.
MILLER	Jos	PTE	23 /1064			SEAHAM HARBOUR				NOV 16, MISSING 27/5/18		TO 27th, 16th, 1/6th(A COY) BNS, CLASS Z RESER	BEAUFORT HOSP BRISTOL 8/7/16.
MILLER	Robt	PTE	23 / 594			BEDLINGTON			23/10/16		RATION FARM MIL CEM		
MILLICAN	Thos	PTE	23 / 611	A		SLEEKBURN			20/3/18		ARRAS MEM		
MINTO	Jos	CPL	23 /1358				2/1/15	9/4/17	BRONCHITIS			TO DEPOT.	
MITCHELL	Ben	PTE	23 / 827										RENUMBERED 90391 STILL SERVING JAN 1923.
MITCHELL	John	PTE	23 /1533			HIRST	5/7/15	12/10/17	WOUNDS	AUGUST 16		TO DEPOT.	AGE 22.
MITCHELL	W	CQM	23 /1339		3 ADOLPHUS STREET	SEAHAM						TO CLASS Z RESERVE.	
MITCHELL	Wm	PTE	23 /1101		10 AUSTRALIA STREE	SEAHAM COLLIERY				SEPT 16, JAN 19.		TO 27th, 18th, 8th BNS, CLASS Z RESERVE.	
MOLE	John	PTE	23 / 154		OLD HALL ST ANTHOI	NEWCASTLE						TO 1st GARRISON BN, CLASS Z RESERVE.	
MOLE	Jos	PTE	23 / 585	C	21 PORTIA STREET	ASHINGTON			1/7/16	MISSING DEC 16	THIEPVAL MEM		AGE 30 BORN PEGSWOOD.
MOLE	Thos	PTE	23 / 576				9/12/14	3/3/18	DEAFNESS	FEB 16		TO ARMY RESERVE CLASS W	AGE 22.
MOLLOY	James	PTE	23 / 262				3/12/14	21/2/18	KR para 392			TO 9th BN, ROYAL DEFENCE CORPS.	
MONTGOMERY	Wm	PTE	23 / 838			BEDLINGTON			25/6/16		ALBERT COM CEM EXT		BORN CHOPPINGTON,
MOODY	John	PTE	23 / 889	D	DUKES COTTAGES	PEGSWOOD			1/7/16	NOV 16, WND+MISSING DEC	THIEPVAL MEM		AGE 31 BORN BOTHELL CUMBERLAND.
MOON	Geo W	SGT	23 / 865			SHIREMOOR			24/10/17		DUNHALLOW ADS CEM YPRES		BORN EARSDON.
MOORE	Linds	CSM	23 /1124	D	45 ADOLPHUS STREE	SEAHAM HARBOUR	29/12/14		23/3/18		SOIGNIES(ZINNIK) COM CEM		AGE 29.
MORALLEE	Geo J	PTE	23 / 940		104 LIDDLE STREET	CORNSAY COLL	21/12/14		27/4/17	OCT 16	BROWNS COPSE CEM		MINER BORN CONSETT, AGE 27, 5'6", BLUE EYES BROWN
MORDUE	Jos	PTE	23 / 681			ASHINGTON	10/12/14	31/3/19	KR para 392	AUG 16,+MISS NOV 17, JULY		TO 16th BN, ARMY RESERVE CLASS P.	
MORGAN	Geo W	SGT	23 / 45			WHEATLEY HILL	24/11/14	31/3/19	KR para 392	APRIL 17		TO ARMY RESERVE CLASS P.	ACTING RSM.
MORGAN	James	PTE	23 /1476			SOUTH SHIELDS			1/7/16	MISSING MARCH 17	THIEPVAL MEM		BORN LEITH SCOTLAND.
MORIARTY	Wm E	PTE	23 /1600			NEWCASTLE	29/7/15	25/7/17	GSW	SEPT 16		TO 3rd BN.	
MORICE	A	SGT	23 / 215							FEB 16.			
MORLAND	And S	PTE	23 /1310			JARROW	4/1/15	7/11/17	WOUNDS	OCT 16		TO DEPOT.	AGE 22.
MORLAND	Geo	PTE	23 / 347	A		NETHERTON COLL			1/7/16	NOV 16, WND+MISSING DEC	THIEPVAL MEM		BORN RIPON AGE 24.
MORRIS	Enoch	PTE	23 / 210	B		BYKER			1/7/16	MISSING DEC 16	THIEPVAL MEM		BORN WREXHAM WALES.
MORRIS	Geo	SGT	23 / 178			BEDLINGTON	1/12/14	3/2/19	KR para 392	AUGUST 16		TO ARMY RESERVE CLASS P.	
MORRIS	Harry	PTE	23 / 601									TO DURHAM LI(12th BN).	DURHAM LI No 45883.
MORROW		CPL	23 /1562	C									
MOULD	John	CPL	23 / 80			MORPETH				NOV 16		TO 20th BN.	
MOUNSEY	John	CPL	23 / 607	D		CHOPPINGTON				SEPT 16		TO 16th, 1/5th, 8th BNS.	2nd STHN GHOSP BRISTOL 8/7/16, BN SPORTS AT ALNWI
MOWBRAY	JohnW	PTE	23 / 105	C	13 OSBOURNE ROAD	CHESTER LE ST			1/7/16	MISSING DEC 16	THIEPVAL MEM		AGE 22 BORN LUMLEY.
MULLEN	Den	PTE	23 / 676						KR para 392			TO DURHAM LIGHT INFANTRY, TRAINING RESER	TRG RES No TR/5/58194.
MULLEN	Jos	PTE	23 / 542										
MULLEN	RobtP	PTE	23 /1378		22 JOHN STREET	TUNSTALL			KR para 392			TO 2nd GARRISON BN.	
MURPHY	Geo	PTE	23 / 646		8 BACK MALING STRE	NEWCASTLE				JULY 16, FEB 18			AWOL 2/8/15
MURPHY	Wm	PTE	23										DESERTED 5/1/15
MURRAY	Ed B	PTE	23 / 276		HEDLEYS BLDGS	EARSDON				AUGUST 16, MISSING DEC 17		TO 1st BN, CLASS Z RESERVE.	PRISONER OF WAR.
MURRAY	Thos	PTE	23 / 963	C		STIRLING SCOTLD			1/7/16	MISSING DEC 16	THIEPVAL MEM		
MURRAY	Thos	PTE	23 / 345		62 MORTIMOR STREE	HARTFORD EAST						TO 1st GARRISON BN, CLASS Z RESERVE.	
MUSHAM	Wm	PTE	23 / 106		43 ORD STREET	GATESHEAD				NOV 16, FEB 17.		TO 13th BN.	
MUTER	Robt	CQM	23 / 546		100 NORTH ROW	BEDLINGTON COLLIEF	7/12/14	15/4/18	GSW			TO DEPOT.	AGE 31.
MUTTON	John	PTE	23 /1284		257 YARD ROW	NETHERTON COLL			1/7/16	NOV 16, WND+MISS DEC 16	THIEPVAL MEM		AGE 36 BORN SHANKHOUSE.
MYERSCOUGH	John	PTE	23 / 545						KR para 392			TO 2nd GARRISON BN.	
NAIL	Edwin	CPL	23 / 203			WEST SLEEKBURN	1/12/14	16/8/17	GSW	JULY 16		TO 3rd BN.	
NAPIER		PTE	23										MENTIONED IN BN SPORTS DAY REPORTS.
NASH	John	PTE	23 / 272	A			3/12/14	26/2/19	KR para 392	MISSING 21/3/18		TO DEPOT.	
NEAL	James	PTE	23 / 392	B		CHOPPINGTON COL				DEC 16, MARCH 18		TO 22nd BN.	AWOL 4/4/15.101 AMBT TO 18 GHOSP 3/7 TO 6 CONV DEP
NEESAM	Thos	PTE	23 / 750	D		CHOPPINGTON			1/7/16	MISSING DEC 16	THIEPVAL MEM		BORN SEATON BURN.
NELSON	Jas K	PTE	23 / 491			NEWCASTLE			1/7/16	MISSING DEC 16	OVILLERS MIL CEM		BORN GLASGOW, AWOL 6/10/15.
NELSON	Jas L	PTE	23 / 747									TO KINGS OWN YORKSHIRE LI(5th BN).	KOYLI No 63198.
NELSON	Wm B	CSM	23 / 249			CHOPPINGTON			1/7/16		THIEPVAL MEM		BORN PETERSBURGH AUSTRALIA.
NESBIT	Wm R	PTE	23 / 617			HIRST			10/6/16		ALBERT COM CEM EXT		
NEVILLE	Mich	SGT	23 /1405		8 INSTITUTE TERR	BIRTLEY			31/5/18		SOISSONS MEM	TO CHESHIRE REGIMENT(9th BN).	CHESHIRE REGT No 52258.
NEVIN	RobtS	PTE	23 / 181									TO KINGS OWN YORKSHIRE LI(5th BN).	KOYLI No 63181.
NEVINS	Jos	PTE	23 /1393			MURTON			7/4/17		BOULOGNE EASTERN CEM		

NICHOL	Andrw	PTE	23	/1597									TO 2nd GARRISON BN, DURHAM LI, CLASS Z RES	DLI No 66623.
NICHOLSON	Geo H	PTE	23	/749			NORTH SHIELDS				SEPT 16		TO 1st, 14th, 1/7th BNS, CLASS Z RESERVE.	
NICHOLSON	Henry	PTE	23	/1519		42 GORDON STREET	SOUTH SHIELDS	20/4/15	29/5/17	WOUNDS	SEPT 16		TO DEPOT.	
NICHOLSON	Henry	PTE	23	/675			CHOPPINGTON	11/12/14	4/3/18	SICK	DEC 16		TO DEPOT.	
NICHOLSON	John	PTE	23	/853			CHOPPINGTON	20/12/14	22/6/17	GSW	AUGUST 16		TO DEPOT.	TO 3 CCS 2/7/16 EVAC 2/7/16.
NICHOLSON	Jos	PTE	23	/1129	D	21 THIRD STREET	NETHERTON COLLIER	29/12/14	7/4/19	KR para 392			TO ROYAL ARMY MEDICAL CORPS. ARMY RESEF	RAMC No 133461.MINER AGE 20 5'5", IN FRANCE 9/1/16-6/
NICHOLSON	Thos	PTE	23	/748									TO 1st GARRISON BN, CLASS Z RESERVE.	
NICHOLSON	Thos	PTE	23	/1351						KR para 392			TO 1st GARRISON BN.	
NICHOLSON	Wm	PTE	23	/1522		42 FRANKLIN STREET	SOUTH SHIELDS	26/4/15	18/2/16	ANAMENIA			TO 29th BN.	DID NOT SERVE OVERSEAS.
NICKALLS	RichP	PTE	23	/903									TO KINGS OWN YORKSHIRE LI(5th BN).	KOYLI No 63196.
NOBLE	Adam	PTE	23	/108	B		NEWCASTLE			1/7/16	NOV 16, WND+MISSING DEC	THIEPVAL MEM		
O'BRIEN	Pat J	PTE	23											AWOL 24/2/15
OLIVER	James	PTE	23	/751			MORPETH				DEC 16		TO 17th, 8th BNS, CLASS Z RESERVE.	
ORD	Jas	PTE	23	/1391		22 MAPLE STREET	ASHINGTON	2/1/15	16/1/19				TO LABOUR CORPS, KINGS ROYAL RIFLE CORPS	LAB CORPS No 397607 25/10/17, KRRC 58450 1/6/18.
ORD	Nath	LCPL	23	/136			CHOPPINGTON				SEPT 16		TO 16th BN.	
ORD	Walt	PTE	23	/1601				28/7/15	18/8/17	SICK			TO 84th TRAINING RESERVE BN.	DID NOT SERVE OVERSEAS.
ORRICK	Robt	PTE	23	/1068		14 RECTORY TERRAC	HETTON LE HOLE	23/12/14	31/3/19	KR PARA 392			TO ARMY RESERVE CLASS P.	
OSBORNE	Archi	PTE	23	/196		8 SALISBURY STREET	BLYTH			1/7/16	NOV 16 WND+MISSING DEC	THIEPVAL MEM		AGE 37 BORN DEARHAM CUMBERLAND.
OSBORNE	James	PTE	23	/413	C		ASHINGTON			1/7/16	MISSING DEC 16	THIEPVAL MEM		
OSBORNE	Wm C	PTE	23	/283			CHOPPINGTON	29/11/14	9/8/17	WOUNDS	AUGUST 16		TO DEPOT.	
OSTLE	Frank	PTE	23	/242	D		ASHINGTON				SEPT 16		TO ROYAL FLYING CORPS.	
OXLEY	Robt	LCPL	23	/1015		3 WIGHAM STREET	PICKERING KNOOK						TO CLASS Z RESERVE.	
PARKER	Jos	PTE	23	/755			WALKER			1/7/16		THIEPVAL MEM		
PARKES	Jos	PTE	23	/758				14/12/14	31/3/19	KR para 392			TO DEPOT.	
PARKINSON	Thos	PTE	23	/213	A		MEDOMSLEY			1/7/16	MISSING DEC 16	THIEPVAL MEM		BORN CONSETT.
PARMLEY	James	PTE	23											DRUNK & DISORDERLY 27/2/15.
PARMLEY	John	SGT	23	/567			BEDLINGTON				DEC 16			
PARRISH	Wm A	PTE	23	/470	C	10 WESLEY TERRACE	ANNFIELD PLAIN			1/7/16	MISSING DEC 16	THIEPVAL MEM		BORN BRANDON AGE 44.
PATTERSON	A	PTE	23	/1538	A									TO 3CCS 2/7 EVAC 2/7 101 AMBT 18 GHOSP 3/7 HSHIP 5/7
PATTERSON	Dixon	PTE	23	/927	D		CHOPPINGTON			1/7/16	MISSING DEC 16	THIEPVAL MEM		BORN OAKENSHAW.
PATTERSON	Jas A	SGT	23	/590	C		CHOPPINGTON			1/7/16	NOV 16, MISSING DEC 16	OVILLERS MIL CEM		IN 10 PLATOON.
PATTERSON	Thos	CPL	23	/266	B	10 DENE ROW	HAMSTERLEY COLL			1/7/16	NOV 16,WND+MISS DEC 16	THIEPVAL MEM		AGE 38 BORN MORPETH.
PATTERSON	Wm J	CSM	23	/318										
PATTISON	G	PTE	23	/234			STANLEY				AUGUST 16			
PATTISON	Jas W	PTE	23	/871		9 GREENFIELD TERR/	AMBLE			1/7/16	MISSING DEC 16	THIEPVAL MEM		AGE 30 BORN CHEVINGTON.
PAXTON	Dan	PTE	23											AWOL 27/2/15.
PEACOCK	Geo	PTE	23	/110			EAST HOLYWELL				JULY 16		TO 8th, 12th BNS.	
PEACOCK	James	SGT	23	/111			SHIREMOOR			2/11/16		RATION FARM CEM		BORN BACKWORTH AGE 28.
PEARCE	Dan	PTE	23	/46		3 DUNSTON STREET	HEBBURN	23/11/14		8/10/18		PROSPECT HILL CEM G	TO 1st, 12/13th BNS.	AGE 24.
PEARCE	James	PTE	23	/1572			NEW DELAVAL				JANUARY 18		TO 16th, 1st, 21st, CLASS Z RESERVE.	DESERTED 7/1/18.
PEARDON	Riddl	PTE	23	/896		61 AUSTRALIA STREE	SEAHAM				POW JULY 17		TO CLASS Z RESERVE.	
PEEL	Thos	PTE	23	/1202		20 DENE STREET	SHOTTON	29/12/14	20/2/18	GASSED	DEC 16, APR 18.		ATTACHED 102 LIGHT TRENCH MORTAR BATTERY, TO DEPOT.	
PERCIVAL	J	CPL	23	/819	C								TO LABOUR CORPS.	ASGT 11 PLATOON.
PERCY	James	PTE	23	/752			BEDLINGTON	15/12/14	23/8/17	GSW	JULY 16		TO DEPOT.	No COULD BE 572??
PERCY	Ralph	PTE	23	/754			BEDLINGTON	15/12/14	24/4/18	SICK	SEPT 16		TO ARMY RESERVE CLASS P.	AGE 41, VA HOSP CHELTENHAM 8/7/16.
PETRIE	C	CQM:	23											BN SPORTS ALNWICK.
PETRIE	JohnC	PTE	23	/1123		335 RECTORY ROAD	GATESHEAD							
POLL	Wm	SGT	23	/1596		53 COOPERATIVE TEF	NEW DELAVAL			6/11/16		RATION FARM MIL CEM		AGE 21.
POPPLETON	JohnA	PTE	23	/400	A		BYKER	7/12/14		1/7/16	WND+MISSING DEC 16	THIEPVAL MEM		AGE 41. ORIINALLY IN 11 PLATOON C COY.
PORTER	Hen D	PTE	23	/64			WILLINGTON NTHB			24/10/18		ROMERIES COM CEM	TO 9th BN.	EMPLOYED BY SMITHS DOCK Co.
POSTINGS	ThosA	PTE	23	/271				27/11/14	25/2/16	KR para 392			TO 29th BN.	DID NOT SERVE OVERSEAS.
POTTS	Thos	LCPL	23	/813									TO 2nd GARRISON BN, CLASS Z RESERVE.	
POULTON	Jos O	PTE	23	/442			SWALWELL			1/7/16	MISSING OCT 16	THIEPVAL MEM		BORN CHESTER LE STREET.
PRATT	JohnC	SGT	23	/756				16/12/14	24/4/18	SKULL FRACTURE			TO 3rd BN.	AGE 25.
PRICE	Harry	PTE	23	/888	D	4 FREEHOLD TERRAC	CHOPPINGTON			1/7/16	MISSING DEC 16	THIEPVAL MEM		BORN SUNDERLAND AGE 31.
PRICE	Wm H	PTE	23	/1396		28 GEORGE STREET	SUNDERLAND	30/1/15	16/8/16	SICK			TO 29th BN.	AGE 42 DESERTED 13/3/15 ,5'6", DID NOT SERVE OVERSE
PRINGLE	Jos	PTE	23	/528	D	181 CHESTNUT STREI	ASHINGTON			1/7/16	MISSING DEC 16	THIEPVAL MEM		AGE 35.
PRINGLE	Wm	CPL	23	/618										
PROCTOR	Jas P	PTE	23	/362			PELTON FELL	5/12/14	7/6/17	WOUNDS	AUGUST 16		TO ARMY RESERVE CLASS P.	AGE 25.
PROUD	JohnE	PTE	23	/112			FENHAM			1/7/16		OVILLERS MIL CEM	TO 20th BN.	
PROUD	Thos	PTE	23	/1306			SCOTSWOOD			KR para 392	AUGUST 16		TO 25th, 1/5th BNS.	RENUMBERED 243183.
PRUDHOE	John	PTE	23	/1485	B		NEWCASTLE			1/7/16	NOV 16, WND+MISSING DEC	THIEPVAL MEM		BORN USWORTH.
PRUDHOE	Wm	PTE	23	/1095				28/12/14	4/3/18	FRACTURES			ATTACHED 102 LIGHT TRENCH MORTAR BATTEF	AGE 26.
PUNTON	David	PTE	23	/582										
PUNTON	EdwdJ	PTE	23	/1261		FRONT ROW	ULGHAM	4/1/15	22/5/18	GSW	JULY 16, APR 17.		TO DEPOT.	AGE 31, TO 3CCS 2/7/16 EVAC 2/7/16 WND LEGS.
PURDY	Wm	PTE	23	/1569			NEW DELAVAL	19/7/15	6/3/18	GSW	AUGUST 16		TO ARMY RESERVE CLASS P.	AGE 21.
PURVIS	Henry	PTE	23	/426				4/12/14	25/11/15	SICK			TO 29th BN.	DID NOT SERVE OVERSEAS.
PURVIS	JohnW	LCPL	23	/999									TO 1st GARRISON, 19th BNS, ATT 5th ARMY HQ, X	SALVAGE COMPANY, CLASS Z RESERVE.
QUINN	James	PTE	23											AWOL 7/6/15, 19/7/15, 21/12/15.
RAFFERTY	J	CSM	23	/921									TO DEPOT.	JOINED DEPOT APRIL 1916 FROM OVERSEAS.
RAFFLE	John	PTE	23	/402				5/12/14	30/3/18	KR para 392			TO DEPOT	DID NOT SERVE OVERSEAS
RAISBECK	Henry	PTE	23	/453		5 QUATRE BRAS	HEXAM							
RAMSAY	Isaac	PTE	23	/1397			SUNDERLAND	30/1/15	25/3/16	6/9/16		BISHOPWEARMOUTH C	TO 20th, 29th BNS.	
RAMSEY	Wm	PTE	23	/446									TO 1st GARRISON BN, CLASS Z RESERVE.	
RAMSHAW	Robt	PTE	23	/14	C		SOUTH SHIELDS			1/7/16	MISSING DEC 16	THIEPVAL MEM		AGE 28.
RAWLINGS	John	PTE	23	/1062				26/12/14	23/10/17	SICK			TO 84th TRAINING RESERVE BN.	DID NOT SERVE OVERSEAS.
REAY	John	PTE	23	/217		7 SHAFTO TERRACE	WASHINGTON						TO 2nd GARRISON BN, CLASS Z RESERVE.	
REAY	Wm	LCPL	23	/1440						KR para 392				IN 11 PLATOON.
REDPATH	Ernst	PTE	23	/975			BEDLINGTON	27/12/14	14/11/18	GSW	SEPT 16		TO DEPOT.	AGE 30, TO 3CCS 2/7/16 EVAC 2/7/16 WND LEGS.
REDPATH	Geo	PTE	23	/1462	A		FOREST HALL			1/7/16	MISSING DEC 16	THIEPVAL MEM		
REDSHAW	FredW	SGT	23	/66									COMMISSIONED YORK & LANCASTER REGIMENT	(1/5th BN) 27/6/17
REED	Geo	PTE	23											AWOL 22/5/15
REES	David	PTE	23	/1070	A		SOUTH SHIELDS			1/7/16	MISSING DEC 16	THIEPVAL MEM		BORN TREGEDAR WALES.
RENNISON	Jos	PTE	23	/956	B	4 LIME TERRACE	LANGLEY PARK			1/7/16	NOV 16, WND+MISSING DEC	THIEPVAL MEM		AGE 35 BORN DURHAM CITY.
REVELEY	Geo	PTE	23	/1092	B	6 ADOLPHUS STREET	SEAHAM			KR para 392	AUGUST 16, MISSING 29/4/1			PRISONER OF WAR.
RICE	Wm	PTE	23	/887			RIPON				SEPT 16		TO 27th, 12/13th , 1st BNS, CLASS Z RESERVE.	
RICHARDSON	AlbtF	SGT	23	/1231						KR para 392			ATT 102 LIGHT TRENCH MORTAR BATTERY, COMMISSIONED 25/9/18.	
RICHARDSON	Aug A	PTE	23	/866	A		NORTH SHIELDS			1/7/16	MISSING DEC 16	THIEPVAL MEM		BORN BELFORD.
RICHARDSON	David	LCPL	23	/381			BEDLINGTON			31/3/18	JULY 16	POZIERES MEM	TO 25th, 1/5th BNS.	RENUMBERED 243185.
RICHARDSON	Ernst	PTE	23	/938			CORNSAY COLL				OCT 16		TO LABOUR CORPS.	TO 3 CCS 2/7/16 EVAC 2/7/16, GSW LEGS.LAB CORPS No !
RICHARDSON	Fred	LCPL	23	/945									TO 25th, 1/5th, 22nd, 20th, 1/7th, 1st BNS, CLASS Z	RENUMBERED 243186.
RICHARDSON	Fredk	PTE	23	/471		49 ELM STREET	NEWCASTLE							
RICHARDSON	John	PTE	23	/916			GOSFORTH			26/6/17	OCT 16	POINT DU JOUR MIL CE	TO 27th BN.	
RICHARDSON	Jos	PTE	23	/803									TO DURHAM LIGHT INFANTRY, TRAINING RESER	TRG RES No TR/5/41415.
RICHARDSON	Olivr	LCPL	23	/867	A		SHIREMOOR			1/7/16	MISSING DEC 16	THIEPVAL MEM		BORN BACKWORTH.
RICHARDSON	Peter	PTE	23	/1000			GATESHEAD			18/7/16	OCT 16	PUCHEVILLERS BRIT CEM		BORN MOFFAT SCOTLAND.
RICHARDSON	Thos	PTE	23	/306	C		BYKER			1/7/16	MISSING DEC 16	THIEPVAL MEM		
RICHARDSON	Thos	PTE	23	/973									TO CLASS Z RESERVE.	
RICHARDSON	Wm	PTE	23	/1273		NORTHUMBRIA TERR.	AMBLE	2/1/15	28/4/19	KR para 392			TO 16th, 1/5th BNS, DEPOT.	
RICHARDSON		PTE	23	/274	C									IN 11 PLATOON.
RIDDELL	Walt	PTE	23	/1638		20 HULL STREET	NEWCASTLE						TO 2nd GARRISON BN.	
RIDDLE	Jas A	PTE	23	/282			BEDLINGTON	29/11/14	3/8/17	WOUNDS	AUGUST 16		TO DEPOT.	
RIDLEY	Geo	PTE	23	/704			WEST WYLAM			19/2/16		SAILLY SUR LYS CAN CEM		
RILEY	Geo	CPL	23	/198			ASHINGTON			1/7/16	NOV 16, WND+MISSING DEC	THIEPVAL MEM		BORN GLASGOW.
RITCHIE	Fred	PTE	23	/1166		26 HENRY STREET	SEAHAM				NOV 16		TO 9th, 1st BNS, CLASS Z RESERVE.	
ROBERTS	John	PTE	23	/1320	A		FELLING			1/7/16	MISSING DEC 16	THIEPVAL MEM		BORN SEATON DELAVAL
ROBERTS	JohnT	PTE	23	/339		5 JOHNSON TERRACE	USWORTH						TO 2nd GARRISON BN, CLASS Z RESERVE.	
ROBERTSON	Hugh	LCPL	23	/316									TO DURHAM LI(15th BN).	DURHAM LI No 46595.
ROBERTSON	John	PTE	23	/523			JARROW				AUGUST 16, DEC 17.			
ROBERTSON	Wm	PTE	23	/252			ASHINGTON	30/11/14	9/1/18	SICK	DEC 16		TO 27th, 1/7th BNS.	AGE 40
ROBERTSON	Wm	PTE	23	/81						KR para 392			TO DURHAM LIGHT INFANTRY, TRAINING RESER	TRG RES No TR/5/58196.
ROBINSON	JohnW	PTE	23	/1164		86 LONGNEWTON STI	DAWDON	28/12/14	30/10/17	WOUNDS	JULY 16		TO 3rd BN.	AGE 46, TO 3CCS 2/7/16 EVAC 2/7/16 WND LEGS.
ROBINSON	Rob D	PTE	23	/6		19 STAVORDALE STRI	DAWDON			1/7/16		THIEPVAL MEM	TO 34th DIV CYC COY, 24th BN.	BORN MOSELEY WORCS, RENUMBERED 24/1711 TYNESI
ROBINSON	Rob P	PTE	23	/460			HULL			5/10/16		THIEPVAL MEM	TO 11th BN.	
ROBINSON	Thomp	PTE	23	/1642		5 BRUNEL STREET	FERRYHILL				JULY 16		TO 20th, 12th, 12/13th, 25th BNS, REENLISTED RO	WND ARM & BUTTOCK, MEDALS FORFEITED FOR LARCEI
ROBINSON	Thos	LCPL	23	/1425			ASHINGTON	4/1/15	30/3/18	GSW	AUGUST 16		TO ARMY RESERVE CLASS P.	AGE 24.
ROBINSON	Wm	PTE	23	/650				9/12/14	31/3/19	KR para 392			TO ARMY RESERVE CLASS P.	
ROBSON	Allan	PTE	23	/841	D		CHOPPINGTON			1/7/16	MISSING DEC 16	THIEPVAL MEM		
ROBSON	Arth	SGT	23	/556									COMMISSIONED.	
ROBSON	John	PTE	23	/322									TO 2nd GARRISON BN, CLASS Z RESERVE.	
ROBSON	John	CPL	23	/836	D		CHOPPINGTON				MARCH 17, MISS 20-23/3/18		TO CLASS Z RES.	IN 8 PLATOON.
ROBSON	John	CPL	23	/914			ASHINGTON			18/9/18		ST SEVER CEM ROUEN	TO ROYAL FUSILIERS(24th BN).	BORN DURHAM, R FUS No G/93163.

ROBSON	Jos	PTE	23	/254	C	963 WALKER ROAD	NEWCASTLE			1/7/16	MISSING DEC 16	THIEPVAL MEM		AGE 19 BORN DURHAM CITY.
ROBSON	Jos	PTE	23	/1242		GRACE VILLA	USHAW MOOR			21/2/16		MERVILLE COM CEM		AGE 29 BORN STANLEY Co DURHAM.
ROBSON	Rich	PTE	23	/843			NETHERTON COLL			10/10/17	SEPT 16	TYNE COT MEM	TO 14th, 10th BNS.	BORN SOUTH HETTON Co DURHAM.
ROBSON	Thos	PTE	23	/1198		25 WEST LANE	MEDOMSLEY				POW DEC 17			
ROBSON	Wm	PTE	23	/589		90 NORTH ROW	BEDLINGTON			1/7/16		THIEPVAL MEM		AGE 19.
ROBSON	Wm D	CPL	23	/300	C		SUNNISIDE			1/7/16	MISSING DEC 16	THIEPVAL MEM		BORN MARLEY HILL.
ROCHESTER	Wm G	LCPL	23	/114	B		NEWCASTLE	23/11/14	1/3/19	KR para 392			TO 16th BN, DEPOT.	3CCS 2/7 EVAC 2/7 101 AMBT 18 GHOSP, 6CON DEP 7/7/1
ROGERSON	J O	SGT	23	/481			BURNHOPEFIELD				OCT 16			
ROGERSON	Robt	PTE	23	/1346						KR para 392			TO 2nd GARRISON BN.	
ROLFE	Albt	PTE	23	/1639			SALISBURY WILTS	10/8/15	12/12/17	GSW	OCT 16		TO DEPOT	AGE 22.
ROONEY	Chas	PTE	23	/1250		21 MARIA STREET	TUNSTALL				AUGUST 16		TO 25th, 16th, 27th, 19th BNS, CLASS Z RESERVE.	
ROSS	Adam	PTE	23	/475			KIRKHEATON COLL				SEPT 16		TO 1/4th BN.	
ROSS	James	PTE	23	/115			FELLING				SEPT 16		TO ROYAL INISKILLING FUSILIERS(6th BN).	R INNIS FUS No 21586.
ROSS	Jos	PTE	23	/762	A		BARRINGTON COLL			1/7/16	MISSING DEC 16	THIEPVAL MEM		BORN BEDLINGTON.
ROSS	Rob W	PTE	23	/1036		3 ADDISON STREET	HENDON			1/7/16	MISSING NOV 16	THIEPVAL MEM	TO 22nd BN(A COY).	AGE 30.
ROUTLEDGE	Adam	PTE	23	/759									TO CLASS Z RESERVE.	
ROUTLEDGE	JohnR	CPL	23	/925			ISABELLA PIT	21/12/14		KR para 392	OCT 16		TO ARMY RESERVE CLASS P.	
ROUTLEDGE	Ramsy	PTE	23	/1566		20 FRONT STREET	BEBSIDE			1/7/16		THIEPVAL MEM	TO 20th BN.	AGE 21.
ROWELL	JohnW	PTE	23											AWOL 24/4/15, 15/6/15.
ROWLEY	James	PTE	23	/1182						KR para 392			TO 22nd BN.	
RUMSBY	Wm	PTE	23	/409			BLYTH	6/12/14	30/10/17	WOUNDS	DEC 16		TO 85th TRAINING RESERVE BN.	
RUSSELL	Alex	PTE	23	/199	D	EAST END FRONT ST	BEDLINGTON			1/7/16	NOV 16, WND+MISSING DEC	THIEPVAL MEM		AGE 22.
RUSSELL	Geo	PTE	23	/188										
RUTHERFORD	Jos	PTE	23	/765	D		BEDLINGTON			1/7/16	MISSING DEC 16	THIEPVAL MEM		BORN HERTFORD
SADLER	Chas	PTE	23	/932			CORNSAY COLL			24/5/18		BOIS GUILLAUME COM	TO LABOUR CORPS(703 AE COY).	LAB CORPS No 407900, AGE 41.
SALKELD	JohnJ	PTE	23	/855		SEATON AVENUE	NEWBIGGIN	20/12/14	15/10/18	GASTRITIS			TO 2nd GARRISON BN.	
SANDERSON	Geo A	PTE	23	/574			ASHINGTON	9/12/14	22/6/17	WOUNDS	OCT 16		TO DEPOT.	
SCHOFIELD	Geo W	PTE	23	/1481		27 BOLAM STREET	BYKER			1/7/16	MISSING OCT 16	THIEPVAL MEM	TO 20th BN(A COY).	AGE 31 BORN SHEFFIELD.
SCOTT	David	SGT	23	/1268			ASHINGTON	4/1/15	12/5/17	GSW	SEPT 16		TO ARMY RESERVE CLASS P.	AGE 40.
SCOTT	G	PTE	23	/299										EMPLOYED SMITHS DOCK.
SCOTT	James	PTE	23	/915	B		CHOPPINGTON			1/7/16	MISSING DEC 16	THIEPVAL MEM		BORN BEDLINGTON.
SCOTT	JohnH	PTE	23	/873			DINNINGTON COLL				JULY 16		TO 25th, 1/5th BNS, CLASS Z RESERVE.	RENUMBERED 243190.
SCOTT	Jos S	PTE	23	/435			RYTON FERRY						TO 2nd GARRISON BN, CLASS Z RESERVE.	
SCOTT	JoshN	CQMS	23	/1127		17 MIDDLE DOUBLE R	NORTH SEATON	29/12/14	1/4/19	KR para392	AUGUST 16		TO NORTHERN COMMAND DEPOT RIPON, ARMY RESERVE CLASS P.	
SCOTT	Rich	PTE	23	/67			WILLINGTON QUAY	25/11/14	19/2/18	SICK	OCT 16		TO 3rd BN.	AGE 47.
SCOTT	Thos	PTE	23	/1344	B		BEDLINGTON			1/7/16	MISSING DEC 16	THIEPVAL MEM		BORN WOOLER.
SCOTT	ThosA	LCPL	23	/277				26/11/14	28/7/15	KR para 392				DID NOT SERVE OVERSEAS.
SCOTT	Walt	PTE	23	/1003	B		LOGIGRIEVE SCTL			1/7/16	MISSING DEC 16	THIEPVAL MEM		BORN ELDON Co DURHAM.
SCOTT	Walt	SGT	23	/1525			HEXAM			KR para 392	MARCH 17, APRIL 17.			
SCOUGAL	Andrw	PTE	23	/837			BEDLINGTON	20/12/14	18/2/18	GSW	AUGUST 16		TO 3rd BN.	
SCURFIELD	James	PTE	23	/204	A	4 RIDGE TERRACE	BEDLINGTON			1/7/16	MISSING DEC 16	THIEPVAL MEM		AGE 30.
SENNETT	John	CPL	23	/120		95 MORRISON STREE	GATESHEAD							
SHANKS	Edwin	PTE	23											AWOL 7/8/15
SHANKS	Geo W	PTE	23	/462			CHOPPINGTON				SEPT 16		TO 8th BN, CLASS Z RESERVE.	
SHAW	Fred	LCPL	23	/564			ASHINGTON				SSHOCK DEC 16		TO ROYAL INNISKILLING FUSILIERS(6th BN).	R INNIS FUS No 21592.
SHAW	James	PTE	23	/1386				2/1/15	31/10/16	SICK			TO ARMY RESERVE CLASS W.	AGE 46.
SHEARVILLE	Thos	CPL	23	/232		4 PINE STREET	SOUTHMOOR	30/11/14	5/9/18	SICK	AUGUST 16		TO 3rd BN.	AGE 38.
SHELL	Wm	PTE	23	/82			SOUTH SHIELDS			KR para 392	AUGUST 16			
SHERWIN	Albt	PTE	23	/454				4/11/14	29/11/16	SICK			TO 2nd GARRISON BN, DEPOT.	AGE 37.
SHERWOOD	Henry	SGT	23	/333	D		HEATON	23/11/14	12/10/18	GSW	JULY 16, NOV 17.		TO 12th, 21st, 4th(RES) BNS.	AGE 39.
SHIELDS	John	PTE	23	/267	C		KIBBLESWORTH			1/7/16	MISSING DEC 16	THIEPVAL MEM		
SHILLAW	Thos	LCPL	23	/1148		28 CASTLEREAGH ST	SILKSWORTH COLL	28/12/14	12/7/18	KNEE INJURY			TO ARMY RESERVE CLASS P.	AGE 38.
SIBBALD	JohnR	PTE	23	/117			GATESHEAD	22/12/14	4/6/18	GSW	JULY 16		TO ARMY RESERVE CLASS P.	AGE 21.
SIMMONETTE	JohnC	PTE	23	/118				23/11/14	25/4/18	GSW			TO 24th, 24/27th BNS.	
SIMPSON	Andrw	LCPL	23	/1074				23/12/14	31/3/19	KR para 392			TO ARMY RESERVE CLASS P.	
SIMPSON	Harld	SGT	23	/1007				28/12/14	22/7/16	KR para 392	FEB 16		TO DEPOT	
SIMPSON	J	PTE	23	/812										DID NOT SERVE OVERSEAS.
SIMPSON	James	PTE	23	/911		23 BACK CLAYTON ST	BEDLINGTON STN	22/12/14	25/2/18	WOUNDS	OCT 16		TO DEPOT.	AGE 35, BORN EAST ORD BERWICK.
SIMPSON	JohnT	PTE	23	/328				24/11/14	4/12/18	SICK			TO DEPOT.	AGE 36.
SIMPSON	Jos	PTE	23	/119			NEWCASTLE				JULY 16			TO 3 CCS 1/7/16 WND BACK, EVAC 18 AMB TRAIN 2/7.
SIMPSON	Wm	PTE	23	/1616			CHOPPINGTON			1/7/16		THIEPVAL MEM	TO 22nd BN.	BORN WEST SLEEKBURN.
SIMPSON	Wm	PTE	23	/288		4 MALTON ROW	BENWELL VILLAGE				JULY 16, OCT 16.		TO 1/4th BN.	
SINCLAIR	Emmnl	PTE	23	/531						KR para 392			TO 1/5th BN.	
SINTON	Jas H	PTE	23	/768				16/12/14	29/1/19	GSW			TO 9th BN, DEPOT.	AGE 26.
SKELTON	JohnB	PTE	23	/1078		5 EASTBOURNE GAR	WALKER			26/2/17		HAUTE AVESNES BRIT CEM		BORN EDINBURGH SCOTLAND.
SKIDMORE	John	PTE	23	/662	D	210 SYCAMORE STRE	HIRST			1/7/16	MISSING DEC 16	THIEPVAL MEM		AGE 31 BORN BEDLINGTON.
SKINNER	Geo	SGT	23	/120										
SLATER	Matt	SGT	23	/774			ASHINGTON	11/12/14	24/5/18	WOUNDS	NOV 17		TO DEPOT.	AGE 20.
SMAILES	Mich	PTE	23	/1754									TO EAST YORKSHIRE REGT(1st GARRISON BN), (	EAST YORKS No 35824.
SMALL	Thos	PTE	23	/504	B	25 ELM PARK TERRAC	SHOTLEY BRIDGE			1/7/16	MISSING DEC 16	THIEPVAL MEM		BORN SOUTH SHIELDS AGE 20, IN 7 PLATOON, AWOL 29/
SMART	Wm R	PTE	23	/1116		22 DERWENT COTTS	MEDOMSLEY	29/12/14		9/4/17		ARRAS MEM		AGE 23.
SMITH	Alf	PTE	23	/1104			SUNDERLAND	28/12/14						FIREMAN, DESERTED 1915 AGE 31, 5'4".
SMITH	Benj	PTE	23	/23			SOUTH SHIELDS				JULY 16, POW JULY 17.			
SMITH	Chas	PTE	23	/1590		14 CHAPEL STREET	BERWICK						TO 21st, 3rd BNS, CLASS Z RESERVE.	
SMITH	Geo	PTE	23	/24		ORCHARD HSE FRON	MONKSEATON	23/11/14	10/3/19	KR para 392	SEPT 16		TO 1/7th, 12/13th BNS, DEPOT.	
SMITH	John	PTE	23	/495			MORPETH			1/7/16	MISSING NOV 16	THIEPVAL MEM	TO 22nd BN(C COY).	AWOL 29/5/15, 7/8/15, 16/9/15.
SMITH	JohnH	PTE	23	/123						KR para 392			TO DURHAM LIGHT INFANTRY, TRAINING RESER	TRG RES No TR/5/41591.
SMITH	JohnR	PTE	23	/427		118 KIRK STREET	NEWCASTLE						TO 2nd GARRISON BN, CLASS Z RESERVE.	
SMITH	Ralph	PTE	23	/1426	B	90 MILL LANE	NEWCASTLE			1/7/16		THIEPVAL MEM		AGE 22.
SMITH	Wm	PTE	23	/1532	C		ASHINGTON			1/7/16	MISSING DEC 16	THIEPVAL MEM		BORN WARKWORTH.
SNOW	Wm F	CPL	23	/1171		1 BEAMISH RED ROW	STANLEY	29/12/14					TO CLASS Z RESERVE.	
SOUTHERN	Robt	PTE	23	/850									TO CLASS Z RESERVE.	
SPARK	John	PTE	23	/1388	D		NEWCASTLE			1/7/16	NOV 16, WND+MISSING DEC	THIEPVAL MEM		BORN GATESHEAD AWOL 17/2/15, 14/7/15.
SPENCER	Walt	SGT	23	/185									TO 2nd GARRISON BN, CLASS Z RESERVE.	
STAFFORD	Alf	SGT	23	/317			RYTON	24/11/14	6/11/18	SICK	SEPT 16		TO 1st, 16th BNS, DEPOT.	
STANGER	Wm M	PTE	23	/265		60 PARKINSON STREE	FELLING				AUGUST 16		TO ROYAL FUSILIERS(24th BN).	FRANCE 23 9/1/16-6/7/16, 23 4/11/16-28/8/18, 24RF-3/10/18.
STEEL	John	PTE	23	/279		5 AIDANS ROAD	SOUTH SHIELDS			15/7/16		ETAPLES MIL CEM		DIED AT No 26 GEN HOSP.
STEEL	Robt	PTE	23	/1347	B									TO 18 GHOSP 3/7/16, BASE DEPOT 9/7/16 AGE 38.
STEEL	Wm	PTE	23	/772	D		BEDLINGTON			1/7/16	NOV 16, WND+MISSING DEC	THIEPVAL MEM		
STEELE	Thos	PTE	23	/775	D	56 CULLERCOATES S	NEWCASTLE			1/7/16	MISSING DEC 16	THIEPVAL MEM		AGE 23.
STEPHENSON	Wm	PTE	23	/72			SOUTH SHIELDS			26/10/17	JULY 16	TYNE COT MEM	TO 25th, 1/5th BNS.	RENUMBERED 243189.
STEPHENSON	Wm	PTE	23	/490		WHITES BUILDINGS	WHICKHAM	23/11/14	22/11/18	GSW	SEPT 16		TO 27th BN, DEPOT.	AGE 31.
STEWART	John	PTE	23	/297			NORTH SHIELDS	28/11/14			JULY 16		TO 20th, 24/27th, 14th, 25th BNS.	AGE 21.
STEWART	Jos	PTE	23	/420	D	11 SOULSBY STREET	BLYTH			1/7/16	NOV 16 WND+MISSING DEC	THIEPVAL MEM		BORN BEDLINGTON.
STEWART	Matt	PTE	23	/766			BEDLINGTON				FEB 18		TO 9th BN, CLASS Z RESERVE.	
STEWART	Robt	PTE	23	/799									TO 9th BN, CLASS Z RESERVE.	
STIMPSON	Law G	PTE	23	/125						KR para 392			TO 21st BN.	
STOBART	Chas	PTE	23	/177			SOUTH SHIELDS			8/9/17		PIETA MIL CEM MALTA	TO 1st GARRISON BN.	
STOBART		PTE	23	/1042	C									IN 11 PLATOON, TO HOSPITAL 14/2/16.
STOBBART	Geo	PTE	23	/1043		2 MINES STREET	HETTON LE HOLE			23/5/17		ARRAS MEM	TO 9th BN	AGE 30.
STOCK	David	PTE	23	/71	C		DINNINGTON COLL			1/7/16	MISSING DEC 16	THIEPVAL MEM		
STOKER	Edwd	PTE	23	/1203		9 WILLIAMSON TERR	MONKWEARMOUTH			KR para 392			TO 2nd GARRISON BN.	
STRAKER	Wm A	SGT	23	/1370									TO CLASS Z RESERVE.	
SUMMERS	Geo B	PTE	23	/856			BEDLINGTON			3/11/16	JULY 16	THIEPVAL MEM	TO CHESHIRE REGIMENT(9th BN).	BORN BEBSIDE, CHESHIRE REGT No 52266.AGE 21.
SUMMERSON	ArthG	PTE	23	/216	C		BURNHOPEFIELD			1/7/16	MISSING DEC 16	THIEPVAL MEM		BORN COCKFIELD Co DURHAM.
SUTHERS	Thos	PTE	23	/1213			SHOTTON	24/11/14	31/10/17	SICK	SEPT 16		TO ARMY RESERVE CLASS W.	AGE 27.
SUTTON	Sam L	LCPL	23	/1249	A		SUNDERLAND			1/7/16	MISSING DEC 16	OVILLERS MIL CEM		BORN ISLE OF DOGS.
SWANSON	Wm	PTE	23	/408				5/12/14	17/11/17	GASSED			TO DEPOT	AGE 39.
SWINBANK	JohnW	PTE	23	/434			DUNSTON	2/11/14	11/5/17	GSW L ARM	OCT 16		TO 3rd BN.	AGE 27.
SWINBURNE	G H	PTE	23	/208		14 BK DAVIDSON ST	HEBBURN NEWTOWN							
SYME	Jos	PTE	23	/296				28/11/14	1/8/16	WOUNDS			TO DEPOT.	
TAIT	Andrw	PTE	23	/783			ASHINGTON	10/12/14	22/5/17	WOUNDS	SEPT 16			AGE 40.
TAIT	Henry	CPL	23	/606	C		BLACKHILL			1/7/16	MISSING DEC 16	OVILLERS MIL CEM		BORN STURTON GRANGE.
TAYLOR	Edwd	PTE	23	/1579			NEW DELAVAL	20/7/15	29/8/17	SICK	12/6/16		TO 20th BN, 84th TRAINING RESERVE BN.	WND HANDS & TOES SHELLSHOCK, AGE 40.
TAYLOR	James	PTE	23	/860		34 KINGS ROAD	BEDLINGTON			1/7/16	NOV 16,WND+MISSING DEC	THIEPVAL MEM		AGE 26 BORN BERWICK.
TAYLOR	James	PTE	23	/1165						KR para 392			TO 2nd GARRISON BN.	
TAYLOR	John	PTE	23	/1478	C	14 TRAFALGAR STRE	CONSETT			1/7/16	MISSING DEC 16	THIEPVAL MEM		
TAYLOR	Lan D	PTE	23	/1264						KR para 392			TO DURHAM LIGHT INFANTRY, TRAINING RESER	TRG RES No TR/5/59094.
TAYLOR	Pet G	PTE	23	/405						KR para 392			TO DURHAM LIGHT INFANTRY, TRAINING RESER	TRG RES No TR/5/41593.
TAYLOR	Robt	PTE	23	/632			ASHINGTON			7/8/16		ALBERT COM CEM EXT		BORN ALNWICK
TAYLOR	Thos	PTE	23	/802						KR para 392				
TAYLOR	Wm	LCPL	23	/1578									TO 2nd GARRISON BN, CLASS Z RESERVE.	

TELFORD	Archi	SGT	23 / 62		BURNSIDE	BELLINGHAM							
TELFORD	Edwd	PTE	23 / 483				7/12/14	9/1/15	KR para 392			TO DEPOT.	DID NOT SERVE OVERSEAS.
TELFORD	Wm J	PTE	23 / 781	C	2 KEPIER CHARE	RYTON			21/3/18	OCT 16	ARRAS MEM		BORN WEST WYLAM, IN 12 PLATOON.
TEMPLETON	Thos	PTE	23 /1596									TO 23rd BN, KINGS OWN YORKSHIRE LI(5th BN).	KOYLI No 63228.
TERNANT	Thos	PTE	23 /1085			NEWCASTLE	30/12/14	4/5/18	GSW	APRIL 17		TO 3rd BN.	
TEW	AlbtE	PTE	23 /1376	B		SUNDERLAND			1/7/16	MISSING DEC 16	THIEPVAL MEM		BORN MANCHESTER.
THIRTLE	James	PTE	23 /1571			BLYTH			1/7/16	MISSING OCT 16	THIEPVAL MEM	TO 20th BN(C COY).	
THOBURN	Alf	PTE	23 /1288			BEDLINGTON	3/1/15	15/2/17	WOUNDS	JULY 16		TO DEPOT.	
THOMPSON	G A	LCPL	23 / 513		9 EMMAVILLE	RYTON	11/11/14	7/10/18		NOV 18			HEWER
THOMPSON	Geo W	PTE	23 / 784				22/12/14	20/7/16	KR para 392	FEB 16			LAY IN NO-MAN'S-LAND THREE DAYS WOUNDED.
THOMPSON	James	PTE	23 / 371				27/11/14	27/9/15	UNFIT			TO 29th BN.	AGE 20 DID NOT SERVE OVERSEAS.
THOMPSON	James	PTE	23 / 568				8/12/14	4/7/17	WOUNDS			TO 3rd BN.	AGE 27.
THOMPSON	James	PTE	23 /1604									TO 2nd GARRISON BN, CLASS Z RESERVE.	
THOMPSON	John	PTE	23 /1582			HARTLEPOOL			30/6/17		RAWLPINDI WAR CEM	TO 2nd GARRISON BN.	
THOMPSON	JohnD	PTE	23 /1611		17 HIGH STREET	BLYTH	1/7/15	8/10/15	23/6/20		BLYTH		DID NOTSERVE OVERSEAS.
THOMPSON	Jos	PTE	23 / 560			NEWCASTLE	8/12/14						LABOURER AGE 25, 5'10", DESERTED 1915.
THOMPSON	Matt	PTE	23 / 278			SOUTH SHIELDS			8/11/17	JULY 16	ST MARTIN CALVAIRE E	TO 25th, 26th BNS.	BORN NORTH SHIELDS AGE 42.
THOMPSON	Thos	PTE	23 / 778	B	12 HATTERS LANE	BERWICK			1/7/16	MISSING DEC 16	THIEPVAL MEM		AGE 35.
THOMPSON	Wm	PTE	23 / 644	C	54 GEORGE ST HUNTI	ABERDEEN			1/7/16	MISSING DEC 16	THIEPVAL MEM		BORN NEWCASTLE, AGE 37.
THOMPSON		PIPR	23 /1357	C									IN 11 PLATOON.
THORNTON	Jos H	PTE	23 /1276			AMBLE	2/1/15	8/6/17	WOUNDS	JULY 16		TO DEPOT.	AGE 31.
THORNTON	Rob P	LCPL	23 / 384			BEDLINGTON	29/11/14	22/12/16	GSW R SHLDF	JULY 16		TO DEPOT.	AGE 31.
TOMLIN	Robt	PTE	23 / 329	B	72 MORRIS ST TEAMS	GATESHEAD			1/7/16	MISSING DEC 16	THIEPVAL MEM		AGE 30 BORN LEICESTER.
TOPPING	Wm	PTE	23 /1018				28/12/14	24/4/15	INEFFICIENT				AGE 47, DID NOT SERVE OVERSEAS.
TOWLER	Albt	PTE	23 /1510			HEBBURN			22/10/17	JULY 16	TYNE COT MEM	TO 16th BN.	BORN ABERDEEN.
TOWNSEND	Wm Ed	PTE	23 / 73			SOUTH SHIELDS			21/3/18		ARRAS MEM	TO 1st BN.	BORN SHREWSBURY.
TRIGG	Edwd	PTE	23 /1345						KR para 392			TO DURHAM LIGHT INFANTRY, TRAINING RESER	TRG RES No TR/5/41592.
TUBMAN	Thos	CPL	23 / 153			FENCEHOUSES	2/12/14	6/4/17	WOUNDS	JULY 16		TO DEPOT.	
TUCK	Ernst	SGT	23 / 870			LEADGATE				MISSING DEC 16, POW FEB 1		TO 20th BN(D COY), CLASS Z RESERVE.	
TUNLEY	Wm	SGT	23 /1372			NEWCASTLE			1/7/16	MISSING DEC 16	OVILLERS MIL CEM		BORN LEOMINSTER HERTFORDSHIRE.
TUNNEY	Robt	PTE	23 /1618		9 DELAVAL STREET	SEATON DELAVAL	9/8/15	25/10/18	SICK	JULY 16		TO 24th, 19th, 25th BNS, NORTHERN COMD DEPO	AGE 40, BEAUFORT WAR HOSP BRISTOL 11/7/16.
TURNBULL	Geo	LCPL	23 / 330		185 NORFOLK ROAD	NEWCASTLE						TO 22nd BN.	
TURNBULL	J	PTE	23 / 432										
TURNBULL	Robt	LCPL	23 /1527			SOUTH SHIELDS			3/7/16		PUCHEVILLERS BRIT CEM		AGE 18.
TURNBULL	Robt	PTE	23 / 459			BURRADON			25/9/18		ANZAC SAILLY SUR LY!	TO 1st, 9th BNS.	
TURNBULL	Thos	PTE	23										AWOL 29/11/15.
TURNBULL	Wm	SGT	23 / 39		152 CAMPBELL STREI	SOUTH SHIELDS			22/10/16		HARTON ST PETERS		
TURNER	Sam	PTE	23 / 906									TO 1st GARRISON BN, CLASS Z RESERVE.	AGE 42, AWOL 5/7/15.
TURNER	Wm	PTE	23 / 634		10 CANNON STREET	GATESHEAD			KR para 392			TO 1st GARRISON BN.	AWOL 1/2/15, 5/7/15, 12/7/15.
TURNER	WmJas	PTE	23 /1197			HORDEN				AUGUST 16		TO CHESHIRE REGIMENT(9th BN).	CHESHIRE REGT No 52267.
TURNEY	Wm	PTE	23 /1580			SEATON DELAVAL	20/7/15	1/4/19	KR para 392	SEPT 16		TO ARMY RESERVE CLASS P.	
TWEEDY	Thos	PTE	23 / 187	B		BLYTH			1/7/16	MISSING DEC 16	THIEPVAL MEM		BORN COWPEN.
TWEEDY	Wm	PTE	23 /1554				16/7/15	23/10/17	SICK			TO 84th TRAINING RESERVE BN.	AGE 41 DID NOT SERVE OVERSEAS.
URWIN	W	LCPL	23 / 172			WALLSEND				JULY 16			
USHER	Wm L	LCPL	23 /1301			SOUTH SHIELDS			14/3/16		ERQUINGHEM CHYD EXT		AGE 46.
WAITE	Wm	PTE	23 / 800			BEDLINGTON			18/8/16	MISSING NOV 16	GUILLEMONT RD CEM	TO 1st BN.	BORN NORTH SHIELDS
WALDOCK	JohnT	LCPL	23 / 410			ASHINGTON				SEPT 16		TO 8th, 1/5th BNS.	
WALKER	J	PTE	23 / 441									TO 1st GARRISON, 26th BNS, LABOUR CORPS(76:	MALTA 17/8/15-30/4/16, 26 1/5/16-30/9/17, 762 COY 1/10/17-
WALKER	J S	PTE	23 / 331	B									101 AMBT TO 18 GHOSP 3/7 HSHIP 7/7 WND R LEG. AGE 4
WALKER	John	PTE	23 / 992			BEDLINGTON			11/7/16	NOV 16	BEDLINGTON ST CUTHBERT CH YD		BORN BISHOP AUKLAND.
WALKER	Wm	PTE	23 / 984	B	4 WHITSUN AVENUE	BEDLINGTON			22/6/16		THIEPVAL MEM		AGE 42.
WALLACE	Chris	PTE	23 /1291			STAKEFORD			1/7/16	MISSING DEC 16	THIEPVAL MEM		BORN SLEEKBURN.
WALLACE	Simps	LCPL	23 / 520		6 BAKER STREET	IVESTON	7/12/14	16/8/18	GSW	29/4/17 GAZ NOV 17		TO DEPOT.	AGE 34, PRISONER OF WAR.
WALLACE	Thos	PTE	23 /1111			SHOTTS SCTLD			12/10/18		INDIA	TO 2nd GARRISON BN.	
WALLACE	Wm	PTE	23 /1286			BEDLINGTON				JULY 16		TO 24th, 21st, 25th, 9th BNS, CLASS Z RESERVE.	
WALLER	Robt	PTE	23 /1031	B		SEAHAM HARBOUR			1/7/16	MISSING DEC 16	THIEPVAL MEM		
WALLS	AlbtC	PTE	23 / 537	D		BIRTLEY			1/7/16	MISSING DEC 16	THIEPVAL MEM		BORN PERKINSVILLE.
WALSH	James	PTE	23 /1130		33 VICTORIA TERRAC	BEDLINGTON	29/12/14	11/12/19	KR para 392			TO 1st, 12/13th BNS, DEPOT.	
WALTON	Anthy	PTE	23 /1201		39 FRANCES STREET	NEW SILKSWORTH			24/11/16		BAILLEUL COM CEM E>	ATTACHED LANCASHIRE FUSILIERS(11th BN).	
WALTON	Matth	LCPL	23 /1051				22/12/14	5/9/16	KR para 392				DID NOT SERVE OVERSEAS
WANDLESS	Thos	PTE	23 / 416	C		ASHINGTON	4/12/14	4/1/17	GSW R ARM	AUGUST 16		TO DEPOT.	TO 18 GHOSP 3/7/16 EVAC HSHIP CALAIS 5/7/16 WND R A
WARD	B	PTE	23 /1136		1 MIDDLE ROW	MEDOMSLEY							
WARD	Wm	PTE	23 /1460	A		SOUTH MOOR			1/7/16	MISSING DEC 16	THIEPVAL MEM		BORN BRANCEPETH AWOL 29/6/15.
WARDLAW	Robt	PTE	23 / 378				29/11/14	26/10/16	WOUNDS			TO 84th TRAINING RESERVE BN.	
WARDLE	Jos	CPL	23 /1610			SEATON SLUICE			12/9/18	AUGUST 16	VIS-EN-ARTOIS MEM	TO KINGS OWN YORKSHIRE LI(5th BN).	BORN NEW HARTLEY, KOYLI No 63080.
WARDLE	Thos	PTE	23 /1368			NORTH SEATON	12/1/15	2/10/16	WOUNDS	OCT 16		TO DEPOT.	AGE 21.
WARDLE	Thos	SGT	23 / 604				14/12/14	17/8/17	SICK			TO DEPOT.	AGE 43.
WARNE	ThosH	PTE	23 /1547			ASHINGTON	3/7/15	8/5/18	GSW	JAN 17, MAR 17 WN+MISS JU		TO DEPOT.	AGE 21.
WARREN	James	PTE	23 /1623									TO 29th BN, ATT YORK & LANCS(8th BN), TO SCO	SCO RIF No 55519.
WARRENDER	Jos	PTE	23 /1083				28/12/14	27/2/19	KR para 392			TO ARMY RESERVE CLASS P.	
WATSON	Alex	LCPL	23 / 500		15 STATION ROAD	CRAMLINGTON							
WATSON	Edw J	PTE	23 /1364	A	28 ADOLPHUS STREE	SEAHAM						TO CLASS Z RESERVE	
WATSON	Frncs	PTE	23 / 823	A		NEWBIGGIN / SEA			1/7/16	MISSING DEC 16	THIEPVAL MEM		BORN MORPETH.
WATSON	John	CPL	23 /1493	B	37 MONK STREET	GATESHEAD				MISSING 29/4/17		TO CLASS Z RESERVE.	PRISONER OF WAR.
WATSON	JohnT	PTE	23 / 404				6/12/14	2/4/19	KR para 392			TO 25th, 1/7th BNS, ARMY RESERVE CLASS P.	RENUMBERED 293340.
WATSON	Robt	PTE	23 /1459					14/12/18		1/7/16		TO ROYAL AIR FORCE.	TO 3CCS 2/7/16 EVAC 2/7/16.RAF No 139110
WATSON	Sim S	PTE	23 / 629			CHOPPINGTON				AUGUST 16		TO 25th, 14th, 9th, 1st BNS.	
WATT	Aaron	PTE	23 / 175			WEST ALLOTMENT	30/11/14	30/11/18	SICK	SEPT 16		TO ARMY RESERVE CLASS W.	AGE 42.
WEAR	John	PTE	23 /1557									TO 24th, 24/27th, 9th, 22nd BNS, CLASS Z RESERVE.	
WEARMOUTH	I	PTE	23 / 415										
WEARS	Frncs	PTE	23 /1098			SEAHAM COLLIERY			8/10/16		THIEPVAL MEM	TO 21st BN, DURHAM LI(13th BN).	DURHAM LI No 46024.
WEARS	Rich	PTE	23 /1103			SEAHAM COLLIERY	28/12/14	30/10/17	GSW	JULY 16		TO 3rd BN.	AGE 23.
WEATHERITT	Robt	PTE	23 / 785			BEDLINGTON	16/12/14	28/8/18	MENTALLY ILL	DEC 18		TO DEPOT.	AGE 22.
WELCH	Geo	PTE	23 / 25			TYNEMOUTH				AUGUST 16		TO 1st, 12/13th BNS	
WELSH	Gordn	PTE	23 /1367		146 CHESTNUT STREI	HIRST	7/1/15	21/11/17	WOUNDS	AUGUST 16		TO 3rd BN.	AGE 22.
WEST	Edmd	PTE	23 / 205										
WEST	Harry	PTE	23 /1524	A	28 GREY STREET	NORTH SHIELDS				MISSING 27/4/17		TO CLASS Z RESERVE.	PRISONER OF WAR.
WESTOE	John	PTE	23 /1359		20 QUARRY SQUARE	TANTOBIE						TO 2nd GARRISON BN, CLASS Z RESERVE.	
WHITE	David	PTE	23 / 807	D		EDINBURGH			1/7/16	MISSING DEC 16	THIEPVAL MEM		
WHITE	Robt	PTE	23 /1428		22 GREY TERRACE	RYHOPE			16/8/17	AUGUST 16	POELCAPEPPLE BRIT C	TO 8th BN.	BORN MURTON COLLIERY, AGE 25.
WHITE	ThosN	PTE	23 /1312	B	1353 WALKER ROAD	NEWCASTLE			1/7/16	NOV 16,WND+MISSING DEC	THIEPVAL MEM		AGE 37 BORN SOUTH SHIELDS.
WHITEHEAD	Geo H	PTE	23 / 994									TO CLASS Z RESERVE.	
WHITEHILL	Thos	LCPL	23 / 221		14 ROCK STREET	NEWCASTLE						TO 1st GARRISON BN, CLASS Z RESERVE.	
WHITELOCK	John	CPL	23 / 307			SUNDERLAND			1/4/17		FAUBOURG DE AMIENS ARRAS		
WHITFIELD	James	PTE	23 /1331			SEAHAM HARBOUR			8/6/17		LIJSSENHOEK MIL CEM	TO 11th BN.	BORN SUNDERLAND.
WHITHAM	Geo W	PTE	23 /1147			SILKSWORTH			11/4/17	AUGUST 16	ROCLINCOURT VALLEY	TO 24th BN.	
WHITNEY	Thos	PTE	23 /1458			DINNINGTON COLL	24/11/14		KR para 392	NOV 16		TO ARMY RESERVE CLASS P.	
WHITTLE	John	LSGT	23 /1387			GLANTON	13/1/15	24/1/17	WOUNDS	JULY 16		TO DEPOT.	
WILFORD	Edwd	PTE	23 /1328			HORDEN				SEPT 16		TO 8th, 9th BNS.	
WILKINSON	Andrw	PTE	23 / 828			CHOPPINGTON	20/12/14	27/12/17	GSW	SEPT 16		TO 3rd BN.	AGE 40.
WILKINSON	Geo W	CPL	23 / 229										
WILKINSON	John	CPL	23 /1214	D		ACKLINGTON			1/7/16	MISSING DEC 16	THIEPVAL MEM		BORN NEWCASTLE.
WILKINSON	Wm	CSM	23 / 655			CHOPPINGTON	13/12/14	31/3/19	KR para 392	FEB 18		TO ARMY RESERVE CLASS P.	
WILLIAMS	Anthy	PTE	23 / 344	B	42 PAPERMILL SQUAF	GATESHEAD			1/7/16	NOV 16, WND+MISSING DEC	THIEPVAL MEM		
WILLIAMS	Geo	PTE	23 /1142	B		SEAHAM HARBOUR			1/7/16	MISSING DEC 16	THIEPVAL MEM		BORN SHOTTON COLLIERY.
WILLIAMS	Goodm	PTE	23 / 666			HIRST	13/12/14	31/10/17	GSW	SEPT 16		TODEPOT.	AGE 38.
WILLIAMSON	James	PTE	23 /1586		FARTHING BANK	THORNHILL DUMFR			31/12/17	SEPT 16	TYNE COT MEM	TO 8th, 26th 1/7th BNS.	BORN GLENCALEN SCOTLAND.
WILLIAMSON	John	PTE	23 / 993	A		SOUTH SHIELDS			1/7/16	NOV 16,WND+MISS DEC 16	THIEPVAL MEM		
WILLIAMSON	Wm J	CSM	23 /1389									TO CLASS Z RESERVE.	
WILLIS	ChasW	SGT	23 / 786			CHOPPINGTON	15/12/14	31/3/19	KR para 392	NOV 16, FEB 18.		TO DEPOT.	REP NOT WND DEC 16.
WILLIS	Ernst	CPL	23 /1278		1 RAILWAY ROW	NORTH SEATON			1/7/16	NOV 16	THIEPVAL MEM		
WILLIS	Gil J	PTE	23 / 829		16 SIXTH ROW	CHOPPINGTON			3/11/18		RUESNES COM CEM	TO KINGS OWN YORKSHIRE LI(5th BN).	KOYLI No 63242.BORN MOSELEY YORKS.
WILSON	Andrw	PTE	23 /1348			CHOPPINGTON			7/4/21		CHOPPINGTON ST PAU	TO 2nd GARRISON BN.	AGE 39.
WILSON	Arch	PTE	23 / 790	D		CHOPPINGTON			1/7/16	MISSING DEC 16	OVILLERS MIL CEM		
WILSON	Geo	PTE	23 / 682			SHIELDFIELD			1/7/16	NOV 16, WND+MISSING DEC	THIEPVAL MEM		
WILSON	Geo R	PTE	23 / 433	A		ASHINGTON			1/7/16	MISSING DEC 16	THIEPVAL MEM		
WILSON	Henry	SGT	23 / 514		35 ROBINSON STREE	NEWCASTLE				SEPT 16		TO 9th BN.	STILL SERVING 1920.
WINSHIP	Wm	PTE	23 /1563			NEWSHAM			5/11/16			TO 20th BN, CHESHIRE REGIMENT(9th BN).	CHESHIRE REGT No 52335. BORN BLYTH.
WINTER	Jos	PTE	23 / 791	C	9 SPEN STREET	WEST STANLEY	12/12/14		1/7/16		THIEPVAL MEM		BORN CONSETT.
WOOD	Albt	PTE	23 / 623	D	6 NEW ROW	CAMBOIS			1/7/16	MISSING DEC 16	THIEPVAL MEM		AGE 23 BORN BLYTH.
WOOD	Geo	PTE	23 / 990			FELLING			31/3/17	JULY 16	AUBIGNY COM CEM EXT		BORN MONKWEARMOUTH.
WOOD	JohnS	PTE	23 /1245			SACRISTON				AUGUST 16		TO 12/13th BN, CLASS Z RESERVE.	

Surname	Forename	Rank	Unit	Number	Coy	Address	Place					Notes
WOOD	Reubn	PTE	23	/233				30/11/14	5/6/18	SICK		ATTACHED LABOUR CORPS, ROYAL ENGINEERS AGE 40.
WOOD	Robt	PTE	23	/637			CHOPPINGTON			9/4/17	FEB 16, SEPT 16.	BAILLEUL RD EAST CEM TO 16th BN.
WOOD	ThosD	PTE	23	/1546			ASHINGTON				SEPT 16	TO 20th, 25th, 1/5th BNS. VOLUNTARY AID HOSP CHELTENHAM 8/7/16. RENUMBER
WOODS	James	PTE	23	/1102								TO 1st BN. STILL SERVING SEPT 1920.
WOODWARD	Chas	PTE	23	/665			FRAMWELLGATE MR	14/12/14	19/1/18	WOUNDS	SEPT 16	TO ARMY RESERVE CLASS P. AGE 39.
WREN	Robt	PTE	23	/227			BURNHOPEFIELD				AUGUST 16	TO 25th, 1/5th BNS, CLASS Z RESERVE. RENUMBERED 243173
WRIGHT	J	PTE	23	/129								
WRIGHT	Jos R	PTE	23	/1271			ASHINGTON			10/6/16		ALBERT COM CEM EXT
WRIGHT	Wm G	SGT	23	/1338		26 MAGDELENE STRE	DURHAM CITY			9/7/16		ST SEVER CEM ROUEN SERVED HUSSARS 1890s, SOUTH AFRICAN CON AGE 36, QSA MEDAL, PUBLICAN IN SHIELDROW 1913-14.
WYLIE	Andrw	PTE	23	/458	B		RYTON			1/7/16		THIEPVAL MEM AGE 40, IN 6 PLATOON, FAMILY FROM Co TYRONE.
WYLIE	John	PTE	23	/642						1/7/16	MISSING DEC 16	TO KINGS OWN YORKSHIRE LI(5th BN). KOYLI No 63243.
YATES	Mark		23	/1093								TO 1st GARRISON BN, CLASS Z RESERVE.
YEATS	Henry	SGT	23	/792			WALKER			1/7/16	MISSING DEC 16.	THIEPVAL MEM
YOUNG	Andrw	PTE	23	/933		156 CHADWICK STRE	CORNSAY COLL					TO 16th BN, CLASS Z RESERVE. TO 3CCS 2/7/16 EVAC 2/7/16 WND LEGS.
YOUNG	Ern J	CPL	23	/411	B	282 YARD ROW	NETHERTON COLL			1/7/16	MISSING DEC 16	THIEPVAL MEM
YOUNG	Ernst	LCPL	23	/130		20 RECTORY ROAD	HETTON LE HOLE			29/6/16		ALBERT COM CEM EXT AGE 23.
YOUNG	Frank	CPL	23	/892		SKINNERS ARMS COT	HEXHAM			7/2/16		SAILLY SUR LYS CAN CEM AGE 29.
YOUNG	G	PTE	23	/131								TO LABOUR CORPS.
YOUNG	Geo G	PTE	23	/ 40								
YOUNG	James	PTE	23	/806			BLYTH			14/10/17		SOLFERINO FARM CEM TO 16th, 23rd BNS.
YOUNG	Listr	CPL	23	/1322			SUNDERLAND			1/7/16		SAILLY SUR LYS CAN CEM
YOUNG	Math	CPL	23	/1306			NEWCASTLE			KR para 392	MARCH 17	TO DURHAM LIGHT INFANTRY, TRAINING RESER TRG RES No TR/5/59129.
YOUNG	RobtC	CPL	23	/554				7/12/14	22/4/17	GSW		TO 80th TRAINING RESERVE BN.
YOUNG	Walt	CPL	23	/1217		27 BOCA CHIA CAMBC	BLYTH			10/9/17		HAGRICOURT BRIT MIL ATTACHED 102nd LIGHT TRENCH MORTAR BATT BORN EAST SLEEKBURN.

Appendix VII

NOMINAL ROLL OF OTHER RANKS 29th (Reserve) NF

Owing to postings and renumbering in the UK it has proved difficult to trace many members of the reserve battalion. Facts and figures are therefore inconclusive.

Surname	Forename	Rank	Number	Address	Town	Enlisted	Discharged	Fate	Notes	Memorial/Cemetery	Postings	Notes
ASHWORTH	Rich	PTE	29 / 358			28/2/16	4/1/19	GSW			TO 1st BN, DEPOT.	
ATKINSON	Geo	SGT	29 / 8		E CRAMLINGTON	11/9/15	31/1/19	KR para 392	JULY 16		TO 20th, 10th, 24/27th BNS, ARMY RESERVE CLASS P.	
BAKER	Edgar	LCPL	29 / 874		MEWSTON YORKS			4/11/17		BOCQOUY ROAD CEM	TO MACHINE GUN CORPS(103 MG COY).	MGC No 58199.
BARRACLOUGH	Harry	PTE	29 / 485								TO 20th, 9th BNS, CLASS Z RESERVE.	
BECK	Wm	PTE	29 / 39	46 KINGS STREET	SOUTHMOOR	23/9/15	21/9/16	GSW	SEPT 16		TO 22nd BN, DEPOT.	WND R ARM.
BEEVERS	Frank	PTE	29 / 572		HUDDERSFIELD			7/10/17			TO GREEN HOWARDS(8th BN).	GREEN HOWARDS No 42618.
BELL	Geo	PTE	29 / 104		ANNFIELD PLAIN			1/7/16	MISS DEC 16	THIEPVAL MEM	TO 22nd, 23rd BNS.	16 PLATOON D COY 23rd BN.
BELL	Geo	PTE	29 / 107	22 FRY STREET	BEARPARK	27/10/15		1/7/16	MISS DEC 16	THIEPVAL MEM	TO 23rd BN(C COY).	AGE 36, BORN WARDLEY.
BELL	J W	PTE	29 / 208	BAGNELLS COTTAGES	WHICKHAM						TO 20th BN, DURHAM LI(13th BN).	DURHAM LI No 46041.
BELL	Randl	PTE	29 / 47		WHITLEY BAY			1/7/16	MISS DEC 16	THIEPVAL MEM	TO 20th, 23rd BNS.	
BENNION	PERCY	RSM	29 / 893								TO 1/5th, 17th BNS, CLASS Z RESERVE.	
BENSON	Robt	PTE	29 / 12		SOUTH SHIELDS			12/2/17			TO KINGS OWN YORKSHIRE LI(2nd BN).	KOYLI No 42355.
BINNS	Geo H	PTE	29 / 539		WILLESDEN			4/10/17			TO 22nd, 12/13th BNS.	
BLACK	JohnG	PTE	29 / 70		WESTMOOR			20/6/17		BAILLEUL RD EAST CEM	TO 20th BN.	AGE 42. ON 20th BN ROLL AS 2nd GARRISON BN.
BLAIR	Geo	PTE	29 /1713	28 EAST STREET	GATESHEAD	30/8/15	24/4/18	DEBILITY	MISSING 27/5/18		TO 3rd BN.	
BLAKENEY	Jos	PTE	29 / 100	16 MITCHELL STREET	RYTON						TO 12/13th(D COY), 11th BNS, CLASS Z RESERVE.	
BRADLEY	Lewis	PTE	29 / 570		HUDDERSFIELD			9/11/18			TO 22nd, 12/13th BNS.	
BRENNAN	JohnW	SGT	29 / 190	7 ARCHER ST KINGS X	HALIFAX			14/10/16		HALIFAX STONEY ROAD C	TO 33rd BN, 84th TRAINING RESERVE BN.	TRAINING RESERVE No TR/5/56977, AGE 41.
BRIER	Percy	PTE	29 / 607		HALIFAX			2/10/17			TO DURHAM LI(15th BN).	DURHAM LI No 53761.
BRIGGS	EllS	PTE	29 / 427	983 TUNCLIFFE	BRADFORD			3/12/18		TERLINCTHUN MIL CEM	TO 20th, 9th, 10th, 1st BNS.	AGE 35 BORN SHELF YORKS.
BROADHEAD	Edmd	PTE	29 / 695			20/6/16	23/8/16	SICK			TO 33rd BN.	DID NOT SERVE OVERSEAS.
BROWN	John	PTE	29									AWOL 29/5/15.
BROWN	Wm	PTE	29 / 959			9/12/15	11/8/16	KR para 392			TO 33rd BN.	DID NOT SERVE OVERSEAS.
BUCKLEY	Jas I	PTE	29 / 612		HUDDERSFIELD			14/10/17			TO 22nd, 12th, 12/13th BNS.	
BULL	RobtW	CSM	29 / 224								TO 12/13th, 1st BNS, CLASS Z RESERVE.	
BUNKER	RichJ	PTE	29 /1182		GOSFORTH			26/8/18		GROVETOWN CEM	TO YORK & LANCASTER REGIMENT(2/4th BN).	Y&L No 57699.
BURGESS	Brook	PTE	29 / 652	3 SPARKS RD LINDLEY	HUDDERSFIELD			10/11/16			TO 23rd, 9th BNS.	AGE 19.
BURN	John	PTE	29 / 77	7 HEDGEHOPE TERR	E CHEVINGTON			27/9/18			TO 25th, 1st BNS.	BORN BROOMHILL NTHBLD.
BURNS	Geo	PTE	29 / 95		HEBBURN	19/10/15	11/8/17	GSW	SEPT 16		TO 23rd BN, DEPOT.	AGE 21.
BURNS	Wm	PTE	29 / 117		HEBBURN				DEC 16		TO 21st BN, CLASS Z RESERVE.	
CAMPBELL	Edw G	CPL	29 / 231		SOUTH SHIELDS			KR para 392	MARCH 17		TO 21st, 11th BNS.	
CAMPBELL	Wm	PTE	29 / 230		SOUTH SHIELDS			7/8/16		THIEPVAL MEM	TO 21st, 11th BNS.	
CARTER	Wm	PTE	29 / 174		WEST BROMWICH			17/2/17		BOULOGNE EASTERN CEM	TO YORK & LANCASTER REGT(6th BN), NF(23rd BN).	Y&L No 12642.
CAWTHORPE	Clem	CPL	29 / 244		NEWCASTLE			KR para 392	MARCH 17		TO 20th, 9th BNS.	
CHARLESWORTH	Stan	SGT	29 / 655								TO 2nd, 12/13th BNS.	
CHIPPENDALE	WaltN	PTE	29 / 883								TO 24/27th BN, MACHINE GUN CORPS(34th BN).	MGC No 152012.
CLARE	Wm	PTE	29 /1027		BILSTON STAFFS			26/7/17			TO WEST YORKSHIRE REGIMENT(2nd BN).	W YORKS No 41071.
CLARKSON	Harry	PTE	29 / 575		HUDDERSFIELD			4/10/17			TO 22nd, 12/13th BNS.	
CLOUGH	Sam	PTE	29 / 397	4 MADDOCK STREET	SHIPLEY			24/6/17		ARRAS MEM	TO 20th, 9th BNS.	BORN SELKIRK.
CLOUGH	Will	PTE	29 / 285								TO 20th, 9th, 25th BNS, KINGS OWN YORKSHIRE LI(2/4t	KOYLI No 63271.
COCKCROFT	Arth	CPL	29 / 487		HALIFAX				JAN 18		TO 20th, 9th, 23rd BNS, CLASS Z RESERVE.	
COLDWELL	Arth	PTE	29 / 701		HUDDERSFIELD			9/11/17		WANCOURT	TO 23rd, 9th, 20th BNS.	BORN MELTHAM YORKS.
COLLINSON	Stan	CPL	29 / 1		NEWCASTLE				JUNE 17		TO 9th BN, CLASS Z RESERVE.	
COOK	Ernst	PTE	29 / 573			11/12/15	31/1/19	GSW			TO 23rd, 9th, 24/27th, 19th BNS.	AGE 34.
COOPER	Fred	PTE	29 / 435		QUEENSBURY			2/7/17	MISSING NOV 17		TO 20th, 9th BNS.	
CRAIG	James	CPL	29 /1227			8/2/16	21/3/19	KR para 392			TO 2nd, 12/13th BNS, ARMY RESERVE CLASS P.	
CRAVEN	Renny	PTE	29 / 432		BRADFORD			14/4/18		NEIUPORT MEM	TO 9th BN.	
CRAVEN	Wm	CPL	29 / 489								TO 20th, 9th, 18th, 23rd, 19th BNS, CLASS Z RESERVE.	DID NOT SERVE OVERSEAS.
CRESWELL	H	CPL	29 / 488									
CROWE	Wm	PTE	29 / 30	HOME FARM	OTTERBURN	18/11/15	20/11/15	UNFIT			TO 20th BN.	BORN MANNINGHAM YORKS.
CUNNINGHAM	Dan	PTE	29 / 436		BRADFORD			24/3/18		ETAPLES MIL CEM	TO 20th, 9th BNS.	
CURRIE	Donld	CPL	29 / 183		JARROW	13/12/15	9/1/18	GSW	APRIL, AUG, SEPT 16.		TO 8th, 16th BNS, KINGS OWN YORKSHIRE LI(8th BN).	AGE 35.
DAVIDSON	Wm	LCPL	29 / 79								TO 20th BN, CLASS Z RESERVE.	
DAVIS	James	PTE	29									AWOL 25/9/15.
DAVIS	Robt	PTE	29 / 145	27 LANDSDOWNE TERR	NORTH SHIELDS			1/7/16	WND+MISSING DE·	THIEPVAL MEM	TO 23rd BN.	AGE 20.

Surname	Forename	Rank	Number	Address	Place	Date A	Date B	Cause	Casualty	Memorial/Cemetery	Service / Transfer	Notes
DEPLIDGE	Chas	LCPL	29 / 437								TO 9th, 1st GARRISON BNS, CLASS Z RESERVE.	
DIXON	David	PTE	29 / 62		HARTFORD COLL	7/10/16			DEC 16, MISS FEB	NIEUPORT MEM	TO 20th BN, ATTACHED DURHAM LI(13th BN).	
DONALD	ThosR	PTE	29									
DONNACHIE	James	PTE	29 / 43									AWOL 6/10/15
DOUGAL	Sam	PTE	29 / 36								TO 11th BN, CLASS Z RESERVE.	
DOWDS	Henry	PTE	29 /1252		ROTHESAY BUTE	10/8/16				GREENOCK CEM	TO 11th, 8th, 14th BNS, CLASS Z RESERVE.	
DUFFIELD	Walt	PTE	29 / 490		TODMORDEN				APR 17, NOV 18.			
DUNCAN	Wm	PTE	29 / 159	11 COACH ROAD	WALLSEND	1/7/16			MISSING DEC 16	THIEPVAL MEM	TO 20th, 9th, 18th BNS, CLASS Z RESERVE.	BORN HEBBURN, AGE 34.
DURRANS	Geo	PTE	29 / 287	7 KING ST LINDLEY	HUDDERSFIELD	9/11/16					TO 23rd BN.	AGE 32.
DYSON	Edwin	PTE	29 / 239		BAILIFFBRIDGE	10/4/18					TO 9th BN.	
DYSON	Hubt	PTE	29 / 438		SALTBURN	19/4/18					TO 23rd, 9th, 16th, 1/4th(C COY) BNS.	
DYSON	Hylt	PTE	29 / 148		SLAITHWAITE	19/10/17				FONCQUEVILLERS	TO 20th, 9th, 14th, 1/7th BNS.	BORN HUDDERSFIELD
DYSON	Percy	PTE	29 / 828		LINDLEY YORKS	31/10/17					TO GREEN HOWARDS(8th BN).	GREEN HOWARDS No 42643.
EARNSHAW	Will	PTE	29 / 257							KIRECHKOL-HORTAKOI MII	TO BORDER REGIMENT(9th BN).	BORDER REGT No 32146. AGE 39.
ECCLES	Percy	PTE	29 / 442								TO 1st, 23rd, 1/5th BNS, CLASS Z RESERVE.	
EDWARDS	Thos	PTE	29 / 75	49 CHEVINGTON CRES	MORPETH	5/6/17			NOV 16	ARRAS MEM	TO 9th, 22nd BNS, CLASS Z RESERVE.	
ELLIOTT	Arth	PTE	29 / 704		HALIFAX	10/7/17					TO 11th, 22nd BNS.	BORN BROOMHILL.
ENGLAND	JoHN	PTE	29 / 441								TO KINGS OWN YORKSHIRE LI(2nd BN).	KOYLI No 42362.
EXON	Jas E	PTE	29 / 433		BRADFORD	4/11/16				THIEPVAL MEM	TO 9th BN, CLASS Z RESERVE.	
FAIRLAMB	Septi	PTE	29 / 169		ALLENDALE	17/11/16				ST SEVER CEM ROUEN	TO 9th BN.	AGE 36.
FARRELL	James	PTE	29 / 10			16/9/15	28/10/17	SICK			TO 23rd BN, 84th TRAINING RESERVE BN.	AGE 41.
FENWICK	Robt	PTE	29 / 177		NEWCASTLE				DEC 16			DESERTED 25/11/16.
FISHER	Tom	PTE	29 / 291	9 SAVILLE STREET	NORTH SHIELDS	28/10/15	26/10/16	KR para 392	AUGUST 16		TO 20th, 9th BNS, CLASS Z RESERVE.	
FLOOD	James	PTE	29 / 109	27 PETERBOROUGH PL	BRADFORD		9/4/18			NEIUPORT MEM	TO 23rd BN.	
FOGDEN	Frank	PTE	29 / 447			18/10/15	31/3/17	MENTALLY ILL			TO 20th, 9th BNS.	AGE 27.
FOOTS	John	PTE	29 / 92								TO DEPOT.	AWOL 1/11,13/11/15,AGE 25,R VIC HOSP NETLEY 11/7/16.
FORREST	Fred	PTE	29 / 59		NEWCASTLE	1/7/16			MISSING NOV 16	THIEPVAL MEM	TO 21st BN.	BORN GATESHEAD.
FORSTER	John	PTE	29 / 83	10 OAK STREET	HEBBURN	1/7/16			MISSING DEC 16	THIEPVAL MEM	TO 23rd BN(C COY).	AGE 18.
FOSTER	Andrw	PTE	29									
FRANCIS	Fred	PTE	29 / 256		LINTHWAITE				APRIL 17			AWOL 25/9/15
GARDINER	James	PTE	29 / 55	61 BIRCHAM STREET	SOUTHMOOR				MISS OCT 16, WND DEC 16.		TO ROYAL DEFENCE CORPS	RDC No 65362.
GARNETT	Geo	PTE	29 / 449								TO 22nd BN.	
GOLDTHORPE	Irv	PTE	29 / 583		HUDDERSFIELD	15/5/16	29/11/18	GSW	JULY 18		TO 20th, 9th, 25th, 23rd BNS, K OWN YORKSHIRE LI(5th	KOYLI No 63146.
GORDON	Wm	PTE	29								TO 23rd, 9th, 13th BNS, DEPOT.	AGE 30.
GORE	Elias	LCPL	29 / 908		ACCRINGTON	16/8/17						AWOL 11/10/15.
GRAHAM	Edwd	PTE	29 / 94	22 WEAR STREET	SOUTHWICK	18/10/15	12/10/17	SICK	OCT 16		TO WEST YORKSHIRE REGIMENT(2nd BN).	W YORKS No 41074.
GRAHAM	John	PTE	29 / 3	15 CANNON STREET	NEWCASTLE		23/10/17	SICK			TO 23rd, 16th, 3rd BNS.	AWOL 13/11/15.
GRAHAM	Jos	PTE	29 / 72	CLESKETT HOLME	BRAMPTON CUMB	1/7/16			MISSING NOV 16	THIEPVAL MEM	TO 84th TRAINING RESERVE BN.	AGE 40.
GREAVES	Jos	PTE	29 / 451								TO 22nd BN(C COY).	AGE 30.
GREENWOOD	Fred	PTE	29 / 448		QUEENSBURY	9/9/17			JUNE 17	HAGRICOURT BRIT CEM	TO TRG RES BN, KINGS SHROPSHIRE LI, ROYAL ENGI	NF 44296, TRG RES TR/5/56682, KSLI 45704, RE WR/550354.
GREENWOOD	Wilf	PTE	29 / 705								TO 9th, 20th, 12th BNS.	
GREENWOOD	Wm J	PTE	29 /1077			13/1/16	31/8/16	KR para 392			TO 23rd, 9th BNS, CLASS Z RESERVE.	DID NOT SERVE OVERSEAS.
HAIGH	EdwnH	PTE	29 / 623								TO 23rd, 9th, 24th, 24/27th, 12/13th BNS, CLASS Z RESERVE.	
HAIGH	Harld	PTE	29 / 955		SOWERBY BRIDGE	15/4/17					TO KINGS OWN YORKSHIRE LI(2nd BN).	KOYLI No 42371.
HALL	ChasE	PTE	29 / 52			KR para 392					TO 23rd, 1/7th, 1/4th, 12/13th BNS.	BEAUFORT HOSP CHELTENHAM 8/7/16, RENUMBERED 292104.
HALL	J H L	PTE	29 /1218		SHIPLEY	20/9/17					TO GREEN HOWARDS(8th BN).	GREEN HOWARDS No 42646.
HALL	Jos	PTE	29 / 106	2 ROSE BANK	WEST KYO	1/7/16			MISSING DEC 16	THIEPVAL MEM	TO 23rd BN(D COY).	AGE 26
HALLIDAY	Fred	PTE	29 / 616	15 LANGDAKLE STREET	ELLAND	15/10/18				HIGHLAND CEM LE CATEA	TO 2nd BN.	AGE 20 BORN HALIFAX.
HARRISON	Wm	PTE	29 / 219			24/1/16	28/7/16	EPILEPSY			TO DEPOT.	AGE 28 SERVED OVERSEAS.
HARRISON	Wm	PTE	29 / 215			KR para 392						
HARTLEY	Percy	PTE	29 / 496		BRADFORD	3/5/16	23/1/19	GSW	DEC 17		TO 20th, 9th, 16th BNS.	AGE 27.
HEALEY	Herbt	PTE	29 / 543		BROUGHTON YORKS	24/7/17					TO MACHINE GUN CORPS.	MGC No 58681.
HEBDEN	Robt	PTE	29 / 618		BARNOLDSWICK	2/4/17				ARRAS MEM	TO 22nd, 12th BNS.	
HEELEY	Harld	PTE	29 / 660								TO 20th, 9th BNS, CLASS Z RESERVE.	
HENDERSON	Robt	PTE	29 / 60			30/9/15	5/7/18	KR para 392			TO 30th BN(TYNESIDE IRISH RES).	DID NOT SERVE OVERSEAS.
HEWITT	Rich	PTE	29 / 38			KR para 392					TO 21st BN, DURHAM LIGHT INFANTRY, TRAINING RES	TRG RES No TR/5/41476.
HINCHCLIFF	Fred	PTE	29 /1031		HUDDERSFIELD	16/4/17					TO WEST YORKSHIRE REGIMENT(2nd BN).	W YORKS No 41076.
HINCHCLIFFE	J	PTE	29 / 838	HILL HEAD	HONLEY YORKS	15/8/16				HONLEY CH YD YORKS	TO 33rd BN.	AGE 38.
HINNELLS	Albt	PTE	29 / 497			3/5/16	21/6/18	KR para 392			TO 9th, 27th, 24/27th BNS, DEPOT.	
HODGSON	Peter	PTE	29 / 454	HILL TOP WENNINGTON	LANCASTER	17/2/17			JUNE 17	GROVETOWN CEM	TO 20th, 9th BNS.	BORN WHITTINGTON WESTMORELAND AGE 25.
HOLDSWORTH	Duke	PTE	29 / 495			3/5/16		VDH			TO 20th, 9th BNS.	
HOLLAND	Jos J	PTE	29 / 5		CRAMLINGTON	4/6/16				ALBERT COM CEM EXT	TO 20th BN.	AGE 26.
HOLROYD	Arth	PTE	29 /1402		TONG YORKS	20/1/17						DIED HOME.
HOLT	Harry	PTE	29 / 294								TO 20th, 12th, 12/13th/ 1/7th BNS, CLASS Z RESERVE.	
HOWARD	Wm	PTE	29 / 207								TO 21st, 11th BNS.	DESERTED 4/5/19.
HUMBLE	ThosW	PTE	29 / 76		HAMSTERLEY	KR para 392			AUGUST 16		TO 23rd BN.	
HUNTER	JohnS	PTE	29 / 152		NORTH SHIELDS	5/6/17				ARRAS MEM	TO 22nd BN.	BORN TYNEMOUTH AGE 24.
HUNTER	JohnT	PTE	29 / 146		NORTH SHIELDS				JUNE 16		TO 22nd BN.	DESERTED 21/7/17.
HUNTER	Wm	PTE	29 / 150		NEWCASTLE	4/8/16			MISS NOV 16	THIEPVAL MEM	ATTACHED DURHAM LI(13th BN), 21st(A COY) BN NF.	AGE 34.
HUTCHINSON	Percy	PTE	29 / 494			3/4/16	27/6/16	SICK			TO 33rd BN.	DID NOT SERVE OVERSEAS.
INGHAM	Arth	PTE	29 / 778		SKIPTON	2/11/17					TO DURHAM LI(15th BN).	DURHAM LI No 201231.
IRVINE	John	PTE	29 / 209			3/9/14	18/10/16	SICK			TO DEPOT.	AGE 47.
IVES	Walt	PTE	29 / 544		ELSHOT YORKS	14/8/18					TO EAST YORKSHIRE REGIMENT(7th BN).	E YORKS No 37861.
JAAP	Wm	SGT	29 /1295								TO TRAINING RESERVE BN, ATT 1st WEST AFRICAN FI	TRAINING RESERVE No TR/5/56092.
JACKSON	Edwin	CPL	29 / 90	96 GILL STREET	BENWELL	16/10/15	31/7/16			ALBERT COM CEM EXT	TO 21st, 11th BNS.	
JACKSON	Frank	PTE	29 / 457						MISSING 20-21/3/18		TO 23rd(B COY), 9th, 10th BNS, CLASS Z RESERVE.	
JACKSON	Frank	PTE	29 / 296								TO 20th, 9th BNS, CLASS Z RESERVE.	
JACKSON	Freem	PTE	29 /1060		TODMORDEN	11/4/18					TO 1/4th BN.	
JAMES	Alf	PTE	29 / 404		LEEK	29/2/16	25/2/19	KR para 392	DEC 17		TO DEPOT.	
JESSOP	Fredy	LCPL	29 / 504								TO 20th, 9th, 10th BNS, CLASS Z RESERVE.	
JOHNSON	Forst	CPL	29 / 138		WARDEN LAW	10/10/17					TO KINGS OWN YORKSHIRE LI(1/4th BN).	KOYLI No 203480.
JOHNSON	H	LCPL	29 / 228								TO 20th BN, DURHAM LI(13th BN).	DURHAM LI No 45992.
JOHNSON	Wm		29									AWOL 21/9/15.
JONES	Henry	PTE	29 / 16	14 MAFEEN TERRACE	NEWBIGGIN / SEA						TO 2nd GARRISON BN, CLASS Z RESERVE.	
JOWETT	Sam	PTE	29 / 716		HALIFAX	26/5/18					TO DURHAM LI(1/5th BN).	DURHAM LI No 44872.
JOWETT	Thorn	PTE	29 / 406		HALIFAX	3/11/16				THIEPVAL MEM	TO 9th BN.	
JUDSON	Thos	PTE	29 / 458		HALIFAX	23/3/18					TO 20th, 9th, 23rd(C COY) BNS.	
KELLETT	Ernst	PTE	29 / 458		NEWCASTLE						TO 9th BN, ROYAL FLYING CORPS.	
KERRIGAN	J	PTE	29 / 201		NEWCASTLE							
KERRISON	Thos	PTE	29 / 68		HEBBURN	10/1/19					TO 23rd, 20th, 10th BNS.	
KING	Fr l	PTE	29 / 505		NOCKBRIDGE	23/4/17				CABERET ROUGE MIL CEM	TO 20th, 9th BNS.	AGE 26.
KITSON	Arth	PTE	29 / 330		ELLAND YORKS	3/4/17					TO KINGS OWN YORKSHIRE LI(2nd BN).	KOYLI No 42397.
KNAPTON	Fred	PTE	29 / 374	21 CHAPER STREET	BRADFORD	5/6/17				ARRAS MEM	TO 9th, 19th, 22nd BNS.	BORN YORK.
KNOX	James	LCPL	29 / 74		INVERKEITHING				SEPT 16		TO 22nd, 11th BNS, CLASS Z RESERVE.	
LANCASTER	Walt	PTE	29 / 299								TO 9th, 27th BNS, CLASS Z RESERVE.	
LAWS	Thos	PTE	29 / 116	34 VICTORIA PLACE	NEWCASTLE	28/10/15	1/7/16		NOV 16, MISS DEC	THIEPVAL MEM	TO 23rd BN(D COY).	
LAYCOCK	Seth	PTE	29 / 725		COWLING YORKS	26/4/18					TO KINGS OWN YORKSHIRE LI(9th BN).	KOYLI No 42368.
LEA	ThosE	SGT	29 /1028	14 LAKE STREET	BRADFORD	3/7/17				SALONIKA ANGLO FRENCH	TO BORDER REGIMENT(9th BN), ATT 60 FLD AMB RAM	BORDER REGT No 32233. AGE 31, BORN ABERGAVENNY.
LEIGHTLEY	Anthy	SGT	29 / 51			KR para 392					TO 20th BN.	
LIVSEY	Fred	PTE	29 / 512								TO 23rd BN, CLASS Z RESERVE.	
LOCKWOOD	Vic	PTE	29 / 508		KIRKBURTON YKS	3/6/17				DRURY CRUCIFIX CEM	TO 20th, 9th, 1st BNS.	AGE 22.
LODGE	Frank	SGT	29 / 864								TO 18th BN, COMMISSIONED 29/9/18 WEST RIDING REGT.	
LOFTHOUSE	Wm H	CPL	29 /1688	GILESGATE	DURHAM CITY	5/7/16	1/7/16			ST NICHOLAS' CH YD DURI	TO SERV BN TS, 34th DIV CYC COY, 24th BN.TI No 24/1	BORN LANGLEY MOOR, DIED ON BOARD HOSP SHIP ST GEORGE.
LONGBOTTOM	Sam	SGT	29 / 376								TO 23rd, 9th, 8th 26th, 23rd BNS, LABOUR CORPS.	RENUMBERED 79345, LAB CORPS No 632430, STILL SERVING 5/21
LONGFIELD	Harry	SGT	29 / 970								TO 12/13th BN.	
LUND	Albt	PTE	29 / 511								TO 20th, 19th, 8th BNS, CLASS Z RESERVE.	
MAIN	Jas	LCPL	29 / 87	18 WOOD STREET	HEBBURN COLL	14/10/15	20/2/18	GSW	OCT 16		TO DEPOT.	BEAUFORT HOSP BRISTOL 8/7/16, AGE 32.
MANN	Wm H	PTE	29 /1204		ROTHERHAM	24/5/17					TO WEST YORKSHIRE REGIMENT(1st BN).	W YORKS No 235275.
MARSHALL	Percy	PTE	29 / 464	193 ROCHDALE RD	TODMORDEN	26/12/16				THIEPVAL MEM	TO 20th, 9th BNS.	AGE 22.
MASKILL	J	PTE	29 /1258								TO 8th, 27th BNS, ROYAL DEFENCE CORPS.	
MAXFIELD	Colin	PTE	29 / 516								TO 9th BN, CLASS Z RESERVE.	
MAXWELL	Chas	PTE	29									AWOL 15/12/15.
McANDREWS	Philp	LCPL	29 / 632		PORTURLIN	16/5/16		KR para 392	APRIL 17		TO 22nd BN, DEPOT.	
McGRANE	Jos E	CPL	29 /1084								TO 1st BN, CLASS Z RESERVE.	
McGRORY	Wm	PTE	29 / 220	43 THOMAS STREET	WEST HARTLEPOOL	5/6/17			DEC 16		TO 20th BN, ATTACHED DURHAM LI, 20th BN NF.	WND ATTACHED DLI.
McKIE	Wm	PTE	29 / 162								TO 9th, 14th BNS, CLASS Z RESERVE.	
McPHERSON	Duncn	PTE	29 /1306		SHIELFOOT ARGYL	29/5/17				SALONIKA	FROM ROYAL GARRISON ARTILLERY, TO BORDER RE	HAD SERVED WITH 2/1st MOUNTAIN BATTERY RGA.
MELLOR	Geo A	PTE	29 / 631	38 VICTORIA INN	HOLMEFIRTH	18/10/18					TO 23rd, 9th, 1st, 12/13th BNS.	AGE 31.
MELLOR	Luthr	PTE	29 / 517			KR para 392			MISSING 21/3/18		TO 9th, 22nd(D COY) BNS.	
METCALFE	Hubt	PTE	29 / 630								TO 23rd, 9th BNS, CLASS Z RESERVE.	
MIDDLETON	Irvin	PTE	29 / 518	48 DARTON STREET	BRADFORD	25/10/18				AWOINGT BRIT CEM	TO 9th BN.	AGE 22.

Surname	Forename	Rank	No.	Address	Place	Enlist	Disch	Cause	Period	Memorial	Transferred To / Notes
MILNER	Dan	PTE	29 / 461		QUEENSBURY						TO 9th, 26th, 22nd BNS, CLASS Z RESERVE.
MILNES	Harry	LCPL	29 / 633		HUDDERSFIELD				4/10/17		TO 22nd, 12th, 12/13th BNS.
MINNIKIN	Alb E	PTE	29 / 516								TO 3rd, 9th, 12/13th, 8th BNS.
MITCHELL	Fost	PTE	29 / 462		ELLAND				9/11/16	MARCH 17, JUNE 1 THIEPVAL MEM	TO 20th, 9th BNS.
MITCHELL	Sydn	PTE	29 / 514		BRADFORD				21/10/17	DOZINGHEM MIL CEM	TO 20th, 9th 25th BNS.
MOLLOY	Frncs	PTE	29 / 173								TO 20th BN, DURHAM LI(13th BN). DURHAM LI No 45995.
MOORE	F	PTE	29 / 552								TO 25th, 1st BNS, ROYAL DEFENCE CORPS. IN FRANCE 25th 17/1/18-20/1/18, 1st 21/1/18-25/3/18
MORRIS	Harld	PTE	29 /1164		HEBBURN COLL	6/12/15	23/8/16	MITRAL DIS			TO 33rd BN. DID NOT SERVE OVERSEAS.
MOSS	Hubt	LCPL	29 / 271		HUDDERSFIELD	14/4/16	20/4/18	GSW	AUGUST 18		TO 20th, 9th, 18th, 22nd BNS, DEPOT. AGE 22.
NADEN	Geo W	PTE	29 / 556			12/5/16	4/12/19	KR para 392			TO 18th, 20th BNS.
NEWCOMBE	Lew J	PTE	29 / 303		HALIFAX				APRIL 18		TO 10th BN, CLASS Z RESERVE. DURHAM LI No 46046.
NIXON	Adam	PTE	29 / 22		COLWELL				25/9/16		TO DURHAM LI(13th BN).
OGDEN	Wilf	PTE	29 / 465								TO 20th, 9th, 24th, 8th, 1st, 14th BNS, CLASS Z RESERVE.
PARKER	James	PTE	29 / 993	DUKE STREET	SETTLE				6/7/18	SALONIKA ANGLO FRENCH	TO BORDER REGIMENT(9th BN, B COY). BORDER REGT No 32179. AGE 32
PARKIN	Edgar	PTE	29 / 730		RIPONDEN				MAY 18		TO 11th BN, CLASS Z RESERVE.
PAVIOUR	Harld	PTE	29 / 339		HUDDERSFIELD				23/3/18		TO MACHINE GUN CORPS(47th BN MGC). MGC No 44351.
PEAKE	Clem	PTE	29 / 557		KEIGHLEY	5/12/15	3/5/18	GSW	APRIL 17		TO 9th BN, DEPOT. AGE 26.
PEARS	Thos	PTE	29 / 313			9/11/14	4/8/16	SICK			DID NOT SERVE OVERSEAS. AGE 27.
PEARSON	Fred	PTE	29 / 520			3/5/16	3/10/17	SICK			TO 20th, 9th, 3rd BNS.
PEARSON	Geo H	PTE	29 / 593					KR para 392			TO 23rd, 9th, 13th BNS.
PEARSON	Morrs	PTE	29 / 634	OUTLANE	HUDDERSFIELD				25/9/17	MENDINGHEM MIL CEM	TO 23rd, 9th, 1st BNS.
PEARSON	ThosS	PTE	29 / 341								TO 9th, 21st, 25th, 12/13th BNS, CLASS Z RESERVE.
PENNINGTON	Ward	PTE	29 / 409	26 INDEPENDANT STREE	BRADFORD				3/10/18	KIRECHKOL -HORTAKOI MI	TO BORDER REGIMENT(9th BN). BORDER REGT No 32242. AGE 27.
PETYT	Henry	PTE	29 / 466	39 STANLEY ROAD	BRADFORD				4/2/18	CHOQUES MIL CEM	TO 20th, 9th, 24th, 8th BNS. AGE 27.
PICKLES	Fred	PTE	29 / 280		HALIFAX	11/12/15	20/11/17	SICK	MAY 17		TO 20th, 9th, 3rd BNS. GREEN HOWARDS No 42617.
PODGSON	Staff	PTE	29 / 732		GOLCAR			2/7/17			TO GREEN HOWARDS(8th BN). DURHAM LI No 45996.
PRESSLIE	Kieth	PTE	29 / 15								TO 20th BN, DURHAM LI(13th BN).
RAMSDEN	Ernst	PTE	29 / 525		HALIFAX				4/11/16	THIEPVAL MEM	TO 20th, 9th BNS. AGE 21.
RAWLINGS	John	PTE	29 / 84		JARROW	11/10/15	14/3/18	GSW	DEC 16		TO ARMY RESERVE CLASS W. BOR BRIGHOUSE.
RAWNSLEY	Arth	PTE	29 / 524		HALIFAX				3/11/16	MISSING MARCH 1 THIEPVAL MEM	TO 20th, 9th BNS. AGE 38.
REED	John	PTE	29 / 161	137 DURHAM STREET	NEWCASTLE				7/7/16	WIMEREUX COM CEM EXT	TO 23rd BN.
RIDSDALE	Geo	PTE	29 / 535					KR para 392			TO 20th, 9th, 21st, 25th BNS.
RILEY	Wm	PTE	29 / 523		BRADFORD				NOV 18		TO 20th, 9th, 11th BNS, CLASS Z RESERVE.
ROBINSON	Leo C	PTE	29 / 637								TO 9th, 21st, 1st, 12/13th BNS, CLASS Z RESERVE.
ROBINSON	Tom	CPL	29 / 671								TO 12/13th, 1st BNS, CLASS Z RESERVE.
ROGERS	JohnW	PTE	29 / 595		LOTHERSDALE				9/4/17	ARRAS MEM	TO 23rd, 21st(A COY) BNS.
ROWELL	HughF	PTE	29 / 193	SOUTHWARD HSE	BURNHOPEFIELD				1/7/16	MISSING DEC 16 THIEPVAL MEM	TO 23rd BN. AGE 20.
RUSBY	John	PTE	29 / 559		DENHOLME YORKS				28/8/18		TO KINGS OWN YORKSHIRE LI(2/4th BN). KOYLI No 63327.
SANDERSON	Arth	PTE	29 / 561		GUISLEY			KR para 392	MAY 17		TO 23rd, 9th, 1st BNS.
SAXTON	John	PTE	29 / 412								TO 9th BN, CLASS Z RESERVE.
SCOTT	John	SGT	29 / 13		BEDLINGTON				9/4/17	HENIN FARM BRIT CEM	TO 20th BN.
SCOTT	Syd	PTE	29 / 192		NEWCASTLE			KR para 392	SEPT 16		TO 23rd, 10th, 11th BNS.
SCULLION	Dan	PTE	29 / 34		BLYTH				23/12/16	INDIA	TO 2nd GARRISON BN.
SCULLION	John	PTE	29 / 81	13 FIR STREET	HEBBURN				1/7/16	MISSING DEC 16 THIEPVAL MEM	TO 23rd BN(C COY). AGE 19.
SENIOR	Norm	PTE	29 / 249			15/4/16	23/8/16	SICK			TO 33rd BN. DID NOT SERVE OVERSEAS.
SHACKLETON	John	PTE	29 / 384		MIDGLEY				24/3/18		TO EAST YORKSHIRE REGIMENT(7th BN). E YORKS No 37852.
SHAW	Walt	PTE	29 / 472		STOCKPORT	1/5/16	15/10/17	WOUNDS	MARCH 17		TO 1st BN, DEPOT.
SHEARD	Percy	LCPL	29 / 385		MIRFIELD				3/10/18		TO GREEN HOWARDS(1/5th BN). GREEN HOWARDS No 42620.
SHIELDS	Wm	PTE	29 / 114	12 MANOR CHARE	NEWCASTLE	28/10/15			JULY 16,SS DEC 16,MISS 21		TO 22nd BN(D COY), CLASS Z RESERVE.
SHOESMITH	Geo	PTE	29 / 473		SOWERBY BRIDGE				11/4/18		TO 20th, 26th, 9th BNS.
SHUTT	Wm S	PTE	29 / 849			12/12/15	2/6/19	KR para 392			TO 1/4th BN, DEPOT.
SINGLETON	Joe	PTE	29 / 673								TO 23rd, 9th BNS, CLASS Z RESERVE.
SMEE	Archi	PTE	29								AWOL 17/12/15
SMITH	Jas W	PTE	29 / 32		ANNFIELD PLAIN				28/3/18		TO DURHAM LI(1/9th BN). DURHAM LI No 46032.
SMITH	Jos	PTE	29 / 777		KEIGHLEY				11/2/17		TO KINGS OWN YORKSHIRE LI(2nd BN). KOYLI No 42377.
SMITH	Wilf	PTE	29 / 424			27/4/16	31/8/16	ALBUMINURE			DID NOT SERVE OVERSEAS.
SMITHIES	Joe H	PTE	29 / 735		HUDDERSFIELD				23/1/17		TO GREEN HOWARDS(7th BN). GREEN HOWARDS No 42657.
SPEIGHT	H	CPL	29 / 640								TO 20th, 9th BNS.
STEAD	Jos	PTE	29 / 243	4 ALBERT ST HILL TOP	BRADFORD				16/4/17	ARRAS MEM	TO 9th BN.
STEPHENSON	Albt	PTE	29 / 123	22 ROBERT STREET	NEWCASTLE				JULY 18.		TO YORK & LANCASTER REGIMENT(2/4th BN). Y&L No 35625.
STEPHENSON	Walt	PTE	29 / 124		NEWCASTLE				22/11/17		
STOREY	JohnJ	PTE	29 / 119	34 STRACHAN STREET	NEWCASTLE				5/6/17	ARRAS MEM	ATTACHED DURHAM LI(13th BN), TO 12th BN NF. AGE 26, TRUE NAME Herbert LOUGHLIN.
STRINGER	Nelsn	PTE	29 / 678		HILLHOUSE				14/9/17	HAGRICOURT BRIT CEM	TO 23rd, 9th BNS. BORN ALMONDSBURY.
SUMMERHILL	Sam	LCPL	29 / 89	48 COCHRANE STREET	BENWELL	16/10/15	27/3/18	GSW	NOV 18		TO 12th, 20th BNS, DEPOT. AGE 29.
SUTCLIFFE	Herbt	PTE	29 / 247		BRADFORD				MARCH 17		TO 20th, 9th, 14th BNS, CLASS Z RESERVE.
SUTCLIFFE	JohnW	PTE	29 / 736								TO 23rd, 9th, 21st, 25th BNS, CLASS Z RESERVE.
SYKES	Geo	LCPL	29 / 476		BARNOLDSWICK				28/6/17	AUBIGNY COM CEM EXT	TO 20th, 9th BNS. BORN SOUTHRAM YORKS AGE 27.
SYME	Wm	LCPL	29 / 58			28/9/15	8/11/18	GSW			TO 20th, 9th, 1/6th BNS, DEPOT. AGE 31.
TAIT	John	PTE	29 / 218				18/4/19				TO 23rd BN, DURHAM LI(12th BN), YORK & LANCASTER CLASS Z RESERVE. Y&L No 55833.
TALLENTIRE	John	PTE	29 / 180		CRAGHEAD				5/11/16		TO KINGS OWN YORKSHIRE LI(1/4th BN). KOYLI No 7136.
TATTERSALL	JohnJ	PTE	29 / 479		ELLAND YORKS				26/9/17		TO 9th, 24th, 1st BNS.
TAYLOR	Fred	PTE	29 / 601		GOLCAR				7/6/17		TO 23rd, 9th, 1st, 11th BNS.
TEAL	Stead	SGT	29 / 564		KEIGHLEY	27/11/15	7/10/18	GSW	NOV 18		TO 18th, 23rd BNS, DEPOT.
THOMAS	Arth	PTE	29 / 168		LLANDUDNO				22/9/16		TO DURHAM LI(13th BN). DURHAM LI No 46008.
THOMPSON	Andrw	PTE	29 / 680		EDINBURGH				27/11/17		TO KINGS OWN YORKSHIRE LI(2nd BN). KOYLI No 42370.
THOMPSON	Thos	PTE	29 / 677								TO 9th, 3rd BNS.
THORNTON	Harry	PTE	29 / 477		BRADFORD	10/12/15	3/5/18	DEAFNESS	MARCH 17		TO 23rd, 9th, 21st BNS, CLASS Z RESERVE. AGE 22.
THORNTON	John	PTE	29 / 681								TO 9th, 1st, 1/4th BNS, CLASS Z RESERVE.
TOLSON	Stan	PTE	29 / 351	16 CHICHESTER RD	KILBURN				1/7/16	THIEPVAL MEM	TO 22nd BN.
TOMLIN	RobtT	CPL	29 / 142						MISSING 28-29/3/18		TO 1st BN, CLASS Z RESERVE.
TWEEDIE	David	LCPL	29 /1312	24 RIVER VIEW	BLACKHALL MILL				25/8/18 SS NOV 16, DEC 1?	VIS-EN-ARTOIS MEM	TO 23rd, 18th, 1st, 12/13th, 1st, 1st, 12/13th BNS. AGE 29.
WALLACE	Alb R	PTE	29 / 64								TO 20th, 9th BNS, CLASS Z RESERVE.
WARBURTON	Willi	CPL	29 / 531								TO 3rd BN.
WARREN	JohnW	PTE	29 / 63			30/9/15	25/4/18	GSW			AWOL 31/8/15.
WATSON	John	PTE	29								AWOL 25/9/15.
WATSON	JohnH	PTE	29								
WATSON	Thos	PTE	29 / 883	1 STANLEY CRES	THIRLWALL						TO 10th BN, AGRICULTRAL COY, WEST YORKS REGT. W YORKS No 48271.
WHITFIELD	Chas	PTE	29 / 423								TO 19th(Z COY), 9th BNS, CLASS Z RESERVE.
WILKINSON	Albt	PTE	29 / 354		HUDDERSFIELD				12/10/17	CEMENT HOUSE CEM LAN	TO 23rd, 9th, 25th BNS.
WILKINSON	Harry	PTE	29 /	28 VICTORIA STREET	LINDLEY HUDDERSFIELD				4/10/17		TO 12/13th BN. RENUMBERED 45920.
WILKINSON	Jos	PTE	29								AWOL 8/10/15, 20/2/16.
WILKINSON	Luthr	PTE	29 /1173		OAKWORTH				16/3/17		TO GREEN HOWARDS(8th BN). GREEN HOWARDS No 42662.
WILLIAMS	John	PTE	29 / 71								TO 20th BN, DURHAM LI(13th BN). DURHAM LI No 45962.
WILLIAMS	JohnW	PTE	29 /1417		BRADFORD				21/7/18	SALONIKA ANGLO FRENCH	TO BORDER REGIMENT(9th BN). BORDER REGT No 32259.
WILSON	Archi	PTE	29 /1247						MISSING 28-29/3/18		TO 1st BN(W COY), CLASS Z RESERVE. DID NOT SERVE OVERSEAS.
WOOD	ThosE	PTE	29 /1199			25/11/15	31/8/16	KR para 392			
WOOD	Verdi	PTE	29 / 686								TO 23rd, 9th, 21st, 11th BNS, CLASS Z RESERVE.
WOODHALL	Sam	PTE	29 / 118					KR Para 392		ALL SAINTS NEWCASTLE	TO LABOUR CORPS(198 LAB COY). LAB CORPS No 118550.
WRIGHT	G	PTE	29 / 44					3/1/19 KR Para 392			TO 12/13th BN.
WRIGHT	Harry	LSGT	29 / 604								TO 23rd, 9th BNS, DEPOT.
WRIGHT	ThosD	PTE	29 / 469		BARNOLDSWICK				7/6/17		TO GREEN HOWARDS(8th BN). GREEN HOWARDS No 42561.
WRIGHTSON	Percy	PTE	29 / 356			30/11/15	21/12/17	SICK			AGE 32.
YOUNG	Nich	CPL	29 / 24	26 CHURCH ROW	HOLYWELL	20/9/15	27/4/18	GSW			TO 9th BN. POSSIBLY POW.

Nominal Rolls

Sources used in compiling Battalion Nominal Rolls

When the work of compiling the battalion nominal rolls was started it was as a hobby, to try and locate as many of the soldiers of the Tyneside Scottish Brigade as possible. When this work became a book, more and more, sources of information were located and used.

Unfortunately Brigadier Ternan did not include nominal rolls in his book about the Tyneside Scottish, therefore the work proved slightly more difficult than that on the Tyneside Irish. The following sources were used:

War Grave Registers, North West Europe, Italy, British Isles, Malta. Published by the Commonwealth War Graves Commission.

Memorials to the Missing registers for, Thiepval, Arras, Tyne Cot, Pozieres, Vise-en-Artois, Nieuport, Soissons, Ploegsteert, Giovera Italy and Kirkee India. Published by the Commonwealth War Graves Commission.

Soldiers Died in the Great War, HMSO re-published 1989. Every volume was consulted, in order to identify men who had been killed or died when serving with other regiments.

Absentee Voters Lists for, Barnard Castle, Bishop Aukland, Blaydon, Chester le Street, Durham City, Houghton Le Spring, Jarrow, Seaham, Sedgefield, Spennymoor, held at Durham County Record Office. Gateshead, Hartlepool, Darlington, Middlesbrough, Newcastle, Held in the various city and town libraries. Hexam shire, Berwickshire, Wansbeck, held at Northumberland County Record Office.

Local Newspapers, recruiting articles and casualty lists, *Alnwick and Northumberland Gazette, County Chronicle, Durham Advertizer, Durham Chronicle, Darlington Evening Despatch, Middlesbrough Evening Gazette, Newcastle Illustrated Chronicle, Newcastle Daily Chronicle, Newcastle Evening Chronicle, Newcastle Journal, Northern Echo, North East Raiway Magazine, North Mail, Northern Daily Mail, Sunderland Echo, South Shields Gazette, St George's Gazette*, the Regimental Journal of the Northumberland Fusiliers. Volumes for 1914, 15, 16, 17, 18, 19, 1920.

Medical Health Records MH/106 PRO Kew, Admission registers for the 3rd and 34th Casualty Clearing Stations and the 2nd and 18th General Hospitals. But not to the extent of Tyneside Irish.

WO/329 PRO Kew First World War.

1914/18 War & Victory Medal Rolls, 1914/15 Star Rolls, Silver War Badge lists, Volumes for many regiments other than the Northumberland Fusiliers were consulted, this enabled large drafts of men to other regiments to be identified. Drafts to the Labour Corps proved difficult owing to the removal of the battalion prefix from the regimental number.

Petty Sessions Registers, for courts in Durham, Newcastle, Sunderland, Gateshead, South Shields, Houghton Le Spring, Blyth, Morpeth, this identified many absentees and deserters who are not mentioned in other sources. Held at County Record Offices in Durham, Tyne and Wear and Northumberland.

Rolls of Honour

Various Battalion, Colliery, Engineering Works, Town/Village Rolls of Honour.

War Diaries, 34th Division, 102nd Brigade, 20th, 21st, 22nd and 23rd Battalions. WO/95 PRO Kew.

Police Gazette 1915, lists of deserters. British Library Colindale.

Red Cross lists of missing for October 1916 and October 1918.

Courts Martial Registers January - September 1916 France

WO 213/7 -12 PRO Kew.

Officers Died in the Great War.

The Army List and Army List Supplements.

The London Gazette.

St Georges Gazette extracts from the 'London Gazette'.

It is very much regretted that these nominal rolls only contain information on the original enlistments to the Brigade. Although some information on reinforcements was traced the work would have been to great to publish, I hope therefore that the reader will excuse the inclusion of those reinforcements who won gallantry awards and the few who I have been lucky enough to obtain a photograph of, to be fair I would have preferred to include every man who served.

NOTES ON THE NOMINAL ROLLS

The first columns are self explanatory, Name, Initials, Rank, Number, Company, Address and Town or Village.

Enlisted, this date comes from the Silver War Badge List, or it is the date that the soldiers name appeared in one of the local newspapers as having enlisted.

Discharged, this date is taken from the Silver War Badge List, the Medal Rolls, or in some cases the soldiers discharge certificate.

Cause of Discharge, in this column the date of death or the cause of discharge is given. Once again this information was extracted from the above sources.

Wounded. generally a month is given, this is the month the casualty was recorded in the Saint George's Gazette. Casualties recorded between July and November 1916 are nearly all from the 1st of July 1916.

Buried, the cemetery or churchyard of burial, this column also records those commemorated on memorials to the missing.

Transfer, other units that the soldier served with. Mainly extracted from the medal rolls, but some information included from Absentee Voters Lists and Soldiers Died in the Great War. Where the battalion of a new regiment is known this is recorded behind the regiment thus:- Kings Own Yorkshire LI(9th BN). This was done for indexing purposes on the computer. eg 1st, 12th, 16th BNS, this shows that the soldier was transferred to and served with the 1st then the 12th and finally the 16th Battalions of the Northumberland Fusiliers'.

Additional information, This column records any extra information noted, especially from Medical Health Records and Petty Sessions Registers.

To included as much information as possible it was found necessary to abbreviate many unit titles, and words thus:

34CCS = the 34th Casualty Clearing Station.

2GENHOSP or 18GHOSP = the 2nd or 18th General Hospitals.

21AMBT = 21st Ambulance Train. WND = Wounded R or L = Right or Left e.g WND R ARM+L BUTTOCK. AWOL = ABSENT WITHOUT LEAVE.

ST BEARER = Stretcher Bearer. EVAC = Evacuated. BN = Battalion.

CONV DEPOT = Convalescent Depot.LAB COY = Labour Company e.g. 101 LAB COY.

No = NUMBER, Where a new regimental number has been allotted e.g.

LAB CORPS No 123456.

SHIP OR HSHIP = casualty has been transferred to a Hospital Ship.

Officers and NCOs of C Company 4th Tyneside Scottish.

Picture Album

Colour of 23rd Battalion paraded through Edinburgh on the dedication of the Scottish War Memorial. On the left is Sergeant William Stokoe.

Private and Mrs Thomas Atkinson.

Men of 20th Battalion at Alnwick. Standing fourth from the right is 20/1310 Private Isaac Johnson from Dawdon Colliery.

Five unidentified soldiers at Alnwick.

Private Dixon

247

Men of 20th Battalion at Alnwick in 1915. The second pattern cap badge is being worn. Standing on the right rank is 20/206 Private Gibson Alexander.

Private Edward Waddell, 21st Battalion, on the right.

23/673 Private John Forrest, A Company, 4th Tyneside Scottish. Seated second row from the front.

Men of 20th Battalion at Alnwick. Rear rank 3rd left stands Private Stephen Kitchin.

Seated, 22/224 Private William Stokoe, St Georges T Newcastle.